PEACE AGREEMENTS AND HUMAN RIGHTS

Peace Agreements and Human Rights

CHRISTINE BELL

OXFORD
UNIVERSITY PRESS

*This book has been printed digitally and produced in a standard specification
in order to ensure its continuing availability*

OXFORD
UNIVERSITY PRESS

Great Clarendon Street, Oxford OX2 6DP

Oxford University Press is a department of the University of Oxford.
It furthers the University's objective of excellence in research, scholarship,
and education by publishing worldwide in

Oxford New York

Auckland Cape Town Dar es Salaam Hong Kong Karachi
Kuala Lumpur Madrid Melbourne Mexico City Nairobi
New Delhi Shanghai Taipei Toronto
With offices in
Argentina Austria Brazil Chile Czech Republic France Greece
Guatemala Hungary Italy Japan South Korea Poland Portugal
Singapore Switzerland Thailand Turkey Ukraine Vietnam

Oxford is a registered trade mark of Oxford University Press
in the UK and in certain other countries

Published in the United States
by Oxford University Press Inc., New York

Oxford is a registered trade mark of Oxford University Press
in the UK and in certain other countries

Published in the United States
by Oxford University Press Inc., New York

ISBN 0-19-927096-1

To Joy and Sloan Bell

Acknowledgements

I would like to thank the following people and institutions who gave me tremendous support during the writing of this book.

Thanks and acknowledgements are due to the Arts and Humanities Research Board of the British Academy, who generously grant-assisted this research, enabling me to take time away from my regular duties to complete it, and to travel to the countries involved. Secondly, thanks and acknowledgement are due to Queen's University, Belfast, who gave me a term of research leave to support the project; and to the University of Ulster, who facilitated its completion through the understanding and generosity of colleagues. Thanks are also due to the British Council for funding a visit to South Africa. Particular thanks are due to Michelle McDowell (Queen's University, Belfast) and Denise McLaughlin (University of Ulster) for administrative assistance throughout the time of writing the book.

Special thanks are due to Kathleen Cavanaugh, Chris McCrudden, and Colin Warbrick for heroic reading of most of the manuscript. Thanks also to Nazreen Bawa, Colm Campbell, Neil Duxbury, Peter Emerson, Marie Fox, Adrien Guelke, Tom Hadden, Colin Harvey, David Kretzmer, Stephen Livingstone, Mustafa M'ari, Fionnuala Ní Aoláin, Emma Playfair, William Schabas, and William Twining, all of whom read drafts of different chapters, and offered invaluable advice and critique. Mistakes which remain are my own.

The following people provided invaluable assistance in collecting and accessing peace agreements: Andy Carl, Conciliation Resources; Ed Garcia, International Alert; Alvie Jaspe; Fernand de Varennes; and Pedro Valenzuela. Elizabeth Craig also did a terrific job in helping me to summarize the agreements and provide thumbnail sketches of the conflicts, together with other valuable assistance.

I would particularly like to thank the following people who befriended me, housed or fed me, and debated and facilitated my research during my travels: Ned Bašić, Nazreen Bawa, Manda Bell, Mary Black, Hugh Corder, Oren Gross, Edy Kaufman, Aida Mehičečić, Keela McConville, John McConville, Henning Moe, Fionnuala Ní Aoláin, Michele Pickover, Ermin Sarajlija, Noel Stott, Charles Shammas, Raji Sourani, Tara, Luka, and Ozren Tošić, and Michael Warshschawski. Research was never before so much fun.

I would like to thank all the national institutions, politicians, and non-governmental organizations who gave me invaluable documentation and analysis and who continued to inspire the project. Particular thanks are due to the following people, and staff at the following institutions, many of whom spent a lot of time explaining their work and the human rights situation, while under the enormous pressures of their day-to-day work.

In Bosnia: Democratic Initiative of Sarajevo Serbs; Council of Europe Secretariat; Federation Ombudsman Office; Hajrudin Hajdarević; Helsinki Committee for Human Rights in Republika Srpska; Human Rights Centre, University of Sarajevo; Human Rights Chamber; Human Rights Office, Tuzla; Human Rights Watch; Sabira Jahić; NGO Information and Support Centre, Sarajevo; Office of the High Representative; Human Rights Department, Organization for Security and Cooperation in Europe; Phare Programme, Technical Assistance to the Constitutional Court of Bosnia and Herzegovina; Haris Silajdžić; United Nations High Commissioner for Refugees; United Nations Mission in Bosnia and Herzegovina.

In Israel and Palestine: Al Haq; Alternative Information Centre; B'Tselem; HaMoked; LAW; Mandela Institute for Political Prisoners; the MATTIN Group; Minerva Center for Human Rights, Hebrew University of Jerusalem; Palestinian Centre for Human Rights; People-to-People Project; Palestinian Independent Commission for Citizens' Rights; Raja Shehadeh; Trueman Institute for the Advancement of Peace, Hebrew University of Jerusalem; United Nations Office of the Special Coordinator in the Occupied Territories, Gaza.

In Northern Ireland: the Committee on the Administration of Justice; Northern Ireland Human Rights Commission.

In South Africa: Alex Boraine; Centre for the Study of Violence and Reconciliation; Commission for Gender Equality; Community Agency for Social Enquiry; Community Law Centre, University of Western Cape; Richard Goldstone; Human Rights Commission; Human Rights Committee; Law Faculty, University of Cape Town; Legal Resources Centre (Cape Town); Albie Sacks; Khehla Shubane, Centre for Policy Studies; Nico Steytler; Truth and Reconciliation Commission; Women's Legal Centre (Cape Town).

Finally, but not least, I would like to thank my family, Robbie, Muireann, and Róise McVeigh, and my parents Joy and Sloan Bell, for their support.

Christine Bell
Belfast
June 2000

Preface

This book was in part motivated by my own experiences of engaging with the peace process in Northern Ireland. In addition to addressing ongoing violations of human rights in the conflict, those of us involved in human rights activism often asserted that as human rights abuses were part of the problem in the conflict, so human rights protections had to be part of its solution. The issue of fairness and just treatment underpinned much of the conflict, and so required to be addressed. It is perhaps surprising to say that as the peace process developed often this argument was not accepted. The conflict was assumed to require nothing other than a comprise between a national dispute as to British and Irish sovereignty. However, as the process developed and negotiations began it became clear that if the parties were to reach agreement at all, human rights issues would have to be addressed. Furthermore, it soon became obvious that human rights issues could provide a less zero-sum context from which to address unresolvable national disputes. However, while the resulting Belfast Agreement proved somewhat of a triumph for those concerned with human rights, and (unlike earlier governmental blueprints) contained substantial human rights provisions. Of course, then the question of how difficult or easy implementation would be reared its head.

This experience, coupled with my own academic interest, led me to explore the situation in other countries with peace processes and with which I had had some contact. As part of this project I also began collecting peace agreements. The book arose as an attempt to document when and why human rights standards made their way into peace agreements, while examining the role of international law which provides domestic non-governmental organisations with a yard stick on which to base interventions. Rather than generalise from my own experience it seemed useful to set up the study as a four-way comparison. This also raised questions that I had been long interested in exploring, around the relationship of principle and pragmatism, or law and politics.

During the course of writing the book each of the peace processes concerned has gone through triumphs and disasters, punctuated by long periods of apparent inactivity. Because the book focuses on peace agreements these changes are not integral to the book's discussions, although of course they begin to tell us about implementation and are mentioned. At time of writing three out of the four processes are in the news almost daily. The Middle East sees daily conflict with so far over one hundred Palestinians and around five Israelis killed, in horrible circumstances and ways on both sides. The peace process is daily announced to be 'on the verge of collapse' although one wonders what total collapse would now look like. In Northern Ireland dispute over policing threatens future progress in a battle that is very much also about the survival, or not, of the Belfast Agreement. With relation to Bosnia Herzegovina, the fallout of the conflict plays out in the Federal Republic of Yugoslavia's mostly 'velvet' revolution against Milosević. While South Africa rarely enters the news and is assumed to be a completed process, the extreme socio-economic disparities in the country and high levels of violence in the form of criminal activity evidence an ongoing conflict, albeit transformed.

The book did not aim to, and nor did it, prophecy such events but it is interesting to note the extent to which the problems in the processes can be better understood by looking at the text of the peace agreements, and examining their human rights component (or lack of it). I myself have found some of the conclusions I have reached surprising and interesting, and have felt during the writing of the book that the comparison across the countries has helped me understand the rhythms of the process in the place where I live, and better address them. I hope that the book will be valuable to others engaged in similar exercises elsewhere.

Preface to the Paperback Edition

This book deals, in essence, with the relationship of justice to transition from conflict. While the term transitional justice is often used to describe how societies emerging from violent conflict deal with past human rights abuses, the book reveals a much broader transitional justice terrain, where law also plays a distinctive role with regard to political accommodation and building institutions for the future. Since this book's initial publication, both the peace processes described herein, and the international legal landscape have changed. These changes have often appeared as dramatic and yet it can be argued that they have served to highlight, rather than diminish, the debates at the centre of the book: in particular, those around the relationship of international law to conflict resolution, and the relationship of justice to peace.

At the local level, the Northern Irish peace process has seen the centre-piece of the Belfast Agreement – the devolved Assembly – suspended four times (one still current), and a failure to progress and implement many other aspects of the Agreement. While peace technically prevails, the political solutions crafted to sustain it remain precarious, raising questions about whether cessation of violence can survive the vacuum. While South Africa appears to be a country that has moved beyond its transitional phase, problems strongly linked to the apartheid era still haunt it, albeit in mutated ways. High levels of violence – physical and structural – prevail, while the appropriate human rights responses are less obvious. In particular, the socio-economic divide and violent crime remain central issues and, interestingly, are shaping types of human rights engagement, with new forms of activism around HIV treatment, but also arguably less central focus on civil and political human rights abuses by the state. Meanwhile, conflict in neighbouring Zimbabwe bears testimony to the phenomenon of return wars that are simultaneously connected to new, and to past, human rights issues. In Bosnia Herzegovina, most dramatically, the overthrow and eventual arrest and trial of Milošević have re-shaped, and continue to reshape, narratives of responsibility for the conflict. Yet the obstacles for fashioning an exit strategy for the international community bear testimony to the continued difficulties of building democracy identified in this book. Furthermore, Bosnia with hindsight, can be seen as part of a pattern relating to both the international community's interventions during conflict and its subsequent peacebuilding efforts which links to Kosova, Afghanistan and ultimately Iraq. While September the 11th has created the rationale for engagement in the last two situations, clear rhetorical and legal precursors can be found in Bosnia. In each situation the Bosnian paradox has become more evident – lack of democracy and human rights abuses are stated to provide a rationale for international intervention which soon itself becomes subject to challenges of lack of democracy and human rights abuses. The Middle East peace process, since first publication, is the most self-evident example of a failed peace process, with tragic results for Israelis and Palestinians. The current road map represents an attempt to return to a drawing board where there are no new solutions to old impasses, only tried, and untried, old solutions. As at time of publication, the Middle East peace process stands testimony, among other things, to the difficulties of fashioning lasting compromises without providing for human rights protections.

Central to the book is an attempt to explore the relationship between international law, and peace processes, and agreements. With regard to international law, the most dramatic and influential intervening event since first publication has been the attacks on the World Trade Centre of September 11th, 2001, and their global repercussions. The resulting challenges to international law are too various to document here but notably have placed the peace v. justice debate at the heart of this book, more clearly at the centre of the geo-political stage. This debate continues to play out in an internally inconsistent way. On one hand, democracy has been placed at the centre of foreign policy rhetoric by the United States and Britain with respect to internal conflict. Attempts to establish multi-ethnic coalitions, however, indicate a clear group rights spin on traditional liberal democratic structures. The language of human rights and democracy is now centrally asserted by the United States and Britain both to justify military interventions and to be the goal of complex reconstructions. On the other hand, pressure from the United States on a myriad of governments dealing with internal conflicts has resulted in increased emergency law and anti-terrorist measures which assume that military strategies justified in the name of human security must trump human rights protections. Thus, military strategies ostensibly aimed at security often conflict with political strategies ostensibly aimed at providing liberal democracy. While the book aimed to start at the other end of the spectrum by asking whether human rights can play a constructive role in the search for peace, it also continues to speak to the context of conflict escalation. The meta-conflicts at the heart of each of the conflicts explored herein, revolve around similar debates regarding the relationship of legal and military strategies for conflict containment and legal and political strategies for conflict transformation. The peace processes documented in this book attempted to find ways beyond these clashes and could be better used to inform current debates.

Regarding attempts to find ways out of entrenched conflicts, the dialectical interactive relationship between internal conflicts and international law demonstrated in the book continues, albeit in a changed way. The book's continued relevance lies in its central assertion that implementation or not of the human rights component of a peace agreement, in effect, determines the nature and direction of transition, and whether or not that direction is towards liberal democracy, towards a new discriminatory hegemony, or towards an unstable limbo, which at best, is less violent than what went before. Any placing of militarily strategies of containment ahead of strategies that address human rights abuses as root causes of violence is not, therefore, neutral regarding peace process outcomes. Moreover, domestic parties aware of this international, legal, and rhetorical shift, are quick to use the new international positions as tools for reworking agreements towards their own ends, thus undermining finely balanced compromises. While much has been made of the impact of any demise of international law on long-term global security, this book bears testimony to the also negative consequences for approaches to resolving or transforming internal conflict. Global and domestic security remain crucially linked in the capacity of injustice to provide a catalyst and a justification for individuals who resort to violence at both domestic and international levels. The relationship of international law to domestic conflict resolution therefore deserves continued attention.

Contents

1

Introduction

Almost every day the lead news stories include an account of a fresh outbreak of 'ethnic' violence, the waxing or waning of a peace process, or even the signing of a peace agreement. Central to the stories is the language of human rights and the moral dilemmas that go with it. What should be done with displaced peoples during and after conflict? Which party are the 'real' human rights violators? Could the international community have better addressed human rights violations that preceded the escalation of the conflict? What should the international community's role be in resolving it? Should war be waged or prolonged on 'humanitarian' grounds? Is human rights language selectively applied by powerful countries out of self-interest? When should political leaders become amenable to war crimes? What is more important—justice or peace? Is there a conflict between the two?

When a peace agreement is reached, often human rights provisions form a central part of its text. Many agreements, such as those of Central America and South Africa, provide for a transition to democracy. They are characterized by a constitutionalism designed to define, protect, and enforce rights, and to replace the arbitrary use of power with its legal regulation through checks and balances. Where the conflict involves a self-determination claim by ethno-national groups, as in Northern Ireland or Bosnia Herzegovina, peace agreements also typically attempt to redefine state structures and the access of these groups to power. This is then coupled with the enforced protection of individual rights, aimed at creating a working polity out of a deeply divided society and reassuring all citizens that they will not be penalized on the basis of their ethnicity.

The typical peace blueprint involves a central deal on democratic access to power (including minority rights where relevant), with a human rights framework including measures such as bills of rights, constitutional courts, human rights commissions, reform of policing and criminal justice, and mechanisms to address past human rights violations.

HUMAN RIGHTS, PEACE AGREEMENTS, AND INTERNATIONAL LAW

This book analyses the human rights component of the peace agreements signed in four conflicts with an 'ethnic' dimension, South Africa, Israel/Palestine, Northern Ireland, and Bosnia Herzegovina. The role that human rights play in negotiated peace agreements is critically examined

to reveal the trade-offs between different human rights provisions including in particular the relationship between group and individual rights.

The human rights component of the peace agreements is also systematically compared with relevant international law provision. This exposes
the extent to which international law regulates or provides guidance for
peace agreements, and conversely the extent to which the solutions fashioned in peace agreements provide lessons for international law.

The purpose of the volume is to illuminate thinking at three levels.
First, to provide some clear analysis of the role of human rights in peace
agreements, including examining the assumptions that put human rights
into an agreement and the factors that shape the provisions chosen.
Secondly, to inform consideration of the relationship between international human rights law and 'protracted social conflict', through the lens
of peace agreements.[1] Finally, to provide a context from which to consider
the relationship between justice and peace more generally, and to draw
some conclusions about the role of international law in peacemaking.

BACKGROUND TO THE STUDY

This comparative study is stimulated by two factors. First, a changing
global politics which has catapulted contemporary 'ethnic conflict' to
centre stage as one of the main challenges for international law's peace-
making ambitions. Secondly, an expanding human rights project that
raises fundamental questions about the relationship between international law and the internal political arrangements of states.

The Role of International Law

This examination of the connections between human rights, peace agreements, and international law takes place against a post-cold war backdrop
that has linked ethnic conflict and international law in a circle of ever
increasing dimensions. The last decade has been characterized by contradictory and yet intimately connected processes of globalization and frag-
mentation. These are epitomized by the parallel attempts to articulate a
'new world order' and the increase in demands for nation statehood and
the proliferation of 'ethnic conflict'. Both developments have their source
in the collapse of a bipolar world, which has enabled the emergence of

---

[1] See Azar (1990: 2) for definition of 'protracted social conflict' as: identity-related conflict
whose focus is 'religious, cultural or ethnic communal identity, which in turn is dependent
upon the satisfaction of basic needs such as those for security, communal recognition and
distributive justice.'

buried national conflicts, and also paradoxically provided new possibilities for resolving old conflicts (such as South Africa, Guatemala, and
Northern Ireland)[2] and indeed new possibilities for international cooperation in general.[3]

The pervasive nature of ethnic conflict and the scale of destruction
wrought by it in situations such as former Yugoslavia and Rwanda pose a
challenge for the effectiveness of international law. However, ethnic conflict does not register as a category in international law and uneasily
straddles the internal–international boundary, making delimitation of the
scope and role of international law difficult.[4] Ethnic conflict exposes an
'internal instability' for international law, whereby it must respond to
ethnic conflict to maintain credibility, but where responding in turn poses
a crisis for legitimacy in so far as it requires reworking traditional
accounts of international law's ambit.[5]

While ethnic conflict is not a new challenge for international law, the
current international legal terrain and post-cold war political climate have
created new possibilities for legal intervention. These are relevant not just
to 'ethnic conflict' (a label which is itself problematic[6]) but to internal conflict more generally.

In particular, international provision for human rights provides a basis
for international involvement in internal arrangements. International
human rights law claims to regulate many of the issues at the heart of ethnic conflict. Most pertinently it claims to regulate the self-determination
claim itself. As Berman argues, 'the decline of the anti-imperialist stress
on formal deference to a formal version of self-determination and sovereignty has made it possible for internationalists to consider systematically
the array of techniques for settling nationalist conflict.'[7] International
human rights law also provides minimum standards for the political,
civil, social, economic, and cultural rights of individuals and groups.
Increasingly, international soft law standards also address the institutional arrangements designed to achieve these rights, such as the judiciary or the police. International human rights law thus provides an

---

[2] See Roberts (1995) (generally); Cox (1997) (Northern Ireland); Guelke (1996a) (South Africa).

[3] See, generally, Bourantonis and Wiener (1995); Evans (1993); Pugh (1997); Roberts and Kingsbury (1998). Cf. also Boutros-Ghali (1992, 1995).

[4] See Wippman (1998a); Esman and Telhami (1995) (noting the difficulties of the distinction for the role of international organizations dealing with ethnic conflict).

[5] The term 'internal instability' comes from critical legal theorist Roberto Unger, who used
it in particular to describe the tensions inherent in liberal order's twin requirements of
generality and specificity (Unger 1975). For critical legal analysis specific to international
law, see Binder (1988) (focusing on Camp David Accords); Kennedy (1987); Koskenniemi
(1989).   [6] See further Ch. 2 at p. 15.

[7] Berman (1998: 55–6).

4   Introduction

expanding mechanism for regulation, whether conflict is international or internal.

In many areas however, international law makes only general or partial provision. It has been argued that the current 'array of international legal responses to ethnic conflict reflects a further step toward the imposition of formal requirements concerning the way in which states are themselves constituted.'[8] However, there is still considerable confusion as to what these formal requirements are. To return to the self-determination example, while major human rights instruments pay little or no attention to group rights, recognition of limited collective rights for ethnic groups has recently emerged as an alternative to self-determination, as part of what is essentially a liberal democratic 'cure' for ethnic conflict. International law has produced programmatic standards that would appear to under-write novel group-oriented arrangements, such as the UN General Assembly Declaration on the Rights of Persons Belonging to National or Ethnic, Religious, and Linguistic Minorities;[9] or the Council of Europe's Framework Convention on the Rights of National Minorities.[10] These, however, do not provide clear guidance as to how the balance with indi-vidual rights should be struck. Political scientists have placed consider-able emphasis on consociational arrangements as a possible way of reconciling incompatible ethnic demands and providing access to govern-ment for minorities.[11] However, although minority rights provisions require the *effective* participation of minorities in public and private life, a requirement which will require something other than majoritarianism, the compatibility of consociationalism with the individual rights of inter-national human rights law cannot be assumed.[12]

The book's comparison between the human rights component of peace agreements and international law will illustrate the extent to which law provides regulation or even guidance to negotiators; or whether inter-national law is struggling to catch up with the mechanisms which nego-tiators turn to. In doing so, the book revisits the well-worn terrain of the nature and role of international law as regards international and domes-tic politics.

Justice, Peace, and the Human Rights Project

The study also operates as a lens through which to examine the interna-tional human rights law project, in more general terms. In particular, it

---

[8] Slaughter (1998: 144).
[9] 18 Dec. 1992, G.A. Res. 47/135, UN Doc. A/Res/47/135 (1992), pub. in (1993) 32 I.L.M. 911.   [10] 1 Feb. 1995 (ETS No. 148) (hereafter 'Framework Convention').
[11] For account of 'consociationalism', see Lijphart (1968, 1969, 1977, 1989).
[12] See Wippman (1998b).

opens up two related fundamental debates crucial to human rights lawyers. First, the connection between justice and peace, and secondly, its jurisprudential restatement as the relationship between law and politics.

At the heart of the human rights order, established after the Second World War, is a contemplated relationship between justice and peace. The UN Charter itself opens with the objective of avoiding war and immediately references the concept of human rights.[13] The Universal Declaration makes the 'just peace' thesis more explicit, claiming that 'it is essential, if man is not to be compelled to have recourse, as a last resort, to rebellion against tyranny and oppression, that human rights should be protected by the rule of law.'[14] More recently, the Council of Europe's Framework Convention notes that 'the upheavals of European history have shown that the protection of national minorities is essential to stability, democratic security and peace in this continent.'[15]

While a connection between human rights and peace may seem obvious and is acknowledged in human rights instruments, in practice the precise nature of the connection is problematic and controversial.[16] Linking of human rights protections with peace-building is often challenged as partisan and/or idealistic. The view that human rights law provides unnegotiable minimum universal standards is often presented as in tension with the need for a pragmatic peace involving compromise, including compromise on human rights. In 1996 an anonymous contribution to the *Human Rights Quarterly* provided a stark example of this argument.[17] In it the writer castigated the human rights community for prolonging the war in former Yugoslavia by insisting on requirements of justice. By judging every peace blueprint primarily in terms of whether it rewarded aggression and ethnic cleansing, human rights 'pundits' and negotiators were accused of rejecting pragmatic deals which, with hindsight, were as good or better than the eventual settlement. The anonymous writer argued that as a result, '[t]housands of people are dead who should have been alive—because moralists were in quest of the perfect peace.'[18]

A number of writers over the years have grappled with trying to

---

[13] Preamble, United Nations Charter 1945.

[14] Preamble, Universal Declaration of Human Rights 1948.

[15] Preamble, Framework Convention 1995.

[16] For direct discussion of the connection between human rights and conflict resolution, see e.g. Akhavan (1996*b*), 1997, 1998); Anonymous (1996); Boyle (1996); D'Amato (1994); Galtung (1994); Kaufman and Bisharat (1998*a*, *b*); Müllerson (1997); Reisman (1995); Rupesinghe (1995, 1998); Tascan (1992). A related 'prior' literature exists, dealing with the question of whether and how domestic protection of human rights (and democratic institutions generally) prevents or reduces inter-state and intra-state conflict: see e.g. Donnelly (1994); Forsythe (1993); Russett (1990, 1993). Walzer's famous account of the 'just war' examines the 'justice leads to peace' thesis in reverse, by examining the connections between injustice and war (1992).   [17] Anonymous (1996).

[18] Anonymous (1996: 258); see response by Boyle (1996).

explore the connection between human rights abuses and internal and international conflict with various conclusions.[19] Less explored is the question of whether protecting human rights through the implementation of human rights mechanisms plays a positive role in conflict management, resolution, or transformation. It is to this more forward-looking project that this book hopes to contribute.

Many contemporary peace processes involving ethnic conflict and culminating in some type of written agreement have included significant provision for protecting human rights as a crucial element. This would suggest that mediators and parties to the conflict find the connection between peace and justice persuasive. Typically, such agreements provide for three human rights aspects: first, some type of self-determination often falling short of secession or statehood, such as autonomy or power-sharing; secondly, a collection of human rights institutions—bills of rights, constitutional courts, human rights commissions, equality commissions, new police and criminal justice structures, and measures providing for social and economic equality; and thirdly, mechanisms to deal with past human rights abuses, such as truth commissions or international tribunals, while simultaneously providing for prisoner release. The unstated backdrop to such provisions is a tension between demands of justice and demands of political accommodation, and when, how, and to what degree one must give way to the other. This book does not aim to provide a theory of the just peace. But by examining peace agreements it does provide an insight into how the relationship between justice and peace plays out during negotiations, and exposes the differing concepts of peace which parties may be working to.

THE SCOPE OF THE BOOK

The book focuses on the content of the 'peace agreement' itself. Peace agreements, whatever the pressures forming them, constitute at least a moment of agreement in a conflict. As such they embody a set of understandings between some of the protagonists to a conflict as to how to resolve or at least manage that conflict. These understandings are not academic theorizations but reflect a realpolitik. The written agreements that embody them provide tangible measures that can be compared with international legal provision. A focus on peace agreements, while in some senses artificial, enables a broad spectrum of issues to be considered. Much of the scholarship on peace processes and human rights has isolated an issue within the peace process—for example, policing or truth

---

[19] See above, n. 16.

commissions—and compared that across several examples.[20] This study aims to cover four key case-studies, examining their human rights component as broadly conceived. This makes it possible to unpack the trade-offs between different human rights components, and to expose the key factors that shaped these trade-offs. In particular, the book attempts to unpick the relationship in both conflict and peace agreement, between the self-determination–minority rights issues which often appear to be at the centre of ethnic conflict, and the civil, political, social, economic, and cultural individual rights issues which are inextricably linked to the conflict. Contextualized comparative analysis is vital to those who seek to make comparisons between and across peace processes.

The texts of peace agreements reveal a tension between the production of peace agreements with their finely balanced trade-offs and ongoing bargaining between different parties to the conflict as to their substantive concerns. Often issues that appear to be about process, or technical in nature, are inextricably intertwined with substantive issues going to the core of the conflict. Process issues range from preliminary issues of who should be at negotiations and the location and format of any talks, to implementation issues of timing, sequencing, and mechanisms for enforcement. Typically these issues determine substantive matters such as whether provisions agreed to as temporary and interim will in effect become permanent; or whether an agreement will be used to extract a party's bottom line, pocket it, and then attempt to force further concessions. While the texts of peace agreements are static, both the conflicts and the peace processes in which they operate are fluid.

The focus on peace agreements serves to contain the comparison but has not been chosen merely for this pragmatic reason. Most peace processes focus on agreeing a text which emerges under the pressure of negotiations in a highly legalistic form. As is addressed in the final chapter, peace agreements have different types of legal status, vary in their nature, and have different types of enforcement mechanism. Some are stated to be constitutions, some are treaties, some are international agreements, and some have no clear legal status despite their legal language. The book focuses on peace agreements to throw light on their role as texts within peace processes. Understanding the place and role of a peace agreement within a conflict is essential to understanding the potential and limits of

[20] See e.g. Gormley and McEvoy (1995), McEvoy (1998) (prisoner release); Brewer *et al.* (1996) (not specifically peace process related), Milton Edwards (1996), Moore and O'Rawe (1997, 1998) (all on policing); Hayner (1994), Rolston (1996) (truth commissions); Roniger and Sznajder (1999) (the 'past' more generally); Institute for Public Policy Research (1998) (Human Rights Commissions, not specifically peace process related); Cassese (1998*b*), Guelke (1985) (self-determination); Wilson (1997) (civic society); Alston (1999) (bills of rights, not specifically peace process related). Cf. also Reilly and Harris (1998) (comparing many of these elements, but not packages of trade-offs).

the human rights provisions (or indeed any provisions) which are built into that agreement.

THE STRUCTURE OF THE BOOK

This first chapter addresses the backdrop and scope of the study, setting out the underlying questions as to the relationship between international law and ethnic conflict, and between justice and peace. Chapter 2 explores a general problem of definitions and what is meant by ethnic conflict, peace processes, peace agreements, and human rights. Part of the difficulty of comparing the human rights components of peace agreements to each other and to international law is that the key terms 'peace process', 'peace agreement', and 'human rights' are contested. This is a problem not of semantics but of boundaries. The chapter also lays out the rationale for the chosen comparisons, and puts the four case-studies in a broader comparative context of other peace processes and peace agreements.

Chapters 3 and 4 provide brief thematic accounts of each of the four conflicts in South Africa, Northern Ireland, Israel/Palestine, and Bosnia Herzegovina, and a short analysis of international law's relationship to each by way of background. While clearly not providing comprehensive histories these highlight significant legal and constitutional developments in order to make subsequent peace agreements accessible. These accounts serve to illustrate how the stance of both state and non-state actors to international human rights and humanitarian law is determined by their analysis of the nature of the problem. The parties to a conflict use human rights and humanitarian law with a view to meta-bargaining as to the nature of the conflict, and this impacts on the ingredients for its resolution. This demonstrates an interactive two-way relationship between international law and conflict. This relationship in turn affects the human rights component of peace agreements. These chapters also provide a brief sketch of the four peace processes with particular reference to their documentary fruits—peace agreements. Chapters 3 and 4 illustrate the role that a peace agreement plays in a process, and the types of human rights issue that are dealt with in pre-negotiation, framework, and implementation agreements.

The following chapters isolate and compare the central human rights aspects of the peace agreements in turn, comparing these with international law provision in the area. Chapter 5 examines how each set of agreements deal with the self-determination and minority rights claims ostensibly at the heart of the conflict. Chapter 6 compares the provision found in the agreements with international law—both its core content and its evolutionary trends. The chapter evaluates the extent to which the self-determination approach taken in the peace agreements is assisted by the legal regulation of self-determination; and, conversely, whether peace agreements have anything to offer the evolution of international law in this area.

Chapter 7 examines provision for future protection of human rights through institutions. This chapter examines mechanisms for entrenching rights, such as bills of rights; measures aimed at providing social and economic justice; mechanisms for rights enforcement (such as courts and national institutions for human rights); and reform of the criminal justice apparatus, including policing. This chapter notes that the relative ease with which these issues can be negotiated, because of their 'win–win' potential, obscures the way in which the self-determination debate tends to re-emerge at the point at which they are implemented. Indicators of how this will happen can be found in the text of the peace agreements. The comparison between human rights packages demonstrates how in a divided society the institutions of democracy aim not merely to police the polity, but to assist in creating the polity. Central to the chapter is analysis of the relationship between the formulation of group rights through self-determination and individual rights protections.

Chapters 8 and 9 examine the provision in the agreements for dealing with past human rights violations. Chapter 8 examines provision aimed at undoing the past, such as return of refugees and land claims. Chapter 9 examines related provisions aimed at the past, including prisoner release, truth and reconciliation commissions, and international criminal tribunals. This latter chapter raises most graphically the justice–peace debate. It demonstrates how provision for dealing with the past is inextricably linked with how the agreement has dealt with self-determination. It also exposes the different place that 'past' issues have in agreements at different stages of the process. As with the self-determination chapter, this chapter considers the possible regulation of this aspect of peace agreements by emerging international legal norms, and the possible lessons from peace agreements for international legal developments.

Throughout the book a picture of the interrelationship between peace agreements, human rights, and international law is built up. Chapter 10 draws this picture together. I suggest that peace agreements are best understood as a form of transitional constitution, and that the human rights provisions must be understood as an integral part of that constitution and as having particular transitional functions. Peace agreements provide a framework which is both constitutional—setting out governmental arrangements and values—but at the same time distinctively temporary, transitional, international, and political. This explains why peace agreements are difficult to classify as legal documents. Understanding peace agreements as transitional constitutions helps to explain the role which human rights protections face in effecting the transition. Human rights protections aim to mediate between a conflict-riven past and a better future. This simultaneously forward- and backward-looking role generates characteristic choices for such institutions, and a distinctive form of 'transitional jurisprudence'.

As regards the relationship with international law—it both shapes and is shaped by ethnic conflict; this interaction impacts on the self-determination deal cut; and the self-determination deal in turn creates or does not create the space for human rights institutions. These human rights institutions will be shaped by the demands of the 'deal' as a whole, and in particular its arrangements as to sovereignty, government and territory, but also will be shaped by international legal criteria. The role of international law is therefore neither irrelevant, as realists would suggest, nor regulatory, in the way that idealists might want. The chapter also demonstrates that just as international law shapes the peace agreement, so the devices found in peace agreements also impact on international law.

WHY THESE FOUR PEACE PROCESSES?

The four peace processes at the centre of the study have been chosen for several reasons. While each conflict is very different and has its own historical, social, (geo)political, and legal context, there are some basic similarities. First, they all involved protracted conflict with deep ethnic division and self-determination claims. In each case any explanation of the conflict is fraught by the existence of a 'meta-conflict'—a conflict as to what the conflict is 'about'.[21] Secondly, these conflicts all attracted the label 'peace process' and resulted in (a) written agreement(s) and reached, at least, a framework–substantive agreement stage. These agreements, unlike some earlier counterparts, included representatives of all the main protagonists to the conflict, including anti-state opposition groups and their armed counterparts, as parties to the negotiation, namely: the African National Congress (ANC) and Umkhonto we Sizwe (MK) in South Africa; Sinn Féin (SF) and the Provisional Irish Republican Army (IRA), the Progressive Unionist Party (PUP) and the Ulster Volunteer Force (UVF), the Unionist Democratic Party (UDP) and Ulster Defence Association (UDA), in Northern Ireland; the Palestinian Liberation (PLO) in the Israeli/Palestinian process; and Croats, Muslims, and Serbs in Bosnia Herzegovina.[22] Thirdly, the written agreements all explicitly attempted to deal, at least partially, with the substantive issues in the conflict, and in particular the differing claims to statehood, governmental power, and self-determination of the protagonists.

---

[21] See further Ch. 2 at p. 15.

[22] Although Bosnian Serb leader Karadžić was excluded from Dayton as having been indicted by the Ad Hoc International Criminal Tribunal for Former Yugoslavia. However, both the Federal Republic of Yugoslavia and the Republika Srpska (both representing 'Serb' interests) signed relevant portions of Dayton.

The differences between the conflicts and peace processes also make the comparison interesting. Aside from differences of detail and context alluded to above, which must be taken into account in any comparative study, the four chosen examples have some key structural differences which contribute to the comparison. They all involve different degrees of legitimacy of self-determination claim.[23] This ranges from the fairly straightforward and internationally accepted claim of the black majority in South Africa, to the more contested claim of (Catholic) Irish nationalists, presented as a minority within the borders of Northern Ireland. The claims of Palestinians fall somewhere in between, while the rival claims in the disintegrating Yugoslavia saw fluctuating and inconsistent international attempts to rework the self-determination norm in order to limit and end the conflict.

Each of the four cases involved different types and degrees of international mediation: from the fully fledged (if chaotic and problematic) legal responses of the international community in former Yugoslavia through the various third-party mediations in Israel/Palestine (most recently by Norway and the United States), to the 'chairmanship' (rather than mediation) of US Senator George Mitchell in Northern Ireland, and the relatively isolated internal processes of South Africa. Each set of agreements is currently at a different stage of implementation, with different problems, and different degrees of 'success', although time alone may give us a measuring stick for what constitutes success, and tell us which processes meet the measurement.

Finally, there are other possible reasons to choose these four cases as a comparison. They have often formed the basis of comparative study and have been mutually referencing.[24] Academic conferences drawing together experts from these conflict situations have abounded. A glance at an account of one process is peppered with references to the others. When the Truth and Reconciliation Commission in South Africa published its report, its chairperson, Archbishop Tutu, presented South Africa as 'a beacon of hope for those places like Northern Ireland, Bosnia and Rwanda . . .'.[25] While considering Bosnia Herzegovina (BiH), John Major warned that intervention might get Western armies embroiled for decades, 'like the British in Northern Ireland.'[26] US negotiator in BiH Richard Holbrooke documents how the Dayton peace negotiations were deliberately modelled on the Camp David process for the Middle East. Holbrooke notes how he distributed to all his team Carter's own account of the thirteen days of Camp David, along with two other accounts.[27] He

[23] Guelke (1985).
[24] See e.g. Akenson (1992); Giliomee and Gagiano (1993); Guelke (1991, 1994*a*, *b*, 1996 *a*, *b*, *c*, 1997); Lustick (1993); McGarry (1998); Taylor (1994); Wright (1987).
[25] *Irish Times*, 30 Oct. 1998, 1.   [26] Thompson (1992: 325).
[27] Holbrooke (1998: 204–5).

later notes how a '"Dayton" has been seriously suggested for Northern Ireland, Cyprus, Kashmir, the Middle East, and other festering problems.'[28] Indeed aspects of the Mitchell Review in Northern Ireland towards the end of 1999 may well have been styled with Dayton in mind. Later Holbrooke illustrates European opposition to a strong international police force for BiH by recounting the opposition of the British, who (somewhat bizarrely) argued that 'British tradition and the legacy of Northern Ireland precluded her government from allowing police officers to make arrests on foreign soil.'[29]

These passing references at the political level have been underwritten by the mobility of local social movements between processes. Women's groups have met across processes, sharing experiences of how to survive and influence the peace process; community and voluntary sector personnel have met frequently and exchanged ideas.[30] Political elites too visited each other, intervening in each other's processes. The ANC intervened in Northern Ireland at different stages in the process, most notably after the Belfast Agreement was signed, when their presence was aimed at helping Sinn Féin sell the deal. Individuals with experience in one process have become involved in another. Brian Currin, a South African lawyer and former chair of an Amnesty Commission involved in the release of politically motivated prisoners in South Africa, made a significant contribution to the thinking of political parties and the British government on prisoner release towards the end of multi-party negotiations in Northern Ireland. After the Belfast Agreement was signed, he was appointed co-chairperson of the Life Sentence Review Board responsible for processing the agreement's prisoner release provisions. Justice Goldstone of the South African Constitutional Court, and former head of the South African Commission of Inquiry into Intimidation and Violence, was also an independent prosecutor for the Ad Hoc International Criminal Tribunals on Former Yugoslavia and Rwanda. Most recently, former secretary-general of the ANC Cyril Ramaphosa and former president of Finland Martti Ahttisaari, both with experience in a number of conflicts, have been nominated as inspectors of Provisional IRA weapons dumps.

The interchange is not of course limited to these four processes, but grows and expands. Shortly after the signing of the Belfast Agreement, for example, on 5 October 1998 Sinn Féin President Gerry Adams travelled to the Basque Country to discuss with Basque nationalist political parties how the shift from armed to non-armed negotiation had been achieved.[31]

---

[28] Holbrooke (1998: 232).   [29] Holbrooke (1998: 251).
[30] See e.g. Cockburn (1998).
[31] Gerry Adams met with all the signatories of the Lizara Garazi Declaration, a declaration of Basque nationalists and some of the Spanish left, on how to resolve the conflict. This declaration was the result of a public debate organized by the Forum on Ireland, the aim of

Euzkadi ta Azkatasuna (ETA) declared a ceasefire on 24 October 1998 shortly after.[32]

These connections form part of the increasing transnational operation of social movements, which itself forms part of the complex tapestry of globalization. As Goodman notes, such social movements often start from the simplest and most obvious connections. The Dublin-based East Timor-Ireland Solidarity Campaign, set up in 1992, forged a connection between two contexts which bore little resemblance in terms of state, society, economy, and culture, by drawing on a common colonial experience. In the words of an organizer,

> Our first challenge was obvious: to link an island on the other side of the world and our own, when there was no historical relationship. The connection that we made was that, like East Timor, we had been invaded and occupied by a larger, more powerful neighbour. We had also suffered colonialism. That was the direct link.[33]

Goodman argues that, regardless of the basis for the connection, the very 'process of articulating national and transnational frameworks can reorient these movements from exclusive to inclusive political categories; it can also force changes in the logic of state policy, with parallel moves from confrontation to negotiation.'[34] Therefore, the fact that a broad range of connections has already been made between the four chosen processes, both conceptually and through the actual exchange of people and ideas, further justifies this detailed comparison of the agreements produced by the processes. It is hoped that the comparison will further inform those involved in the ongoing processes of exchange, in particular human rights lawyers, international organizations, and non-governmental human rights organizations.

---

which was to examine the Irish peace process with a view to drawing lessons for resolution of the conflict in the Basque Country.

[32] This ceasefire was officially ended in Nov. 1999.
[33] Goodman (1998: 57), citing Steele (1998: 180).
[34] Goodman (1998: 57). Cf. Burgerman (1998).

2

Peace Processes, Peace Agreements, and Human Rights: What are They?

THE THEMES OF THE BOOK: A PROBLEM WITH DEFINITIONS

So far the terms 'human rights', 'peace processes', and 'peace agreements' have been used without explanation. One of the problems in comparing peace agreements and human rights is that both are difficult to define. Any comparison must make clear what is being compared, but two factors make this difficult in the present case.

First, the scope of human rights law is constantly expanding and is increasingly fuzzy around the edges. International instruments contain a clear statement of basic rights. However, increasingly questions can be asked as to how prescriptive international law is as to how rights should be delivered. Questions arise as to what extent human rights standards require provision for groups rights, specific institutional arrangements (such as power-sharing, a functioning criminal justice system, an independent judiciary, and national institutions for protecting rights), or the punishment of individuals for past abuses.

Secondly, ethnic conflict is often characterized by 'multiple disagreements over what kind of conflict it is, and about whether it is "one" or "many".'[1] That is, there is a 'meta-conflict' or 'conflict about what the conflict is about'. This makes the term 'ethnic conflict' itself problematic. Disagreement as to what the conflict is about leads to disagreement on how it can best be resolved. If the conflict is about lack of democracy for example, that leads to one set of solutions; if it is about inter-group ethnic hatred, then that leads to others.[2] The very existence of a meta-conflict in cases of ethno-national conflict raises a host of related micro-conflicts over when a peace process exists, what can be classified as a peace agreement, and indeed what can rightfully be considered as a 'human rights' issue.

This chapter deals with the terms 'peace process', 'peace agreement', and 'human rights' in turn. The point is less to provide semantic definitions of each than to illustrate how the difficulties with definition are due to the fluid nature both of conflict (and therefore peace processes) and of human rights, and indeed their interactive evolutionary relationship with each other.

---

[1] McGarry and O'Leary (1995: 1).
[2] See further McGarry and O'Leary (1993, 1995); Horowitz (1985, 1991: 1–41).

WHAT IS A PEACE PROCESS?

While political scientists have long analysed the dynamics of politics and conflict, they have proved singularly unsuccessful at predicting turbulent change, including the onset of conflict and breakthroughs towards its resolution.[3] Not surprisingly, after-the-fact analyses aim to unpick what 'caused' the peace processes, and the post-cold war global shift is often one prevalent, partial explanation.[4] However, for the purposes of this inquiry there is a prior question to be asked and answered. That is the question of 'when is a process a peace process?' The short and flippant answer might be, whenever it suits one of the parties to the conflict to so describe it. In other words, the term 'peace process' can be understood as a value judgement attached to efforts to resolve a conflict at a particular time. Just as one person's freedom fighter is another's terrorist, so one person's peace process is another's 'ceasefire agreement', or yet another's 'victory' and another's 'sell-out' or 'capitulation to terrorists'.

As Mitchell notes, the very concept of what constitutes a resolution of a conflict is inextricably tied up with a party's perceptions of the causes of the conflict and its own end goals. He distinguishes five basic 'solutions':

  (a) Victory for one party with all goals achieved, and defeat for the other.
  (b) Destruction of one party, or the incorporation of its remnants in another entity, probably the victor.
  (c) Isolation, withdrawal or disengagement, whereby conflict behaviour is suspended and inter-action between the parties ceases, although the situation of goal incompatibility remains.
  (d) Settlement, or accommodation, whereby some compromise solution is achieved 'splitting the differences', and allowing both parties to achieve some of their objectives, even if on an unequal basis.
  (e) Resolution, whereby the sources of the conflict situation itself are removed, rather than the behavioural or attitudinal components being altered. Both parties achieve mutual gains, or a new range of benefits.[5]

Therefore, paradoxically, the entire process of conflict can be regarded as an attempt to achieve a solution, even though this 'solution' may involve the enforced submission or even annihilation of the opposing party. The difficulty of when to use the term 'peace process' plays out yet another version of the 'meta-conflict'. At its starkest, war is often described by those who wage it as a process designed to lead to peace.

Although Mitchell's list is not specific to ethnic conflict, it is worth noting the similarity with the strategies that political scientists identify as

---

[3] See Cox (1997: 671–8).

[4] See Brewer (1998), outlining three types of explanation based on social structure, individual biographical experience, and political process.   [5] Mitchell (1981: 253–4).

used to address ethno-national disputes. As Table 2.1 indicates, only some of these strategies are permitted under international human rights law, although this is a position which is evolving all the time. International law's human rights standards and its prohibition on acquisition of territory by use of force attempts to outlaw (a) and (b) of Mitchell's list, by outlawing

TABLE 2.1. *Political strategies for dealing with minorities*

Strategy	Methods of implementing	International law prescription
Elimination	• genocide • expulsion • voluntary expatriation	• specifically outlawed • specifically outlawed • unclear (little guidance as to what is voluntary)
Domination	• discrimination against the minority • hegemonic control (differences tolerated)	• specifically outlawed • in effect prohibited through protection for individual rights
Assimilation	• elimination of communal differences	• moving towards prohibition (in recent minority rights instruments)
Recognition and accommodation	• making special provision for separate but equal treatment in relevant spheres	• unclear status (depends on the balance between individual- and group-oriented rights provisions)
Self-determination	• granting internal autonomy • consociational governmental arrangements • accepting partition–dissolution or secession	• unclear status (depends on group–individual balance) • unclear status (depends on group–individual balance) • unclear status (neither mandates recognition nor prohibits; yet provides for seemingly inconsistent rights of territorial integrity and rights of peoples to predetermine their political status)

Notes: This table is adapted from one produced in Hadden (1996: 13); for a more detailed discussion of a slightly different set of strategies from a political science viewpoint, see McGarry and O'Leary (1990: 269–89).

conquest, genocide, and ethnic cleansing, and (c) by outlawing discrimination and increasingly assimilation.

Despite the fact that parties to a conflict may view their war efforts as aimed at achieving peace, colloquial use of the term 'peace process' usually attaches to an attempt to resolve the process through dialogue rather than direct violence. The peace processes in South Africa, Northern Ireland, and the Middle East were so named because they involved a shift from primarily violent forms of interaction towards increasingly non-violent forms. Yet, even this definition of a peace process does not pin the creature down. In any ethnic or internal conflict there are likely to have been many attempts, either official or unofficial, governmental or community-based, local or international, to resolve that conflict, with different initiatives often taking place at the same time. To give an example, a Kennedy School of Government review of proposals for reaching a settlement in Chechnya between 1995 and 1996 alone lists sixteen peace initiatives proposed by politicians, members of the Russian government, and internationally convened groups.[6] In contrast, the label 'peace process' is most often attached to attempts to bring political elites, particularly those directly involved in violent conflict, to some sort of mutual agreement. This may or may not include face-to-face talks.

Even when the term 'peace process' is used with this meaning, the meta-conflict will still play out in the micro-conflicts of when the peace process started (or when to use the label), who started the peace process, and who owns the peace process. Sometimes parties choose to describe a stage in the conflict as a peace process, and sometimes it serves them better not to use this language. Thus, in Chechnya the 1996 Khasavyurt Accord reached by Russia's General Lebed is often referred to as a 'ceasefire agreement', although the agreement claims to deal with substantive issues such as providing a timetable for possible autonomy. In Bougainville (Papua New Guinea) the terminology 'peace process' has been used for many years. However, the key Lincoln Agreement on Peace Security and Development on Bougainville 1998 did little more than declare a ceasefire and provide some measures aimed at ameliorating the consequences of the conflict (although groundwork on substantive issues had been laid in preliminary agreements; see Table 2.2).

The cases of Israel/Palestine and Northern Ireland illustrate conflict over who started the peace process and who owns it. Israel's Foreign Ministry claims the process leading to Oslo as 'Israel's peace process' and has linked it to Shamir's 1989 proposals for Palestinian elections and negotiations and preceding Israeli-backed initiatives through to the Camp

---

[6] Curran *et al.* (1997: 81–91).

David Accords.[7] Palestinians trace the peace process to the intifada's emergence in 1988, Palestinian Liberation Organization (PLO) and Palestinian National Council policy shifts around that time, and Arafat's peace initiative as presented to the UN in December 1988. With the subsequent difficulties in the peace process, the response of many Palestinians and some Israelis has often been to question immediately whether a peace process exists at all.

In Northern Ireland the peace process was initially called 'the Irish peace process', 'the British–Irish peace process', and (then British Prime Minister) 'John Major's peace process' or the 'Northern Ireland peace process', depending on who was talking about it. Similarly, its start was variously linked to the Hume–Adams talks, to secret talks between the British government and the Irish Republican Army (IRA), to the Brooke–Mayhew talks between some political parties, and the IRA ceasefire (to name a few). The difficulties of the term 'peace process' are further illustrated by the short accounts of the four peace processes and their peace agreements provided in Chapters 3 and 4. These accounts demonstrate the ongoing nature of both conflict and attempts to resolve it.

The existence of a few much publicized 'peace processes' in some highly visible cases of seemingly intractable social conflict obscures the fluid nature of conflict and attempts to resolve it, the multiplicity of initiatives which can be ongoing at any point in time, and the sheer number of formal peace processes and peace agreements which have been negotiated since 1990. The Appendix to this book provides a surprisingly long list of the many processes of the last decade and a summary of their many written agreements between political elites aimed at reducing and resolving conflict.[8]

WHAT IS A PEACE AGREEMENT?

Just as there are certain high-profile 'peace processes', so there are certain high-profile 'peace agreements'. In particular, the agreements focused on in this book, the Israel–Palestinian Declaration of Principles (Oslo I),[9] the South African Interim Constitution,[10] the Belfast Agreement,[11] and the General Framework Agreement for Peace in Bosnia and Herzegovina (Dayton Peace Agreement),[12] provide examples. Yet, a wider comparative

---

[7] See www.israel-mfa.gov.il/mfa.go.asp?MFAHOOOcO (last visited 9 May 2000). These documents available in Abdul Hadi (1997a: 248–51 and 341 respectively).

[8] The tables of agreements below are drawn from this Appendix, where the full range of agreements are given along with general sources.   [9] (1993) 32 I.L.M. 1525.

[10] Constitution of the Republic of South Africa Act 200 of 1993.

[11] Agreement Reached in the Multiparty Negotiations, Belfast, 10 Apr. 1998.

[12] (1996) 35 I.L.M. 89.

study indicates that just as the term 'peace process' is contested, so is the term 'peace agreement'.

High-profile 'peace agreements' which receive media attention often mark a particular breakthrough in a process, rather than a definitive 'solution'. They are inevitably preceded and succeeded by other peace agreements. Most peace processes leave a complex documentary trail, as different issues are dealt with at different stages, as political actors come and go, as agreements are accepted and rejected, and as agreements themselves shape a conflict, and its central issues mutate accordingly.

Towards a Classification of Peace Agreements?

In order to facilitate comparison of peace agreements, it is worth attempting a classification of the different types of agreement which emerge at different stages of a peace process. An overview of a number of agreements would suggest that peace agreements can loosely be categorized into three stages: pre-negotiation agreements, framework–substantive agreements, and implementation agreements.[13]

Pre-Negotiation Agreements

Parties move from violent to less violent forms of addressing the conflict when they perceive that they can potentially gain more at the table than they can away from it. However, often, from the point of moving towards the negotiating table, the process is one of 'trial and error' for each actor, and the process is characterized by stops and starts, progress and breakdown. The pre-negotiation stage typically revolves around who is going to negotiate and with what status.[14] Often pre-negotiation agreements are not inclusive but form bilateral agreements between some of the players. Indeed, the 'pre-' pre-negotiation stage often includes attempts to exclude a key 'militant' party to the conflict in an attempt by those in power to broker a deal with the perceived moderates on the other side. Examples of such attempts include the Anglo-Irish Agreement in Northern Ireland,[15] the 1983 Constitution in South Africa,[16] and, more arguably, the 1995 Devolution Proposals in Sri Lanka.[17] At a later stage the non-inclusive

---

[13] This follows the typical pattern of talks, see Mitchell (1981: 207). Cf. also Du Toit (1989).

[14] Mitchell (1981: 206–16).

[15] Agreement between the Government of the United Kingdom of Great Britain and Northern Ireland and the Government of the Republic of Ireland 1985 (British version) Cmnd. 9690; Agreement between the Government of Ireland and the Government of the United Kingdom (Irish version) Prl. 3684; published in McGarry and O'Leary (1990, app. 304–10).   [16] Republic of South Africa Constitution Act 110 of 1983.

[17] Available at www.lacnet.org/devolution (last visited 1 Dec. 1999). See also subsequent revisions in 1996 Legal Draft of devolution proposals, and 1997 Draft Constitution, also available at this web site.

nature of the agreement usually arises as a result of different parties exploring the possibility of setting a mutually agreeable agenda. Examples include the Groote Schuur, Pretoria, and Royal Hotel Minutes in South Africa, where the African Nationalist Congress (ANC) drew up bilateral agreements with the National Party, South African government (NP/SAG), and the Inkatha Freedom Party (IFP), respectively.[18] In Northern Ireland they include the Hume–Adams proposals and the British–Irish Framework Document.[19] As these initiatives (often secret) develop, are published, and begin to be supported by other parties, those who continue to remain outside the process tend to do so by choice, in an attempt to outbid those within the process and so influence or destroy the compromises taking place there.

For face-to-face or proximity negotiations to take place each party must also be assured that their attempts to engage in dialogue will not be used by the other side to gain a military advantage. In order to get everyone to the negotiating table, agreement needs to be reached on matters such as the return of negotiators from exile, or their release from prison; safeguards as to future physical integrity and freedom from imprisonment; and limits on how the war is to be waged while negotiations take place. Pre-negotiation peace agreements can include mechanisms such as amnesties for negotiators; temporary ceasefire agreements; human rights protections; and monitoring of violations both of ceasefires and of human rights. Pre-negotiation agreements also typically begin to set the agenda for talks as the parties begin to bargain and sound out each other's positions on substantive issues. Often this takes the form of attempts to set preconditions on the negotiating agenda.

Where international mediation takes place while conflict is ongoing, the pre-negotiation agreements can be understood as including the various blueprints and attempts to structure ceasefires which precede any agreement eventually assented to by all the relevant parties. This trial-and-error settlement process takes place simultaneously with the war in which the parties continue to strive for military victory. Ongoing attempts to find possible frameworks for a settlement are engaged in by all parties in the shadow of their prospects for military victory. Examples of such agreements include the peace blueprints brokered by the international community, which were put on the table during the conflict in former Yugoslavia between 1992 and 1995.[20] Table 2.3 sets out two sets of pre-negotiation agreements as an illustration. The pre-negotiation agreements of the four case-studies can be found in Chapters 3 and 4, with the Appendix providing additional examples.

---

[18] See further Ch. 3, pp. 46–7.   [19] See further Ch. 3, pp. 62–4.
[20] See Ch. 4, pp. 108–9, 110–11, 112–14.

TABLE 2.2. *Examples of pre-negotiation agreements*

Place	Pre-negotiation agreements
Bougainville The present conflict on Bougainville, an island under the jurisdiction of Papua New Guinea (PNG), began in 1987 as a dispute over compensation for the use of land by Bougainville Copper Ltd, a subsidiary of an Australian company. The underlying issue of independence soon emerged and conflict escalated, waged between the government of PNG and islanders, spearheaded by the Bougainville Revolutionary Army (BRA). Since 1989 an estimated 20,000 lives have been lost in the conflict. The following pre-negotiation agreements culminated in an agreement to a 'permanent and irrevocable' ceasefire, and a framework for normalization, including elections **(The Lincoln Agreement on Peace, Security, and Development on Bougainville, Lincoln, Christchurch, New Zealand, 23 January 1998)**	**Namaliu Peace Agreement, May 1989** **Bougainville Ceasefire Initiative, March 1990** **Endeavour Accords, 5 August 1990** The PNG had begun to restrict services to the island. After a declaration of independence by BRA in May 1990 an agreement was signed aboard a New Zealand warship aiming to restore services but was never implemented after arguments over whose responsibility delivery of the services was **Kavieng Agreement** **The Honiara Declaration, 23 January 1991** Signed by both the PNG and factions of the BRA, this declaration sought to annul the unilateral independence of the BRA, to restore services cut off by the blockade of Bougainville, to introduce a Multinational Supervisory Team, and to supervise the truce and handover of BRA arms and to offer an amnesty to the BRA. The deal broke down almost immediately amidst confusion over whether the BRA had accepted it or not. **Agreement between Papua New Guinea and Fiji, Tonga, Solomon Islands, Vanuatu, Australia, and New Zealand, concerning the Status of Elements of the Defence Forces of those Countries Deployed in the North Solomon Province of Papua New Guinea as Part of the South Pacific Peacekeeping Force, Suva, 28 September 1994** Agreement was reached on a ceasefire and holding of a peace conference with security by the South Pacific regional peacekeeping force. BRA leaders did not attend and in response a strong moderate movement emerged and attempted to form a bridge between the BRA and the PNG government **Charter of Mirigini for a New Bougainville, 25 November 1994** The PNG and a group which had broken away from the BRA (who boycotted the talks) signed

Place	Pre-negotiation agreements

this charter. It was agreed to form a Transitional Government for Bougainville (BTG) with power to review the Constitution. The charter was to signify a commitment to consultations and negotiations.

Waigani Communiqué, 19 May 1995
Following on from the Mirigini Charter, this agreement between PNA and members of the new BTG provided for an amnesty for surrendered BRA; for a future 'restoration programme' aimed at rehabilitation of the Bougainville economy; and for negotiations over the reopening of the coppermine. It committed to considering packages addressed at resistance forces and to establishing the permanent Bougainville government as soon as possible

Cairns Joint Communiqué, 1 December 1995
Constituted an agreement between the BTG and the Bougainville Interim Government (BIG) (a political party associated with the BRA) on how to form a joint basis for negotiations with the PNG which would lead to a comprehensive political settlement.

Memorandum of Understanding, 4 June 1996
Extended the term of the BTG and committed to discussing autonomy.

The Burnham Declaration by Bougainville Leaders on the Re-establishment of a Process for Lasting Peace and Justice on Bougainville, 5–18 July 1997, 18 July 1997 (Burnham I)
Leaders committed to a negotiation process, to ending the war, and declared a ceasefire. An agreement on the location and timing of a first meeting between Bougainville leaders and the government of PNG was agreed. The following were suggested as ingredients of the process: a UN peacekeeping force, lifting of blockade and restrictions of donors and humanitarian agencies, and ensuring that the people of Bougainville can 'freely and democratically exercise their right to determine their political future'.

TABLE 2.2. *Continued*

Place	Pre-negotiation agreements
	Burnham Truce, signed at Burnham Military Camp, New Zealand, 19 October 1997 (Burnham II) Reaffirmed and reviewed Burnham I and reached agreement on the deployment of a neutral Truce Monitoring Group to Bougainville, involving personnel from Australia, New Zealand, and other Pacific Island nations. Set an agenda for a future meeting
	Cairns Commitment on Implementation of the Agreement concerning the Neutral Regional Truce Monitoring Group (TMG) for Bougainville, 24 November 1997 Provided for operation of TMG and agreed a multi-party Peace Consultative Committee to review and assess 'implementation adherence' by signatories to the truce
Sri Lanka Ethnic–national conflict has been a feature of Sri Lankan politics since independence in 1948. In 1983 it escalated into a war fought between the government and militant Tamil nationalism, spearheaded by the Liberation Tigers of Tamil Eelam (LTTE). The war has claimed around 50,000 lives. In 1994 the new government negotiated with LTTE, and a series of understandings was reached and documented in public letters between government and LTTE. In 1995 these culminated in a 'cessation of hostilities' agreement. Talks stalled and the ceasefire broke down. While direct negotiations are no longer publicly taking	**1994–5 Correspondence between the government and the LTTE** Deals with LTTE violence, cessations of hostilities, lines of communication, how to reduce the military apparatus of the government, reconstruction of Tamil north-east areas. **Declaration of cessation of hostilities, 8 January 1995, signed by LTTE leader and president of Sri Lanka for the government** Provides for 'no offensive operations' and suggests that jointly appointed committees with international and local representation could be set up to monitor violations, seventy-two-hour notice to be given of termination of cessation **1995 Devolution proposals** **1996 Legislative draft of devolution proposals** **1997 Draft Constitution** Based on the devolution proposals, provides for establishment of regional councils, approved by local referendums, to which power would be devolved

Place	Pre-negotiation agreements
place, and no further agreement has been signed, the government has promoted devolution proposals aimed at addressing the conflict. However, Sri Lanka seems to have stalled at the pre-negotiation stage.	**The Constitution of Sri Lanka – A Bill to Repeal and replace Constitution of Sri Lanka [Bill No. 372] 3 August 2000** Again includes proposals for Tamil autonomy

Note: For sources and surrounding agreements, see Appendix.

Framework or Substantive Agreements

The second type of peace agreement can be termed 'framework or substantive' agreements. These agreements tend to be more inclusive of the main groups involved in waging the war by military means. Their emergence is often marked by a handshake moment, signifying a 'historical compromise' between enemies.

Framework–substantive agreements begin to set out a framework for resolving the substantive issues of the dispute. The agreement usually reaffirms a commitment to non-violent means for resolving the conflict; acknowledges the status of the parties in the negotiations; begins to address some of the consequences of the conflict (such as prisoners, emergency legislation, and ongoing human rights violations); provides for interim arrangements as to how power is to be held and exercised; and sets an agenda, and possibly a timetable, for reaching a more permanent resolution of substantive issues such as self-determination, democratization, armed forces–policing, rights protection, and reconstruction.

These frameworks may or may not hold. Even when signed up to by all parties, they may come to an abrupt standstill due to the death or assassination of one of the parties, as in Rwanda in 1994 and Israel in 1995, and/or a change in those in power, or a party reneging on its commitments. This triggers renegotiation as parties attempt to rework the timing or sequencing of the framework, or even start afresh. Peace processes may thus have a number of framework agreements so that the distinction between pre-negotiation agreements and framework agreements may be unclear and to some extent artificial. Examples of these framework-continuation agreements include the series of agreements in Angola, as illustrated in Table 2.4, where a series of framework agreements failed to be implemented in full, and were superseded by fighting and then by new agreements. These new agreements built on the earlier ones, but amended and expanded the framework and its timetables.

TABLE 2.3. *Examples of framework–substantive agreements*

Place	Framework agreements
Chittagong Hills Tract A conflict between indigenous–tribal peoples of the Chittagong Hills Tract region of Bangladesh and the Bangladesh government over development, respect for indigenous ways of life, and self-government. The agreement began to be implemented in 1998 when the JSS began to disarm. But anti-agreement parties opposing the Bangladesh government sparked crisis and riots, and led to the government stalling implementation of the agreement, and a peace that is at best uneasy	**Agreement between the National Committee on Chittagong Hill Tracts Constituted by the Government, and the Parbattya Chattagram Jana Samhati Samiti (JSS) 1997** Provides an affirmation of the sovereignty and territorial integrity of Bangladesh and commitment to upholding 'the political, social, cultural, educational and economic rights of all the citizens of the Chittagong Hill Tracts region' and expediting 'their socio-economic development process and preserving and developing the respective rights of all the citizens of Bangladesh.' Agreement has four main parts: (A) recognizing the region as 'tribe-inhabited', agreeing on an implementation committee to amend laws in accordance with agreement; (B) establishing a Hill District (local government) Council with specified numbers of tribal, non-tribal, male, and female members; (C) establishing a Regional Council also with specified make-up; (D) dealing with rehabilitation, general amnesties, government reparations, return of displaced persons, a mechanism for land claims, education quotas, education facilities, development assistance, non-discrimination, bank loans priority, JSS disarmament, and phased removal of government armed forces
Mindanao The conflict on this island under the jurisdiction of the Philippines began in 1970, when Philippine President Marcos declared martial law, and the Moro (or Muslim) Liberation Front (MNLF) resorted to a war of independence. Approximately 120,000 people are estimated to have died in the civil war. The Final Peace Agreement, 1996,	**Final Peace Agreement, Manila, 2 September 1996** Implements a much earlier framework agreement—1976 Tripoli Agreement between the Government of the Republic of the Philippines and the MNLF—which had unravelled within six months of being signed, but still formed a key background document. This 1996 agreement sets up a two-stage process. Phase I, lasting three years from signing, provides for the joining of MNLF elements with the Armed Forces of the Philippines. It provides for the establishment of a zone of peace which is to become the focus

Place	Framework agreements
provided a framework for autonomy, but did not end the conflict as the MNLF was not the only armed group. Later agreements were made with the Moro Islamic Liberation Front (MILF).	of intensive peace and development efforts and have investments channelled towards it. A Southern Philippines Council for Peace and Development (SPCPD) with inter-communal representation is established and government agencies responsible for peace and development are to be supervised by it. A Consultative Assembly is provided for with multi-party government, and MNLF and civic society representation. It is to address concerns, hold public hearings, and recommend policies to the SPCPD. A Joint Monitoring Committee with government and MNLF membership is to review and implement agreements. Phase II deals with the setting-up of a new regional autonomous government and provides the detail of its legislative and executive branches and its administrative system, and devolved matters. The Autonomous Area is to have a Special Regional Security Force, a multicultural integrated education system, and a Regional Economic and Development Planning Board, and can establish shariah courts

Note: For sources and surrounding agreements, see Appendix.

Implementation Agreements

The final category of peace agreements is implementation agreements, as Table 2.5 indicates. These begin to take forward and develop aspects of the framework, fleshing out their detail. The Israeli–Palestinian Interim Agreement (Oslo II) filled out and partially implemented the framework in Oslo I; the South African Final Constitution filled out and implemented the Interim Constitution.[21] By their nature implementation agreements involve new negotiations and in practice often see a measure of renegotiation as parties test whether they can claw back concessions made at an earlier stage. Implementation agreements typically include all of the parties to the framework agreement. Sometimes implementation agreements are not documented, and sometimes agreement takes other forms, such as agreed legislation.

[21] For description of agreements, see Chs. 4 (pp. 89, 84–5) and 3 (pp. 52, 50) respectively.

TABLE 2.4. *Examples of framework–continuation agreements*

Place	Framework–continuation agreements
Angola In 1991 accords were signed by the main warring parties in a thirty-year civil war between the (then government) Popular Movement for the Liberation of Angola (MPLA) and the National Union for the Total Independence of Angola (UNITA). The ceasefires and agreement did not last. The resulting conflict was temporarily brought to an end by the UN-mediated **Lusaka Protocol, 15 November 1994.** This also failed to end fighting and a new set of timetables was agreed in January 1998. Sporadic breaches of the ceasefire escalated dramatically in 1998, resulting in both parties abandoning the peace accord. But a split in UNITA led to government negotiations with UNITA-Renovada, a	**Accordos de Paz para Angola, Lisbon, 31 May 1991 (Bicesse Accords)** Ratified ceasefire and called for UNITA forces to be integrated into the Angolan Armed Forces (FAA). Prohibited both sides from purchasing new weapons; established MPLA as legitimate interim government; set a date for elections; set up UN monitoring **Lusaka Protocol, Lusaka, 15 November 1994** Formally brought an end to the third war. The protocol was mediated by the UN and was signed by MPLA and UNITA. It referred to the need for a just and lasting peace. A series of annexes dealt with the agenda of the peace talks; reaffirmation by both sides of the relevant legal instruments; military issues; police; national reconciliation; completion of the electoral process; UN mandate and role of observers; timetable for implementation **Government–UNITA Agreement on Implementation of the Lusaka Protocol, 9 January 1998** Provides a timetable for ten matters: the completion of UNITA demobilization; determination of numbers of UNITA bodyguards; demilitarization of UNITA; legalization of UNITA; promulgation of UNITA's special status; state administration; appointment of UNITA-nominated political appointees; disarming of civilians; establishment of UNITA leadership in UNITA area; ending of UNITA 'Voran' broadcasts **Agreement with UNITA-Renovada Updating the Lusaka Protocol concerning the Appointment of UNITA Cadres to Government Positions, 18 February 1999** Parties expressed new readiness to comply with Lusaka Protocol and described the current situation. Documents an agreed position that the Lusaka Protocol broke down as a result of the actions of UNITA Chairman Jonas Savimbi, and notes the election of a new UNITA leadership. The government and UNITA agreed to accept new names proposed by UNITA as governors in three provinces. Parties also agreed to allow the officials to take office as soon as circumstances allowed it

Place	Framework–continuation agreements
breakaway group, in an attempt to revive the **Lusaka Protocol** in 1999	**1999 Agreement with UNITA-Renovada Updating the Lusaka Protocol concerning a Second Round of Presidential Elections, 18 February 1999** Notes that, while elections were held on 29 and 30 September 1992, the winning candidate did not gain the requisite weighting of votes, and the second candidate prevented the second round of elections from being held. Given that a second round of elections was impossible due to the conflict, and that the UN had withdrawn from the peace process, government and UNITA agreed to consider the electoral process as concluded. Parties also agreed that the National Assembly would approve the amendments regulating this issue
	Agreement with UNITA-Renovada Updating the Lusaka Protocol concerning the Reinstatement of Government Administration over the National Territory, 18 February 1999 Agreed to consider areas not under government or UNITA control as being in the hands of organized armed groups under the leadership of Jonas Savimbi and outside the framework of the Lusaka Protocol. It was agreed that the normalization of the administration of the state under the terms of the Lusaka Protocol was concluded and that obligations should be undertaken to ensure full respect for the Angolan Constitution and for human rights. Also agreed that the organs of the state must assist populations held captive by groups under Savimbi

Note: For sources and surrounding agreements, see Appendix.

The Difficulties with the Classification

Agreements do not, of course, fit neatly into the above classification. As noted, pre-negotiation agreements often include an 'agenda-setting' element which begins to create the framework for how the process will be continued. Agreements which were intended to be substantive, but where a key party was excluded or reneged from signing, or signed and was later ousted from power, may be better thought of as pre-negotiation agreements. In some processes, for example Guatemala, the framework is very basic, and a more detailed framework and agreement is signed issue by issue, leading to a more detailed and final framework.[22] In such cases,

---

[22] See Conciliation Resources (1997). See further Appendix.

TABLE 2.5. *Examples of implementation agreements*

Place	Implementation agreements
Liberia	**Akosombo Agreement, 12 September 1994**
In 1989 the National Patriotic Front of Liberia (NPFL) launched an attack on border posts as part of a campaign to oust the dictatorship of President Samuel Doe. This triggered a war which by 1995 had killed an estimated 150,000 and displaced an estimated 850,000. The outbreak of war is attributed to the domestic socio-economic and political environment of the 1980s, such as poverty and discrimination and repression. However, its sustenance is also related to past discrimination against indigenous Liberians by 'Americo-Liberians', and deep ethnic divisions. A dozen peace accords have been acceded to, but none has established a lasting cessation of hostilities.	Clarifies and expands the definition of terms such as 'cessation' and 'disarmament' found in the Cotonou Agreement. The agreement provides much more detail on the role of the governmental branches. Remaining provisions of the Cotonou Agreement are incorporated into it.
	Accra Acceptance and Accession Agreement and Accra Clarification, 21 December 1994
	In this agreement additional parties who did not sign the Cotonou or Akosombo Agreements commit themselves to its terms. The agreement further clarifies the Akosombo Agreement. In places the clarification expands the earlier agreement. For example, the Accra Agreement sets up safe havens and buffer zones as part of the implementation of the earlier agreements
The Cotonou Accord, 25 July 1993 provided a framework for resolving the dispute, dealing with ceasefire, disarmament, demobilization, the structure of transitional government, election modalities, repatriation of refugees, and a general amnesty. Subsequent accords clarify and amend this. While fighting resumed, another ceasefire was agreed on 26 May 1996, and elections took place in 1997. The accords are framed as implementation accords, but often restate commitments, indicating the incapacity of the process to progress, owing to lack of commitment, regional instability, and factionalism	**Abuja Accord, 18 August 1995**
	Commits parties to a specific timetable for implementation of the Accra clarification. It also deals with a delay in elections by making provisions for a transitional executive for the period prior to elections, and sets limits on the tenure and mandate of the transitional government
	Supplement to the Abuja Accord, 17 August 1996
	Changes the leadership of the Council of State 'in order to enable it to perform more efficiently and creditably.' Modifies timetable to take account of delays in implementation of Abuja Accord

Note: For sources and surrounding agreements, see Appendix.

it may be a matter of debate as to whether these agreements are better classified as framework–substantive or implementing agreements. Conversely, agreements clearly aimed at implementing an earlier framework agreement may include a measure of renegotiation of the framework, and it may be a matter of dispute as to whether the new agreement primarily implements or renegotiates.

Further, as we have seen, peace processes come and go, or at least wax and wane. Today's framework agreement may become the future's prenegotiation stage. The peace agreements of Liberia, for example, while apparently being implemented and expanded on, do not seem to have addressed the root causes of the conflict, and do not have mechanisms to deal with proliferating warring factions who then need to be brought on board in subsequent agreements.[23] Past peace agreements may form a basis for incremental progress towards peace, or another approach entirely may be needed. Peace agreements seldom, however, become entirely irrelevant, forming, as they do, an important part of the history of the conflict. In Mindanao, for example, the 1976 Tripoli Agreement set out a framework for agreement which lasted approximately six months before breaking down. In 1996, in a later 'peace process', a 'Final' agreement was reached which explicitly stated the 1976 agreement to be its basis. In Northern Ireland Seamus Mallon, a long-term leading nationalist politician, famously described the Belfast Agreement as 'Sunningdale for slow learners' in a reference to a similar (unsuccessful) agreement signed in 1973.[24]

The classification is idealized. The Appendix indicates the sheer diversity of peace agreements in terms of both their context and also their form. The agreements documented include agreements in classical ethnonational disputes, transition to democracy agreements, agreements with indigenous peoples, and agreements in inter-state conflict. They come in different shapes and sizes: treaties, international agreements, constitutions, and general pacts with no clear legal status but which read more like a type of inter-group contract.[25]

Even a broad approach to peace agreements does not provide a comprehensive account of the fruit of a peace process. Agreements can be secret or unwritten. In the Israel/Palestine peace process, for example, the letters of assurance from the United States to Israel and associated newspaper reports made reference to prisoner release and US Central Intelligence Agency (CIA) involvement, as part of the deal reached at Wye.[26] However, the Wye Memorandum, which documents this deal, contains

---

[23] See Sesay (1996: 75–9).   [24] Bew and Gillespie (1999: 361).
[25] The question of the legal nature of peace agreements is returned to in Ch. 10 at pp. 304–11.   [26] See further Ch. 4, p. 90.

no references to either, and these provisions must be surmised to be secretly documented or made orally. In Northern Ireland the 'Mitchell Understanding', which led to a temporary devolution of power to the governmental structures of the Belfast Agreement in January 2000, was not released as a written agreement, but took place as a series of pre-agreed statements and actions made by the parties independently over a number of weeks.

Moreover, agreements and the issues dealt with in them are often taken forward, or implemented, in forms other than further multi-party agreements. A framework agreement may delegate an issue to a commission or independent working group (such as the Commissions on Policing and Criminal Justice established in the Belfast Agreement). Implementing legislation may contain the detail of how an issue is to be resolved in practice, as with the laws governing the electoral period from December 1993 to April 1994 in South Africa.[27]

A fuller understanding of the interrelationship of peace agreements with the broader peace process is provided by the account of the peace processes and agreements of the four case-studies provided in Chapters 3 and 4. These chapters provide a more detailed description of both agreements, other documents, and legislation, which goes some way towards illustrating the chronological relationship of agreements, legislation, and other implementing mechanisms. These chapters establish the scope of the comparison as focusing primarily on the framework agreements of the four conflicts, namely the South African Interim Constitution, the Belfast Agreement, the Israel/Palestine Declaration of Principles and successor Interim Agreements, and the Dayton Peace Agreement.

WHAT IS THE 'HUMAN RIGHTS' COMPONENT OF A PEACE AGREEMENT?

International law relates to internal conflict with an ethnic component in two main ways. First, it addresses the human rights abuses that are part and parcel of the conflict, through the application of human rights and humanitarian law standards which seek to limit how the conflict is waged. Secondly, international law's self-determination provisions, and more recently its minority rights provisions, address the issues of sovereignty, territory, and access to government which are at the heart of the conflict. The two are of course connected. A crisis as to the legitimacy of a state often leads to a cycle of repression, violent response, and repression, in which the use of force escalates and self-sustains. This type of dynamic often leads such conflicts to be protracted.

---

[27] Ch. 3, p. 47.

Examination of the human rights component of an agreement could therefore mean several things. Given that peace agreements are aimed at reducing violent conflict, in one sense the entirety of the agreement is concerned with human rights through ending the violence which took life and injured limb, and which went hand in hand with a panoply of human rights abuses. From a slightly narrower approach, in agreements which provide for a transition to democracy or an attempt to deal, at least partially, with the self-determination claims of an ethno-national group, the political arrangements for how power is to be held and exercised would seem to be a part of the 'human rights component' of the agreement.[28] Most clearly, parts of the agreement setting up specific protections of straightforward civil, political, social, economic, and cultural rights or addressing past human rights abuses are part of the human rights component of any agreement.

The difficulty in deciding what constitutes the 'human rights component' of an agreement reflects not only the intermeshing of issues in practice, but also the currently expanding remit of international human rights law. The original conception of human rights evidenced in the Universal Declaration of Human Rights has been expanded significantly. Any primacy for civil and political rights, and the liberal model of rights protection on which it is implicitly premissed, no longer stand as a good account of human rights in theory or practice.[29] A series of challenges, many arising out of 'the politics of cultural recognition', have caused shifts in the ambit of human rights law. These challenges parallel and are related to challenges made to domestic Western constitutions which, as Tully asserts, have made cultural diversity 'the characteristic constitutional problem of our time.'[30]

A few examples will illustrate. With the International Covenant on Economic, Social, and Cultural Rights 1966 came rights which required positive state action for their protection, in contrast to the primarily negative enforcement of civil and political rights. In addition to demanding new mechanisms for enforcement, these rights gave substance to Southern arguments around a right to development, which could not be housed within a civil and political rights framework. During the 1960s decolonization and self-determination were given flesh through General Assembly Resolutions and state practice. A legal right to self-determination was then included in the 1966 International Covenants.[31] The right to self-determination is a group right pertaining not to individuals but to peoples:

---

[28] While this may be more obvious with relation to ethno-national disputes (given international human rights provision for minority rights), it has also been argued that the present human rights regime in effect has moved towards granting a right to democracy; see Franck (1992), Crawford (1993). [29] Cassese (1986, 1990).
[30] Tully (1995: 1–2). [31] See Cassese (1998*b* 69–70); see further Ch. 6.

its enforcement takes human rights law more obviously and directly into the field of politics than either civil and political or even social, economic, and cultural rights. The recent proliferation of instruments relating to minorities and indigenous peoples similarly breaks down the distinction between rights as requiring discrete action, and rights as requiring particular internal institutional arrangements.

During the last decade in particular, the assertions of rights by women and racial minorities have continued to undermine the public–private divide so as to expose the politics inherent in the traditional primacy of civil and political rights.[32] These efforts, in seeking an increased role for state action, have also promoted a connection between rights and specific institutional arrangements, with the development of soft law standards that provide best practice in relation to a whole range of domestic legal matters, from domestic violence to policing structures. Finally, recognition that the state is no longer the only, or even the primary, international actor has led to attempts to subject power, wherever it lies, to human rights standards. Thus, international corporations and institutions, non-state paramilitary actors, and even individual political leaders are increasingly being brought within human rights law's ambit. Current trends show human rights law becoming more specific in its application, with increasingly specialist treaties proliferating.[33]

The expansion of human rights means that its discourse increasingly calls to account state, non-state, and individual action, increasingly comments on internal political arrangements, and increasingly provides specialist legal regimes. The expansion has in part come about as an attempt to broaden rights discourse in response to claims of cultural diversity. However, paradoxically, one consequence of the expansion has been to fuel assertions of cultural relativism which try to limit the reach of human rights. Indeed, expansion of rights discourse has fuelled human rights theory generally. Many of the philosophical debates as regards the relationship between rights and politics, long rehearsed at domestic level, have now been written large, as the relationship between human rights and new world order is interrogated.[34]

Philosophical problems aside, the expansion of human rights discourse makes it difficult to isolate the human rights component of peace agree-

[32] See e.g. Cook (1994); Romany (1993); but cf. Engle (1993).

[33] See e.g. Convention for the Protection of Human Rights and Dignity of the Human Being with regard to the Application of Biology and Medicine: Convention on Human Rights and Biomedicine 1997 (ETS No. 164); Additional Protocol on the Convention for the Protection of Human Rights and Dignity of the Human Being with regard to the Application of Biology and Medicine, on the Prohibition of Cloning Human Beings 1998 (ETS No. 168).

[34] See e.g. An-Na'im (1992); Donnelly (1989, 1994); Dunne and Wheeler (1999); Shestack (1998).

ments. In particular the inclusion of self-determination and group 'rights' blurs any distinction between the rights component of an agreement and its broader political arrangements. The very process of attempting to isolate and compare the human rights component of the chosen peace agreements serves to inform future comparative work.

It is important, however, to clarify the basis which will be used to identify 'the human rights component of a peace agreement' in this study. Human rights will be identified using customary law, and international instruments relating to first, second, and third generation rights: reference will also be made to international humanitarian law standards where relevant. The book will not be structured primarily around those divisions, but rather will deal with three types of human rights provision figuring in peace agreements: rights to self-determination or minority rights ('the deal'), building for the future (institutional protection for civil, political, social, economic, and cultural rights), and past human rights violations. Self-determination and 'minority rights' provision are fully considered, not to further debates as to whether these are properly rights or not, but because it is argued that individual rights provision can only be understood in the light of the deal's political arrangements, and because international law talks of such 'rights'.

A SITUATED COMPARATIVE ANALYSIS

The attempt to define the terms 'peace agreement', 'peace process', and 'human rights' does not end here. The remainder of the book continues to grapple with untangling the role of human rights in peace processes by examining the chosen peace agreements. The above discussion provides an initial framework for understanding the types of dilemma inherent in the project—dilemmas that are illustrative of the fraught relationship between law and politics, domestically and internationally, which the project brings under scrutiny. It also serves to set down a basis for understanding the limits of the comparison. With that in mind, we now turn to the four case-studies in question.

3

From Conflict to Peace?
South Africa and Northern Ireland

The conflicts and peace processes in South Africa and Northern Ireland were both largely internal in the sense that the international community did not directly intervene to limit the conflict or to negotiate an overall settlement.[1] The international community did of course take positions in both conflicts, and international individuals and groups played time-limited roles in negotiating discrete issues.

The process in South Africa lasted several years and followed a 'step–break–gesture–step' pattern. Concessions were made by both sides in stages, punctuated by high levels of violence and instability which at times brought public negotiations to a standstill, although behind-the-scenes negotiations often continued until a new set of compromises was reached. In Northern Ireland a similarly long, drawn-out, and halting process was concluded with a contrasting intense period of negotiations under pressure of a deadline imposed by US Senator George Mitchell, who had been brought in to chair the talks. In both South Africa and Northern Ireland the agreement reached produced a constitutional document which claimed to provide the way forward, but which required to be implemented through legislation and ongoing negotiations.

SOUTH AFRICA

The roots of the modern South African conflict are found in the British and Dutch colonization of Southern Africa, which resulted in the introduction of a white minority who soon held power in the region. The modern South African state emerged as part of a pact between the British government and the white Afrikaner minority in South Africa, creating the South African Union in 1910.[2] Its Constitution excluded all black people[3] from Parliament and denied most of them the right to

---

[1] The term 'international community' is being used to mean the action of international and regional organizations or other concerted state action.

[2] For useful histories, see Beinart (1994); Davenport (2000); de Kiewiet (1950); Nuttal *et al.* (1998); Price (1991). For specific histories of resistance, see Davis and Johns (1991); Lodge and Nasson *et al.* (1991); Mandela (1995); Marx (1992); Mayibuye Centre for History and Culture in South Africa (1994); Meli (1988).

[3] Racial terminology is problematic. In this account the term 'black' is used to mean all people of colour, and 'white' to mean non-black people. Where apartheid legislation is

vote.[4] Discrimination and white domination permeated accompanying legislation.[5] 'Apartheid'—the Afrikaans word for separateness—officially became a legislative tool after 1948 when the Afrikaner-dominated National Party (NP) came to power and extended previous policies of racial segregation and discrimination through proliferating legislation.[6] Most notably, the Population Registration Act 30 of 1950 assigned every person to a racial category, underpinning the apartheid system. By 1999 approximately 77 per cent of the population were African, 11 per cent White, 3 per cent Indian–Asian, and 9 per cent Coloured.[7]

The apartheid system was 'refined, perfected and enforced' in the 1960s under the prime ministership of H. F. Verwoerd (1958–66).[8] In particular, a homelands policy—'grand apartheid'—was developed under the pressure of international expectations with relation to self-determination and human rights.[9] The Promotion of Bantu Self-Government Act 46 of 1959 initiated a policy of consolidating eight 'homelands'.[10] Ostensibly predicated not only on separating black and white, but on separating different (black) ethnic groups from each other, the homeland system was justified as embodying a form of self-determination and being capable of leading to independent statehood. In practice, land ownership outside the homelands became virtually impossible for blacks, all of whom were ultimately intended to become citizens of their respective homelands only, and

being described, its terminology of 'Indian', 'Coloured', 'Black–African', and 'White', will be used.

[4] A small number of African and Coloured people had votes in certain regions and for certain places in the Senate and House of Assembly which formed the Parliament (although they could only vote for White people). They were gradually stripped of these. For a full explanation of the franchise and 'Constitutional development' for White male, White female, Indian, Coloured, and Black persons, see Marais (1989); for a shorter summary, see Mbeki (1992).

[5] See e.g. Mines and Works Act 1911 (institutionalized discrimination in the workplace by reserving certain jobs for whites only) and the Land Act 1913 (barred blacks from buying land outside the reserves and thereby laid the foundations for racial separation on a territorial basis).

[6] For detailed discussion of apartheid, see Ngcokovane (1989); O'Meara (1996); Posel (1991).   [7] Forgery *et al.* (1999: 6).

[8] Horowitz (1991: 11).

[9] See statement of then Prime Minister P. W. Botha, *Hansard*, 6 Feb. 1975, col. 293 ('We stand by the principle of the right to self-determination and that we want to give the peoples in Southern Africa the opportunity, without interference in the domestic affairs of one another, to come to live in a spirit of détente, each exercising its own right of self-determination'). See also then Foreign Minister Dr H. Muller, *House of Assembly Debates*, vol. 62, col. 5434 (26 Apr. 1976), cited in (1976) 2 *South African Journal of International Law* 303. For description of evolution of the homeland policy in response to international pressure, see Dugard (1980: 12–15); on the homeland policy and international law generally, see Dugard (1994: 77–9).

[10] The terminology 'homelands' was later changed to 'self-governing territories' and 'national states' depending on the degree of independence. See further, Venter (1985); Marais (1989).

foreign workers in South Africa 'proper'. The policy was expanded to ten homelands, and by 1981 through a series of incremental legislative initiatives, four of these—Transkei, Bophuthatswana, Venda, and Ciskei ('the TBVC states')—had accepted a form of independence. The other six homelands refused to accept 'full' independence, preferring to remain an essential part of South Africa.[11]

Resistance to apartheid had many faces and strategies; as Lodge writes, 'the dividing lines in Black South African politics have been as much over strategy as principle.'[12] Most famously, the African National Congress (ANC) was formed in 1912 to push for reform. During the 1950s the ANC worked in particular with the Indian Congress Movement and the South African Communist Party, which was formally banned in 1950. In 1959 a number of 'Africanists', who opposed the ANC's strategies of reform to assert policies based on a notion of 'Africa for the Africans', broke away from the ANC to form the Pan Africanist Congress (PAC). After the Sharpeville massacre in 1960, when sixty-nine people (including women and children) were shot dead by state security forces and a state of emergency was imposed, members of the ANC and their allies formed an armed wing, Umkhonto we Sizwe (Spear of the Nation, MK), stating that their only options were to 'submit or fight'.[13] During the 1960s and 1970s new organizations and movements proliferated. In particular the Black Consciousness Movement emerged in the late 1960s, and was articulated by the South African Students' Organization (SASO) with Steve Biko as its president. After its banning and the death of Biko in 1977, this movement was taken forward through the Azanian People's Organization (AZAPO), its armed wing, the Azanian National Liberation Army (AZANLA), and the Black Consciousness Movement of Azania (BCMA). The 1980s and resistance to the tricameral parliament proposed by Botha saw the emergence of the United Democratic Front (UDF), a coalition of over 600 anti-apartheid civil, church, labour, and women's organizations which organized mass mobilization.[14]

Moving towards a Peace Process?

During the 1980s President P. W. Botha (1979–89) attempted to move from policies of complete exclusion to ones of limited political and institutional accommodation, in particular through the promulgation of the 1983

---

[11] The other self-governing territories reaching various degrees of autonomy were: Gazankulu, previously known as Mashangana Territorial Authority, Kangwange, KwaNdebele, KwaZulu, Lebowa, and QwaQwa. See further, Marais (1989: 240) and Venter (1985). For a detailed list of the 'homeland' legislation for the TBVC states, see Interim Constitution Schedule 7.   [12] Lodge and Nasson *et al.* (1991: 27).
[13] Lodge and Nasson *et al.* (1991: 6).   [14] Lodge and Nasson *et al.* (1991).

Constitution with a tricameral Parliament.[15] This Parliament established three houses, for White, Coloured, and Indian groups respectively, each of whom would legislate on its 'own' affairs with 'general' legislation subject to the veto power of the White House of Assembly.[16] These reforms left untouched the central pillars of the apartheid system and were predicated on racial classification. Most fundamentally they did not address the denial of access to government of black Africans. The tricameral system did not dissipate opposition to apartheid but rather galvanized it. Boycotts of the elections were effective, and the new Constitution precipitated widespread revolt against the South African government of the mid-1980s. The remainder of the 1980s saw increasing cycles of revolt, repression, and increasing violence. While the ANC set about making the country 'ungovernable', the government responded with states of emergency. Towards the end of the 1980s most commentators were pessimistic about the possibilities for effective change.[17] Unknown to them at that time, the initial steps of what was to become the peace process had already occurred.

The Positions of the Domestic Players

Immediately prior to the peace process at the end of the 1980s there were four main positions reflected by the major players which required to be negotiated.[18] First, the official view of the South African government, as exhibited above. Under this view, South Africa was a society divided into four racial groups (Whites, Coloureds, Indians, and Africans), and within these groups into a number of distinct ethnic groups or nationalities. The government's proposed solution included the idea of an element of participation in politics of most, and perhaps even all, of the ethnic groups at the centre, with some form of power over 'separate' matters devolved to each racial (and perhaps ethnic) group. This devolution of power could be linked to specific territory, in the form of self-governing, or perhaps federated, homelands. The government view can only be stated vaguely as from the 1980s, and in particular after the experiment of the 1983 Constitution, it began to mutate in its detail.[19]

The second position was the Charterist position exhibited by the ANC, as broadly reflected in the language of its Freedom Charter adopted in 1955. Under this view the problem with South Africa was apartheid,

[15] Republic of South Africa Constitution Act 110 of 1983.
[16] See further Marais (1989: 252–71).
[17] Azar and Burton (1986); Guelke (1991).
[18] Horowitz (1991: 1–41). In fact Horowitz documents twelve South Africas, which he suggests can be reduced to the four mentioned above, although this oversimplifies the positions adopted.   [19] Ibid.

which both created and sustained ethnic divisions and denial of human rights. The Freedom Charter proclaimed that 'South Africa belongs to all who live in it, black and white.'[20] The central plank of the ANC solution was the abolition of apartheid and its replacement with a non-racial and non-ethnic multi-party democracy.

The third position was the Africanist view, which was reflected by the PAC and later the black consciousness movement. From this perspective the problem of South Africa was 'settler colonialism' and racially based capitalism. The prescription was anti-colonial revolution leading to a socialist state, and the return of land to indigenous African owners. In the new state 'settlers' would either have no role, or in some formulations could become Africans 'by means unspecified.'[21]

The fourth position was a consociational view exhibited most strongly in the policies of Inkatha and Chief Mangosuthu Buthelezi. Under this view, South Africa was a divided society with both racial and ethnic divisions. While democracy was not impossible, it could only be achieved by designing an elaborate consociational pact between these groups. Centrally, this would include elites from various groups sharing executive power and abiding by a system of mutual vetoes, with spheres of communal authority.

The International Community and International Law

Even prior to the NP government of 1948, the United Nations had begun to address apartheid from the viewpoint of discrimination against citizens of Indian origin.[22] As the modern law of self-determination evolved, so the international community repeatedly endorsed its application to South Africa. Both the General Assembly and the Security Council passed repeated resolutions endorsing the rights of self-determination of the South African people, and rejecting the establishment of 'bantustans' as contrary to that right, and calling for their non-recognition.[23] Dugard notes that while the TBVC states arguably met the criteria for statehood, no state other than South Africa gave them recognition. He notes four

[20] Freedom Charter, June 1955, repr. in Amien and Farlam (1998: 158–61).

[21] Horowitz (1991: 6).

[22] GA Res 44(I), 8 Dec. 1946 (a resolution of the General Assembly after considering a request of the government of India). This item was examined regularly until 1962, when it was merged with the question of apartheid, GA Res 1761(XVII), 6 Nov. 1962. See Dugard (1994a: 201).

[23] See e.g. UN GA Res 31/6, 26 Oct. 1976; UN GA Res 2775 E (XXVI), 28 Nov. 1971; UN SC Res 392, 19 June 1976; UN SC Res 402, 22 Dec. 1976; UN SC Res 407, 25 May 1977; UN SC Res 417, 31 Oct. 1977; see also S/13549 (1979) 16/6 *UN Monthly Chronicle* 32. For self-determination and South Africa, see generally Cassese (1998b: 124–5); Klug (1990: 253–76); McCorquodale (1992, 1994b).

principal reasons: first, that TBVC state independence violated the territorial integrity of South Africa as a whole; secondly, that this political status was not determined 'freely' by the people of South Africa by election; thirdly, that the policy furthered the goal of apartheid which had been characterized as contrary to international law; and finally, that the policy's implementation involved further denial of human rights.[24] While the international community had a clear position on the right to self-determination for South African people and what would *not* satisfy it, it did not prescribe precisely what *would* satisfy the right.[25] Examination of the evolutionary trends in self-determination law, however, led commentators to suggest the types of formula which would at least be consistent with the norm, if not mandated by it.[26]

The laws and practices of apartheid also brought South Africa into conflict with international law's individual rights norms.[27] However, until 1994 the South African government did not sign any international human rights conventions and was only party to one treaty dealing with human rights, namely the Charter of the United Nations, which provides only very general references to human rights.[28] This meant that the only way of holding the South African government accountable was under the UN Charter and such customary law standards as existed. Domestically, under South Africa's dualist approach, treaties and customary law were not directly incorporated into domestic law, but were supposedly to be used as an interpretative aid. However, in practice, as Dugard noted, 'International Law received no constitutional recognition and was largely ignored by courts and lawyers' although it was occasionally applied in 'politically neutral' matters.[29] Therefore, internal legal strategies against apartheid were limited to working within the deeply problematic apartheid legal system, a matter which generated ongoing moral dilemmas for anti-apartheid lawyers as to whether and how to participate, or not.[30]

Internationally the most effective enforcement machinery for human rights at the UN's disposal would have been under Chapter VII of the UN Charter. This requires denial of human rights to reach such proportions that it constitutes a threat to international peace.[31] Under Chapter VII the

[24] Dugard (1994a: 79–81). It can further be argued that this form of 'decolonization' violated the *uti possedetis* rule; see Dugard (1980); McCorquodale (1992, 1994b).

[25] See Cassese (1998b: 319–20, 331).

[26] See McCorquodale (1994b: 14–20). For further description, see below Ch. 6, p. 171.

[27] See Dugard (1992b, 1994a: 198–230; 1997c: 270–5).

[28] Articles 13, 55, 56 Charter of the United Nations 1945.

[29] Dugard (1997a: 77); see further Dugard (1986, 1994a, 1998).

[30] See Abel (1995); Corder (1989); Dysenhaus (1998); Hajjar (1997).

[31] Article 39 ('The Security Council shall determine the existence of any threat to the peace, breach of the peace, or act of aggression and shall make recommendations, or decide what measures shall be taken in accordance with Articles 41 and 42, to maintain or restore international peace and security').

Security Council could have made legally binding directions to states to take non-force- (such as sanctions) and force-based actions. However, this was always unlikely, owing to the veto power of the most powerful nations, and indeed the United States and Britain, in particular, repeatedly vetoed such moves. In fact, the Security Council, with the exception of one resolution in 1977 (limiting sale of arms to South Africa), adopted its resolutions under Chapter VI of the charter, which empowers it to make recommendations to address disputes which do not threaten international peace but which are likely to do so if continued.[32] Therefore, UN human rights redress was left to more piecemeal devices. In addition to the Chapter VI Security Council Resolutions, these devices included repeated resolutions of the General Assembly and, where the matter came before it, judgments of the International Court of Justice.[33]

The South African situation did, however, produce new international legal reponses. In 1973 the General Assembly adopted an International Convention on the Suppression and Punishment of the Crime of Apartheid, which denounced apartheid as a crime against humanity in violation of international law. As the South African government (unsurprisingly) did not ratify the convention, and no prosecutions were instituted under it, its effect was symbolic. In 1974 the General Assembly excluded South Africa from participation in its work, after a finding that the NP government was not representative of the people of South Africa and therefore did not have credentials to represent South Africa at the General Assembly.[34] The South African situation further influenced international law in 1977 when additional Protocol I to the Geneva Conventions of 1949 extended the application of the conventions to include within their definition of international conflict, 'armed conflicts in which people are fighting against colonial domination, and alien occupation and against racist régimes in the exercise of their right of self-determination'.[35] This provision was directed largely at South Africa and Israel, who did not sign the protocol. However, both the ANC and the PLO attempted to accede to the protocol. The ANC deposited declarations of acceptance with the president of the International Red Cross.[36]

[32] SC Res 418 (1977) was made under Chapter VII; see further Dugard (1994a: 297–329).

[33] South Africa appeared before the court six times over South-West Africa–Namibia; see Dugard (1973, 1994a: 279–96).

[34] In a decision of 5 Oct. 1973 the General Assembly decided to reject the credentials of the representatives of South Africa (72 for, 37 against, 13 abstentions). The Assembly acted by adopting a Syrian amendment to a report by the Credentials Committee, which had stated that the credentials of South Africa were in order. Official Records of the General Assembly, Twenty-Eighth Session, Supplement No. 30 (A/9030) at 10, item 3.

[35] Article 1(4) Protocol Additional to the Geneva Conventions of 12 August 1949, and relating to the Protection of Victims of International Armed Conflicts (Protocol I), 1977.

[36] (1981) 220 *International Review of the Red Cross* 20; Article 96(3) Protocol I provides for national liberation movements to deposit declarations of acceptance with the Swiss Federal Council. For PLO and accession, see Ch. 4, p. 77.

Although the international community's anti-apartheid bark was worse than its bite, its bark was still important. As Asmal *et al.* point out, the international law positions had a normative quality which was 'independent of the international community's actual resources of enforcement, or its fluctuating inclination to enforce them.' They argue that '[e]ven in rare periods, when, for whatever reasons of *realpolitik* or simple distraction, global anti-apartheid forces flagged, the laws and norms still spoke clearly.'[37] In particular, the international community's clear articulation (if not enforcement) of a moral position helped to underwrite the ANC's effective international boycott campaign, and engender the support of other governments for it.[38] The international illegitimacy of the South African government affected its status and ultimately its bargaining power when it responded by pursuing a path of negotiations.

The Peace Process and its Agreements

The minutiae of the South African peace process are well documented and what follows is merely a broad map.[39] The peace process had its beginnings in the late 1980s with a series of secret meetings between ANC leader Nelson Mandela, then a prisoner, and the NP government of the time.[40] These talks focused on creating a degree of agreement about the parameters of any talks and the requirements necessary for them to take place. In 1989 the ANC had adopted a set of principles setting out their conditions for direct negotiations with the government in the Harare Declaration.[41] This position was broadly similar to the one adopted by

---

[37] Asmal *et al.* (1997: 203).

[38] See ANC web site discussion of boycotts: www.anc.org.za/ancdos/history/#Boycotts (last visited 19 Nov. 1999); see also McCrudden (1999a) (detailed discussion of the Sullivan Principles in the United States); and the US Comprehensive Anti-Apartheid Act 1986.

[39] For fuller accounts, see African National Congress Department of Political Education (1996); Ebrahim (1998); Friedman (1993); Friedman and Atkinson (1994); Guelke (1999); Hough and Du Plessis (1994); Sisk (1995); Southall (1990); Sparks (1996); Waldmeir (1997).

[40] See 'A document presented by Nelson Mandela to P. W. Botha before their meeting on 5 July 1989' ('Mandela Document') (available at www.anc.org.za/ancdocs/history/transition, last visited 1 Dec. 1999).

[41] 'Harare Declaration': Declaration of the Organization of African Unity Ad-Hoc Committee on Southern Africa on the Question of South Africa, Harare, Zimbabwe, 21 August 1989 (available at www.anc.org.za/ancdocs/history/transition, last visited 1 Dec. 1999). This declaration was based on an earlier draft of ANC President Oliver Tambo. It set out the following conditions for negotiation: unconditional release of all political prisoners and detainees without restriction; lifting all bans and restrictions on all proscribed and restricted organizations and people; removing all troops from townships; ending the state of emergency and repealing all repressive legislation; ceasing all political executions. It also stated the goals of the Organization of African Unity (and the ANC) for a negotiated settlement, and proposed a process whereby 'talks about talks' would try to 'achieve the suspension of hostilities on both sides by agreeing to a mutually binding ceasefire' followed by

Mandela in the secret talks and was subsequently used by him in articulating his position to then President F. W. de Klerk.[42] Several years of these secret talks led to the public emergence of the peace process, most notably on 2 February 1990, when in the opening session of Parliament de Klerk dramatically announced a package of measures meeting some of the ANC's concerns, such as: the lifting of bans and restrictions from many organizations (including the ANC, the PAC, and the SACP), indemnities for returning exiles, and a stated intention to release Nelson Mandela unconditionally.[43] This speech, while not fully complying with the Harare Declaration, enabled the ANC to meet the government to talk about the preconditions for negotiations, and thus marked the beginning of direct government–ANC negotiations.

The peace process from this point can be loosely categorized in three stages. First, the 'talks about talks', which had begun during the secret meetings and were negotiated with public knowledge from February 1990 to December 1991. This period saw a 'stop and start' process during which a number of bilateral accords were reached between the ANC and the government, and one between the ANC and the IFP. These agreements culminated in the National Peace Accord of 14 September 1992, signed by over forty groups. These agreements are summarized in Table 3.1. They were aimed at limiting violence and preventing either side from using negotiations to achieve military advantage; but also served to shape and scope the talks to follow.

The second phase was the multi-party talks, first at the Convention for a Democratic South Africa (CODESA I), which met from December 1991 until its second round (CODESA II) broke down in May 1992; and then at the multi-party negotiating talks commencing in March 1993, which culminated in the adoption of the Interim Constitution in November 1993, paving the way for the first democratic elections. Although the multi-party talks broke down several times in the face of violence, a number of preliminary agreements were reached, some formally documented, some not. These talks operated using an NP–ANC agreed device known as 'sufficient consensus', which meant that where consensus decision-making proved impossible the chair could judge whether there was sufficient agreement among opposing parties to allow negotiations to move forward. In practice this meant that at least the NP and the ANC had to

---

a process to agree a new Constitution and an interim government which would effect the transition to democracy and elections.

[42] 'A document to create a climate of understanding, document forwarded by Nelson Mandela to F. W. de Klerk', 12 Dec. 1989; pub. in Ebrahim (1998: 458–65).

[43] Address by the State President, Mr F. W. de Klerk, DMS, at the Opening of the Second Session of the Ninth Parliament of the Republic of South Africa, Cape Town, 2 Feb. 1990; pub. in Ebrahim (1998: 466–84).

TABLE 3.1. *Written pre-negotiation agreements*

Agreement and parties	Parties	Content
Groote Schuur Minute, 4 May 1990	ANC and South African government (SAG)	Common commitment to ending violence. SAG committed to moving towards Harare Declaration demands. ANC committed to language curtailing its ability to use armed action (but not to withdrawal of the armed struggle). Established working group to take issues forward[a]
Pretoria Minute, 6 August 1990	ANC and SAG	SAG accepted report of working group and moved towards a plan for release of prisoners and granting of indemnity. ANC suspended 'all armed actions with immediate effect.' Agreement also addressed violence in Natal, state of emergency, and review of security legislation. Affirmed joint commitment to negotiations
Royal Hotel Minute, 29 January 1991	ANC and IFP	Aimed to address increasing violence in Natal region and tensions between IFP, ANC, and SAG security forces. Both parties committed to ending violence. Grass-roots committees established to implement this.
DF Malan Accord, 12 February 1991	ANC and SAG (accord was produced by working group set up in Pretoria Minute and endorsed by Mandela and de Klerk)	Both parties committed to non-violent, democratic process. Main role of agreement was to further define the ANC ceasefire. Unable to agree on detail, so liaison committee set up to continue working
National Peace Accord, 14 September 1991	ANC, SAG, IFP, trade unions, and over forty diverse organizations	Aimed at 'stabilization' and the 'common goal' of establishing 'multi-party democracy in South Africa.' Detailed provision was made in ten chapters to address ongoing violence, and in particular the role of the police. The package also included socio-economic reconstruction; a Commissionof Inquiry regarding the

Agreement and parties	Parties	Content
		Prevention of Public Violence and Intimidation; a National Peace Secretariat, and Committee; regional and local dispute resolution committees; and special criminal courts

Note: The following agreements are published in Cooper *et al.* (1993, apps. A, 512; B, 513–15; E, 519–21; and F, 522–56 respectively). Agreement was also reached in Mar. 1991 between the South African government and the United Nations High Commissioner for Refugees (UNHCR) that UNHCR would have a role in repatriation of political exiles. The UNHCR facilitated the signing of an agreement by the SAG for the repatriation of 'any South African refugee and/or political exile who returns voluntarily to South Africa as an unarmed civilian.' The agreement contained detailed definitions and procedures; Memorandum of Understanding on the Voluntary Repatriation and Reintegration of South African Returnees, 4 Sept. 1991; pub. in (1992) 31 I.L.M. 526.

[a] Text of working group report pub. in Ebrahim (1998: 488–92).

agree.[44] Of interest also is that in March 1992 de Klerk held a whites-only referendum on the pursuit of negotiated settlement, to stave off a right-wing challenge that he was acting without mandate.[45] He won with a 69 per cent majority, but immediately the NP toughened its negotiating stance, contributing to the breakdown of CODESA.

By June 1993 a framework had begun to emerge which was to evolve into the Constitution of the Republic of South Africa 1993 often known as the Interim or Transitional Constitution. This Constitution was to govern the interim period until the drafting of a Final Constitution. The drafting of this Final Constitution would be constrained so as to accord with agreed Constitutional Principles, which were laid out in the Interim Constitution. In September 1993 Parliament enacted the package of legislation dealing with elections and transitional governance, providing impetus to the negotiations.[46] On 17 November 1993 a rush of bilateral agreements led to endorsement of the Interim Constitution, which was adopted into statute by the tricameral Parliament in December 1993.

The agreement had not, however, been complete. The increasing desire

[44] This model of decision-making was challenged by the IFP in the Transvaal Division of the Supreme Court, which found that 'it would be inappropriate for the court to interfere in a political process which is still far from being completed.' *Kwazulu Government* v. *Mahlangu* 1994 (1) SA 626 (T).

[45] The question asked was 'Do you support the continuation of the reform process which the state president began on 2 February 1990 and which is aimed at a new constitution through negotiation?' (Cooper *et al.* 1993: 418).

[46] The Transitional Executive Council Act 151 of 1993, the Independent Media Commission Act 148 of 1993, and the Independent Electoral Commission Act 150 of 1993; the Independent Broadcasting Authority Act 153 of 1993 and the Electoral Act 202 of 1993.

TABLE 3.2. *Preliminary agreements reached in multi-party negotiations*

Agreement	Parties	Content
CODESA Declaration of Intent, 21 December 1991	ANC, South African Communist Party, NP/SAG, Democratic Party, and twelve other homeland governments or political groupings. (Not signed by AZAPO, Conservative Party, IFP, or PAC)	Stated goals of talks to be 'a united democratic, non-racial, non-sexist state in which sovereign authority is exercised over the whole of its territory.' Set out six broad principles which prefigured a broad framework for agreement
Record of Understanding, 26 September 1992	ANC and SAG	Agreement to recommence negotiations after breakdown and ANC withdrawal. Agreed the beginnings of a blueprint for agreement. In particular, agreed that an elected, democratic constitution-making body bound by constitutional principles negotiate a constitution within a fixed time frame. This body would also act as an interim Parliament with no constitutional hiatus. Further matters related to limiting violence were also agreed
SAG and ANC joint proposal, 12 February 1993	SAG and ANC	Joint proposal for power-sharing and the establishment of a five-year interim Government of National Unity after election of a Constituent Assembly. The interim government proposal was later endorsed by ANC National Executive Council, which rejected the NP proposal of consensus executive decisions or veto powers for minorities

Note: First three published in Ebrahim (1998: 529–31, 588–94). NP/SAG joint proposal described and analysed in Battersby (1993); the precursor to ANC thinking on this can be seen in Slovo (1992).

and cooperation of the South African government and the ANC to reach agreement had alienated in particular Buthelezi and the IFP, who during the multi-party negotiation talks had formed an alliance with the right-wing white Conservative Party and two of the four nominally independent homelands, Ciskei and Bophuthatswana. They called themselves Concerned South Africans Group (COSAG) and in particular demanded 'federalism' and 'self-determination' in what seemed to amount to a claim for secession. Until the elections on 27 April 1994 the ANC and the NP continued efforts to persuade these groups to become involved in the elections. After a violent and tense March a series of amendments was passed aimed at accommodating the demands of these groups by providing for more extensive provincial legislative and revenue-raising powers; for further restraints on a future Parliament's competence to legislate concurrently in areas of provincial competence; and for a Volkstaat Council and a further constitutional principle enshrining a right to self-determination.[47] As the election date approached, all but the IFP and the Afrikaner Volksfront agreed to participate. At the eleventh hour a further undertaking by the ANC and the NP to 'recognize and protect the institution status and role of the constitutional position of the king of the Zulus and the Kingdom of KwaZulu' enshrined in a constitutional amendment, and to provide a double ballot system (provincial and national), induced the IFP to enter fully into the electoral process.[48] After failed white right-wing military action, General Constand Viljoen of the Afrikaner Volkstaat at the last minute registered the Freedom Front as a party for the elections.

South Africa's first democratic elections were held as planned on 27 April 1994. The ANC won 62.7 per cent, the NP 20.4 per cent, IFP 10.6 per cent while other parties made up around 7 per cent. The NP won a majority in Western Cape Province, and the IFP in KwaZulu–Natal, with the ANC winning a majority in the other seven provinces.

The final stage in the process was the implementation stage. After the elections the democratically elected Constitutional Assembly drafted a Final Constitution in accordance with Constitutional Principles agreed in the Interim Constitution, and after an extensive public consultation exercise.[49] The resulting Final Constitution required to be 'certified' by the new Constitutional Court as complying with Constitutional Principles set out in the Interim Constitution. The first time around, the court rejected the Constitution as not complying with the Constitutional Principles in eight respects, most significantly through its over-reduction of provincial

[47] Constitution of the Republic of South Africa Amendment Act 2 1994. See further Ch. 5, pp. 132–4.
[48] Constitution of the Republic of South Africa Second Amendment Act 3 of 1994.
[49] See Ebrahim (1998: 189–221, 239–50); Nicol (1997).

TABLE 3.3. *Written substantive–framework agreements*

Agreement	Parties	Content
Constitution of the Republic of South Africa, 1993 (200 of 1993) (Interim Constitution)	All major political stakeholders and parties excluding (until after agreements below) right-wing Afrikaner groups and IFP	Complex document (255 pages), which provided for universal adult suffrage in a quasi-federal state, with a justiciable Bill of Rights and an institutionalized multi-party system of government designated as a Government of National Unity and guaranteed to last a period of five years. The detail provided for eleven official languages, and language rights; constitutional supremacy; citizenship and the franchise; a bill of individual rights; and an integrated defence and centralized police force. The Constitution was established as transitory in nature and provided for a final constitution to be drafted subject to agreed Constitutional Principles. It delineated the interim structures of government (national, provincial, and local and traditional authorities); structure of judiciary; finance; public service; policing; and defence. The Constitution also contained copious detail on transitional matters
Accord on Afrikaner self-determination, 23 April 1994 (already incorporated as Constitution amendment)	Freedom Front (newly formed), ANC, and SAG	Agreement to address Afrikaner self-determination including the concept of a Volkstaat
Memorandum of agreement for reconciliation and peace between the IFP/KwaZulu government and the ANC and the South African government/NP, 16 April 1994 (incorporated as Constitutional amendment)	IFP, SAG, and ANC	Agreement to 'recognise and protect the institution, status and role of the constitutional position of the King of the Zulus and the Kingdom of KwaZulu' and to provide for this in a constitutional amendment. Statement that all parties reject violence and 'will therefore do everything in their power to ensure free and fair elections'

Note: Copies of the two accords are published in Ebrahim (1998: 613–18).

powers.[50] The Constitution was duly amended and successfully certified.[51] During the period between Interim and Final Constitutions, legislation was designed implementing many of the structures as agreed to in the Interim Constitution, such as the Commission for Gender Equality, the South African Human Rights Commission, and new policing structures.[52] The Government of National Unity, however, collapsed in June 1996, when the NP withdrew. The Final Constitution of the Republic of South Africa 1996 (108 of 1996) reads as an elegant and 'constitutional' document, laying down the broad principles which inform the institutions but leaving their specifics to legislation; it stands in contrast to the contract-like, all-inclusive detail of the Interim Constitution.

NORTHERN IRELAND

The history of the conflict in Northern Ireland reaches back to the colonial military conquest of Ireland by England in 1169 and subsequent 'plantation' in the early 1600s, during which hundreds of thousands of (Protestant) settlers were offered land to move from England and lowland Scotland to Ireland, where they displaced native Irish (Catholics) predominantly in the north-east of the country.[53] However, the story can be started, as in the case of South Africa, in the early twentieth century. During the late nineteenth century Irish pressure for home rule and independence had led the British government to respond in the form of home rule bills.[54] By the early twentieth century large numbers of Protestants, in particular from the north-east of Ireland, where they were in greatest numbers, mobilized militarily to oppose home rule. Events in the rest of Ireland, notably the Republican Easter Rising of 1916 and the general election of 1918 (in which Sinn Féin won a majority of votes on an independence platform), had made it clear that the demands of Irish nationalists could not be effectively resisted. The British government, under pressure from conflicting communal and paramilitary demands, decided to partition the island. They established six of the counties of the north-east province of Ulster as a unit of government. Northern Ireland's borders

---

[50] *Ex Parte Chairperson of the Constitutional Assembly: In re Certification of the Constitution 1996*, 1996 (4) SA 744 (CC); 1996 (10) BCLR 1253 (CC).

[51] *Ex Parte Chairperson of the Constitutional Assembly: In re Certification of the Amended Text of the Constitution of the Republic of South Africa, 1996*, 1997 (2) SA 97 (CC); 1997 (1) BCLR 1 (CC). The amended text is Act 108 of 1996. See also Butler (1997); Henderson (1996).

[52] Pan-South African Language Board Act 59 of 1995; South African Police Service Act 68 of 1995; Commission on Gender Equality Act 39 of 1996; Human Rights Commission Act No. 54 of 1994.　　　　　　　　　　　　　　　　　　[53] Foster (1988); Stewart (1977).

[54] For history and accounts of the conflict, see Bardon (1992); Bew *et al.* (1996); B. O'Brien (1995).

TABLE 3.4. *Final Constitution as implementation agreement*

Agreement	Parties	Content
The Constitution of the Republic of South Africa Act 108 of 1996 ('Final Constitution')	Passed by Constituent Assembly according to interim constitution provisions	Many provisions are similar to Interim Constitution, but detail is left to legislation with general principles provided by Constitution. Bill of Rights contains additional social and economic rights. Details of provincial–central powers are slightly different. Second chamber (Senate) is renamed National Council of Provinces

were essentially determined to ensure the largest area geographically which could be comfortably held with a (mainly Protestant) majority of around 66 per cent in favour of the union with Britain, although it also contained a (mainly Catholic) minority of around 34 per cent, who did not wish to be separated from the rest of the island. Since that time demographic changes have meant that by 1991 there were approximately 38 per cent Catholics, 50.5 per cent Protestants, 0.5 per cent 'other' and 11 per cent who did not state, or stated no religion.[55]

The Government of Ireland Act 1920, which legislated partition, made detailed provision for a regional Northern Ireland Parliament and government modelled on the Westminster Parliament, but with legislative powers limited and subject to review in the courts.[56] It had been contemplated that this would be paralleled by a Parliament in the South, but events, including partition itself, overtook this. Instead, a treaty was signed between Britain and Ireland which led to the establishment of the twenty-six-county Irish Free State, with dominion status.[57] The signing of this treaty led to bitter civil war within the Free State counties between pro- and anti-treaty forces. In 1937 the Irish Free State established a Constitution which laid claim to the entire territory of Ireland.[58] Articles 2 and 3 effectively claimed sovereignty over the entire country, providing that the 'national territory consists of the whole island of Ireland, its islands and the territorial sea', but that 'pending the reintegration of the national territory' the laws of the Dáil (Irish Parliament) would apply within the

---

[55] Department of Health and Social Services Registrar-General (1993) xvi. 1991 Census for Republic of Ireland showed religious breakdown in that jurisdiction to be 92% Catholic, 3% Protestant, 1% other, and 4% did not state or stated 'no religion' (see www.cso.ie/ , last visited 9 May 2000). Island-wide there are approximately 75% Catholics, 18% Protestants, 9% others, and 6% did not state or stated 'no religion'.

[56] See generally Hadfield (1989, 1992: 1–12).

[57] Articles of Agreement for a Treaty between Great Britain and Ireland, 21 Dec. 1921, Cmnd. 1534.   [58] Constitution of Ireland 1937.

MAP 3.1. Ireland, showing Northern Ireland and the Republic of Ireland

Irish Free State. In 1949 the Irish Free State left the Commonwealth, becoming a republic.

The partition arrangement, still the subject of intense historical controversy, resulted in almost fifty years of unionist government in Northern Ireland with Irish Republican Army (IRA) campaigns in the 1920s, 1930s, 1940s and 1950s. Relative political stability was at the expense of the interests and aspirations of Northern nationalists, whose political and economic interests were subordinated to those of the dominant Protestant–British unionist community through gerrymandering and other inequalities in access to voting; unfairness in the allocation of public housing; discrimination in public and private employment, policing, and emergency law; and political bias on the part of (particularly) the magistrates and county court judges.[59]

The failure of the Northern Ireland state to provide equally for Protestants and Catholics culminated in 1967 in the establishment of the Northern Ireland Civil Rights Association, which pushed for reform of state

[59] A series of commissions was established over a number of years to investigate these claims and address the rising violence; see *Disturbances in Northern Ireland: Report of the Cameron Commission*, Cmnd. 532 (Belfast: HMSO, 1969); Hunt Report, *Report of the Advisory Committee on Police in Northern Ireland*, Cmnd. 535 (Belfast: HMSO, 1969); Scarman Report, *Violence and Civil Disturbances in Northern Ireland in 1969*, Cmnd. 566 (Belfast: HMSO, 1972); Diplock Report, *Report of the Commission to Consider Legal Procedures to Deal with Terrorist Activities in Northern Ireland*, Cmnd. 5185 (London: HMSO, 1972); *Report and Recommendations of the Working Party on Discrimination in the Private Sector of Employment* (Belfast: HMSO, 1973).

structures, using the model of the civil rights campaign in the United States. Responses by the Northern Ireland Parliament, on its own initiative or prompted by Westminster, to reform state institutions such as local elections, policing, and local government, proved too little too late for much of the Catholic/nationalist population and a bridge too far for much of the Protestant/unionist one. As inter-communal violence escalated and the state neared collapse, the British army was deployed on 12 August 1969, and soon added impetus to the revival of the republican movement and the IRA, and later the Provisional Irish Republican Army (IRA). By the end of 1972, having introduced 'internment' (detention without trial) in 1971 and against a rising death toll, the Northern Ireland Parliament was suspended by the British government, and all legislative and executive powers were transferred to Westminster for 'direct rule'.[60] In 1973 the Sunningdale Agreement was reached between unionists and nationalists together with the British and Irish governments, providing for devolution with power-sharing, and also an Irish dimension to government in Northern Ireland through a Council of Ireland and a North–South Consultative Assembly.[61] In 1974 a Northern Ireland Assembly with a power-sharing executive was established, but lasted only five months before a unionist workers' strike and related events led to its downfall and the reimposition of direct rule.

Moving towards a Peace Process?

Throughout the next twenty years a war of attrition developed. British attempts to address issues seen to be at the heart of the conflict, such as discrimination against Catholics, were combined with different 'anti-terrorist' strategies, including the extensive use of emergency legislation which impacted disproportionately on the (Catholic) nationalist population.[62] Perhaps one of the most significant constitutional developments during this time was the signing of the 1985 Anglo-Irish Agreement between the British and Irish governments, which gave the Republic of Ireland government a limited consultative role in the administration of the North.[63] Despite a strong unionist backlash, it formed the starting-point for joint British–Irish policy initiatives on the North. This began to lay the framework for the 'three-strand' approach which was to underpin the Belfast Agreement, whereby agreement was sought on (i) relation-

[60] Northern Ireland (Temporary Provisions) Act 1972.

[61] The Northern Ireland Constitution Act 1973 provided the legislative framework for the Northern structures, reaffirming in section 1 the Constitutional commitment of section 75 of the Government of Ireland Act 1920.

[62] See Livingstone (1990) (arguing that the efforts to inspire positive social change of the former were undermined by the counter effects of the latter). Cf. also McCrudden (1994).

[63] Boyle and Hadden (1989). This had similarities with the Sunningdale Agreement's Irish dimension.

ships within Northern Ireland, (ii) relationships between Northern Ireland and the Republic of Ireland, and (iii) relationships between the British and Irish governments.

The Positions of the Domestic Players

While the British and more recently the Irish governments have presented themselves as mediators in the conflict, they are clearly also participants. Prior to the current process the British government position regarding Northern Ireland, as stated in both the Government of Ireland Act 1920 and the Northern Ireland Constitution Act 1973, was that Northern Ireland was a part of the United Kingdom, and should remain so as long as a majority wanted it to.[64] In contrast, the Irish government continued its sovereign claim on the territory of Northern Ireland through Articles 2 and 3 of its Constitution.

These conflicting British and Irish constitutional claims underwrote the conflicting national aspirations of Irish nationalists (mostly Catholic) and British unionists (mostly Protestant), which were seen as the key positions to be negotiated in any settlement.[65] Unionists, represented mainly through the Ulster Unionist Party (UUP) (current leader David Trimble) and the more extreme but smaller Democratic Unionist Party (DUP) (leader Ian Paisley), wanted to keep the union with Britain although both were divided on whether the better structure was full political integration with Britain, or some form of regional devolution such as existed prior to direct rule.[66] Neither Ulster Unionists nor DUP put forward power-sharing or other constraints as desirable in any new devolved structures (although both deemed a Bill of Rights as acceptable). Loyalist paramilitaries also supported union with Britain, although at times they contemplated an independent Ulster, or a redefinition of the border to increase the Protestant majority, as alternatives. All these groups viewed IRA violence, coupled with British government lack of interest and (at least tacit) Irish government support, as the problem at the heart of the conflict. Immediately prior to the peace process two political parties, the

[64] See McCorquodale (1995: 315) (arguing that the people of Northern Ireland are not a people in the same sense as those of England, Wales, or Scotland, but two peoples, and that this position was therefore problematic in self-determination terms); but cf. Bell and Cavanaugh (1999: 1360 n. 50) (suggesting that the reference is not to 'the people' but to 'a majority of the people', in what is effectively code for the 'Protestant peoples').

[65] For a detailed review of the explanations and political prescriptions for Northern Ireland, see Boyle and Hadden (1985, 1994); McGarry and O'Leary (1990, 1995); Whyte (1990). For a short overview, see Livingstone and Morison (1995). Terminology is also problematic in Northern Ireland. Here the terms 'Irish nationalist' and 'British unionist' will be used, rather than Catholic and Protestant. At times Irish nationalists will be broken down into ('constitutional') nationalists and Irish republicans, and British unionists into unionists and loyalists.   [66] See Guelke (1985) for a short overview of main positions.

Ulster Democratic Party (UDP) and the Progressive Unionist Party (PUP), associated with the main loyalist paramilitary groups~~the~~ Ulster Defence Association (UDA) and the Ulster Volunteer Force (UVF)~~came~~ to the fore, and although electorally small came to play an important role in the peace process.

Nationalists, represented by the Social Democratic and Liberal Party (SDLP) (leader John Hume) and after 1981 also by Sinn Féin (leader Gerry Adams), aspired to Irish unity. However, while the SDLP adopted a position that this should be achieved through consent rather than political violence, earning the label 'constitutional' nationalists, Sinn Féin were closely allied with the Provisional IRA whose armed struggle they supported as fellow Irish Republicans. Both groupings saw the national question as at the heart of the conflict, but also viewed human rights abuses as part and parcel of the failure of the state to provide equality and democracy to Catholics. For republicans particularly, this constituted evidence that Northern Ireland was undemocratic and unreformably so, and that the only solution was the end of British involvement.

The British government analysis, while largely similar to that of unionists, had one important difference. It viewed a key part of the problem as inter-ethnic hatred between Catholics and Protestants and itself as the neutral mediator.[67] Accordingly, the government provided 'community relations' strategies for bringing Catholics and Protestants together, and under international pressure produced measures to address (what it usually termed 'perceived') inequality for Catholics in jobs and public life.

The International Community and International Law

Unlike the cases of South Africa, Israel/Palestine, and Bosnia, the international community did not intervene, even rhetorically, on the issue of self-determination in Northern Ireland. In 1969, when the British government sent troops to Northern Ireland, the Irish government sought to raise the question of Northern Ireland before the UN Security Council, appealing for the dispatch to the area of a UN peacekeeping force.[68] The British opposed this as interference in an internal matter. The Security Council adjourned without taking a decision on whether or not to adopt the agenda, and never again considered the question.[69] That year Irish government representatives also raised the matter before the UN General

[67] Miller (1994); O'Dowd *et al.* (1981).

[68] UN doc. S/9394 (1969); see Boyle (1995); McCoubrey and White (1995: 38).

[69] UN SC meeting 1503: S/9394, Letter of 17 Aug. 1969 from Ireland (request to convene council); S/9396, Letter of 18 Aug. 1969 from Ireland (representation in Council's discussions); S/INF/24/Rev.1 Resolutions and Decisions of Security Council, 1969. Decisions, p. 8. See (1969) 23 *Yearbook of the United Nations* 179–81.

Assembly.[70] However, the Irish government did not mount an international law challenge to British rule itself. Neither did the British government take international legal action to challenge the Irish Constitution's assertion of sovereignty, an action that in and of itself would have given credence to the Irish self-determination claim.

The failure of Britain, Ireland, or any of the local actors to take international legal action reflects a multitude of political considerations. These certainly included the question mark over which position the law supported. The silence of the international community on the issue, together with its apparent acceptance of Northern Ireland's borders as legitimate, could be taken as support for unionist and British government claims that Northern Ireland had territorial integrity and that the people who should self-determine its future were the majority (de facto Protestants) within that territory.[71] However, nationalist appeal to underlying principles of self-determination based on a lack of 'representative' government were not without legal basis.[72] This gave nationalist self-determination claims a rhetorical power which contributed to a situation in which 'Northern Ireland as a political entity . . . lack[ed] international legitimacy' at least politically.[73] As Guelke argued, this illegitimacy was evidenced, not in the tangible external support (although Irish Americans and the Libyan government have provided material support for the IRA), but in more oblique ways. First, it shaped expectations, internally and externally, that Northern Ireland's future was temporary, making any compromise seem to be transitional and undermining unionist incentive to negotiate. Secondly, it legitimized political violence by providing a justification for it and creating ambivalence in regard to the need for unionist consent, even among 'constitutional' nationalists. Thirdly, it affected the balance of forces in the conflict, both directly, by constraining the British government's military response to IRA violence; and indirectly, by creating a violence-sustaining assumption by domestic and international actors that a united Ireland would be the only viable option if the British were to withdraw.[74]

[70] On 5 Sept. 1969 the permanent representative of Ireland addressed a letter to the secretary-general requesting inclusion in the agenda of the twenty-fourth session of the General Assembly of an item entitled 'The Situation in the North of Ireland'. The request for inclusion was considered by the Assembly's General Committee on 17 Sept. A decision was deferred and not returned to. A/7651 and Corr. 1 Letter of 5 Sept. 1969 from Ireland, requesting inclusion in agenda of item entitled: 'The situation in the North of Ireland'; A/7700/ First Report of General Committee, para. 11; A/7360, Resolutions Adopted by General Assembly during its 24th Session, 16 Sept.–17 Sept. 1969. Other decisions, p. 7. See (1969) 23 *Yearbook of the United Nations* 181.
[71] See e.g. Hadden (1988). For different views, see also *Broken Covenants: Violations of International Law in Northern Ireland* (Report of Northern Ireland Human Rights Assembly 6–8 Apr. 1992) London (1993) 140–50.   [72] See Harvey (1990); Boyle (1995); Carty (1996).
[73] Guelke (1985: 38).   [74] Guelke (1985).

Unlike South Africa, international intervention was forthcoming in the individual rights sphere. This was because the British government had signed and ratified all the major human rights treaties and purported to comply with them in Northern Ireland. This gave international bodies a clear basis on which to evaluate the British government's human rights practices. These bodies' record in changing law or practice, whilst peppered with successes, was nevertheless uninspiring. Domestically the conventions were not directly incorporated into law, and in practice instances of domestic courts actually using or even referring to such instruments were few and far between.[75] The strongest convention enforcement mechanism was the individual and inter-state case mechanism of the European Convention on Human Rights and Fundamental Freedoms (ECHR). This formed an outside avenue of appeal. Most famously in *Ireland* v. *UK* (1978) the Irish state challenged British interrogation practices as constituting torture and inhuman and degrading treatment, the European Court finding that such practices had indeed constituted the latter.[76] Between 1969 and 1994 cases from Northern Ireland contributed to the United Kingdom being found in violation of the convention more than any other Council of Europe country.

Despite this, the ECHR's effect in curbing human rights violations in Northern Ireland was strikingly ineffective, raising doubts about the effectiveness of human rights standards in situations of conflict.[77] The convention repeatedly proved incapable of significantly curbing a number of persistent patterns of human rights abuse, including use of plastic bullets, continuance of emergency legislation, and use of lethal force by security forces.[78] The British government successfully pushed to the limits of the convention in a number of different ways. These included gaining deference to the fact-finding processes of domestic courts;[79] adopting narrow interpretations of the remedial action required after an adverse finding;[80] and use of a derogation under Article 15 of the ECHR to avoid compliance completely. This derogation was justified by a British government assertion of the existence of an emergency threatening the life of the nation (running somewhat counter to a crimi-

---

[75] Dickson (1996, 1999).   [76] (1978) 2 E.H.R.R. 25.

[77] See Hadden (1999) (arguing that the assumptions incorporated in these standards—of a functioning liberal democracy—makes them defective in conflict situations). Cf. Ní Aoláin (1995); Fitzpatrick (1994) (critique of implementation and enforcement of the standards by international agencies).

[78] For accounts of cases, see Dickson (1997, 1999); Livingstone (1995).

[79] See *McCann* v. *United Kingdom* (1996) 21 E.H.R.R. 97.

[80] For example, in *John Murray* v. *United Kingdom* (1991) 13 E.H.R.R. 157 the court found a violation of the right to trial which was not addressed for three years, and then through Attorney-General guidelines rather than legislative change, see [1998] *Bulletin of Northern Ireland Law* para. 41. See generally Churchill and Young (1992).

nalization strategy) and was subsequently upheld as lawful by the European Court of Human Rights.[81]

While human rights instruments were acceded to, this was with a backward glance at the non-applicability of the 1977 Protocols to the 1949 Geneva Conventions (the protocols were not ratified until 28 January 1998, when the Belfast Agreement was close). After the early 1970s, when the Northern Ireland problem had become internationalized through the use of repression on the streets and policies such as internment, the British government became determined to represent the conflict as an internal criminal problem which they were addressing by modernizing anachronistic social and political structures. Their assertion that neither the 'war of national liberation' regime of Protocol I, nor the 'civil war' regime of Protocol II, nor even the 'internal armed conflict' standards of Common Article 3 of the 1949 Geneva Conventions were applicable fitted with this analysis.[82] At the time that it signed and entered reservations to the protocols, the British government made it clear that it viewed the Northern Ireland situation as outside Protocol I in particular.[83] From the late 1970s the British government moved to a policy known as 'Ulsterization, criminalization, and normalization', whose central emphasis was to contain the conflict within the rubric of a (modified) criminal justice system with the primacy of local police rather than British army. This policy both depended on avoiding any analysis of the conflict as a 'war' of any kind, and operated to bolster that analysis.[84]

In contrast, the IRA rhetorically claimed national liberation movement status and fought against straightforward criminalization through non-recognition of modified (Diplock) courts and demands for prisoner-of-war status in prisons. They resisted the symbols of 'criminalization' such as wearing prison uniforms, through the blanket protest and ultimately the hunger strikes, when ten republican prisoners starved to death.[85] The

---

[81] The case after which the derogation was implemented was *Brogan* v. *United Kingdom* (1989) 11 E.H.R.R. 117. The derogation was unsuccessfully challenged in *Brannigan and McBride* v. *United Kingdom* (1993) 17 E.H.R.R. 539. (A previous derogation enabling 'internment' had been considered valid in *United Kingdom* v. *Ireland* (1978) but had been withdrawn on 22 Aug. 1984.) [82] See further Ní Aoláin (2000: 218–47).

[83] Evan Luard MP stated in the House of Commons in Dec. 1977 that '[n]either in Northern Ireland nor in any other part of the United Kingdom is there a situation which meets the criteria laid down for the application of either Protocol. Nor is there any terrorist organisation operating within the United Kingdom that fulfils the requirements which a national liberation movement must meet in order to be entitled to claim rights under Protocol I. There is, therefore, no question of any of the provisions of either Protocol benefiting the IRA or any others who may carry out terrorist activities in peacetime.' *Hansard*, H.C. Debates, vol. 941, col. 237 (written answers) (14 Dec. 1977). Cf. also Ní Aoláin (2000: 234–8).

[84] In contrast Ní Aoláin (2000: 218–47) argues that, while it is unlikely that the status of a 'war of national liberation' could have been satisfied, the levels of violence for Common Article 3, and possibly even Protocol II, were present at least in particular phases of the conflict. [85] See Beresford (1987); Campbell *et al.* (1994); O'Malley (1990).

IRA did not, however, push their point legally by attempting to file a declaration of accession under Protocol I, as the Palestine Liberation Organization (PLO) and ANC had done. This seems largely due to lack of a coherent international legal strategy, including a lack of knowledge of humanitarian law and lack of access to international lawyers versed in it. By 1992, however, a number of non-governmental organizations had taken the approach of using standards from Common Article 3 of the 1949 Geneva Conventions as a baseline in trying to monitor the violent actions of loyalist and republican paramilitary organizations.[86]

The Peace Process and its Agreements

The peace process in Northern Ireland can also be described as having three stages, the final stage of which is still uneasily playing out, at time of writing.[87] As in South Africa, the pre-negotiation stage began with secret talks. These were between John Hume (SDLP) and Gerry Adams (Sinn Féin) and also apparently between the British government and the IRA directly. On 15 December 1993 the British and Irish governments responded in the form of the Downing Street Declaration, an intergovernmental agreement between Prime Minister John Major and Irish Taoiseach Albert Reynolds on 15 December 1993 (see Table 3.5).[88] After some months the IRA called a ceasefire[89] and loyalist parties followed suit on 13 October 1994.[90] In February 1995 the two governments produced a joint report entitled *Frameworks for the Future* intended to help 'carry the Talks forward.'[91] This was cautiously welcomed by nationalists and categorically rejected by unionists as a basis for negotiation. Their rejection, coupled with wrangling between Sinn Féin and the British government (in tandem with unionist concerns) about the permanence of the IRA ceasefire and IRA decommissioning, developed into an impasse. This lasted until 1997 and saw the involvement of US Senator George Mitchell to try to resolve the impasse in January 1996, and the breakdown of the IRA ceasefire in February 1996. In May 1996 elections were held to a Northern Ireland Forum and all-party negotiating talks, in which Sinn Féin got 15.5 per cent of the vote.[92] Talks commenced without Sinn Féin in

---

[86] See e.g. Helsinki Rights Watch (1991, 1992); Amnesty International (1994).

[87] For chronologies and summary of peace process see: www.cain.ulst.ac.uk/events/peace/peace.htm (last visited 11 May 2000); see also Bew and Gillespie (1999); Boyle and Hadden (1995, 1999); Cox (1997). For detailed accounts focused mainly on the events leading to the ceasefires, see Coogan (1996); McKittrick (1996); Mallie and McKittrick (1996); B. O'Brien (1995); Rowan (1996).   [88] Published in Bew and Gillespie (1999: 282–3).

[89] IRA Ceasefire Statement, 31 Aug. 1994; pub. in Bew and Gillespie (1999: 293).

[90] Combined Loyalist Military Command Ceasefire Statement, 13 Aug. 1994; pub. in Bew and Gillespie (1999: 297).   [91] *Frameworks for the Future* (Belfast: HMSO, 1995), p. iii.

[92] Results were as follows: UUP 24.17%, SDLP 21.36%, DUP 18.8%, Sinn Féin 15.47%, Alliance Party of Northern Ireland (APNI) 6.54%, United Kingdom Unionist (UKU) 3.69%,

June 1996, and their exclusion was not remedied until the landslide Labour majority in the House of Commons in the United Kingdom (May 1997) freed Tony Blair's government from the influence of the Ulster Unionists, on whose votes John Major's prior government had come to depend for their majority. After meetings between Sinn Féin and the new Blair government, the IRA declared a renewal of its ceasefire on 20 July 1997. On 9 September 1997 Sinn Féin signed up to the 'Mitchell Principles', developed by George Mitchell's international body as a response to the decommissioning impasse (see Table 3.5), and entered the multi-party talks at Stormont. The pre-negotiation stage agreements are set out in Table 3.5.

Little progress was made until January 1998, when the British and Irish governments produced a document containing their 'best guess at what could be a generally acceptable outcome.'[93] This 'Propositions of Heads of Agreement' paper marked an attempt to add impetus to the talks. It set out an embryonic version of the Belfast Agreement. In the following months more detailed discussion papers were produced on each of the three strands.[94] As in South Africa this period of intense negotiations took place against a backdrop of violence, and both Sinn Féin and the small UDP were expelled temporarily from the talks after both the IRA and the Ulster Freedom Fighters (UFF) were implicated in killings. The talks ended in an intense frenzy, on 26 March 1998 George Mitchell set a deadline of 9 April for reaching agreement; on 6 April he gave the parties a possible draft agreement based on the negotiations up to that point. The midnight deadline of 9 April came and went and negotiations continued into the night. Agreement was finally reached on 10 April 1998, which happened to be Good Friday of Easter, giving rise to the christening of the agreement by some commentators as the 'Good Friday Agreement', while others preferred the 'Belfast Agreement' (the terminology used throughout this book) (see Table 3.6).

The final stage in the process, still unfolding, is implementation. On 22 May 1998 a referendum on the agreement took place simultaneously

Progressive Unionist Party (PUP) 3.47%, Ulster Democratic Party (UDP) 2.22%, Northern Ireland Women's Coalition (NIWC) 1.03%, Labour 0.85%, and others 2.4%. While elections to the Forum were allocated by seat to gain, the top ten parties were guaranteed to be at the negotiations, in an election designed to ensure that the small political parties close to loyalist paramilitary groups were represented. Interestingly, this formula led to the formation of the Women's Coalition, which secured a place at the talks.

[93] Text of Joint Statement by British and Irish Governments, 12 Jan. 1998 (available at cain.ulst.ac.uk/events/peace/soc.htm, last visited 11 May 2000).

[94] British Irish Government Discussion Paper: Strand 3East/West Structures, 27 Jan. 1998; British and Irish Government Discussion Paper: Strand 2North/South Structures, 27 Jan. 1998; Paper Presented by British Government to Northern Ireland Talks on Proposed Northern Ireland Assembly, 2 Feb. 1998 (all available at cain.ulst.ac.uk/events/peace/soc.htm, last visited 11 May 2000).

TABLE 3.5. *Pre-negotiation agreements*

Agreement	Parties	Content
Hume–Adams Agreement (*c.* 1993–4)	Hume–Adams in the broadest sense amounted to a series of drafts circulated between John Hume (SDLP) and Gerry Adams (Sinn Féin), Albert Reynolds (Irish Taoiseach), and the British government	These agreements culminated in the Downing Street Declaration, which Mallie and McKittrick (1996) suggest was 'the final draft in a process that had been underway for years.' The elements of the agreements were broadly similar to the Downing Street Declaration, focusing on getting British–Irish agreement on self-determination language, the possibility of the British government becoming persuaders of unionists for a united Ireland, or at least acknowledge that they had 'no selfish, strategic or economic interest' in Northern Ireland
Downing Street Declaration, 15 December 1993	John Major (British prime minister), and Albert Reynolds (Irish Taoiseach)	The British government accepted the concept of self-determination for people of Ireland 'North and South' in an ambiguous phrase. The Irish government accepted the need for unionist consent to a united Ireland. The agreement stated that the British government had 'no selfish strategic or economic interest in Northern Ireland.' It included a commitment by British and Irish governments to accept 'democratically mandated parties' (a definition which included Sinn Féin) as legitimate participants in all-party talks on a new constitutional settlement, on the basis of 'a permanent end to the use of, or support for, paramilitary violence'
Frameworks for the Future, February 1995	British government and Irish government	Two-part document. First, 'A Framework for Accountable Government in Northern Ireland', spelling out British government proposals for devolving power to a local Assembly, including power-sharing. Secondly, 'A New Framework for Agreement' setting out a 'shared understanding' between the

Agreement	Parties	Content
		British and Irish governments to assist negotiations, and including provision for cross-border bodies with executive powers. Together the documents addressed all three strands of relationships
Joint Communiqué, 28 November 1995	British government and Irish government	Launched a 'twin track' process aimed at breaking the decommissioning–all-party talks impasse. Set up two tracks to make progress in parallel on the two issues. The 'political track' was 'to invite the parties to intensive preparatory talks with a remit to reach widespread agreement . . . to bring all parties together for substantive negotiations aimed at a political settlement based on consent.' The decommissioning track was addressed by setting up an International Body to assess the issue and report
Report of the International Body on Arms Decommissioning, 22 January 1996	Not strictly an agreement, but was produced as a statement of the possible way forward after extensive consultations with political parties and others	Set out a compromise between a position of no decommissioning and decommissioning prior to all party talks. Parties were to sign up to six principles of democracy and non-violence, and decommissioning was then to take place 'during all-party negotiations.' A number of other matters, such as a cessation of 'punishment beatings and shootings' by paramilitary groups and problems in state policing, were addressed under the heading 'Further Confidence Building', signalling that decommissioning was part of a package of larger issues
Rules of Procedure, 29 July 1996	Produced by British government (after the new IRA declaration of a ceasefire)	Rules providing the broad format and decision-making process of the talks. They set up four main sections: a plenary (all participants); strand one (British government and politicians); strand two (all participants); and strand three (British and Irish governments)

TABLE 3.5. *Continued*

Agreement	Parties	Content
Procedural Motion, 24 September 1997	Plenary session of talks (including all parties elected to talks apart from Sinn Féin, who were excluded due to absence of IRA ceasefire)	Established two all-party 'Liaison sub-committees' on Decommissioning and 'Confidence Building Measures' as identified in the Mitchell Report. These provided that talks should be confidential unless otherwise agreed, that they would work 'on a basis of consensus' or if none, on 'sufficient consensus'. Borrowed from the South African process, this was defined as satisfied when 'supported by participating political parties which . . . represent a majority of both the unionist and nationalist communities in Northern Ireland respectively and which also constitute a majority of the participating political parties'

Note: For text of various drafts of 'Hume–Adams', see Mallie and McKittrick (1996: 118–19, 371–80); for texts of others see cain.ulst.ac.uk/events/peace/soc.htm (last visited 11 May 2000).

North and South as stipulated by the agreement. Endorsement was given in both jurisdictions: in Northern Ireland by 71.2 per cent (a figure which included a majority of nationalists and a slimmer majority of unionists) and in the Republic by 94 per cent of those voting. Following this the various commissions established under the agreement were set up; prisoner release commenced; elections to the new Assembly were held; and David Trimble (UUP) and Seamus Mallon (SDLP) were selected as (shadow) first minister and deputy first minister, respectively.[95]

However, by November it had become clear that the formation of the power-sharing executive had become stalled, and with it the agreement's centrepiece—the operation of three-strand-based devolution. Devolution stalled over dissension among unionists over whether to support the agreement, and in particular a demand that IRA decommissioning take place prior to executive formation. This was temporarily resolved in November 1999 after George Mitchell conducted a review of the process leading apparently to an unwritten agreement. Devolution to the Northern Ireland Assembly and a power-sharing government took place on 2 December 1999, but was suspended on 11 February 2000 by the British

[95] The election produced the following results: SDLP 21.99%, UUP 21.28%, DUP 18.03%, Sinn Féin 17.65%, APNI 6.5%, UKU 4.52%, PUP 2.55%, NIWC 1.51%, UDP 1.07%, others 5%.

TABLE 3.6. *Substantive–framework agreement*

Agreement	Parties	Content
Agreement Reached in Multi-party Negotiations, 10 April 1998 (Belfast Agreement)	All parties except DUP and UK Unionists (very small unionist party)	Agreement in two parts: an agreement of the parties, and annex containing an agreement between the British and Irish governments. The first agreement opens with a declaration of support which sets out common understandings. Opens with Constitutional Issues, which has language dealing with self-determination. Then the agreement is detailed over the three strands. Strand one: Northern Ireland Assembly with power-sharing and proportionality. Strand two: a new British–Irish Agreement and North–South Ministerial Council, with cross-border implementation bodies. Strand three: a British–Irish Council and a council made up of representatives from Ireland, Northern Ireland, Scotland, Wales, Isle of Man, and Channel Islands, and others from the United Kingdom. The remaining sections deal with rights, safeguards, and equality of opportunity; decommissioning; security; policing and criminal justice; prisoners; and validation, implementation, and review. The second agreement embodies the inter-governmental commitments made in the document

Note: Cmnd. 3883 (Apr. 1998).

government, who cited lack of progress by the IRA on decommissioning, under threat of unionist withdrawal. On 5 May 2000 a similar, apparently unwritten, agreement to a new choreography was reached and the UUP (by a narrow majority) agreed to re-enter the Assembly institutions. Power was once again devolved on 30 May 2000. These two sets of unwritten agreements can be found in Table 3.7.

CONCLUSIONS

Both the accounts of South Africa and Northern Ireland demonstrate the interaction of international law and conflict alluded to in Chapter 1, whereby each shapes the other. This interactive evolutionary relationship

TABLE 3.7. *(Unwritten) implementation agreements*

Agreement	Parties	Content
Unwritten agreement apparently reached, November 1999 ('Mitchell Understanding')	Parties to the original agreement (and perhaps IRA itself)	A sequence of events was apparently agreed to which would see different parties (including the governments) making a series of statements aimed at addressing the concerns of opponents. Ulster Unionists agreed to devolution in advance of IRA decommissioning, but apparently believing that it would follow soon after
Unwritten agreement apparently reached, May 2000	Parties to the original agreement (and perhaps IRA itself)	Again a sequence of events was apparently agreed. The British and Irish governments made statements of commitment to implementation. The IRA made a statement committing to opening some arms dumps to international witnesses as a beginning of a process which would 'completely and verifiably put IRA arms beyond use.' Ulster Unionists agreed (after a narrow internal vote) to re-enter devolved institutions

Note: Copies of the different statements made are available at www.cain.ulst.ac.uk/events/peace/soc.htm (last visited 11 May 2000).

prefigures the relationship between international law and peace agreements.

The conflicts in both South Africa and Northern Ireland in different ways helped to shape the international legal standards which claimed to regulate the conflicts. In the case of South Africa this was at times direct, with new legal standards being created to address the conflict. These included the Convention on the Crime of Apartheid, the National Liberation Movement concept of 1977 Protocol I to the 1949 Geneva Conventions, and customary law on self-determination and racial domination. In the case of Northern Ireland it was more intangible. International law's refusal to challenge the borders of Northern Ireland or to recognize the claims of Irish nationalists as anything other than those of minorities contributed to establishing the limits of self-determination claims. The human rights jurisprudence created by the Northern Irish conflict, particularly at the European Court of Human Rights, also helped create a jurisprudence of how such law applies in situations of conflict.

Conversely, both conflict accounts illustrate the difficulties inherent in the notion of international legal regulation of internal conflict. In the application of self-determination's group-oriented rights, and the individual rights of human rights and humanitarian law, there are gaps which mean that different domestic parties to the conflict and different international players can assert an international law position to back up their meta-conflict stance. As regards international law on self-determination, the gaps revolve around the central conundrum of who are the relevant people to decide the future, and what is the relevant territory within which to decide it. In South Africa self-determination provision was used both by the government to justify bantustans and apartheid, and by the ANC and the international community to oppose them. In Northern Ireland self-determination law and principles can be used to support both the claims of British unionists and Irish nationalists. The gaps and lack of clarity in the international legal standards translate the issues at the heart of the conflict into abstract legal language, rather than resolving them.

As regards individual rights standards, the meta-conflict plays out in debate over which legal regimes are applicable to the conflict (humanitarian law and/or human rights regimes). The meta-conflict also plays out with regard to the extent to which these legal regimes can, and should, be externally enforced. Thus in South Africa human rights conventions and Protocols I and II to the Geneva Conventions of 1949 were not ratified, while in Northern Ireland human rights standards were ratified but the protocols were not.

Despite these limitations both South Africa and Northern Ireland do provide a basis for arguing that international law can play a crucial role in limiting the conflict (although other factors are of course important). In both it would seem that international illegitimacy played some role in bringing an end to the conflict, and certainly to the types of solution which were on the table at that point. In doing so, it impacted on their peace processes and resulting agreements. A full demonstration of how this operated would require further treatment than given above. In short it was not through direct enforcement, but through more long-term less dramatic but no less real ways.

In South Africa the international community's clear position on self-determination and human rights abuses made sanctions and other campaigning pressures sustainable. These campaigns were clearly significant in reaching a 'mutually perceived stalemate'. The international community's positions also influenced the type of solution that could prevail. For the South African government negotiating a solution only made sense if it brought international legitimacy. The international community's position put limits on the type of solution which would achieve this. Anything that looked like white minority domination in another guise would not do. Between bantustans and white-weighted government and majority rule, there were not too many options.

In Northern Ireland the international legal regime forced the British government either to address the conflict within a broadly liberal democratic framework, and therefore apply international human rights standards which they had acceded to, or to jettison these commitments and in doing so acknowledge that Northern Ireland required a high level of conflict to sustain the British presence. This latter analysis was not possible after the decolonization period without a total forfeiting of Britain's democratic liberal and international credentials (as Britain had begun to discover with their policies of the early 1970s). The British government's stated commitment to human rights instruments can therefore be seen as integral to their broader meta-conflict stance—that of the neutral arbitrator of an inter-ethnic conflict—every bit as much as was the South African government's refusal to commit to such instruments.

It can be argued that the British government's commitment to human rights instruments (however partial) limited the conflict, by limiting the government's capacity to wage war militarily. However, the relatively low number of deaths (in particular civilian deaths) as compared with other situations would indicate that this policy served to limit the conflict as a whole. Just as the government were constrained by human rights standards in how they waged war, so reciprocity constrained the IRA not to appear to kill 'civilians' indiscriminately through increasingly inclusive definitions of 'legitimate' (supposedly military) targets.[96] The role of human rights measures in creating the 'mutually perceived hurting stalemate' which brought the British government and the Provisional IRA to negotiations has undoubtedly been under-explored.

The international community's relative silence on self-determination paradoxically also served to set broad parameters for the conflict's resolution. The failure to weigh in, even rhetorically, in support of nationalist–Republican self-determination analysis while providing broad sympathy to the Irish nationalist predicament meant that the international community underwrote as crucial to settlement both unionist consent to any solution and radical reformation of the state to provide full and equal participation for nationalists. By the 1990s the international community viewed the Irish nationalist position as classically one of minorities. However, by this decade, as Boutros-Ghali put it, creative efforts were required to ensure that the demands of 'territorial integrity and independent statehood' were 'not permitted to work against each other.'[97] This set a context for a creative synthesis of international law with domestic politics and negotiations, which resulted in the Belfast Agreement.

---

[96] Although clearly questions of what was morally acceptable within their immediate communities also determined this approach.   [97] Boutros-Ghali (1992, para. 19).

4

From Conflict to Peace?
Israel/Palestine and Bosnia Herzegovina

The conflicts in Israel/Palestine and Bosnia had much clearer international dimensions than those in South Africa and Northern Ireland. Both contained the potential for regional and ultimately global instability; and both had created a refugee problem for other countries. Also, unlike Northern Ireland and South Africa, the parties' claims to separate statehood meant that the conflicts much more clearly straddled international law's internal–international boundary. No categorization of the conflicts as internal or international could be made without adjudicating on the self-determination issues at the heart of the conflicts.

The international dimension of both conflicts gave the international community a clearer reason for being involved than with the previous two examples, both legally and in terms of self-interest. As a result, the internal conflict dynamics and the international responses are impossible to isolate from each other. Furthermore, the international law positions of the international community were more directly implicated in creating (or not) the necessary precursor for negotiations—a 'mutually perceived hurting stalemate'. In other words, international actors were in essence party to the conflict, and therefore an ongoing factor relevant to resolution.

This level of internationalization tends to affect peace processes and their agreements in two main ways. Most obviously, the carrots and sticks which the international community use to induce settlement become part of the equation of any resulting deal, and therefore an ongoing factor in implementation. Secondly, the international community's involvement influences when and how peace negotiations take place, and through that, any resulting peace agreement's content.

ISRAEL/PALESTINE

While both Arab and Jewish peoples claim long historic ties to the land of Palestine, the origins of the contemporary conflict are linked to events in the early part of this century.[1] Until 1917 Palestine had been part of the

---

[1] As with all the conflicts, terminology is particularly difficult and 'neutral' terminology impossible to find. The term 'Palestine' will be used to describe the territory under dispute until 1948, when the term 'Israel' will be used to describe territory in which the state of Israel was established. From 1967 onwards the term 'Israel' will be used to describe the land

Ottoman empire. During the First World War Britain made incompatible commitments to both Arab and Jewish peoples. To Arab peoples, through promises of help in achieving independence made in exchange for the support of Sharif Hussein of Mecca in the war;[2] and to Jewish peoples, through the Balfour Declaration, in which the British promised to 'view with favour the establishment in Palestine of a national home for the Jewish people.'[3] Thus the land was effectively promised to two groups of people, both of whom asserted historical ties with it, with no clear plan for how their conflicting interests could be reconciled. This took place against a backdrop of British intent to retain control over Palestine. By 1914 Jewish people formed approximately 12 per cent of the population and Arab people the remainder.

After the war Britain was later given the Mandate for Palestine under the new League of Nations system.[4] The official Mandate document declared that 'the Mandatory should be responsible for putting [the Balfour Declaration] into effect.'[5] A process of incremental Jewish immigration was supported by the British against increasing Arab opposition. Nazi atrocities against Jews in Europe before and during the Second World War had a profound effect on Jewish understanding of the need for a homeland, fuelling Jewish claims to Palestine and legitimizing them internationally. In 1947, against the backdrop of escalating hostilities between Arabs, Jews, and the British, the Palestine situation was turned over to the United Nations. The UN established a Special Committee on Palestine (UNSCOP) to investigate and propose a solution.[6] This Committee recommended the partition of Palestine into a Jewish and an Arab state with an international enclave comprising Jerusalem and Bethlehem.[7]

excepting 'the Occupied Palestinian Territories'. The terms 'Jews' and 'Arabs' will be used to describe Jews and Arabs within Palestine until 1948. After that point the term 'Palestinians' will be used to describe Arabs who identify as Palestinian within the state of Israel and the Occupied Territories, and the diaspora. For references to the historic conflict of interests, see Abdul Hadi (1997*a*: 11–14) (extracts from Omar Ibn Al-Khattab Covenant, AD 638; T. Herzl, *The Jewish State* (1896)). For histories, accounts, and documents of the conflict, see Cattan (2000); Chomsky (1983); Laquer (1969); Laquer and Rubin (1984); Lustick (1990); Pappé (1994); Said (1995*b*); Tessler (1994). For a concise, primarily legal account see Malanczuk (1995). For copies of the key historical documents, see Abdul Hadi (1997*a*); Lapidoth and Hirsch (1992); www.israel-mfa.gov.il/mfa.go.asp?MFAHOOOcO (last visited 9 May 2000). For a comprehensive research guide to the Occupied Territories and International Law prior to 1990, see Vincent-Daviss (1989).

[2] See MacMahon–Hussein Correspondence, 1915–16, and Sykes–Picot Agreement, 16 May 1916; excerpts pub. in Abdul Hadi (1997*a*: 17–21).

[3] The Balfour Declaration 1917; pub. in Abdul Hadi (1997*a*: 21–2).

[4] For a brief description of the Mandate system, see Rauschning (1987).

[5] Council of the League of Nations' Confirmed Text on Terms of the British Mandate, 24 July 1922; pub. in Abdul Hadi (1997*a*: 52–5).

[6] See Summary of the Report of the UN Special Committee on Palestine (UNSCOP) regarding the Partition Plan, 31 Aug. 1947; excerpts pub. in Abdul Hadi (1997*a*: 155–72).

[7] UN GA Res 181 (Partition Plan) on the Future Government of Palestine, 29 Nov. 1947.

This was then endorsed by UN General Assembly Resolution 181. While the Arabs rejected the plan, the Jewish Agency (then representing the Jewish population) accepted it. Britain left, and Zionist leaders made a Proclamation of Independence establishing the state of Israel.[8] Israel's declaration of independence set out two principles on which the constitutional system of the state was to rest. First, Israel was declared to be a 'Jewish state' (in Eretz Israel, or 'the Land of Israel, Palestine') that would 'open . . . [its] gates . . . to every Jew and confer upon the Jewish people the status of a fully privileged member of the comity of nations.'[9] Secondly, despite this, Israel claimed to be a democratic state committed to 'foster[ing] the development of the country for the benefit of all its inhabitants' and undertook to 'ensure complete equality of social and political rights to all its inhabitants, irrespective of religion, race or sex', and to 'guarantee freedom of religion, conscience, language, education and culture', to 'safeguard the Holy Places of all Religions', and 'be faithful to the principles of the Charter of the United Nations.'[10]

After the Proclamation of the State of Israel neighbouring Arab states intervened militarily, precipitating the first Arab–Israeli war. This war and resulting armistice agreement left historic Palestine divided into three parts. Jewish forces captured much of the territory assigned to the Arab state. Jordan took control of the West Bank (East Jerusalem and the central country of Palestine), while the Gaza Strip was held by Egypt. As a result Palestinians were divided into four communities: those within the Israeli state, those within Jordanian and Egyptian administration respectively, and refugees in neighbouring Arab countries and beyond. These four populations were to retain four sets of interlocking yet discrete interests until the present day. The UN responded to the refugee crisis created by the conflict, setting up the United Nations Relief and Works Agency (UNRWA) for the Palestinian refugees created by the conflict, and establishing 'temporary' refugee camps in the region, many of which exist to this day.[11] UN General Assembly Resolution 194 of 14 December 1948 asserted the right of Palestinians to return and/or to be compensated for their losses.

---

[8] Israeli Proclamation of Independence, 14 May 1948; excerpts pub. in Abdul Hadi (1997a: 185–6).

[9] Preamble, The Declaration of the Establishment of the State of Israel, 14 May 1948, available at www.israel-mfa.gov.il/mfa.go.asp?MFAHOOOcO (last visited 9 May 2000).

[10] Preamble, The Declaration of the Establishment of the State of Israel, 14 May 1948. A formal Constitution was never adopted, instead the Harari Resolution committed the Knesset (Israeli Parliament) to draw up the Constitution through a series of basic laws, which have now largely been completed but do not include a full bill of rights as such; see Kretchmer (1996: 39, 1999); see further Gavison (1985).

[11] UN GA Res 194, 11 Dec. 1948; UN GA Res 302(IV): Assistance to Palestinian Refugees, 8 Dec. 1949.

In 1964 the Arab League established the Palestinian Liberation Organization (PLO) as a basis for the mobilization of the Palestinian people. The PLO's Charter repudiated Zionism and Jewish claims to a homeland in (Mandate-defined) Palestine and committed Arabs to establishing Palestine as an Arab homeland by mobilizing 'military, spiritual and material potentialities.'[12] In 1967 Israel, fearing that hostile Egyptian actions indicated imminent attack and annihilation by combined Arab states, responded militarily. In what has become known as the Six Day War (or June War) Israel went on to occupy the West Bank (including East Jerusalem) from Jordan; the Gaza Strip, together with the Sinai Peninsula (from Egypt); and the Golan Heights (from Syria). The UN condemned this occupation[13] with UN Security Council Resolution 242, emphasizing 'the inadmissibility of the acquisition of territory by war and the need to work for a just and lasting peace in which every State in the area can live in security,' and setting out two principles as a framework.[14] First, the 'withdrawal of Israel armed forces from territories occupied in the recent conflict'; and secondly the

[t]ermination of all claims or state of belligerency and respect for and acknowledgement of the sovereignty, territorial integrity and political independence of every State in the area and their right to live in peace within secure and recognised boundaries free from threats or acts of force.[15]

The lack of the definite article before the phrase 'territories occupied in the recent conflict' (territories, rather than 'the' territories) in the English text, was ambiguous as to whether withdrawal from all or merely some of the territories was contemplated, giving rise to immediate controversy and contributing to the rejection of Resolution 242 by the PLO.[16] The Arab defeat in 1967 enabled the PLO to gain a measure of independence. In 1968 the PLO amended its covenant, providing for the continuation of armed struggle against Israel. Yasser Arafat was elected chairman and set about changing it into an umbrella organization with membership open to all Palestinian factions.[17]

[12] National Covenant of the Palestine Liberation Organization, First Arab Palestine Congress, Jerusalem, 28 May 1964; pub. in Abdul Hadi (1997a: 203–5, para. 14).
[13] UN GA Res 237, 14 June 1967; UN GA Res 2253 on Jerusalem, 4 July 1967; UN GA Res 2254 on Jerusalem, 14 July 1967.   [14] UN SC Res 242, 22 Nov. 1967.
[15] UN SC Res 242, 22 Nov. 1967, para. 1.
[16] The definite article was present in the French text. For Palestinian rejection, see Statement Issued by the Palestine Liberation Organization Rejecting UN Resolution 242, Cairo, 23 Nov. 1967; pub. in Abdul Hadi (1997a: 212). ('[Resolution 242] may be interpreted as permitting her to withdraw from such territories as she chooses to withdraw from and to retain such areas as she wishes to retain.') The omission of the word 'the' seems to have been deliberate; see Statements Clarifying the Meaning of UN Security Council Resolution 242; pub. in Abdul Hadi (1997a: 210–12).
[17] The Palestinian National Charter: Resolutions of the Palestinian National Council, 17 July 1968; pub. in Abdul Hadi (1997a: 213–15).

MAP 4.1. Israel and Palestinian occupied territories of West Bank and Gaza Strip after 1967

Moving towards a Peace Process?

In 1978, under the Carter administration in the United States, the Camp David Frameworks for Peace were signed between Egypt and Israel, leading to the Egyptian–Israeli Peace Treaty (Camp David Accords).[18] These accords, which provide the most obvious precursor to the more recent peace process agreements, worked out two main agreements: a framework for peace between Egypt and Israel; and a general framework for resolution of the Middle East crisis—or the 'Palestinian question'. Under this latter agreement it was proposed to grant autonomy to Palestinians in the West Bank and Gaza Strip, to install a local administration for a five-year interim period, and to decide the ultimate status of the territories after that period. Only the Egyptian–Israeli agreement was implemented. The Arab governments rejected the accords, suspending Egypt's membership in the Arab League, and the PLO continued its confrontation with

---

[18] Camp David Frameworks for Peace, Text of the Agreements signed on 17 Sept. 1978 (signed by A. Sadat and M. Begin); Framework for the Conclusion of Peace Treaty between Egypt and Israel, 17 Sept. 1978; Exchanges of Letters; pub. in Abdul Hadi (1997a: 248–54).

the Israeli army.[19] Again, however, peace initiatives continued to be attempted.

After two decades of occupation, internally organized resistance to the Israeli army arose through the 'intifada' (literally 'the shaking-off' or 'uprising').[20] This affected the course of the conflict in two key ways. First, it gave rise to a new leadership from those Palestinians living inside the Occupied Palestinian Territories, rather than in exile. Secondly, it provided new impetus for Palestinians, Israelis, and external players and mediators to clarify their positions and work towards dialogue. Citing the consolidation of a distinct and separate Palestinian identity, Jordan renounced any interest in the West Bank, in favour of the PLO.[21] On 15 November 1988 the Palestinian National Council proclaimed independence of the state of Palestine and accepted UN Security Resolutions 242 and 338 as the basis for statehood, thereby in effect limiting demands for a Palestinian state to the pre-1967 borders.[22]

By 1990, however, a war of attrition had developed and world attention was focused on the events of the Gulf War. The current population of the Occupied Territories (including East Jerusalem) is approximately 1 per cent Israeli and 99 per cent Palestinian–Arab. The population of Israel within pre-1967 boundaries is approximately 80 per cent Jewish, 15 per cent Arab, and 5 per cent other or unclassified.[23]

The Positions of the Domestic Players

The key positions which the peace process attempted to negotiate between were those of the PLO to independent statehood and those of the Israeli government to some resolution of the conflict falling short of that. Behind these broad negotiating positions are a wide variety of others, but

[19] See Final Statement of the Arab League Summit Conference, Baghdad, 5 Nov. 1978; Arab League Summit Conference Resolution, Baghdad, 31 Mar. 1979; both pub. in Abdul Hadi (1997a: 260–2, 277–9). See further Binder (1988).

[20] See Lockman and Beinin (1990); Robinson (1997).

[21] King Hussein, Speech on Jordan's Disengagement from the West Bank, Amman, 31 July 1988; pub. in Abdul Hadi (1997a: 312).

[22] Palestinian Declaration of Independence II, 15 Nov. 1988 (adopted by 85% for and 15% against); Palestinian National Council, 'Political Communiqué', Algiers, 15 Nov. 1988; pub. in Abdul Hadi (1997a: 331–6). For differing views on the international legal validity of the declaration, cf. Boyle (1990) with Crawford (1990).

[23] This means that the Palestinian–Arab population within the entire area under Israeli jurisdiction amounts to around 40%. Accurate statistics are difficult to access given the overlapping jurisdictional scope of Israel and Palestinian census surveys, and structural factors which mean that under-counting of Palestinians by Israel, and non-counting of Israelis by Palestinians seems to take place. See Israeli Statistics, www.cbs.gov.il (last visited 9 May 2000) and Palestinian Statistics, www.pcbs.org (last visited 9 May 2000). The population percentages given do not include the substantial numbers of Palestinian refugees outside the borders of Israel or the Occupied Territories.

perhaps most important are the key 'outbidders' of peace process proponents. On the Palestinian side these are Palestinian groupings such as the
Islamic Resistance Movement (Hamas), who do not favour any peace settlement with Israel, or indeed acknowledge the right of the state of Israel
to exist.[24] On the Israeli side outbidders of the liberal 'peace settlement'
politicians exist in the form of the Israeli right, who conversely claim the
entire territory as 'Eretz Israel' and as a rightful part of the Jewish state.[25]

Both Palestinian and Israeli positions are of course more complex, and
fluctuate depending on events and upon which precise coalition holds
power within Israel.[26] Indeed, one of the features of conflict and peace
process is the meta-conflict which takes place within Israeli society itself
as to the causes of the conflict and its prescriptions for resolution. The
Jewish Israeli population is itself diverse both politically and ethnically.
Democratic elections ensure that this meta-conflict determines both negotiators and negotiating positions. This means that the Israeli position can
only be stated very generally, as different consecutive governments have
adopted both different approaches to the peace process, and different
interpretations of the peace agreements negotiated by previous governments, giving the process its 'stop and start' quality.

Both the Israeli government and the PLO have articulated their positions using international law, and these positions have changed incre-
mentally as conflict and law have developed. In particular the 1967 war
and subsequent international rooting of the Palestinian self-determination
claim in a prohibition on use of force and ongoing occupation rather than
within a colonial–racist domination framework has enmeshed self-
determination arguments with debate about the applicable humanitarian
law regime and standards.

Both before and after 1967 Israel consistently refused to accept the self-
determination claim of Palestinian people to independent statehood.
After 1967 they argued that there was no legitimate sovereign in West
Bank or Gaza prior to 1967, but that Jordan's status in West Bank was one
of an occupying state, while the Gaza Strip involved at most Egyptian
administration. Israel could not therefore be considered as merely an
'occupying power' with regard to these territories. This connects to a
denial that Palestinians constitute a 'peoples' within the terms of international law, on the grounds that Palestinians cannot be separated ethnically
from the larger category of 'Arab' and that territorially their ties are with

---

[24] Charter of the Islamic Resistance Movement (Hamas) of Palestine, 18 Aug. 1988, pub.
in Abdul Hadi (1997*a*: 314–25).
[25] For descriptions of contrasting Israeli positions of 'disengagement' and 'incorporation',
see Lustick (1993: 7–25); Abdo and Yuval-Davis (1995) (describing what they term as 'the
Zionist settler project').
[26] For an overview of theories of the conflict and positions in it, see Feste (1991).

the land of Jordan rather than the Occupied Territories. Finally, an argument that Israel needs to retain these areas to preserve its security has also been used to deny Palestinian self-determination claims with little reference to international law.[27]

The official Israeli position, as argued by Professor Blum in 1980, asserted that Palestinian Arabs had already 'achieved their self-determination' through the establishment of Jordan; that prior to 1967 there had been 'no demand for the establishment of a "Palestinian State" in those areas'; and that to create such a state would amount to requesting the creation of 'a second Palestinian Arab State.'[28] Blum further asserted that 'full autonomy' to the inhabitants of these areas in accordance with the Camp David Framework of 1978 would provide a 'dignified solution for the needs of the Arab population' of the West Bank and the Gaza Strip.[29] This analysis of Palestinian claims played out both in Israeli control of land through law and settlement-building patterns, and in Israeli approaches to peace negotiations.[30]

As regards humanitarian law, Israel is a party to the 1949 Geneva Conventions but not to 1977 Protocol I.[31] However, Israel has consistently argued that it is not bound to apply the Fourth Geneva Convention providing humanitarian standards for civilian persons in times of war (and during occupation).[32] With a sideways glance to its self-determination position, Israel argues that this convention does not merely protect the civil rights of the local population, but also has the function of safeguarding the status and reversionary rights of the legitimate sovereign ousted by the occupant. Israel argues that if it were to agree to the application of the Fourth Geneva Convention, this would be tantamount to recognition of Jordanian and Egyptian sovereignty over these territories, a sovereignty which, as we have seen, it does not accept.[33] Israel does claim to respect voluntarily 'the humanitarian provisions' of the Fourth

---

[27] See e.g. Halberstam (1989).

[28] GAOR, XXXVth Session, Plenary Meetings, 77th Meeting, 1318 as cited in Cassese (1998b: 235–7).   [29] Ibid.

[30] Shehadeh (1997) (arguing that the peace agreements 'came as the culmination of a legal process that began much earlier.' This process was the body of law by which settlements were planned and legalized, which Shehadeh argues shows a legal continuity with the political 'solutions' which the peace agreements enshrine). See also Shehadeh (1988).

[31] Israel is a party to the 1954 Hague Cultural Property Convention, but not to the 1907 Hague Convention, although Israel accepts that it is bound by the Hague Regulations in so far as they reflect norms of customary international law.

[32] See Shamgar (1971) (arguing this position while attorney-general of Israel).

[33] For a good overview of the 'for' and 'against' positions, see A. Roberts (1992). On the different justifications of the Israeli position, see particularly Blum (1968) (arguing the missing reversioner thesis); Gerson (1973, 1978) (arguing that Israel is in the position of a 'trustee-occupant'); Rostow (1979) (arguing that the position is one of lease for life by Israel on the Palestinian Mandate). For critiques of this argument that Geneva IV does not apply, see essays in Playfair (1992: 25–238).

Geneva Convention, but has never defined this term or specified which of the convention's provisions it considers to fall within this category. Review of the impact of humanitarian law in Israeli courts indicates that it has been largely ineffective in curbing abusive practices.[34]

The PLO position has changed over the years, in particular around the legal status of the Occupied Territories and the territorial scope of the Palestinian self-determination claim. As Roberts writes, 'for a long time the PLO was reluctant to draw clear legal distinctions between the lands controlled by Israel before and after June 1967', claiming a right to Palestinian statehood in both.[35] This affected the PLO's interaction with humanitarian law, and, as Roberts noted, the PLO position on Geneva IV was at times incoherent.[36] The PLO did of course accept Protocol I. Indeed in 1989, after its declaration of statehood, an attempt was made to deposit Palestine's instrument of ratification of the 1949 Geneva Conventions, an attempt which failed.[37] However, as Palestinian lawyer Raja Shehadeh asserts, Palestinian attempts to build a consensus around the applicability of Geneva IV, particularly during intifada years, helped to develop a 'legal narrative' among Palestinians living within the Occupied Territories which provided a basis for critiquing Israeli actions.[38] Legal strategies used humanitarian law and human rights standards both to argue in domestic cases, and to build coalitions with lawyers in Israel and the international community more generally.[39]

The International Community and International Law

The international legal response has been complex and is difficult to summarize. Like the responses of the parties to the conflict, it has evolved and its evolution is tied up with the very evolution of the body of international law which is applicable to the conflict. The self-determination claim of Palestinians asserted around the granting of the Mandate to Britain was in essence based on anti-colonialism, although at this time no legal right

[34] See Kuttab (1992); Qupty (1992).
[35] See A. Roberts (1992: 49). Cf. Article 2, Palestinian National Charter: Resolutions of the Palestinian National Council, 17 July 1968; pub. in Abdul Hadi (1997a: 213–15).
[36] A. Roberts (1992: 50–1).
[37] Letter claiming to ratify Geneva Conventions and protocols from Permanent Member of Palestine to the UN Office at Geneva to Swiss Federal Department of Foreign Affairs on 21 June 1989 stating decision of the PLO to adhere to the four Geneva Conventions and the two additional protocols. Swiss Federal Council responded on 13 Sept. 1989 indicating that they were not in a position to decide whether it constituted an instrument of accession because of uncertainty within the international community regarding status. See www.icrc.org (last visited 3 Dec. 1999).   [38] Shehadeh (1996).
[39] Dugard (1992a); Hajjar (1997); Kuttab (1992); Qupty (1992); Shehadeh (1996). Cf. Falk and Weston (1991); Quigley (1989) (who use humanitarian law to justify the intifada's use of force).

to self-determination existed.[40] As we have seen, the international community, both through the terms of the Mandate for Palestine and later through the UN partition plan, contemplated partition as satisfying mutually incompatible, but equally legitimate, self-determination claims for both Jews and Arabs.[41]

Since then the emergence of the Jewish state of Israel and Israel's acquisition of territory by force in 1967 (at which time self-determination existed not just as a principle but as a binding legal norm) has shifted the basis of the Palestinian self-determination claim to one based on repudiation of acquisition of territory through force and a ban on military occupation.[42] The international legal position can be summarized as a 'slow and uneven' movement towards acceptance of three propositions: that there is a Palestinian people; that it has a right of self-determination; and, that this right is to be exercised in the West Bank and Gaza, rather than in the whole of the former Mandatory Palestine.[43] This position has been stated in many General Assembly Resolutions, from 1970 onwards.[44] As Roberts notes, none of these positions were 'self-evident' in terms of the law on self-determination.[45] The emergence of a distinct Palestinian identity, the renouncing by Jordan of any claim to the West Bank, together with the PLO's acceptance of UN Resolution 242 in 1988, all contributed to the situation where 'by the late 1980s neither the complete abolition of Israel nor complete Israeli settlement and domination of the Occupied Territories could be presented with the same conviction.'[46]

Gaps, however, remain. As Cassese asserts, the international consensus around a Palestinian right to self-determination does not extend to agreement 'on the exact territory in which the right to self-determination is to be exercised (for instance should it include East Jerusalem?).'[47] Further, even more than was the case in South Africa, there is no international legal consensus on what the political arrangements capable of fulfilling the Palestinian right to self-determination are; in particular, whether simple withdrawal of the occupying power is sufficient, or whether there are

[40] Indeed, the underlying purpose of the Mandate system of the League of Nations was to create a move towards self-determination and independent government (see Musgrave 1997: 29–30), although, as we have seen, the terms of the Palestine Mandate were ambiguous as Arab self-determination claims.

[41] In an interesting aside Musgrave suggests that this assumption regarding Palestine was also pertinent in preventing an explicit reference to self-determination in Chapters XI, XII, and XIII of the United Nations Charter (setting up the trusteeship of non-self-governing territories which was to subsume the mandate system); Musgrave (1997: 65–6).

[42] See Cassese (1998*b*: 230–47); A. Roberts (1992); but cf. Drew (1997).

[43] A. Roberts (1992: 60).

[44] See e.g. GA Res 2672/C (XXV), 8 Dec. 1970. Security Council resolutions have been more ambiguous.   [45] A. Roberts (1992: 60).

[46] A. Roberts (1992: 61); Cassese (1998*b*: 238–9).   [47] Cassese (1998*b*: 240–1).

further requirements as regards the internal arrangements of the emancipated territory.[48]

The international community has with 'a remarkable degree of unanimity' repeatedly and consistently affirmed that the Fourth Geneva Convention is applicable, and should be applied in all the territories occupied by Israel since 1967.[49] Despite this unanimity, as with South Africa, the record on enforcement is less convincing. In the case of Israel/Palestine, UN Security Council direct enforcement of human rights and humanitarian law under Chapter VII of the UN Charter premissed on a finding that the situation in the Occupied Territories constituted a threat to international peace, was not used and was always unlikely, given the veto power of the United States, who rely on Israel in terms of their Middle East foreign policy.[50] Indirect enforcement through the International Court of Justice Advisory Opinions was not pursued, and faced legal obstacles.[51] However, the United Nations did use a variety of actions aimed at enforcement reminiscent of its actions in South Africa. These included repeated use of non-recognition (of the annexation of East Jerusalem), economic coercion, and attempts to exclude Israel from international organizations.[52] In 1974 the UN General Assembly recognized the PLO as 'the principal party to the question of Palestine' and invited the PLO to participate in deliberations of the General Assembly on the question of Palestine.[53] Soon after, it invited Yasser Arafat to address a plenary session of the Assembly[54] and granted the PLO observer status in the Assembly.[55] As noted in Chapter 3, Protocol I to the 1949 Geneva Conventions 'internationalized' internal wars involving national liberation movements partly in recognition of the PLO's position. Unlike South Africa, as

---

[48] Cassese (1998*b*: 331).

[49] A. Roberts (1992: 52). Cf., however, Bayefsky (1995) for a critique of UN actions against Israel's human rights abuses as excessive to the point of violating the principle of equality of nations.   [50] Dugard (1992*a*: 463).

[51] See generally Dugard (1992*a*).

[52] See e.g. UN SC Res 476, 30 June 1980 (declaring as null and void measures taken by Israel to change the character of Jerusalem and calling on states to withdraw their diplomatic missions from Jerusalem); UN GA Res ES-91, 5 Feb. 1982 (declaring Israel's decision to impose its laws, jurisdiction, and administration on the Golan Heights to be null and void); UN GA Res 37/88, C, 10 Dec. 1982 (on Israeli practices affecting human rights in the Occupied Territories). Israel has been excluded from its regional group within the UN system, and thereby from membership to a large number of UN posts and bodies (see Bayefsky 1995: 448–9).

[53] UN GA Res 3210, inviting the PLO to participate in the UN debates on Palestine, 14 Oct. 1974.

[54] PLO Chairman Yasser Arafat addressing the UN General Assembly, 13 Nov. 1974; pub. in Abdul Hadi (1997*a*: 226–34).

[55] UN GA Res 3237, Granting Observer Status to the Palestine Liberation Organization, 22 Nov. 1974.

Dugard notes, all the methods of enforcement 'suffer[ed] from an absence of a clear statement of the law on the status of the Occupied Territories.'[56]

While human rights conventions provide their own enforcement mechanisms, the question of the applicability of international law's human rights standards in the Occupied Territories is a complicated one.[57] First, there arises a general problem of the applicability and relevance of human rights standards with regard to situations of prolonged military occupation. This cannot be dealt with fully here, but raises difficult questions regarding the relationship between human rights law and humanitarian law.[58] While Israel has at times argued that human rights standards cannot be applied to a situation of occupation, the international community is increasingly coming to view the two sets of standards as conceptually different but complementary, and both applicable in most situations of internal or international conflict.[59] Important as this might be, it does not solve many of the practical problems in applying human rights standards in such a situation. These include the relevance of such standards to situations of violent conflict, alluded to with relation to Northern Ireland; and also difficulties arising from the difference between human rights and humanitarian law standards with respect to issues such as use of lethal force and right to fair trial.[60]

Practically speaking, a convention needs to have been ratified to be applicable. Although Israel has currently ratified the main international human rights conventions, as with South Africa and Northern Ireland, they are not technically part of domestic law until enacted into domestic law, and this has not happened. Israeli courts have therefore been reluctant to rely on them.[61] However, even when ratified, there are questions as to whether the Israeli ratification covers the Occupied Territories.[62] This would seem to be a matter to be ascertained from the wording of each individual treaty as to its scope.[63] However, while acknowledging applicability of some, at times Israel has denied applicability of the treaty to the Occupied Territories,[64] or the treaty itself is silent on scope.[65] The responses of international enforcement bodies as to scope of application

---

[56] Dugard (1992*a*: 476).   [57] See Bevis (1994); A. Roberts (1992: 53–7).

[58] See generally A. Roberts (1987).

[59] Kälin (1994: 26–7). See Statute of the International Tribunal [for former Yugoslavia] 1993; Statute of the International Tribunal for Rwanda; Rome Statute of the International Criminal Court 1999.

[60] While human rights law provides for a right to life and a right to be tried fairly, humanitarian law provides for a right to shoot combatants, and for a right not to be tried in certain conflict circumstances.   [61] Benvenisti (1994*a*).

[62] See Bevis (1994).   [63] Bevis (1994).

[64] See e.g. Office of the Legal Advisor, memorandum (12 Sept. 1984), written for, and contained in, A. Roberts *et al.* (1984: 80–1), as cited in A. Roberts (1992: 55 n. 89).

[65] See in particular Convention on the Elimination of All Forms of Discrimination against Women 1979.

have tended to affirm that Israel is responsible for all areas where it maintains geographical, functional, or personal jurisdiction.[66] However, Israel has entered a notice under Article 4 of the International Covenant on Civil and Political Rights derogating from Article 9.

The Peace Process and its Agreements

The contemporary Middle East peace process commenced under the impetus of the end of the cold war, the break-up of the Soviet Union, and the Gulf War.[67] After months of diplomacy by the United States, Russia and the United States issued an invitation to a peace conference in Madrid on 30 October 1991 (the Madrid Invitation).[68] The invitation affirmed UN Security Council Resolutions 242 and 338 as the basis for the process. The governments of Israel, Syria, Lebanon, Jordan, and Egypt were invited, together with a number of other parties.[69] The PLO were not invited, neither were Palestinians invited in their own right (which Israel would have seen as a concession) but 'as part of a joint Jordanian–Palestinian delegation.'

The Madrid process in effect formed a pre-negotiation stage to the secret talks eventually held directly between the PLO and representatives of the Israeli government, through what became known as 'the Oslo Channel'. During Madrid no agreements were reached, although the agreement to talk within the Madrid Framework indicated possible parameters for the talks, parameters which were further explored during the tortuous negotiations (see Table 4.1).

The Israeli/Palestinian negotiations continued without any serious breakthrough for twenty-two months. The main logjam centred around the exact nature of interim government, and the extent to which this would predetermine final status negotiations. Although Israeli draft agreements used language which stated that final status negotiations

[66] See e.g. Concluding Observations of the Committee against Torture: Israel 18/05/98, A/53/44, para. 232–42 (deals with application in the Occupied Territories); Concluding Observations of the Committee on Economic, Social, and Cultural Rights: Israel, 04/12/98, E/C.12/1/Add/27, para. 6 (affirms applicability of covenant to all areas of Israeli jurisdiction). The Committee on the Elimination of Racial Discrimination on 7 Mar. 1994 requested an urgent report on 'the safety and protection of the Palestinian civilians in the occupied Palestinian territory and to bring to an end the illegal action of Israeli settlers and to disarm them.' Israel submitted a report (Report on Measures Taken to Guarantee the Safety and Protection of the Palestinian Civilians in the Occupied Palestinian Territory: Israel 03/05/95, CERD/C/282). [67] For account, see Ashrawi (1995).

[68] Letter of Invitation to Madrid Peace Conference, 30 Oct. 1991; pub. in Abdul Hadi (1997b: 10).

[69] These were the European Community; Gulf Cooperation Council (GCC); UN secretary-general (observer only, with GCC member states invited to participate in organizing negotiations on multilateral issues); the UN (observer representing the secretary-general).

TABLE 4.1. *Madrid Invitation as Middle East pre-negotiation agreement*

Agreement	Parties	Content
Letter of Invitation to Madrid Peace Conference, 30 October 1991	All parties to conference (not PLO)	Established a framework of a number of bilateral negotiations: Israeli–Palestinian, Israel–Jordan, Israel-Syria, and Israel–Lebanon. A parallel multilateral negotiation was to address common issues of concern such as water, environment, and refugees. The Israel–Palestine dimension, as per Camp David, contemplated a two-phase process for Israeli/Palestinian negotiations: 'negotiations will be conducted in phases, beginning with talks on interim self-government arrangements. These talks will be conducted with the objective of reaching agreement within one year. Once agreed, the interim self-government arrangements will last for a period of five years; beginning the third year of the period of interim self-government arrangements, negotiations will take place on permanent status'

Source: Abdul Hadi (1997b: 10).

would not be prejudiced, Palestinians asserted that Israeli concepts of autonomy in effect predetermined a solution whereby large amounts of land within the pre-1967 borders would be annexed to Israel.[70] Conversely, the Israeli team rejected Palestinian models of autonomy as basically 'represent[ing] a Palestinian State in all but name, considered by Israel a mortal security threat.'[71]

By the eleventh round it became apparent that the process had become deadlocked. However, the PLO and then Israeli Prime Minister Rabin, under a range of pressures externally and internally, were searching for new ways forward outside of the Madrid process. This gave rise to the secret Oslo negotiations, in which the PLO and the Israeli government negotiated face to face in Norway. These negotiations took place in a series of talks over nearly a year, with early rounds forming exploratory pre-negotiation understandings before reaching the substantive stage.[72]

[70] Palestinian Delegation Press Conference with Hanan Ashrawi, Official Spokesperson, 25 Feb. 1992; excerpts pub. in Abdul Hadi (1997b: 67–9); see generally Ashrawi (1995).

[71] Israeli Delegation, Memorandum to the Palestinians regarding Autonomy, 21 Feb. 1992; pub. in Abdul Hadi (1997b: 66–7).

[72] Accounts of these negotiations and some of the draft documents can be found in Abbas (1995); Aburish (1998: 230–61); Makovsky (1996).

While the official delegations continued their negotiations at Washington, an agreement was directly negotiated between the PLO and the Israeli government. This Declaration of Principles (DoP) was initialled on 20 August 1993, and formally signed on 13 September 1993 at a ceremony with President Clinton on the White House lawn. Although negotiated separately, it drew on the drafts flated during the Madrid talks, and similarities can be seen with the Israeli and, to a lesser extent, the Palestinian documents there. A day later a Jordanian–Israeli agreement was signed, rooted in UN SC Resolutions 242 and 338 (affirming 242), providing for a mutual commitment to help back up the Declaration of Principles (see Table 4.2).

Implementation of the DoP was not easy, and, as with Northern Ireland, took place in fits and starts. The DoP had set out a structure for future negotiations, contemplating further agreements to fill out the detail of its broad framework. These were to culminate in final status negotiations and final agreement. However, these agreements did not take place on schedule, often due to intervening violence and disputes over interpretation. The distinction between framework agreements and substantive agreements is in this case particularly difficult to draw, as subsequent agreements both expand the framework in anticipation of final status negotiations and implement the DoP. Furthermore, the implementation stage was characterized by parties, in particular the Israelis, trying to claw back what had been earlier conceded by exploiting the constructive ambiguities of the DoP, and later by simple refusal to implement.[73] It is therefore a matter of debate which agreements actually implemented the DoP and which renegotiated it. The first three agreements in Table 4.3 were contemplated by the DoP and fill out its framework. They also represent the result of continued negotiations and deal with the consequences of the failure to implement earlier agreements, with issues such as prisoner release appearing in different forms in consecutive agreements.

Just after the signing of Oslo II, on 4 November 1995, Israeli Prime Minister Yitzhak Rabin was assassinated by a Jewish extremist, Yigal Amir. During the year that followed, Israeli redeployment took place from the major towns in the West Bank, and Palestinian elections to the Palestinian Legislative Council took place. On 6 May 1996 the first session of the final status talks between Israel and the PLO was held in Taba. However, on 29 May 1996 the Israeli electorate returned the conservative Likud to power, with Benjamin Netanyahu as prime minister, signalling opposition to the peace process. This effectively froze the peace process. The only agreements signed during Netanyahu's prime-ministership

---

[73] For a comprehensive account of the destructive effect of 'constructive ambiguity' in the peace process and historically, see Klieman (1999). For detailed evaluation of both Israeli and Palestinian compliance and non-compliance with the peace agreements, see Watson (2000).

TABLE 4.2. *Substantive–framework peace agreements*

Agreement	Parties	Content
Israel/PLO Recognition, 9–10 September 1993	A mutual exchange of letters between Yasser Arafat (PLO) and Prime Minister Rabin of Israel. (Letter from Yasser Arafat to Norwegian foreign minister confirmed PLO commitments)	PLO recognized 'right of the State of Israel to exist in peace and security.' It committed itself to peaceful resolution of the conflict through negotiation and announced as 'inoperative' inconsistent articles of the Palestinian Covenant, which it undertook to change. PLO renounced 'use of terrorism and other acts of violence.' The letter from Rabin stated 'in the light of the PLO commitments included in your letter, the Government of Israel has decided to recognise the PLO as the representative of the Palestinian people and commence negotiations with the PLO within the Middle East Peace Process'
Declaration of Principles, 13 September 1993	Israeli government and PLO (witnessed by US and Russian Federation)	Creates a two-stage process. First, an interim period of up to five years during which a form of Palestinian self-government is to be established. Secondly, 'permanent status' negotiations based on UN SC Resolutions 242 and 338. The agreement sets out the framework for the interim period, including elections to a Palestinian Council (PC) with international supervision, and provision for an interim Palestinian Authority (PA). The powers of the PA are delimited, functionally (not to cover 'final status' issues), territorially (Gaza and parts of West Bank), and personally (Palestinians, not Israelis). The five-year transitional period is to start upon Israeli 'withdrawal' from the Gaza Strip and Jericho (West Bank) area. The subsequent permanent status negotiations are to cover 'remaining issues', including Jerusalem, refugees, settlements, security arrangements, borders, relations and cooperation with other neighbours, and other areas of common interest. Authority provided to be 'immediately' transferred in education and culture, health, social welfare, direct taxation, and tourism.

Agreement	Parties	Content
		Palestinians are also to commence building a Palestinian police force. Provision is made for an interim agreement to be negotiated, further specifying the make-up and powers of the future Palestinian Council. A joint Israeli–Palestinian Liaison Committee is established to deal with implementation; a Continuing Committee, including the governments of Jordan and Egypt, is to examine refugee issues; and an economic development plan is to be initiated by G7. Protocols provide for agreements to be made on elections and withdrawal of Israeli forces. Protocols also provide for Israeli–Palestinian cooperation in Economic and Regional Development Programmes. Agreed minutes to the agreement provide further details on its interpretation
Israel-Jordan Common Agenda, 14 September 1993	Jordan and Israel	Provides for mutual commitment not to use force against each other. For reaching agreement on water, refugees and displaced persons, and borders and territorial matters. Also provides for bilateral cooperation with reference to natural resources, human resources, infrastructure, economic areas, and implementation

Note: Agreements can be found at <u>www.israel-mfa.gov.il/mfa.go.asp?MFAHOOOcO</u> (last visited 9 May 2000). The agreements, or excerpts of them, up to Wye are also published in Abdul Hadi (1997*b*).

were the agreement on redeployment from Hebron, and the Wye Memo-randum, both of which attempted to deal with Israeli redeployment which should have followed from Oslo II. This latter agreement was not fully implemented.

Not until May 1999, when Israeli elections saw Netanyahu replaced with Labour's Ehud Barak on a platform supportive of a peace process, did the process begin to move again, with new agreements being signed. Negotiations recommenced, and on 4 September 1999 a new agreement was signed, providing for the 'Implementation Timeline of Outstanding Commitments of Agreements Signed and the Resumption of Permanent Status Negotiations'. The post-Rabin agreements much more clearly constitute renegotiation agreements than implementation ones, as they were not contemplated by the framework of the DoP and in places they redefine and amend the DoP commitments.

The Sharm el Sheikh Memorandum provided that final status negotiations would resume on 13 September 1999 and aim to conclude within a year. This commitment also revived the multilateral negotiations. In January 2000 talks took place in Shepardstown, West Virginia, between Israel and Syrian delegations, as part of the Israeli–Syrian track, to little result. At the beginning of February the Steering Committee of the multilateral negotiation process met at ministerial level in Moscow, officially renewing the multilateral track. Dates were set for convening plenary meetings for its five working groups on water, economic development, refugees, the environment, and regional security. A summit between Arafat and Barak broke down over issues relating to further Israeli redeployment.

Towards the end of March and beginning of April Palestinian–Israeli talks commenced at Bolling Air Force Base in the United States and lasted one week, but continued in the following months in different locations. These talks dealt with the implementation of Interim Agreements and also began to touch on permanent status issues. On 5 July 2000, after the Israeli decision to withdraw from Lebanon in March and the death of President Al-Assad of Syria in June, President Clinton announced that Barak and Arafat had accepted an invitation to come to Camp David on 11 July 2000 to continue final status negotiations. The talks finally ended on 25 July 2000 having failed to reach agreement, with Clinton criticizing Arafat's failure to move as far as Barak. The parties did, however, release a trilateral statement wherein Arafat and Barak affirmed that the aim of negotiations was to achieve 'a just and lasting peace' based on UN Security Council Resolutions 242 and 338, and pledged to continue efforts to conclude agreement.[74] Both sides also affirmed the importance of 'avoiding unilateral actions' and of the United States' role as a 'partner in the search for peace.' However, behind these commitments lay Arafat's stated intent to unilaterally declare a Palestinian state on 13 September 2000 (the day by which final status agreement should have been reached), and Israel's probable response to any such declaration of formally annexing large portions of the West Bank.

At the time of writing it remains unclear if or when final agreement will be reached. While both leaders, but at present particularly Barak, need a settlement to consolidate their leadership, a settlement which involves major concessions will undermine the leader concerned and consequently

---

[74] Trilateral Statement on the Middle East Summit at Camp David, available at www.israel-mfa.gove.il/mfa/go.asp?MFAHohn10 (last visited 2 Aug. 2000).

any agreement reached. International and in particular United States' interests require a settlement, not least to facilitate free trade agreements.

Camp David II gave some indication of the negotiating parameters of the parties, and the type of final status agreement which might emerge.[75] Barak apparently agreed to recognize a Palestinian state on up to 94 per cent of the West Bank, while some of the largest settlements in the West Bank (around Jerusalem and containing approximately 80 per cent of West Bank settlers) would be annexed to Israel, in exchange for a land transfer to Palestinians of some areas within the 1948 borders of Israel. However, according to Israeli sources the land transfer would be 'symbolic' (for example, some desert areas near Gaza Strip) rather than equal in size, significance, and resources.[76] Commentators had previously mooted that a raised road linking West Bank and the Gaza Strip could become part of the transfer, and that annexation could be presented as a long-term lease, thus saving face for Palestinian negotiators, who could claim sovereignty had been preserved.

As regards refugees, Barak apparently agreed to the resettlement of about 100,000 refugees within the 1948 borders of Israel, but with the stipulation that this take place under family reunification schemes and that Israel admit no 'moral or legal responsibility, for the creation of Palestinian refugees.' For those refugees not admitted, a large international rehabilitation fund would be established with Israeli contributions, to help with resettlement issues (with Palestinians reputedly accepting that displaced Israelis could also benefit).

While it seemed that these types of compromise would be accepted by Palestinian negotiators (with the exception perhaps of the refugee provisions), commentators agreed that it was the issue of Jerusalem that caused negotiations to founder. Israeli proposals apparently focused on relinquishing controls of northern Palestinian-dominated suburbs, and devolving administration in central areas of East Jerusalem to Palestinian bodies, in exchange for overall Israeli sovereignty and security control over East Jerusalem including the Old City, and the main sites sacred to Christianity, Judaism, and Islam. This proposal was unacceptable to Palestinians, who already in practice undertake such administration in East Jerusalem and also in significant sections of the Old City, and to whom Jerusalem has equally important symbolic, cultural, and religious importance.

---

[75] See generally Beinin (2000); Dumper (2000); Normand (2000).
[76] See A. Benn, *Israel will Pay, but Deny Responsibility, for Refugees*, Ha'aretz Special for the on-line edition, 14 July 2000.

TABLE 4.3. *Implementation agreements*

Agreement	Parties	Content
Protocol on Economic Relations, 29 April 1994 (Paris Protocol)	Israeli government and PLO	Described as a 'contractual agreement that will govern the economic relations between the two sides' and 'cover the West Bank and the Gaza Strip during the interim period.' Establishes a joint economic committee. Deals with import taxes and policy, and monetary matters, direct and indirect taxation, labour, agriculture, industry, tourism, and insurance
Gaza–Jericho Autonomy Agreement, 4 May 1994		This is the further agreement contemplated in Art. 13 and Annex II of the DoP. In addition to providing the technical detail of how (military) withdrawal is to take place, this agreement details how authority is to be transferred from the Israeli military government and its Civil Administration to a Palestinian Authority, together with the structure, composition, powers, and functions of that authority, and the establishment of the Palestinian police force. It also provides for 5,000 Palestinian prisoners to be released. Annexes set out the detail of arrangements for security, civil affairs, and legal matters. A final annex incorporates the above Economic Protocol. An exchange of letters between Rabin and Arafat providing for additional undertakings
Agreement on the Preparatory Transfer of Powers and Responsibilities, 29 August 1994 (Early Empowerment Agreement)	Israeli government and PLO	This provides for transfer of power and responsibilities from Israel to the PA in the areas of education and culture, health, social welfare, tourism, direct taxation, and value added tax on local production. It commits to ongoing exploration of 'possible expansion of the transfer of powers and responsibilities to additional spheres.' The scope of the powers and responsibilities transferred in each sphere are set out in the protocols attached as Annexes I to VII. The PA is given legislative power to promulgate secondary legislation with relation to the powers and responsibilities transferred. All powers are transferred within the terms of the DoP, and do not encroach on final status issues

Agreement	Parties	Content
Protocol on Further Transfer of Powers and Responsibilities, 27 August 1995	Israeli government and PLO	Transfers powers in the additional spheres of labour, commerce and industry, gas and petroleum, insurance, postal services, local government, and agriculture. The agreement essentially applies the mechanisms and scope of the above agreement to these additional spheres.
Interim Agreement between Israel and the Palestinians, 28 September 1995 (Taba, Oslo II, or Interim Agreement)	Israeli government and PLO (witnessed by United States, Russian Federation, Arab Republic of Egypt, Hashemite Kingdom of Jordan, Kingdom of Norway, and EU)	Incorporates and supersedes the two above agreements. Comprises over 300 pages of detailed provision for the transfer of authority, which both restates and expands earlier agreements within the DoP framework. Includes provision for elections; the structure and powers of the Palestinian Council; redeployment of Israeli forces; security and policing; and cooperation over issues such as economic relations. With regard to the division of powers the agreement establishes three different arrangements for 'internal security and public order' in three different types of area: area 'A' comprising named cities, or parts of cities, where the Palestinian Council is to have full responsibility; area 'B' comprising Palestinian towns and villages where the Palestinian Council has responsibility subject to overriding Israeli security authority; and area 'C' comprised of 'unpopulated areas, areas of strategic importance to Israel and Jewish settlements' where Israel retains full responsibility for security and public order, and the Palestinian Council for civil responsibilities not related to territory. Protocols provide for detail on these issues, and also for Palestinian prisoner release. Israeli redeployment from A areas is provided for
Agreement on a Temporary International Presence in Hebron, 17 January 1997	Israeli government and PLO	Fulfils an article of the Interim Agreement, providing for a Temporary International Presence (TIPH) in the city of Hebron made up of Norwegians. This is to stay in place until Israeli deployment from Hebron, when it is to be replaced by a new TIPH, to be agreed

Table 4.3. *Continued*

Agreement	Parties	Content
Protocol concerning the Redeployment in Hebron, 17 January 1997	Israeli government and PLO	Although the Interim Agreement provided that redeployment in Hebron should have taken place within six months of its signing, by then the process had begun to disintegrate. This protocol was the first agreement signed by Netanyahu's government. It provided the detail of agreement of a transfer of powers in (part of) Hebron
Wye River Memorandum, 23 October 1998	Israeli government and PLO (witnessed by William J. Clinton, United States)	Negotiated under US pressure and in a hothouse environment, the Wye Memorandum aimed to start the 'peace process' again. It provided for Israeli redeployments from 13% (1% to Area A and 12% to Area B, with, in a later phase, 14.2% to move from Area B to Area A) of the remaining 72% of West Bank land then remaining under Israeli control. It also committed parties to resuming final status negotiations and complete by 5 May 1999. The bulk of the agreement dealt with placing a security onus on Palestinians, who were to use US cooperation. A timeline shows the timetable for the commitments. Letters from US Secretary of State Madeleine Albright to Prime Minister Netanyahu provide US undertakings concerning Palestinian security. After an initial phase of redeployment the process broke down, and was suspended by the Israeli cabinet as Netanyahu moved towards early elections
The Sharm el-Sheikh Memorandum on Implementation Timeline of Outstanding Commitments of Agreements Signed and the	Israeli government and PLO, witnessed by the Arab Republic of Egypt, the United States, and the	The first agreement negotiated by Barak, this provides commitment to resume permanent status negotiations 'in an accelerated manner' to 'lead to the implementation of Security Council Resolutions 242 and 338.' These negotiations are to commence after the release of prisoners and the second stage of first and second redeployments and be completed not later than 13 September

Agreement	Parties	Content
Resumption of Permanent Status Negotiations, 4 September 1999	Hashemite Kingdom of Jordan	2000. Israeli redeployment in three phases: September 1999, 7% from area C to area B; November 1999, 2% from Area B to area A, and 3% from area C to area B; and January 2000, 1% from area C to area A and 5.1% from Area B to Area A. This left 17.2% of land in A Areas, 23.8% of land in B areas, and 59% in C Areas. Release of 300 prisoners is provided for. The DoP committees are to resume their work. Provision is made for an agreement to be reached by 30 September 1999 on safe passage. Provision of a sea port at Gaza is made, and also security provisions
Protocol concerning Safe Passage between the West Bank and Gaza Strip, 4 October 1999	Israeli government and PLO	Detailed agreement dealing with modalities of Palestinian movement between the West Bank and Gaza Strip. It provides for safe passage to be facilitated by Israel, but also that passage can be 'temporarily' halted or modified for 'security or safety reasons.' Safe passage may be denied for persons 'who have seriously or repeatedly violated the safe passage provisions.' Cards applying for passage have to be submitted to Israelis for approval. Details for the mechanics of how safe passage is to operate are provided.

Note: Agreements can be found at www.israel-mfa.gov.il/mfa.go.asp?MFAHOOOcO (last visited 9 May 2000). The agreements, or excerpts of them, up to Wye are also published in Abdul Hadi (1997*b*).

BOSNIA AND HERZEGOVINA

Yugoslavia was first created after the First World War in 1918, as the outcome of struggles against the empires of Austria, Hungary, and Turkey.[77] It was proclaimed as the Kingdom of Serbs, Croats, and Slovenes, and renamed Yugoslavia (meaning 'South Slav') in 1929. This particular formation broke down during the Second World War when Yugoslavia

[77] For histories of Yugoslavia (dealing with different periods), see Banac (1984); Doder (1979); Ramet (1985, 1992); Rusinow (1977); Singleton (1976, 1983). For a summary of the history of the conflict, the conflict and peace plans, see International Commission on the Balkans (1996).

surrendered to the Axis powers and was occupied by Germany and Italy. In 1944 the (mainly Serbian) Partisans led by Josip Broz (Tito), a Croat, with Soviet assistance, took Belgrade and established a communist regime. A federal system was constructed after the Second World War consisting of six republics: Serbia, Croatia, Slovenia, Bosnia Herzegovina, Macedonia, and Montenegro. Serbia included two autonomous provinces, each containing a high concentration of an ethnic minority: Kosovo (ethnic Albanians) and Vojvodina (ethnic Hungarians). This arrangement was ultimately codified in the 1974 Constitution, which set out the balances in the federation, explicitly using the language of self-determination.[78] Its opening language asserts:

> The nations of Yugoslavia, proceeding from the right of every nation to self-determination, including the right to secession, on the basis of their will freely expressed . . . have together with the nationalities with which they live, united in a federal republic of free and equal nations and nationalities and founded a social-ist federal community of working people—the Socialist Federal Republic of Yugoslavia . . .[79]

Thus the Socialist Federal Republic of Yugoslavia (SFRY) consisted of 'a state community of voluntarily united Nations' with a right to self-determination and secession. The Constitution made a distinction between nations and republics: nations being defined as peoples (with no territorial criteria attached) such as Croats, Macedonians, and Serbs; and republics being the six geographically defined federal units. A second distinction was made between 'nations' and 'nationalities', nationalities being 'members of nations whose native countries border on Yugoslavia.' Thus, the Albanians of Kosovo and the Hungarians of Vojvodina were regarded as 'nationalities' and did not have the right to self-determination or secession under the Constitution.[80]

The Constitution, while providing a right to secession, did not provide a mechanism for achieving it; this indicated the difficulties inherent in any dissolution of the federation. These were difficulties of reaching a satisfactory accommodation of nations and nationalities within republics and provinces—the people/territory problem at the heart of any self-determination dispute. The language of voluntary association, and the carefully crafted balance of powers among republics, and between

---

[78] After the Second World War there were four Constitutions, 1946, 1953, 1963, and 1974, before the constitutional reforms which began in the late 1980s. They differed in 'the details of the voting systems, distributive rules, and governmental distributions' (Woodward 1995). For extracts from the 1946 and 1974 Constitutions, see Trifunovska (1994: 212, 224).

[79] Preamble, The Constitution of the Socialist Federal Republic of Yugoslavia, promulgated on 21 Feb. 1974; pub. in Trifunovska (1994: 224).

[80] Glossary of Terms, The Constitution of the Socialist Federal Republic of Yugoslavia, promulgated on 21 Feb. 1974, as cited in Rich (1993: 37–8).

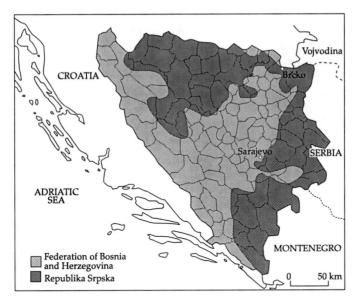

MAP 4.2. Republic of Bosnia Herzegovina post-conflict, showing the two Entities

republics and the SFRY, left it unclear how these problems were to be resolved in the event of dissolution.

Explanations as to the genesis and escalation of conflict vary and can be traced to different points in time.[81] What is clear is that by 1989 indicators of the violent conflict ahead had clearly begun to emerge. During the 1980s Western powers represented by the International Monetary Fund, in an attempt to address the failing Yugoslav economy, had conditioned aid on the imposition of drastic austerity measures, including cuts in the public sector. Economic reforms implicated the balance of power relations, both within the republics and between the republics and the federal authorities, in complex ways.[82] In particular, economic reforms forced the federal government to constrain the republics, tightening control over banking, taxation, budgets, investment, and foreign trade. This was accompanied by proposed constitutional amendments tipping the balance of powers towards centralization.

The resulting pressures led to quarrels between the leaders of the rival republics, and between them and the federal authorities, with the result

[81] There are numerous explanations or accounts of the conflict, from different points of view, focusing on slightly different time periods and emphasizing different analysis. See e.g. L. J. Cohen (1995); Gleny (1996); Gow (1997); Kumar (1997); Owen (1996); Ramet (1996); Silber and Little (1996); Thompson (1992); Woodward (1995).

[82] See Woodward (1995, esp. 47–81).

that 'communist ideology progressively lost its hold . . . [as] Serbian and Croatian nationalisms [surged] back to life, feeding off each other.'[83] Slobodan Milošević, who had come to power in 1987 as the leader of Serbia, made a series of constitutional amendments to the Serbian Constitution, among other things eliminating Kosovan autonomy. He played on Serbian nationalism and attempted to bolster federal powers by moving towards a majoritarian rather than a consensus mode of decision-making among the federation (also recommended by the International Monetary Fund). This was matched by Slovenian and Croatian demands for greater autonomy in republic decision-making. By January 1990 the Federal Communist Party had collapsed, and between April and December the republics held competitive multi-party elections, where nationalist parties swept the board.[84] At this time Slovenia and Croatia declared republic sovereignty, after majority-based referendums, claiming their right to national self-determination.[85] This was followed by similar declarations of sovereignty by the other republics. The move towards separate-state status in turn sparked autonomy claims by minorities within those republics (in particular Serbs within Croatia and Bosnia) and also in Kosovo (ethnic Albanians), that the right to national self-determination belonged not to the republics but to ethnically defined nations.

As Ullman introduces it, the resulting conflict can be understood as four wars: first, the brief and successful struggle for independence waged against the federal army (the so-called Yugoslav People's Army, JNA) by the republic of Slovenia.[86] Secondly, Croatia's more protracted but ultimately successful similar effort to achieve independence. Thirdly, the attempt by the Serbs who were a majority in the Krajina district of Croatia to avoid Croatian sovereignty by joining their lands to Serbia, an attempt which had failed by August 1995, when the Croatian army overran this area, killing or displacing the Serbian community. And fourthly, the war in the Republic of Bosnia and Herzegovina which was both the largest and the most devastating. To this, a fifth war in Kosovo can now be added, which in fact involved two conflicts, that between the Federal Republic of Yugoslavia (or Serbia) and ethnic Albanians, and that between NATO and the Federal Republic of Yugoslavia.[87]

---

[83] Cockburn (1998: 31).

[84] Although, as Emerson (1998: 62–7) notes, this was in part because of the 'first past the post' electoral system in which leaders were elected on what were in fact a minority of votes cast.

[85] Republic of Slovenia Assembly Declaration of Independence, Ljubljana, 25 June 1991; Constitutional Decision on the Sovereignty and Independence of the Republic of Croatia, Zagreb, 15 June 1991; both pub. in Trifunovska (1994: 286–90, 301–4).

[86] Ullman (1996: 1–8).

[87] Ullman (ibid.) notes the possibility that these will not be the only wars, and notes the potential for conflict in Macedonia. More recently, the spectre of conflict relating to Montenegro has also been raised.

The length and scale of the first four wars was proportionately related to how homogeneous (or not) the area in question was. The war in Bosnia Herzegovina was exacerbated by two main factors. First, that any ethnic map-drawing was impossible. While the population in Slovenia was largely homogeneous, and that of Croatia involved a geographically discrete 'Serb' area, Bosnia Herzegovina involved a fairly mixed territory of Croats, 'ethnic Muslims', and Serbs. The April 1991 census recorded a population which was 43.77 per cent Muslim, 31.46 per cent Serb and 17.34 per cent Croat (although interestingly Bosnia Herzegovina had the highest proportion of mixed marriages). The spread of these populations seemed to indicate that any partition of the country was out of the question. In 1991:

There were especially large concentrations of Serbs in western Bosnia—far from the Republic of Serbia—and of Muslims in eastern Bosnia, along the Serbian border. But the picture was rendered even more complex by the fact that in only 32 of Bosnia-Herzegovina's 109 districts did one of the three ethnic groups constitute 70% or more of the local population.[88]

The second complicating factor was that the international community's actions and inactions before and during the Bosnian stage of the conflict operated, not to limit the conflict, but to exacerbate it.[89] As with the case of Israel/Palestine, it is impossible to separate the story of the conflict from the accounts of the international attempts to contain and resolve it.

The Positions of the Domestic Players

Throughout the conflict the Serbian authorities claimed that the dissolution of Yugoslavia had been caused by the illegal secession of Slovenia and Croatia, and that this had resulted in an 'inter-ethnic and civil war' in Bosnia.[90] Their view that Slovenian and Croatian independence was unlawful was based on the constitutional argument that no nation could secede without the consent of all the nations. Serbian authorities also argued in terms of international law, that the requisite territorial unit was that of Yugoslavia as a whole and that any attempt to proclaim independence by the republics was in violation of the international law prohibition on disrupting territorial integrity. As a corollary of this, the

---

[88] Ramet (1996: 244). Again terminology is difficult. Before the conflict the terms 'Croat', 'ethnic Muslim', and 'Serb' will be used to refer to those groups within former Yugoslavia. After 1995 the terms 'Bosniac', 'Croat', and 'Serb' will be used to talk of the ethnic divisions in Bosnia Herzegovina.

[89] See particularly Gow (1997); Woodward (1995).

[90] See e.g. Assessments and Positions of the SFRY Presidency concerning the Proclamation of the Independence and Sovereignty of Slovenia, Belgrade, 11 Oct. 1991; pub. in Trifunovska (1994: 353–5).

Republics of Serbia and Montenegro started to call themselves the Federal Republic of Yugoslavia (FRY), and claimed this to be the successor state to the Socialist Federal Republic of Yugoslavia.[91]

Croatia and Slovenia claimed a converse case, namely that, in declaring independence from former Yugoslavia, they were exercising a right to self-determination and independent statehood consistent with both the Constitution and international law.[92] They subsequently argued that all the emerging states, rather than the FRY alone, had to be regarded as successor states to the SFRY.[93]

The Bosnian government was caught in a bind. It was clear that the dissolution of Yugoslavia would cause tremendous difficulties and violence in Bosnia, were it not to take place 'in the framework of an overall settlement.'[94] Furthermore, Bosnia had a long history of pluralism in the face of diversity, and this had influenced its government. While the elections in Bosnia Herzegovina in 1990 had been fought by three parties organized on ethnic lines (Croatian, Muslim, and Serbian), the government which resulted was dominated by the Muslim Party of Democratic Action (SDA), led by Alija Izetbegović. This party had played two 'contradictory cards', that of strengthening Muslim political representation, while simultaneously emphasizing the multinational, multi-religious character of BiH.[95] As the conflict in Croatia escalated, it became clear that lack of recognition for Bosnia Herzegovina as an independent state would leave the Bosnian claims to territorial integrity vulnerable to Serbian and Croatian expansionist claims. By 23 December 1991 Bosnia had applied for international recognition as a state along with Croatia and Slovenia. Unsurprisingly, perhaps, it was the eventual act of recognition which was to mark the descent into war.

The International Community and International Law

As with Israel/Palestine, the conflict in Bosnia both shaped and was shaped by international law. The international community's self-determination analysis varied according to the development of the conflict. At the begin-

---

[91] See e.g. Positions of the Government of the Federal Republic of Yugoslavia in Reply to the Letter of 27 May 1992, 5 June 1992; pub. in Trifunovska (1994: 589).

[92] See e.g. Republic of Slovenia Assembly Basic Constitutional Charter, Ljubljana, 25 June 1991; Constitutional Decision on the Sovereignty and Independence of the Republic of Croatia, Zagreb, 25 June 1991; both pub. in Trifunovska (1994: 286–90, 299–300).

[93] See Letter from the Minister for Foreign Affairs of the Republic of Slovenia Addressed to the Secretary General of the United Nations, 27 May 1992; pub. in Trifunovska (1994: 586–9).

[94] See Letter from the Secretary General of the United Nations Addressed to the Minister for Foreign Affairs of the Netherlands, 10 Dec. 1991; pub. in Trifunovska (1994: 428–9).

[95] Cockburn (1998: 32).

ning of the conflict the international community, acting at that stage through the European Community (EC), tried to contain violence and to mediate a package settlement, which would recognize the independence of republics but preserve some supra-republic 'Yugoslav' structure. As the conflict developed, making this arrangement redundant, so the self-determination analysis shifted to a debate around the integrity of republic borders, and the fate of 'new' minorities created by their independence. The shifting 'solutions' proffered to address the self-determination issues can be traced through what have been labelled the pre-negotiation agreements (that is, the failed peace blueprints) illustrated in Tables 4.4 and 4.5.

The international community's international law positions also varied, depending on which particular configuration of international players was involved. Among these players a meta-conflict raged over what were the causes of the conflict, and consequently the parameters of any solution. These variously impacted on the use of international law to contain the conflict, often making legal responses incoherent. As noted by Woodward, there were two main competing views.[96] On the first view, the war in Bosnia was an act of aggression by Serbs against the legitimate government of a sovereign member of the United Nations, and part of a pattern of Serb nationalism begun by Slobodan Milošević earlier in Slovenia and Croatia. This view was mainly identified with the United States, and the prescription was the post-cold war formula used with other 'renegade' states and 'new Hitlers', namely a 'package of indirect measures, designed to turn such leaders into international pariahs and to reduce their military advantage . . .'[97] These included incremental punishments from arms embargoes, economic isolation by means of withdrawal of trade privileges, through trade sanctions, political exclusion from international bodies, and diplomatic isolation, to a no-fly zone, and the threat of air power against attempts to attack civilians with heavy weapons.[98]

The second view, most often associated with Europe and Canada, saw the Yugoslav and Bosnian conflicts as a type of civil war between long-time ethnic rivals, unleashed by the death of Tito and the fall of communism.[99] This view did not exclude the use of sanctions to change Serbian behaviour. Neither did it deny that international norms on the sanctity of international borders could apply to the borders of the republics. However, it did view as impossible any solution which was not based on political settlement among the three parties over their territorial disputes.

These two broad positions waxed and waned at different times in the conflict, with the latter 'European approach' peaking during the

---

[96] Cf. also Albert (1997: 3–4).   [97] Woodward (1995: 7).
[98] These strategies arguably reached a peak in the subsequent conflict in Kosovo with NATO air bombing of Serbia.   [99] Woodward (1995: 8).

European initiatives towards the start of the conflict and into the London Conference period, and the 'US approach' becoming dominant as the conflict continued.

Self-Determination and Deal-Making

On 7 July 1991, after the Croatian and Slovenian Declarations of Independence, the EC assumed the principal mediation role in the conflict.[100] When initial agreements broke down, the EC announced that it was setting up a Conference on Yugoslavia in the Peace Palace in The Hague, chaired by Lord Carrington, and a simultaneous arbitration procedure to deal with the self-determination issues, whose results would be put back to the Conference.[101] This arbitration procedure was to outlast EC attempts to mediate, and interestingly provided a unique mechanism for interchange between international law and conflict.

The arbitration procedure comprised a Commission of five presidents from among the various Constitutional Courts of the EC countries, and became known as the Badinter Commission after its president.[102] This Commission was to issue fifteen 'opinions' in total, relating to the application to the Yugoslav situation of international law regarding sovereignty, recognition, self-determination, and state succession.[103] These opinions attempted to apply international law to the facts pertaining at different points during the conflict. These opinions then informed international action. As Craven notes, the opinions provided both a legal rationalization for otherwise incoherent and contradictory elements of state practice, and a legal framework for its development.[104]

On 29 November 1991 the Badinter Commission issued its first opinion, addressing whether the claims of independence by the republics constituted secession from the SFRY, 'which would otherwise cease to exist'; or whether the question was 'one of a disintegration or breaking-up of the SFRY as the result of the concurring will a number of republics' who

---

[100] Joint Declaration of the EC Troika and the Parties Directly Concerned with the Yugoslav Crisis ('Brioni Accord'), Brioni 7 July 1991; pub. in Trifunovska (1994: 311–15). For an overview of EC actions, see Gow (1997: 46–98).

[101] [EC] Declaration on Yugoslavia, Adopted at the EPC Extraordinary Ministerial Meeting, The Hague, 3 Sept. 1991; pub. in Trifunovska (1994: 342–3).

[102] See generally Craven (1995); Pellet (1992). The composition and terms of reference of the Commission were revised in Jan. 1993, (1993) 31 I.L.M. 1572.

[103] Opinions 1–10 pub. in (1992) 31 I.L.M. 1494 (No. 1) , 1497 (No. 2), 1499 (No. 2), 1501 (No. 4), 1503 (No. 5), 1507 (No. 6), 1512 (No. 7), 1521 (No. 8), 1523 (No. 9), 1525 (No. 10). Opinions 11–15 pub. in (1993) 32 I.L.M. 1586 (No. 11), 1589 (No. 12), 1591 (No. 13), 1593 (No. 14), 1595 (No. 15). The Commission also gave an 'interlocutory decision' prior to its eighth opinion following a challenge from Serbia and Montenegro to its competence; (1992) 31 I.L.M. 1518.　　　　　　　[104] Craven (1995: 334–5).

would consequently be 'equal successors to the SFRY.'[105] After clarifying terms, the arbitration committee formed the opinion that:

- the Socialist Federal Republic of Yugoslavia is in the process of dissolution;
- that it is incumbent upon the Republics to settle such problems of State succession as may arise from this process in keeping with the principles and rules of international law, with particular regard for human rights and the rights of peoples and minorities;
- that it is up to those Republics that so wish, to work together to form a new association endowed with the democratic institutions of their choice.

The open-endedness of this determination, apparently crafted so as to avoid a direct answer, tended towards the position of the Slovene and Croatian republics that the process was one of dissolution rather than secession, while emphasizing the desirability of negotiated agreement.

During this same period the EC also grappled with similar self-determination issues relating to the dissolution of the former Soviet Union. The two processes became linked through timing and the need for consistency.[106] On 16 December 1991 the EC set out guidelines for the 'Recognition of new States in Eastern Europe and the Soviet Union' (Annex 1) together with a 'Declaration on Yugoslavia' (Annex II).[107] These articulated guidelines incorporated self-determination concerns. The guidelines set out a list of the following requirements for recognition:

- respect for the provisions of the Charter of the United Nations and the commitments subscribed to in the Final Act of Helsinki and in the Charter of Paris, especially with regard to the rule of law, democracy, and human rights
- guarantees for the rights of ethnic and national groups and minorities in accordance with the commitments subscribed to in the framework of the CSCE
- respect for the inviolability of all frontiers which can only be changed by peaceful means and by common agreement
- acceptance of all relevant commitments with regard to disarmament and nuclear non-proliferation as well as to security and regional stability
- commitment to settle by agreement, including where appropriate by recourse to arbitration, all questions concerning state succession and regional disputes

The guidelines concluded by stating that EC countries 'will not recognize entities which are the result of aggression' and that 'they would take

---

[105] Opinion No. 1 of the Arbitration Commission of the Peace Conference on Yugoslavia, 29 Nov. 1991 (1992) 31 I.L.M. 1494.

[106] See Rich (1993) for discussion of the interrelationship between these two processes.

[107] EC Declaration concerning the Conditions for Recognition of New States, Brussels, 16 Dec. 1991; pub. in Trifunovska (1994: 431–2).

account of the effects of recognition on neighbouring states.' As Rich notes, while purporting to retain 'normal standards of international practice' these standards for recognition add a series of new requirements such as protections for minorities which 'have tended to supplant the previous practice which was largely based on meeting the traditional criteria for statehood.'[108] These new criteria in part aimed to harmonize the criteria on recognition with self-determination requirements.

Further criteria were then added for states emerging from Yugoslavia, and a process for applying the guidelines to Yugoslavia was established. The republics were invited to apply for recognition, upon which the Badinter Commission would adjudicate on whether they complied with guidelines and criteria. These criteria required that:

- they wish to be recognised as independent states
- they accept the commitments contained in the above-mentioned guidelines
- they accept the provision laid down in the draft Convention under consideration by the Conference on Yugoslavia—especially those in Chapter II on human rights and rights of national or ethnic groups
- they continue to support
  - the efforts of the Secretary General and the Security Council of the United Nations
  - the continuation of the Conference on Yugoslavia[109]

In response Slovenia, Croatia, Bosnia, and Macedonia requested recognition, and consequently Badinter opinions were proffered. Badinter decided that Slovenia had met the guideline conditions, but that Croatia had not sufficiently fulfilled the commitments with relation to 'special status' protection of minorities embodied in Chapter 2 of the Carrington Draft Convention (produced in the peace conference track).[110] Badinter also found that Macedonia had satisfied the guideline conditions, but its recognition was to become complicated by Greek concerns regarding the use of the name, and possible claims of Macedonia in Greece.[111] This will not be further considered here.

As regards Bosnia, Badinter found that guideline criteria had been substantially met, but that Serbian people in Bosnia and Herzegovina (BiH) had not associated themselves with the relevant undertakings, having formed a separate Serbian Assembly and later republic; and further, that as recently as October 1991 the Assembly of BiH had agreed conditions by

---

[108] Rich (1993: 43).

[109] EC Declaration concerning the Conditions for Recognition of New States, Brussels, 16 Dec. 1991; pub. in Trifunovska (1994: 431–2).

[110] Opinions No. 7 and No. 5 (respectively) of the Arbitration Commission of the Peace Conference on Yugoslavia, Paris, 11 Jan. 1992; pub. in (1992) 31 I.L.M. 1503, 1512.

[111] Opinion No. 6 on the Recognition of the Socialist Republic of Macedonia by the European Community and its Member States, Paris, 11 Jan. 1992; pub. in (1992) 31 I.L.M. 1507.

which it would remain a member of 'a new Yugoslav community'; and that the Constitution provided for testing of the will of the people through referendums.[112] Given these findings, Badinter found that 'the will of the peoples of Bosnia-Herzegovina to constitute [the republic] as a sovereign and independent State cannot be held to have been fully established.'

At the same time Badinter offered opinions on two related self-determination questions. First, it considered: '[d]oes the Serbian population in Croatia and BiH, as one of the constituent peoples of Yugoslavia, have the right to self-determination?' Badinter decided that the Serbian people were entitled to 'all the rights accorded to minorities and ethnic groups under international law and under the provisions of the [Carrington Draft Convention]', to which both republics had undertaken to give effect; and that the republics had to protect these rights and also the right of individuals to choose their nationality.[113]

The second question asked: '[c]an the internal boundaries between Croatia and Serbia and between Bosnia and Herzegovina and Serbia be regarded as frontiers in terms of public international law?' Noting that their opinion was given in the context of 'a fluid and changing situation', Badinter set down principles which were to govern the dissolution period, namely that the boundaries could not be altered except by free agreement; that any attempt to alter by use of force would be devoid of legal effect; and that, except where otherwise agreed, 'the former boundaries become frontiers protected by international law' as following from the principle of *uti possedetis*.[114]

These two opinions, while avoiding direct answers, implied that indeed the borders were international, or in the process of so becoming, and that Serbians within Croatia, BiH, and the Albanians of Kosovo were entitled to equality and full protection of rights (with a possible group dimension), but not secession or unilateral border redrawing.[115]

Croatia gave guarantees of compliance on minority rights, and although these seemed to fall short of what Badinter had required, the EC

[112] Opinion No. 4 on International Recognition of the Socialist Republic of Bosnia and Herzegovina by the European Community and its Member States, Paris, 11 Jan. 1992; pub. in (1992) 31 I.L.M. 1501. The then declared Serbian 'Republika Srpska' voted for independence on 9 Nov. 1991, when a turnout of 87% voted overwhelmingly (98%) to endorse independence. This was declared unconstitutional by others in the Bosnian government.

[113] Opinion No. 2 of the Arbitration Commission of the Peace Conference on Yugoslavia, Paris, 11 Jan. 1992; pub. in (1992) 31 I.L.M. 1497.

[114] Opinion No. 3 of the Arbitration Commission of the Peace Conference on Yugoslavia, Paris, 11 Jan. 1992, (1992) 31 I.L.M. 1499.

[115] Badinter effectively ignored referendums in which the minority groups had supported secession: the Serbs of the Krajina in Croatia, on 17 Aug. 1990, with a 99% majority of a 95% turnout, in support of autonomy; Krajina Serbs on 12 May 1991, with a majority of 90% of a 95% turnout, in favour of remaining part of a Federal Republic of Yugoslavia; and Albanians in Kosovo on 22 Oct. 1991, in which a majority of 99% of an 87% turnout voted for independence. See Emerson (2000: 62–3).

recognized Croatia and Slovenia on 15 January 1992. A last-minute attempt to find political accommodation in Bosnia through a blueprint proposing an independent state divided into three autonomous and largely ethnically defined entities, loosely held together by a weak central government (Statement of Principles, Cutilheiro Plan see Table 4.4), failed. Instead, the proposed referendum was held on 11 March 1992. The Serb minority, forming 31 per cent of the population, boycotted the vote, which then resulted in a positive vote of over 99 per cent (of a voter turnout of 63 per cent). Despite the Serb boycott (which undermined Badinter's rationale in suggesting a referendum), recognition was given by the EC on 6 April 1992, with other states and eventually the UN following suit, and the country descended into violence.

Debate has since raged on the role that recognition of Bosnia played in confirming the conflict there. Was it too late, leaving the initiative with the Serbs, who had already begun preparing for war? Or was it too early, pre-empting any attempt to negotiate agreement? Gow suggests that the timing of recognition ensured the worst of both worlds:

It would have been better, having failed to act decisively and recognise in January, to allow the talks more time. Recognition in April, in one sense too late, was also precipitate—not because it caused a war which negotiations could have prevented but because deferred recognition would have bought a little time both for the Bosnian government to prepare for the inevitable armed hostility and for the international community to prepare a co-ordinated follow through to the act of recognition [including lifting the arms embargo on Bosnia].[116]

As the war developed, the international community, through the EC, the (then) Conference on Security and Cooperation in Europe (CSCE, later OSCE), the ministers of foreign affairs of the Organization of the Islamic Conference, the UN General Assembly, and the UN Security Council repeatedly stated the following principles as relevant to any proposed 'solution' to the conflict:

- recognition of the sovereignty, territorial integrity, and political independence of Bosnia Herzegovina
- the need for a negotiated solution freely arrived at
- the unacceptability of the acquisition of territory by force
- the right of refugees to return home
- the principle of personal culpability for crimes against humanity (eventually)[117]

Peace plans purporting to comply with such principles were developed and rejected, most often by the Bosnian Serbs.[118] By 4 July 1992 Badinter

---

[116] Gow (1997: 90).
[117] See e.g. UN SC Res 859 of 24 Aug. 1993.   [118] See Table 4.5.

opinions affirmed that the process of the dissolution of Yugoslavia was complete and that FRY was not the sole successor state.[119] Shortly after, it was decided that the FRY could not automatically assume the SFRY place on the UN Security Council, General Assembly, and Economic and Social Council, and must apply for UN membership in its own right as the other republics had done.[120]

The eventual self-determination position arrived at in Yugoslavia developed the international law, much in the same way as that of South Africa and Israel/Palestine. As with those cases, the definition was somewhat incomplete or unclear. While the traditional phrases of 'territorial integrity' and 'inviolability of borders' were frequently repeated, this did little to resolve the central question of which territory and which borders? As in Northern Ireland and Israel/Palestine, the self-determination norm stands accused, not merely of failing to prevent the conflict, but of causing it.[121]

The case of former Yugoslavia apparently evidences a principle that dissolution is permitted, subject to the application of *uti possedetis* and provision of minority rights. 'Referendum mania' ensued, promoted in part by the international community. But the referendums were used less as a way of finding an accommodation, and more to justify the independence of republics within pre-existing borders (even when boycotted by minority groups); referendums were ignored when they expressed minority demands for autonomy or secession.

The legal principle apparently established raises a host of questions, such as: What is the difference between 'dissolution' and 'secession'? Are the above principles only applicable to federal states? Is former Yugoslavia *sui generis* given the particular constitutional relationship between centre and republics? Or is the case of Eastern Europe more generally *sui generis* owing to the 'grand transformation' wrought by the cold war?[122]

---

[119] Opinion Nos. 9 and 10 of the Arbitration Commission of the Peace Conference on Yugoslavia, Paris, 4 July (1992) 31 I.L.M. 1523, 1525. A year later they dealt with questions of succession of states, Opinion Nos. 11–15.

[120] UN SC Res 777 of 19 Sept. 1992; UN GA Res 47/1 of 22 Sept. 1992; UN SC Res 821 of 28 Apr. 1993; GA Res 47/229 of 29 Apr. 1993.

[121] Cf. below. See further, Basic *et al.* (1999) (sketching out the rational choice model whereby the legal principles can force a minority and a government to 'make rational choices that result in armed conflict').

[122] See further Dugard (1992*b*); Rich (1993: 60–5); Weller (1992). The Badinter opinions themselves evidence some inconsistencies in the application of this principle. For example, some of the dates established by the Commission in its Opinion No. 11 as the dates at which statehood was acquired by the different republics are earlier than the date at which the Commission (in that same opinion) decided that dissolution had commenced, suggesting that secession had taken place (in conflict with their very first opinion); (1993) 32 I.L.M. 1586; see Craven (1995: 377).

Human Rights and Humanitarian Law

There was little disagreement during the conflict in Bosnia that human rights and humanitarian law standards applied and were being violated. The conflict was addressed by many different international actors, in particular, the EC, the CSCE, and the UN. The International Court of Justice (ICJ) also became involved when the Republic of Bosnia and Herzegovina filed a complaint against the FRY, accusing it of committing genocide, and of incitement, conspiracy, and complicity in genocide, with relation to Bosnia Herzegovina. Two successive requests for indications of provisional measures were refused, although the ICJ did state that the government of the FRY should take all measures within its power to prevent commission of the crime of genocide.[123]

While the enforcement actions ultimately taken may seem robust as compared with the previous three examples, in the light of the intensity of the conflict they often appeared ineffective and incoherent.[124] As with Israel/Palestine, the enforcement actions were intimately related to a fluctuating international analysis of self-determination claims, and mutated with that analysis. Only a brief summary is possible here, by way of sketching out how enforcement measures evolved, as the self-determination analysis moved towards the (US) view that an internationally recognized state was being attacked.[125] This was accompanied by a transition from European intervention to UN intervention, with NATO ultimately becoming involved in air strikes. In the first phase, until late November 1991, the EC had primacy. As violence began, the initial response of the EC was to

---

[123] See *Case concerning Application of the Convention on the Prevention and Punishment of the Crime of Genocide* (1993) I.C.J. 3, 325 (both requests then focused on trying to get the court to recommend a termination of the arms embargo against Bosnia, with the latter also inviting the court to intervene in the then ongoing political negotiations concerning the future structure of BiH). See further *Case concerning Application of the Convention on the Prevention and Punishment of the Crime of Genocide (Bosnia and Herzegovina v Yugoslavia) Preliminary Objections and Counterclaims,* 115 *International Law Reports* 1, 207 (where preliminary objections of FRY were rejected but its counter-claims allowed to go forward). On 2 July 1999 Croatia also initiated proceedings before the ICJ against FRY for violations of the 1948 Convention on the Prevention and Punishment of the Crime of Genocide alleged to have been committed between 1991 and 1995. FRY has also recently initiated proceedings in the ICJ against the ten states involved in the NATO bombing.

[124] For a detailed review of UN intervention, see Economides and Taylor (1996); for an overview of the role of the international community in the conflict, see Gow (1997). See also McGoldrick (1999); Szasz (1995); Weller (1992).

[125] For example, the principal efforts of the international community amounted to increasingly desperate efforts to alleviate the effects of the conflict, coordinated by the UN High Commissioner for Refugees and other organizations such as the World Food Programme, UNICEF, the World Health Organization, the Food and Agriculture Organization of the United Nations, UNESCO, the International Committee of the Red Cross, and non-governmental organizations such as Médecins sans Frontières. These will not be considered further.

put an embargo on sending armaments and military equipment to Yugoslavia, and to suspend trade cooperation agreements.[126] The UN at this stage largely operated to back up EC action, for example by underwriting the arms embargo through UN Security Council Resolution 713, an action taken under Chapter VII of the UN Charter.

From November 1991, as EC peace making initiatives failed, the EC became replaced by the UN in its peace keeping role, but with 'the peacemaking function of the EC remain[ing] intact.'[127] UN Secretary-General Cyrus Vance put forward a blueprint for a UN peace keeping operation which was to result in the establishment by UN Security Council Resolution 743 of a UN protection force (UNPROFOR). The original form of the peace keeping mandate did not claim to be Chapter VII based. It also made reference to the request of the Yugoslav government. These factors seemed to indicate that UNPROFOR was to undertake the consensual peace keeping function rooted in Chapter VI of the UN Charter. However, the mandate stated the force's aim as 'to create the conditions of peace and security required for the negotiation of an overall settlement of the Yugoslavia crisis,' indicating a possible extension into enforcement and Chapter VII. Recognition of the republics as independent states meant that the conflict was now clearly defined to be an international one, and had to be dealt with as such.

As violence escalated by the summer of 1992, the UNPROFOR mandate evolved, at first to a more active security role with regard to protection of Sarajevo airport after the withdrawal of the Bosnian Serb forces.[128] Then, in SC Resolution 770 of 13 August 1992, the mandate was expanded to include the delivery of humanitarian assistance and to use 'all measures necessary' to do this, becoming UNPROFOR II in the process. The pretence for consent of the parties to the conflict was gone, with UN Security Council resolutions clearly rooted in Chapter VII of the UN Charter.

As the peace making functions were transferred from the EC to the 'London Conference' the UN was pushed into a more active role.[129] About the same time a consensus emerged (similar to the US position) that Serbia Montenegro was the violating state. Trade sanctions were extended by the UN, under Chapter VII, to the Federal Republic of Yugoslavia (Serbia and Montenegro).[130] From late 1992 indications of a greater willingness to use force became evident, with increasingly strident Security

---

[126] [EC] Declaration on the Situation in Yugoslavia, The Hague, 5 July 1991; pub. in Trifunovska (1994: 310–1); EC Declaration on the Suspension of the Trade and Cooperation Agreement with Yugoslavia, Rome, 8 Nov. 1991, (1991) 42 *Review of International Affairs* 26–7.
[127] Economides and Taylor (1996: 70).
[128] UN SC Res 758 of 8 June 1992 (passed pursuant to an Agreement on the Opening of Sarajevo Airport for Humanitarian Purposes, 5 June 1992).
[129] See Economides and Taylor (1996: 71).   [130] UN SC Res 757 of 30 May 1992.

Council resolutions. The mandate for UNPROFOR was extended first until March 1993 and then until June 1993, with the relevant resolutions affirming that the Security Council was acting under Chapter VII of the charter.[131] A fight ban was instituted in Bosnian airspace, and then extended.[132]

As evidence of mass graves, concentration camps, and the practices of ethnic cleansing emerged, humanitarian law obligations were increasingly emphasized by the international community, and monitoring processes facilitated.[133] In 1992 the UN Commission on Human Rights appointed a special rapporteur on human rights, who submitted a well-documented series of reports on abuses to the General Assembly and/or UN Security Council. In October 1992 the Security Council asked the secretary-general to establish an impartial Commission of Experts, informally known as the Yugoslav War Crimes Commission.[134] On 25 May 1993 this culminated in UN SC Res 827, which established an ad hoc criminal tribunal, following hot on the heels of Serbian refusal to accept the Vance–Owen plan which had emerged from the London Conference—a clear peace blueprint with a chance of success. Interestingly the references to humanitarian law made no attempt to state the basis of its application, a matter which would have involved deciding whether the conflict was international, internal, or even (more unlikely) one of national liberation by any one of a number of parties. This would have required consensus both on the cause of the conflict and on the path to its resolution—a consensus that was missing.

As Bosnian Serbs continued to reject peace plans, UN 'punishment' action strengthened further. The UN extended UNPROFOR's mandate to enforce 'safe areas';[135] considered lifting the arms embargo as regards the Bosnian government (although ultimately it did not[136]); periodically increased UNPROFOR's number and length of mandate;[137] and sanctioned the use of air power to enforce the safe areas.[138]

The 'mission-creep' approach to enforcement led to incoherence, as past analysis hindered changes in direction. As the ('European') approach of conflict containment and negotiation later gave way to the ('US') attempts to punish 'baddies', the strategies of the former hobbled the latter. To give

---

[131] UN SC Res 807 of 19 Feb. 1993; UN SC Res 815 of 30 Mar. 1993.

[132] UN SC Res 781 of 9 Oct. 1991; UN SC Res 816 of 31 Mar. 1993.

[133] See e.g. UN SC Res 764 of 13 July 1992.

[134] Formally known as the Commission of Experts established pursuant to Resolution 780 (1992); set up under UN SC Res 780 of 6 Oct. 1992.

[135] UN SC Res 836 of 4 June 1993.

[136] Draft Resolution (not adopted) of 29 June 1993.

[137] See e.g. UN SC Res 847 of 30 June 1993; UN SC Res 869 of 30 Sept. 1993; UN SC Res 908 of 31 Mar. 1994; UN SC Res 914 of 27 Apr. 1994.

[138] UN SC Res 836 of 4 June 1993; UN SC Res 958 of 19 Nov. 1994 (extending to Croatia).

some examples, the presence of UNPROFOR in an extended peace keeping role limited more robust enforcement action, such as air strikes. Similarly, the ban on arms to all parties, initially designed to limit conflict, soon appeared to escalate the conflict by leaving 'goodies' (read Bosnian government) unfairly disadvantaged and vulnerable. Given the continued failure of the UN to protect Bosnia, an arms embargo on the Bosnian army became increasingly inconsistent with the recognition of Bosnia as a state, and its consequent right to defend its territorial integrity.

In the summer of 1994 the United States secured agreement between the Croatian and Bosnian governments to a Federation of Bosnia and Herzegovina (see Table 4.6). By 1995 factors such as Croatian–Bosnian gains against Bosnian Serbs in Bosnia Herzegovina, greater US involvement, and Milošević's distancing from Bosnian Serbs had produced a stalemate.[139] The United States began strong diplomatic initiatives. In August 1995, after the massacre of Bosnians in the UN 'safe area' of Srebrenica which the UN had failed to prevent, and a bomb in Sarajevo which killed many civilians, NATO began a sustained bombing campaign to force the withdrawal of Bosnian Serb forces from around Sarajevo. This was in effect complemented by the success of joint Croatian–Bosnian initiatives, and paved the way for the Dayton Peace Agreement.[140]

The Peace Process and its Agreements

While the term 'peace process' seems peculiarly inappropriate to be applied to any stage of the conflict prior to Dayton, as with Israel/Palestine, unsuccessful peace plan blueprints were agreed to by some parties, and can be viewed as pre-negotiation agreements. Whilst unsuccessful, these blueprints began to sketch out possible formulas for resolution, which influenced the final deal agreed to. As noted above, these agreements also provide a picture of evolving international analysis as to what would best accommodate the differing self-determination claims. Tables 4.4–4.6 divide the pre-negotiation agreements into three phases. First, agreements prior to the escalation of hostilities in BiH, which aimed to find an overall framework agreement for former Yugoslavia, and end with a plan for a tripartite state in BiH aimed at preventing conflict (Table 4.4). With the failure of these plans by March 1992, the stage was set for the conflict in BiH. The second phase (Table 4.5) includes peace plans developed to address this conflict, which played (unfortunately only) a pre-negotiation role. Table 4.6 includes plans which emerged from late 1994 until 1995 under US mediation, which were agreed to by most of the

---

[139] Croatian gains in BiH were preceded by Croat ethnic cleansing of the Serbs in the Knin Krajina in Croatia, with the connivance of the United States.   [140] Gow (1997: 276).

TABLE 4.4. *Pre-negotiation agreements: peace blueprints aimed at mediating process of dissolution of former Yugoslavia*

Agreement	Parties	Content
Joint Declaration of the EC Troika and the Parties Directly Concerned with the Yugoslav Crisis, Brioni, 7 July 1991 (Brioni Accord)	EC Troika statement, referencing agreements reached by 'representatives of all parties directly concerned by the Yugoslav crisis'	General principles provided, namely: it is only up to peoples of Yugoslavia to decide upon their future; a new situation has arisen which requires monitoring; negotiations should begin urgently on basis of Helsinki Final Act and Paris Charter for a new Europe; parties should refrain from unilateral action, particularly acts of violence. Two annexes deal with military matters mainly relating to establishing a ceasefire and monitoring of the agreed ceasefire
Peace Conference on Yugoslavia: Arrangements for General Settlement, The Hague, 18 October 1991 ('Carrington Draft Convention'); expanded in Peace Conference on Yugoslavia: Treaty Provisions for the Convention, The Hague, 1 November 1991	Accepted by Republics of Croatia, Bosnia Herzegovina, Macedonia, Montenegro, and Slovenia, but rejected by Slobodan Milošović and Republic of Serbia	Provided a constitutional framework of sovereign and independent republics (according to existing borders unless otherwise agreed) within a 'free association with international personality.' Provided detailed human rights provision, referencing international human rights instruments and emphasizing the importance of applying them to national and ethnic groups. Also made provision for autonomy of minority groups within republics, with autonomous legislative, administrative, and judicial structures, to apply 'in particular to the Serbs living in areas in Croatia where they form a majority'
Statement on Principles for New Constitutional Arrangement for Bosnia and Herzegovina, Lisbon, 23 February 1992 (Cutilheiro plan);	Accepted by Serbian, Croatian, and Bosnian negotiators, but later repudiated by Bosnians and Croatians	In an attempt to reach settlement prior to independence of BiH, this plan proposed an independent BiH 'composed of three constituent units' wherein the three nations, 'Muslims, Serbs and Croats and those belonging to other nations and nationalities would realise their sovereign rights.' Provided for human rights and structures of

Agreement	Parties	Content
later supplemented by human rights principles, March 1992		government similar to those of Carrington Draft Convention

Note: The three agreements are published in Trifunovska (1994: 311–15, 357–63, 517–19). Further agreements relating to the former Yugoslavia focusing on Croatia's Krajina area will not be considered here, but are discussed in International Commission on the Balkans (1996) and the Appendix to this book.

main parties to the conflict and formed the building-blocks for Dayton. These include the Washington Peace Agreement, which ended the war between Bosnian Croats (supported by Croatian President Tudjman) and Bosnian armed forces.

With the above broad principles containing the embryonic structure of a final settlement, negotiation continued to intensify, and culminated in twenty-one days of intense talks in Dayton Airbase, Ohio.[141] This resulted in the General Framework Agreement for Peace in Bosnia and Herzegovina or Dayton Peace Agreement (Table 4.7).

Implementation of Dayton has been largely supervised by the international community through a Peace Implementation Conference and continued Contact Group Meetings. While the mechanisms specified in Dayton have been established, they have been sustained chiefly through the involvement of the international community, and through the coordination of the Office of the High Representative established by Dayton. This Office has had its power gradually increased by the Peace Implementation Conference.[142] The post-Dayton landscape is characterized by a multi-agency international approach that has been likened to a protectorate or League of Nations mandate.[143] In particular Dayton's mechanisms are sustained by the work of the OSCE, the UN Mission to Bosnia and Herzegovina, the Council of Europe, and of course, the Office of the High Representative. Despite the establishment of many of Dayton's mechanisms, the actual record of implementation remains poor and difficult, as will be discussed further in Chapter 7 with reference to the human rights mechanisms.

[141] For account, see Holbrooke (1998).

[142] Political Declaration from Ministerial Meeting of the Steering Board of the Peace Implementation Council, Sinatra, 30 May 1997, para. 92; Peace Implementation Conference: Bosnia and Herzegovina 1998—Self-Sustaining Structures Bonn, 9–10 Dec. 1997, Conclusions XI(2); both pub. in Office of the High Representative (1998: 157–63, 188–203).

[143] See e.g. Pajić (1998: 126).

TABLE 4.5. *Pre-negotiation agreements: key peace blueprints aimed at ending the conflict in BiH*

Agreement	Parties	Content
Vance–Owen Peace Plan, January 1993–May 1993 (put forward initially as Agreement Relating to Bosnia and Herzegovina, Geneva, 30 January 1993)	Both agreements signed by Bosnian Croats, Bosnian Serbs, and Bosnian government. However, the accompanying map was not signed by either the Bosnian Serbs or the Bosnian government. The Bosnian government eventually signed the map. The Bosnian Serb leader eventually signed, but subject to the ratification of the Bosnian Serb Assembly, which it failed to do (5 May 1993)	Plan comprised three components: a military agreement, a constitutional document, and a provisional map. The constitutional document provided for a weak unitary structure for BiH, with ten provinces, most of which would have ethnic majorities, but were designed as 'multicultural' through proportionality in their governments
Owen–Stoltenberg Plan, July 1993–November 1993 (a plan put forward on 20 September 1993 and known as the *Invincible Acquis*)	Agreed to by Bosnian government leadership, Bosnian Serb leadership and Bosnian Croat leadership, who agreed to put it to their respective assemblies to be ratified, which the Bosnian Croat and Bosnian Serb Assemblies did. The Bosnian	A plan for a 'union of three Republics' which amounted to *de facto* tripartite partition, similar to the earlier Carrington and Cutilheiro plans. It incorporated a constitutional agreement, with provision for human rights courts; agreed arrangements for making the union 'work', such as an access authority; a draft agreement guaranteeing the Muslim republic access to the Adriatic; and an agreement on military aspects of implementation. Agreement to leave some territorial issues to be resolved by a future mechanism

Agreement	Parties	Content
	presidency informed that their Assembly had not ratified the plan	

Note: The initial drafts of the Vance–Owen plan are set out in UN Documents S/24795, Annex VII; pub. in (1992) 31 I.L.M. 1584. The Vance–Owen plan continued to be developed, often through shuttle diplomacy for the next eight months, in an attempt to reach agreement. For a summary of where the plan got to before being abandoned, see Report of the Co-Chairmen of the Steering Committee on the Activities of the International Conference on the Former Yugoslavia, 20 Aug. 1993 (S/26337.Add.1 (Constitution) and Add.2 (Map)). The Owen–Stoltenberg or *Invincible* Acquis (which became modified by the end of 1993 into the European Union Action Plan) is discussed in detail in S/26486, 23 Sept. 1993; see also International Commission on the Balkans (1996: 52). Maps showing the territorial divisions of all the major peace plans are reproduced in International Commission on the Balkans (1996: 50–1).

The international role in a situation of distrust means that implementation agreements are signed on an ongoing basis between the parties to on-the-ground disputes.[144] Other agreements provided for the normalization of relations between different republics. Furthermore, agreements between international actors may be just as significant to implementation as agreements between local actors, in particular with respect to regional approaches. Important in this regard is the Stability Pact for South Eastern Europe, Cologne, 10 June 1999.[145] Given this, a full record of implementation agreements is beyond the scope of this book, but a record of agreements as far as January 1998 can be found in a publication of the Office of the High Representative established under Dayton.[146]

CONCLUSIONS

Similarly to the cases of South Africa and Northern Ireland, the cases of Israel/Palestine and Bosnia illustrate both the relationship of interchange between international law and conflict, and the malleability of international law standards and their potential for fuelling the meta-conflict. The parties to each conflict used international law to articulate opposing positions, and as international legal responses to the conflict were developed

---

[144] See e.g. Agreed Measures, Geneva, 14 Aug. 1996, whereby signatories to the Dayton Peace Agreement agreed further measures as regards implementation.

[145] Available at www.stabilitypact.org/ (last visited 16 Aug. 2000).

[146] Office of the High Representative (1998). See also Office of the High Representative web site at www.ohr.int/ (last visited 3 Dec. 1999).

TABLE 4.6. *Pre-negotiation agreements: preliminary agreements between the parties to the conflict*

Agreement	Parties	Content
'Washington Peace Agreement': (1) Bosnia and Herzegovina–Croatian: Preliminary Agreement concerning the establishment of a Confederation, 18 March 1994	Agreement was signed by BiH government and Bosnian Croat leaders on behalf of republic of BiH and Croatia, respectively	Agreement led to end of Croatian–Bosniac military activities. Preliminary agreement provides for a confederation to operate 'in the territories with a majority of Bosniacs and Croat population in the Republic of BiH.' Two annexes deal with granting BiH access to the Adriatic through Croatia, and granting Croatia transit through BiH. The detail of how the federation was to be achieved was provided for in a Federation Constitution
(2) Constitution of the Federation of Bosnia and Herzegovina, 18 March 1994		The Constitution stated that 'decisions on the constitutional status of the territories of BiH with a majority Serb population shall be made in the course of negotiations toward a peaceful settlement and at the ICFY.' The Federation consisted of cantons, whose boundaries were to be agreed. The Constitution provided for flags and anthem, and had a substantive human rights chapter, including provision for a Federation Ombudsman. The Federation was given some powers, but many powers were left at the cantonal level and (where cantonal populations are mixed Croat and Bosniac) even at municipal level. Election to a Federation House of Representatives and House of Peoples was to be proportional, as was the membership of the executive. Minority vetoes were to operate in areas of 'vital interest'. Provision was made for a human rights court, a Constitutional Court, and a Supreme Court. Judges were

Agreement	Parties	Content
		to be proportionally (equally) Croat and Bosniac. Detailed provision was made for cantonal and municipal government
Contact Group Plan April 1994–Summer 1995 (eventually paved the way for the following agreements)	Accepted by parties except Bosnian Serbs (resulting in Milošović cutting off links with them)	Based on *Invincible* Acquis and Washington Peace Agreement. Aimed to create an internal partition along political and constitutional lines already agreed. Unlike the earlier agreements it was 'delivered as an ultimatum in the form of a map; constitutional arrangements would be refined *after* the acceptance of the territorial deal' (International Commission on the Balkans 1996). Although this plan was declared by US negotiator Richard Holbrooke to be a failure in February 1995, it continued to hover in the background until NATO air strikes and Croatian–Bosnian victories brought the parties to agreement in Geneva in September 1995
Agreed Principles, Geneva, 8 September 1995	Foreign ministers of BiH, Croatia, and FRY (on behalf of those parties, FRY also representing Bosnian Serbs)	Agreed principles to govern negotiations. BiH will continue its legal existence with present borders and continuing international recognition. It will consist of two entities, the Federation of BiH as established by the Washington Agreements, and the Republika Srpska. The parties agree in principle to establish a Commission for Displaced Persons; a Human Rights Commission; joint BiH public corporations, financed by the two entities; a Commission to Preserve National Monuments; and the design and implementation of arbitration for the solution of disputes between the two entities

TABLE 4.6. *Continued*

Agreement	Parties	Content
Joint Statement and Further Agreed Basic Principles, New York, 26 September 1995	Foreign ministers of BiH, Croatia, and FRY (on behalf of those parties, FRY also representing Bosnian Serbs). Witnessed by France, Germany, Russia, United Kingdom, United States, and European Union special negotiator for former Yugoslavia	Further principles agreed to govern negotiations. Establishes that BiH will have a Parliament or National Assembly, a presidency, and a Constitutional Court. Establishes that both Parliament and presidency will be proportionally selected by two-thirds from the federation, and one-third from Republika Srpska. Sets up involvement of OSCE in verifying conditions for 'free and fair elections'

Note: The preliminary agreement can be found in (1994) 33 I.L.M. 609–18; the federation Constitution can be found in (1994) 33 I.L.M. 740. The Contact Group Plan is discussed in International Commission for the Balkans (1996: 53–4); and remaining agreements can be found in Office of the High Representative (1998: 14, 15).

and addressed these positions, law evolved and new mechanisms were created. To give some examples: both confcts reworked and extended the definition of self-determination with implications for other confct situations. The Israeli/Palestinian confct also posed difficult questions for the enforceability of Geneva IV, and its relevance to extended occupation. At the same time the international community created some specific mechanisms for the confct, and the confct inflenced some general responses. The Bosnian confct saw a variety of innovative mediation efforts, raised questions about the role of UN peacekeepers, and created an ad hoc international criminal tribunal in an attempt to enforce individual responsibility for human rights and humanitarian law violations. The existence and experience of these responses all have implications beyond the Yugoslav context.

TABLE 4.7. *Substantive–framework peace agreements*

Agreement	Parties	Content
Dayton Agreement on Implementing the Federation of Bosnia and Herzegovina signed in Dayton 10 November 1995	Signed by Alija Izetbegović, president of the Republic of BiH, Kresimir Zubak (Croat BiH leader and president of the Federation of BiH), Dr Haris Silajdžić (deputy prime minister), and Jadranko Prlić (deputy prime minister). The president of the Republic of Croatia also endorsed the provisions of the agreement and committed to assisting in its full implementation. Witnessed by FRG, US, Spanish EU presidency, and EU administrator of Mostar	Deals with the transfer of responsibilities to the federation and provides a timetable, which aims to mesh the earlier agreement on the federation with the subsequent supra-state BiH structure agreed to in Dayton. An annex sets out agreement principles for an Interim Statute for the city of Mostar (a divided city with a mainly Muslim Bosniac and Croat population)
The General Framework Agreement for Peace in Bosnia and Herzegovina, 4 December 1995 ('Dayton Peace Agreement')	The parties to the agreement are the Republic of BiH, the Republic of Croatia, the Federal Republic of Yugoslavia. Witnessed by European Union special negotiator, French Republic, Federal Republic	The general agreement at its heart divides BiH into two separate entities, the (Serbian) Republika Srpska (RS) and the Federation of BiH (between mainly Muslim Bosniacs and Croats), to be bound together in a unitary federal state with very limited powers. Eleven annexes provide agreements on military aspects of the peace settlement, providing for

TABLE 4.7. *Continued*

Agreement	Parties	Content
	of Germany (FRG), Russian Federation, the United Kingdom, and United States	the mechanics of a ceasefire; on regional stabilization; on the inter-entity boundary line; on elections; on a Constitution for BiH; on arbitration; on human rights; on refugees and displaced persons; on BiH public corporations; on civilian implementation; and on an International police task force
	The annexes are for the most part signed by the Entities and BiH. Exceptions are: Annex 1-B (Agreement on Regional Stabilization) and Annex 10 (Agreement on Civilian Implementation), which are signed by the Entities, BiH, FRY, and the Republic of Croatia	

Note: Agreements can be found in Office of the High Representative (1998: 16–52, 53–4, 56).

[a] The agreement is backed up by UN SC resolutions establishing the international forces and organs set out in the agreement: UN SC Res 1021 of 22 Nov. 1995, (1996) 35 I.L.M. 257; UN SC Res 1022 of 22 Nov. 1995, (1996) 35 I.L.M. 259; UN SC Res 1026 of 30 Nov. 1995, (1996) 35 I.L.M. 251.

In the previous chapter it was argued, with reference to South Africa and Northern Ireland, that the application of international law created conditions which both limited the conflict and provided a normative framework, so that when the parties came to negotiate, the legitimate parameters of any solution were relatively clear. The cases of Israel/Palestine and Bosnia illustrate the other side of the coin.

In these cases the international community's inability to agree on the parameters of the solution hampered attempts to limit the conflict by enforcing human rights protections and preventing ethnic population shifts. Conversely, the inability of the international community to enforce basic human rights and humanitarian law protections created a fluid numbers game in which parties to the conflict could further their self-determination claims through illegitimate 'fact creation' on the ground. In the Occupied Palestinian Territories this was most obviously through Israeli land appropriation and settlement-building, which runs counter to

Article 49 of Geneva IV. In Bosnia Herzegovina it was through the murderous practices labelled 'ethnic cleansing'.

In both cases, an imbalance of power meant that one party was militarily weaker—the Bosnian government and the Palestinians, respectively. In such a situation, only the intervention of international actors could produce the mutually hurting stalemate that would make negotiations a better option than continued military activity. Du Toit has argued that central to achieving a peace agreement is a process of 'bargaining about bargaining' or meta-bargaining.[147] In order to agree on future structures and measures to resolve the conflict, parties need to come to some sort of compromise on what the nature of the conflict is. The very decision to bargain often indicates a move towards such a meta-bargain, as it indicates agreement that both sides stand to lose in continued conflict.

Where, however, the move towards negotiations is primarily as a result of international pressure, then the negotiations have a different dynamic. Any resulting deal and its implementation will have an ongoing international dimension. While the peace negotiations and agreements in South Africa and Northern Ireland were largely sustained (or not) through a notion of reciprocity and self-interest, the processes in Israel/Palestine and BiH required, and require, to be sustained through continued international pressure. The deals were driven and forged, not by a mutual acceptance of the parties to the conflict that the conflict could not be won by either party on its own terms, but by international intervention. This crucially impacts on implementation. As Horowitz notes, without a joint commitment of parties to a negotiated solution, 'the antagonists will see the choice as being merely to dominate or to be dominated and so will engage in behaviour that aims at hegemony.'[148]

The failure of the international community and international legal standards to limit the conflicts and provide clear parameters for their solution meant that the conditions necessary for a meta-bargain were largely missing. The absence of such a meta-bargain crucially helps to explain the ambivalent nature of the agreements struck, the role of human rights provisions within them, and the problems with implementation, as will be seen in later chapters. International law's failure to provide for a clear normative application of legal standards during the conflict is therefore just as influential in shaping the negotiations and peace agreement as its articulation of such standards.

---

[147] Du Toit (1989).   [148] Horowitz (1991: 34).

5

Getting to Yes?
Negotiating Self-Determination

In each of the four case-studies the peace agreements signed at the framework–substantive stage attempted to address the self-determination claims at the heart of the conflict, at least implicitly. Each deal involved an agreement between political elites of majority and minority populations on how to reconcile their seemingly incompatible demands for access to power, government, and territory. This required compromise not just on the issues of equality, sovereignty, territorial integrity, and secession–partition, but on the meta-conflict underlying these issues. This chapter will lay out the nuts and bolts of how this was done. The following chapter will evaluate the deals in the light of international law on self-determination and minority rights.

POLITICAL SCIENCE DISCOURSE: A FRAMEWORK FOR ANALYSIS

Political scientists have provided models for resolving 'ethnic conflict' which can provide a useful framework from which to understand the deals reached in the four case-studies. The 'solutions' for ethnic conflict of political science, as synthesized by Sisk, have revolved around two distinct models of how to tailor democratic institutions to cope with ethnic division, and in particular the permanent exclusion of minorities which can occur with straightforward majoritarianism.[1] These models comprise a *consociational* model of democracy, and an *integrative* (or pluralist) model of democracy. Authoritarianism and/or partition are rejected by political scientists, less for normative reasons and more because there are relatively few examples where either of these approaches lead to successful management or resolution of ethnic conflict.

The consociational model focuses on cooperation between political elites as a mechanism of managing ethnic conflict. Political elites, usually in an ethnic-based party system, cooperate through governmental structures with four central characteristics, as its main proponent, Lijphart, has suggested.

1. Broad-based parliamentary coalitions, which ensure that the minority is not permanently excluded from political power. Here political elites

---

[1] Sisk (1996).

representing the ethnic divisions among the population thrash out their differences while making decisions in government.

2. Minority or mutual veto. This gives each group 'a guarantee that it will not be outvoted by the majority when its vital interests are at stake.' These interests include language, cultural rights, or education rights.
3. Proportionality. This is introduced at every level: through electoral systems using proportional representation, and through the allocation of resources.
4. Segmental group autonomy. This can be through territorial autonomy or conceptual autonomy over spheres of life (sometimes called 'corporate federalism').[2]

In contrast to the consociational model stands a more *integrative* approach to conflict management. While there are common elements, such as an advocacy of federalism, proportionality, and ethnic balance, the crucial difference of the integrative model is that it focuses on creating incentives for politicians to appeal beyond their own ethnic group for support. While consociational models rely on constraints against immoderate politics, integrative approaches focus on designing political institutions which encourage or induce integration across the communal divide, through five central mechanisms:

1. Dispersions of power, often territorial, through, for example, federal arrangements. These 'proliferate points of power so as to take the heat off a single focal point.'
2. Devolution of power and separation of offices on an ethnic basis in an effort to foster intra-ethnic competition at the local level.
3. Inducements for inter-ethnic cooperation, such as electoral laws that effectively promote pre-election electoral coalitions through vote-pooling.
4. Policies to encourage alternative social alignments, such as social class or territory, by placing political emphasis on cross-cutting cleavages.
5. Reducing disparities between groups through managed distribution of resources.[3]

Both models aim to promote governing coalitions that are broadly inclusive of all ethnic groups in a deeply divided multi-ethnic society.[4] However, they are based on fundamentally different opinions as to how and when such coalitions are formed, and what specific institutions and practices better manage ethnic conflict. However, Sisk suggests that the two approaches should not be considered an either/or choice, but rather as providing a

---

[2] See further Lijphart (1968, 1969, 1977, 1989); see also Sisk (1996: 36–8).

[3] See Horowitz (1985: 597–600); see also Sisk (1996: 40–1).

[4] Reilly and Reynolds (1999) in their analysis of electoral systems posit four different approaches: consociationalism, centripetalism, integrative consensualism, and explicit recognition of communal groups. This points to the fact that when a specific mechanism such as an electoral system is addressed, different systems within the framework may significantly affect issues such as coalition-forming and the stage at which it happens, in even more permutations than this simple two-model account allows for.

Box 5.1. *Summary of consociational and integrative options*

Consociational practices: territorial divisions of power
  1. Granting autonomy and creating confederal arrangements
  2. Creating a polycommunal federation (i.e. where internal boundaries closely correspond to ethnic–racial divisions)

Consociational practices: decision rules
  3. Adopting proportional representation and consensus rules in executive, legislative, and administrative decision-making
  4. Adopting a highly proportional electoral system

Consociational practices: state–ethnic relations
  5. Acknowledging group rights or corporate federalism (i.e. autonomy over spheres such as language or culture)

Integrative practices: territorial divisions of power
  6. Creating a mixed or non-communal federal structure (that is, where federal boundaries do not primarily relate to ethnic division)
  7. Establishing a single inclusive unitary state

Integrative practices: decision rules
  8. Adopting majoritarian but integrated executive, legislative, and administrative decision-making
  9. Adopting a semi-majoritarian or semi-proportional electoral system
  10. Adopting ethnicity-blind public policies

'menu of options from which policymakers might choose as they confront the complexities of any given ethnic conflict.'[5] Drawing from the two models, he produces a list of ten conflict-regulating practices and institutions. He presents these in terms of three sets of variables: territorial divisions of power; rules for how decisions are made; and practices and institutions which define the relationship between the state and ethnic groups. His resulting typology is presented in Box 5.1, and is expanded on in the next chapter.

The case-studies draw on the 'menu' in this box, but also cut across integrative and consociational practices as Table 5.1 summarizes.

SOUTH AFRICA

In South Africa the Interim Constitution provided that every South African citizen over the age of 18 years be enfranchised with regard to elections at all levels of government. Furthermore, it provided for the Constitution as supreme law of the land, binding all the legislative, executive, and judicial

---

[5] Sisk (1996: 8).

TABLE 5.1. *Self-determination arrangements in case-study peace agreements*

	South Africa	Northern Ireland	Bosnia Herzegovina	Israel/Palestine
Territorial divisions of power	• Unitary state with universal franchise • Mixed provincial structure (with some polycommunal significance)	• Single inclusive unitary state • 'Confederal' cross-border arrangements with North–South emphasis	• Nominal unitary state • Autonomy of ethnic 'Entities' (almost 'confederal') • Entities able to make cross-border connections to ethnic counterparts	• Palestinian autonomy • No common state structure • But ambiguity as to whether final outcome will lead to two-state solution, with an independent and viable Palestinian state
Decision rules	• Constitutional principles constraining majoritarian constitution drafting (transitional in effect) • Time-limited consociationalism practices for government followed by majoritarian integrative practices • Weighted voting for significant decisions	• Indefinite consociational practices for government structures	• Consociational practices for Entity and republic government structures	• No joint government • Complex rules delimiting powers, functions, and territory between Israel and Palestinian Authority
State–ethnic relations	• Little provision • Individual human rights protections • Self-determination language addressing right-wing white claims	• Self-determination language • Human rights protections (with possible group rights dimension) • Emphasis on 'equality' between groups	• Individual human rights protections • Right of return of refugees and displaced persons (with significance for ethnic make-up for Entities) • International involvement in key institutions (mediating ethnic disputes)	• Some minor provision for a 'spirit of peace and reconciliation' and 'people-to-people' Israeli–Palestinian contacts

organs of the state at all levels of government.[6] These unexciting statements of constitutional supremacy and universal franchise replaced years of apartheid with one person one vote, and replaced illegitimate government with constitutional democracy, thus responding to both domestic and international anti-apartheid and self-determination demands. The Interim Constitution does not use the language of self-determination to achieve this.

However, this is not the whole story. The deal encapsulated in the South African Interim Constitution involved compromises on access to power, between the (African National Congress) majority and other minority 'ethnic' groups—both white and black, although nowhere in the Constitution are labels of ethnicity used. These compromises were twofold in nature: temporary and permanent. The temporary compromises were designed to facilitate a transfer of power from the ruling South African government–National Party (NP/SAG) to the African National Congress (ANC) majority government. The permanent compromises related to the particular structure of government agreed, whose basic form the Constitutional Principles aimed to ensure would be translated into the Final Constitution.

The two-stage arrangement of transitional mechanisms and permanent structures owes its explanation to the interrelationship of self-determination issues with process issues, which was a particularly strong feature of the South African peace process. Some of the most difficult issues to resolve concerned the mechanisms by which transition from minority white rule to multi-party democracy was to be achieved. These issues were, as process issues generally are, intrinsically bound up with how the end-result would be influenced by the processes adopted. Process debate therefore constituted indirect negotiation of the self-determination issue.

Transitional Decision-Making Rules: 'Constitutional Assembly', Constitutional Principles, and Weighted Voting

The central example of the entanglement of process with substance was the agreement on a Constitutional Assembly to draft a Final Constitution after the elections, subject to constraining Constitutional Principles.[7] This was an arrangement produced from a compromise between two main differing visions of how transition would take place, and what type of future arrangements this would dictate.

The first was a NP/SAG position that it should remain in government until negotiations on a new Constitution began. The second was the ANC

---

[6] See generally Articles 4–6 Constitution of the Republic of South Africa 200 of 1994 (hereafter Interim Constitution).

[7] Agreement that a Transitional Executive Council would govern prior to democratic elections was another; see Sarakinsky (1994).

demand that a transitional government be established before elections were held for a new democratically elected assembly which would *then* write a new Constitution. The Inkatha Freedom Party (IFP) went further than the NP, wanting elections only after a new Constitution was agreed, and only then if it ensured a robust form of federalism. The (white) Conservative Party (CP) similarly opposed elections until a separate Afrikaner Volkstaat was agreed. At the other end of the spectrum the Pan-African Congress (PAF), outbidding the ANC, demanded *immediate* elections for an assembly.

As Sarakinsky demonstrates, these disputes were not just about the principle of a one-stage process (continued rule by the present government until after election) versus a two-stage process (the creation of an interim body, then an election). They were also about the underlying power dynamics and self-determination outcome.

The ANC position would ensure that it would gain a share of power before elections, preventing the NP from using the levers of government to influence the result. Its view, and that of the PAC, that elected representatives should write the constitution ensured that the majority could do so alone. The NP, IFP and CP had a stake in preventing this. It was important to the NP to remain the government; vital to the IFP, whose support was concentrated in Natal, both to continue administering KwaZulu until an election and to guarantee that Natal would have maximum power before it agreed to an election; and crucial to the white right not to leave the fate of a *volkstaat* in the hands of a hostile majority. And since all three represented minorities, it was vital to all that the constitution should be written before an election.[8]

By the Convention on a Democratic South Africa (CODESA) the NP/SAG had accepted that an elected Constitutional Assembly should draft the Final Constitution. However, the self-determination dispute over the relative power of black majority and white minority played out in the form of a dispute (stalemating CODESA) between the NP/SAG and the ANC on the size of majority necessary for the adoption of the new Constitution. On entering the negotiating process, the NP had focused on how to entrench a measure of white minority power through specific power-sharing mechanisms and vetoes. The ANC had rejected any form of entrenched white power as negating majority rule.

By CODESA the NP/SAG had relinquished its earlier claim for an automatic veto, and accepted that means should be found to ensure that a non-racial Constitution would not be indefinitely delayed by negotiations.[9] Although the parties were agreed that a weighted majority be required for

<hr>

[8] Sarakinsky (1994: 69–70).

[9] Atkinson (1994: 94), states that this NP concession was partly a result of talks with the PAC and the PAC's decision to give up 'armed struggle', a decision urgently needed by the NP to reassure the white electorate.

adoption of the Constitution, they disagreed on what the precise weighting should be. The NP wanted a weighting that would in practice require their support, while the ANC wanted a lesser weighting that would prevent the NP from stalling the process. The ANC were also concerned that a deadlock-breaking device be agreed to, especially in the event of a high weighting, again so that the drafting of the Final Constitution could not be frustrated by the NP, thus making the Interim Constitution with its power-sharing arrangements effectively permanent.

Compromise was eventually arrived at in the context of violent events outside the negotiations which had made agreement vital, and produced a 'package' approach which made an exchange of compromises possible. The end-result provided that an elected Constitutional Assembly, consisting of both houses of the new Parliament, the National Assembly and the Senate, would become the body authorized to draft the Final Constitution.[10] The new Constitution would have to comply with the Constitutional Principles (which could not be amended or repealed) and the newly established Constitutional Court would certify that it did so.[11]

The new Constitution was to be passed by a two-thirds majority of all the members of the Constitutional Assembly (at that stage it was assumed that this would require support of more than the ANC but not necessarily require NP support). But matters dealing with the boundaries, powers, and functions of the provinces also had to be approved by a majority of two-thirds of all the members of the (provincially elected) Senate.[12] A time limit of two years from the first sitting of the National Assembly was set for the Final Constitution to be passed by the Assembly and a number of deadlock-breaking devices provided for the event that the requisite majority was not forthcoming in the requisite time.[13]

The Constitutional Principles, as we have seen, were one of the key safeguards negotiated by the NP/SAG in conceding that a democratically elected body draft the Constitution. They were a device whereby '[i]n effect the transitional government agreed in advance to certain curbs on

[10] Section 68 Constitution of the Republic of South Africa Act No. 200 of 1993 (hereafter 'Interim Constitution').   [11] See sections 71, 73, 74 Interim Constitution.
[12] Section 73 Interim Constitution.
[13] If the draft failed to gain a two-thirds majority, but did gain a majority, it was to be put to a panel of experts to propose amendments. These amendments if passed by a two-thirds majority would then become incorporated in the Constitution. If this did not resolve matters, then a majority of the Constitutional Assembly could approve the draft, but after certification the president would have to put it to the national electorate for approval in a referendum by a 60% majority. If this mechanism failed, and a Constitution was not forthcoming within two years, then Parliament was to be dissolved, a new national election held, and a Constitutional Assembly formed and empowered to pass a Constitution by a 60% majority within a year of the election. In essence this meant that if progress had not been negotiated within two years, an ANC majority would be given power to draft the Constitution (section 73(9) Interim Constitution).

its future constitution-making powers in order to persuade those formerly in government to relinquish their political power.'[14] The thirty-four Constitutional Principles have been described as laying down 'an almost complete picture, though not the exact wording of the new constitutional text.'[15] Francis Venter has analysed the principles as establishing five essential attributes of the new constitutional arrangements:

- Constitutional foundations: setting out the 'essence' of the Constitution: equality (on grounds of race and sex), fundamental rights, democracy, diversity (in particular of language and culture), and self-determination (both internal and external)
- Characteristics of the state: one sovereign state; separation of powers; accessibility (with freedom of information and fair administration); formal legislative procedures
- Characteristics of the Constitution: justiciable supreme law; rigidity ('special procedures involving special majorities')
- Constitutional structures: vertical distribution of competencies (between national, provincial, and local legislatures); independent, professional, and impartial institutions
- Transitional nature: the transitional Government of National Unity and second elections in five years time[16]

They therefore ensured a basic 'deal' would be translated into the Final Constitution, while leaving the detail of drafting and some scope for expansion and revision for the elected Constitutional Assembly. The Constitutional Principles were enforceable with the newly established Constitutional Court to 'certify' the Final Constitution as compatible with them.[17] This mechanism appeared more than cosmetic when the court rejected the first draft of the Final Constitution, in part due to its failure to ensure adequate provincial powers.[18]

Yet the balance of power achieved by the ANC in the 1999 elections means that now they alone hold more than the two-thirds majority needed to amend the Final Constitution. While the Constitutional Principles may have constrained the initial design of the Final Constitution and given the white minority an accentuated influence, they do not constrain its future amendment. Notions that the Constitutional Principles could have a lasting constraint on the design of the Constitution anticipated erroneously a different balance of political forces than currently pertains.[19]

---

[14] Corder and Du Plessis (1994: 14).   [15] Venter (1995: 32).   [16] Venter (1995).
[17] Section 71(1) Interim Constitution.
[18] *Ex Parte Chairperson of the Constitutional Assembly: In Re Certification of the Constitution 1996*, 1996 (4) SA 744 (cc), 1996 (10) BCLR 1253 (cc).
[19] See further Guelke (1999). For debate on whether the Constitutional Principles can and should indirectly influence constitutional adjudication, see Henderson (1996); Butler (1997).

Transitional 'consociationalism'

Proportionality

The Interim Constitution provided for a national legislature to be elected by proportional representation from both regional and national lists.[20] A measure of proportionality was to pertain in the membership of key institutional positions. The Judicial Service Commission responsible for some Constitutional Court appointments had mechanisms to ensure cross-party representation.[21] Presidential Constitutional Court appointments were to be made 'in consultation with [the power-sharing] Cabinet.'[22] Furthermore, a form of transitional proportionality between apartheid regime (white) judges and new appointments was provided for, through provision that four of the ten Constitutional Court judges be appointed from 'among the judges of the Supreme Court.'[23] The length of tenure was seven years, meaning that this proportionality was temporary, although significant given the Constitutional Court's role in certifying the Final Constitution. The Public Protector and Human Rights Commission members were all to be nominated by cross-party committees and approved by a weighted majority of 75 per cent of the National Assembly and Senate.[24]

Executive Power-Sharing

The Interim Constitution provided for national executive authority to vest in a president, who is to exercise and perform his or her powers and functions subject to and in accordance with the Interim Constitution.[25] This president is head of state, and elected by the National Assembly by a majority of members.[26] These provisions are retained largely unchanged in the Final Constitution.[27]

However, in what amounted to a crucial compromise between minority power and majority rule, the Interim Constitution contained provision for power-sharing at executive level for a maximum of five years following the elections. Under these provisions, every party holding at least eighty seats out of 400 in the National Assembly (a threshold the NP was expected to meet) was entitled to designate an executive deputy president from among the members of the National Assembly.[28] The Cabinet was to consist of the president, the executive deputy presidents, and a maximum

---

[20] Section 40 and Schedule 2 Interim Constitution.
[21] Section 105 Interim Constitution.   [22] Section 99 Interim Constitution.
[23] Ibid.   [24] Sections 110, 115 Interim Constitution.
[25] Section 75 Interim Constitution. See generally, Ch. 7 below.
[26] Section 77 and Schedule 5 Interim Constitution.
[27] Sections 83–6 The Constitution of the Republic of South Africa Act No. 108 of 1996 (hereafter 'Final Constitution').
[28] Section 84 Interim Constitution (there are fallback provisions for when this number is not reached by any party).

of twenty-seven ministers appointed by the president in accordance with a system of proportional representation.[29] Any party holding at least twenty seats in the National Assembly (a threshold low enough to accommodate the NP and the IFP) and deciding to participate in the executive was entitled to have Cabinet portfolios allocated to it in proportion to the number of seats held by it in the National Assembly.[30] The allocation (and removal) of portfolios was to be 'implemented in the concept of a government of national unity' and the president and others concerned had to 'endeavour to reach consensus at all times.'[31] If consensus was not possible, then the president or the leader of the party whose representative held the relevant portfolio was to take the decision.[32]

National Party arguments for enforceable in-Cabinet voting mechanisms were given up towards the final stage of negotiations. Instead the Interim Constitution adopted informal decision-making mechanisms, which provided that the Cabinet was to function 'in a manner which gives consideration to the consensus-seeking spirit underlying the concept of a government of national unity as well as the need for effective government.'[33]

This mechanism was not to last beyond 30 April 1999, although in fact the Government of National Unity collapsed long before this, when the NP withdrew on 30 June 1996. In contrast to the Interim Constitution the provisions of the Final Constitution (effective after 30 April 1999) merely provide that the Cabinet is to consist of the president, deputy president, and ministers selected by the president,[34] with provision for two ministers to be selected from outside the Assembly.[35] As Atkinson writes:

The agreed form of 'mixed government' in the executive was a masterpiece of political compromise. It gave the NP a role in the cabinet and presidency. It gave the ANC the majority party right to take decisions if consensus could not be reached. And, by relying on formulae which were, in principle, available to any party which could achieve a required share of the vote, it reconciled 'mixed government' with democratic constitutionalism.[36]

While process issues had masked self-determination issues, conversely self-determination issues were ultimately resolved by turning them into process issues. The device of the Constitutional Principles and a Government of National Unity which would continue even after multi-party elections gave interim safeguards to the white minority during which their interests could be protected, and their contribution to South Africa's future accentuated. This took the place of any permanent minority veto which would have sustained protection of white minority

---

[29] Section 88 Interim Constitution.   [30] Ibid.
[31] Section 88(5) Interim Constitution.   [32] Ibid.
[33] Section 89(2) Interim Constitution.   [34] Section 91 Final Constitution.
[35] Ibid.   [36] Atkinson (1994: 107; footnotes omitted).

interests and insulated them more effectively and indefinitely against majority decision-making. In fact, in contrast to the consociational model of government adopted in the Belfast Agreement in Northern Ireland or the Dayton Peace Agreement in Bosnia Herzegovina, the Final Constitution has adopted what is essentially a traditional liberal-democratic framework,[37] with individual rather than group rights protections, and where weighted majorities entrench (to different degrees) separation of powers, national–provincial balance, fundamental rights provisions, and the Constitution itself.[38]

Permanent Provisions

Although dressed up by the consociational transitional arrangements, the lasting constraints on majority power were to be through two main arrangements. First, a territorial division of power involving a compromise between unitary and federal structures with powers given to provincial governments. Secondly, the traditional safeguards of constitutionalism in particular: an entrenched, judicially enforceable bill of rights, and weighted majorities for important issues. A further nuance was provided for by the language conceded to immediately prior to negotiations, which encapsulated a notion of internal self-determination addressed at right-wing white Afrikaners.

Territorial Divisions of Power: 'provincialism'

The Interim Constitution provided for provincial representation in the second chamber of the Parliament, the Senate, which of course is also part of the national legislature. It also provided for delimited power to be exercised by provincial and local governments.[39]

The regionalism of the Interim Constitution took shape under the pressures of the different interests amongst those who were destined to become political minorities upon majority rule. These were interests such as those of homeland leaders, which had been vested by apartheid. In particular, the NP and the IFP, both of whom stood to gain provincial power in one province (and in the first elections did the NP in Western Cape Province and the IFP in KwaZulu-Natal), saw potential for insulating such power from an ANC-dominated national government through forms of

---

[37] Although as Corder and Du Plessis point out in their analysis of the Interim Constitution's Bill of Rights, the framework reconciled competing traditions of liberalism and liberationist (and to a lesser extent feminist) visions (1994: 22–39).

[38] See further Guelke (1999) (arguing that South Africa's 'miracle' is misunderstood as a triumph of cooperation between ethnic groups, when that cooperation is intended only as a transitional device).   [39] Chapter 9 Interim Constitution.

federalism. However, these parties were also somewhat ambivalent about their goals. The NP approach to federalism fluctuated with gains won or lost around the issue of how central power would be held.[40] IFP concerns about federalism centred less on the design of a general system than on how the region they dominated—KwaZulu-Natal—would fare.[41]

The resulting provisions of the Interim Constitution established nine provinces, delimited their territory,[42] and provided for legislature, executive, and possible limited tax-raising powers.[43] The legislative power encompassed a finite list of competencies and was to be exercised only within that provincial territory.[44] Central government was not prohibited from legislating in these areas, but if it did, such legislation was only to prevail in specified circumstances. However, some of these circumstances were enumerated vaguely, giving wide scope to central intervention. For example, national legislation was to prevail when it dealt with 'a matter that cannot be regulated effectively by provincial legislation'.[45] Thus flexibility in the centre–province relationship was retained, together with the potential for disputes, and in effect this meant that the detail of the interim division of powers was ultimately left to the Constitutional Court to fill in.[46] The provincial legislatures were also empowered to pass a Provincial Constitution by resolution of a majority of at least two-thirds of its members.[47] As with the Final Constitution, the Constitutional Court was empowered to adjudicate on any Provincial Constitution's compliance with the Constitutional Principles.[48] Proportionality and transitional

---

[40] Humphries *et al.* (1994).   [41] Ibid.

[42] Section 124 and Part 1, Schedule 1, Interim Constitution. The provinces are: Eastern Cape, Eastern Transvaal, Natal, Northern Cape, Northern Transvaal, North-West, Orange Free State, Pretoria-Witwatersrand-Vereeniging, and Western Cape. Provision is made for disputed delimitations to be resolved by holding referendums in certain areas, section 124, and Part 2, Schedule 1 Interim Constitution.

[43] Chapter 9 Interim Constitution (as amended by Constitution of the Republic of South Africa Amendment Act No. 2 of 1994).

[44] Chapter 9 and Schedule 6 Interim Constitution (as amended by Constitution of the Republic of South Africa Amendment Act No. 2 of 1994). The list comprises abattoirs; agriculture; airports (other than international and national airports); animal control and diseases; casinos, racing, gambling and wagering; consumer protection; cultural affairs; education at all levels, excluding university and technical education; environment; health services; housing; indigenous law; language policy and the regulation of the use of official languages within a province, subject to section 3 (Interim Constitution); aspects of local government; aspects of nature conservation; aspects of police; provincial public media; provincial sport and recreation; public transport; regional planning and development; road traffic regulation; roads; soil conservation; tourism; trade and industrial promotion; traditional authorities; urban and rural development; and welfare services.

[45] Section 126 Interim Constitution.

[46] Indeed Sarkin (1997: 139), examining the relevant cases which subsequently arose under the Interim Constitution, notes how, indeed, 'disputes of a constitutional nature between political parties are often played out as constitutional conflicts between the national and provincial governments'.   [47] Sections 160–2 Interim Constitution.

[48] During the Interim Constitution's lifetime the only province to produce a Constitution was KwaZulu-Natal, and this failed to be certified based on its encroachment into the area

power-sharing at provincial executive level were provided for in what was in essence a microcosm of the mechanisms at national level.[49]

The future of provincial government was safeguarded as regards the Final Constitution in a number of ways. First, the Transitional Constitution provided that 'the development of a system of provincial government was to receive 'priority attention' from the Constitutional Assembly, which was to be advised by a 'Commission on Provincial Government.'[50] This Commission was to be appointed by the president.[51] In addition, ten out of thirty-four Constitutional Principles entrenched provincial government, together with a basic level of powers and competencies for it.[52] In particular CP XVIII provided that the powers, boundaries, and functions of the national government and provincial governments were to be defined in the Constitution; and that any future amendment to these should require the approval of

a special majority of the legislatures of the provinces, if there is such a chamber, a two-thirds majority of a chamber of Parliament composed of provincial representatives, and if the amendment concerns specific provinces only, the approval of the legislatures of such provinces will also be needed.

Both the Interim and the Final Constitutions opted for a provincial second chamber, giving provinces an additional role in national legislation.[53] Further layers of government were provided with provision for both local government[54] and traditional authorities who were to observe a system of indigenous law.[55]

Decision-Making Rules: Weighted Decision-Making

The Interim Constitution required weighted majorities for Constitutional Amendment, for certain pieces of legislation, and for other important decisions, such as removal of the president. Weighted decision-making is a

---

of national powers; see Ex *Parte Speaker KwaZulu-Natal Provincial Legislature: In Re Certification of the Constitution of the Province of KwaZulu-Natal* (1996) 1996 (11) BCLR 1419; 1996 (4) SA 1098 (CC). The Final Constitution also gives provinces the power to pass their own constitution by a two-thirds majority of the provincial legislature. Any such Constitution is to be consistent with the Final Constitution, and in particular to respect its delimitation of national and provincial powers, the values of section 1 of the Constitution, and the Bill of Rights in Chapter 3 (Section 143 Final Constitution).

[49] Sections 149–50 Interim Constitution.   [50] Sections 161–73 Interim Constitution.
[51] Section 165 Interim Constitution.
[52] In particular CPs XVI, XVII, XVIII, XIX, XX, XI, and XII; however, see also XXIII, XXV, and XXVI (Schedule 4 Interim Constitution).
[53] In the Final Constitution the name is even changed from the 'Senate' to the 'National Council of Provinces' composed of a single delegation from each province, with ten delegates, allocated according to party proportionality in the legislature. Final Constitution sections 60 and 65.   [54] Chapter 10 Interim Constitution.
[55] Chapter 11 Interim Constitution.

traditional constitutional device which ensures a measure of entrenchment of the Constitution itself, and a greater degree of political consensus for particularly important matters. However, as illustrated earlier, in a divided society such weightings can also (depending on how the weighting is set) provide a measure of group protection by ensuring that the political consensus requires the support of non-majority parties. Such weightings are therefore not just a matter of 'constitutionalism' (itself a matter of self-determination broadly conceived), but are also relevant to minority rights and ensuring the effective participation of minority groups in decision-making.

In both Interim and Final Constitutions in South Africa, weighted decision-making also provided for limits on the ability of national and provincial houses to legislate on each other's concerns (although the precise mechanism differed from Interim to Final Constitutions).[56] Thus, the mathematics of weighted voting facilitate future tilting of power in the direction of a unitary or a 'federal' structure, also forming part of the complex tapestry of the self-determination deal.

State–ethnic relations

Human Rights Protections

Human rights protections will be considered further in Chapter 7. However, the supremacy of a justiciable bill of rights, with independent judiciary and a Human Rights Commission to enforce it, should be noted here as a significant constraint on majority power.[57] As with weighted majorities, human rights protections are a part of the self-determination arrangement, both as a matter of constitutionalism, but also as a protection for minorities in a divided society. Even though the South African Bill of Rights includes only individual rights and not group rights, it can be regarded as having a role in defining state–ethnic relations. The individualist model itself indicates that it is as a citizen rather than through a group that the individual asserts his or her rights against the state.

Self-Determination Language

Although self-determination claims were satisfied through the establishment of a non-racial, multi-party democracy within the framework of a written Constitution and Bill of Rights, nowhere in the body of the Interim Constitution was the term 'self-determination' expressly used. However,

---

[56] See sections 60–1 Interim Constitution; sections 75–7 Final Constitution.
[57] Chapter 3 Interim Constitution; Chapter 2 Final Constitution.

the term was used in two of the Constitutional Principles.[58] Constitutional Principle XII provided for '[c]ollective rights of self-determination in forming, joining and maintaining organs of civil society, including linguistic, cultural and religious associations.' Although using the term 'self-determination' this Constitutional Principle does little more than assert in stronger language a right to freedom of association to form non-state groups.

Last-minute negotiations with the Afrikaner Volksfront led to Constitutional Principle XXXIV being inserted into the Interim Constitution. This CP provides:

1. This Schedule and the recognition therein of the right of the South African people as a whole to self-determination, shall not be construed as precluding, within the framework of the said right, constitutional provision for a notion of the right to self-determination by any community sharing a common cultural and language heritage, whether in a territorial entity within the Republic or in any other recognised way.

2. The Constitution may give expression to any particular form of self-determination provided there is substantial proven support within the community concerned for such a form of self-determination.

3. If a territorial entity referred to in paragraph 1 is established in terms of this Constitution before the new constitutional text is adopted, the new Constitution shall entrench the continuation of such territorial entity, including its structures, powers and functions.[59]

As Venter has pointed out, the language is slightly confusing.[60] While the principle refers to 'recognition of the right . . . of self-determination', there is no such express recognition of the right and, as has been mentioned, the term 'self-determination' does not appear in the main text of the Constitution or Schedule. However, such a right could be found implicitly in Constitutional Principle I, which entrenches 'the establishment of one sovereign state, a common South African citizenship and a democratic system of government committed to achieving equality between men and women and people of all races.' It would therefore seem that the concept of self-determination being referred to is an 'internal' one, as is backed up by the Constitutional Principle's reference to self-determination 'within the

---

[58] As Venter (1995: 36–9) points out, there are therefore three slightly confused notions of self-determination in the Interim Constitution and the Constitutional Principles: self-determination of the national population; right to self-determination of a community sharing a common cultural and language heritage; and recognition and protection of 'collective rights of self-determination' established by CP XII and the establishment of the Volkstaat Council.

[59] The wording of section 1 was incorporated in section 235 Final Constitution. Sections 30–1 Final Constitution also provided for rights for cultural, religious, and linguistic communities.   [60] Venter (1995: 36).

Republic.' The next part of the phrase, which adds 'or any other recognised way', while sounding ambiguous as regards secession, in the light of Constitutional Principle I must be read as contemplating other forms of self-determination. Interesting also is the identification of the relevant group as one which shares 'a common cultural and language heritage', thus avoiding racial classifications, clearly so problematic in the South African context. This formulation does, however, admit the main groups which in the past were categorized as 'ethnic' groups, such as Afrikaners, Zulus, or Xhosa.

Late amendments to the Constitution also provided for the establishment of a Volkstaat Council, which is to 'serve as a constitutional mechanism to enable proponents of the idea of a Volkstaat to constitutionally pursue the establishment of such a Volkstaat.'[61] The Volkstaat Council was conceded to by the ANC in the knowledge that there was no geographically ethnically homogeneous area in which a Volkstaat could easily be established; and that the broader human rights framework, by preventing any 'fixing of the numbers' through population transfer and denial of rights, would ensure that such an area could not be established. Nevertheless, this constituted an important symbolic concession to right-wing Afrikaner self-determination demands.

NORTHERN IRELAND

State–ethnic Relations

Self-Determination Language

In Northern Ireland the self-determination deal at its heart aimed to set in place structures which would form a compromise between nationalist claims to United Ireland and unionist claims to continued union with Britain. This issue is ostensibly dealt with at the beginning of the agreement. Explicit references to self-determination are found in the first substantive section of the Belfast Agreement, entitled 'Constitutional Issues', although the mechanism for affirming the parties' support for the provisions is a little convoluted.[62]

---

[61] Section 9 Constitution of the Republic of South Africa Amendment Act No. 2 of 1994.

[62] The participants to the talks endorse the commitment made by the British and Irish governments to make a new British–Irish Agreement which will replace the Anglo-Irish Agreement, and incorporate the new self-determination language of the Belfast Agreement. The actual text of this 'British–Irish Agreement', which unlike the rest of the document has treaty status, is set out at the end of the 'Belfast Agreement' document. This British–Irish Agreement restates and incorporates the self-determination language in its first article. Article 2 goes on to affirm the commitment to set up the 'cross-border' institutions—the North–South Ministerial Council, cross-border implementation bodies to be set up by the Council, and the British–Irish Council, and the British–Irish Inter-Governmental Conference.

Essentially the self-determination language is deliberately ambiguous, designed to be read by both sides as endorsing their position even though these are polar opposites. Paragraph 1 of the Belfast Agreement is a masterpiece of ambiguity, violating all rules of legal drafting. In sub-paragraph (i) it would seem that the self-determination issue is settled. The governments will recognize '*the legitimacy* of whatever choice is freely exercised by a *majority of the people of Northern Ireland*, whether they prefer to continue to support the Union with Great Britain or a sovereign united Ireland' (emphasis added). The unit commanding territorial integrity would appear to be Northern Ireland, and 'the people' all of its people (which at present would mean a Protestant majority).

However, sub-paragraph (ii), using language from the Downing Street Declaration, goes on to

recognise that it is for the people of the island of Ireland alone, by agreement between the two parts respectively and without external impediment, to exercise their right of self-determination on the basis of consent, freely and concurrently given, North and South, to bring about a united Ireland, if that is their wish, accepting that this right must be achieved and exercised with and subject to the agreement and consent of a majority of the people of Northern Ireland.

In its opening this paragraph suggests that the unit for self-determination is 'the island of Ireland' and 'the people' the people of that island 'alone'. Then the ambiguity re-enters. The mechanism for determining the will of the people reintroduces Northern Ireland as a unit. It becomes clear that 'consent' includes 'consent of a majority of the people of Northern Ireland' and that Irish unity is 'subject' to this consent (the latter half of the paragraph's last sentence being an add-on to the Downing Street Declaration). This conclusion is reinforced by sub-paragraph (iii), which notes that

the present wish of a majority of the people of Northern Ireland, freely exercised and legitimate, is to maintain the Union and, accordingly, that Northern Ireland's status as part of the United Kingdom reflects and relies upon that wish; and that it would be wrong to make any change in the status of Northern Ireland save with the consent of a majority of its people.

Thus while the language of self-determination appears to support Irish republican analysis, the mechanism of implementation appears to entrench unionist analysis.

While the Belfast Agreement and Northern Ireland Act arguably provide

An annex to the Constitutional Issues section of the Belfast Agreement provides the actual text of legislative and constitutional changes to be made by the British and Irish governments to the Government of Ireland Act 1920, and the Irish Constitution, respectively.

little change from earlier statements on Northern Ireland's constitutional status, such as in the Northern Ireland Constitution Act 1973 and the Anglo-Irish Agreement 1985, they do provide a clear procedure whereby union with Britain could be ended.[63] Sub-paragraph (iv) provides that if the current situation changes, with 'the people of the island of Ireland' choosing a united Ireland, then 'it will be a binding obligation on both Governments to introduce and support in their respective parliaments legislation to give effect to that wish.' The remaining two paragraphs affirm that whatever choice is freely exercised, all 'the people' of the entity should be entitled to equality and rights, and that people in Northern Ireland can identify as, and hold citizenship as, Irish or British or both.

The agreement's self-determination rhetoric is supported by the repeal of the conflicting constitutional claims of Britain and Ireland. Articles 2 and 3 of the Irish Constitution, which claimed territorial sovereignty over the 'island of Ireland' including the North, are to be replaced by a right to all 'persons born in the island of Ireland' to be 'part of the Irish Nation' and a recognition that 'a united Ireland shall be brought about only by peaceful means with the consent of a majority of the people, democratically expressed, in both jurisdictions in the island.'[64] Similarly, the British government, in provisions now adopted in the Northern Ireland Act,[65] commit to repealing the Government of Ireland Act 1920.

Although the ambiguous self-determination provisions may seem largely symbolic, they have some substantive effect. It can be argued that the holding of a referendum on the agreement as a package has reshaped the parameters of the sovereignty question. If the all-Ireland vote itself is an act of self-determination, then 'union with Britain' has a new meaning and now requires the limitations on majoritarianism and the cross-border cooperation also included in the agreement (discussed more fully in the next section).[66] Indeed the contingency of devolution was underlined by the contingency of the changes to the Irish Constitution which were not to be confirmed until the Northern Ireland Assembly and cross-border bodies were set up.[67]

Furthermore, while the clear reference to the 'people of the island of

[63] See section 1 and Schedule 1, Northern Ireland Act 1998. As Hadfield (1998: 609) notes, 'section 1 is a provision which, at the least, would delight those of a Scottish nationalist persuasion if an equivalent had been included in the Scotland Act 1998'.

[64] Belfast Agreement (BA) Constitutional Issues, Annex B.

[65] Sections 1 and 2, and Schedule 1 Northern Ireland Act 1998.

[66] Note the objections of Conor Cruise O'Brien to the agreement, on the very grounds that the options open to unionism have now been unjustifiably limited to the agreement or Irish unity (1998: 435–47).

[67] The Irish government had to make a declaration in order to confirm the changes to the Irish Constitution. Under the British–Irish Agreement section of the Belfast Agreement, the Irish government is not obliged to 'ensure that the amendments to the Constitution of Ireland . . . take effect' until the British–Irish Agreement comes into force, and in effect

Ireland alone' may, in practical terms, seem irrelevant to the exercise of self-determination (given the need for the consent of a majority in the North), it has immense symbolic importance, particularly given the all-Ireland referendum. Both provision and referendum reaffirm the continued involvement of the people of the Republic of Ireland, and not just its government, in future major decisions on the constitutional status of the North. Indeed it could be argued that the clear location of self-determination in an all-Ireland framework goes beyond the purely symbolic. It addresses one of the very problems created by the international law of self-determination—the perpetuation of two irreconcilable self-determination claims which both have validity. In doing so it addresses Guelke's lack of international legitimacy to the current borders and status of Northern Ireland as discussed in Chapter 3.[68]

The all-Ireland vote also addresses a lack of internal legitimacy alleged by Irish republicans to be the source of a just war of national liberation, a position not entirely without support in international documents, as we have seen.[69] The dynamics of this can be illustrated by examining the role of the vote on the Belfast Agreement itself. After the breakdown of the first IRA ceasefire in February 1996 John Hume in public statements challenged the Provisional IRA directly to let 'the people of Ireland' self-determine not just their future, but the means they would choose to reach that future—violence or dialogue.[70] At that time he asked for a vote on the issue of violence. Although this was not taken up at that time, John Hume continued to push for an all-Ireland vote on any agreement, a matter which had also been addressed in the Downing Street Declaration, and the Framework Document.[71] The eventual all-Ireland pro-agreement vote in effect strongly endorsed negotiation (within this particular framework) over return to political violence.

While the self-determination language is not therefore without effect, the

this did not happen until after power was devolved to the Northern Irish Assembly, whereupon the Irish government made the declaration. See further Bell and Cavanaugh (1999: 1359–60).

[68] Guelke (1985).

[69] The symbolism of the vote addressed, for example, the vote in 1918 in which Sinn Féin won over 70% on an Irish independence platform, and which formed in part a basis for present-day legitimacy.

[70] For example, in a BBC radio interview on 10 Feb. 1996 (the day after the breach of the 1995 IRA ceasefire by the Canary Wharf bomb) John Hume stated: 'My strong message to the leadership of the IRA is that since you say you believe in the right of the Irish people to self-determination, the Irish people also have the right to self-determine their methods,— particularly during the visit of President Clinton, and particularly since the cease-fire—they have made their self-determination on methodology very, very, clear.' As quoted in Bew and Gillespie (1996: 164).

[71] The Republic of Ireland Constitution requires a referendum for its amendment, in any case.

crux of the deal is found in the institutional arrangements for governing Northern Ireland. These have two main aspects: a consociational form of government, and a cross-border dimension which provides for cooperation between Britain and Ireland in governing Northern Ireland. Unlike South Africa the consociational mechanisms are indefinite rather than temporary.

Human Rights

Human rights provisions (considered further in Chapter 7) are also relevant to self-determination in providing a constraint on government, whether devolved or not. The human rights component of the agreement aims to provide values to underpin the new governmental arrangements. The agreement provides for protection of individual human rights through incorporation of the European Convention on Human Rights, and a possible bill of rights with a Human Rights Commission to enforce it. The agreement also provides for reviews of policing and criminal justice. The agreement emphasizes equality particularly between Catholics and Protestants, but also as regards a broader range of groups. A group right element is hinted at in several places. The Human Rights Commission is tasked with consulting and advising on the Bill of Rights, and in particular to consider equality and 'parity of esteem' between the two communities. Furthermore, specific provision is made for cultural and language rights development.

Consociational Mechanisms

Proportionality

The agreement establishes a Northern Ireland Assembly to be elected using proportional representation by single transferable vote.[72] Indeed, proportionality is extended to the whole of government. Assembly committees established to review the operation of each government department and their chairs and deputies are all to be selected in proportion to party strength.[73] The make-up of the Human Rights Commission is to 'reflect community balance.'

Executive Power-Sharing

The agreement provides for a power-sharing executive in which both unionists and nationalists will share power in proportion with their legislative rep-

---

[72] Reilly and Reynolds (1999: 36–40) note that this device is not typical of consociationalism, and thus label the overall package of which it is typically a part as 'integrative consensualism'. In theory the single transferable vote is meant to encourage a reorganization of politics around cross-cutting cleavages other than ethnicity. In practice, it has been used in Northern Ireland for some time where it has not done so.

[73] Belfast Agreement (BA) Strand One, 'Democratic Institutions in Northern Ireland', para. 8. Cf. section 29 Northern Ireland Act 1998.

resentation. The agreement establishes first minister and deputy first minister in a devolved Northern Ireland Assembly. These two persons are to be elected into office by the Assembly voting on a cross-community basis, which means that 50 per cent of registered unionists, 50 per cent of registered nationalists, and a majority of the Assembly as a whole must elect them, giving an incentive for both these groupings to nominate a candidate for one of these positions who is acceptable to at least a majority of the other group. While ethnic criteria are not specified for either post, the voting system also practically ensures that a unionist and a nationalist will share them. The Northern Ireland Act provides that 'if either the First Minister or the deputy First Minister ceases to hold office, whether by resignation or otherwise, the other shall also cease to hold office.'[74] Thus the posts are interlinked, and indeed their functions are essentially the same, with a difference in name only. Both are to convene and preside over an Executive Committee, and coordinate its work and the 'response of the Northern Ireland administration to external relationships.'[75]

The Executive Committee itself is made up of ministers whose posts are allocated to parties in proportion to their strength, according to a mathematical formula known as the 'd'Hondt rule'.[76] In practice this has resulted in two out of ten ministerial positions for Sinn Féin.

Mutual Vetoes

Further safeguards against abuse of power are provided for both the work of the power-sharing executive and the Assembly itself by the cross-community voting procedures, or mutual veto system. Certain key decisions require cross-communal support, either by a majority of members representing each main community, or by a weighted majority of 60 per cent including at least 40 per cent of members representing each community.[77] These include the appointment of a chief minister and a deputy; the establishment of cross-border bodies; or any other matter on the petition of at least thirty Assembly members. Each party must opt to be counted as 'unionist', 'nationalist', or 'other', for the purposes of voting.[78]

[74] Section 14(6) Northern Ireland Act (1998).
[75] Sections 17, 18 Northern Ireland Act (1998).
[76] BA Strand One, 'Democratic Institutions in Northern Ireland', para. 16; section 18, Northern Ireland Act 1998.
[77] BA Strand One, 'Democratic Institutions in Northern Ireland', para. 5; section 4(5) Northern Ireland Act 1998.
[78] BA Strand One, 'Democratic Institutions in Northern Ireland', para. 6; section 4(5) Northern Ireland Act 1998.

Territorial Divisions of Power: Cross-Border Links and Supra-National Structures

The second component to the 'internal self-determination' package is the provision for British–Irish cooperation with relation to Northern Ireland (which O'Leary has called the 'plus' factor).[79] This goes to the heart of the territorial aspect of the self-determination claim of nationalists. Although the legitimacy of Northern Ireland and the need for consent of a majority of its people (a unionist position) is affirmed by the agreement, provision is made for embryonic all-Ireland joint structures of government, which aim to accommodate nationalist claims to united Ireland.

There are several elements. The most obvious are the Strand Two North–South Ministerial Council and implementation bodies for cross-border cooperation, and the Strand Three British–Irish Inter-Governmental Conference. In addition an 'all-Ireland' dimension is provided by the island-wide referendum on the agreement as already discussed, and provision for a joint Human Rights Committee of the two new Human Rights Commissions, which is addressed further in Chapter 7.[80]

A North–South Ministerial Council, composed of those with executive responsibilities in Northern Ireland and the Irish government (represented by the relevant ministers), is to operate 'by agreement between the two sides', although ultimately each side is 'to remain accountable to the Assembly and Oireachtas [Irish legislature] respectively.'[81] Participation in the Council is an 'essential responsibility attaching to relevant posts in the two administrations.' The Council is to have four primary functions:

- to exchange information, discuss and consult with a view to cooperating on matters of mutual interest
- to use best endeavours to reach agreement on the adoption of common policies, in areas where there is a mutual cross-border and all-island benefit . . . making determined efforts to overcome any disagreements
- to take decisions by agreement on policies for implementation separately in each jurisdiction, in relevant meaningful areas
- to take decisions by agreement on policies and action at an all-island and cross-border level to be implemented by the cross-border bodies[82]

In addition the Council is to undertake a work programme covering at least twelve subject areas for cooperation, six of which must be matters for existing bodies to deal with, and six where 'co-operation will take place through agreed implementation bodies on a cross-border or all-island level.'[83]

[79] See generally BA Strand Two. See O'Leary (1999).
[80] BA Rights Safeguards and Equality of Opportunity, 'A Joint Committee', para. 10.
[81] BA Strand Two, North–South Ministerial Council, paras. 2, 6.
[82] BA Strand Two, North–South Ministerial Council, para. 5.
[83] BA Strand Two, North–South Ministerial Council, para. 9.

The agreement makes it clear that the North–South Ministerial Council and the Northern Ireland Assembly are 'mutually inter-dependent, and that one cannot successfully function without the other.'[84] This interdependence is constructed so as to ensure that nationalists and unionists cannot 'cherrypick' the aspects of government which they particularly want to implement. Thus, unionists only get the Assembly and devolved power if they operate the cross-border mechanisms, and for nationalists the situation is reversed. What the agreement did not contemplate was union-ist refusal to participate in the Assembly's establishment (which long frus-trated the agreement's implementation).

Possibilities for future expansion of this cooperation are contemplated through the provision that 'the Northern Ireland Assembly and the Oireachtas [are] to consider developing a joint parliamentary forum, bringing together equal numbers from both institutions for discussion of matters of mutual interest and concern'.[85] There is also provision for a possible North–South 'independent consultative forum' which would be 'representative of civil society, comprising the social partners and other members with expertise in social, cultural, economic and other issues.'[86]

The British–Irish Council and British–Irish Inter-Governmental Conference

Membership of a British–Irish Council is to comprise representatives of the British and Irish governments, devolved institutions in Northern Ireland, Scotland, and Wales, and, if appropriate, elsewhere in the United Kingdom, together with representatives of the Isle of Man and the Channel Islands.[87] The contemplated role of the British–Irish Council is to 'exchange information, discuss, consult and use best endeavours to reach agreement on co-operation on matters of mutual interest within the competence of the relevant Administrations.'[88] Transport links, agricultural issues, environmental issues, cultural issues, health issues, education issues, and approaches to EU issues (a list similar to that of the North–South bodies) are mentioned as '[s]uitable issues for early discussion'.[89] Decision-making is to be by consensus, and agreement and can be multilateral or bilateral.[90] This paves the way for East–West cooperation between any permutation or number of the participants, raising the possibility, for example, of Irish–Scottish, or Northern Irish–Welsh initiatives.

The British–Irish Inter-Governmental Conference is to bring together British and Irish governments 'to promote bilateral cooperation at all levels

---

[84] BA Strand Two, North–South Ministerial Council, para. 13.
[85] BA Strand Two, North–South Ministerial Council, para. 18.
[86] BA Strand Two, North–South Ministerial Council, para. 19. See further Ch. 10 below.
[87] BA Strand Three, British–Irish Council, para. 2.
[88] BA Strand Three, British–Irish Council, para. 5.   [89] Ibid.
[90] BA Strand Three, British–Irish Council, paras. 6, 7, 10.

on all matters of mutual interest within the competence of both Governments.'[91] The Conference can meet at summit level (prime minister and Taoiseach), or the governments can be represented by appropriate Ministers and attended by advisers.[92] The Conference therefore establishes a clear mechanism for communication and cooperation directly between Dublin and London. While decisions are to be 'by agreement between both Governments',[93] a stronger right for Irish government intervention than the formula for the British–Irish Council is provided. It is specifically provided that

[i]n recognition of the Irish Government's special interest in Northern Ireland and of the extent to which issues of mutual concern arise in relation to Northern Ireland, there will be regular and frequent meetings of the Conference concerned with non-devolved Northern Ireland matters, *on which the Irish Government may put forward views and proposals*.[94]

Cooperation in 'security matters, rights, justice, prisons and policing in Northern Ireland (unless and until responsibility is devolved to a Northern Ireland administration) *will* be addressed'.[95] While the emphasis is on the Dublin–London governmental relationship, Northern Ireland executive members are to be involved in meetings of the Conference and in the reviews of the new British–Irish Agreement and the machinery and institutions established under it which the Conference is to undertake.[96]

Together the Strand Two and Three institutions give government in Northern Ireland overlapping, innovative supra-state structures which O'Leary has described as 'confederal' in nature, with both all-Ireland and British–Irish confederal relationships.[97] These structures do not explicitly use self-determination language, but clearly the North–South elements were designed to accommodate nationalist demands for Irish sovereignty and to build on the 1985 Anglo-Irish Agreement. The British–Irish element was further designed to this end, as is evident from the earlier Frameworks for the Future, British–Irish proposal of February 1995 (Annex B, para. 2).[98] However, unionist concern to widen this body into an 'East–West' Council, a clear departure from earlier blueprints facilitated by the intervening United Kingdom-wide devolution project, changed both its scope and its symbolism. Rather than a further North–South mechanism whose focus is Northern Ireland, a much broader and more complex set of relationships is enabled.

---

[91] BA Strand Three, British–Irish Inter-Governmental Conference, para. 1.

[92] BA Strand Three, British–Irish Inter-Governmental Conference, para. 3.

[93] BA Strand Three, British–Irish Inter-Governmental Conference, para. 2.

[94] BA Strand Three, British–Irish Inter-Governmental Conference, para. 5 (emphasis added).

[95] BA Strand Three, British–Irish Inter-Governmental Conference, para. 6 (emphasis added).   [96] BA Strand Three, British–Irish Inter-Governmental Conference, para. 9.

[97] O'Leary (1999: 1645–9).   [98] See Ch. 3 at pp. 60, 62–3.

Furthermore, in self-determination terms, the Irish government is given a relationship not just with Northern Ireland but also with all the other parts of the United Kingdom. On a bold view it is possible to see this element as symbolically hinting at the pre-partition concept of the 'British Isles of Britain and Ireland' in a way that either transcends pre-partition colonialism or harkens back to it (another constructive ambiguity).[99] While full analysis of the negotiation dynamics surrounding the 'regional' aspects of the agreement is beyond the scope of this chapter, it is important to note that the British–Irish Council was for unionists a mechanism which mitigated and changed the significance of the North–South cross-border bodies, so crucial to settlement for nationalists and Irish republicans. By having cooperation which was not only North–South, but East–West, unionists could present the British–Irish structures not as diminishing British sovereignty, but as a matter of common-sense cooperation with a variety of forums.

BOSNIA HERZEGOVINA

The first article of the Dayton Peace Agreement (DPA) in essence reiterates the self-determination principles which supposedly underlie its framework, and which were stated by the international community during the conflict to be non-negotiable. That is, that the parties are to conduct their relations in accordance with the principles of the UN Charter, the Helsinki Final Act, and other Organization for Security and Cooperation in Europe (OSCE) documents, and that they shall:

fully respect the sovereign equality of one another, shall settle disputes by peaceful means, and shall refrain from any action, by threat or use of force or otherwise, against the territorial integrity or political independence of Bosnia and Herzegovina or any other state.[100]

While the first two annexes provide for the military implementation of a ceasefire, Annex 3 DPA marks a more ambitious agenda for reconstruction and transition to democracy. It provides for 'free, fair and democratic elections' designed 'to lay the foundation for representative government and ensure the progressive achievement of democratic goals throughout Bosnia and Herzegovina, in accordance with relevant documents of the OSCE.' Provision is made for OSCE involvement in ensuring that the elections are free and fair.[101] The annex provides that '[a]ny citizen of Bosnia and Herzegovina aged 18 or older whose name appears on the 1991

---

[99] Cf. Guelke (1985).
[100] Article I The General Framework Agreement for Peace in Bosnia and Herzegovina, 14 Dec. 1995 (hereafter 'Dayton Peace Agreement' or 'DPA').
[101] See further Annex 3 DPA.

census for Bosnia and Herzegovina shall be eligible, in accordance with electoral rules and regulations, to vote.'[102] The significance of the 1991 census reference is that it recorded the population distribution prior to widespread shifts due to the war and ethnic cleansing. Citizens can apply to the Commission to cast their ballot elsewhere. An exercise of a right to vote is to be interpreted as confirmation of a person's intention to return to Bosnia and Herzegovina.[103]

Territorial Divisions of Power

As in the Belfast Agreement, while the self-determination language is important, it is the governmental arrangements found in the Constitution in Annex 4 of the DPA which encapsulate the central self-determination deal. Article I(1) provides that: 'The Republic of Bosnia and Herzegovina . . . shall continue its legal existence under international law as a state, with its internal structure modified as provided herein and with its present internationally recognized borders.' Thus the unity of the state is affirmed. BiH is to be a 'democratic state, which shall operate under the rule of law and with free and democratic elections.'[104]

However, Article I(3) provides that 'Bosnia and Herzegovina shall consist of the two Entities, the Federation of Bosnia and Herzegovina and the Republika Srpska.' A large part of the Constitution then sets out the different spheres of operation and powers of Entities and republic. It is in the detail of the delimitation of powers between republic and Entities that the nature of the compromise between separatist claims of Serbs and Croats, on one hand, and the claims of Bosniacs and the international community, on the other, can be ascertained. Contract-like provisions, reminiscent of the detail of the South African Interim Constitution, make allowance for the fact that neither Entity's allegiance to the common structures can be taken for granted. For example, the provision of citizenship notes that '[a]ll citizens of either Entity are *thereby* citizens of Bosnia and Herzegovina.'[105] Conversely, no person 'shall be deprived of Bosnian and Herzegovina or Entity citizenship arbitrarily or so as to leave him or her stateless.'[106] This amounts to a safeguard against ongoing discrimination, or Entity attempts to in effect dissolve BiH.

General clauses aim to provide for the physical and symbolic existence of the unitary state. Freedom of movement between the Entities is provided for with neither Entity being allowed to establish entity boundary controls.[107]

---

[102] Article IV, Annex 3 DPA.
[103] Ibid. The election system subsequently chosen was a list PR system. See further Ch. 6, pp. 178–9.   [104] Article I(2), Annex 4 DPA.
[105] Article I(7)(a), Annex 4 DPA.   [106] Article I(7)(b), Annex 4 DPA.
[107] Article I(4), Annex 4 DPA.

Sarajevo is established as 'a common capital', and provision is made for common state symbols.[108] Citizenship of BiH is provided for, although there is also to be 'a citizenship of each Entity, to be regulated by each Entity.'[109] Both Entities are to 'ensure the highest level of internationally recognized human rights and fundamental freedoms, as policed by the Human Rights Commission', a matter addressed further in Chapter 7.[110]

Beyond this the common space created by the BiH institutions is minimal. Its institutions are responsible only for a defined and limited list of areas: foreign policy, foreign trade policy; customs policy; monetary policy; finances of the institutions and for the international obligations of BiH; immigration, refugee, and asylum policy and regulation; international and inter-entity criminal law enforcement, including relations with Interpol; establishment and operation of common and international communications facilities; regulation of inter-entity transportation; and air traffic control.[111]

There are, however, possibilities written into the agreement for the republic's competencies to grow as (or if) inter-ethnic trust grows. Article III(4) provides that '[t]he Presidency may decide to facilitate inter-Entity coordination on matters not within the responsibilities of Bosnia and Herzegovina as provided in this Constitution, unless an Entity objects in any particular case.' Given that the presidency is itself comprised of three people representing Bosniacs, Croats, and Serbs, as we shall see below, such a decision would itself involve a degree of inter-ethnic trust and cooperation. The Constitution also provides that BiH can assume responsibility for other matters as agreed by the Entities; either as provided for (in Annexes 5–8 DPA) or as 'are necessary to preserve the sovereignty, territorial integrity, political independence, and international personality of Bosnia and Herzegovina, in accordance with the division of responsibilities between the institutions of Bosnia and Herzegovina'.[112] Additional institutions can be established to carry out any additional responsibilities created under this article.[113]

In contrast to the limited powers of the republic, the Entities have 'all governmental functions and powers not expressly assigned in [the] Constitution to the institutions of Bosnia and Herzegovina'.[114] Indeed, they potentially also have an overlapping role in some areas. Although not responsible for foreign policy, trade, or international persons, Entities 'shall have the right to establish special parallel relationships with neighboring states consistent with the sovereignty and territorial integrity of Bosnia and Herzegovina.'[115] They can also 'enter into agreements with states and international organizations with the consent of the Parliamentary Assembly'

---

[108] Article I(5), (6), Annex 4 DPA.   [109] Article I(7), Annex 4 DPA.
[110] Article II(1), Annex 4 DPA.   [111] Article III(1), Annex 4 DPA.
[112] Article III(5), Annex 4 DPA.   [113] Ibid.
[114] Article III(3), Annex 4 DPA.   [115] Article III(2)(a), Annex 4 DPA.

or where it so provides, without its consent.[116] For the most part the entity powers are not expressly enumerated, testifying to their residual width. However, criminal justice does receive specific mention: the Entities are 'to provide a safe and secure environment for all persons in their respective jurisdictions, by maintaining civilian law enforcement agencies' operating in accordance with international human rights standards.[117]

A quick glance at the Constitutions of the two Entities reveals the coincidence of Entity and ethnicity which underlies the map-drawing accompanying the agreement. The Federation Constitution (produced prior to Dayton as the 'Washington Peace Agreement') provides for 'Bosniacs and Croats, as constituent peoples';[118] while that of Republika Srpska provides that 'Republika Srpska shall be the State of Serb people and of all its citizens'.[119] In other words, while the DPA affirms the unitary structure of the BiH Republic, it does so by creating highly autonomous, ethnically divided Entities with many of the attributes of statehood.

The Federation Constitution further reveals ethnic border-drawing between Croats and Bosniacs at the sub-entity level. The Federation is a federation of cantons. The Federation government has an exclusive jurisdiction over a limited list of matters: Federation defence, citizenship, economic policy, regulation of finance, financial institutions and fiscal policy, combating crime, allocating radio and television frequencies, energy policy, and raising finance.[120] The Federation and cantons have overlapping competence in a further list of areas, comprising human rights, health, environmental policy, communications infrastructure, social welfare policy, implementation of citizenship laws, regulations on passports and foreigners, tourism, and use of natural resources.[121] And the cantons, like the Entities, have 'all responsibility not expressly granted to the Federation Government'.[122] This is explicitly stated to include: 'establishing and controlling police forces', education policy, cultural policy, housing policy, public service provision, regulating local land use, regulating local business and charity, regulating local energy, radio and television policy,

---

[116] Article III(2)(b), Annex 4 DPA.   [117] Article III(2)(c), Annex 4 DPA.

[118] Article 1(1) The Constitution of the Federation of Bosnia and Herzegovina 1994 (hereafter 'Federation Constitution'); pub. in *Ustavi* (Sarajevo: Federalno Minisarstvo Pravde, 1998), 137–65.

[119] Article 1 Constitution of Republika Srpska (as amended by Amendment XLIV) (hereafter 'RS Constitution'); pub. in *Ustavi* (Sarajevo: Federalno Minisarstvo Pravde, 1998), 209–37. About 4 July 2000 the BiH Constitutional Court issued a decision addressing the compatibility of the provisions of the entity Constitutions with the BiH Constitution. At the time of writing the decision had not been published.

[120] Article 3(1) Federation Constitution (as amended by Amendment VIII adopted 5 June 1996).

[121] Article 3(2) Federation Constitution (as amended by Amendment IX adopted 5 June 1996).   [122] Article 3(4) Federation Constitution.

implementing social welfare policy, cantonal tourism, and financing including tax-raising powers.[123]

In practice, eight out of the ten cantons have majority populations from one or other ethnic group. While this leaves two 'mixed' cantons, the Constitution provides a mechanism for a possible further devolution of their powers to autonomous municipal governments, so facilitating ethnic autonomy even in these mixed cantons. Each canton is authorized to 'transfer its authorities to a municipality or city in its territory, or to the federal authority'.[124] More specifically, each canton can 'transfer the authorities concerning education, culture, tourism, local business and charity in its territory, and *is obliged to do so if the majority of population in the municipality or city is not a majority population in the entire canton*'.[125]

Consociational Mechanisms

Proportionality in BiH State Structures

The accommodation of ethnic division is as much a feature of the governmental structures designed to operate at the level of the shared republic as it is of the territorial divisions. The BiH governmental structures are consociational in design, with many similarities to the Northern Irish institutions, although they are more explicitly based on ethnic criteria.

The BiH government is to comprise a Parliamentary Assembly with two chambers: a House of Peoples and a House of Representatives.[126] Each is to be elected proportionally from the Entities, with Federation representation also being proportional between Croats and Bosniacs. The House of Peoples is to comprise fifteen delegates, with two-thirds from the Federation (five Croats and five Bosniacs) and one-third from the Republika Srpska (five Serbs).[127] The delegates are to be selected by the relevant delegates to the Federation House of Peoples (Croat and Bosniac delegates respectively) and the National Assembly of the Republika Srpska.[128] Nine members comprise a quorum, provided they are in the proportions three Bosniac, three Croat, and three Serb.[129]

The House of Representatives is to comprise forty-two members, again with two-thirds from the Federation and one-third from the Republika Srpska.[130] All legislation 'shall require the approval of both chambers'.[131] Each house is to have one chair and two deputies, a Serb, a Croat, and a

---

[123] Ibid.

[124] Article 5(2)(1) Federation Constitution (as amended by Amendment XV adopted 5 June 1996).

[125] Article V(2)(2) Federation Constitution (as amended by Amendment XV adopted 5 June 1996) (emphasis added).   [126] Article IV, Annex 4 DPA.

[127] Article IV(1), Annex 4 DPA.   [128] Ibid.   [129] Ibid.

[130] Article IV(2), Annex 4 DPA.   [131] Article IV(3), Annex 4 DPA.

Bosniac, with the position of chair rotating among the three.[132] The house can be dissolved by the presidency, or by the house itself, provided that the house's decision 'is approved by a majority that includes the majority of Delegates from at least two of the Bosniac, Croat, or Serb peoples'.[133]

Bosniac–Croat–Serb proportionality is a feature all the BiH Republic institutions set up, as Table 5.1 illustrates. Furthermore, the Federation Constitution ensures similar Bosniac–Croat proportionality in its institutions, and also in the institutions of the cantons through detailed and complicated provisions.[134] Where the canton is 'mixed' Bosniac and Croat, full consociational cantonal government is provided for (although here the cantonal powers are only residual to the municipalities).[135]

Mutual vetoes

Legislative voting at the BiH Republic level also has a mutual veto mechanism similar to that in Northern Ireland, although with slightly different procedures. The Constitution provides that '[a]ll decisions in both Chambers shall be by majority of those present and voting'.[136] However, the delegates and members are to 'make their best efforts' to see that the majority includes at least one-third of the votes of the delegates or members from the territory of each Entity. If it does not, then the chair and deputy chairs are to meet as a commission and attempt to obtain approval within three days of the vote.[137] If they fail, then 'decisions shall be taken by a majority of those present and voting, providing that the dissenting votes do not include two-thirds or more of the Delegates or Members elected from either Entity' (which seems to be the original veto power in any case).[138] There is no procedure stated to overcome this final veto.

In what seems to be an exception to these procedures and weighting, '[a] proposed decision of the Parliamentary Assembly may be declared to be destructive of a vital interest of the Bosniac, Croat, or Serb people by a majority of, as appropriate, the Bosniac, Croat, or Serb Delegates.'[139] Where this happens, the decision must be approved by 'a majority of the Bosniac, of the Croat, and of the Serb Delegates present and voting'.[140] Where a second party objects to another party's declaration of vital interest, the House of Peoples is immediately to convene a Joint Commission comprising three delegates, selected by the three groups respectively, to resolve the issue. If this Commission fails to resolve the issue, then the matter is to be referred to the Constitutional Court, which

---

[132] Article IV(3)(b), Annex 4 DPA.

[133] Article IV(3)(g), Annex 4 DPA (this provides that the first house may not be so dissolved).   [134] See generally Federation Constitution.

[135] See e.g. Article V(12) as inserted by Amendment 1, Federation Constitution.

[136] Article IV(3)(d), Annex 4 DPA.   [137] Ibid.   [138] Ibid.

[139] Article IV(3)(e), Annex 4 DPA.   [140] Ibid.

shall 'in an expedited process review it for procedural regularity'.[141] Again, there is no further provision on how 'vital interest' disputes should be resolved if the Constitutional Court's procedural review fails to resolve the matter.

Power-Sharing Executive

The presidency of Bosnia and Herzegovina is to 'consist of three Members: one Bosniac and one Croat, each directly elected from the territory of the Federation, and one Serb directly elected from the territory of the Republika Srpska'.[142] Members of the presidency are to be directly elected in each Entity (with each voter voting to fill one seat only). The term of office for the first members of the presidency is two years, and thereafter four. The presidency is to have a chairperson, and this is to rotate among its members. It is to 'endeavor to adopt all Presidency Decisions' by consensus.[143] Where this fails, two members can adopt the decision unless the dissenting member claims the decision to be destructive of a 'vital interest' of the Entity from which he or she was elected.[144] In this case, the decision is referred to the relevant delegates of the relevant entity government and if confirmed by two-thirds of them, then 'the challenged Presidency Decision shall not take effect'.[145]

The executive arm of government is the Council of Ministers.[146] A chair of the Council is appointed by the presidency, and this chair then nominates a foreign minister, a minister for foreign trade, and 'other Ministers as may be appropriate'. Again, membership is to be proportional with 'no more than two-thirds of all Ministers' to be appointed from the territory of the Federation and therefore one-third to be from Republika Srpska.[147]

StateEthnic Relations

There are other elements of the deal which go to the heart of the relationship between the state, ethnic groups, and citizens. In particular, these include measures which seek to build the fragile space shared between the two Entities and three peoples. First, there is the constraint of constitutionalism, including built-in human rights protections with enforcement mechanisms. Secondly, there is provision for international involvement in the shared institutions aimed at making them work. Lastly, there is provision aimed at reversing the ethnic cleansing which led to the Entity and Federation's cantonal structures in the first place.

---

[141] Article IV(3)(f), Annex 4 DPA.   [142] Article V, Annex 4 DPA.
[143] Article V(2)(c), Annex 4 DPA.   [144] Article V(2)(d), Annex 4 DPA.   [145] Ibid.
[146] See generally Article V(4), Annex 4 DPA.   [147] Article V(4)(b), Annex 4 DPA.

Human Rights and Constitutionalism

As with the last two case-studies, human rights and constitutionalism aim to provide a constraint on government, but also aim to cement the unitary state by providing shared values across the two Entities, and enabling the reversing of ethnic cleansing through return of refugees and displaced persons. The BiH Constitution has primacy over Entity and cantonal Constitutions and other laws and judgments; a Constitutional Court with ethnically proportional, and international, membership is to be its guardian.[148] In particular the court has the role typical of any federal system, of policing boundaries between the different governmental structures.

The court also has jurisdiction over issues referred by any court in BiH, relating to whether a law is compatible with the Constitution (which includes human rights protections), and with the European Convention for Human Rights and Fundamental Freedoms and its protocols.[149] Article II of the BiH Constitution provides that 'Bosnia and Herzegovina shall ensure the highest level of internationally recognised human rights and fundamental freedoms'. This article, together with Annex I, specifically enumerates lists of rights to be protected, and these will be considered further in Chapter 7. Decisions of the court are to be final and binding. Thus, the human rights standards listed several times in Dayton constitute an attempt to create some common principles and a basis for shared allegiance. While the Constitution can be amended, amendment cannot diminish human rights commitments.[150]

International Involvement

In imposing consociational mechanisms on BiH, the deal had to make provision not only for the ethnic division, but for the fact that the prior institutions had been those of a socialist federation. A key part of cementing the BiH-wide institutions in the face of both the lack of democratic tradition and the recent ethnic conflict was time-limited international involvement. The main BiH structures not only involve proportionality between Bosniacs, Croats, and Serbs, but also have an overall weighting of international members who are not to be citizens of the Republic of Bosnia Herzegovina or any neighbouring state. International appointments are either to be internalized after five years or to be continued by agreement. Table 5.2 illustrates who makes appointments and the balance between Federation, Republika Srpska, and international community.

In addition to this international presence in BiH institutions a High Representative is established by the Dayton Peace Agreement, to 'mobilise

---

[148] See generally Article VI, Annex 4 DPA.   [149] See generally Article II, Annex 4 DPA.
[150] Article X, Annex 4 DPA.

TABLE 5.2. *Make-up of BiH institutions*

Institution	Federation	Republika Srpska	International organizations	Total
Provisional Election Commission	Parties	Parties	Head of OSCE mission (chair); High Representative; other persons as OSCE head shall decide in consultation with parties	
Constitutional Court	4	3	Three members selected by president of European Court of Human Rights in consultation with the presidency	10
Human Rights Chamber	4	2	Eight members appointed by the Committee of Ministers of the Council of Europe.	14
Commission for Displaced Persons and Refugees	4	2	Three members appointed by the president of the European Court of Human Rights (one to be designated chairperson)	9
Commission to Preserve National Monuments	2	1	Two appointed by the director-general of UNESCO (one to be chairperson)	5
Commission on Public Corporations	2	1	Two appointed by president of the European Bank for Reconstruction and Development (one to be chairperson)	5

and, as appropriate, coordinate the activities of the organisations and agencies involved in the civilian aspects of the peace settlement'.[151] These civilian activities are very broadly conceived and include continuation of the humanitarian aid; rehabilitation of infrastructure and economic reconstruction; the establishment of political and constitutional institutions in BiH;

---

[151] Article I(2), Annex 10 DPA. See further Joulwan and Shoemaker (1998: 26–45) for an argument that the Office of the High Representative (OHR) mandate and lines of responsibility were unclear and that this has impeded the implementation of the agreement.

promotion of respect for human rights and the return of displaced persons and refugees; and the holding of free and fair elections according to the specified timetable.[152] In essence these activities amount to implementation of most of the DPA, apart from the military aspects in Annex 1A and B, and policing as addressed in Annex 11. However, even in these areas the High Representative has some input. The High Representative or his or her designate is to 'remain in close contact with IFOR' (the multinational military Implementation Force of Annex 1A), exchanging information and liaising regularly.[153] The High Representative is also to attend or be represented at meetings of the Joint Military Commission and offer advice 'particularly on matters of a political-military nature'.[154] The all-inclusive role of the Office of High Representative is underlined by Article V, Annex 10, which provides that '[t]he High Representative is the final authority in theater regarding interpretation of this Agreement on the civilian implementation of the peace settlement'.

Reversing Ethnic Cleansing?

While the one-state–two-entity structure appears to underwrite ethnic cleansing, in one of its central paradoxes the DPA also makes provision designed to reverse that situation. The concept of a 'right to return' for refugees and displaced persons runs through the agreement.

The right of return is provided for indirectly in the election provisions. As noted above, these provide for BiH citizens to cast their votes in the municipality in which they resided in 1991 'by person, or by absentee ballot', although an application to vote elsewhere can be made.[155] The DPA confidently asserts that '[b]y Election Day, the return of refugees should already be underway, thus allowing many to participate in person in elections in Bosnia and Herzegovina'.[156] The human rights provisions of the Constitution also state that

All refugees and displaced persons have the right freely to return to their homes of origin. They have the right . . . to have restored to them property of which they were deprived in the course of hostilities since 1991 and to be compensated for any such property that cannot be restored to them.[157]

Annex 7 of the DPA makes further detailed provision for the conditions required to facilitate return. These will be considered further in Chapters 7 and 8.

---

[152] Annex 10 DPA.   [153] Article II(5) and (6), Annex 10 DPA.
[154] Article II(7), Annex 10 DPA.   [155] Article IV, Annex 3 DPA.   [156] Ibid.
[157] Article II(5), Annex 4 DPA.

ISRAEL/PALESTINE

Territorial Divisions of Power

Self-Determination Language

The Declaration of Principles (DoP) and later Interim Agreements, unlike the other three examples, are explicitly stated to be interim only. They do not explicitly claim to address Palestinian self-determination claims; indeed this word is studiously avoided (for its use in itself would amount to an Israeli concession in the direction of Palestinian statehood).[158] Palestinian self-determination or statehood is not even listed on the agenda for permanent status negotiations, an agenda which includes Jerusalem, refugees, settlements, security arrangements, borders, relations and cooperation with other neighbours, and other issues of common interest.[159]

There is, however, language that hints at self-determination. The DoP sets out the end goal as to achieve 'permanent status' agreements on Gaza and West Bank on the basis of UN Resolutions 242 and 338, noting that 'the outcome of the permanent status negotiations should not be prejudiced or preempted by agreements reached for the interim period'.[160] Cassese has argued that fundamental objectives of the UN resolutions, such as withdrawal of Israeli armed forces, 'logically presuppose' an unspecified form of external self-determination including 'independent international status'.[161] Given that the DoP is grounded in these resolutions, Cassese has argued that the DoP also logically presupposes 'independent international status' albeit 'in an oblique and roundabout way', although the next chapter explores the idea that the agreements have come to predetermine quite a different outcome.[162]

The DoP also states that provision of elections is 'a significant *interim preparatory* step toward the realisation of the *legitimate rights* of the Palestinian people and their *just requirements*'.[163] This would again seem to suggest that the issue of self-determination, broadly defined, is implicitly on the final status agenda, although the ambiguity of the language (used before in the Camp David Accords[164]) hides deep disagreement over what the legitimate rights or just requirements are. Article IV of the DoP, using

---

[158] Agreements after the DoP, however, do state in general terms that the process is bound by international human rights standards, which of course include self-determination. See The Agreement on the Gaza Strip and the Jericho Area, 4 May 1994 (hereafter Gaza–Jericho Agreement), Article XIV; Israeli–Palestinian Interim Agreement on the West Bank and Gaza Strip, 28 Sep. 1995 (hereafter Interim Agreement), Article XIX. [159] Article V(3) DoP.
[160] Articles I and V(4) DoP. [161] Cassese (1998*b*: 569). [162] Ibid. cf. Cotran (1996).
[163] Article III(3).
[164] Section A 1(C), A. Framework for Peace in the Middle East Agreed at Camp David, Text of Agreements signed on 17 Sep. 1978; pub. in Abdul Hadi (1997*a*: 248–50). See also Klieman (1999).

terminology from international law on self-determination, states that '[t]he two sides view the West Bank and the Gaza Strip as a single territorial unit, whose integrity will be preserved during the interim period'. This language (reused in later agreements) was seen by Palestinians as implicitly acknowledging their self-determination claim, but also as capable of offsetting the exclusion of Jerusalem, settlements, military locations, and Israelis from the scope of Palestinian Authority powers. As Shehadeh writes, 'Palestinians were hoping to be able to argue that the two Palestinian areas of the West Bank and the Gaza Strip should be linked and that Israeli settlements break the areas' integrity and violate this provision'.[165] In practice, not only did this strategy fail, but Israeli policies of absolute closure, instituted after bomb attacks on Israeli civilians, moved beyond previous closure strategies and prevented all movement of Palestinians and goods in and out of the Occupied Territories, and frustrated Palestinian passage between West Bank and Gaza.[166] The detailed provisions of the recent 'safe passage' agreement of 4 October 1999 bears witness to these difficulties.

Despite the nebulous ambiguity of the self-determination language, it can be argued that the DoP substantively moves the Israel–Palestine conflict towards resolution of the self-determination issue in the following ways.[167] The accompanying letters of recognition exchanged between Rabin and Arafat begin to move the parties towards mutual acknowledgement of the clash of self-determination claims and a mutual right to exist side by side on the land. The letters of recognition move Palestinians towards limiting their self-determination claims to pre-1967 borders acknowledging the right of the state of Israel to exist;[168] they move Israelis towards recognition of Palestinian peoplehood, and through that 'implied recognition of the right of that people to determine freely its political status, and to pursue freely its economic, social, and cultural development'.[169] Secondly, Malanczuk argues that Arafat's renunciation of terrorism and use of force 'renders moot the controversial issue of the extent to which international law and the principle of self-determination permits the use of armed force in

[165] Shehadeh (1997: 19).

[166] See B'Tselem (1998a); Democracy and Workers' Rights Center (1996); Palestinian Center for Human Rights (1995).

[167] See further Benvenisti (1993); Cotran (1996); Malanczuk (1996).

[168] Although arguably this shift had already been made unilaterally in 1988.

[169] Benvenisti (1993: 543–4) (suggesting that this flows from Israel's ratification on 18 Aug. 1991 of the International Covenant on Civil and Political Rights 1966, and the International Covenant on Economic, Social, and Cultural Rights 1966, both of which provide for such rights in their common Article 1). Benvenisti goes further in his analysis of the self-determination import of the DoP. He argues that by relinquishing 'effective control' in Gaza and Jericho, Israel is no longer an occupying power there, and thus has 'no right to reoccupy those areas' meaning that 'the Declaration establishes an *irreversible step* towards the settlement of the conflict (1993: 546; emphasis added). This argument is not shared by the author and will be addressed in Ch. 6, pp. 183–5.

so-called wars of national liberation, and the intervention by third states in support of such wars'.[170] He argues conversely that if the PLO respects its obligations, Israel can 'no longer invoke the right to use armed force, Article 51 of the UN Charter, or any customary international law right of self-defence vis-à-vis the PLO.[171] These points may, however, be somewhat academic, in that Israel may still attempt to justify force against Palestinians other than the PLO, and breach of any of the obligations in the agreements by either side may negate the undertakings by the other.

Thirdly, although it may seem almost too obvious to state, the agreements begin (or continue) to build separate Israeli and Palestinian institutions and government, rather than designing ways to share both. Although the context makes any other focus almost inconceivable, it is worth pointing out as a key difference between the DoP and Interim Agreements and the agreements of South Africa, Northern Ireland, and even Bosnia Herzegovina. Israeli/Palestinian cooperation is contemplated in certain areas and arrangements made for such cooperation. These cooperation mechanisms are very different from the complex attempts to design common institutions for sharing day-to-day decision-making found in the other three examples. Cooperation is to take place in economic related fields such as water, energy, finance, transport and communication, trade and industry, labour relations, human resources development, and environmental protection.[172] Further cooperation also including Jordan and Egypt is provided for generally, and is, in particular, to include 'the modalities of admission of persons displaced from the West Bank and Gaza Strip in 1967, together with necessary measures to prevent disruption and disorder' in an implicit reference to a certain category of Palestinian refugees.[173] All the cooperation is allocated to committees and is vaguely delimited, with no procedures for resolving difficult decisions.

Perhaps the most significant self-determination dimension of the Declaration of Principles is its deafening silence on what the end goal of the negotiations is to be. Ultimately, its language is consistent with two radically different underlying visions of the possible end-game: that of Palestinians to statehood within pre-1967 borders; and that of Israelis to something falling short of that, perhaps as far short as clumps of limited Palestinian autonomy in (mostly urban) centres of high Palestinian density.[174] The legal significance of this will be explored in the next chapter.

Palestinian Autonomy

The DoP claims to provide a measure of Palestinian autonomy for the interim period. It provides for elections to a Palestinian Council, which is

---

[170] Malanczuk (1996: 492–3).   [171] Ibid.
[172] Articles XI, XII, and XVI, and Annexes III and IV, DoP.   [173] Article XII DoP.
[174] See generally Shehadeh (1997).

to have some jurisdiction over the West Bank and Gaza Strip.[175] Power is to be transferred to this Council gradually, in terms of both its territorial ambit, and its spheres of operation. Prior to the elections to the Council, power is to be transferred to an interim Palestinian Authority, which is to be appointed by the PLO with Israeli approval.[176] The DoP provides for an immediate transfer of authority to an interim Palestinian Authority in the areas of education and culture, health, social welfare, direct taxation, and tourism, all of which are transferred 'with the view to promoting economic development in the West Bank and Gaza Strip'.[177] A Protocol to the DoP provides that within two months of the signing of the DoP an agreement will be signed on the withdrawal of Israeli military forces from the Gaza Strip and Jericho area.[178] The DoP states that a future Interim Agreement will provide further detail on the Palestinian Council and the arrangements for transferring power to it. Furthermore, the DoP provides that 'transfer of powers and responsibilities to the Palestinian police will be accomplished in a phased manner, as agreed in the Interim Agreement'.[179]

The DoP provides stringent limits to the jurisdiction of Palestinian power. The jurisdictional scope of the Authority and the subsequent Council are spelt out in agreed minutes to the DoP, where language is included which Palestinian negotiators would not agree to in the text of the DoP itself. These minutes move towards a definition of Palestinian jurisdiction as limited territorially, functionally, and personally.[180]

Territorially the jurisdiction of the Council is to cover areas of the West Bank and Gaza Strip as hinted at by the missing definite article before 'West Bank' (not 'the West Bank'). Functionally, the Council's jurisdiction is only to extend to the spheres transferred to it. The agreed minutes make it clear that '[t]he withdrawal of the [Israeli] military government will not prevent Israel from exercising the powers and responsibilities not transferred to the Council'.[181] Even in these areas the Council's jurisdiction is limited and does not cover 'issues that will be negotiated in the permanent status negotiations: Jerusalem, settlements, military locations and Israelis'.[182] This also makes it clear that the jurisdiction is limited personally to Palestinians and is not to include Israelis.

The subsequent Interim Agreement plays out and confirms the limits of

[175] Article III DoP.
[176] Section B, Article VI(2) Agreed Minutes to the Declaration of Principles on Interim Self-Government Arrangements.   [177] Article VI DoP.
[178] Annex II DoP.
[179] Article VIII Agreed Minutes to the Declaration of Principles on Interim Self-Government Arrangements.   [180] Shehadeh (1997: 35).
[181] Article VII(5) Agreed Minutes to the Declaration of Principles on Interim Self-Government Arrangements.   [182] Article IV DoP.

the transfer of power.[183] The first part of the agreement provides for the detail of the elected Palestinian Council.[184] This provides that the Council is to have both legislative and executive power in all the areas transferred to under the agreement. Authority is to be transferred to the Council from the Israeli Civil Administration in a long list of spheres.[185] However, authority is still limited functionally, territorially, and personally as foreshadowed by the DoP. Functionally, Palestinian jurisdiction only covers the spheres devolved to it; Israel is to have residual authority.[186] The jurisdiction is not to include:

a. issues that will be negotiated in the permanent status negotiations: Jerusalem, settlements, specified military locations, Palestinian refugees, borders, foreign relations and Israelis; and
b. powers and responsibilities not transferred to the Council.[187]

Territorially the jurisdiction is to encompass Gaza Strip territory, except for the settlements and the military installation area detailed on maps. In the West Bank the territorial jurisdiction is further complicated by the Interim Agreement's provision for three different types of territory, each with different applicable provisions and jurisdictions. In Area A, comprising six West Bank cities and parts of the city of Hebron, the Palestinian Council is to have 'full' responsibility for internal security and public order, as well as full responsibility for civil affairs, subject to the personal and functional limits above. In Area B, comprising mainly Palestinian towns and villages, civil authority is to be transferred as in Area A. But as regards security authority the Council is charged with maintaining 'public order', while Israel has overriding security responsibility. Israeli and Palestinian police are to coordinate their movement, as confirmed by Israel. In Area C, comprising the Israeli settlements and large areas around them (described by the Israeli government as 'unpopulated' or of 'strategic importance to Israel and the Jewish settlements'), Israel is to retain 'full responsibility for security and public order' while transferring 'powers and responsibilities not relating to territory' to the Palestinian Council.[188] The agreement then contemplates

---

[183] The picture is built up through the intervening agreements which the Interim Agreements supersede. See generally Interim Agreement.
[184] Articles I–IX Interim Agreement.
[185] The list comprises: agriculture, archaeology, assessments, banking and monetary issues, Palestinian employees of the Israeli civil administration, commerce and industry, comptrol, direct taxation, education and culture, electricity, employment, environmental protection, fisheries, forests, gas, fuel, and petroleum, government and absentee land and immovables, health, indirect taxation, insurance, interior affairs, labour, land registration, legal administration, local government, nature reserves, parks, planning and zoning, population registry and documentation, postal services, public works and housing, quarries and mines, religious sites, social welfare, statistics, surveying, telecommunications, tourism, transportation, treasury, and water and sewage. Annex III Interim Agreement.
[186] Article I(1) Interim Agreement.   [187] Article XVII Interim Agreement.
[188] Article XI Interim Agreement.

a phased withdrawal of Israeli military and civil administration and transfer to the Palestinian Council, although always subject to the issues to be negotiated at permanent status negotiations.[189] It bears repeating that this means that in the interim period Palestinian Council jurisdiction in all areas is not to cover Israelis.

CONCLUSIONS

If reduced to generalizations, there is a very loose pattern across the four 'deals' found in the peace agreements. It can be put somewhat cynically. A central compromise is achieved on the 'peoples–territory', self-determination issue, through permutations of federalism, autonomy, power-sharing in central government, and inter-governmental relations with kin groups in neighbouring states. The word 'self-determination' is rarely used in the agreements to describe these arrangements. The arrangements are, however, often coupled with explicit language on self-determination which is vague in order to have different meanings to different parties. The vagueness or 'constructive ambiguity' of the self-determination language contrasts with enumerated detail of the maps, mathematics, and measurements which delineate how power will actually be held and exercised. Here broad rhetoric is replaced by numbers: how many police, of which ethnic background, policing precisely where? How many votes of which ethnic block for which issue? Head-counting is vital, with referendums, mutual vetoes, weighted voting mechanisms, and membership of institutions all having numbers precisely agreed to. These numbers may be explicit ethnic headcounts or not, but in either case they reflect an ethnic balance.[190] The next chapter further explores this pattern and the extent to which it is consistent with, falls short of, or moves beyond international law provision regarding self-determination and minority rights.

However, it is worth noting that the detailed description of the deals begins to reveal a twofold role for human rights institutions, which will be explored more thoroughly in Chapters 7, 8, and 9. The institutionalized human rights protections found in the deals result not from an abstract commitment to ensuring domestic protection for human rights, but as part of a complex self-determination bargain. Human rights are responsive to the claims of one or more parties that mechanisms are

---

[189] Article XI(3) Interim Agreement.
[190] In South Africa it could be argued that the institutional balance is more about a balance between pre-democracy membership and post-democracy membership, although this is obviously overlaid with ethnicity.

needed to ensure that the human rights violations of the past are not repeated.

Claims of past human rights abuses are often asserted by one side more than the other, and indicate a particular meta-conflict stance. However, the insertion of human rights mechanisms into a peace agreement requires their acceptance by parties holding opposing positions on what their functions and role should be, and therefore a meta-bargain as to the nature of the conflict by those involved. This acceptance usually comes about as a quid pro quo of the agreement on sovereignty and territorial division. In Northern Ireland, for unionists, human rights and equality for nationalists were the price of retaining a Northern Ireland state within its present boundaries. For nationalists, human rights institutions could contribute to changing the nature and meaning of the state in a practical way. In Bosnia Herzegovina overarching human rights protections and minority rights were the price for nationalist entity mini-states. For the international community, they provided legitimacy to a deal which, in territorial terms, underwrote the gains of the human rights violations of ethnic cleansing; they also provided a mechanism for ongoing international involvement in reconstruction. In South Africa human rights institutions were a crucial part of legitimizing the new regime, and creating a new order of democracy and the rule of law. Given that whites were destined to be a minority, they had an interest in seeing that human rights were protected, as an anti-majoritarian device. In Israel/Palestine the point is illustrated through an absence. Here the focus of the deal on territorial division meant that human rights were largely irrelevant to the deal's content.

The deals described above begin to suggest an ambitious dual role for human rights institutions. First and most obviously, human rights protections are designed to ensure that rights are protected. Through this, at a deeper level, they aim to legitimize the new regime established by the peace agreement, by providing institutions which will respond to rights abuses in a way that the previous regime did not. Thus human rights institutions have a legitimizing role: they constitute a flagship of democratic credentials.

Secondly, the human rights institutions emerge not from a (fictional) social contract between individual and state, but as part of an (actual) ethnically based group bargain. They are designed and agreed to, with the idea that such institutions can provide a common framework of justice through which ongoing ethnic divisions can be mediated. Often the general wording of rights means that different sides to a conflict can sign up relatively easily to the same list, while having very different notions of what the consequences of application and enforcement would be. Despite the fact that the very concept of what constituted a human rights abuse was contested during the conflict, the institutional protections emerge bearing an integrative burden. The language of human rights is put forward as a possible common language through which ongoing ethnic disagreement can be mediated. Chapters 7, 8, and 9 will provide further illustration, by examining specific peace agreement provisions, to explore how these ambivalent ambitions are translated into institutional responses.

6

But What was the Question?
Evaluating the Deal

In the last chapter the self-determination deal found in each peace agreement was described. This chapter evaluates each deal in the light of international law on self-determination and minority rights. One of the immediate problems with this comparison is that the international legal standards lack clarity. Moreover, evaluating peace agreements in the light of the law can seem somewhat circular, given that the normative standards of the law cannot be ascertained without reference to at least three of the conflicts being considered.

Detailed distillation of the normative basis of international self-determination law is beyond the scope of this book. This chapter begins by setting out the issues that make the law unclear and difficult to apply, and then looks at the new legal approaches which are emerging from dissatisfaction with its failures, particularly in relation to ethnic conflict.

This chapter moves on to evaluate the four deals in terms of international legal provision. This evaluation illustrates a complex interaction of law and conflict. It also builds up the picture of how the self-determination provision in the peace agreements impacts on their other human rights provisions. In particular, the chapter begins to demonstrate how the capacity of individual rights institutions to deliver is determined in practice, by the precise balance between those institutions and any group autonomy agreed to. The dynamics of this are then further explored in Chapter 7's more detailed account of human rights institutions.

INTERNATIONAL LAW ON SELF-DETERMINATION

As we began to see in Chapters 3 and 4, international law on self-determination provides a series of conundrums about the precise relationship between peoples, nations, minorities, territory, human rights, and statehood.[1] A terse statement of the law confirms that '[a]ll peoples have the

---

[1] Comprehensive accounts of the law on self-determination are provided in Cassese (1998*b*); Cristescu (1981); Epseill (1980); Musgrave (1997); Pomerance (1982). Comprehensive accounts focusing on minority rights are provided in Caportorti (1991); Hannum (1990); Thornberry (1991).

right of self-determination . . . to freely determine their political status and freely pursue their economic, social and cultural development.'[2]

However, any attempt to apply the law immediately raises a series of difficult questions to which the law has few definitive answers: who constitutes a 'peoples'? Are they to be defined with reference to shared characteristics such as national identity, or territorially? What remedies to the right to self-determination are permissible: independent statehood; secession; participation in government? A short examination of legal norms illustrates the problems.

Who are the Peoples?

All the international documents which set standards in the area of self-determination refer to it as a right of 'peoples'.[3] That said, nowhere in international law is a peoples defined. After 1960 the classically accepted application of self-determination as a *legal* principle was the straight-forward decolonization situation, where the peoples seeking independence were typically the whole people of a territory (with the principle of *uti possedetis* limiting independence to colonial boundaries).

Technically, however, the concept of peoplehood is not necessarily limited to a predetermined territory: none of the international instruments limit self-determination in this way, with some seeming to contemplate decolonization as only one of a number of examples.[4] State practice also reflects a broader application, as the case-studies themselves illustrate. In Southern Africa self-determination was established as a requirement that racial groups be given access to government. In Israel/Palestine

[2] Common Article 1 UN International Covenant on Civil and Political Rights 1966 (ICCPR) and UN International Covenant on Economic, Social, and Cultural Rights 1966 (ICESCR).

[3] The United Nations Charter refers to self-determination of peoples in Article 1(2), stating that one of the purposes of the United Nations is to 'develop friendly relations among nations based on respect for the principle of equal rights and self-determination of peoples.' Articles 1 of the ICCPR and the ICESCR as noted above refer to it as a right of 'peoples'. The two foundational UN General Assembly resolutions dealing with self-determination provide further articulation of the right to self-determination as belonging to 'peoples'. See Declaration on the Granting of Independence to Colonial Countries and People, GA Res 1514 of 14 Dec. 1960 (hereafter Colonial Declaration 1514), para. 2; Declaration on Principles of International Law concerning Friendly Relations and Co-operation among States in accordance with the Charter of the United Nations, GA Res 2625, adopted without vote on 24 Oct. 1970 (hereafter Declaration 2625). See also Article 2(4) and Article 55 United Nations Charter; Article 1(3) of both ICCPR and ESCR; Article 2 para. 1 The Vienna Declaration and Programme of Action; pub. by the United Nations Department of Public Information, doc. DPI/1394–39399, Aug. 1993 (hereafter Vienna Declaration).

[4] McCorquodale (1994a: 859–66). See also Thornberry (1993: 124–31); Brilmayer (1991) (who in essence argues that the link between self-determination and territoriality is not close enough, in part because 'peoples' are defined as holders of the right and this does not require a connection with territoriality).

it was established as a ban on foreign occupation.[5] In former Yugoslavia the right of self-determination appeared to attach to the peoples of its constituent republics rather than the federation as a whole (or minority groups within the republics).

The argument that the concept of 'peoplehood' is not limited to the entire people of a predetermined territory is further indirectly supported by instruments relating to indigenous peoples. These have blurred the distinction between peoples and minorities by their use of the term 'peoples' for indigenous groups who are almost always minorities within states.[6]

Despite the above evidence for a wider concept of peoplehood, international instruments seem to draw a distinction between peoples who are entitled to self-determination, and ethnic minorities, who are not.[7] As Epseill, a special rapporteur of the Sub-Commission on Prevention of Discrimination and Protection of Minorities, argued in his report to the United Nations, '[i]t is peoples as such which are entitled to the right to self-determination. Under contemporary international law minorities do not have this right.'[8]

What is the Remedy?

Inextricably intertwined with the 'peoples' debate is the 'territory' debate. If a peoples are entitled to self-determination, in which territory are they permitted to exercise that right? Classically ethno-national claims involve disputes around territory, borders, and the proper unit for defining and determining the will of the 'people'. This can also be framed as a question of remedies. To what does a right to self-determination entitle the holder: independent statehood, representative government, secession, autonomy, or other remedies?

While self-determination in the decolonization period was often associated with independent statehood as an outcome, this is only one of a number of possibilities contemplated in international instruments. The Friendly Relations Declaration 2625 identifies several possible means of

---

[5] Cassese (1998b: 319).

[6] For example, Article 1(1)–(2) International Labour Organization, Convention Connecting Indigenous and Tribal Peoples in Independent Countries, 1989 (No. 169) (although Article 1(3) denies that this has any implications for rights, in an oblique reference to self-determination). The 1994–5 Draft United Nations Declaration on the Rights of Indigenous Peoples (E/CN.4/Sub.2/Res/1994/45) also refers to the holders of rights as 'peoples'. As Tomuschat points out, 'at least verbally, it brings indigenous populations close to peoples that are undeniably holders of the right of self-determination' (1993: 13).

[7] For example, while Article 1 ICCPR (and ICESCR) establishes a right to self-determination for 'peoples', Article 27 ICCPR gives members of minority groups only 'the right, in community with the other members of their group, to enjoy their own culture, to profess and practise their own religion, or to use their own language.'

[8] Epseill (1980: 9, para. 56).

exercising the right of self-determination: emergence as a sovereign independent state, free association with an independent state, integration with an independent state, and 'any other political status freely determined.'[9] The key is that the choice should be free and voluntary and 'expressed through informed and democratic processes.'[10] International practice has also established that varieties of territorial change by consent can occur. Examples include the dissolution of the Union of Soviet Socialist Republics in 1991, the 'velvet divorce' of Czechoslovakia into its two constituent republics, and the reunification of Germany.

However, both Declarations 1514 and 2625 establish self-determination explicitly with the caveat that its exercise should not disrupt territorial integrity. As Declaration 2625 puts it:

Nothing in the foregoing paragraphs [dealing with self-determination] shall be construed as authorising or encouraging any action which would dismember or impair, totally or in part, the territorial integrity or political unity of sovereign and independent States . . .[11]

This would seem to rule out secession by a minority group within established borders, without consent of the entire people within those borders. The combination of the commitment to the political choice of peoples with a prohibition on the disruption of territorial integrity has been described as the 'central paradox' of the self-determination norm: it claims to grant both peoples and states seemingly incompatible rights. The cases of Northern Ireland and Bosnia Herzegovina, in different ways, illustrate the potential for conflict.

External and Internal Self-determination

This indeterminacy of the self-determination norm evidences its historical contingency and different underlying conceptions of its role. Put briefly, at play are two quite different notions of what self-determination is designed to achieve: often contrasted as external self-determination and internal self-determination. The predominant notion of external self-determination defines 'the status of a people in relation to another people'.[12] External self-determination underwrites change in the status of states, for example, from colonial to independent, or from one state to two or more. The emergence of self-determination as a legal norm was closely

---

[9] Cf. also UN GA Res 1541 (XV), 15 Dec. 1960 Annex (principles which should guide members in determining whether or not an obligation exists to transmit the information called for in Article 73e of the Charter of the United Nations).

[10] Principle IX, UN GA Res 1541 (XV), 15 Dec. 1960.

[11] Colonial Declaration 1514 states that '[a]ny attempt aimed at the partial or total disruption of the national unity and the territorial integrity of a country is incompatible with the purposes and principles of the Charter of the United Nations.'

[12] Thornberry (1993: 101).

associated with the decolonization period, when it underwrote transition from colonialism to independence. External self-determination remains as a tool for managing change in status as evidenced more recently through its use in dismantling the USSR and reshaping Eastern Europe. However, while well established in the decolonization context, the exact perimeter of external self-determination in other contexts remains unclear, as the example of former Yugoslavia illustrates.

Internal self-determination focuses on the 'relationship between a people and "its own" state or government.'[13] It lifts the veil of the state to question its legitimacy, and whether it represents all of its people. As Thornberry writes, in contrast to the once-off exercise of external self-determination, internal self-determination aims to 'translate the achievement of freedom by a people into a continuing process of authentic self-rule, to anchor their liberation in the culture of democracy.'[14] While once a lesser-known (and less well-established) form of self-determination, its roots can be found in most of the legal articulations of self-determination.[15] The UN Charter itself can be understood to acknowledge choice of government in its articulation of the self-determination principle; in Article 55 it links 'equal rights' and self-determination to promotion of human rights, and social and economic development.[16] Internal self-determination also finds a basis in international human rights conventions. Common Article 1 of the UN International Covenants on Civil and Political Rights (ICCPR) and on Economic, Social, and Cultural Rights provides for peoples to 'freely determine' the political, social, and cultural policies of the state. Taken together with their other provisions, in particular the individual rights to freedom of association, assembly, and speech, they arguably provide for a measure of internal self-determination. Article 1(1) together with the other rights require 'that people choose their legislators and political leaders free from any manipulation or undue influence from the *domestic* authorities themselves.'[17] Article 27, while implicitly making a distinction between 'minorities' and peoples, provides rights relating to the internal organization of the state for certain minorities.

Both the Friendly Relations Declaration 2625 and the 1993 Vienna Declaration and Programme of Action provide some support for the concept of internal self-determination, by linking the principle of territorial integrity to the conducting of representative government. Declaration 2625 states that territorial integrity attaches to

[13] Ibid.   [14] Thornberry (1993: 102).
[15] For a comprehensive review of these roots, see Thornberry (1993). Cf. also Crawford (1993).
[16] See Articles 1(2) and 55 UN Charter 1945. See also Thornberry (1993: 107–9).
[17] Cassese (1998b: 53) (emphasis in original).

sovereign and independent States conducting themselves in compliance with the principle of equal rights and self-determination of peoples as described above and thus possessed of a government representing the whole people belonging to the territory without distinction as to race, creed or colour.[18]

This seems to suggest that where such government does not exist, then disruption of territorial integrity, for example through secession, may be permitted. However, as Thornberry writes, 'international law is not a suicide club for states' and unsurprisingly they have not applied it so as to dismantle themselves.[19] The provision remains ambiguous and can plausibly also be taken to support a measure of internal self-determination—a right to more representative government.[20]

Where customary law is concerned, there has been resistance to accepting a similar broad right to internal self-determination, beyond the right of some racial groups to an (undefined) amount of access to government, which is evidenced by state practice with regard to South Africa (and Southern Rhodesia).[21]

However, this is a situation which is rapidly changing. The attempt in the situation of former Yugoslavia to condition statehood to referendums and the demonstrable protection of minority rights in essence was an attempt to connect external self-determination to internal self-determination. Interesting also is the increasing use of internal self-determination by human rights monitoring bodies. For example, the Human Rights Committee's most recent concluding observations with relation to Canada clearly envisage the treatment of aboriginal peoples to fall within the self-determination provisions of Article 1 of the ICCPR. The Committee took note of the concept of self-determination as applied by Canada to the aboriginal peoples and regretted that 'no explanation was given by the delegation concerning the elements that make up that concept'.[22] It urged Canada to 'report adequately on implementation of article 1 of the Covenant in its next periodic report.'[23] The concept of internal self-determination provides a way to harmonize the group right basis of self-determination with individual human rights protections.[24]

---

[18] This is effectively restated in Article 2(3) Vienna Declaration.

[19] Thornberry (1993: 118).

[20] See Cassese (1998*b*: 122–4). See also McCorquodale (1994*a*).

[21] Cassese (1998*b*: 101–40).

[22] Concluding observations of the Human Rights Committee: Canada 7/4/99. CCPR/C/79/Add. 105, para. 7.   [23] Ibid.

[24] Cf. Committee on the Elimination of Racial Discrimination, *Right to Self-Determination*, 15 Mar. 1996. CERD General Recommendation XXI (forty-eighth session, 1996) (noting importance of internal self-determination recommending implementation of the rights in the International Convention on the Elimination of All Forms of Racial Discrimination, as one way to promote it).

Evolutionary Trends: Expanding Internal Self-Determination

An expanding notion of internal self-determination is increasingly coming to the fore as a possible way of transcending the self-determination paradox, according to which the norm 'both supports and challenges statehood.'[25] If self-determination is thought as a principle which requires that groups, as well as individuals, should be able to choose their own forms of government, then creative ways of facilitating that choice can be imagined which do not disrupt territorial integrity. Internal self-determination can be contemplated not merely as a right to vote, but as a right to *effective participation* in government. For minority groups permanently locked out of power in a majoritarian democratic system, this requires proactive measures to ensure representation in governmental structures and political institutions.

In divided societies it is suggested that this notion of expanded internal self-determination supports the development of policies of group accommodation such as autonomy regimes, consociationalism, or other minority protections less than secession.[26] Although it is too early to talk of a legal 'right' to this broad concept of internal self-determination, the notion does find support in proliferating international instruments on minority rights and, as noted above, is increasingly referred to by international bodies.

Minority rights protection is most fully articulated and extended in the recent UN Declaration on the Rights of Persons Belonging to National or Ethnic, Religious and Linguistic Minorities (1992), and by the Council of Europe's Framework Convention on the Protection of National Minorities (1994) and Conference on Security and Cooperation in Europe (now OSCE) documents that preceded it.[27] These documents clearly contemplate policies of recognition and accommodation as opposed to assimilation, as illustrated by continual reference to 'the right to participate effectively.'[28] States have obligations not just to prevent discrimination, but 'to create favourable conditions to enable persons belonging to minorities to express their characteristics and to develop their culture, language, religion, traditions and customs.'[29] Interestingly, as well as preserving inter-group contacts within the territory, the convention and the declaration refer to the

---

[25] Koskenniemi (1994: 249).   [26] Cf. McCorquodale (1994*a*).

[27] e.g. Report of the CSCE Committee of Experts on National Minorities, adopted on 19 July 1991.

[28] Article 1(1) Declaration on the Rights of Persons Belonging to National or Ethnic, Religious, and Linguistic Minorities (as approved by the Commission on Human Rights at the forty-eighth session (resolution 1992/16 of 21 Feb. 1992) (hereafter 'UN Declaration'). Article 5(2) Framework Convention for the Protection of National Minorities, 1 Feb. 1995 (ETS No. 148) (hereafter 'Framework Convention').

[29] UN Declaration Article 4(2); see also, Framework Convention *passim*.

right of ethnic groups to maintain cross-border contacts with ethnic counterparts in other jurisdictions. Article 2(5) of the UN Declaration provides
a right of minorities to maintain 'contacts across frontiers with citizens of
other States to whom they are related by national or ethnic, religious or linguistic ties.' In Article 17(1) of the Framework Convention states undertake

> not to interfere with the right of persons belonging to national minorities to establish
> and maintain free and peaceful contacts across frontiers with persons lawfully
> staying in other States, in particular those with whom they share an ethnic, cultural,
> linguistic or religious identity, or a common cultural heritage.

More proactively Article 18 states that 'Parties shall endeavour to conclude,
where necessary, bilateral and multilateral agreements with other States, in
particular neighbouring States, in order to ensure the protection of persons
belonging to the national minorities concerned.'

There are indications that these frameworks may become more specific
over time. In September 1999 the Lund Recommendations on the Effective
Participation of National Minorities in Public Life were published. These
recommendations were produced by a group of experts to assist the OSCE
in policy development, and are much more specific as to the types of
mechanism that can ensure 'effective participation' by providing access to
decision-making and self-government.[30] As regards access to decision-
making the Lund recommendations suggest

- informal and formal types of power-sharing at governmental level
- minority-oriented electoral systems, including proportional representation, preference voting, low numerical thresholds for representation, and sensitive electoral boundary-drawing
- state encouragement of minority participation at regional level
- the establishment of advisory or consultative bodies 'to serve as
  channels for dialogue between governmental authorities and national
  minorities.'

As regards self-governance, the recommendations note that territorial and
non-territorial self-governance may be called for. Self-governance is to be
'based on democratic principles to ensure that they genuinely reflect the
views of the affected population.' Non-territorial measures include the right
of minorities to have a measure of control over language, religion, education,
and cultural expression. Territorial arrangements are recommended to be
considered where they 'would improve the opportunities of minorities to
exercise authority over matters affecting them.' Finally the recommendations suggest that effective participation is established through a constitutional and legal framework, and interestingly that this framework be

---

[30] Available at www.osce.org/henm/documents/lund.htm (last visited 11 Aug. 2000).

implemented in a step-by-step, or trial-and-error way, and should be subject to periodic review.

These instruments and recommendations all suggest the development of creative institutional arrangements aimed at accommodating minorities, and also transnational arrangements which may provide a way for minorities to transcend the confines of an 'alien' sovereignty, while formally remaining within the state.

Examples of Evolving Legal Blueprints

Expansive notions of internal self-determination can be used to develop blueprints for dealing with ethnic conflict. Cassese, for example, has developed a blueprint which involves seeing self-determination as 'a principle mandating the recognition of group rights and regional autonomy . . . [and] a basis for the development of *alternative constitutional frameworks*, affording those with a right to self-determination a meaningful measure of autonomy.'[31] He argues that internal self-determination for the population as a whole within the territory should be established. Then positive action, participatory rights, and a wide measure of autonomy should be granted to minorities. Both elements should fulfil and be consistent with the mostly individual rights protections of international human rights conventions.[32]

Eide (also one of the Lund experts) describes a similar framework as incorporating two domains: a common domain, in which all citizens participate under conditions of equality and non-discrimination as specified in international standards.[33] And secondly, a separate 'pluralist' domain which aims to provide minorities with access to government and public life. This second domain can be achieved in two quite different ways. First, through a range of devices which boost minority access to decision-making ('pluralism in togetherness'), such as consociational democracy or special institutions providing for protection of minority culture, religion, language, and education. Alternatively, pluralism can be achieved by 'territorial subdivision' such as local self-government, federalism, autonomy, and regional and municipal local government, all with protections for minorities within the minority-controlled area. Again, however, individual rights play a crucial role in policing equality among ethnic groups in the common domain which they simultaneously help to carve out.[34]

---

[31] Cassese (1998b: 350) (emphasis in original).

[32] Cassese acknowledges the possibility of permitting secession or dissolution in extreme circumstances.   [33] See e.g. Eide (1993, 1995, 1996).

[34] See also Hannum (1990) (arguing for a right to autonomy); and Thornberry (1993, 1991) (arguing for 'participation rights' and suggesting federalism as a possible option).

The internal self-determination approach sketched out by Cassese, Eide, and the Lund experts (and others) is similar to the types of options posited by political scientists and set out in Chapter 5 above. However, these types of blueprint raise a series of normative questions.

First, there is the question of the extent to which the emphasis on groups is *in practice* compatible with individual rights protection found at the heart of international human rights law.[35] Secondly, while a new evolutionary direction for the law is tempting, where does it leave past clear normative statements on the application of self-determination in specific cases (such as Israel/Palestine)? Finally, there is a lurking normative question as to whether it is useful to move towards a *right* to internal self-determination as requiring specific institutional arrangements and measures directed at groups, or whether such measures are better left as a possible 'menu' of solutions for those interested in pursuing them.[36] These are questions which form the background to the following evaluation of the case-studies.

INTERNATIONAL LAW AND THE DEALS

The self-determination analysis laid out above provides a basis for evaluating the deals described in Chapter 5. Several related questions can be asked of the negotiated agreements, to facilitate comparison between these deals and international law. Namely:

- To what extent did the four sets of agreements produce an arrangement which complied with the international law provisions which claimed to govern the conflicts?
- To what extent did the agreements find solutions to fill in the gaps where international law ended?
- Did these solutions play out the emerging trends in how international law should deal with ethnic conflict?

South Africa

As noted in Chapter 3, the parameters set by international law for resolution of the self-determination dispute in South Africa were relatively clear. While silent on what precisely would satisfy the claim, it was

---

[35] See e.g. Wippman (1998*b*).

[36] See P. Jones (1999) (on conceptual difficulties with rights asserted by 'groups'). Note also the difference between Hannum (1990) (arguing for a group 'right to autonomy' in certain cases) with Thornberry (1991) (in effect suggesting robust application of essentially individual rights together with some more group-oriented procedures).

clear that self-determination had to include access by all racial groups to government, and that white-weighted parliaments and bantustans would not constitute such access. McCorquodale, writing prior to settlement, noted the type of solution compatible with international law as possibly including limitations to protect individual human rights; provision for ongoing free and fair elections; possible federal structures; limited minority rights provisions (with a question mark as to whether whites were a minority); and an entrenched constitutional self-determination clause.[37] The Interim Constitution embraced aspects of all these elements, and thus filled in the gaps where the law of self-determination ended.[38]

When compared with Sisk's table of 'options',[39] the constitutional model provided by the South African deal can be seen as primarily integrative, incorporating a unitary state with a primarily non-communal federal element, a proportional electoral system, and robust protection of individual rights. Consociational devices play a role in transition, and there are tinges of corporate federalism in the limited provision for cultural rights and the role of traditional leaders.

Given the present evolutionary direction of self-determination law, it is interesting to ask why a more permanent consociational arrangement was not forthcoming for minorities, and in particular the white minority. Although consociational arrangements were included, these were strictly time-limited. Wippman states that in deeply divided societies 'consociationalism is not only compatible with self-determination but may be the only way to give effect to self-determination that is consistent with the rights of minorities to effective political participation'.[40]

However, in the case of South Africa, it would seem that the international community did not back a consociational solution and indeed was wary of such solutions as possibly perpetuating apartheid in another form. While the reason for this probably lies chiefly in the respective bargaining power of the negotiators, there is an interesting convergence with international legal standards. From a legal point of view there is a question as to whether white people constitute a minority group. Although nowhere is there a precise legal definition of what constitutes a minority group, attributes of common origins, culture, religion, and language are usually taken as indicators. According to these criteria, white people do not comprise a unitary ethnic group.[41] International law provision may not have directly prevented a group-oriented consociationalism, but it did not encourage it, suspicious as it was of past race-based 'solutions' and attempts to use minority rights to perpetuate privilege. Guelke documents in detail how

---

[37] McCorquodale (1994*b*: 14–20).   [38] Cf. Strydom (1993–4).
[39] See Ch. 5, pp. 120–1.   [40] Wippman (1998*b*: 230).
[41] McCorquodale (1994*b*: 25–6 n. 123), citing Mohamed (1991: 66).

the international community shaped the deal: 'in helping to establish the terms under which the negotiations took place, the international community indirectly influenced their outcome.'[42] In particular, he argues that the international community's rejection of consociationalism helped to shape settlement in the mould favoured by the ANC.

One of the consequences of the integrative approach was that it created common ground around the need for strong human rights institutions. For minority groups, the integrative design meant that human rights protections formed the main safeguard against future majority excesses. For the ANC majority, strong human rights protections were an essential part of legitimizing the new regime, providing a break with the abusive practices of the past, and setting up an exemplary multiracial democracy. These human rights protections were clearly consistent with, and even necessary to fulfilling, international human rights law standards. Of course, agreement in principle did not prevent deep disagreement over particular rights, most notably social, economic, and property rights, as will be touched on in subsequent chapters. These disagreements themselves indicate that a key issue for ANC–SAG negotiations was the extent to which any transfer of political power would be accompanied by a transfer of economic power. While the issue of economic power is rarely discussed as part of a self-determination debate, in a world of global economies it is clearly central to the meaningful realization of self-determination in many other situations.

Northern Ireland

The situation in Northern Ireland throws up the classic minority–territorial integrity conundrum of international self-determination law. While a black-letter international law position would define (Catholic) nationalists within Northern Ireland as a minority group within a unit commanding territorial integrity, the international community also showed concern over the legitimacy of Northern Ireland given continuing denial of rights and equality to (Catholic) nationalists. The Belfast Agreement attempts to find a way out of self-determination conundrums, drawing on current trends towards an expanded notion of internal self-determination.[43] It is of great significance for international lawyers as it both complied with the legal requirements of international law and creatively transcended their paradoxes. Moreover, international law was self-consciously used in this process.

Self-determination is dealt with in the Belfast Agreement ostensibly by using the imprecise language of international law. This is then coupled

---

[42] Guelke (1999: 151; and see generally 135–58).
[43] See further Bell and Cavanaugh (1999).

with institutional mechanisms which move away from absolute notions of statehood, sovereignty, and territorial integrity through devices of consociational government, cultural provision, human rights protections, and cross-border connections. First, effective participation of all groups in decision-making is guaranteed by a consociational arrangement (with proportionality, power-sharing, and mutual vetoes). Secondly, human rights are guaranteed to all groups equally, regardless of where borders are or how they might change in the future, taking the sting out of whichever constitutional arrangement might prevail. Thirdly, the agreement establishes 'regional' mechanisms which reassure competing nationalisms, and potentially offer new ways of thinking about sovereignty and, indeed, new ways of 'getting government done'.

These structures, with their many symbolic and practical possibilities, tap into the 'new trends currently emerging in the world community' of greater political and economic integration at the 'supranational' level coupled with growing emphasis on the ethnic and cultural distinctiveness of groups, at the internal level.[44] Together the combination of supra-state structures and local consociational structures mark a move away from traditional notions of democracy and sovereignty. The Belfast Agreement illustrates how this move can enable self-determination solutions which begin to transcend the sovereignty–territorial integrity versus minority rights divide. Northern Ireland retains its territorial integrity in what unionists claim is an 'internal' solution, but British sovereignty and the nature of the state is also changed through the cross-border bodies and regional dimension.

The compatibility of the agreement with international law developments was not a coincidental convergence of political pragmatism with international law standards.[45] This was not just as a result of the intangible guidance of the parameters set by international law during the conflict. It is clear from analysis of contributing paragraphs, phrases, and ideas to the agreement that international law formed an important backdrop to negotiations. At key moments parties felt they had to address international law, and on other occasions it gave parties new ways of relating to the conflict.

For Irish republicans agreement could only have been reached when their self-determination claims were addressed. The history of the self-determination paragraph is beyond the scope of this book, save to say that the formulation as first accepted by the British government in the

---

[44] Cassese (1998b: 362).

[45] See Eide (1996), published during the peace process, on the request of the Irish government's Forum for Peace and Reconciliation, suggesting how a solution might be fashioned using international law standards. This publication itself is evidence of the use of international law in the process.

Downing Street Declaration was vital to reaching the first IRA ceasefire.[46] As pointed out in Chapter 5, John Hume also saw the value of making non-violent method itself a self-determination issue. This answered the Provisional IRA's national liberation agenda, which drew support from international standards and conflicts elsewhere.

Similarly, however, in debating whether to enter talks, unionists reframed their claim in self-determination terms. Rather than frame their claim purely in terms of democratic majoritarianism (and count on the majority being a Protestant one), unionists began to adopt the term 'consent', claiming that they should not be forced into a form of government or a different state against their freely determined choice. This in essence reframed their claim as that of a distinctive group to a form of self-determination. They simultaneously used international in- struments to argue for an internal solution. In particular Ulster Unionists made reference to C/OSCE standards, taking comfort from their refer- ences to 'the integrity of borders.'[47] But this was not without consequence. Along with territorial integrity these standards also promoted human rights protections and robust minority rights. Arguably, international law played some part in moving key Ulster Unionist elites to a position where they accepted that affirmation of Northern Ireland's legitimacy as a political entity could be secured by conceding increased human rights protection and even group rights to nationalists. International legal stan- dards also gave progressive unionists a tool for engaging in internal nego- tiation with more traditional party members, who saw unionism's claims as claims to a unionist nation-state, rather than to pluralism. Under this traditional view Northern Ireland is comprised of loyal British citizens, and those who dissent from this position constitute the disloyal 'other', whose disloyalty cannot be accommodated, and who do not therefore reg- ister as a relevant part of the polity.[48] International human rights stan- dards reveal this position as illegitimate, and movement from it could therefore be argued by liberal unionists to be internationally necessary rather than (merely) a concession to nationalists or Irish republicans.

The Framework Convention was of course a child of CSCE documents and therefore also relevant. It was only in January 1997 that the British government exhibited a serious intent to bring the talks to an end-game by publishing the heads of agreement documents. Interestingly, this was also the month in which they ratified the Framework Convention, despite the fact that British governments had traditionally denied the need for

[46] The Downing Street Declaration, 15 Dec. 1993, para. 4. For a fuller account of the influences on the IRA ceasefire, see Mallie and McKittrick (1996).

[47] Ulster Unionist Party (1994: 6–7).

[48] This view still characterizes, for example, current Democratic Unionist Party rhetoric of 'ordinary citizens' as including only those with a pro-union allegiance.

minority rights, on the grounds that protection for individual rights was sufficient.[49] Indeed, one Ulster Unionist Party politician has claimed in private that ratification took place on their insistence. To the extent that unionists used the convention, it was to claim that it underwrote the territorial integrity of Northern Ireland. But of course the convention also refers to cross-border linkages and rights to effective participation in all aspects of public life. Unionists insisted that cross-border linkages were purely cultural and did not imply any 'right' to executive power for a neighbouring state with a kin group, such as was being contemplated in the North–South cross-border bodies. Yet it does seem that when a crucial republican–unionist logjam over the role and scope of cross-border bodies was reached, discussion of Framework Convention requirements came into play. However, when the Belfast Agreement approach to internal self-determination is viewed as a package, it can also be argued that it develops, rather than jettisons, the traditional UK approach to self-determination.[50]

International law also, of course, affected the other human rights aspects of the agreement, such as the Bill of Rights, policing and criminal justice provision, equality, and the mechanisms for enforcement.[51] While this will be dealt with more fully in the next chapter, it is worth pointing out one interesting dynamic. The articulation of rights protection as flowing from international law commitments rather than just the history of the conflict opened up arguments for Irish government reciprocity which were difficult to resist. The agreement ultimately included an overarching commitment to 'ensure at least an equivalent level of protection of human rights as will pertain in Northern Ireland' and to consider incorporating the European Convention on Human Rights, the establishment of a Human Rights Commission in the Republic of Ireland, and provision for an all-Ireland Charter of Rights.[52] This came about as a result of a common interest of republicans and unionists, based paradoxically in their entirely different self-determination perspectives. While republicans saw mutuality in rights protection as part of the all-Ireland dimension, unionists saw it as saying, 'if you're going to shove this down our throats you're going to have it as well.'[53]

The Belfast Agreement demonstrates a reconciliation of political pragmatism and international law. International lawyers can, with some excitement, point to a deal that has harmonized minority rights with self-determination. This was achieved through creative mechanisms that build on notions of 'internal' self-determination for groups. Yet this

---

[49] Ratified 15 Jan. 1998. [50] See McCorquodale (1995).
[51] See Mageean and O'Brien (1999); McCrudden (1999*b*).
[52] Belfast Agreement, Rights, Safeguards, and Equality of Opportunity, Comparable Steps by the Irish Government.
[53] Stephen King of the Ulster Unionist Party, as quoted in Ann Marie Hourihane, 'King of the Hill', *Sunday Tribune*, 27 Dec. 1988.

internal self-determination has external elements which do not disrupt territorial integrity, but yet transcend traditional notions of sovereignty and statehood.

Bosnia Herzegovina

The deal found in the Dayton Peace Agreement (DPA) goes to some length to assert its compatibility with international law standards on self-determination. Thus, the territorial integrity of a unitary Bosnia Herzegovina (BiH) within its pre-war boundaries is affirmed.[54] It can be further argued that, as with the Belfast Agreement, the detail of the deal is fashioned around international law's evolutionary trends as identified above. Autonomy in the two Entities provides for a form of internal self-determination, while the common structures embrace a consociationalism designed to ensure *effective* participation of all three main ethnic groups to government. Furthermore, relationships with kin groups in neighbouring states are enabled by giving a power to the Entities to 'establish special parallel relationships with neighboring states consistent with the sovereignty and territorial integrity of BiH', even though BiH retains the power to conduct foreign policy.[55]

However, the Dayton Peace Agreement can be viewed more negatively. It can be argued that rather than endorsing the international community language around the importance of a sovereign BiH within pre-war territorial boundaries, the deal in fact involves a compromise between this position and the separatist demands of Croats and Serbs. While the self-determination language and common BiH structures evidence the presence of a unitary republic, the detail of the constitutions of both BiH and the Entities indicates a messy three-way division of territory, with the three constituent peoples largely self-governing from homogeneous ghettos: '[t]he Constitution makes the entities de facto mini-states within an imaginary central state.'[56] The tiny common sphere found in the BiH structures is only sustainable with a large international presence in all its institutions, and in particular through the powers of the Office of the High Representative (OHR), powers which have required to be increased since Dayton. Given that the OHR lacks a clear enforcement mechanism, implementation of decisions is often a matter of negotiation.[57] The fragile common BiH institutions, together with their international components, have the immense task of expanding the BiH state spheres of power and of reversing ethnic cleansing by enforcing the right to return.

---

[54] See Article I The General Framework Agreement for Peace in Bosnia and Herzegovina, 14 Dec. 1995 (hereafter 'Dayton Peace Agreement' or 'DPA'). Cf. Article I, Annex 4 DPA (Constitution proclaims a unitary BiH within its pre-war boundaries).

[55] Article III(2)(a), Annex 4 DPA.   [56] International Crisis Group (1999: 19).

[57] International Crisis Group Report (1999: 42–3).

Herein lies the problem at the heart of the Dayton deal. The very Croatian and Serbian parties charged with cooperating to reverse ethnic cleansing are those which practised it to achieve separatist demands. The territorial divisions are based around territory won by these groups through ethnic cleansing. The danger for the international community was that by selling territorial autonomy in exchange for a 'right to return' and a largely symbolic unitary state, the implementation of both could in fact be frustrated by the autonomous structures. Indeed, the fear contemplated by the detail of Dayton has been realized. Rather than working to solidify BiH, Bosnian Serbs and Croats persist in their goals of union with Serbia and Croatia respectively. As a recent report puts it, '[b]oth parties are attempting to now realize by peaceful means the goals they could not achieve through force of arms.'[58]

Two main factors assist these separatist claims. First, the structural problems inherent in Dayton itself; and secondly, its lack of enforcement mechanisms to implement the civilian aspects of the agreement. Both are a product of the international community's ambivalence as between enforcing its self-determination demands and negotiating a pragmatic end to the war. This ambivalence has been translated into the deal fashioned. While ongoing (re)negotiation is a feature of any implementation phase, the DPA contains the potential seeds of its own demise in its failure to resolve the central self-determination issue. In the DPA the international community in effect gives itself the job of winning through implementation what it did not clearly secure in the text of the agreement.

As regards the structures of the DPA, the centrality of ethnic head-counts vies against attempts to assert the primacy of constitutionalism and individual rights, and undermines their role in reversing ethnic cleansing. Complicating the matter is the DPA's attempt not only to accommodate incompatible self-determination claims, but also to effect a transition to a specific form of institutionalized democracy in a country without these democratic traditions. The results are that different aspects of the agreement tend to work against each other in a series of paradoxes, as the following discussion illustrates.

---

[58] International Crisis Group (1999: 51), referring to remarks of Zivko Radišić, 'moderate' Serb member of the tripartite BiH presidency, at an election celebration dinner in Doboj, 25 Oct. 1998 ('It is through Republika Srpska that we will open the door to our own statehood. But for the time being it is in our best interest to act within the institutions of BiH'). Cf. European Stability Initiative (1999: 2) (asserts that, '[f]ollowing the collapse of the former Yugoslavia, three nationalist parties in Bosnia . . . became the local successors to the communist party, taking over its tools of social and economic control . . . So long as these illegal power structures remain intact, the new institutions created under the Dayton Agreement will not acquire real authority.' Holbrooke (1998: 352) (documents the comments of Krajišnik (Serbian member of presidency) that he had been wrong to oppose Dayton, and notes that his interpretation of Dayton was as 'a way station on the path to partition').

Both the electoral system and consociational form of government at the BiH level encourage ethno-national stances by political parties. This provides support to the parties most resistant to the DPA, while simultaneously providing disincentives to working towards the democratic pluralistic unitary state that the agreement is supposedly designed to achieve. The DPA contemplated elections as crucial in establishing the legitimacy of the republic and provided for elections 'on a date . . . no later than nine months after entry into force [of the Agreement].'[59] However, in practice all post-war elections have returned nationalist leaders and parties to office, and in many cases mirrored the 1990 election results in which ethno-national parties dominated. The reasons for this are complicated, but include the group imperatives of the Constitution, the electoral system chosen (list PR), and failure to achieve fully free and fair voting conditions within the specified time-frame.[60] Where voting registration requirements did result in a minority candidate being elected, implementation of the election results proved difficult, with elected officials unable to take office or sidelined in real decision-making.[61]

The nationalistic voting patterns have been further solidified since. In 1997 an OSCE Provisional Electoral Commission (PEC) rule interpreted the DPA residency requirements to provide that anyone who could prove that he or she lived in his new municipality prior to 31 July 1996 could cast a ballot for elections in that new municipality. Given that many ethnically motivated movements occurred prior to this date, this in effect underwrote and reinforced ethnic cleansing. As the International Crisis Group note,

The message to [displaced persons] and refugees was clear: you could vote either for your pre-war municipality, where you were now in the ethnic minority, or you could vote in your new municipality in order to nullify the voting power of the majority groups ethnically-cleansed from your new region [who still retain the capacity to vote there].[62]

Scheffer has noted a post-1994 shift in UN policy, whereby it pursues enhancement of the effectiveness of periodic and genuine elections and promotion of democratization. He argues that this has become a key post-conflict policy, 'eclipsing the old rhetoric of self-determination as the bedrock principle of UN practice toward ethnic conflict.'[63] However, the case of Bosnia illustrates the dangers of assuming that the very act of voting has a democratizing effect on a non-democratic country. Here the elections, which the international community pushed for in such a hurry, in practice became a counter-productive 'ethnic headcount' which gave those with

---

[59] Article II(4), Annex 3 DPA.   [60] International Crisis Group (1996, 1999: 11–18).
[61] Ibid.   [62] International Crisis Group (1999: 13).
[63] Scheffer (1998: 153–6) (Scheffer notes as evidence of this shift US UN Press Release No. 233–(94), 23 Dec. 1994; UN GA Res 50/185 (1995); UN GA Res 50/133 (1995)).

reputations as ethnic cleansers a stamp of legitimacy, and undermined a broader, longer-term democratic project.

In practice the consociational form of government with its mutual veto system has not led to cooperation between ethnic groups, and again the structure of the agreement predestines this outcome. With the central government sphere weak, and at least two groups resisting its relevance, its consociational system means that decision-making can easily be blocked, and such central government as exists effectively shut down.[64]

The consociational form of government has similarly raised tensions between individual rights and group claims in the Constitution. The rigid ethnic criteria for governmental make-up is difficult to marry with the long list of primarily individual rights also incorporated in the Constitution. For example, the requirement of Bosniac, Croat, and Serb proportionality would seem to permanently exclude the 'others' (including other minority groups) acknowledged by the Constitution to exist.[65] The 'two Entities–three nations' formula leaves the connection between the two Entities, three nations, and the (almost forgotten) individual 'citizen' ambiguous. In doing so, it contravenes international anti-discrimination standards incorporated as part of the Constitution.

Paradoxically, international attempts to move beyond these ethnic group–individual conundrums stand to undermine the longer-term parallel democratization project of the DPA. The common institutions can only be made to work through increased international intervention. Since Dayton the OHR has been given more power to impose decisions, including sacking elected officials and imposing legislation (subject to eventual ratification). Since 1996 the House of Representatives has forced the High Representative to impose eight national-level laws on an interim basis, only four of which have been passed since by both House of Representatives and House of Peoples, in one case more than eighteen months later.[66] Indeed there is evidence that such parties prefer to wait for the intervention of the OHR, rather than appear to compromise on their own accord. A list of decisions of the OHR shows that in the years 1999 and 2000 the OHR has removed twenty elected politicians from office, such as ministers and mayors of cantons, and has even removed the Serbian

---

[64] Despite the unsatisfactory operation of majority and consociational mechanisms, few academics pay attention to the promising notion of multi-option voting mechanisms in the form of preferenda; neither do international notions of 'free and fair' elections promote this mechanism, despite its seeming advantages. See further Emerson (1998).

[65] The Preamble to the Constitution states that 'Bosniacs, Croats, and Serbs as constituent peoples (along with Others), and citizens of Bosnia and Herzegovina hereby determine that the Constitution of Bosnia and Herzegovina is as follows . . .'; Annex 4 DPA. Neither is the position of women specifically addressed; cf. Dolgopol (1997).

[66] International Crisis Group (1999) 23.

member of the BiH presidency.[67] The preservation of both deal and 'democracy' requires to be sustained through the trumping of elected officials, and legislature by unelected international actors. In the ultimate paradox, it appears that the price of democracy is democracy. A similar paradox hovers over the problems of internal inconsistencies of Constitutions. Rewriting of the Constitutions to eliminate these inconsistencies becomes difficult for an international community which is also concerned to foster the primacy of democratic constitutionalism.

Exacerbating these structural weaknesses are weaknesses in the enforcement mechanisms at the disposal of the international community. Robust enforcement of the human rights mechanisms designed to achieve a unitary pluralist democratic state has not taken place. As more fully addressed in the next chapter, the difficulties lie in the willingness of the multinational military implementation force (IFOR, now SFOR) to take on a clear enforcement role; the lack of any alternative executive enforcement mechanism for the OHR; and lack of clarity regarding who is to implement what.[68]

The DPA illustrates the danger of broad blueprints for ethnic conflict. Although the DPA seems to comply formally with international law and build on its evolutionary trends, the devil is hidden in the detail. That detail reveals deep tensions between individual and group rights and an ongoing failure to resolve a bitter self-determination dispute. These questions are coming increasingly to the fore with the question of when and how the international community can fashion an exit strategy.

Israel/Palestine

In Israel/Palestine the creation of an interim stage claims to postpone resolution of the self-determination issue. Ostensibly the agreements are neutral as to end outcome and therefore consistent with international law's normative application. Writing in 1998, Cassese argued that while the agreements left unclear how external self-determination would be implemented, international lawyers should be satisfied with emphasizing two things:

firstly, that at long last, the path suggested by international norms, that is, a peaceful process of negotiation between the parties concerned, has been taken; secondly, that as an initial measure, provision has been made for the exercise of *internal* self-determination by the Palestinians, as a stepping stone to external self-determination.[69]

[67] Decisions by the High Representative available at www.ohr.int/decisions.htm (last visited 7 Aug. 2000).

[68] See generally International Crisis Group (1999); Joulwan and Shoemaker (1998).

[69] Cassese (1998b: 249–50).

However, on the eve of permanent status agreement, lack of clarity regarding how, or if, external self-determination is to be exercised, raises questions as to whether its form has been preordained by the Declaration of Principles (DoP) (as amended by subsequent agreements and events). Furthermore, the increasingly repressive actions of the Palestinian Authority (PA) raises serious questions as to whether devolution of power is capable of producing internal self-determination.

As regards external self-determination, the most pressing question for Palestinians currently is whether the two-stage process contemplated by the DoP has, in practice, created a situation in which the temporary compromise of Palestinian islands of authority within an Israeli state is, in effect, to become permanent. Commentators had noted that this 'solution' was prefigured in the DoP and Interim Agreements, and in the Israeli settlement-building patterns which had preceded them.[70] They argued that given that the agreements explicitly avoided addressing ongoing settlement-building, the Israeli vision of the end outcome was not only left open by the agreements, but its creeping implementation was facilitated by them. Detractors from this analysis have faded as the difficulties with implementation of Israeli withdrawal specified in the DoP and Interim Agreements have continued. Rather than entering final status negotiations with approximately 80 per cent of West Bank land under Palestinian control, it has been a struggle to obtain control of 17.2 per cent of the land in A areas and 23.8 per cent in B areas. In the meantime, Israeli settlement-building and construction of roads to link Israeli-populated areas while bypassing Palestinian areas has further destroyed the possibility of a future independent Palestinian West Bank with territorial integrity.[71]

A plan leaked by Netanyahu in 1997 indicated that Likud foresaw handing over about 40 per cent of the West Bank, divided into four areas with no territorial contiguity, plans which Barak and Labour did not express objections to.[72] In 1999 it was reported that Barak was to propose a Palestinian state on 18 per cent of the West Bank.[73]

In the negotiations of Camp David II in July 2000 Israel seemed to contemplate a Palestinian state in over 90 per cent of the West Bank and perhaps all of Gaza. However, in return West Bank settlements containing 80 per cent of current settlers were to be annexed to Israel. With the detail and map-drawing remaining secret the exact shape and contiguity of any proposed Palestinian state is unclear. Furthermore, this comparative 'generosity' of Israel as compared to earlier positions may well have been dependent on Palestinian concessions on Jerusalem, although proposed

[70] Shehadeh (1997); Said (1995a, b).
[71] Aronson (1996); LAW (1998a); Shah (1997); Shehadeh (1997).   [72] Beinin (1999).
[73] *Ma'ariv*, 22 Oct. 1999.

options may now be difficult to row back from. While final status agreement seems likely to create a Palestinian state, it is this state's capacity for independence from Israeli policies and decision-making which will determine whether nominal statehood is in fact functional autonomy operating in a manner not dissimilar to interim agreement arrangements. Such independence will be crucially affected by the extent of Israel's ability to control entry to and exit from Palestinian territory and the extent to which such territory is contiguous.

As with BiH, it can be argued that autonomy arrangements of the interim agreements and indeed any attenuated statehood which might result from final status negotiations draw on the evolutionary direction of self-determination law. The interim agreements and Israeli proposals for final status solutions move towards a situation where the labels 'sovereignty' and 'state' may be given to arrangements which rework both concepts into a divisible package of differentiated powers and functions for different issues, areas, and people, rather than territorially based unitary concepts. The Israeli/Palestinian interim agreements (while refusing to deal explicitly with sovereignty or statehood) separate out territorial, functional, and geographic jurisdiction in devolving power, so as to simultaneously devolve power for urban centres to Palestinians, while retaining such Israeli control as is perceived necessary to Israel's security. More explicitly the Camp David II Israeli proposals on Jerusalem would seem to be based on ideas of international lawyers (among others) to take this division of powers further with regard to Jerusalem, and begin to think of functional, geographical, and personal sovereignty, as an alternative to unified territorial control.[74]

As discussed above, evolving self-determination proposals focus on precisely these types of innovative divisions of power, territory, and government, in an attempt to achieve a measure of group self-determination regardless of where state borders officially lie. Current self-determination trends usually conceive of minority self-governance taking place within the larger state structures (to preserve state integrity). However, it can be argued that if the parties agree to label an entity which has a high level of territorial and functional control of an area, as a 'state', then they should be allowed to do so. Even if the entity's functions, powers, and territorial control are not as absolute as those of many states, concepts of sovereignty have traditionally been diverse, and even the most 'traditional' states are losing accepted attributes of statehood as global economies and

---

[74] See N. Shragai, *Sovereignty and Power-Sharing: How is Jerusalem Likely to be Shaped by a Final Status Agreement?*, Ha'aretz Special for the on-line edition, 13 June 2000 (which attributes the development of such ideas for Jerusalem to the Jerusalem Centre for Israel Studies, and in particular international lawyer and expert on autonomy regimes Professor Ruth Lapidoth).

governance expand.[75] The distinction between state and non-state entity is therefore increasingly one of degree rather than principle.

However, as with BiH, there are problems with analysing these arrangements as moving in parallel with international self-determination law's evolutionary direction. The difficulty is twofold. First, any arrangement which seeks to make permanent either autonomy or attenuated statehood will not give continuity to international self-determination law by filling in its gaps, but will in effect trump the clear normative demands of international law as understood prior to the peace process. Secondly, the arrangements in the interim agreements effectively bypass the rationale for developing the new approaches to self-determination which underwrite mechanisms such as autonomy in the first place.

Rewriting International Law?

The gradual rewriting of international law's normative demands for Palestinian self-determination can be illustrated by examination of the questions that the interim agreements posed for international lawyers. The notion of differentiated jurisdiction in the interim agreements posed difficult questions for the application of international law and in particular Geneva IV. These were questions such as, Did the agreements end Israeli occupation or not, and if so, to what extent and in what areas? Or, put another way, Did Geneva IV cease to apply in any areas?

Common sense would seem to indicate that occupation cannot end as long as Palestinian powers and territories do not add up to statehood. Neither Palestinian Liberation Organization (PLO) nor PA are sovereign governments under the interim agreements, and Israel retains all residual powers. However, Benvenisti argues a contrary position. Given that Israel had derived its status in the Occupied Territories as an occupying power, with its powers as occupier flwing from its effective control of the area, [76] Benvenisti argues that, having relinquished control through the agreements, Israel has no right to reoccupy the areas relinquished, and that the DoP therefore constitutes an 'irreversible step' towards the settlement of the conflt.' [77] In contrast, Malanczuk doubts these conclusions for two reasons. First, because in the event of the agreements breaking down, Israel might well reoccupy released territories, and then, whether occupation was justified or not, the laws of war would apply, although this surely would also be the case were statehood conceded. Secondly, because Israel retains jurisdiction over Israelis and Israeli settlements; because it

---

[75] See e.g. Falk (1995: 79–103).

[76] Effective control being a necessary component of occupation; see Article 42 of the Regulations Respecting the Laws and Customs of War on Land, Annex to the Convention (IV) Respecting the Laws and Customs of War on Land, signed at the Hague, 18 Oct. 1907; cited in Benvenisti (1993: 5456 n. 25).   [77] Benvenisti (1993: 5456).

controls security and external relations; and because it has retained 'residual power', Malanczuk suggests that:

In effect, Israel is therefore still an occupant with regard to the fields which it has
not transferred to the Palestinians for self-government. A different conclusion
would lead to the absurd result of legalising the current status quo, including the
Israeli settlements, from the view-point of international law.[78]

Yet, it would seem that the very difficulties of applying international law
to interim agreement arrangements has indeed furthered a process of de
facto 'legalization' of the status quo, including Israeli settlements. This
was a process begun by international inaction in enforcing Geneva IV,
and by the sheer length of Israeli occupation. However, the creation of
Palestinian autonomy and the existence of a 'peace process' has further
contributed to undermining international legal consensus that withdrawal of Israel from all of the Occupied Territories is called for, as
apparently contemplated by UN Resolution 242, and that building of
settlements is an impermissible violation of Geneva IV.

There remains a further international legal problem with the likely
shape of final status agreement. International law of occupation appears
to set limits on the type of arrangement which Israel can achieve through
negotiation. It has been suggested that the application of Geneva IV
should preclude a settlement which in effect involves repartition of the
West Bank with clumps of settlements remaining in Israeli control. This
would raise problems under Article 49 of Geneva IV, which provides that
an occupying power 'shall not deport or transfer parts of its own civilian
population into the territory it occupies'; and Article 47, which provides
that

[p]rotected persons who are in occupied territory shall not be deprived in any case
or any manner whatsoever, of the benefits of the present Convention by any
change introduced as the result of the occupation of a territory, into the institutions
or government, nor by any agreement concluded between the authorities of the
occupied territories and the Occupying Power, nor by any annexation by the latter
of the whole or part of the occupied territory.

It could be argued, as Campbell has, that any solution attenuating
Palestinian sovereignty of the Occupied Territories 'would seem to fall
foul of article 47 since it would deprive the local Palestinian population of
their right to be free from settlements and thus of the benefits of the Convention.'[79] While a sovereign authority can cede territory, this is very different from 'the representatives of an occupied people ceding part of
occupied territories to the Occupying Power.'[80] Benvenisti argues a
contrary position that Israeli deployment and granting of authority to the

---

[78] Malanczuk (1996: 487).   [79] Campbell (1996).   [80] Campbell (1996: 53).

PA in certain areas means that these areas are already 'not "occupied" in the sense of the international law of occupation.'[81] Malanczuk takes something of a middle course, suggesting that the situation described in Article 47 does not really fit the situation created by the DoP and Interim Agreements. He argues that these are agreements not with local authorities but with the PLO as 'an entity recognised as representing the people in the occupied territories as a whole.'[82] This entity has agreed to these institutions as a stepping-stone to a much broader self-determination claim. As Malanczuk puts it, 'there is no autonomy, possibly as a pre-stage to independence, without delegation of authority and responsibility.'[83] However, a question remains regarding the extent to which Geneva IV limits Israeli–PLO negotiations, and the extent to which it constitutes *ius in bello*, only preventing settlement-building and annexation during occupation prior to negotiations. Given international ambivalence about enforcing Geneva IV or clarifying permissible self-determination outcomes, this argument may be fairly academic. Article 47's application to final status compromises would be even further complicated by a land transfer, if, for example, final status agreement saw Israeli annexation of settlements accompanied by a land transfer of non-occupied territory to Palestinians. Such an arrangement would appear to be a lawful exchange rather than an unlawful annexation. Yet, if such an exchange was unequal and accepted only owing to an imbalance of power between occupier and occupied, and the 'fact' of illegal settlements, then it would seem that the Article 47 prohibition on annexation might still be relevant.

Internal or External Self-Determination?

Geneva IV aside, the 'clumps of autonomy' approach to Palestinian statehood, built through the interim agreements, does not seem consistent with satisfaction of Palestinian claims to self-determination. While autonomy would seem to be a key tool in the current emphasis on internal self-determination for groups, its use as a 'solution' in the Israel–Palestine conflict does not play out the underlying rationale which has created this emphasis.[84] The essence of autonomy as a device for management of ethnic conflict is that it provides for a territorially based internal self-determination for minorities in areas where they predominate. However, the underlying rationale of autonomy regimes is supposedly to ensure access to government and the adequate protection of the minority rights likely to be trampled in a majoritarian system. In the words of Hannum,

---

[81] Benvenisti (1996: 57).   [82] Malanczuk (1996: 498).

[83] Ibid. Although it should be noted that Malanzcuk argues that Israel is still an occupant as regard autonomous areas.

[84] On models of autonomy see generally Hannum (1990); Lapdioth (1997).

autonomy should not be an end in itself, but a 'political tool to ensure that other rights and needs are appropriately addressed.'[85]

Evaluated in terms of this underlying rationale, the design of Palestinian autonomy as found in the interim peace agreements is problematic, with implications for any final status settlement. The contours of interim autonomy arrangements revolve around the relationship between Israel and the PLO–PA, dealing with questions of power, control, and status. These are more typically the subject-matter of external self-determination concerns than internal self-determination concerns. Yet external self-determination is supposedly not being dealt with.

But neither is internal self-determination being dealt with. As examined further in the next chapter, both sides had reasons not to negotiate into the peace agreements, a package which would harmonize Palestinian autonomy with internal self-determination requirements. As a result the contours of Palestinian autonomy are prescribed by Israeli security concerns. Indeed by the Wye Memorandum, Human Rights Watch were arguing that the security obligations on the PA on which Israeli with-drawal was conditioned would in implementation require the PA to commit human rights abuses against Palestinians.[86] After the interim agreements it has become unclear who is responsible for human rights violations within areas of Palestinian autonomy. It has even become unclear whether anyone can sign human rights conventions with regard to these areas.[87] Furthermore, the interim agreements set up an auton-omy which then justifies differential standards of living and access to water, jobs, and other socio-economic benefits as between Israelis and Palestinians, rather than ensuring equality between these groups, as is a usual objective of using internal self-determination as a conflict man-agement device.

The paradox of the interim agreements is that they use the language and mechanisms of internal self-determination to move towards a change of status, or external self-determination, rather than to deliver internal self-determination as substantively understood. Yet, the precise resulting sta-tus of Palestinian areas remains, and may well continue to remain, unclear. The concepts of internal and external self-determination are played off against each other so that neither is delivered in a coherent form. This runs contrary to the human-rights-based rationale for developing innovative approaches to statehood and sovereignty in the first place. A narrow focus on how to change the status of the Occupied Territories so as to 'end occupation' as the route to satisfaction of Palestinian self-determination should not bypass the overarching principle of self-determination, which,

---

[85] Hannum (1990: 474); cf. also Steiner (1991).   [86] Human Rights Watch (1998).
[87] Cf. Benvenisti (1994*b*).

Cassese argues, 'transcends, and gives unity to' customary rules, 'casting light on borderline situations.'[88] This is a principle of self-determination as a free and genuine expression of the will of the people concerned. This principle seems to point to procedural requirements on how a solution is negotiated, including answers to a series of crucial questions. Namely, against a backdrop of a negotiating power imbalance, are there any legal limits on what deal the PLO can accept, in terms either of Geneva IV or of self-determination law? Are there any requirements on the PLO to ensure that they are the legitimate representatives of the people, and that negotiated solutions are popularly accepted? Or does PLO accession to any permanent status agreement itself amount to satisfaction of the self-determination claim, regardless of either PLO legitimacy or the content of what is agreed to? These pertain, regardless of any more substantive self-determination content that might apply.[89]

The interim agreements present a complex set of interlocking conundrums for international lawyers. They provide for a change of status of territory but not external self-determination. They provide for Palestinian autonomy but not internal self-determination. They devolve power and remove some Israeli forces, but do not end occupation. Or they end Israeli occupation but do not create a Palestinian state. They are interim and transitional but may become permanent if negotiations do not succeed. Paradoxically, if negotiations do succeed, substantially the same arrangements may be asserted to comprise a Palestinian state, even while the ability of political elites, and even more so ordinary Palestinians, to self-determine their future is limited.

Before looking to the international community to solve these conundrums it should be noted that the difficulties in evaluating the self-determination provided for in the interim agreements in terms of international law merely reflect back international law's gaps with regard to Palestinians. As with Bosnia Herzegovina, it can be argued that the failure of international law and the international community to set down clear parameters for resolution of the self-determination claim, or to limit the numbers game played in the interim through settlement-building and population transfer, has become transcribed into the deal. Lack of agreement on, or commitment to, a common end goal for negotiations, and a negotiating focus on separation, means that internal self-determination has become lost in the unresolved battle over external self-determination, even as external self-determination has been redefined.

[88] Cassese (1998b: 319).   [89] See e.g. discussion in Drew (1997).

CONCLUSIONS

International law on self-determination raises as many questions as it answers. It has singularly failed to prevent conflict, and in many cases, including Northern Ireland, Bosnia Herzegovina, and Israel/Palestine, stands accused of having exacerbated the conflict. The dilemma is that if the people's only right is to statehood, then this right is at variance with international law principles of territorial integrity. On the other hand, defining a people's rights purely in terms of individually asserted rights such as right to vote and to equality ignores the more fundamental prior challenge asserted by minorities concerning the legitimacy of the state.

As described in this chapter, the current evolutionary trend is to move from concern with defining who a 'people' is in the self-determination context, to a greater concern with what the people have a right to. This involves reconsidering the ends of self-determination and attempting to find new means to implement them and thereby transcend the 'people v. territory' self-determination conundrum. The ends are taken from what apparently lies at the heart of self-determination claims—the right for individuals and groups to shape government and play a meaningful and equal part in public life. In divided societies possible means of achieving this include autonomy regimes, ethnically based federalism, power-sharing and consociational models of government, cross-border government, and robust protection for individual rights.

There are two main prongs to this attempt to refashion international law in the light of ethnic conflict. First, an emphasis on the institutions of liberal democracy, as the '"ideal polity" almost mystically endowed with an array of characteristics that are supposed to assure both domestic and international peace and prosperity.'[90] Mechanisms for protecting individual rights are at the heart of this polity. Secondly, the increasing introduction of minority–group rights as a component of that liberal democracy, which, as Slaughter points out, 'may be international law's long-term response to ethnic conflict.'[91]

This dual emphasis raises in particular the question of the relationship between individual and group rights, and, through that, the relationship between law and politics. As Slaughter suggests, '[t]he rise of group rights may be understood as the further colonisation of the political by the legal.'[92] Indeed, the programmatic nature of new minority rights standards indicates this straddling of politics by law. However, Slaughter has also noted that 'the relative success of informal efforts at mediating simmering ethnic conflicts suggests the value of expanding the repertoire of political

[90] Slaughter (1998: 129).   [91] Slaughter (1998: 134).   [92] Slaughter (1998: 129).

solutions rather than searching for new rights and remedies.'[93] And so the question must be posed as to whether international lawyers should strive to produce a normative response at all, or merely police the law–politics divide, acknowledging that where law ends, politics begin.

When the four deals are turned to, they would seem to move in tandem with the law's current evolutionary direction (with the possible exception of South Africa). All four use the mechanisms and/or language of both democracy and group rights. However, the detail of the deals reveals very different balancings between democratic legitimacy, individual, and group participation.

The political arrangements of South Africa and Northern Ireland, while addressing groups, do this within an overarching structure which emphasizes the primacy of individual rights, and indeed these rights were integral to the respective deals. In South Africa individual rights protections spliced the integrative structures and simultaneously legitimized the new state structures as democratic. In Northern Ireland individual rights and equality provisions operate as a control mechanism on a consociational form of government. Here also human rights formed an area of common ground where different sides could agree on a common set of governing values.

In contrast, the deals in Bosnia and Israel/Palestine evidence tensions between group-oriented governmental structures and protection of individual rights. In both, provision for group autonomy leaves little or no space for a common sphere in which individual rights would have primacy. If the solution is primarily about separation of ethno-national groups, then individual rights may be irrelevant to the deal cut (as in Israel/Palestine), or be left to the feeble institutions of an emaciated common sphere, whose power to enforce rights within autonomous spheres is negligible (as in Bosnia).

Clearly the precise reasons for the different balances struck between individual and group rights are contextual, multi-layered, and complex. Some of that context has been explained in these last two chapters. However, international law should not be ignored as a key part of that context.

International law's normative claims impact on processes in two ways. Negotiating self-determination in a peace agreement is not just a matter of getting agreement to a suitable recipe from a menu of conflict resolution devices, as accounts of possible devices unintentionally suggest. International law will inevitably have had something to say regarding the legal basis for self-determination claims during the conflict, even if through silence. This will shape the types of option on the table. An alien from Mars (with an interest in political science) would be hard-pushed to understand why 'bantustanization' was internationally unacceptable in

---

[93] Ibid.

South Africa, but perhaps acceptable in Palestine; or why consociational government was considered vital internationally in the divided society of Bosnia Herzegovina, permissible in Northern Ireland, but unnecessary in South Africa. These questions can only be answered with reference to the normative standards of international law as applied during the conflicts, and the actions of the international community in enforcing them.

Secondly, in a less tangible way, the willingness of the international community to set limits on how the conflict is waged, or to set out and enforce clear parameters for its resolution, shapes the resulting accommodation of self-determination claims found in the agreements. In this sense, also, the self-determination 'solution' is prefigured in international law attempts to deal with the conflict.

A form of legal regulation is visible in South Africa and Northern Ireland, where international law parameters concerning resolution of the conflicts provided a constructive context for negotiations. In both places it is true that, at the time of signing the agreement, different groups had quite different understandings of where the future would lead in self-determination terms. It is also true that these underlying differences will continue to be negotiated with subtlety for many years, through the various institutions set up by the agreements. However, both agreements do contain a meta-bargain which attempts a practical accommodation of the self-determination claims as a medium- or long-term solution. While the eventual outcome may remain uncertain (particularly in Northern Ireland), the meta-bargain aims to provide closure on what was seen as the central cause of the conflict.

In the cases of Bosnia Herzegovina and Israel/Palestine, the failure to set such parameters was just as significant in shaping the peace agreements reached, albeit in a negative way. The willingness of the international community to force settlement without enforcing limits on how the conflict was waged, and without stating what the parameters for their resolution should be, has led to agreements which continue to be ambiguous about the underlying self-determination analysis. The peace processes established by these deals are not just subject to the normal pressures of implementation. By incorporating rather than accommodating the self-determination dispute, they become the new forums for waging the old self-determination conflicts. The ability of parties to continue practices of population transfer during negotiations and during the post-agreement 'peace-building' stage indicates the failure of these agreements to resolve the underlying conflicts. This makes the agreements in these two situations entirely different in nature from those in South Africa and Northern Ireland.

The last chapter concluded by noting the connection between the self-determination deal and the role for human rights institutions. This chapter has begun to add another layer to that connection. The success or failure of the deal to move towards resolution of the self-determination issue has important implications for the role of human rights and democratic institution-building. Put bluntly, it is difficult to establish democratic legitimacy for the state when the deep questions as to what the nature of that state is remain completely unresolved. This connection forms a basis for the exploration of human rights institutions in the next chapter.

7

Building for the Future: Human Rights Institutions

In the previous two chapters the nature of the political settlement in each of the four case-studies was examined and compared with international law on self-determination. These chapters began to explain why and how human rights protections find their way into peace agreements. This chapter begins by summarizing and expanding that analysis. I then examine the specific institutional design of human rights protection in each of the four case-studies by way of illustration.

INSTITUTIONALIZED HUMAN RIGHTS PROTECTIONS AND PEACE AGREEMENTS

In three of the four case-studies (Bosnia, Northern Ireland, and South Africa) human rights institutions were an integral part of the deal arrived at in the peace agreements. In the fourth example—that of Israel/ Palestine—human rights protections were largely non-existent, for reasons that will be explored later. The protection across the first three examples indicates a superficial similarity between the chosen institutions. They all address to different degrees:

- overarching justiciable rights (e.g. bills of rights)
  - civil and political rights
  - social and economic rights (and/or policy alternatives)
  - cultural rights (and/or policy alternatives)
- constitutional or human rights courts
- independence of the judiciary
- national human rights enforcement institutions (e.g. human rights commissions, ombudspersons)
- rights-based reform of criminal justice system
- rights-based reform of policing

As would be expected, the detail of agreements reveals different mandates, different strengths of enforcement mechanism, and different relationships between the various institutions. This chapter does not aim to produce a detailed institutional comparison.[1] Rather, the chapter aims to examine

---

[1] See Watson (1993: 10–15) (on dangers of such comparisons). See also Alston and Darrow (1999: 470) (on need for political, social, cultural, and institutional context).

and compare how the different institutions fit into the constitutional–peace processes as documented in the peace agreements.

Three main factors can be suggested to influence the precise institutional structures agreed to therein. First, the dynamics of the bargaining process and in particular the self-determination deal agreed to by political elites. Secondly, international law standards which inform institutional design of any institutions agreed to. And thirdly, the legacy of the past, including pre-agreement institutional structures and experience.

Meta-Bargaining and Human Rights Protections

The nature of the deal and the assumptions which underlie it shape the treatment of human rights institutions, as previous chapters have begun to illustrate. In the last chapter a dichotomy between primarily consociational and primarily integrative political mechanisms was examined. Rights play a different role in each because each model has different underlying assumptions about how ethnic conflict is best managed. In each model, individual rights have a role in underlining democratic legitimacy, but beyond this the role of rights differs. In the consociational model, with its emphasis on group accommodation, group rights may be used to give conceptual autonomy in areas such as culture or language, while individual rights aim to consolidate a common ethnic space. The role of human rights will depend on the precise consociational tools chosen, and in particular the balance struck between pluralism–individual rights and autonomy–group rights. In the integrative model, with its emphasis on pluralism, individual rights have a heavier burden of ensuring inclusiveness and minority participation given that typically the context is that of a unitary state with a majoritarian government, rather than group protections with ethnic balancing.

However, as discussed in the last chapter, self-determination provision in peace agreements does not often fit neatly into the models offered by political scientists. Furthermore, it is perhaps the territorial division at the heart of the deal, rather than the precise model of government, which most starkly affects the role of human rights institutions. Where the deal underwrites and solidifies a physical, geographic separation of populations, through mechanisms such as autonomy, ethnically based federalism, or partition, then inter-group cooperation ('sharing') will be limited to the conceptual space of common institutions. If these institutions are limited, then sharing is limited. Conversely, where the deal establishes a unitary territory with shared governmental institutions, then group autonomy ('separation') can only be facilitated, if at all, conceptually in spheres of life such as language, education, and culture (sometimes known as 'corporate federalism').[2]

As a deal moves towards or away from geographic separation, so the incentives of parties to build in rights are affected. Where institutions are to be shared by different groups, then all sides may have an interest in ensuring that these institutions operate within a rights framework. Thus, in South Africa and Northern Ireland human rights came to form a centrepiece of the deal, because, as the deal began to take shape, opposing parties came to see that individual rights protections could address mutual concerns of domination. In South Africa a Bill of Rights took on increasing importance for the white minority as it became clear that the deal was moving towards majority rule without minority vetoes. This is not to say that there was consensus on what should be in the Bill of Rights. While many generally framed core rights were accepted by both African National Congress (ANC) and the South African government/National Party (NP/SAG) as necessary, the meta-conflict re-emerged with regards to whether certain rights, such as a right to property, should be protected, and, if so, what the content of that right should be. This was in essence a negotiation over the transfer, or not, of economic power as touched on in the last chapter.

In Northern Ireland what became known as 'the equality agenda' came to form an area of common ground between Sinn Féin and the various fringe loyalist parties, especially the Progressive Unionist Party (PUP), who particularly emphasized social inclusion. This was supported by pluralist parties such as the Women's Coalition, and by civic society operating in parallel outside the talks process.[3] As McCrudden writes, for Sinn Féin and the PUP,

a failure to address human rights and equality issues of importance to their communities would make it much more difficult to 'sell' any agreement. Once human rights was identified as an area that was important, particularly to Sinn Féin, it then became important for those who wanted to keep Sinn Féin 'on board' to include it for reasons of strategy as well as for reasons of principle in the final Agreement.[4]

For Ulster Unionists, human rights and equality issues could be conceded more easily than areas which implicated sovereignty, such as cross-border bodies. They could even be traded against these bigger concessions. Furthermore, as mentioned in the previous chapter 'rights for nationalists' could be sold to constituents as a concession necessary to underwriting the international legitimacy of Northern Ireland within its present borders.

---

[2] For similar use of the terms 'separation' and 'sharing', see Boyle and Hadden (1994).
[3] See further McCrudden (1999b: 1724–7).   [4] Ibid.

In contrast, in Israel/Palestine the focus on a 'separation' approach aimed at accommodating Palestinian claims for external self-determination with Israeli demands for security meant that, unlike the other examples, there was no reciprocal interest to see human rights protections instituted as part of the deal. Indeed, quite the opposite: the focus on separation provided a distinct disincentive to incorporate human rights protections within the text of the deal. With Israelis excluded from the ambit of Palestinian authority, there was no Israeli self-interest to protect human rights. Rather, the granting of a measure of autonomy to Palestinians brought with it Israeli security concerns as to whether autonomy would facilitate or decrease Palestinian attacks on Israelis.

Conversely, for the Palestinian Liberation Organization (PLO), although building in human rights institutions could have provided the Palestinian Authority with a buffer against unreasonable Israeli security demands, there were clear disincentives to do this. Having failed to secure Geneva IV as governing the interim period, there was no reason to limit Palestinian autonomy further by conditioning it on human rights as policed by Israel. Not only would this have been offensive to underlying claims of Palestinian statehood, it would also have reinforced Israeli arguments that Israel no longer had responsibility for human rights violations in the Occupied Territories. More cynically, it would have limited PLO capacity to control dissident political forces. Discussion of human rights and institution-building in the Israeli Palestinian Agreements is therefore short, as such provision is virtually non-existent.

In Bosnia Herzegovina (BiH) the deal itself must be understood as a compromise between opposing demands of separation and sharing. The role of the human rights institutions can only be understood with reference to this compromise. It is through human rights institutions that the international community tries to claw back the unitary state from the separate Entities to which it devolves power. The formal powers of the BiH government as compared with those of the Entities are extremely limited. In contrast, the BiH human rights institutions stand superior to the governments and institutions of the Entities. The human rights institutions are aimed at reversing the ethnic cleansing which resulted in the Entity division. With their international membership they also give the international community an ongoing role in implementation. Yet the territorial concessions underlined by the deal through the devolution of power to the Entities create difficulties for the implementation and effectiveness of those human rights protections.

International Standards and Human Rights Protections

While the 'deal' may determine when and how human rights institutions emerge in an agreement, international standards also play an important role in pressing the need for human rights institutions, and in influencing their design. As Alston notes, rights protections preceded the internationalization of the concept, with 82 per cent of national constitutions drafted between 1788 and 1948 including some form of protection for human rights.[5] In recent times, however, there has been increased emphasis on a specific set of human rights institutions as a necessary part of constitutionalism. Indeed some commentators have gone as far as to suggest that rather than being merely one part of constitutionalism, a human rights framework with judicial review is 'the prime component of constitutionalism providing a normative legal framework within which politics operates'; in other words, 'constitutionalism has come to mean nothing more than a system of legally entrenched rights that can override, where necessary, the ordinary political processes.'[6] As Alston notes, this view, although strongly contested, finds support in international law. Increasingly, it can be argued that the rights found in international instruments require specific institutional arrangements for their implementation.[7]

International human rights conventions do not explicitly claim to prescribe how states are to fulfil their human rights obligations. The details of human rights protection are ostensibly to be left to the domestic arena. But it can be argued that they implicitly require institutions such as a court system with independent judiciary if the obligations are to be met. Proliferating soft law standards and the responses of convention committees underline this institutional expectation and in effect set out a 'best practice' blueprint for these institutions. Loosely speaking, soft and hard law international standards address national institutions for human rights protection,[8] the judiciary,[9] policing,[10] and criminal justice.[11]

---

[5] Alston (1999: 3), citing Van Maarseveen and van der Tang (1978: 191–5).

[6] Alston and Darrow (1999: 467), citing Bellamy (1996: 24).

[7] Reisman (1994: 190); Crawford (1993).

[8] See e.g. Principles Relating to the Status of National Institutions 1992; see generally United Nations (1995).

[9] See e.g. UN Basic Principles on the Independence of the Judiciary, 1985; UN Procedures for the Effective Implementation of the Basic Principles on Independence of the Judiciary, 1989; UN Basic Principles on the Role of Lawyers, 1990; see generally the compilation of standards in Centre for the Independence of Judges and Lawyers (1990).

[10] See e.g. UN Code of Conduct for Law Enforcement Officials 1979; UN Guidelines for the Effective Implementation of the Code of Conduct for the Effective Implementation of the Code of Conduct for Law Enforcement Officials 1989; UN Basic Principles on the Use of Force and Firearms by Law Enforcement Officials; see generally United Nations (1997); Crawshaw *et al.* (1998).   [11] See e.g., UN Guidelines on the Role of Prosecutors, 1990.

Examination of international human rights standards evidences movement towards a situation in which it can grandly be claimed not only that international law implicitly requires democratic structures, but that it prescribes a particular set of human rights institutions, and that it even sets down a detailed blueprint for each institution. The new formulas for internal self-determination have accentuated this process by moving the focus of self-determination law itself from concern over who are 'the people' and what is 'the territory' to concern around what the people are substantively entitled to. This further evidences the tapestry of interchange between international law and ethnic conflict which is a recurring theme of this book.

The Legacy of the Past

A third factor shaping the design of human rights institutions is the legacy of the past. The experience of past human rights abuses and the debate about what in the past constituted a human rights abuse shapes institutional protection for the future. Secondly, the experience of past institutional responses and reform which takes place during the peace process also shapes the institutional provision found in peace agreements. As mentioned earlier, the current discussion does not aim to provide a detailed comparison of the institutional arrangements found in the different agreements. Theoretical issues aside, this is because the institutions are often only partially provided for in the agreements, either because some of what came before is retained, or conversely because institutional detail is to be provided by post-agreement negotiations. In the descriptions of the arrangements below some of this context is given as background to understanding where the peace agreement provision connects to both prior and subsequent processes of social change.

The Legitimizing and Integrating Roles of Human Rights Institutions

The above discussion indicates the twofold role for human rights institutions touched on towards the end of Chapter 4. Human rights protections, institutionalized for example through a bill of rights and an independent judiciary, are intended to do two quite different things: to *legitimize* the deal and new governmental structures established by it, and to *integrate* the divided polity.[12] Janus-faced, they look to both the past and the future.

As regards legitimization, human rights institutions signal the stamp of democratic legitimacy on the deal arrived at: they constitute part of the '"politically correct" approach to constitutionalism.'[13] This does not mean

[12] Cf. de Búrca (1995) (looking at this dual function with regard to the Charter of Rights debate in the European Union).   [13] Alston (1999: 4).

that their role is purely symbolic, or even cynical. They arrive in peace agreements as a result of instrumental demands. Those who have suffered human rights abuses in the past often successfully win human rights protections in the deal as an element crucial to resolving the conflict, as South Africa and Northern Ireland demonstrate. Human rights protections legitimize the deal internationally, but also may legitimize it in the eyes of a significant party.

As regards their integrative ambition, human rights protections form part of the peace agreement's attempt to redefine state–ethnic relations. They claim to ensure that in the new regime created no one should be penalized on the basis of ethnicity. Human rights protections supposedly take the sting out of the sovereignty issue. If everyone's rights are equally protected no matter who is in power, then the issue of sovereignty should become much less important. Thus human rights institutions aim not merely to police the division between law and politics found in the polity, as in the classic liberal-democratic state, but also to *create* the polity by mediating communal divisions. This is perhaps most striking in the case of Bosnia Herzegovina, where the human rights protections aim to undo ethnic cleansing, and rewrite the bargain at the heart of the deal.

This integrative ambition is a vital part of the institutional protection. As Reilly and Reynolds note, 'institutional design takes on an enhanced role in newly democratising and divided societies because, in the absence of other structures politics becomes the primary mode of communication between divergent social forces.'[14] While pluralist Western democracies have a variety of channels through which to carry on these conversations, such as civil society, social and sporting clubs, and churches, in divided societies with fledgling democracies these institutions are characterized by rigid separation of communities. Therefore, 'political institutions take on even greater importance' and 'become the most prominent, and often the only, channel of communication between disparate groups.'[15] This is no less true of the human rights institutions than the institutions of government. Indeed where, as in Bosnia, the government institutions are designed to facilitate group separation, then the human rights institutions may take on this role largely unaided.

ISRAEL/PALESTINE

The approach of the Israeli/Palestinian peace agreements to institution-building provides the starkest and most negative example of how the self-determination deal can impact on human rights provisions.[16] The

---

[14] Reilly and Reynolds (1999: 3).   [15] Reilly and Reynolds (1999: 4).

[16] Much non-governmental organization material has been published dealing with specific human rights violations. For some overviews on Human Rights and the Oslo Accords, see B'Tselem (1999); LAW (1999c); Mar'i (1997).

separation nature of the deal meant that the institutions identified in international instruments as crucial to human rights protections, such as police or the criminal justice system, are provided for with barely a mention of human rights or any grounding principles. The focus of the institutional provision in the agreements is the transfer of power and the precise delimiting of Palestinian Authority (PA) spheres and powers.

Overarching Rights

The agreements do not include an explicit list of rights, provision for a Bill of Rights or incorporation of international instruments, and therefore do not include human rights enforcement institutions.[17] There is no attempt to provide any overarching rights framework.

Human rights are not mentioned in the Declaration of Principles (DoP). They are first mentioned in the Gaza–Jericho Agreement; Article XIV, entitled 'Human Rights and the Rule of Law', states that 'Israel and the Palestinian Authority shall exercise their powers and responsibilities pursuant to this Agreement with due regard to internationally-accepted norms and principles of human rights and the rule of law.'[18] This is repeated in the later Interim Agreement (Oslo II).[19] However, both the Interim Agreement and subsequently the Wye Memorandum which reiterate this language suggest that internationally accepted norms are to be subject to the agreement, rather than vice versa.[20] While some specific rights receive a scattered mention throughout the agreement, this does not amount to even an embryonic rights framework.[21]

Social and Economic Rights

Economic issues are addressed in the Israeli/Palestinian Agreements as one of their 'cornerstones' but not as 'rights' issues, and without a reference to equality.[22] Rather, mechanisms for development and economic cooperation are established. Economic cooperation is addressed by the DoP,[23] and subsequently by the Protocol on Economic Relations, 29 April

[17] Although 'an independent judiciary' is mentioned in the context of Palestinian Authority–Council administration of justice, Article VI Gaza Jericho Autonomy Agreement, 4 May 1994 (hereafter Gaza–Jericho Agreement).   [18] Gaza–Jericho Agreement.
[19] Article XIX Interim Agreement between Israel and the Palestinians, 28 Sept. 1995 (hereafter 'Interim Agreement').
[20] Article XI, para. 1, Annex 1 Interim Agreement; cf. also Article II(4) Wye Memorandum.
[21] See e.g. the right not to be tried twice for same crime (in the context of Israeli-retained jurisdiction over offences committed against Israelis), Article 1(7), Annex III Gaza–Jericho Agreement; restriction on use of capital punishment, Article 2(7)(g), Annex III Gaza–Jericho Agreement.
[22] The only convergence of an economic issue and mention of a 'right' is in the term 'water rights', which the Israeli–Palestinian Continuing Committee for Economic Cooperation is to focus on, Article 1, Annex III DoP.   [23] See Annex III and IV DoP.

1994 (later incorporated in the Gaza–Jericho Agreement), which provides many of the administrative mechanisms for economic cooperation. These mechanisms are supplemented or implemented by the Interim Agreement,[24] Wye Memorandum,[25] and Sharm el Sheik Memorandum, and Safe Passage Protocol.[26]

The agreements provide for economic matters within a framework of Israeli–Palestinian cooperation,[27] and a development plan consisting of two elements: an Economic Development Programme for the West Bank and the Gaza Strip, and a Regional Economic Development Programme.[28] As Fassberg notes, the framework suggests that Israeli–Palestinian economic relations are to contribute to the establishment of some form of regional economic union.[29]

The history of Israeli economic policies with regard to Palestinian Occupied Territories has been analysed as one of 'de-development' of the Palestinian economy so as to serve Israeli strategic and economic interests.[30] It is into the context of this pre-existing relationship that the agreements arrive and must be judged. When the detail of the agreements is explored, the economic relationship therein is exposed as lopsided. Detail of provision for customs, monetary affairs, movement of persons and services, and even the mechanics of the legal facilitative arrangements reveals ambivalence between two aims: 'to establish the Palestinian Authority as an economic actor, and to limit its power in order to protect the Israeli economy.'[31] In examining the potential of the agreements to improve the Palestinian economy, Elmusa and El-Jaafari argued in 1996 that two broader political factors would be determining:

the degree to which Israel allows the free movement of goods, labour, and capital into and out of West Bank, and Gaza . . . and the ability of the . . . PNA [PA] to set up the prerequisite institutions and regulatory framework as well as to pursue the appropriate economic policies.[32]

In implementation, the broader power-political concerns of Israel and the PA have often frustrated both.[33]

---

[24] See generally Annex III and Articles V and VI, Annex VI Interim Agreement.

[25] See Article III Wye Memorandum (restarting the DoP committees dealing with economic cooperation, and dealing with the establishment of an international airport, a business park, and a sea port at Gaza).

[26] See Article 5 (dealing with safe passage) and Article 6 (dealing with building Gaza Sea Port) Sharm el Sheik Memorandum. See also Protocol concerning Safe Passage, 5 Oct. 1999.

[27] Annex III DoP.   [28] Annex IV DoP.   [29] Fassberg (1996: 157).

[30] Roy (1995, 1996).   [31] Fassberg (1996: 164).

[32] Elmusa and El-Jaafari (1996: 189).

[33] See e.g. Arnon and Spivak (1998) (noting a severe decline in Palestinian standards of living between 1993 and 1996, largely owing to Israeli closures, which deprived many Palestinians of work in Israel).

Cultural Rights

Cultural rights as such are nowhere mentioned in the agreements. However, it can be argued that the provision of autonomy for a Palestinian Council is itself designed to ensure Palestinian cultural rights. The matters devolved immediately by the DoP to the PA include education and culture.[34] The Gaza–Jericho Agreement and the Interim Agreement mention cultural and educational cooperation with specific reference to its particular role in fostering 'peace between Israel and the Palestinian people', 'peace in the entire region', and 'mutual understanding and tolerance'.[35] However, the underlying thread of Israeli security concerns emerges here and there in tiny details. For example, the devolution of postal services to the PA notes that Palestinian stamps must be designed 'in the spirit of peace.'[36]

Policing and Criminal Justice

While policing and criminal justice both receive detailed treatment, unlike South Africa and Northern Ireland this detail deals with logistics rather than principle. As regards policing, provision is made for how many police, where, and when? As regards criminal justice, provision deals with the scope of Palestinian jurisdiction.

The DoP provides that

[i]n order to guarantee public order and internal security for the Palestinians of the Gaza Strip and the Jericho Area, the Palestinian Authority shall establish a strong police force, while Israel will continue to carry the responsibility for defending against external threats, as well as the responsibility for overall security of Israelis for the purpose of safeguarding their internal security and public order.[37]

In the Gaza–Jericho Agreement the duties of the police are listed in a functional way as:

1. performing normal police functions, including maintaining internal security and public order;
2. protecting the public and its property and acting to provide a feeling of security and safety;
3. adopting all measures necessary for preventing crime in accordance with the law; and,
4. protecting public installations and places of special importance.[38]

---

[34] Article VI DoP.

[35] Article II(9), Annex II Gaza–Jericho Agreement; Article VII, Annex VI Interim Agreement. See also Article VIII, Annex VI Interim Agreement establishing a 'people-to-people' programme.

[36] Article 29(c), Annex III Interim Agreement; cf. also Article II(26)(b), Annex II Gaza–Jericho Agreement.   [37] Article VIII DoP.

[38] Article III(2), Annex I Gaza–Jericho Agreement; cf. Article II, Annex I Interim Agreement.

The agreements progressively provide the detail of how many police, their relationship to Israeli security forces, recruitment, number of arms, ammunition and equipment, and specific areas of deployment.[39] Explicit or implicit references to human rights protections are virtually impossible to find.

As with policing, the fairly extensive criminal justice provisions deal with the delimitation of Palestinian jurisdiction as regards Israeli jurisdiction, and also impose obligations regarding security issues.[40] Apart from a passing reference to an 'independent judiciary',[41] there are no mechanisms for ensuring rights protection.

Implementation Prefigured

The agreements preserve the status quo wherein Israeli human rights abuses take place: they neither provide new rights mechanisms nor address the issues which underlie many human rights abuses, such as settlement-building and population transfer.[42] While the absence of confrontation between intifada and Israeli security forces has reduced certain types of human rights abuses, such as deportation and the overall number of deaths in the conflict, other types of abuse have stayed the same (for example, percentage of Palestinian prisoners tortured) or even increased (for example, the revocation of residency rights in Jerusalem).[43] The agreements mean that the PA can also commit human rights abuses.

On closer examination the lack of an overarching human rights framework, either in the agreements, or to which the agreements are subject, does not merely preserve a status quo, but has led to a dynamic whereby rights have simply disappeared. This dramatic statement can be illustrated by a few examples on different levels.

The Palestinian autonomy provided for in the agreements has muddied the question of responsibility for international human rights obligations, as was discussed in Chapter 5. While legally Israel arguably retains responsibility for human rights violations in the absence of a Palestinian state, as a practical matter human rights advocacy must also be addressed at the PA. Although the PA has affirmed its (moral) commitment to international human rights standards[44] and even set up a national institution for human rights—the Palestinian Independent Commission for Citizens'

---

[39] See e.g. Articles XIII, XIV Interim Agreement, and Article II, Annex I Interim Agreement.
[40] See generally Shuqair (1994).   [41] Article VI Gaza–Jericho Agreement.
[42] See e.g. B'Tselem (1999).   [43] Ibid.
[44] Arafat stated in a meeting with Amnesty International that 'human rights would be a high priority for [the Palestinian Authority] and that international human rights standards will be incorporated into new legislation.' See Amnesty International News Service 23/96, dated 8 Feb. 1996.

Rights (PICCR)[45]—in practice the PA has been responsible for a broad range of human rights abuses.[46] This of course must be blamed on the PA itself. As a regime it has failed to make a transition 'from behaving like a liberation army of soldiers and commandos to one of bureaucrats and civil servants, who put the law above political expediency.'[47]

But the structure of Palestinian autonomy found in the agreements also militates against Palestinian attempts to build a society based on rule of law and human rights.[48] In addition to its inability to ratify international instruments, PA domestic jurisdiction is limited and the Interim Agreement makes clear that legislation

which exceeds the jurisdiction of the Council or which is otherwise inconsistent with provisions of the DoP, this Agreement, or any other agreement that may be reached between the two sides during the interim period, shall have no effect and shall be void ab initio.[49]

All legislation has to be communicated by Palestinians to Israel, and the Israeli side can refer any legislation which it views as incompatible with the DoP and other agreements to a joint Legal Committee established by the agreements.

This makes Palestinian state-building more difficult. For example, a Palestinian draft basic law prepared by the Palestinian Legislative Council (PLC) and containing a Bill of Rights is arguably inconsistent with the agreements and would automatically exceed PLC authority.[50] Although the law has in fact become a casualty of PA reluctance to enact it, the agreements provide a buffer to the PA against the demands of civic society. While a significant amount of international money has been channelled in the direction of Palestinian democracy and rule of law projects, this cannot make up for the flaws in the framework through which these issues must be addressed.[51] State-building is difficult without a state.

At a deeper level the agreements build in disincentives for the PA to

---

[45] Established on 30 Sept. 1993 by Presidential Decree No. 59/1994; pub. in *Palestinian Gazette* 2 (Jan. 1995), 33. See further Azzam (1998) for description of mandate and operation in first four years.

[46] See e.g. Palestinian Independent Commission for Citizens' Rights (1996, 1997, 1998, 1999). [47] Azzam (1998: 344).

[48] Cf. Aruri (1995). [49] Article XIII Interim Agreement.

[50] Palestinian Legislative Council, The Basic Law, 2 Oct. 1997 (non-official translation by Jamal Aabu Kadijeh). For further background and context on the draft law, see Al Qasem (1996).

[51] For recent audit of funding, see Office of the United Nations Special Coordinator in the Occupied Territories (1999). In an interesting illustration, when this very report was published, a PA official misrepresented it as demonstrating that human rights non-governmental organizations (NGOs) were working to an externally funded agenda, and were corrupt; this appears to have been part of a broader attempt of the PA to attack the work of human rights NGOs and frustrate attempts to provide a basic law governing the role of Palestinian NGOs.

develop a culture based on the rule of law. The political dynamic means that Israel and the United States emphasize Israeli security concerns above other considerations. The agreements, most overtly illustrated by the Wye Memorandum, focus on PA needs to prevent dissident Palestinian violence against Israelis and subject human rights obligations to this over-riding obligation. The central bargain of 'land (for Palestinians) for peace (for Israelis)' often asserted to underlie the peace process means that the PLO must be seen as trying to deliver 'peace' to Israel, even if that is at the expense of Palestinian human rights. Paradoxically, this 'security-based' approach undermines long-term peace-building based on the elimination of root causes of violence. It leads to a dangerous dynamic where the fail-ure of the peace process to deliver change on the ground for Palestinians diminishes Palestinian grass-roots support for the PA, resulting in attempts at coercion which further reduce that support. This establishes a vicious circle whereby Palestinian-on-Palestinian repression and the fail-ure of the peace process reinforce each other.

The division of powers between Israel and the PA has also erased some 'principled struggles' in domestic law. Matters which prior to the DoP had some principled basis for struggle between the individual and the Israeli state are now a matter of bargaining between the PA and the Israeli state. For example, as regards family reunification, the previous procedure of petitioning the Israeli High Court against revocation of residency for those who returned to the territories after their exit permits expired has now been adjudicated to be beyond the jurisdiction of the High Court because authorities in this matter have been transferred from Israel to the PA.[52]

In summary, in both their text and their implementation the Israeli/ Palestinian peace agreements demonstrate an almost complete divorce between the concept of peace and the concept of justice. The concept of peace embodied in the agreements is a concept of managed separation, whose contours are shaped by Israeli security concerns. The negotiating dynamics between the parties mean that it was always unlikely that the agreements between them would include human rights constraints on Palestinian autonomy. However, it would have been possible for the entire process to have been subject to overarching international law con-straints, although imagining this is difficult, and involves reimagining the entire process and international context.

[52] HCJ 2151/97 *Shaqir et al. v. Commander of the IDF in the West Bank Region et al.*, 6 Nov. 1997 (unpub.). See further HaMoked (1998: 10–11). Note, as a further example attempts to limit Israeli liability for security force actions during the intifada period through a draft Law concerning Handling of Suits Arising from Security Force Activities in Judea, Samaria and the Gaza Strip (Exemption from Liability and Granting of Payment), 1997.

SOUTH AFRICA

In South Africa the deal or peace agreement itself was formulated as a written Constitution due to acceptance among the major political players that this was the best 'arena within which the handover of formal power and transformation of the substance of social relations was to take place.'[53] The Constitution with its human rights provisions was to provide the future 'rules of the game' for managing both transition to democracy and also ethnic and other differences. The particular form of government agreed to meant that the Bill of Rights in particular was to become one of the key mechanisms for minorities to challenge majority rule. It was also to form one of the central planks in the new constitutional democratic order. Thus there was a common interest between the ANC and the NP/SAG in establishing strong rights protections, although not necessarily agreement on what should be included.[54]

Overarching Rights

The first three chapters of the Interim Constitution addressed the primacy of the Constitution (Chapter One), common citizenship and universal franchise (Chapter Two), and a justiciable Bill of Rights which was to 'bind all legislative and executive organs of state at all levels of government' (Chapter Three). The Bill of Rights formed a centrepiece of the Interim Constitution's human rights protection.[55] Aside from the limitations clause and state of emergency exceptions, no law, whether a rule of the common law, customary law, or legislation, could limit any right entrenched in the Bill of Rights. The Bill of Rights drew on but reworded a basic list of mainly civil and political rights, similar to those found in international documents.[56]

As Corder and Du Plessis explain, the Bill of Rights aimed to guarantee rights denied by the apartheid government, but it was also influenced by

---

[53] Corder (1998: 3).

[54] For discussion of human rights and South African Transition, see wa Mutua (1997).

[55] For a detailed analysis of the Interim Bill of Rights, see Corder (1994, 1996); Corder and Du Plessis (1994); Davis (1996); Dugard (1994b); Erasmus and de Waal (1996); Mureinik (1994); Van Wyk (1994).

[56] In particular, it provides for equality, life, human dignity, freedom and security of the person, protection from servitude and forced labour, privacy, religion, belief and opinion, freedom of expression, assembly demonstration and petition, freedom of association, freedom of movement, residence, citizen's rights (to enter and leave the republic, and not to be deprived of citizenship), political rights (to form parties, campaign, make political choices, and vote), access to court, access to information, administrative justice, rights relating to detention and arrest of accused persons, economic activity, labour relations, property, environment, children, language and culture, and education.

existing foreign bills of rights and international human rights conventions.[57] International instruments often operated as a tool for achieving compromise. As Corder and Du Plessis note: '[i]n the case of some controversial provisions in [the Bill of Rights] the Technical Committee sought to expedite compromise by following certain of the wordings in international instruments quite closely.'[58] The precise formulation of rights, however, resulted from what was essentially a *political* compromise.

The resulting Interim Bill of Rights reflected a balance between different meta-conflict positions: first, competing libertarian and egalitarian (or liberationist) traditions,[59] the former emphasizing rights protecting individual liberty, and the latter normally arguing for a fuller bill of rights which would provide mechanisms for second and third generation rights; and secondly, competing minimalist (only those rights necessary for transition) and optimalist (fullest possible bill of rights) positions. Minimalist positions were held by those who favoured reserving the drafting to the elected Constitutional Assembly. Optimalist positions were held by those such as the NP/SAG, who feared marginalization in a proportionally representative constitution-making process. The negotiating process produced a fairly optimalist bill of rights but one with significant gaps.

Social and Economic Rights

The main gap was in the area of social and economic rights. For the most part these were not catered for, and when they were, they enjoyed restricted recognition only.[60] Many of the deficits of the Interim Bill of Rights were corrected in the Final Constitution, where rights were refined after a lengthy public participation and consultation process. While the Final Constitution's Bill of Rights is broadly similar to the Interim Bill of Rights, it also reflects the more open negotiation process, in particular with the addition of possible horizontal application and more substantive protection for socio-economic rights.[61]

---

[57] See Corder and Du Plessis (1994: 47–8).

[58] For example, section 8(3)(a) of the Constitution of South Africa 200 of 1993 (hereafter Interim Constitution) dealing with affirmative action was modelled on a similar provision in Article 1(4) of the International Convention on the Elimination of All Forms of Racial Discrimination; see ibid.   [59] See Corder and Du Plessis (1994: 40–1).

[60] See Corder and Du Plessis (1994: 45–6), who cite section 29, which protects every person's 'right to an environment which is not detrimental to his or her health or well-being' but makes no reference to any duty to act so as to protect the environment. They note, however, that attempts to similarly restrict second-generation children's rights were unsuccessful.

[61] For differences between Interim and Final Constitutions, see further Du Plessis (1996); Heaton (1997).

Cultural Rights

There were no 'group rights' as such in the Interim Bill of Rights.[62] However, section 31 of the Bill of Rights stated that '[e]very person shall have the right to use the language and to participate in the cultural life of his or her choice.' Provision for education rights provided a right 'to instruction in the language of his or her choice where this is reasonably practicable' and 'to establish, where practicable, educational institutions based on a common culture, language or religion, provided that there shall be no discrimination on the ground of race.'[63] Cultural rights were also provided for elsewhere in the Constitution with provision for traditional authorities, the establishment of a Volkstaat Council, and Constitutional Principles XII and XXXIV, both of which dealt with a collective right of self-determination of 'linguistic, cultural and religious' communities, as discussed in Chapter 5.

Constitutional Court and Independent Judiciary

A new Constitutional Court was to have jurisdiction as a court of final instance over 'all matters relating to the interpretation, protection and enforcement of the provisions of this Constitution.'[64] Particularly identified for its jurisdiction were alleged violations of the Bill of Rights; the constitutionality of executive or administrative acts or conduct; the constitutionality of national and provincial legislation; and constitutional disputes between the organs of government.[65] In the event of the Constitutional Court finding any law or provision inconsistent with the Constitution, it was to declare such law or provision invalid to the extent of its inconsistency or give the relevant authority a specified time to correct the defect.[66] With regard to administrative action, the Constitutional Court could declare it to be unconstitutional and order the relevant organ of state to refrain from or correct such conduct within a specified time.[67] Decisions of the Constitutional Court were to bind all persons and all legislative, executive, and judicial organs of state.[68]

The Interim Constitution provided that judicial authority was to be vested in the courts established in the Constitution and any other law; that the judiciary be 'independent, impartial and subject only to this Constitution and the law, and shall not be interfered with in the performance of their functions.'[69]

A Constitutional Court consisting of a president and ten other judges

---

[62] In the Final Constitution a right similar to the minority rights provided for in Article 27 of the ICCPR was inserted, although the term 'minority rights' is not explicitly used; Article 31 The Constitution of South Africa Act 108 of 1996 (hereafter Final Constitution).
[63] Section 32 Interim Constitution.   [64] Section 98 Interim Constitution.   [65] Ibid.
[66] Ibid.   [67] Ibid.   [68] Ibid.   [69] Section 96 Interim Constitution.

was established to enforce the Constitution. Given the Constitution's primacy in reconstruction, the issue of who would appoint these judges was a matter of intense negotiation focusing around opposing demands for continuity with the apartheid judicial system versus demands for complete transformation.[70] The result was a twofold compromise. First, a compromise between old- and new-order judges, and secondly, a compromise on the degree of control which politicians would have over judicial appointments.

As regards the former compromise, four of the judges were to be appointed from among the judges of the Supreme Court (old order) by the president (of state) in consultation with the Cabinet and the chief justice.[71] Seven judges, including the president of the court and any subsequent vacancies, were to be appointed under the new procedures.[72]

The second compromise was dealt with by establishing a Judicial Service Commission with political and legal representation to make recommendations from which the president (of state) was to make the appointments under the new procedures.[73] In making its recommendations, the Judicial Service Commission was to have regard to the 'need to constitute a court which is independent and competent and representative in respect of race and gender.'[74]

While the Constitutional Court as a new creation could incorporate both old- and new-order judges, as regards the lower courts, transformation was to be incremental. Judicial Service recommendation followed by presidential appointment was to govern all future appointments, but no provision was made for automatic removal of existing judges who reflected the political and racial make-up of the apartheid order. Furthermore, neither Interim nor Final Constitution provided a new mechanism for the magistrates, who deal with a very large volume of work. In 1993 in anticipation of multi-party democracy the apartheid Parliament had passed the Magistrates Act 90 of 1993, which established a Magistrate's Commission with eleven members, appointed by the state president with five-year terms. It was not until 1996 that the process was amended to provide for a mechanism similar to the Judicial Service Commission which would ensure more representative appointments.

---

[70] See Corder and Du Plessis (1994: 191–200); Bawa (1998: 35–50).

[71] Section 99(3) Interim Constitution.

[72] The question of transition from old- to new-order judges continued to be played out in the Final Constitution as regards length of tenure questions (which would affect the persistence of old-order judges in the court).

[73] Section 105 Interim Constitution. Cf. section 178 Final Constitution (which saw changes in the composition of the Judicial Service Commission which in effect marked a swing from appointees of the legal community, to appointees of the politicians).

[74] Section 99(5)(d) Interim Constitution.

Again there is no specific mechanism for automatic removal of apartheid magistrates.[75]

One additional element designed to address the under-representation of blacks and women on the bench was the provision of an additional criterion of having lectured in law at a university; or being 'a person who, by reason of his or her training and experience, has expertise in the field of constitutional law relevant to the application of this Constitution and the law of the Republic.'[76] This provided a non-practice route for judicial appointments.

National Human Rights Institutions

A number of other institutions relating to the enforcement of human rights were also established by the Interim Constitution.[77]

Public Protector

The public protector's office dealt with maladministration of public servants.[78] The main functions and powers of the public protector were to investigate and deal with maladministration in connection with the affairs of government at any level; abuse or unjustifiable exercise of power, or unfair, capricious discourtesy or other improper conduct or undue delay by a person performing a public function; dishonesty; improper enrichment or advantage; and acts or omissions which result in improper prejudice.[79] Provincial legislatures also had powers to appoint public protectors at provincial level, provided their powers did not derogate from those of the national post.[80]

Human Rights Commission

The Interim Constitution established a Human Rights Commission (HRC), to consist of a chairperson and ten members, who are South African citizens and 'broadly representative of the South African community'.[81]

---

[75] See wa Mutua (1997).

[76] Section 99 Interim Constitution; although only two of the Constitutional Court judges can be qualified by virtue of this latter section, section 99(4) Interim Constitution.

[77] Chapter 8 Interim Constitution. For the background to the negotiation of some of these institutions see Corder and Du Plessis (1994: 191–205).

[78] Corder and Du Plessis (1994: 200–4) (noting that attempts were made in negotiations to include human rights as more broadly conceived of, within this mandate).

[79] Section 112 Interim Constitution.   [80] Section 114 Interim Constitution.

[81] Section 115 Interim Constitution. The president makes the appointments, but the nominations are made by a joint committee of the houses composed of one member of each party represented in Parliament and willing to participate in the committee, and approved by the National Assembly and Senate by a resolution adopted by a majority of at least 75% of the members.

The HRC was given power to

- promote the observance of, respect for, and the protection of fundamental rights
- develop an awareness of fundamental rights among all people of the republic
- make recommendations to organs of state at all levels of government where it considers such action advisable
- undertake studies for report on or relation to fundamental rights
- request any organ of state to give information on human rights measures adopted[82]

The Commission was also to give advice on the compliance of draft legislation with human rights. The Commission was given investigative powers, which include helping the persons adversely affected to secure redress such as taking a court case if a rights abuse is found.[83]

Commission on Gender Equality

A Commission on Gender Equality was established in outline only.[84] Its objects were broadly defined as 'to promote gender equality and to advise and to make recommendations to Parliament or any other legislature with regard to any laws or proposed legislation which affects gender equality and the status of women.'[85]

In addition to these institutions two additional institutions touched on rights issues: a Volkstaat Council was established, as noted above, to act 'as a constitutional mechanism to enable proponents of the idea of a Volkstaat to constitutionally pursue the establishment of such a Volkstaat.'[86] Secondly, provision was made for the establishment of a Commission on the Restitution of Land Rights to investigate, mediate, and report on land claims.[87]

Final Constitution

The human rights institutions of the Interim Constitution are retained in a more or less similar fashion in the Final Constitution. The Final Constitution re-presents six key institutions as 'State Institutions Supporting Constitutional Democracy.'[88] These are: the Public Protector, the Human Rights Commission, the Commission for the Promotion of and Protection of the Rights of Cultural, Religious, and Linguistic Communities (which replaces the former Volkstaat Council), the Commission for Gender

---

[82] Section 116 Interim Constitution.   [83] Section 116(3) Interim Constitution.
[84] Section 119 Interim Constitution.   [85] Section 119(3) Interim Constitution.
[86] Section 184B Interim Constitution (as amended).
[87] Sections 121–2 Interim Constitution. See further Ch. 8, pp. 243–5.
[88] Chapter 9 Final Constitution.

Equality, the Auditor-General, and the Electoral Commission. The Final Constitution also provides for the establishment of an independent authority to regulate broadcasting. These are provided for in terms of general principles, detail being left to legislation (which in most cases had been enacted prior to the Final Constitution). Functions and mandate are largely similar to Interim Constitution.

Police, Defence, and Criminal Justice

The Interim Constitution established the South African Police Service, which was to be structured at both national and provincial levels and to function under the direction of the national government as well as the various provincial governments.[89] The Interim Constitution did not address the human rights aspects of policing explicitly, apart from providing that provincial legislation regulating police cannot 'detract from the rights which citizens have under an Act of Parliament.'[90] The Interim Constitution did set up clear lines of democratic accountability through police commissioners at national and provincial level, community–police fora, and an independent complaints mechanism under civilian control.[91] Effective coordination of the services and cooperation between the various commissioners was to be ensured through a committee of the responsible ministers and members of the Executive Councils and a Board of National and Provincial Commissioners. The Constitution also provided for an Act of Parliament to be passed which would provide much of the detail for the future police service. The broad functions of the service were identified as the prevention of crime, the investigation of any offence or alleged offence, the maintenance of law and order, and the preservation of the internal security of the republic.[92]

The Interim Constitution further established a National Defence Force 'as the only defence force for the Republic'.[93] The minister responsible for defence was to be accountable to Parliament for the National Defence Force.

Issues important to human rights and policing such as recruitment, symbols, and training were addressed subsequently in legislation.[94] Some of these matters then found their way into the general principles for security services laid out in the Final Constitution. These include compatibility of policing with

the resolve of South Africans, as individuals and as a nation, to live as equals, to live in peace and harmony, to be free from fear and want and to seek a better

---

[89] Section 214 Interim Constitution. [90] Section 217(4)(b) Interim Constitution.
[91] Sections 218–22 Interim Constitution. [92] Section 215 Interim Constitution.
[93] Section 224 Interim Constitution. [94] South African Police Service Act 68 of 1995.

life; and that security services are conducted in accordance with law and the Constitution.[95]

The Interim Constitution did not contain specific provision for criminal justice; however, the Bill of Rights contained lengthy provision for the rights of 'Arrested, Detained and Accused Persons'. The Bill of Rights also contained detailed provision controlling the declaration of a state of emergency and consequent suspension of rights, which was criticized by the Constitutional Court in its certification judgment, and subsequently further limited.[96] The provisions for judicial and policing reform are, of course, also significant for criminal justice.

Implementation Prefigured

While democratic constitutionalism and a human rights culture were apparently placed at the centre of the Interim Constitution, a detailed examination reveals compromises in the make-up of the institutions charged with implementation. Police, judiciary, and civil servants are to retain their pre-apartheid make-up virtually unchanged but with provision for incremental reform. This is the same compromise which lies at the heart of the self-determination deal—sharing between old and new for an interim period, followed by a more fully fledged new order. Lurking beneath the surface is also continued conflict over how socio-economic justice and equality are to be achieved, whether as policy commitments (in which radical measures may be balanced against the risk of capital flight) or through a more rights-based framework.[97]

NORTHERN IRELAND

In Northern Ireland human rights form a key part of the Belfast Agreement and interestingly this was a departure from earlier peace blueprints.[98] However, many of the rights issues are not dealt with substantively.

[95] Chapter 11, Security Services, Final Constitution (this chapter additionally deals with intelligence services).

[96] See *Ex Parte Chairperson of the Constitutional Assembly: In Re Certification of the Constitution of the Republic of South Africa, 1996*, 1996 (4) SA 744 (CC), 1996 (10) BCLR 1253 (CC) (the emergency law provision did not technically contravene or fail to implement a Constitutional Principle, and therefore the court's criticisms did not have the force of law, but did in fact result in changes being made to the Final Constitution).

[97] See Chanock (1999: 426) (arguing that while the Bill of Rights provisions for redistributing socio-economic resources are important, that in practice 'South Africa will be reconstructed by administrators.' And so reform of administrative law may be a more relevant legal undertaking.)

[98] On human rights and the Belfast Agreement, see generally Harvey and Livingstone (1998); McCrudden (1999b); Mageean and O'Brien (1999); Moore (1999).

Instead general principles for the institutions are agreed and a series of commissions established to work to agreed remits and recommend ways forward. Thus the agreement provides only a broad framework which establishes processes for how detail is to be filled out. Where rights issues do receive more substantive treatment in the agreement, this is generally because there were clear initiatives prior to the peace process which became incorporated and sometimes reshaped therein.

An Overarching Rights Framework

The rights section of the agreement begins with an affirmation by the parties of their commitment to mutual respect for 'the civil rights and the religious liberties of everyone in the community.'[99] The agreement provides for overarching enforceable rights by providing for 'complete incorporating into Northern Ireland law of the European Convention on Human Rights (ECHR), with direct access to the courts, and remedies for breach of the Convention, including power for the courts to overrule Assembly legislation on grounds of inconsistency.' The Human Rights Act 1998, which fulfils this commitment (to come into force on 2 October 2000), had been drafted and debated independently of peace process documents, as part of a UK-wide pre-election commitment to constitutional reform by the Labour Party.[100] It provides for the ECHR to be directly applicable to public bodies, and to be directly enforceable through United Kingdom courts. The Human Rights Act 1998 and any future bill of rights are to constrain law-making and provide a safeguard against Assembly abuse of power.

Provision is also made to move towards a more comprehensive bill of rights.[101] The Human Rights Commission which the agreement establishes is tasked with consulting and advising on a bill of rights.[102] This Bill of Rights is to form a set of 'add-ons' to the ECHR, in order to address the 'specific circumstances of Northern Ireland.' While the agreement

[99] Belfast Agreement (BA), Rights Safeguards and Equality of Opportunity, para. 1.
[100] Boeteng and Straw (1997).
[101] The agreement can be unpicked to reveal different conceptions of what a bill of rights is, an enforceable constitutional piece of legislation (some parties and civic society), or an aspirational symbolic charter (a government view). Both these visions contributed to the different provision which resulted.
[102] The Human Rights Commission will 'be invited to consult and to advise on the scope for defining, in Westminster legislation, rights supplementary to those in the European Convention on Human Rights, to reflect the particular circumstances of Northern Ireland, drawing as appropriate on international instruments and experience. These additional rights to reflect the principles of esteem, and—taken together with the ECHR—to constitute a Bill of Rights for Northern Ireland'. BA, Rights, Safeguards, and Equality of Opportunity United Kingdom Legislation, para. 4.

itself singles out eight rights for affirmation, these have no enforcement mechanism in the agreement, and seem to have been inserted for symbolic reasons and chosen because they most easily garnered nationalist–unionist consensus.[103]

The agreement also provides that the Northern Ireland Human Rights Commission will be involved in setting up a 'joint committee' with members of the similar Human Rights Commission to be established in the Republic of Ireland.[104] This joint committee is to be 'a forum for consideration of human rights issues in the island of Ireland', and in particular is to consider 'the possibility of establishing a charter, open to signature by all democratic political parties, reflecting and endorsing agreed measures for the protection of the fundamental rights of everyone living in the island of Ireland.'[105] Thus, as regards overarching human rights frameworks, the door is propped firmly open.

Socio-Economic and Equality Rights

The ECHR deals mainly with civil and political rights. However, its socio-economic equality deficit is somewhat redressed elsewhere in the agreement. First, equality and group rights matters are highlighted as issues for inclusion in the Bill of Rights:

[a]mong the issues for consideration by the Commission will be:

- the formulation of a general obligation on government and public bodies fully to respect, on the basis of equality of treatment, the identity and ethos of both communities in Northern Ireland; and
- a clear formulation of the rights not to be discriminated against and to equality of opportunity in both the public and private sectors.[106]

The Belfast Agreement also provides immediate measures addressed at socio-economic rights and equality.[107] Provisions governing a pledge of office for ministers in the power-sharing executive required them to 'serve all the people of Northern Ireland equally, and to act in accordance with the general obligations on government to promote equality and prevent discrimination.'[108]

The agreement provides for innovative 'mainstreaming' of equality in

---

[103] These rights comprise: right of free political thought; right to freedom and expression of religion; right to pursue democratically national and political aspirations; right to seek constitutional change by peaceful and legitimate means; right to freely choose one's place of residence; right to equal opportunity in all social and economic activity, regardless of class, creed, disability, gender, or ethnicity; right to freedom from sectarian harassment; and the right of women to full and equal political participation.   [104] See below, p. 218.

[105] BA, Rights, Safeguards, and Equality of Opportunity, A Joint Committee, para. 10.

[106] BA, Rights, Safeguards, and Equality of Opportunity, United Kingdom Legislation, para. 4.

[107] For a full account of the history and context of these provisions, see McCrudden (1999*b*).   [108] BA, Strand One, Annex A: Pledge of Office.

public decision-making.[109] It provides that '[s]ubject to the outcome of public consultation underway' the government intends 'to create a statutory obligation on public authorities in Northern Ireland to carry out all their functions with due regard to the need to promote equality of opportunity in relation to religion and political opinion; gender; race; disability; age; marital status; dependants; and sexual orientation.'[110]

Public bodies are to be required to draw up statutory schemes showing how they will implement this obligation. These schemes are to cover 'arrangements for policy appraisal, including an assessment of impact on relevant categories, public consultation, public access to information and services, monitoring and timetables.'[111]

As with incorporation of the ECHR, these latter provisions had a history independent of the Belfast Agreement, with their genesis in the five-year review of operation of the Fair Employment Act 1989 and resulting government White Paper of March 1998[112] (although with its reference to impact assessment the agreement goes further).[113]

In addition to this legal framework for 'mainstreaming' equality, the British government commits to pursuing 'broad policies for sustained economic growth and stability in Northern Ireland and for promoting social inclusion, including in particular community development and the advancement of women in public life.'[114] In particular the agreement mentions consultation and progress on a new regional development strategy; a new economic development strategy; and further anti-discrimination measures. These last are to include 'a new more focused Targeting Social Need initiative and a range of measures aimed at combating unemployment and progressively eliminating the differential in unemployment rates between the two communities [greater Catholic unemployment] by targeting objective need.'[115]

Cultural Rights

The remaining rights provisions deal with language rights and cultural diversity, although these operate as a policy commitment, rather than at a constitutional level. In particular, linguistic diversity is affirmed with specific reference to 'the Irish language, Ulster-Scots and the languages of the

---

[109] See McCrudden (1999*b*).
[110] BA, Rights, Safeguards, and Responsibilities, United Kingdom Legislation, para. 3.
[111] Ibid.
[112] *Partnership for Equality: The Government's Proposal for Future Legislation and Policies on Employment Equality in Northern Ireland*, Mar. 1998, Cm. 3890 (Belfast: HMSO).
[113] McCrudden (1999*b*).
[114] BA, Rights, Safeguards, and Equality of Opportunity, Economic, Social, and Cultural Issues, para. 1.
[115] BA, Rights, Safeguards, and Equality of Opportunity, Economic, Social, and Cultural Issues, para. 2.

various ethnic communities'.[116] The British government makes further specific commitments to the Irish language, in particular providing that '[i]n the context of active consideration currently being given to the UK signing the Council of Europe Charter for Regional or Minority Languages' they will undertake a list of initiatives which reflect the charter's scope.[117] Reference is also made to 'the sensitivity of the use of symbols and emblems for public purposes and the need in particular in creating the new institutions to ensure that such symbols and emblems are used in a manner which promotes mutual respect rather than division.'[118]

Constitutional Court and Independent Judiciary

The Belfast Agreement does not make provision for a special court entrusted with enforcement of rights or indeed for reformation of the judiciary (beyond training them on the Human Rights Act 1998). The only reference to judicial reform appears in the section on criminal (rather than constitutional) law, where the issues detailed in the Criminal Justice review's terms of reference include 'the arrangements for making appointments to the judiciary and magistracy, and safeguards for protecting their independence.'[119]

National Human Rights Institutions

In Northern Ireland, two institutions are established with a role in enforcement—the Northern Ireland Human Rights Commission (NIHRC) and an Equality Commission. The NIHRC according to the agreement is to have 'membership from Northern Ireland reflecting the community balance.'[120] It is to be established by Westminster legislation 'independent of Government, with an extended and enhanced role beyond that currently exercised by the Standing Advisory Commission on Human Rights.'[121] The Northern Ireland Act makes it clear that the Commission will consist of a chief commissioner and other commissioners 'appointed by the Secretary of State'.[122] In addition to its above-mentioned role advising on a bill of rights, its functions are to include:

[116] BA, Rights, Safeguards, and Equality of Opportunity, Economic, Social, and Cultural Issues, para. 3.
[117] BA, Rights, Safeguards, and Equality of Opportunity, Economic, Social, and Cultural Issues, para. 4.
[118] BA, Rights, Safeguards, and Equality of Opportunity, Economic, Social, and Cultural Issues, para. 5.
[119] For the result of the criminal justice review, see Criminal Justice Review Group (2000).
[120] BA, Rights, Safeguards, and Equality of Opportunity, New Institutions in Northern Ireland, para. 5.
[121] A previous body with a limited remit and powers; see Livingstone (1999: 1470–7); Maguire (1981). [122] Section 68(2) Northern Ireland Act 1998.

- keeping under review the adequacy and effectiveness of laws and practices
- making recommendations to government as necessary
- providing information and promoting awareness of human rights
- considering draft legislation referred by the new Assembly
- in appropriate cases, bringing court proceedings or providing assistance to individuals doing so[123]

The Equality Commission for Northern Ireland is to replace the pre-existing Fair Employment Commission, the Equal Opportunities Commission (NI), the Commission for Racial Equality (NI), and the Disability Council (enforcement bodies for anti-discrimination legislation dealing with religion–political belief, sex, race, and disability respectively). The functions of the Equality Commission are to enforce anti-discrimination legislation. In addition to these functions, the Commission is to have an important role in the implementation of the new equality duties imposed on public authorities; it is to 'advise on, validate and monitor the statutory obligation and will investigate complaints of default.'[124] The make-up of the Equality Commission is not addressed at all in the Belfast Agreement (or indeed the earlier government White Paper). However, the Northern Ireland Act provides that the Commission shall consist of fourteen to twenty commissioners, including a chief commissioner and a deputy chief commissioner, all to be appointed by the secretary of state, who 'shall as far as practicable secure that the Commissioners, as a group, are representative of the community in Northern Ireland.'[125]

Irish Government Parity

The Irish government commits to human rights provision to ensure 'at least an equivalent level of protection of human rights as will pertain in Northern Ireland', in wording which hints at incorporation of the European Convention on Human Rights. It also commits to:

- establishing a Human Rights Commission with a mandate and remit equivalent to that within Northern Ireland
- proceeding with arrangements as quickly as possible to ratify the

---

[123] BA, Rights, Safeguards, and Equality of Opportunity, para. 5. The implementing Northern Ireland Act provides additional functions to 'promote understanding and awareness' of human rights, educational and research activities, a power to conduct investigations (but no concurrent powers of discovery or subpoena), and a duty to review its own work after two years; section 69 Northern Ireland Act 1998.
[124] BA, Rights, Safeguards, and Equality of Opportunity, New Institutions in Northern Ireland, para. 6.   [125] Section 73(4) Northern Ireland Act 1998.

Council of Europe Framework Convention on National Minorities (already ratified by the UK)
- implementing enhanced employment equality legislation
- introducing equal status [anti-discrimination] legislation; taking further active steps to demonstrate its respect for the different traditions in the island of Ireland[126]

Policing and Justice

The agreement states an aim to provide 'a new beginning to policing in Northern Ireland with a police service capable of attracting and sustaining support from the community as a whole.'[127] It lays out a series of principles which are asserted to be a shared basis for policing among the participants. These are:

- that the police service is professional, effective and efficient, fair and impartial, free from partisan political control
- that the police service is accountable, both for its actions and under law, to the community it services
- that the police service is representative of the society it polices, and operates within a coherent and cooperative criminal justice system, which conforms to human rights norms
- that the police service is capable of maintaining law and order including responding effectively to crime and to any terrorist threat and to public order problems[128]

The new arrangements are to 'be based on principles of protection of human rights and professional integrity and should be unambiguously accepted and actively supported by the entire community.'[129]

The agreement provides for an independent Commission to be established to 'make recommendations for future policing arrangements in Northern Ireland including means of encouraging widespread community support for these arrangements within the agreed framework of principles.' A more detailed term of reference which expands on the underlying principles is provided in an annex to this section. These terms of reference make it clear that the Commission is to look into 'composition, recruitment, training, culture, ethos and symbols' and 'should include recommendations covering any issues such as re-training, job placement and educational and professional development required in the transition to policing in a peaceful society.'[130]

The Commission is to 'consult widely', including with non-governmental

---

[126] Ibid.　　[127] Ibid.　　[128] BA, Policing and Justice, para. 2.　　[129] Ibid.
[130] BA, Policing and Justice, Annex A Commission on Policing for Northern Ireland.

expert organizations, and through such focus groups as they consider it appropriate to establish. It is to publish its final report by summer 1999.[131] The make-up of the Commission is to be 'broadly representative with expert and international representation among its membership.'

Criminal justice is similarly dealt with, by setting out broad principles and setting up a special commission to review criminal justice provision. The parties state four shared aims of the criminal justice system as to deliver a fair and impartial system of justice to the community; to be responsive to the community's concerns, and encourage community involvement where appropriate; to have the confidence of all parts of the community; and to deliver justice efficiently and effectively. A wide ranging review of criminal justice, excluding emergency legislation, is to be conducted by the British government 'through a mechanism with an independent element', in consultation with the political parties and others. The review is to report by autumn 1999. Again more detailed terms of reference are provided, which address the independence of the judiciary, magistracy, and prosecution service, and issues of accountability.

Implementation Prefigured

The particular institutions which come to be addressed by the Belfast Agreement do not constitute a principled overhaul of human rights provision, but rather reflect an uneasy compromise over the 'nature of the problem' or the meta-conflict. The institutional arrangements can best be seen as a hotchpotch of fairly ad hoc mechanisms, which spring from the pattern of human rights abuses during the conflict, and which are presented for the most part as 'safeguards' for the new governmental structures (replacing the 'confidence-building' language of earlier documents).

The lack of agreement at the heart of 'the agreement' plays out in an inability to deal quickly or in detail with new institutional arrangements. This results in a pattern in which difficult human rights issues are fielded out to a number of commissions (some temporary, some permanent) to consult and propose ways forward. In practice, this in effect phases the peace process negotiations into constituent blocks (although the text of the agreement does not make this staged approach explicit and the time scales for reporting are loosely stated and so left flexible). It also takes institution-building largely out of the hands of elected politicians. The advantage of this is the capacity for civil society to become more involved in the processes of reform. The disadvantage is that the Belfast Agreement definitively delivers very few concrete human rights changes. In many

---

[131] The Policing Commission, headed by Christopher Patten, published its report in Oct. 1999; Independent Commission on Policing for Northern Ireland (1999).

areas the British government alone is left with the ultimate decision-making power with respect to further change. The question of implementation of Commission recommendations will also be subjected to ongoing inter-communal bargaining which may have less to do with delivering a workable human rights framework than political point-scoring linked to other aspects of the peace process, prolonging and perhaps postponing or negating delivery of human rights commitments.

BOSNIA HERZEGOVINA

In the Dayton Peace Agreement (DPA) different institutional protections are found in different parts of the agreement.[132] While human rights institutions and mechanisms abound, their remit and jurisdiction is overlapping and confused and the mechanisms for enforcement are unclear. The central institutional protections for human rights are found in Annex 4, which provides the BiH Constitution. However, it is Annex 6 which provides for the human rights mechanism of a Human Rights Commission comprised of a Human Rights Ombudsman and a Human Rights Chamber. Further institutional protection for human rights is also found in Annex 7, on Refugees and Displaced Persons. This section provides specific rights designed to enable return of these persons. Other institutions with a role in rights protection are established elsewhere in the DPA, such as the International Police Task Force of Annex 11. The different annexes have different signatories and different levels of commitment by the parties, meaning that human rights provisions found in different parts of the agreement apparently have different weights.[133]

OVERARCHING RIGHTS

The preamble to the BiH Constitution in Annex 4 provides that it is '[b]ased on respect for human dignity, liberty, and equality' and dedicated to

---

[132] See General Framework Agreement for Peace in Bosnia and Herzegovina (hereafter 'Dayton Peace Agreement' or DPA). See generally Benedek (1999); Pajić (1998); Sadiković (1999); Sloan (1996).

[133] As Sloan (1996: 21243) notes, 'the parties must " *fully respect and promote fulfilment of the commitments*"[emphasis added] contained in all the Annexes; however the only commitments to which the Parties agree to *"fully comply"*[emphasis added] are those set forth in Annex 1-B (Agreement on Regional Stabilization) and Chapter One of each of Annexes 6 . . . and 7.' While Chapter One of each annex contains the human rights, the implementation commissions are established in other parts of the annexes and are, 'apparently, therefore subject to the lower fully respect and promote fulfillment of'standard' (footnotes omitted).

'peace, justice, tolerance, and reconciliation.' These words begin a Constitution which claims human rights principles as its guiding principles.

Article II of the Constitution provides that 'Bosnia and Herzegovina and both Entities shall ensure the highest level of internationally recognised human rights and fundamental freedoms.' It provides that '[t]he rights and freedoms set forth in the European Convention for the Protection of Human Rights and Fundamental Freedoms and its Protocols shall apply directly in Bosnia and Herzegovina' and shall 'have priority over all other law.' In addition to this, Article II(3) provides a list of rights drawn from the European Convention and whose specific reiteration, as with the list enumerated in the Belfast Agreement, seems designed chiefly to place fundamental rights symbolically in the text of the Constitution.[134]

An annex to the Constitution also provides a list of international human rights instruments which are 'to be applied in Bosnia and Herzegovina.'[135] This wording is different from the wording incorporating the ECHR, indicating a lesser form of incorporation. However, the Constitution states that both the ECHR and this list of international agreements 'shall be secured to all persons in Bosnia and Herzegovina without discrimination on any ground such as sex, race, color, language, religion, political or other opinion, national or social origin, association with a national minority, property, birth or other status.'[136]

---

[134] These rights are the right to life; right not to be subjected to torture or to inhuman or degrading treatment or punishment; the right not to be held in slavery or servitude or to perform forced or compulsory labour; rights to liberty and security of person; right to a fair hearing in civil and criminal matters, and other rights relating to criminal proceedings; the right to private and family life, home, and correspondence; freedom of thought, conscience, and religion; freedom of expression; freedom of peaceful assembly and freedom of association with others; the right to marry and to found a family; the right to property; the right to education; the right to liberty of movement and residence.

[135] The listed agreements are 1948 Convention on the Prevention and Punishment of Genocide; 1949 Geneva Conventions I–V on the Protection of the Victims of War, and the 1977 Geneva Protocols I–II thereto; 1950 European Convention for the Protection of Human Rights and Fundamental Freedoms and its Protocols; 1951 Convention Relating to the Status of Refugees and its 1966 Protocol; 1957 Convention on the Nationality of Married Women; 1961 Convention on the Reduction of Statelessness; 1965 International Convention on the Elimination of All Forms of Racial Discrimination; 1966 International Covenant on Civil and Political Rights and its 1989 Optional Protocols; 1966 International Convenant on Economic, Social, and Cultural Rights; 1979 Convention on the Elimination of All Forms of Discrimination against Women; 1984 Convention on the Prevention of Torture and Inhuman or Degrading Treatment or Punishment; 1987 European Convention on the Prevention of Torture and Inhuman or Degrading Treatment or Punishment; 1989 Convention on the Rights of the Child; 1990 International Convention on the Protection of the Rights of All Migrant Workers and Members of their Families; 1992 European Charter for Regional or Minority Languages; and the 1994 Framework Convention for the Protection of National Minorities.

[136] Article II(4), Annex 4 DPA. The Agreement on Human Rights provided in Annex 6 of the DPA reiterates the commitment to the ECHR and its protocols, the enumerated rights, and the list of international human rights and humanitarian law instruments.

A third set of rights is provided for in Article II(5) of the Constitution, which provides for a right to return home for all refugees and 'to have restored to them property of which they were deprived in the course of hostilities since 1991 and to be compensated for any such property that cannot be restored to them.' Annex 7 (considered further in Chapter 8) provides more detail on the right to return and places proactive obligations on the parties necessary to facilitating this.

Economic, Social, and Cultural Rights

Little explicit attention is given to economic, social, or cultural rights, although the International Covenant on Economic, Social, and Cultural Rights 1966, and other specific conventions with socio-economic dimensions, such as the Convention on the Elimination of All Forms of Discrimination against Women 1979, are included on the list of international conventions to apply within the jurisdiction. The provisions relating to right to return, including assistance with repatriation, housing, and compensation, form a type of economic provision. Annex 8 provides an Agreement on Commission to Preserve National Monuments, which is directed at ensuring cultural protection. The Commission's mandate is to 'receive and decide on petitions for the designation of property having cultural, historic, religious or ethnic importance as National Monuments.'

Independent Judiciary

There are no specific provisions in the DPA for an independent judiciary. However, provision is made for a new Constitutional Court. The Constitutional Court is to have nine members, four selected by the House of Representatives of the Federation, two by the Assembly of the Republika Srpska, and three by the president of the European Court of Human Rights after consultation with the presidency (these judges not to come from BiH or any neighbouring state).[137] The judges are to be 'distinguished jurists of high moral standing.'

The court has jurisdiction over three matters. First, exclusive jurisdiction to decide any dispute under the Constitution between the Entities, or between BiH and an Entity or Entities, or between institutions of BiH. This specifically includes whether an Entity's decision to establish a special parallel relationship with a neighbouring state is consistent with the Constitution, 'including provisions concerning the sovereignty and territorial integrity of Bosnia and Herzegovina.' These disputes can only be referred to the court by specified politicians.[138] Secondly, the court has appellate jurisdiction over issues under the Constitution arising out of a judgment of any other court in BiH. Thirdly, it has jurisdiction over cases

---

[137] Article VI, Annex 4 DPA.   [138] Article VI(3), Annex 4 DPA.

referred by any court in BiH, concerning whether a law on whose validity that court's decision depends is compatible with the Constitution, the
ECHR and its protocols, the laws of BiH, or a general rule of public international law. It is unclear what its relationship is to the Human Rights
Chamber of the Human Rights Commission, which has an apparently
overlapping jurisdiction.

National Human Rights Institutions (with an International Element)

In addition to the Constitutional Court, other institutions to enforce
human rights are established. Annex 6 establishes a Commission on
Human Rights. This Commission consists of two parts: the Office of the
Ombudsman and the Human Rights Chamber. These two bodies are
divided in terms of the type of action they undertake in a manner not dissimilar to the Council of Europe's former European Commission and
Court of Human Rights. The Ombudsman fulfils an investigative and
screening role and the Chamber a more adjudicative role. They are both
to deal with the same subject-matter:

alleged or apparent violations of human rights as provided in the European Convention for the Protection of Human Rights and Fundamental Freedoms and the
Protocols thereto and,

Alleged or apparent discrimination on any ground such as sex, race, color, language, religion, political or other opinion, national or social origin, association
with a national minority, property, birth or other status arising in the enjoyment of
any of the rights and freedoms provided for in the international agreements listed
in the Appendix, where such violation is alleged or appears to have been committed by the parties, including by any official or organ of the Parties, Cantons,
Municipalities, or any individual acting under the authority of such official or
organ.[139]

The internationally appointed Ombudsman is generally to receive
'[a]llegations of violations of human rights received by the Commission.'[140] The Ombudsman is to investigate the alleged or apparent violations specified above, and issue findings and conclusions upon
concluding an investigation. The Ombudsman can also present special
reports 'at any time to any competent government organ or official.'

Those receiving such reports are to reply within a specified time. In the
event of non-compliance the report is to be forwarded to the High
Representative, and to the presidency of the appropriate party. The
Ombudsman can also initiate proceedings before the Human Rights

---

[139] Article II(2), Annex 6 DPA.   [140] Article V, Annex 6 DPA.

Chamber based on such report, and can intervene in proceedings before the Chamber.[141]

The Human Rights Chamber is to receive referrals from the Ombudsman or directly from any party or person, non-governmental organization, or group of individuals claiming to be the victim of a violation by any party or acting on behalf of alleged victims who are deceased or missing, for resolution or decision applications concerning alleged or apparent violations of human rights as defined in Annex 6. In particular the Chamber is to 'endeavour to, and to give particular priority to allegations of especially severe or systematic violations and those founded on alleged discrimination on prohibited groups.'[142] The Chamber has the power to facilitate amicable resolution (to be forwarded to the Office of the High Representative). Otherwise, when the Chamber concludes its proceedings it is to issue a decision promptly; this decision to address steps to be taken by the party to remedy the breach.[143] The Chamber is to give reasons for its decisions, and to forward them to the High Representative.

In addition to these institutions specifically created with reference to the human rights commitments in the DPA, Annex 8 establishes the Commission to Preserve National Monuments referred to above, and Annex 7 establishes a Commission for Displaced Persons and Refugees whose mandate is to 'receive and decide any claims for real property in Bosnia and Herzegovina.'

The Human Rights Agreement (Annex 6) also provides that the parties 'shall promote and encourage the activities of non-governmental and international organizations for the protection and promotion of human rights.' These parties are to monitor the human rights situation, and the parties to the DPA are to allow them 'full and effective access to non-governmental organizations for the purposes of investigating and monitoring human rights conditions' and are to 'refrain from hindering or impeding them in the exercise of these functions.'[144]

Criminal Justice and Policing

Criminal justice is barely mentioned in Dayton. Its omission from the list of BiH spheres means that it is clearly a matter for the Entities, and this is affirmed in provision for the Entities' powers. The Constitution and human rights provisions make it clear that criminal law should be compatible with human rights standards, and can be adjudicated by the Constitutional Court and the Human Rights Chamber.

Criminal law is also affected by Annex 7 on Refugees and Displaced

---

[141] Ibid.   [142] Article VIII(2), Annex 6 DPA.
[143] Article XI, Annex 6 DPA.   [144] Article XIII(3), Annex 6 DPA.

Persons, which obliges parties to repeal domestic legislation and administrative practices with discriminatory effect; to prevent and promptly suppress any written or verbal incitement through media, or otherwise, of ethnic or religious hostility or hatred; to prevent and suppress acts of retribution; to protect ethnic and/or minority communities; and to dismiss or transfer persons in military, paramilitary, and police forces, and other public servants, responsible for serious violations of basic rights of persons belonging to ethnic or minority groups.

While the BiH Constitution empowers the Entities to undertake their own policing, there is an international dimension to policing with Annex 1-A, Agreement on the Military Aspects of the Peace Settlement, and Annex 11, Agreement on International Police Force. Annex 1-A provides for a multinational military Implementation Force (IFOR, later SFOR) which is to implement the military aspects of the annex. However, in Article VI(3) other supporting tasks are agreed to. These include helping 'to create secure conditions for the conduct by others of other tasks associated with the peace settlement, including free and fair elections'; helping 'the UNHRC and other international organizations in their humanitarian missions'; and to 'observe and prevent interference with the movement of civilian populations, refugees, and displaced persons, and to respond appropriately to deliberate violence to life and person'.

Annex 11 provides an Agreement on International Police Force to assist domestic policing. Article I affirms the constitutional provision that Entities should establish their own police forces, 'operating in accordance with internationally recognized standards and with respect for internationally recognized human rights and fundamental freedoms, and by taking other such measures as appropriate.' Through the annex the parties request the UN to establish through the mechanism of the Security Council a UN International Police Task Force (IPTF) to carry out a programme of assistance as laid out in the annex. This assistance is specified to include monitoring, advising, training, and facilitating and assisting local law enforcement. While these are all directed at supporting domestic policing, the IPTF also has a direct enforcement role with respect to human rights. When the IPTF learns of 'credible information concerning violations of internationally recognised human rights or fundamental freedoms or the role of law enforcement officials or forces in such violations', it is to provide the information to the Human Rights Commission, the International Criminal Tribunal for Former Yugoslavia (ICTFY) or 'other appropriate organisations.'

The parties are to cooperate fully with the IPTF and to provide the IPTF with information on their law enforcement agencies. The IPTF is to notify the High Representative and the IFOR commander of failures to cooperate, and request that the high representative take appropriate steps upon receiving such notifications, including calling such failures to the attention of the parties, convening the Joint Civilian Commission, and consulting with the UN, relevant states, and international organizations on further responses.

The IPTF itself is to 'at all times act in accordance with internationally recognized standards and with respect for internationally recognized human rights and fundamental freedoms, and shall respect, consistent with the IPTF's responsibilities, the laws and customs of the host country.'[145]

Implementation Problems Prefigured

While lists of rights, incorporation of international instruments, and enforcement mechanisms abound throughout the DPA, there are structural problems. First, the institutional mechanisms are overlapping and confused. The Ombudsman, the Human Rights Chamber, and the Constitutional Court all have jurisdiction over human rights issues with no clear delimitation between them. Further complicating this are the institutions at the entity level, such as the Federation Ombudsman, Federation Constitutional Court, Federation Human Rights Court (whose establishment is now opposed by the international community),[146] the Republika Srpska Constitutional Court, and the more recently established Republika Srpska Ombudsman.[147] In practical terms the Human Rights Chamber has dealt with a majority of human rights cases, and has received substantially more funding than the Constitutional Court. Exit strategies now have to address how best to support the development of the BiH Constitutional Court, and whether to merge different institutions.[148]

Most crucially, mechanisms for implementing human rights decisions are strikingly missing. Neither the Office of the High Representative, I/SFOR, nor the IPTF has an explicit mandate to arrest, necessary in the last resort to enforcing human rights. Holbrooke describes this 'security gap' as a result of several factors. First, North Atlantic Treaty Organization (NATO) reluctance to make arrests and expose itself to the possibility of the 'mission-creep' which had dogged United Nations Protection Force (UNPROFOR)'s efforts. And secondly, NATO and EU unwillingness to support a strong international police task force with an arrest power.[149] While NATO was not prepared to assume a robust implementation role with associated risk to NATO personnel, neither was it prepared to let the

[145] Article II(5), Annex 11 DPA.
[146] Chapter II, section B; Chapter IV C(4); Chapter IV C(5), respectively, of The Constitution of the Federation of Bosnia and Herzegovina.
[147] Chapter IX Constitution of Republika Srpska. The Republika Srpska passed the law establishing the Ombudsman office on 8 Feb. 2000 after negotiations with the OSCE and Venice Commission.
[148] For proposals, see European Commission for Democracy through Law (Venice Commission) (1999).   [149] Holbrooke (1998: 251–2).

IPTF, placed under the auspices of a discredited and marginalized UN, assume these powers. A similar dynamic with NATO appears to have limited the enforcement powers of the Office of the High Representative.[150]

In practice this has led to a situation where decisions and recommendations are issued but not implemented. The figures are startling: by 15 September 1999 only seven out of thirty-seven decisions of the Human Rights Chamber had been fully implemented; only twenty-seven out of fifty-seven final reports of the BiH Ombudsperson had been fully complied with.[151] In March 1999 the Federation Ombudsman also noted that 'authorities did not show political will to comply with recommendations.'

Were Dayton being implemented in good faith, the entity police forces and other implementation mechanisms might have taken on enforcement. But given that the Entities are pulling against the multi-ethnic unitary BiH which the human rights provisions aim to create and enforce, then this absence is fatal to realizing the rights incorporated.

Finally, the DPA human rights institutions exhibit a lack of understanding of the deep reconstruction necessary to implementing human rights commitments. Fundamental issues such as the infrastructure of policing and criminal justice are left almost completely unaddressed. The ready incorporation of lists of rights appears cavalier when contrasted to the approach of the new South African government (and most Western governments), who do not ratify such instruments until they can assert with some basis that existing laws and practices comply. While there was a need to start somewhere in providing a human rights framework, the way in which it was done suggests that negotiators either gave little thought to institutional questions of implementation, or did not appreciate the difficulties, or were not overly concerned with implementation of these aspects of the agreement. This would be less problematic in an agreement which purported to be the first stage in a process of institutional development. However, the DPA claims to provide a complete and final package.

Since Dayton these last two factors have come to be partially addressed by a huge evolution in the mandate of the UN under Annex 11 providing for the IPTF. The IPTF, together with the Office of the High Representative, has now moved from low-level monitoring to taking more robust action to reform, restructure, democratize, and ensure the independence and impartiality of local police forces, the judiciary, and criminal justice systems.[152]

---

[150] Holbrooke (1998: 362) (noting the initial opposition of the United States to *any* form of civilian or political, as opposed to military, authority); Pajić (1998).

[151] Figures supplied by the Office of the High Representative Human Rights Department, Sept. 1999.

[152] See e.g. Framework Agreement on Police Restructuring and Democratization in the Republika Srpska, 9 Dec. 1998; United Nations Mission in Bosnia and Herzegovina (1999*a*, *b*). For critique of IPTF, see International Crisis Group (1999: 43–50).

CONCLUSION

In summary this chapter has expanded the pattern which had begun to emerge in the previous chapters. It further illustrates the importance of the self-determination deal in shaping what institutions emerge. It illustrates the importance of institutional context to what appears in the peace agreement—the agreement will address what has come before, and institutional detail will be developed in the future. Finally, the case studies show the role of international human rights standards in shaping institutional design.

The case-studies show that the institutions which emerge, while guided by international law, find their way into agreements as a direct result of a political bargaining process rather than principled design. Thus, particular institutional arrangements, and indeed even their existence, depend on the territorial division agreed to. Their function and role is also dictated by the self-determination deal as more broadly conceived. Are human rights protections trying to create a more inclusive state and agenda-set for the future (Northern Ireland)? Are they trying to build democracy (South Africa)? Are they holding together a fragile middle ground in the face of a largely group-oriented solution (BiH)? While in each deal one role may predominate, often in practice the human rights institutions seem to undertake several, at times contradictory, roles at once. This is because institutional design as found in the peace agreement is a product of negotiation between parties who have different reasons for putting human rights institutions there, and different roles in mind for them.

The negotiation process produces institutions with a view to both legitimizing and integrating the polity. However, given that the very notion of human rights has been contested during the conflict, their dual ambitions may prove mutually negating during implementation. Particularly in situations where the self-determination deal is still to be resolved, as in Israel/Palestine or Bosnia Herzegovina, and to a lesser extent in Northern Ireland, then the role of human rights in integrating the polity is likely to be difficult and controversial. Who is appointed to the institutions, how they define human rights, and how they prioritize their work can all become micro-versions of the meta-conflict.

Perhaps for this reason peace agreements tend to provide for ethnic balance in human rights commissions, the police, and the judiciary, and for the symbols of each to be neutral as between competing ethnic/national groups. This reflects the fact that while these institutions are set up as separate from the institutions of government, they are still 'political' in a broader sense. In contrast, the many international soft law standards relating to institutional best practice do not address the question of ethnic balance in such institutions.[153] This is also in contrast to minority rights standards which address balance in institutions of government through the idea of 'effective participation'.[154] Clearly, an overemphasis on inter-communal representation for human rights institutions could lead to party-political pressures which could detract from legitimizing functions. However, conversely, if institutions in a divided society are completely unrepresentative of the different communities from which their make-up is drawn, this also inhibits their work and particularly their integrative function.

The negotiation dynamics behind the creation of the institutions continue to affect implementation issues. Human rights institutions negotiated as part of a peace agreement daily face decisions where integration tactics run counter to legitimization tactics. Should bill of rights provisions on equality vindicate the right of a relatively wealthy white person in South Africa not to pay metered water bills, because impoverished residents of the neighbouring black township are charged on a cheaper flat rate?[155] Should the Human Rights Commission in Northern Ireland prioritize the hard edge of state human rights abuses (most often committed against nationalists), the abuses of paramilitary groups (a unionist focus with difficult international law basis), or find areas such as old persons' rights where Catholic–Protestant consensus is fairly easy?[156]

Human rights institutions are not only aimed at the future, they are produced as a product of past experience of human rights abuses. As regards institutional design they have some characteristic problems, as the different case-studies demonstrate. First, institutions tend to be defined around strategic negotiation issues as shaped by past experience, rather than the most coherent institutional design. Often not very far into implementation, reworking or amalgamating the human rights institutions is called for.[157] Secondly, human rights institutions usually take second place to

---

[153] A possible exception is the Principles Relating to the Status of National Institutions 1992. These principles provide that selection procedures shall 'afford all necessary guarantees to ensure the pluralist representation of the social forces (of civilian society) in the promotion and protection of human rights . . .' (although this seems to relate to balance of professional and human rights background rather than of ethnicity).

[154] See e.g. UN General Assembly Declaration on the Rights of Persons Belonging to National or Ethnic, Religious, and Linguistic Minorities, 18 Dec. 1992, GA Res 47/135, UN doc. A/Res/47/135 (1992), (1993) 32 I.L.M. 911; and Council of Europe's Framework Convention on the Rights of National Minorities, 1 Feb. 1995, ETS No. 148.

[155] See *City Council of Pretoria* v. *Walker* 1998 (2) SA 363 (CC); 1998 (3) BCLR 257 (CC) (where this was held not to be *unfair* discrimination in violation of Article 8(2) Interim Constitution).

[156] Of course, these approaches are not mutually exclusive; to see how the Northern Ireland Human Rights Commission has begun to prioritize, see Northern Ireland Human Rights Commission (1999).

[157] See Pityana (1996) (South Africa); European Commission for Democracy through Law (Venice Commission) (1999) (Bosnia).

governmental arrangements in terms of negotiators' priorities. They can end up almost hastily tacked on to an agreement without the institutional detail which would make them effective. This can be because this detail was ignored, or because it was explicitly postponed to a later stage of the process. This can produce institutions with serious gaps which leave them largely rhetorical and symbolic, rather than capable of effecting real change. Sometimes these gaps are deliberate and strategic, such as with the creation of a weak IPTF in the DPA. However, often it seems to be a by-product of negotiations which focus on bringing party-political elites together with negotiators who are themselves diplomats, with neither group particularly concerned about, or expert in, the mechanisms required to ensure that human rights commitments are deliverable and delivered.

A quick glance at the human rights provision in the four case-studies would suggest (rather superficially) that the more internal a deal, the greater its human rights sophistication; and the more international, the less human-rights-friendly it is. If the human rights measures in the deal were quickly ranked according to detail and capacity to deliver change, the ranking would be South Africa, Northern Ireland, Bosnia Herzegovina, Israel/Palestine. This apparent inverse relationship between international involvement and effective human rights provision in peace agreements has its explanation in the pressures producing a deal. Where there is a 'mutually perceived hurting stalemate' then the parties will craft ways to redefine their positions in terms of shared interests, and the language of human rights may help them to do this. The more the international community is driving the deal, the more the negotiation process is merely another forum for waging the old conflict, and the very process of 'winning the war' typically involves violating rights rather than protecting them.

However, the inverse relationship also has its explanation in the more mundane but related question of who was at the negotiations. Internally mediated processes tend to have mechanisms for including civil society, while internationally mediated processes working out of traditional international relations and violence-focused paradigms do not. Internally driven processes by their nature must preserve the link between politicians and their constituents. Internationally facilitated processes often focus on bringing together those who have directly waged the war, often in secret and isolated locations, while the skills of those who have waged peace through churches, voluntary associations, women's groups, and trade unions are left at home. This can mean that key experience and expertise in how to fashion workable mechanisms for achieving social goals is missing.

Finally, and most controversially, negotiated human rights protections can be particularly vulnerable to attack from the very peace process which created them. Where an agreement is at least partially successful in creating a 'new dispensation', emerging areas of political consensus in turn can begin to undercut human rights commitments. In South Africa the rising crime rate and the difficulty of addressing socio-economic factors has led to pressure coming from both black and white communities and also from the flight of international capital, to begin to scale back human rights commitments, such as the Bill of Rights and South Africa's pro-union labour law. In Northern Ireland a dramatic example also occurred less than six months after the signing of the Belfast Agreement. A devastating bomb in Omagh, Northern Ireland killing 29 people, brought a consensus between Irish and British governments on implementing what the Irish government boasted of as 'draconian measures' in what could amount to a form of administrative detention, albeit a form which operated so as to use (and therefore taint) the courts.[158] Ironically, this legislation, which almost certainly violates the European Convention on Human Rights, politically could not have been passed North or South prior to the adoption of the Belfast Agreement, with all its human rights language.

[158] Criminal Justice (Terrorism and Conspiracy) Act 1998. See further Campbell (1999).

8

Undoing the Past: Refugees, Land, and Possession

In one sense, all the human rights aspects of a peace agreement attempt to deal with the past. To cut a deal on self-determination and minority rights is to attempt to address the reality of conflict and provide a basis for future cooperation and even reconciliation. To design institutions to protect civil and political rights is to acknowledge the connection between past abuses of human rights and conflict, and to attempt to prevent this cycle in the future. Although negotiated with a backward glance to past violence, these components of peace agreements are, however, essentially forward-looking. They aim to deal with future events.

In each situation there is a question which is inherently backward-looking. Broadly put, it is the question of how to deal with the legacy of the conflict. There are two types of past-focused issues which typically need to be dealt with. The first is the extent to which aspects of the past can be undone. Can and should population shifts and changes in land ownership occurring as a result of the conflict be reversed? The second issue is that of 'transitional justice'—can and should individuals be made accountable either for the worst abuses of the conflict, or for the conflict itself? Although the two issues are connected, the first will be addressed in this chapter, the second in the next chapter.

This chapter begins by setting out the international legal framework relevant to 'undoing the past', a framework which is partial and at times unhelpful to peace process dilemmas. The provisions in the four sets of peace agreements addressed at undoing the past are then examined.

INTERNATIONAL LAW FOR UNDOING THE PAST: REFUGEES, LAND, AND POSSESSION

International law provides only piecemeal provision relating to the issues which arise when negotiators consider how, or whether, to undo the past. That provision was not designed with the context of ethno-political conflict particularly in mind, and therefore largely leaves difficult post-conflict questions without answers or much guidance at all.

These questions include: Do displaced persons have a right to return to their home country? Do they have a right to return to their specific localities and homes? Do local and/or international authorities have positive obligations to ensure the conditions which are necessary to this return?

How extensive are these? If conditions are unsafe, do displaced persons have a right *not* to return? What are the property rights to land and houses which refugees and displaced persons abandoned in flight from the conflict? What is to happen to the property rights of those people (usually from the 'other side') who have come to occupy the property during the conflict, often under sanction of law? When is there a right of compensation in lieu of return, and for land lost?

There is also another set of possible questions which can impact on considerations of return and resettlement, or operate independently of them. These are questions revolving around the notion of 'sharing' of public and private space between divided groups. Given that, without a proactive approach, ethno-political communities will tend towards remaining spatially separated, are there any rights to pluralism which can require policies towards this end? Or, put another way, can those who do not wish to live in a divided society assert rights to 'sharing'?

International law provides very little in the way of individual land rights and next to nothing about 'sharing', and these two can be dealt with quickly.

Land Rights

As regards land, Article 17 of the Universal Declaration of Human Rights provides for a right to own private property and not to be arbitrarily deprived of that property.[1] However, neither the International Covenant on Civil and Political Rights 1966 (ICCPR) nor that on Economic, Social, and Cultural Rights 1966 (ICESCR) provide such a right.[2] The ICESCR does, however, provide for a limited right to adequate housing, although this is clearly not a property right.[3] The property rights provisions do not address the practical problems which accompany conflict, such as how to balance the property rights of those who have fled, against those who occupy the properties at the time of the peace process, sometimes having been displaced from their own land; sometimes having owned them for many years; and sometimes a line of owners removed from the original dispossession. Such protection as exists is against 'arbitrary' deprivation.

---

[1] Article 17, Universal Declaration of Human Rights 1948 (UDHR).

[2] Regional conventions do provide property rights. A right to own property is provided by Article XXIII American Declaration of the Rights and Duties of Man 1948. A right to use and enjoyment of private property and not to be arbitrarily deprived of that property, and a right to be paid compensation when appropriately deprived, are provided for by Article 21 American Convention on Human Rights 1969. A right to property and to protection from arbitrary deprivation is also provided by Article 14 African Charter on Human and Peoples' Rights 1981. Other specialist international human rights conventions have provisions relating to how the right of property is to be held and accessed. For a detailed overview of international legal provision, see Rodríquez (1993).

[3] Article 11 International Covenant on Economic, Social, and Cultural Rights 1966.

Thus compensation in lieu of property, or an adjudication procedure which balances rights but does not return land in all cases, probably suffices to satisfy the right. These limited land rights clearly do not contemplate or address the problems which mass movements and dispossession create, and thus do not provide much guidance on the parameters of regimes designed to address these problems.

Rights to Sharing

As regards 'sharing' or a right to togetherness, while there are some hints of the need for sharing in provision for education, for the most part human rights law does not provide explicitly for such a right.[4] Indeed the Framework Convention for the Protection of National Minorities 1995 provides programmatic rights aimed at accommodating national minorities rather than assimilating them, and these rights tend to underwrite the provision of separate institutions in areas such as education and culture.

Rights of Refugees and Displaced Persons

International law does address the right of refugees and displaced persons to return, through several different branches. However, it is worth noting at the outset that both international law and debate in this area have been more concerned with the right of refugees *not* to return to their country of origin than with their right to return.

The Right to Return

Human rights conventions provide for a right for those who have had to leave their country to return; they also provide for freedom of movement within a country which could provide some support for internally displaced persons who wish to return to pre-conflict home areas.[5] The ICCPR, for example, provides in Article 12(4) that 'No one shall be

---

[4] There is the barest hint of such a right in some education provisions. Several covenants stress that parents should be able to choose schools which are in accordance with their own religious and moral convictions, which presumably could include preference for 'integrated' or 'multi-ethnic–religious' education; see e.g. Article 13(3) and (4) ICESCR; Article 2 UNESCO Convention against Discrimination in Education 1960 (UNESCO-CADE) ('The establishment or maintenance . . . of separate educational systems or institutions offering an education which is in keeping with the wishes of the pupil's parents or legal guardians' is not discrimination 'if participation in such systems or attendance at such institutions *is optional. . .*' (emphasis added). Cf. *Brown* v. *Board of Education* 347 US 483 (1954) (which suggested that education in its fullest sense could only take place in a racially integrated context, at least where separation stigmatized one racial group of students (in that case African Americans)).

[5] See e.g. Articles 9 and 13 UDHR; Article 5 Convention on the Elimination of All Forms of Racial Discrimination 1965; Article 12 ICCPR.

arbitrarily deprived of the right to enter his own country.' A right to return also finds some basis in nationality law, and humanitarian law.[6] As with international land rights, these rights are individually framed and do not address the problems presented by mass movements. However, there is little to suggest that such rights are inapplicable in the context of a mass movement, as some have argued.[7] A right to compensation seems to exist as an alternative to return, not by virtue of any special provision, but as a necessary alternative remedy for violation of the right, as a matter of customary law. The fact that the ICCPR provides a right only against 'arbitrary' deprivation of the right, for example, indicates that compensation may in certain circumstances be an acceptable alternative to return. As no specific convention provision exists, there is no framework to govern exactly when and how compensation should take place.[8] A right to compensation for refugees, in conjunction with a right to return, has been repeatedly affirmed in the Palestinian context.[9] However, in this context, compensation is not contemplated as a remedy which can be imposed in lieu of return being permitted, but a remedy which is to pertain in the event of the refugee exercising his or her 'free choice' not to return.

As a practical matter, those fleeing war and persecution will not feel able to return home until they are convinced that the situation giving rise to their flight has changed. The human rights provisions relating to return merely state a right to enter a country or not to be excluded. They do not place explicit obligations to ensure that conditions enable return. Neither

---

[6] International nationality law provides an obligation that a state must admit its own nationals (rather than a right for individuals to be admitted); this may be difficult to assert when the state sovereignty changes. International humanitarian law arguably also talks of 'repatriation', seemingly underwriting a right of return. The conventions cannot be denounced until repatriation, (among other things) has occurred (see Article 63 Geneva Convention for the Amelioration of the Condition of the Wounded and Sick in the Armed Forces in the Field 1949 (Geneva I); Article 62 Geneva Convention for the Amelioration of the Condition of Wounded, Sick, and Shipwrecked Members of Armed Forces at Sea (Geneva II); Article 142 Geneva Convention Relative to the Treatment of Prisoners of War 1949 (Geneva III); Article 158 Geneva Convention Relative to the Protection of Civilian Persons in Time of War 1949 (Geneva IV). Repatriation is also mentioned in Article 5 Geneva I; Article 6 Geneva II; Articles 5, 108–19 Geneva III; and Articles 6, 36, and 134 Geneva IV. For fuller discussion of the right of return and mass movements, and the international legal basis of the right to return, see Quigley (1997: 67–72).

[7] This argument focuses on Article 12(4) of the ICCPR, which states that '[n]o-one shall be *arbitrarily* deprived of the right to enter his own country' (emphasis added). Several writers have argued that para. 4 is structured as an individual and not a collective or group right and therefore gives no right of return to members of displaced groups. For discussion and rebuttal of this view, see Quigley (1997: 75–82); Takkenberg (1998: 235–9).

[8] The International Law Association developed guidelines to govern provision of compensation to refugees; see Declaration of Principles of International Law on Compensation to Refugees, approved by consensus by the International Law Association (ILA) at its 65th Conference in Cairo, Apr. 1992 (text in International Law Association, *Report of the Sixty-Fifth Conference: Cairo* (1992)).   [9] See UN GA Res 194 (III), 11 Dec. 1948.

do they provide an explicit right to return to specific home localities. Other human rights protections such as rights to non-discrimination and equality and freedom of movement could of course help to bring about favourable conditions for return to specific localities, and assist those who have returned to stay, if robustly implemented.

The Convention Relating to the Status of Refugees, 1951 (Refugee Convention), and the Protocol Relating to the Status of Refugees, 1967, which provide the core international legal regime for refugees, do not provide a right to return as such. The context of the Refugee Convention as both a product and a tool of cold war politics meant that resettlement rather than return was contemplated as the norm.[10]

The Right Not to Return

The Refugee Convention provides protections for refugees in the host country, and for a right *not* to return to the conditions which gave rise to the flight. This is imposed as an obligation on contracting states, rather than operating as an individual right belonging to the refugee. For enforcement the refugee must rely on the power of the judiciary in each jurisdiction to interpret the Convention, and there is no international enforcement mechanism. It does not, therefore, have the same juridical nature as rights found in human rights conventions.

Article 33(1) of the Refugee Convention provides that

No Contracting State shall expel or return (*refouler*) a refugee in any manner whatsoever to the frontiers of territories where his life or freedom would be threatened on account of his race, religion, nationality, membership of a particular social group or political opinion.

However, protection against refoulement only applies to those who satisfy the convention's limited definition of 'refugee' which excludes many within the mass population movements caused by modern ethnic conflict. The Refugee Convention and the 1967 Protocol define refugees as people who have fled across an international boundary as a result of a well-founded fear of persecution for reasons of race, religion, nationality, membership of a particular social group, or political opinion.[11] Those who have committed some serious crime are not included.[12]

This definition deals with individuals. Those who do not classify as formal refugees under the Convention and Protocol are generally referred to

[10] See generally, Hathaway (1991: 1–27).

[11] Article 1, Convention Relating to the Status of Refugees 1951; Article 1, Protocol Relating to the Status of Refugees 1967 (extending the application of the definition to refugees from new conflicts).

[12] Article 1(F) (disapplying the convention to any persons who may have committed serious crimes); Article 33(2) (removing the non-refoulement protection from persons who are dangerous or who have committed serious crimes) Convention Relating to the Status of Refugees 1951.

as non-status refugees or displaced persons (for example, where they cannot satisfy the 'well founded fear of persecution' on specific grounds test) and internally displaced persons (for example, where they have fled 'internally' rather than across an international border). The convention's narrow refugee definition has been redressed by regional conventions and other state practice, but as yet the argument that there is an expanded concept of the 'refugee' in customary international law remains controversial.[13]

Those fleeing ethnic conflict often do not satisfy the convention's definition of refugee and therefore do not fall within its protection against non-refoulement.[14] In such conflicts mass movements of people flee both internally and across international borders, and indeed the very question of which borders are international and which are not may itself be at the heart of the conflict.[15] People flee both as a result of attack and also in anticipation of attack, raising factual problems as to whether they had a well-founded fear of persecution on the relevant grounds.[16] In practice, the scale of mass movements has reinvigorated a notion of 'temporary protection' which in effect bypasses the technical application of 1951 Convention (even when some of those fleeing could avail of it). For example, the huge number of refugees from former Yugoslavia led the United Nations High Commissioner for Refugees (UNHCR) in 1992 to request governments to give 'temporary protection' to persons in flight, rather than wait to process applications for asylum individually.[17] Although this was designed to speed up entry and bypass the limits of the convention definition, the concept of temporary protection raises the question of how long temporary should be and what the concept of non-refoulement means in practice.[18]

Protection against non-refoulement has also proved difficult because even when the Refugee Convention and 1967 Protocol refugee definition is satisfied, the right to non-refoulement arguably persists only as long as the conditions in the country of origin do not improve and the reasons for fleeing continue to evidence an ongoing need for protection.[19] There is no formal right of resettlement in the country of refuge, no formal right of

[13] See generally Hathaway (1991: 11–27). See also Goodwin-Gill (1996: 1–32); but cf. Hailbronner (1986: 867–73).

[14] Although it has also been argued that the right to non-refoulement constitutes a norm of customary law; Goodwin-Gill (1996: 167–8).

[15] NB: Article 73, Protocol I to the Geneva Conventions of 1949, applying to international armed conflict and conflicts of national liberation, extends the protections of Parts I and III of the Geneva IV to refugees and stateless persons 'under the relevant international instruments accepted by the Parties concerned or under the national legislation of the State of refuge or State of residence.'   [16] See e.g. Gilbert (1993: 417).

[17] Conclusion No. 22 (XXXII) Executive Committee of the UNHCR, 'Protection of Asylum Seekers in Situations of Large-Scale Influx'. See further Bagshaw (1997).

[18] Cf. Bagshaw (1997).

[19] Under Article 1(C)(5) Convention Relating to the Status of Refugees 1951 (Refugee Convention), the definition of refugee ceases to apply if 'the circumstances in connection

resettlement elsewhere, and no formal right not to be returned to the state of origin once the situation permits. In practice the 1990s have seen renewed debate about the temporary nature of protection, the extent of protection from non-refoulement, and the permissibility of mandatory return under the Refugee Convention. A concept of 'safe return' has come to replace the notion of voluntary return long promoted by the UNHCR.[20] As Goodwin-Gill notes, 'safe return' has been posited as in effect 'an interim position' between voluntary return and de facto expulsion.[21] Under this concept return can be imposed once the conditions in the home country are 'safe'. This approach can be justified as being in conformance with the non-refoulement requirements of the Refugee Convention, which, as noted above, on a literal interpretation contemplate the definition of refugee as attaching only as long as the conditions which bring the person within the convention's definition of refugee apply.[22] Under this interpretation once conditions permit return, a person is no longer a 'refugee' and therefore not under the convention's protection from refoulement. Such an interpretation does not stand unchallenged.[23]

The development of a concept of 'safe return' evidences pressures to repatriate which in practice can lead to involuntary or forced repatriation in violation of non-refoulement. As the UNHCR notes, 'it is quite clear that a large proportion of the world's recent returnees have been repatriated under some form of duress. . . . such duress has in many instances been deliberate, exercised by host governments, host communities and other actors with the specific intention of forcing refugees to go back to their homeland.'[24] Chimni notes that in practice a doctrine of involuntary repatriation is emerging which is presented as a necessary evil in the case of 'unavoidable exceptions' to the standard of voluntary repatriation.

It is worth noting that human rights law also provides what is in essence a right not to return through, in particular, its torture jurisprudence.[25] Article 3 of the European Convention on Human Rights (ECHR) prohibiting torture and inhuman and degrading treatment has been found to include protection against being returned to a place where such treatment would follow.[26] Similarly, Articles 2 and 3 of the Convention

---

with which he has been recognised as a refugee have ceased to exist' (unless classified under previous conventions and arrangements, and still able to 'invoke compelling reasons arising out of previous persecution for refusing to avail himself of the protection of the country of his nationality').

[20] See e.g. Coles (1988); see also United Nations High Commissioner for Refugees (1996c) for an examination of the principles of voluntary return.

[21] Goodwin-Gill (1996: 275–6).   [22] Hathaway (1991, 1997).   [23] See Chimni (1999).

[24] See United Nations High Commissioner for Refugees (1997: 147–8).

[25] See generally Lambert (1999); Gorlick (1999).

[26] See e.g. *Chahal* v. *United Kingdom*, 15 Nov. 1996, Reports of Judg. and Dec. (1996-V) No. 22, para. 80. See generally Lambert (1999).

against Torture 1984 and Article 7 of the ICCPR provide similar protection. Unlike the Refugee Convention, this protection applies regardless of whether the refugee has committed a serious crime. However, again these provisions may be logistically difficult for individuals to avail themselves of *en masse* and may do little to help individuals after a peace process, when future country of origin conditions are largely unknown and unknowable.

Clearly, in practice, pressures for return to still-dangerous home countries can trump protections against return for those who formally classify as refugees. Those who do not so classify are even more vulnerable. In the case of internally displaced persons, the difficulties with even a practical working definition of internal displacement[27] form a precursor to the difficulties of deciding when a person ceases to be internally displaced. Is it when they return to their actual home, or when they enjoy sufficient protection of the state wherever they may be within its borders? While pressure for return usually springs from receiving states, this pressure will be all the greater if return is vital to implementing an internationally negotiated peace agreement, as in Bosnia Herzegovina.

Increasing Emphasis on Home Country Conditions

The pressure for mere temporary protection as a response to modern-day conflict has forced a greater engagement with the conditions awaiting the returnee in his or her home locality.[28] As the UNHCR has noted, the return of displaced persons to their place of origin creates needs for physical, social, psychological, legal, and material security. The UNHCR itself has seen its own role evolve so as to address the political, social, economic, and legal cultures of countries of origin in response to the mass movements of the 1990s.[29] This has been in response to a combination of factors, including the scale of the mass movements; the reality that return is regularly (often under duress) to unstable or unresolved political situations; the reality that the needs of returning refugees and other categories of displaced persons are mostly the same, even if their legal entitlements and the incentives of host country donors to support return financially are not; and the reality that government bodies and development organizations by and large are unwilling or unable to cater for the broader rehabilitation needs of returnee-populated areas.

---

[27] See e.g. United Nations High Commissioner for Refugees (1997: 99–104). See also Deng (1993).

[28] As Gilbert argues, the logic of this engagement is of course that international intervention should aim at the 'root causes' of such flows, aiming to prevent them (1993).

[29] See United Nations High Commissioner for Refugees (1997: 164–9).

Palestinian Refugees

The unique international legal status of Palestinian refugees deserves a special mention at this point. While Palestinians displaced by the 1948 wars potentially fit within the Refugee Convention's refugee definition, an exception to that definition is provided which, although framed in general terms, was drafted 'specifically and exclusively with the Palestinian refugees in mind.'[30] Article 1D of the 1951 Convention excludes from protection those who are receiving protection or assistance 'from other organs or agencies of the United Nations other than the [UNHCR]'.[31] This was an implicit exclusion of Palestinian refugees, who were being assisted by the United Nations Relief and Works Agency (UNRWA) established by the General Assembly.[32] Takkenberg suggests that Palestinian refugees are probably best thought of as 'an additional category of so-called "statutory refugees" '.[33] In 1948 the General Assembly considered the displacement issue in a comprehensive resolution on the conflict. Paragraph 11 of UN GA Res 194 provided that Palestinians 'wishing to return to their homes and live at peace with their neighbours should be permitted to do so at the earliest practicable date.'[34] Compensation was also called for, but not it seems as an alternative to return. The right to return was reaffirmed in 1967 in Security Council Resolution 237 (1967), and this was also endorsed by the General Assembly.[35] Since that time a right to return has continued to be endorsed.[36] However, since 1970 the UN emphasis on the right of the organized Palestinian people to establish a territorial entity has led to assertions that the right of return is part and parcel of such a collective right, rather than a right of individual Palestinians, and therefore cannot be redressed as an individual right, although this is disputed.[37] Other legal issues also impinge on the right to return of Palestinians, such as the family reunification issues and the laws of nationality.[38]

[30] Takkenberg (1998: 86–130) (Takkenberg notes that the intention of drafters was not to exclude Palestinians from refugee status and protection but to *suspend* the application of the 1951 Convention and the involvement of UNHCR in respect of those refugees being assisted by UNRWA).
[31] Similar provisions were inserted in paragraph 7(c) Statute of the Office of the UNHCR 1950 and Article 2(I) of the Convention Relating to the Status of Stateless Persons 1954.
[32] UN GA Res 302(IV), 8 Dec. 1949.   [33] Takkenberg (1998: 348).
[34] UN GA Res 194 (III), 14 Dec. 1948, para. 11. This resolution also established a three-member commission which took up the displacement question as one of its first orders of business. See further Quigley (1997: 182–93).
[35] UN SC Res 247 (1967); UN GA Res 2452A (1969).
[36] See e.g. UN GA Res 51/124 of 1996.
[37] See Quigley (1997: 75–82; 1998: 211–12); Takkenberg (1998: 235–9).
[38] See generally Quigley (1997, 1998).

Summary

In summary while human rights instruments clearly establish a right to return, they are silent on the need for positive state action to facilitate return, and do not formally establish a right to return to a specific locality. Compensation may in certain (unspecified) circumstances be paid as an alternative remedy.

As regards the right *not* to return, international law concerning refugees provides protection against refoulement (return to a situation of persecution) for those who formally classify as refugees, but leaves ambiguous who is to define when those conditions pertain, thereby leaving protection precarious. International refugee law provides no formal protection against involuntary return for those who do not formally classify as refugees. This has particular consequences for those who flee *en masse* as a result of ethnic conflict, who often do not fit the individualistic/cross-border definition of 'refugee'. However, human rights law provides some protection against return for those who would be at threat of torture or inhuman and degrading treatment in their home country.

While international refugee law offers little formal protection against enforced return to difficult post-conflict situations to those who flee ethno-political conflict, this has had the dubious benefit of forcing increased international focus on how to change the conditions in the home country. In practice the UNHCR attempts to address such conditions in an increasingly holistic way, although as the case of Bosnia Herzegovina indicates, this is not always successful. Moreover, human rights protections provide objective standards against which to judge the concept of 'safe', providing a possible principled grounding to the notion of 'safe return' at least in theory.

PEACE AGREEMENTS

International law operates at a high level of generality with respect to the right of return and the redistribution of land. Provision for 'sharing' is virtually non-existent. The refugee regime suffers from the limitations summarized above. In contrast, the peace agreements provide specific legal regimes for many of these issues which are aimed at undoing aspects of the past conflict. The conflicts in South Africa, Israel/Palestine, and Bosnia Herzegovina all produced substantial numbers of refugees and displaced persons, and enduring land rights claims, some of which were addressed in their peace agreements and some of which were not. The conflict in Northern Ireland did not produce these issues in the same way, for reasons that will be briefly explained.

South Africa

The conflict in South Africa, in particular the homelands policy, saw thousands of people deprived of land and/or internally displaced, as outlined in Chapter 3. The issue of those exiled during the conflict was partially addressed in the pre-negotiation stages of the peace process as a matter necessary to enabling talks.[39] The UNHCR facilitated the signing of an agreement for the repatriation of 'any South African refugee and/or political exile who returns voluntarily to South Africa as an unarmed civilian.'[40]

During the negotiations process itself, political violence also saw people displaced from their homes, and the ongoing negotiation process tried to address this. The National Peace Accord made provision for return of those displaced by ongoing violence.[41] The Interim Constitution also attempted to deal with the historical legacy of land dispossession more broadly.

Restitution of Land Rights

The Interim Constitution provided a framework for addressing land rights, which it specified was to be implemented through an Act of Parliament.[42] The framework contemplated a cut-off date for claims being set (subsequently nominated as 19 June 1913, this being the date of the dispossession of black South Africans through the Land Act of 1913).[43] Criteria for the type of dispossession to be remedied were set out. These included any dispossession 'effected under or for the purpose of furthering the object of a law which would have been inconsistent with the prohibition of racial discrimination'.[44] This form of wording was designed to cover apartheid legislation in all its forms.

The Interim Constitution framework provided for restoration of land to a claimant whether that land was publicly or privately owned.[45] The claims of current owner and claimant were to be balanced according to whether it was 'just and equitable' to return the land. This balancing act between owner and claimant was to take into account matters such as 'the history of the dispossession, the hardship caused, the use to which the

---

[39] See Ch. 3, p. 47.

[40] Memorandum of Understanding on the Voluntary Repatriation and Reintegration of South African Returnees, 4 Sept. 1991, South Africa—UNHCR; pub. in (1992) 31 I.L.M. 526 (in his introductory note Dugard estimates the number of potential returnees at 30,000).

[41] Chapter 5 National Peace Accord 1991 (which addresses reintegration of displaced persons).

[42] Section 121 Constitution of the Republic of South Africa 200 of 1993 (hereafter Interim Constitution).

[43] See 2(3) Restitution of Land Rights Act 22 of 1994; Cf. Article 25(7) The Constitution of the Republic of South Africa Act 108 of 1996 (hereafter Final Constitution).

[44] Section 121(2)(b) Interim Constitution.   [45] Section 123 Interim Constitution.

property is being put, the history of its acquisition by the owner, the interests of the owner and others affected by any expropriation, and the interests of the dispossessed.'[46] Where restoration of the land was not possible, then alternative state land could be made available to the claimant if possible, or compensation or other relief given, providing for a less zero sum set of interests.[47] The Interim Constitution established a Commission on Restitution of Land Rights to investigate the merits of claims, mediate, draw up reports on unsettled claims, and take on any other powers or functions as added by the Act.[48]

In addition to the land rights provisions, the Interim Constitution Bill of Rights contained a property rights clause, which had proved one of the most difficult to negotiate.[49] This clause provided a right 'to acquire and hold rights to property' (rather than a right to property as such). The property clause contained a similar balancing exercise for cases of expropriation. Expropriation of land could only take place as provided for by law where necessary for public purposes, and was subject to payment of compensation which if not otherwise agreed was to take into account factors such as the use of the property, the history of its acquisition, its market value, the value of the investments in it by those affected, and the interest of those affected.[50]

It is important to note that the roots of the negotiation on land rights were in the bill of rights debate, and in particular African National Congress (ANC)/National Party, South African government (NP/SAG) differences over its property and economic clauses. As noted in Chapter 7, the Bill of Rights was a document negotiated among parties with opposing visions of the role and nature of a bill of rights.[51] The differences between the ANC and SAG approaches and their underlying politics came into relief with respect to the property and economic clauses as evidenced by earlier bill of rights drafts by the ANC and the Law Commission. As Chanock notes, the Law Commission drafts contained the lineaments of a bargain: '[w]hites would recognize black political rights, if blacks recognized white property rights.'[52] ANC versions rejected this trade-off, putting forward extensive social, economic, and

---

[46] Section 123(2) Interim Constitution.   [47] Section 123(3) Interim Constitution.
[48] Section 122 Interim Constitution.   [49] Section 28 Interim Constitution.
[50] Ibid. The Final Constitution does not contain the same detailed provision for land restitution, as this is provided by the intervening Restitution of Land Rights Act 22 of 1994. However, in this Constitution the final Bill of Rights property clause is reformulated. There is no stated right to property or to 'rights in property'. Instead protections against arbitrary deprivation of property are given; these protections allow for expropriation for a public purpose or when in a public interest. 'Public interest' is specifically defined as including 'the nation's commitment to land reform, and to reforms to bring about equitable access to all South Africa's natural resources'; Section 25 Final Constitution.
[51] African National Congress (1991); South African Law Commission (1989, 1991).
[52] Chanock (1999: 410).

educational rights together with a direction that the state use its resources to achieve these rights. ANC versions also worked to reverse the 'great dispossession' of land through the creation of a tribunal to adjudicate on land claims with the power to order restoration of land with no priority to existing rights and no tangible principle of compensation. These differences were at the heart of whether the Bill of Rights was to provide merely a new avenue of judicial review (NP/SAG) or underwrite a fundamentally new set of political priorities (ANC and others).

The resultant Interim Constitution Bill of Rights and land rights provisions constituted a largely symbolic compromise between these different visions. The compromise was largely symbolic because substance had largely been addressed elsewhere in the Constitution. As Chanock notes, the 'property' held by the NP's main constituency was in jobs in the public service and in pension rights, both of which were protected in other parts of the Interim Constitution. As regards the ANC, while reversal of the 'great dispossession was an important goal, the main economic interest of the ANC's constituency centred around housing, employment and education and reconstruction more generally, rather than peasant farming.' Thus Chanock argues, 'once the debates about a Bill of Rights were connected to the world of politics and economics, some of the differences seemed less irreconcilable.'[53] However, it can also be argued that the differences were not fully resolved and continue to play out in ANC government attempts to deliver socio-economic benefits to a large number of impoverished people without alienating the vested minority interests which are important to the country's economic base.

Northern Ireland

While people were displaced during the Northern Ireland conflict as a result of violence, and this has left ongoing hurt and grievances, it has not left a legacy of enduring and conflicting land claims or a lingering refugee population as with the other conflicts.

While historically colonial dispossession and use of land was a key factor in conflict between Ireland and Britain, land use and dispossession was not a key issue in the current phase of the conflict, although allocation of public resources, including housing and jobs, was. Neither did the conflict produce a mass refugee problem. Any displacement of persons tended to be fairly isolated and numerically small; people who did relocate tended to stay within the Republic of Ireland or United Kingdom.

---

[53] Chanock (1999: 422–3) (footnotes omitted). In implementation to date Carey Miller (1999) notes that the most striking aspect of land reform has been, not reversal dispossession in the sense of changing ownership of land, but the enhancement of various forms of possessory right at the expense of ownership.

Displacement occurred as a result of violence rather than state appropriation or population transfer; even this displacement was not on the scale of the other case-studies. Where displacement was from public (state-owned) housing, people were often rehoused. Where displacement was from private housing, compensation was often paid by the state at the time. Since the Belfast Agreement a small number of people who would wish to live in the jurisdiction remain outside it, either because they have been threatened by paramilitary groups and this threat is outstanding, or because they are wanted by British authorities with relation to activities during the troubles.[54]

Neither refugee nor land rights issues have therefore been at the forefront of the peace process, although some issues have been raised. For example, families of Protestant members of the security forces killed by the Provisional IRA in some rural border areas left family homes and farmland. While ownership of the land is retained, the land is let, meaning that certain improvements grants could not be availed of, leading to claims of unfairness.[55] In the nationalist–republican area of Crossmaglen, South Armagh, the British army continues to occupy Gaelic Athletics Association lands with military installations and equipment, the land claim adding to pressure to remove this army base. This has recently begun to be addressed through British government commitments to removal of army bases as 'demilitarization'. The only other peace-process-related piece of land reform has been the extension of the Fair Employment Act 1989, which outlaws discrimination based on religion or political belief, to goods and services and therefore to the sale of land. This effectively outlaws a traditional practice of selling only to those in the same communal group, even to the detriment of price.[56]

While conflict-related population shifts have not left many lingering land claims, they have created an increasingly spatially divided society. This has raised claims for a right to communal sharing or 'integration' in areas such as education, housing, and workplaces. Although not addressed in the text of the agreement, the issue of sharing came to be addressed in the Northern Ireland Act 1998, which implements much of the agreement.[57] In addition to mainstreaming equality considerations in public decision-making, the Northern Ireland Act 1998 imposes a duty on public authorities to pay regard to 'good relations between persons of dif-

---

[54] The provisions on early prisoner release do not cover the case of those not yet convicted.

[55] See generally Bloomfield (1998: 38–9).

[56] Section 29 Fair Employment (Northern Ireland) Order 1998.

[57] Although not directly mentioned in the Belfast Agreement, the government had suggested some form of 'community relations' duty in an earlier White Paper which was referenced in the Belfast Agreement. See *Partnership for Equality, The Government's proposals for future legislation and policies on Employment Equality in Northern Ireland Presented to Parliament by the Secretary of State for Northern Ireland by Command of Her Majesty, March 1998*, Cm. 3890.

ferent religious belief, political opinion or racial group.'[58] In implementation this could begin to move public bodies towards considering whether their decisions would be likely to separate further or to bring together the divided communities, and provides an embryonic example of how sharing could be legislated for.[59] The potential conflict between 'integration' and equality is dealt with by prioritizing equality.[60]

Israel/Palestine

Refugees

The refugee dimension of the Israeli/Palestinian conflict is complex.[61] The complexities include:

1. that Palestinian refugee populations exist in many different countries and are treated differently by different countries.
2. that different populations of refugees and displaced persons were created at different points in the conflict (most notably in 1948 and 1967).
3. that the self-determination claim and the refugee issue have been increasingly intertwined.
4. that international law, as we have seen, has treated Palestinian refugees as a distinct category for the purposes of legal regulation.
5. that while for many years the issue of *non-refoulement* has been the focus of international law, Palestinian refugees have sought to assert a right to return, and this right was emphasized by the General Assembly.

These complexities affect the negotiation process in the following ways. There are multiple possible players who must be involved in any attempt to negotiate the issue. There are many host countries and similarly groups of refugees with very different contexts; neither parties can easily be represented in a unitary way. The overlap with self-determination issues means that progress on return is related to resolution of that issue: the question of refugees is difficult to agree outside an overall negotiated package. These factors form a backdrop to understanding the treatment (and non-treatment) of the issue in the peace agreements, and ongoing attempts to address the issue outside them. In short, agreements establish different negotiating forums but do not substantively deal with the issue,

---

[58] Section 75(2) Northern Ireland Act 1998.
[59] Boal *et al.* (1996); Craig and Hadden (2000).
[60] See section 75(2) Northern Ireland Act 1998. The potential for conflict had made the insertion of the 'sharing' provisions somewhat controversial. There was a fear among many human rights promoters that they would be used to trump hard-won equality protections, either in law or in practice, by virtue of civil service minimalism, based on the alleged difficulty of implementing the dual burden.
[61] For overviews, see e.g., Morris (1987); Nur (1992).

although they do suggest that 1948 refugees and 1967 displaced persons will be dealt with differently.[62]

Bilateral and Quadrilateral Negotiating Processes

The Declaration of Principles (DoP) ostensibly postponed the issue of refugees until final status negotiations.[63] However, the issue of persons displaced in 1967 did receive attention in the DoP. Annex I notes that the future status of displaced Palestinians who were registered for election purposes on 4 June 1967 'will not be prejudiced because they are unable to participate in the election process due to practical reasons.'[64] Article XII of the DoP also provides that a Continuing Committee comprising representatives of the governments of Israel, Jordan, Egypt, and Palestinians shall 'decide by agreement on the modalities of admission of persons displaced from the West Bank and the Gaza strip in 1967, together with necessary measures to prevent disruption and disorder.' This commitment is repeated in both the Cairo and the Interim Agreements. The reference to 'modalities of admission' for post-1967 displaced persons seems to further accept implicitly that they have a right to return, although this disguises deep disagreement over who should be regarded as displaced. The reference does not address the 1948 refugees. This Continuing (or Quadripartite) Committee first met in May 1995 and until 1997 a further five meetings were held until the deterioration of the peace process brought the work almost to a halt. However, the Sharm el Sheikh Memorandum provided that it would resume its activity on 1 October 1999.[65] By March 2000 it was agreed to reconvene the Continuing Committee with the supporting technical experts committee.

The October 1994 peace treaty signed between Jordan and Israel in Article 8 also dealt with refugees and displaced persons. The parties agreed to seek to resolve the refugee problem through the DoP and multilateral Refugee Working Group (RWG), and also created the possibility of direct bilateral refugee negotiations between Jordan and Israel.[66] Some provisions addressing discrete issues of residency and family reunification were addressed in the Gaza–Jericho and Interim Agreements, and in May 1994 in the wake of the Gaza–Jericho Agreement a joint Israeli/

---

[62] On the refugee issue and the peace process, see generally Brynen (1997); Brynen and Tansley (1995); Quigley (1998); Tamari (1996); Takkenberg (1998: 32–40). See also www.arts.mcgill.ca/MEPP/PRRN/ (last visited 16 Aug. 1999).

[63] Article V Declaration of Principles (hereafter DoP).   [64] Article III, Annex 1 DoP.

[65] Article 1c, The Sharm el Sheik Memorandum on Implementation Timeline of Outstanding Commitments of Agreements Signed and the Resumption of Permanent Status Negotiations, 4 Sept. 1999.

[66] Article 8 Treaty of Peace between Israel and Jordan, 26 Oct. 1994.

Palestinian committee was established to coordinate work on family reunification.[67]

Multilateral Negotiations

In addition to the bilateral and quadrilateral fora established under the peace agreements, another forum for negotiation exists. This is the multilateral committee with a regional focus, established during the Madrid Process.[68] This multilateral negotiating forum arose prior to the Oslo process in the less secret Madrid Process, in which the PLO were not officially present. At the Moscow Middle East Peace Conference arising out of the Madrid framework a Refugee Working Group (RWG) was established in the multilateral track to deal with the overall refugee problem. This committee was mandated to treat the refugee problem as a regional issue; to develop common points of reference for studying the issue; and to recommend practical steps for mobilizing international resources towards improving the immediate circumstances of the most destitute of the refugees, pending the completion of negotiations on their permanent disposition. Between 1992 and 1995 this group had eight plenary sessions.[69] It dealt with six different issues: databases; an inventory of assistance to Palestinian refugees; human resources; training, job creation, economic and social infrastructure; public health; child welfare and family reunification. In 1997 the Arab League called for a boycott of the multilaterals in protest over Israeli policies, although lower-level work by the RWG continued. In February 2000 the multilateral track steering committee set a date in May 2000 for the RWG to be reconvened in plenary. While this group has instituted a number of practical initiatives, it was intended to complement bilateral negotiations, and in practice this also served to limit its actions.[70]

---

[67] Article II (27)(l) Gaza–Jericho Autonomy Agreement, 4 May 1994 (hereafter Gaza–Jericho Agreement) (providing that the Palestinian Authority may grant permanent residency within the Gaza Strip and Jericho Area with prior approval by Israel). Annex II Interim Agreement between Israel and the Palestinians, 28 Sept. 1995 (hereafter Interim Agreement) provides a mechanism for gaining residency through electoral law which is not linked to prior approval; Article 28, Annex III, Appendix 1 Interim Agreement provides for Palestinian Authority granting of entry in certain situations; residency subject to Israeli approval for investors and family reunification; residency for children whose parents are residents; visiting rights and work permits; and residency for those who had lost their residency because they exceeded the time limit imposed by Israelis for returning to the territories. In addition to this, the multilateral Refugee Working Group reached an agreement with the Israelis on a new quota for reunification numbers (which was below Oslo Accord Palestinian expectations). See further Tamari (1996).

[68] For overview of the three levels of diplomacy, see Takkenberg (1998: 32–40).

[69] Israel boycotted the first session in May 1992, and in Nov. 1992 its participation was delayed by a dispute over the presence of Palestinian National Council members and cut short by the inclusion of family reunification on the agenda.

[70] See Brynen (1997); Tamari (1996).

The Difficulties

Substantive consideration of refugees and displaced persons in these different forums has been fraught with tension between framing refugee rights in a humanitarian aid paradigm (which Israel can to some extent accept) or a political rights one which would link to Palestinian self-determination claims. As regards the RWG, this tension has played out with respect to the issue of family reunification which can be framed within either paradigm with different implications. As regards the Continuing Committee, difficulties have revolved around the definition of 'persons displaced in 1967'. Lying at the heart of both these sub-debates are differing Israeli and Palestinian views on the numbers of Palestinians who might ultimately be admitted; on the parts of Israel and the Occupied Territories to which they would be admitted (or compensated in lieu of admission); and on whether Palestinians or Israelis would control admission. These issues go to the heart of the self-determination dispute as broadly conceived, and it is precisely because of this linkage that little progress towards a comprehensive long-term solution to the issue of displaced persons and refugees has been made. The refugee issue has become a way of restating the self-determination dispute through different language, as will be examined further in the conclusions below. However, it is worth pointing out at this stage that these negotiating dynamics are at odds with any individualized notion of the right to return, as provided for in human rights standards and resolutions of the General Assembly.

Land Claims

The issue of communal control over land is of course at the heart of the self-determination claims of both Palestinians and Israelis. Communal claims to territory in part play out through issues such as revocation of residency rights, disputes over private ownership, evictions, house demolition and sealing, the legal recategorization of land through zoning, and associated Israeli settlement-building.[71] As Shehadeh notes, Israeli settlements in the broadest sense include the web of legal and administrative arrangements which has facilitated their building and sustenance.[72]

The peace agreements do not provide any means for adjudicating on the human rights issues which settlement-building have given rise to. Indeed the postponement of the 'settlements' issue (for which there is no definition provided in the agreements) to final status negotiations has perpetuated property disputes, particularly in Jerusalem. Despite the illegality under Geneva IV of building settlements in occupied territory, this postponement

---

[71] See e.g. B'Tselem (1997*a, b*, 1998*b*); LAW (1998*a, b* 1999*a, b*); Oyediran (1997); Palestinian Centre for Human Rights (1996); Shuqair (1996, 1997); Welchman (1993).

[72] Shehadeh (1988, 1997).

has built-in ambiguity relating to whether further settlement-building through expansion of existing settlements or completely new developments is permitted by the agreements during the interim period or not.[73] Article XXXI(7) of the Interim Agreement provides: 'Neither side shall initiate or take any step that will change the status of the West Bank and the Gaza Strip pending the outcome of the permanent status negotiations.' While a very formalistic reading of the word 'status' might support Israeli arguments that the accords do not prohibit the construction of new Jewish housing in these areas, there are good arguments that such construction does indeed change the status of the land as it makes it more likely to remain in Israeli hands as Camp David (II) has confirmed.

As Watson points out, the agreements implicitly limit settlement activity in other aspects. The redeployment process itself implies that Israel will stop building settlements in the West Bank as the purpose of those provisions is 'to shrink, not expand, the Israeli presence in the West Bank.'[74] Furthermore, given that the Interim Agreement makes reference only to existing settlements, it can be argued that 'to add new settlements, or expand existing ones, is to alter the factual foundations of the parties' agreement.'[75] Legal arguments aside, the provision on settlements is another example of the ambiguity which characterizes the agreements and which results in different interpretations by Israelis and Palestinians which often derail the process.

In conclusion, as with the forward-looking human rights provisions, mechanisms to 'undo the past' are absent. Although some forums for considering the issues have been established, the dynamics of the agreements and their linkage to the issue of self-determination (not to be resolved until final status negotiations) serve to make some of these issues ongoing and more difficult to resolve. They also reduce issues of rights to political bargaining chips.

Bosnia Herzegovina

Refugees

The conflict in Bosnia Herzegovina resulted in the largest displacement of people to occur in Europe since the Second World War. In 1996 UNHCR estimated that over 2 million people had been displaced, with approximately 1 million displaced within BiH, half a million living in the neighbouring constituents of the former Yugoslavia, and approximately 700,000 receiving temporary protection in other countries, of which half that number are in Germany.[76] In response to the large numbers fleeing

---

[73] See generally Watson (2000, ch. 7).   [74] Watson (2000: 284).   [75] Ibid.
[76] United Nations High Commissioner for Refugees (1996*b*).

the conflict, recourse was made to temporary protection schemes, as mentioned above, which bypassed the individualized protection of international refugee law. While these regimes provided basic protections for the human rights of refugees and non-refoulement, the emphasis on the temporary nature of protection left unclear when, how, and under what authority protection would be terminated.[77]

Return of displaced persons is centrally provided for in the Dayton Peace Agreement (DPA) as a practical response to this crisis. But it is important to note the significance of return for the self-determination deal through the assumption that large-scale returns would change the power balances and territorial realities of the separate Entities and unitary state structure agreed to in the DPA, as discussed in Chapters 5 and 6.

Annex 7 provides an Agreement on Refugees and Displaced Persons. It contains two parts, the first relating to protection and the second to a Commission for Displaced Persons and Refugees, and providing for land rights. Article 1 of this agreement, as described in Chapter 5, provides in part that:

All refugees and displaced persons have the right freely to return to their homes of origin. They shall have the right to have restored to them the property of which they were deprived in the course of hostilities since 1991 and to be compensated for any property that cannot be restored to them.

The annex provides detail on the positive obligations on the parties (who in this annex are the BiH Republic, the Federation, and Republika Srpska) aimed at securing the right to return. These include a commitment by parties to repeal domestic legislation and administrative practices with discriminatory intent or effect; and 'the prevention and prompt suppression of any written or verbal incitement, through media or otherwise, of ethnic or religious hostility or hatred.'[78] As noted in Chapter 5, the annex on elections provides that 'as a general rule' a person shall be expected to vote in the municipality in which he or she resided prior to 1991.[79]

Returning refugees and displaced persons charged with a crime other than a serious violation of international humanitarian law as defined in the Statute of the Ad Hoc International Criminal Tribunal for Former Yugoslavia (ICTFY), or a common crime unrelated to the conflict, 'shall upon return enjoy an amnesty.' The agreement provides that 'in no case shall charges for crimes be imposed for political or other inappropriate reasons or to circumvent the application of the amnesty.'[80]

---

[77] See United Nations High Commissioner for Refugees (1996a) for details of the scheme.
[78] See Articles I, II, Annex 7 DPA.   [79] Article IV, Annex 3 DPA.
[80] Article VI, Annex 7 DPA. Subsequent agreement provided that domestic war crimes trials had to be agreed to by the ICTFY; Procedures and Guidelines for Parties for the

The right to return is specifically stated to be to 'homes of origin' although Annex 7 also provides that '[c]hoice of destination shall be up to the individual or family, and the principle of the unity of the family shall be preserved.'[81] The UNHCR is called on to 'develop in close consultation with asylum countries and the parties a repatriation plan' to allow for 'early' return of refugees and displaced persons.[82] The Parties undertake to cooperate with and give unrestricted access to UNHCR, the International Committee of the Red Cross, and the United Nations Development Programme and other relevant international, domestic, and non-governmental organizations. The parties are also to facilitate the provision of 'adequately monitored, short-term repatriation assistance on a non-discriminatory basis to all returning refugees and displaced persons.'[83]

Although Annex 7 most explicitly deals with refugees, the human rights protections found in the Constitution (Annex 4) and the human rights institutions of Annex 6 were also designed with the issue of return and home conditions particularly in mind, evidencing the interlinking of forward-looking and backward-looking human rights provisions.

Land Claims

A Commission for Displaced Persons and Refugees is established to deal with land claims.[84] The Commission is composed of nine members, with four appointed by the Federation, two by Republika Srpska, and remaining members appointed by the president of the ECHR. This Commission is to 'receive and decide any claims for real property in Bosnia and Herzegovina' or claims for compensation in lieu. A procedure for addressing the claims is set out and the Commission given extensive powers to 'effect any transactions necessary' with regard to title to the property.[85]

A Refugees and Displaced Persons Property Fund is established in the Central Bank of BiH to be administered by the Commission. It is to be replenished 'through the purchase, sale, lease and mortgage of real property which is the subject of claims before the Commission' and by direct payments from the parties, by states, or international or non-governmental organizations.'[86]

The Failure of Implementation

In implementation, the Repatriation Plan developed by UNHCR, as mandated by Annex 7, incorporated a notion of 'safe return' based on defining

---

Submission of Cases to the International Criminal Tribunal for the Former Yugoslavia under Agreed Measures of February 18, 1996 ('Rules of the Road' Agreement), see further Ch. 9 p. 284.

[81] Article I(4), Annex 7 DPA.   [82] Article I(5), Annex 7 DPA.
[83] Article IV, Annex 7 DPA.   [84] See generally Ch. 2, Annex 7 DPA.
[85] See further Waters (1999) (comprehensive overview of property disputes since Dayton).
[86] Article XIV, Annex 7 DPA.

'safe' with reference to benchmarks which largely replicated the conditions set out in Annex 7 as necessary to facilitating return.[87] Despite this setting of benchmarks, countries such as Germany moved towards ending temporary protection before the benchmarks had been achieved.[88] The figures for return repeat the implementation pattern of the other human rights provisions. UNHCR figures as of 31 August 1999 showed that only 340,919 refugees have returned to BiH since the signing of the DPA. Of these 93.3 per cent returned to the Federation and only 0.7 per cent were non-Serbs returning to Republika Srpska. Within the same period a further 270,001 displaced persons 'returned' to municipalities within BiH, over 70 per cent returning to the Federation.

These figures fall far short of the estimated 2 million plus displaced by the conflict. Furthermore, as the International Crisis Group (ICG) claim the 'vast majority of these 600,000 returnees are not returns to pre-war homes, but returns to areas where their ethnic group exercises military control.'[89] The ICG suggest that a better measure of return to homes of origin as provided for by the DPA is the amount of 'minority returns'; that is, return of people to areas where they do not constitute a majority. The figure for minority returns is 100,714 throughout the whole of BiH (less than 5 per cent of all the refugees and persons displaced by the war).[90] With regard to the actions of the Commission for Displaced Persons and Refugees (now renamed the Real Property Commission) by September 1999, while over 60,000 property decisions had been issued, only an unspecified fraction have been implemented.[91] The fund for Refugees and Displaced Persons has not materialized.

UNDOING THE PAST VERSUS UNDOING THE DEAL

All three cases show the indivisibility of the backward-looking and forward-looking human rights protections. They illustrate that just as the design and implementation of the forward-looking human rights mechanisms are intimately shaped by the central meta-bargain or 'deal', so too are the mechanisms which seek to undo the past. In Israel/Palestine and BiH where this meta-bargain failed to resolve the central conflict, the conflict has continued to be waged through issues of return and access to land. However, in South Africa also, although the issue of return did not

---

[87] See generally Bagshaw (1997).   [88] Bagshaw (1997); Andersen (1996).
[89] International Crisis Group (1999: 32).   [90] Ibid.
[91] Figures supplied by the Office of the High Representative Human Rights Department, Sept. 1999. For a detailed account of the work of the Real Property Commission, the legislative context in which it works, and its difficulties see Waters (1999). See further Appendix 1.

have the same demographic impact on the negotiations, the issue of land rights was negotiated as a dimension of the central meta-bargain. Land and economic rights were capable of reshaping the respective access to power of the NP/SAG and the ANC, which were at the centre of the negotiations. Trade-offs between political and economic power, or between a radical new order, on one hand, and stability and continuity, on the other, were explored. Although the context was therefore very different from that of Israel/Palestine or BiH, the relationship between measures intended to undo the past and the central meta-bargain was similar.

The case of Northern Ireland stands apart because the dynamics of the conflict were different. However, it should be noted that part of this difference was no doubt due to the fact that human rights were articulated by the British government as applicable to the conflict. No matter how difficult to implement, or partial or even cynical this commitment may have been, it left the post-conflict landscape with fewer past human rights abuses to undo.

The UNHCR in a recent publication has noted the importance of repatriation of refugees, or 'return', to post-conflict peace-building processes.[92] UNHCR notes that since 1987 'almost every major peace agreement concluded around the world, whether in Bosnia, Cambodia, Mozambique or Namibia, has included specific provisions relating to the return of displaced populations.'[93] They argue that return of displaced people contributes to peace-building in four main interlocking ways. First, return of refugees is an important signifier of peace and the end to the conflict. As long as refugees are displaced, the conflict is in essence continuing in the sense that 'the state is unable to protect its citizens.'[94] Return can have an important impact on public confidence in the peace-building process and conversely lack of return can disrupt transition. Secondly repatriation plays an important part in validating the post-conflict political order. For example, it helps legitimize subsequent elections and the democratic process itself. Thirdly, return of refugees may be a precondition for peace if the refugees are politically and militarily active. Finally, return of displaced populations can make an important contribution to the economic recovery of war-torn states, or can even be 'a pre-requisite for that objective to be achieved.'[95]

These arguments state the positive case—in effect a refugee-specific 'just peace' thesis. However, to each argument there are 'pragmatic peace' counter-arguments which in practice can prevent return being addressed substantively in peace agreements, or prevent implementation of return

---

[92] United Nations High Commissioner for Refugees (1997: 159–64).
[93] United Nations High Commissioner for Refugees (1997: 159).
[94] United Nations High Commissioner for Refugees (1997: 159–60).
[95] United Nations High Commissioner for Refugees (1997: 163).

provisions even when they are clearly agreed to and written down. The issues of refugees and land ownership, while often framed in terms of individual rights, go to the heart of communal claims to territory and power. Mass return of refugees to an area can significantly affect the 'numbers game', that is the ethnic balance of a region, and even its sovereignty. Return can undo one side's territorial gains of the conflict. If those refugees are further entitled to repossess land, then their return may displace those who came to possess the land during the conflict, further undermining an (ethnic) territorial gain. In short, return of refugees and land justice can begin to rewrite the territorial compromises at the heart of the deal, and this crucially affects bargaining over them. Even if return is provided for in a peace agreement, implementation will not necessarily follow. If return of refugees is a signifier of peace, then conversely, where the deal has failed to resolve the conflict (rather than just the violence), the conflict will continue to be waged not least through whether, how, and to where refugees and displaced persons are returned.

The cases of BiH and Israel/Palestine illustrate this. In BiH the agreement contemplates a right of return as not merely reversing the population movements of the past, but as consolidating a fragile unitary state, so creating a possible pluralist future. It is not surprising, therefore, that in Bosnia provision for right of return and land claims is extensive. Neither is it surprising that the Entity governments, and in particular that of Republika Srpska, who most reluctantly agreed to the unitary state, resist the Annex 7 (right to return) imperatives. Given the imbalance of power between centre and Entities, as with the forward-looking human rights institutions, Annex 7 has been largely ineffective.

Paradoxically this situation is exacerbated by the actions of host states. Successful implementation of Annex 7 should mean that refugees are enabled to return and that host state protection is indeed only 'temporary'. However, early enforced return by host states of refugees to parts of the country which are safe, even though original home areas are not, in effect consolidates the ethnic carve-up of BiH rather than reversing it.[96] This undermines the very Dayton Peace Agreement which is the framework for ending the conflict which caused the refugee flows. The effective implementation of Annex 7 falls further from reach as time passes and refugees and internally displaced persons build lives away from their homes of origin. The combined failure of forward-looking and backward-looking human rights provisions operate to reinforce each other. Return becomes more difficult if the human rights institutions are not functioning effectively, while human rights institutions cannot function effectively until the territorial power of ethno-nationalist Entity governments is

---

[96] See Bagshaw (1997); Andersen (1996).

watered down through return of refugees. The overall dynamic operates to ensure a permanently emasculated central state. Pragmatic decisions such as that of host states to return refugees, and of the Organization for Security and Cooperation in Europe's (OSCE) Provisional Electoral Commission to allow people to vote not just in their pre-1991 localities but where they presently live,[97] respond to the reality of the stalemate, but in doing so rewrite the contract at the heart of Dayton.

In the case of the Israeli/Palestinian conflict also, refugees and land possession are negotiated in the shadow of territorial claims and sovereign aspirations. The evolution of international law towards acceptance of Palestinian self-determination saw the refugee issue come to be recast 'not as an exclusively humanitarian issue as it was in the 40s, but as part of a conception of restoring the right of self-determination for the Palestinian people.'[98] As Takkenberg notes, '[i]n this context the question has arisen as to whether there is a friction between focus on the refugee issue as opposed to the issue of self-determination; Palestinian refugees versus Palestinian people; individual rights versus group rights?'[99]

While the connection to self-determination puts the issue of return clearly on the peace process negotiating-table, there are negative consequences to working within the self-determination paradigm.[100] As Tamari argues, rolling refugees into a package of Palestinian demands asserted in bilateral and multilateral forums can dilute the established legal imperative for return of individual Palestinian refugees into a series of political compromises. This dynamic in practice creates a new dichotomy within Palestinian politics 'between the contingencies of state building, and the demands of the Diaspora for representation and repatriation', or, put another way, between the rights of refugees and the negotiating power and internal needs of the PLO. Moreover, as Israelis move towards the possibility of a Palestinian state somewhere within 1967 boundaries, so the issue of return of Palestinian refugees gains greater ideological opposition within Israel as linked to the demographic endgame. This plays out in sub-issues such as family reunification or how to define the relevant group of displaced persons.

Relationship with International Law

Finally, the human rights measures aimed at undoing the past, as with those in other areas, exhibit the capacity of both conflict and peace process to shape and be shaped by international law. In BiH the temporary protection schemes both enabled protection during the conflict and

---

[97] See discussion in Ch. 7 pp. 178–9.   [98] Tamari (1996: 2).
[99] Takkenberg (1998: 346–7).   [100] See generally Tamari (1996: 2).

lifted displaced persons beyond the full protection of international law after the conflict.[101] Yet temporary protection operated within a quasi-legal framework which drew on concepts such as non-refoulement. Interestingly, Bagshaw argues that after the war the DPA, together with the UNHCR's consequent Repatriation Plan, create a new form of legal order.[102] He argues that, as the DPA is itself an international treaty, both the failure of parties to implement their obligations under Annex 7, and mandatory return by them before they have fulfilled these obligations, constitute violations of international law. Bagshaw also suggests that the fact that three European states, Germany, France, and the United Kingdom, witnessed the DPA's conclusion and entry into force, while technically only of political significance, can also be seen as an endorsement of its aims, including the right of refugees to return freely and safely to their homes of origin. These states may of course also be bound by requirements of non-refoulement if it constitutes a norm of customary law.

Israel/Palestine also illustrates the interactive relationship of conflict and law. The particular circumstances of 1948 refugees meant that they were not included in the 1951 Convention regime, which at that time did not contemplate return as the primary model. In contrast General Assembly resolutions dealing with Palestinian refugees confirmed their right of return. However, as the peace process has developed, the package approach to refugees means that the 'right of return' increasingly becomes subject to barter, effectively overwriting a plethora of General Assembly resolutions.

---

[101] While the concept of temporary protection should not have necessarily precluded individual applications for asylum, in practice it can tend to; Bagshaw (1997); Andersen (1996).   [102] Bagshaw (1997: 584–9).

9

Dealing with the Past: Prisoners, Accountability, and 'Truth'

The question of accountability for the past cannot be completely separated from attempts to undo the past, and this is perhaps best illustrated by the issue of prisoner release. While some parties may see prisoners as a consequence of the conflict that should be undone at its end, others may see the prisoner release as raising broader questions about the rights and wrongs of the conflict.

As regards questions of accountability for past human rights violations, international law has inconsistencies, and interfaces uncomfortably, and at times unhelpfully, with the questions facing peace negotiators. In summary these questions are: when should those who fought in the conflict be released, and when should they continue to be prosecuted and punished? How should the 'truth' about responsibility for the conflict and its worst abuses be established? What is the nature of the 'truth' to be sought—individual or communal? What right do victims have to information, 'truth', retribution, and compensation? This chapter summarizes current international law provision before comparing how the four case-studies approached 'the past' in their peace agreements.

INTERNATIONAL LAW

The internal legal regime from which the answers to the above questions can be sought is complex and developing, not least in response to ethnic conflict, and can only be summarized here. This legal regime is the subject of a large and expanding literature.[1] Debates over international legal

---

[1] For example, on international legal dimensions, see Akhavan (1996*a*, *b*, 1997, 1998); Bassiouni (1999); S. Cohen (1995); Dinstein and Tabory (1996); Goldstone (1995*a*, *b*, 1996, 1997*a*, *b*,); MacCormack and Simpson (1997); Meron (1998); Orentlicher (1991); Robertson (1999); Roht-Arriaza (1995); Weiner (1995). For theoretical analysis and transitional justice case-studies, see Ash (1997); Asmal (1992); Asmal *et al.* (1997); Boraine and Levy (1995); Brysk (1994: 63–88); Burgenthal (1994); Dysenhaus (1998); Ensalaco (1994); Hamber (1998*a*, *b*); Hayner (1994); Human Rights Program, Harvard Law School (1996); Huyse (1995); Kritz (1995); McAdams (1997); Malamud-Goti (1990, 1996); Nino (1991); Parker (1996); Reisman (1995); Rolston (1996); Rosenberg (1995); Siegel (1998); Stotzky (1993); Weschler (1991). This literature does not include comprehensive citations of the many books and articles dealing with the criminal tribunals in former Yugoslavia and Rwanda, and the genesis and development of the International Criminal Court, much of which deals with the law and practice of 'dealing with the past'.

regulation for 'dealing with the past' tend to focus on when there is a 'duty to prosecute' human rights abusers, and who has that duty. However, the legal regime also provides for prisoner release and victims' rights.

There are three dimensions to the relevant legal framework regarding a duty to punish for past abuses. First, international humanitarian law, as found primarily in the 1949 Geneva Conventions and their 1977 Protocols, much of which it can now be asserted constitute customary law;[2] secondly, international human rights law—both treaty-based and customary law; and thirdly, 'crimes against humanity' jurisprudence dating primarily from the Nuremberg Tribunals held after the Second World War, as reinvigorated by the ad hoc criminal tribunals for former Yugoslavia and Rwanda, and even more recently by the jurisdiction of the proposed International Criminal Court.[3] These complex and overlapping legal regimes do not provide clear and comprehensive answers to questions of accountability, although a trend towards an expanding notion of individual criminal responsibility with universal jurisdiction to prosecute can be identified. The account below will focus less on the difficult questions of universal jurisdiction and more on when a post-transition state can and should prosecute and punish those within its jurisdiction for human violations committed during the conflict. Humanitarian law also makes provision for prisoner release at the end of conflict, and international (soft law) standards are beginning to address the treatment of victims of the conflict, and a broader notion of 'truth-telling'. However, the legal approaches to questions of accountability, prisoner release, and victims' rights are not always consistent with each other.

Humanitarian Law

Humanitarian law imposes duties both to prosecute violations and to release prisoners. The question of when the law imposes a 'duty to prosecute' raises the question of who owes such a duty, and to whom it is owed. The question of when humanitarian law requires or permits prosecution for violations is therefore better understood with reference to three questions: Is the act in question outlawed by the law ('the question of substance')? If so, does the law impose individual responsibility for the act ('the question of criminality')? If so, who must or may prosecute and punish for the act ('the question of jurisdiction')?[4] The answers to these

---

[2] Although the much longer history of this branch of law should be noted, see e.g. 1907 Hague Convention, Geneva Convention for the Amelioration of the Condition of the Wounded and Sick in Armies in the Field, 6 July 1906. See generally Kalshoven (1987).

[3] This branch of law can also trace its roots much further back to the earlier conventions; see generally Bassiouni (1999: 41–88).   [4] Cf. Greenwood (1996: 277).

questions vary with regard to whether the conflict is international or internal (artificial as this distinction may be). The discussion will focus on the duties on a state after a conflict more than on broader questions of universal jurisdiction.

International conflict

The Geneva Conventions, which apply in their entirety only to international conflicts, impose a duty to punish 'grave breaches', which include

any of the following acts, if committed against persons or property protected by the Convention: wilful killing, torture or inhuman treatment, including biological experiments, wilfully causing great suffering or serious injury to body or health, and extensive destruction and appropriation of property, not justified by military necessity and carried out unlawfully and wantonly.[5]

High Contracting Parties 'undertake to enact any legislation necessary to provide effective penal sanctions for persons committing, or ordering to be committed' any of the grave breaches, and to prosecute grave breaches or hand over persons to another signatory state for prosecution.[6] Provision is made to safeguard trial and defence rights.

Protocol I to the Geneva Conventions provides a broader list of grave breaches, thereby extending the duty to provide effective penal sanctions to this list.[7] Protocol I also brings more conflicts into the fold of the Geneva Convention definition by extending the definition of international armed conflict to include 'armed conflicts in which peoples are fighting against colonial domination and alien occupation and against racist régimes in the exercise of their right of self-determination.'[8]

States are to exercise jurisdiction over persons suspected of committing

---

[5] Article 50 Geneva Convention for the Amelioration of the Condition of the Wounded and Sick in Armed Forces in the Field 1949 (hereafter Geneva I). See also grave breaches listed in Article 51 Geneva Convention for the Amelioration of the Condition of the Wounded, Sick, and Shipwrecked Members of the Armed Forces at Sea 1949 (hereafter Geneva II); Article 130 Geneva Convention Relative to the Treatment of Prisoners of War 1949 (hereafter Geneva III); Article 147 Geneva Convention Relative to the Protection of Civilian Persons in Time of War 1949 (hereafter Geneva IV).

[6] Article 49 Geneva I; Article 50 Geneva II; Article 129 Geneva III; Article 146 Geneva IV.

[7] The new extended list covers attacks on civilian populations and non-defended localities; attacking a person who is *hors de combat*; and perfidious use of the distinctive emblems of the International Committee of the Red Cross; transfer by occupying power of parts of its own civilian population into the territory it occupies, or the deportation or transfer of all or parts of the population of the occupied territory within or outside this territory; unjustifiable delay in the repatriation of prisoners of war or civilians; practices of apartheid and other inhuman and degrading practices involving outrages upon personal dignity, based on racial discrimination; attacking or destroying clearly recognized historic monuments, works of art, or places of worship; and depriving a person of fair trial rights; Article 85(3) and (4) Protocol Additional to the Geneva Conventions of 12 August 1949, and relating to the Protection of Victims of International Armed Conflicts (hereafter Protocol I).

[8] Article 1(4) Protocol I.

grave breaches when such persons are found on their territory, regardless of the nationality of the offender or the place where the crime was committed. Much of both the Geneva Conventions and Protocol I can be asserted to constitute customary law, and therefore to be applicable not just to those who were High Contracting Parties at the time of the violations, but also to states which have not ratified conventions or protocol.[9] The duty to punish therefore applies to states post-transition, as regards the human rights violations of a past regime. And it is now also clear that all state parties to the conventions and protocols and international bodies may also undertake prosecutions.[10] This opens up the possibility that domestic deals on amnesty can now be undone internationally, as such an amnesty is not a bar to prosecution elsewhere and, further, is itself in violation of the conventions and Protocol I.

Other (non-grave) breaches are merely to be 'suppressed'. While there is no explicit obligation on parties to prosecute or punish individuals for such breaches, it seems that individual criminal responsibility is not precluded, and that state parties therefore *may* undertake prosecution.[11] Common Article 1 of the conventions underwrites this, in providing that all the contracting parties must respect and *'ensure respect'* for the conventions (my emphasis).

Prisoner Release

The Geneva Convention Relative to the Treatment of Prisoners of War 1949 (Geneva III) provides that prisoners 'shall be released and repatriated without delay after the cessation of hostilities.'[12] The definition of prisoners of war includes all those who take up arms for one side in a conflict or are civilian members in any branch of armed forces, whether official or informal.[13] The Geneva Convention Relative to the Protection of Civilian Persons in Time of War 1949 (Geneva IV) also provides that each interned person 'shall be released by the Detaining Power as soon as the reasons which necessitated his internment no longer exist,' and certainly after the end of hostilities.[14] It commits parties to try to conclude agreements for the release and repatriation of such internees.

This obligation to release prisoners and internees does not apparently conflict with the duty to prosecute grave breaches. As regards internees, Article 133 of Geneva IV suggests that the release provisions do not apply

---

[9] See e.g. Meron (1989: 41–70).   [10] Meron (1998: 249).

[11] The Geneva Conventions provide that each state party 'shall take measures necessary for the suppression of all acts contrary to the provisions of the present Convention other than the grave breaches.' Meron argues that all states therefore have the right to punish such breaches and 'in that sense nongrave breaches may fall within universal jurisdiction' (1998: 250).   [12] Article 118 Geneva III.

[13] Article 4 Geneva III.   [14] Article 132 Geneva IV. See also Articles 133–5 Geneva IV.

to those who are subject to penal proceedings (unless exclusively for disciplinary offences). As regards prisoners of war, Article 4.A.2(d) of Geneva III provides that combatants who do not respect the laws and customs of war (that is commit grave breaches) are not entitled to prisoner of war status.

Internal Conflict

Thus far the discussion only relates to international armed conflicts (and conflicts involving national liberation movements, which are included in the international conflict regime by virtue of Protocol I). As regards internal conflicts, the situation is less clear. Common Article 3 of the Geneva Conventions, applying to conflicts not of an international character, and Protocol II, applying to internal conflicts (at a seemingly higher threshold of violence than the Common Article 3 conflicts), do not use the notion of 'grave breaches'. Neither, therefore, directly impose an obligation to prosecute, and commentators are divided on whether they provide a basis for individual criminal responsibility at all, and, if so, who is entitled to enforce it. Some commentators argue that without a clear duty to prosecute, there is no individual criminal responsibility and no universal jurisdiction. Others, such as Meron, argue that the absence of a duty to prosecute does not mean that such prosecution is not permitted.[15]

Arguments that Common Article 3 and Protocol II impose individual criminal responsibility have been bolstered by the statutes establishing the Ad Hoc International Criminal Tribunal in Rwanda and the more recent Rome Statute of the International Criminal Court.[16] They have also been bolstered by the decision of the Appeals Chamber of the International Criminal Tribunal for Former Yugoslavia (ICTFY) in the case of *Tadić*.[17] These all contemplate individual criminal responsibility for certain crimes committed in the course of internal conflict. Article 4 of the Statute of the International Tribunal for Rwanda provides that the tribunal 'shall have the power to prosecute persons committing or ordering to be

[15] Meron (1998: 252) (although as Meron acknowledges not all non-grave breaches can and must be treated as potential offences. Different types of obligation are contemplated by the convention regime, for example Article 94 Geneva III requires notification on recapture of an escaped prisoner of war and Article 96 Geneva III requires that a record of disciplinary punishments be kept by camp commanders. Neither of these types of obligation are relevant to individual responsibility).

[16] Statute of the International Tribunal for Former Yugoslavia 1993 (as amended) (hereafter ICTFY Statute), Statute of the International Criminal Tribunal for Rwanda 1995 (hereafter Rwanda Statute), Rome Statute of the International Criminal Court, 1999 (hereafter Rome Statute).

[17] *Prosecutor v. Tadić* appeal and trial chamber judgments available at www.un.org/icty/ (last visited 25 May 2000). Also reported in (1997) 105 ILR 419 (Trial Chamber judgment at 427; Appeals Chamber judgment at 453).

committed serious violations' of both Common Article 3 and Protocol II.[18] The Rome Statute of the International Criminal Court provides jurisdiction for the court for 'war crimes'.[19] These are defined as including '[i]n the case of an armed conflict not of an international character, serious violations of [Common Article 3]' and a list of such serious violations is provided.[20] While the Rome Statute does not explicitly incorporate Protocol II itself into the definition of war crimes, it incorporates a Protocol II-based list of serious violations in 'conflict not of an international character' directly into the text of the statute.[21] Although the statute of the ICTFY does not have a similar provision, in the case of *Tadić* the Appeals Chamber of the ICTFY found that its jurisdiction under Article 3 of the statute (violations of the laws or customs of war) was not confined to international armed conflicts but included violations of humanitarian law applicable to internal armed conflicts.[22] The Appeals Chamber held unequivocally that such violations 'entail individual criminal responsibility regardless of whether they are committed in internal or international armed conflicts.'[23]

In summary, it seems that, while prosecution and punishment of individuals for serious violations of Common Article 3 and Protocol II is not mandated, the state of which the person is a national may (and possibly should) pursue individual criminal responsibility.[24] Furthermore, arguments that these violations provide a basis for universal jurisdiction are gaining strength.[25]

---

[18] Article 4 lists the following violations as included: violence to life, health, and physical or mental well-being of persons, in particular murder as well as cruel treatment such as torture, mutilation, or any form of corporal punishment; collective punishments; taking of hostages; acts of terrorism; outrages upon personal dignity, in particular humiliating and degrading treatment, rape, enforced prostitution, and any form of indecent assault; pillage; lack of fair trial; and threats to commit any of the foregoing acts. While some considered the Rwanda statute's criminalization of Common Article 3 an innovation, the Security Council apparently considered itself complying with the principle of *nullem crimen sine lege* when establishing the tribunal. See further Meron (1998: 244–8) on the problems in this regard.

[19] Article 8 Rome Statute.   [20] Article 8(2)(c) Rome Statute.
[21] Article 8(2)(e) Rome Statute.

[22] The Appeals Chamber's analysis of precisely which rules were applicable to internal armed conflict seemed to go beyond Protocol II and Common Article 3 and resembles the key provisions of Protocol I. This part of its analysis (*obiter dicta*) is somewhat controversial; see Greenwood (1996).

[23] *Prosecutor v. Tadić* 105 ILR 507–20, 520. For detailed explanation of the case, see Greenwood (1996: 277–8).

[24] Meron (1998: 252) argues that national states should be regarded as having an obligation to prosecute, as 'a failure to prosecute violators of clauses other than grave breaches would call into question a state's good faith compliance with its treaty obligations.' It can be argued, however, that if a discretion to prosecute exists, then it is the exercise of this discretion which must be done in good faith.

[25] See Meron (1998: 235–44); see also Bothe (1996).

Prisoner Release

The concept of individual culpability for Protocol II violations is apparently undermined elsewhere in its text by provision for prisoner release. As regards prisoner release, Article 6(5) of 1977 Protocol II states that

[a]t the end of hostilities, the authorities in power shall endeavour to grant the broadest possible amnesty to persons who have participated in the armed conflict, or those deprived of their liberty for reasons related to the armed conflict, whether they are interned or detained.

There is a possible way to reconcile this provision with individual criminal responsibility. The International Committee of the Red Cross (ICRC) has interpreted Article 6(5) narrowly, concluding that it is inapplicable to amnesties that extinguish penal responsibility for persons who have violated international law. It interprets the article's provision for 'the broadest *possible* amnesty' as providing only for 'combatant immunity' and not applying to those who violate international humanitarian law.[26] The interpretation is further supported by Article 6 itself, which in subsection (2) claims to regulate penal prosecutions in providing for due process for defendants, something which would be unnecessary if the protocol were intended to require the giving of amnesties in all circumstances. Thus, the amnesty requirements of Protocol II and the Geneva Conventions can be argued not to apply to grave and serious violations, although this is left somewhat unclear by the terms of Protocol II itself.

Human Rights Law

Although international human rights law has traditionally allowed a certain amount of discretion to states to determine the means by which they will protect rights, increasingly 'international law has required states to punish certain human rights crimes committed in their territorial jurisdiction.'[27] Some treaties explicitly require a state to criminalize certain abuses, investigate violations, and seek to punish the perpetrators. For example, the Genocide Convention commits party states to 'prevent and to punish' genocide.[28] The Convention against Torture provides that '[e]ach State Party shall ensure that all acts of torture are offences under its criminal law.'[29] Others, such as the International Covenant on Civil and Political Rights 1966 (ICCPR), do not on their face impose such

[26] Position cited to in Roht-Arriaza and Gibson (1998: 865 n. 166). See further Domb (1996: 319). [27] Orentlicher (1991: 2551).
[28] Articles 1 and 5 Convention on the Prevention and Punishment of the Crime of Genocide 1948.
[29] Article 4 Convention against Torture and Other Cruel, Inhuman or Degrading Treatment or Punishment 1984.

obligations. However, even with these conventions it has been authoritatively affirmed that the state fails in its duty to protect certain rights if a functioning system for accountability is not in place. These obligations apply after transition to states which had ratified the conventions prior to the conflict, and seemingly also to those who only ratify after transition, when suspects are still at large.

As regards customary law applicable to all states, while it is unclear precisely which human rights are protected, there is agreement on some, including the prohibition on torture, disappearances, and extra-legal executions.[30] As Orentlicher notes, even when the status of a human right is clear, there is still debate over whether a single violation of a right protected by customary law engages international responsibility or whether rights have to be denied on a systematic basis, or as a matter of state policy.[31] However, this is another source of obligation on a state to punish past human rights violators.

Prisoner Release

Human rights conventions say nothing about prisoner release at the end of conflict. Fair trial standards implicitly require that those convicted without such a trial be released or (re)tried.[32] Conversely, where a trial has been found to be fair despite the operation of emergency legislation, then it would logically seem that it is fair for all time. However, a third category exists, of convictions in violation of fair trial standards but where a derogation from those standards was permitted. It can be argued that post-emergency detention of persons convicted under emergency legislation requiring (permitted) derogation infringes Article 17 of the European Convention on Human Rights 1950 (ECHR) and Article 5 of the ICCPR (no limitation on rights greater than provided for in the Convention), taken together with Articles 14 and 4 (providing for derogation only in times of public emergency) of these instruments.[33]

The relative silence of human rights instruments and bodies on post-conflict prisoner release is particularly significant given the tendency of states to deal with internal conflict, at least in its early stages and often throughout, through criminal justice systems modified by emergency

---

[30] See e.g. Dugard (1997c); Orentlicher (1991).   [31] Orentlicher (1991: 2582).

[32] As Stavros notes (1992: 363–4), permissible derogations from rights to speedy trial, which facilitate use of administrative detention for short periods, do not mean that such detention can continue as a punitive measure. Such imprisonment can only follow a trial with due process. Cf. also the Inter-American Commission which has stated that emergency courts may only impose a sentence of a length consistent with the exceptional nature of the emergency situation (see 1981 Report on Columbia, Conclusion 3); and called upon governments to review convictions imposed by military or special courts under emergency rule (see e.g. 1983 Report on Guatemala, Recommendation 2, p. 133).

[33] See further Stavros (1992: 356–8).

legislation. While Protocol II provides that those imprisoned for participating in the conflict should be released at its end, often the very question
of who has 'participated in the conflict' is a difficult one. The state will
often have refused to draw a distinction between 'political' and 'ordinary'
crime, and a very broad range of actions will have been justified under the
banner of the conflict, by both state and non-state actors. Post-conflict
moves to release prisoners often involve re-creating the distinction
between the 'political' prisoners (which it was often denied existed) and
'ordinary' prisoners—a distinction which goes to the heart of the meta-
conflict. Often extradition jurisprudence around 'political offences' is
turned to in the search for a formulation.[34] This debate tends to focus
around the nature of the offence, but questions of seriousness of offence
are often also relevant, evidencing an overlapping with humanitarian and
human rights law.

Crimes against Humanity: The Evolutionary Directions of International Law

The concept of a post-transition duty to prosecute serious human rights
violations is also underwritten by a jurisprudence of 'crimes against
humanity', which finds its roots in the Nuremberg Tribunals established
after the Second World War.[35] Article 6(c) of the Nuremberg Charter (as
amended by the 'Berlin Protocol') defined crimes against humanity as

> murder, extermination, enslavement, deportation, and other inhumane acts com-
> mitted against any civilian population, before or during the war, or persecutions
> on political, racial or religious grounds in execution or in connection with any
> crime within the jurisdiction of the Tribunal, whether or not in violation of the
> domestic law of the country where perpetrated.[36]

These crimes had to be committed on a mass scale, and have a nexus
(somewhat ambiguously understood) to war. The 'crimes against humanity' jurisprudence overlaps significantly with customary law protection of
human rights.

The concept of crimes against humanity has more recently been used in
the Rwanda, ICTFY, and Rome Statutes. The jurisdiction of the ICTFY, the
Rwanda Tribunal, and the International Criminal Court (ICC) confirm the
evolution of international law in the direction of a duty to punish, by
providing further evidence of international principles of international

---

[34] For discussion of such jurisprudence, see Keightley (1995: 339–47). Cf. also her discussion of the Norgaard factors used in Namibia and South Africa (1995: 344–6).
[35] For a detailed discussion of the legal history of crimes against humanity and their content, see Bassiouni (1999).
[36] Article 6(c) Charter of the International Military Tribunal (hereafter 'Nuremberg
Charter').

individual responsibility for 'crimes against humanity'. In former Yugoslavia the international tribunal is given power to prosecute persons responsible for crimes against humanity 'when committed in armed conflict, whether international or internal in character, and directed against any civilian population.'[37] These crimes are listed as murder, extermination, enslavement, deportation, imprisonment, torture, rape, persecutions on political, racial, and religious grounds, and 'other inhumane acts'. In Rwanda the list is the same, but while a nexus to conflict is not required, jurisdiction only applies when the crimes against humanity are 'committed as part of a widespread or systematic attack against any civilian population on national, political, ethnic, racial or religious grounds.'[38] Both statutes thus lift the concept of crimes against humanity out of the unhelpful international–internal–civil disturbance categorization violations, but the Rwanda Statute has been criticized as requiring evidence of widespread and systematic attack on grounds which may be difficult to prove.

The Rome Statute of the ICC provides an extensive definition of crimes against humanity as

> any of the following acts when committed as part of a widespread or systematic attack directed against the civilian population, with knowledge of the attack:
>
> (a) Murder;
> (b) Extermination;
> (c) Enslavement;
> (d) Deportation or forcible transfer of population;
> (e) Imprisonment or other severe deprivation of physical liberty in violation of fundamental rules of international law;
> (f) Torture;
> (g) Rape, sexual slavery, enforced prostitution, forced pregnancy, enforced sterilisation, or any other form of sexual violence of comparable gravity;
> (h) Persecution against any identifiable group or collectivity on political, racial, national, ethnic, cultural, religious, gender [or other recognized grounds];
> (i) Enforced disappearance of person;
> (j) The crime of apartheid;
> (k) Other inhuman acts of similar character intentionally causing great suffering, or serious injury to body or to mental or physical health.[39]

While the Rome Statute provides a threshold test that crimes against humanity must be committed as part of a 'widespread or systematic attack', there is no further requirement of nexus to either internal or international conflict.

As Orentlicher notes, while UN action in ratifying the law applied at

---

[37] Article 5 ICTFY Statute.
[38] Article 3 Rwanda Statute. For criticism that this requirement is difficult to prove, see Meron (1998: 232–3).   [39] Article 7 Rome Statute.

Nuremberg on the whole emphasized the permissive nature of international jurisdiction, developments since then have 'underscored the international community's resolve to ensure that crimes against humanity are punished.'[40] She argues strongly that there is now a duty to punish such crimes which requires that states prosecute past human rights violators after a conflict. It can further be argued that increasingly prosecution and punishment for gross human rights abuses is subject to universal jurisdiction.[41]

A Word on Criminal Law and Due Process Issues

While a duty to punish can be established in international law, it is also clear that prosecution and punishment must accord with due process requirements of international human rights and humanitarian law. The issue of dealing with the past raises specific due process and criminal justice dilemmas whose study is beyond the scope of this book. These issues are worth mentioning as including the principles of 'no crime without a law' (*nullem crimen sine lege*); 'no punishment without law' (*nulla pena sine lege*); non-retroactivity; individual responsibility; the age limit for prosecution; irrelevance of official capacity; responsibility of commanders and other superiors (and the issue of prescription of law); non-applicability of statute of limitations; the requisite mental element for a crime; possible grounds (for example, mental incapacity) for excluding criminal responsibility; and mistakes of fact and of law.[42]

Victims' Rights and Compensation

In peace processes questions of the rights of victims, and in particular the question of compensation, are to the fore in discussions of how to deal with the past. While international law and some past peace treaties involving international conflict have made some provision for reparations, this has traditionally been in terms of state-to-state payments.[43] However, with the case of Iraq the UN Security Council provided for Iraqi reparations to be paid to 'victim states *and their nationals*.'[44] As regards reparations for individual victims, many human rights conventions provide a right to an 'effective remedy' which has often been interpreted to

---

[40] Orentlicher (1991: 2593).

[41] It can be argued that the Preamble of the Rome Statute itself suggests universal jurisdiction over the crimes in the statute.

[42] This list is taken from Part 3 of the Rome Statute. See further Saland (1999).

[43] On reparations, see generally Seidl-Hohenveldern (1982a, b). On compensation, see Roht-Arriaza (1995: 37–8).   [44] UN SC Res 687 1991 (emphasis added).

include a right to compensation,[45] and in some instances an explicit right to compensation is provided.[46] This is also the case in humanitarian law.[47] In contrast compensation has often not been provided for 'crimes against humanity'. There was no provision for compensation in either the Nuremberg or Tokyo Charters and neither were the Criminal Tribunals for Former Yugoslavia and Rwanda empowered to make compensation orders.[48] The Rome Statute of the ICC, however, makes detailed provision for reparations to victims.[49] Declarations of the General Assembly, the reports of special rapporteurs, working groups, and specially commissioned reports into reparations for victims of grave violations of human rights and fundamental freedoms have all affirmed a right to financial reparation as one component of reparation more generally.[50] Such reparation is increasingly being broadly conceived to include a range of initiatives for victims.

PEACE AGREEMENTS AND PAST VIOLATIONS

While the law on individual culpability and duty to prosecute has been developing, countries emerging from repression and conflict have devised various arrangements to deal with 'the past'. These have often taken the form of amnesties, or 'truth commissions', and/or (less frequently) prosecutions. The mechanism chosen often reflects a tension between the requirements of justice for past acts and a demand for information ('truth') about their perpetration, with the requirements of what is sometimes asserted to be the realpolitik—that fragile stability can be

[45] See e.g. Article 3 ICCPR, Article 13 ECHR, and Article 25 American Convention. See also e.g. Human Rights Committee Case No. 45/2979 *Pedro Pablo Camargo* v. *Colombia* (payment of compensation to a husband for the death of his wife); Case No. 84/1981 *Barbaro* v. *Uruguay* (appropriate compensation to the family of the person killed).

[46] See e.g. Article 9(5) ICCPR (right to compensation for unlawful arrest or detention); Article 14(6) (compensation for miscarriages of justice); Article 5(5) ECHR (compensation for unlawful arrest or detention); Article 3 Protocol 7 ECHR (compensation for miscarriage of justice); Article 10 American Convention (miscarriage of justice).

[47] Article 68 Geneva III (compensation in certain circumstances for prisoners of war); Article 55 Geneva IV (occupying power 'shall make arrangements to ensure that fair value is paid for any requisitioned goods'); Article 91 of Protocol I (a party to the conflict which violated the provisions of the conventions or of the protocol shall 'be liable to pay compensation').

[48] Article 23 Rwanda Statute; Article 24 ICTFY Statute (both providing that the penalty to be imposed is 'limited to imprisonment' although provision is also made to 'order the return of any property and proceeds acquired by criminal conduct').

[49] Article 75 Rome Statute. For negotiating history, see Muttukaumaru (1999).

[50] For a good overview of these initiatives, see Bassiouni (1998). See also *The Right to Restitution, Compensation and Rehabilitation for Victims of Grave Violations of Human Rights and Fundamental Freedoms*, Commission on Human Rights Resolution 1999/33, UN DOC. E/CN.4/RES/1999/33. See also Joinet (1997).

undermined by allocating blame through prosecutions. In many aspects this tension restates the 'justice–peace' dilemma outlined in Chapter 1.[51]

In summary, the following arguments are raised in favour of pursuing accountability through prosecution and punishment:

1. It is necessary to address the needs of victims.
2. It is necessary to provide a future deterrent within the jurisdiction and beyond.
3. It is necessary to provide new political arrangements with legitimacy: impunity will undermine claims of legitimacy, while accountability and punishment will legitimize them.
4. It can provide a mechanism for 'lustration' or 'weeding out' of past human rights abusers of the old regime from new institutional arrangements.
5. It can promote inter-communal reconciliation by substituting individual guilt for collective guilt.
6. It is an international legal requirement and necessary to upholding a universal notion of human rights and the rule of law.

Those against a rigid notion of accountability and a duty to punish raise the following main arguments:

1. Fragile democracies may be undermined by politically charged trials. They may increase rather than decrease the possibility of renewed conflict.
2. After transition such trials may be politically motivated against opponents of the new regime (so-called 'victor's justice').
3. Transitional democracies may not have the capacity to ensure that such difficult trials take place consistently with the full exercise of civil and political rights.
4. The particular nature of crimes committed during conflict raise especially difficult due process problems which cannot be satisfactorily addressed, particularly by fragile democracies.
5. Prosecution, lustration, and other punitive measures in practice fail to achieve the extensive moral, legal, and political ends sought in the successor polity.
6. Guilt and responsibility in a conflict are widely shared, often with a large part of the population being recruited into active or passive collaboration. In such a context, national reconciliation is not best served by settling past scores. Rather, as Siegel puts it, it is better to aim to accept 'a measure of truth-telling, and acknowledgement that

---

[51] These arguments are synthesized from the literature cited in n. 1. For good summaries of the arguments, see S. Cohen (1995); Huyse (1995); Siegel (1998).

violation of rights occurred while making a fresh start with all sides eligible to participate in the work ahead.'[52]

These debates form the backdrop to many peace negotiations; they interface uneasily with international law's current direction towards a duty to punish serious violations of human rights and humanitarian law. However, the emerging international imperative has impacted on the mechanisms adopted through peace processes and their agreements in a number of ways. First, there is evidence that the demands of international law for accountability have increasingly shaped domestic initiatives such as the establishment of truth commissions. As Roht-Arriaza and Gibson note, over time the trend for such commissions 'has been from broader to more tailored, from sweeping to qualified, from laws with no reference to international law to those which explicitly try to stay within its strictures.'[53] Secondly, international bodies have adjudicated on attempts to provide transitional justice and found them to be wanting in their failure to prosecute.[54] Finally, the growing concept of universal jurisdiction for crimes against humanity has also threatened to undo domestic deals on truth, justice, and amnesty. This has perhaps most recently been illustrated by the Pinochet case, where Spanish attempts to extradite Chilean General Pinochet from Britain to Spain for human rights abuses found a measure of success, despite the fact that amnesties had been granted Pinochet after a truth process in Chile.[55] While the Chile amnesty procedure was perhaps more vulnerable to international legal challenge than some later examples, the possibility of legal challenges to more sophisticated models such as that in South Africa cannot be ruled out. The South African Truth and Reconciliation Commission showed themselves aware of this possibility in their report, while suggesting that it would not be helpful if their decisions were trumped by external international legal processes.[56]

---

[52] Siegel (1998) 439.   [53] Roht-Arriaza and Gibson (1998: 884).

[54] See e.g. Decisions of the Inter-American Commission on Human Rights that the amnesty laws in Argentina and Uruguay were contrary to the American Convention on Human Rights (Report No. 28/92 in respect of Argentina, and Report No. 29/92 in respect of Uruguay, 13 *Human Rights Law Journal* 336). See further Weiner (1995).

[55] *R v. Bow Street Metropolitan Stipendiary Magistrate and others, Ex Parte Pinochet Ugarte* [1998] 3 WLR 1456 (hereafter Pinochet 1) (deciding that Pinochet, as a former head of state, was not entitled to claim immunity from prosecution); see also *R v. Bow Street Metropolitan Stipendiary Magistrate and others, Ex Parte Pinochet Ugarte* (No. 2) [1999] 2 WLR 272 (hereafter Pinochet 2) (ruling that the previous decision could not stand on grounds of appearance of bias); also *R v. Bow Street Metropolitan Stipendiary Magistrate and others, Ex Parte Pinochet Ugarte* (No. 3) [1999] 2 WLR 827 (hereafter Pinochet 3) (finding that Pinochet had no immunity from prosecution for the offences of torture and conspiracy to torture, albeit on different reasoning from Pinochet 1). See further Woodhouse (2000).

[56] Truth and Reconciliation Commission (1998, vol. 5, ch. 8, para. 114).

The Case-studies

Interestingly the framework agreements in all four case-studies have one feature in common—the past does not figure centrally in any of them. This observation reveals a common sequencing for issues relating to the past. Issues of prisoner release often occur at the pre-negotiation stage, or are resolved by the framework–substantive agreement at the latest. This is because those negotiating may be prisoners or potential prisoners who may need release or immunity from prosecution to even enter into the process (as in the case of the African National Congress, ANC). Also, the peace process becomes difficult to sell if a key constituency of those affected—those imprisoned as a result of their part in the conflict—are not released. However, the question of a more holistic mechanism which would provide some form of accountability for the conflict is often something which can only be dealt with in the post-agreement implementation stage, if at all. The reasons for this sequencing will be revisited after briefly considering the examples and the specific contexts in which the past was addressed.

The case-studies show different approaches to the past and reveal how the debates on justice and peace, and the role of international law, have played out in practice. The most elaborate mechanisms are those in South Africa, where a fairly complex Truth and Reconciliation Commission was established, and in Bosnia Herzegovina (BiH), where the ICTFY, established during the conflict, remained the main mechanism for dealing with the past after the negotiation of Dayton. As we shall see, in neither case was the mechanism constructed in the framework peace agreement. In contrast, the situations of Northern Ireland and Israel/Palestine have no comprehensive 'past-oriented' mechanisms, although there are piecemeal measures for dealing with discrete issues.

South Africa

The legal basis for what became the Truth and Reconciliation Commission was negotiated between the ANC and the South African Government (SAG) at a late stage in negotiations. It was added in an unnumbered section to the end of the Interim Constitution entitled 'National Unity and Reconciliation'.[57] This section provided that '[i]n order to advance . . . reconciliation and reconstruction, amnesty shall be granted in respect of acts, omissions and offences associated with political objectives and committed in the course of the conflicts of the past.' The new Parliament was man-

---

[57] Constitution of the Republic of South Africa Act 200 of 1993 (hereafter Interim Constitution).

dated to adopt a law determining a firm cut-off date between 8 October 1990 and 6 December 1993, and provide for procedures for dealing with amnesty. This provision for amnesty gave birth to the Promotion of National Unity and Reconciliation Act, 1995 (PNU) establishing the Truth and Reconciliation Commission (TRC) after the first democratic elections, in which the ANC won a majority.[58]

What is important to note is that the TRC as a mechanism was not a product of the peace negotiations, but an ANC interpretation of the (negotiated) Interim Constitution provision on amnesty, enacted once they were in power as the new government.

The establishment of the TRC should be seen as the culmination of a process of prisoner release that had preceded the negotiations. As Parker notes, there were two prior phases to this process.[59] For face-to-face negotiations to begin opposition groups had to be protected from prosecution. During the pre-negotiation phase of the peace process, the issue of indemnities for those not charged and amnesty for political prisoners were both seen 'less as protecting agents of the state from subsequent prosecution for human rights abuses, and rather more as a necessary precondition for talks about talks.'[60] This phase saw the ANC and government agree that by 1991 all political prisoners would be freed, exiles would return home without fear of prosecution, and the armed struggle would end.[61] Agreement on the definition of 'political offence' for these purposes was reached, and legislation enacted.[62]

The second phase began in October 1992. The SAG unilaterally passed a Further Indemnity Act 151 of 1992 in the face of opposition, ostensibly to free political prisoners who did not qualify for amnesty under the previous definition of political offence. However, part of the motivation for the legislation had been the Goldstone Commission's inquiry into

---

[58] The Act continued to be amended. See Promotion of National Unity and Reconciliation Amendment Act 1995, No. 87 of 1995 (made improvements in the English and Afrikaans texts). Promotion of National Unity and Reconciliation Amendment Act, No. 18 of 1995 (increased size of Amnesty Committee). Promotion of National Unity and Reconciliation Second Amendment Act No. 84 of 1997 (further regulated the composition of the Committee on Amnesty and extended the period within which the Commission was to complete its work).   [59] Parker (1996); see also Berat (1995).

[60] Parker (1996: 2).   [61] Paragraphs 2–3 Pretoria Minute 1990; see Ch. 3, p. 46.

[62] Indemnity Act 35 of 1990. The criteria for political offence were closely modelled on the criteria developed by Professor Norgaard as an independent jurist in the Namibian negotiations. He identified the relevant factors as being motivation of the offender; whether the offence was committed 'in the course of or as part of an uprising or political disturbance' (the South African criteria added 'or in reaction to'); the nature of the political objective (whether aimed at overthrowing the government or forcing a change in policy); the legal and factual nature of the offence with specific reference to its gravity; the objective of the offence and its targets (civilian or military); the relationship between the offence and the political objective being pursued. The South African criteria replaced the term 'government' with 'political opponent'. See further Keightley (1995: 339–47).

government and non-government violence, and the Act's main benefici-
aries seemed likely to be state agents.[63]

As part of bolstering opposition to this latter piece of legislation by
showing its own accountability and openness, the ANC published a
report of an ANC Commission of Inquiry into ANC atrocities committed
in ANC refugee camps in Zambia, Angola, Tanzania, and Uganda.[64] In
January 1993 the ANC appointed a further commission to examine allegations of human rights abuses in its detention centres, which found that
members of the ANC's security department had been involved in violations including torture, execution, arbitrary detention, and various types
of inhuman treatment.[65] Both of these reports (but particularly the former)
used international law standards (humanitarian and human rights),
together with the ANC's own Codes of Conduct and Freedom Charter, as
a basis for determining what was permissible treatment of detainees and
what was not.

Despite the fact that an attempt had been made to reach a definition of
'political offences' in the indemnity legislation, as Keightley notes, other
mechanisms for release proliferated during the negotiation process, operating outside this definition. These included blanket indemnities for certain categories of offences and fast-tracked remission based on sentence
length. In practice, given the magnitude of the number of applications for
release, the proliferation of release mechanisms, and the ongoing political
negotiations on the matter, the clear application of criteria for political
offences broke down. As a result it became 'extremely difficult to know
whether the release of prisoners was always as a result of a straight application of the indemnity criteria or whether it was the result of political
manoeuvring between the negotiating parties.'[66]

The establishment of the Interim Constitution, the elections of April
1994, and the subsequent establishment of the TRC therefore marked the
third and final phase of amnesty mechanisms. The resulting Promotion of
National Unity Act provided for the establishment of a Truth and Reconciliation Commission with four main objectives:

(a) establishing as complete a picture as possible of the causes, nature and
    extent of the gross violations of human rights which were committed dur-
    ing the period from 1 March 1960 to the cut-off date [6 December 1993, later
    extended to 11 May 1994] including the antecedents, circumstances, factors
    and context of such violations, as well as the perspectives of the victims and

---

[63] Parker (1996: 2). This legislation removed objective assessment of the nature of the
deed, meaning that where the offender believed or was told that he was promoting or combating a political objective, an indemnity was forthcoming. The Act also removed the
requirement of investigation before indemnity and public disclosure of the crime for which
disclosure was sought.   [64] Skweyiya Commission (1992).
[65] Motsuenyane Commission (1993).   [66] Keightley (1995: 353).

the motives and perspectives of the persons responsible for the commission of the violations, by conducting investigations and holding of hearings[67]

(b) facilitating the granting of amnesty to persons who make full disclosure of all the relevant facts relating to acts associated with a political objective and comply with the requirements of this Act[68]

(c) establishing and making known the fate or whereabouts of victims and by restoring the human and civil dignity of such victims by granting them an opportunity to relate their own accounts of the violations of which they are the victims, and by recommending reparation measures in respect of them[69]

(d) compiling a report providing as comprehensive an account as is possible of the activities and findings of the Commission . . . and which contains recommendations of measures to prevent the future violations of human rights[70]

Gross violations were defined as

violations of human rights through (a) the killing, abduction, torture and severe ill-treatment of any person; or (b) any attempt, conspiracy, incitement, instigation or command or procurement to commit an act referred to in paragraph (a). . . the commission of which was advised, planned directed, commanded or ordered by any person acting with a political motive.'[71]

International law played a part in designing this definition, although it was also designed to make the TRC's task manageable and yet meaningful.[72]

The Truth and Reconciliation Commission's amnesty and indemnity process set out an apparent trade-off between truth and punishment. Those members of political organizations, liberation movements, law enforcement agencies, and security forces who were involved in political crimes could apply to the TRC for amnesty and indemnity. However, the TRC was only to recommend amnesty or indemnity on the basis of full disclosure of the applicant's involvement in the crime, and where the action claimed had a political motive that was capable of being realized.[73] As Hamber notes, the TRC, like other parts of the negotiated agreement, 'walked the narrow line between fundamental change and the maintenance of stability. It promised the survivors of apartheid violence accountability, reparations and truth. And by not prosecuting, the TRC ensured that the fragile peace could be sustained.'[74]

Early on this TRC trade-off was challenged before the new South African Constitutional Court by relatives of state violence, Steve Biko, Griffiths and Victoria Mxenge, and Dr and Mrs Fabian Ribeiro. The case primarily concerned the argument that section 20(7) of the PNU Act 1995, which authorized amnesty, was inconsistent with section 22 of the Interim

[67] Section 3(1)(a) PNU.   [68] Section 3(1)(b) PNU.   [69] Section 3(1)(c) PNU.
[70] Section 3(1)(d) PNU.   [71] Section 1(1)(ix) PNU.
[72] See Truth and Reconciliation Commission (1998, vol. 1, ch. 4).
[73] Section 20 PNU.   [74] Hamber (1998b: 10).

Constitution, which provided that every person should have the right to have justiciable disputes settled by a court of law or, where appropriate, another independent or impartial forum.[75] However, interestingly for this study, the applicants also argued that the state was obliged by international law to prosecute those responsible for gross human rights violations and that the amnesty provisions of section 20(7) PNU 1995 therefore also breached international law.

In brief, the Constitutional Court held that the epilogue to the Constitution trumped Interim Constitution section 22, and section 20(7) PNU 1995 was therefore constitutional. The court also addressed the international law attack on the provision, although its analysis of international law was incomplete and disappointing (especially in the light of the supposed grounding of the Interim Constitution in international human rights principles). The court held that the 1949 Geneva Conventions and Protocol I were not applicable to the internal conflict in South Africa[76] and that, if Protocol II was applicable, it was no bar to amnesty given Article 6(5). The court did not consider possible international customary law obligations to prosecute crimes against humanity. Although the Constitutional Court acknowledged transitional justice mechanisms from other countries, it failed to consider the international legal challenges to them.

At a more rhetorical level the TRC response to those who claimed that the trade-off was between truth and justice was that the Commission itself was designed to give a model of 'restorative justice' whereby a strict notion of 'punishment' was substituted with an approach which sought to reconcile victim with the offender, and compensate the victim, and that this did not amount to impunity.[77]

The final TRC report presented to President Mandela on 29 October 1998 ran to five volumes dealing with the key concepts used by the Commission; the commission of gross violations of human rights on all sides of the conflict from 1960 to 1994; the perspective of the victims of the conflict of that time; the nature of the society in which gross violations took place, including a report on 'institutional' hearings which focused on matters such as health and media; and the conclusions reached by the Commission. The report cannot be fully considered here, except to note

---

[75] *Azapo v. President of the Republic of South Africa* 1996 (4) SA 562 (CC). This was one of a number of legal challenges to the TRC all of which are clearly set out in the Truth and Reconciliation Commission (1998, vol. 1, ch. 7, 174–200)

[76] As Dugard notes, the court did not consider the Appeals Chamber of the ICTFY decision of *Tadić* which blurred the distinction between international and non-international conflicts for the purpose of international humanitarian law (1997b: 265).

[77] Truth and Reconciliation Commission (1998, vol. 1, ch. 5, paras. 80–100) (for an interesting discussion of the relationship between the concepts of truth, reconciliation, amnesty and justice, see generally vol. 1, ch. 5).

that in addition to the very specific findings as regards specific cases, the TRC made a general finding that

gross violations of human rights were perpetrated or facilitated by all the major players in the conflicts of the mandate era. . . At the same time, the Commission is not of the view that all parties can be held to be equally culpable for violations committed in the mandate period. . . The preponderance of responsibility rests with the state and its allies.[78]

Among its many recommendations for the future the TRC noted that, having given careful consideration to lustration, they decided 'not to recommend it' as it was 'inappropriate in the South African context.'[79] An entire chapter of its conclusions was devoted to arguing for reparations, including financial reparations.[80]

Northern Ireland

The Belfast Agreement does not provide a 'past-specific' mechanism for resolving issues of culpability, accountability, and truth-telling. However, the issues of 'victims of violence' and 'prisoners' do receive discrete treatment.

The Agreement provides for acknowledgement of the 'suffering of the victims of violence as a necessary element of reconciliation.'[81] A commitment is made to remember and address the concerns of victims, and to support groups who are working with them. Reference is made to the outcome of the work of the Northern Ireland Victims' Commission, set up by the British government prior to the Belfast Agreement.

The agreement's section on prisoners commits the government to 'put in place mechanisms to provide for an accelerated programme for the release of prisoners.'[82] The release process is to happen within a fixed time frame and to 'set prospective release dates for all qualifying prisoners' with 'any qualifying prisoners who remained in custody two years after the commencement of the scheme' being released at that point. Thus, prisoners are to be released within a categorical two-year time frame (there is no provision for those not yet convicted). Further, the agreement provides

[78] Truth and Reconciliation Commission (1998, vol. 5, ch. 6, paras. 66–8).

[79] Truth and Reconciliation Commission (1998, vol. 5, ch. 8, para. 19).

[80] Five components to reparations were identified: urgent interim reparation to those in urgent need; individual reparation grants to each victim; symbolic reparation, for example, through days of remembering and money for commemoration; community rehabilitation programmes; and institutional reform. Truth and Reconciliation Commission (1998, vol. 5, ch. 5).

[81] Belfast Agreement (hereafter BA) Rights, Safeguards, and Equality of Opportunity, Reconciliation, and Victims of Violence.

[82] See generally BA Prisoners, for all quotations in this section.

that '[g]overnments continue to recognise the importance of measures to facilitate the reintegration of prisoners into the community by providing support both prior to and after release, including assistance directed towards availing of employment opportunities, retraining and/or re-skilling, and further education.' Legislation was subsequently provided to implement this commitment. The need to agree an explicit definition of political offences was avoided by including those prisoners who had been convicted of an offence scheduled under emergency legislation, provided that the paramilitary group was on ceasefire.[83] While this in practice provided a way of distinguishing between 'political' or conflict-related convictions and 'ordinary' convictions the terminology of 'political offence' was avoided, and with it any difficult debate about the nature of the conflict.

In addition to these past-oriented provisions in the Belfast Agreement, other measures were introduced by the government, paramilitary groups, and civic society both before and after agreement was reached. In the run-up to negotiated agreement, ad hoc initiatives responding to discrete campaigns on aspects of the past were made by the government in what can be broadly identified as their 'confidence-building strategy'. The Victims' Commission mentioned in the agreement was part of a pre-agreement initiative, following hard on the heels of Sinn Féin's participation in talks, probably in an attempt to address the concerns of unionists and security force members. The Commission's establishment was announced on 24 October 1997, and tasked to 'look at possible ways to recognise the pain and suffering felt by victims of violence arising from the troubles of the last 30 years, *including those who have died or been injured in the service of the community*' (in an implicit reference to security force members). The Commission reported on 29 April 1998, and while the report was welcomed, it was also criticized for largely ignoring those who had been victims at the hands of security forces.[84] The report touched on the idea of a more wide-ranging Truth and Reconciliation Commission, with the statement that '[i]f any such device were to have a place in the life of Northern Ireland, it could only be in the context of a wide-ranging political accord.'[85] In the Republic of Ireland a similar Commissioner was appointed on 21 May 1998, which reported in July 1999.[86] In a similar vein, on 29 January 1998 the government established a judicial inquiry into 'Bloody Sunday' (an incident in which security forces killed fourteen unarmed civilians in 1972).[87]

After the Belfast Agreement the IRA under public pressure released

[83] The Northern Ireland (Sentences) Act 1998. See further McEvoy (1999).
[84] Bloomfield (1998).   [85] Bloomfield (1998: 38).   [86] Wilson (1999).
[87] See further www.bloody-sunday-inquiry.org/ (last visited 9 Mar. 2000).

bodies of some of those people whom it was alleged had 'disappeared'—that is, were murdered and buried without acknowledgement. Other non-governmental, non-paramilitary attempts to account for and classify civilian or military status, religion, and political belief of those killed in the troubles are beginning to be produced.[88] Victims' groups have also proliferated since the signing of the agreement, or found a more public voice since then, but often have membership drawn from primarily one side of the community or the other, reflecting the focus of their mandate.

At the time of writing, while ad hoc governmental responses in the form of inquiries into specific instances of alleged state abuse (such as the killing of defence lawyers Pat Finucane in 1989 and Rosemary Nelson in 1999) seem likely to continue, as do non-governmental attempts to 'cost' the conflict in human terms, there is no coherent proposal from any sector on how to 'deal with the past' in any comprehensive or holistic way. Nor have recommendations for lustration mechanisms for past human rights abusers been made by any of the commissions set up under the agreement.

Israel/Palestine

As with Northern Ireland, the Israeli/Palestinian agreements do not provide any holistic mechanism to 'deal with the past'. This is unsurprising given the interim status of the agreements. As with Northern Ireland, elements of the past are addressed.

Prisoner Release

At the start of the process there were approximately 12,337 Palestinian prisoners in Israeli detention facilities. Although prisoner release was not dealt with in the text of the Declaration of Principles (DoP), Israeli government statements indicated that there would be a mass release of Palestinian prisoners.[89] This was to include stipulations. The cut-off arrest date for prisoners who could be released was the date of the DoP, 13 September 1993. Members of political parties that opposed the agreement were to be excluded, no release would take place unless the Palestinians declared an amnesty for collaborators, and release would be conditional on progress on the issue of missing Israeli soldiers.

Prisoner release is dealt with as a 'confidence-building measure' in several of the later agreements, although there were in practice often difficulties with implementation. The Gaza–Jericho Agreement of 4 May 1994 stated that, upon signing, 'Israel will release, or turn over, to the

---

[88] Fay *et al.* (1999); McKittrick *et al.* (1999); Ní Aoláin (2000).   [89] See McEvoy (1998: 39).

Palestinian Authority within a period of 5 weeks, about 5000 Palestinian detainees and prisoners, residents of the West Bank and the Gaza Strip.'[90] By the end of July 1994 4,500 prisoners had been released, although release was conditional upon signing an individual declaration to support the peace process, a condition not in the agreement, which was the subject of much protest.[91]

The Interim Agreement, also under the heading of 'Confidence Building Measures', provided for three phases of prisoner release: on signing, prior to elections, and at a later stage.[92] Palestinians from abroad who were permitted to enter the West Bank and the Gaza Strip were not be prosecuted for offences committed prior to 13 September 1993.

An Annex (VII) set out criteria for selection for release. The provisions were in part based on general humanitarian criteria based on the status of the prisoner: the old, the young, the sick, women, and those who had already served a considerable length of time in prison; and in part were reminiscent of humanitarian and human rights standards relating to seriousness of offence. There was no attempt at a generic description of 'political offence', and indeed the terms 'security offence' and 'non-security offence' seem to blur any distinction between 'political' and 'non-political' offences, rather than attempt to create the distinction. The provisions provided for the release of

- all female detainees and prisoners (to be released in the first stage of releases)
- persons who have served more than two-thirds of their sentence
- detainees and/or prisoners charged with or imprisoned for security offences not involving fatality or serious injury
- detainees and/or prisoners charged with or convicted of non-security criminal offences
- citizens of Arab countries being held in Israel pending implementation of orders for their deportation

Four categories of person meeting these criteria were then to be 'considered for release':

- prisoners and/or detainees aged 50 years and above
- prisoners and/or detainees under 18 years of age

---

[90] Article XX Gaza–Jericho Autonomy Agreement, 4 May 1994 (hereafter Gaza–Jericho Agreement). [91] See McEvoy (1998: 39).
[92] Article XVI Interim Agreement between Israel and the Palestinians, 28 Sept. 1995 (hereafter Interim Agreement). The Note for the Record, which accompanied the later Hebron Protocol, also made reference to the third phase of prisoner release, noting that it should be dealt with in accordance with the Interim Agreement. Note for the Record prepared by Ambassador Dennis Ross at the Request of Prime Minister Benjamin Netanyahu and Ra'ees Arafat, 15 Jan. 1997, para. 2.

- prisoners who have been imprisoned for ten years or more
- sick and unhealthy prisoners and/or detainees

The agreement does not include a systematic release mechanism for adjudicating on individual prisoners, suggesting a political, rather than a systematic legal, application of the criteria.

In practice, the assassination of Yitzhak Rabin, Palestinian suicide bombings, and the election of Netanyahu's Likud-led coalition government eventually led to the Israeli government unilaterally freezing all discussions on prisoner release at the beginning of 1996. As McEvoy notes, the prisoner situation was further complicated by other factors. These included continued use of administrative detention, including detention of those who had completed their prison sentences and were immediately rearrested, and the view among some sections of the Palestinian community that the Palestinian Authority (PA) had been unenthusiastic in their pursuit of prisoner release, given that many prisoners had come to oppose the peace process publicly.[93]

While the text of the Wye Memorandum agreed between the PA and Netanyahu's government did not appear to provide for prisoner release, surrounding publicity indicated that prisoner release had been agreed as part of the package. Newspapers reported that an agreement on prisoner release had been made as part of a security agreement. Around 500 prisoners were to be released, as identified by the PA on a list passed to Israel through the US Central Intelligence Agency (CIA).[94] In the event, approximately 250 prisoners were released, but according to Palestinians they were 'normal criminals' rather than those imprisoned as a result of their part in the conflict. Resulting Palestinian protests and allegations of Israeli bad faith were one of the factors ensuring that the peace process stayed at a standstill despite the memorandum. As of 20 June 1999 an estimated 2,261 Palestinian prisoners were still held in Israeli detention facilities (many of these imprisoned post-DoP).[95]

The Sharm el Sheik Memorandum, agreed between the PLO and Barak's government, provided that the two sides would establish a joint committee to follow up on issues of prisoner release.[96] The Israeli government agree to release 'Palestinian and other prisoners who committed their offences prior to September 13, 1993, and were arrested prior to May 4, 1994.' Two phases of release are provided for. The first is to consist of 200 prisoners and the second, 150 prisoners, all of whose names are to be agreed by the joint committee. This committee is then to recommend further lists of names for release to the 'relevant Authorities' through a

---

[93] McEvoy (1998: 39–40).   [94] See e.g. Segal (1998).
[95] Figures supplied by Mandela Institute, Ramallah, West Bank.
[96] The prisoner release provisions are in Article 2 Sharm el Sheik Memorandum, 4 Sept 1994.

Monitoring and Steering Committee. The section concludes with the statement that '[t]he Israeli side will aim to release Palestinian prisoners before next Ramadan.' However, the absence of the indefinite article indicates that this may not mean the release of all remaining prisoners.[97]

Limited Truth and Reconciliation

Only two other aspects of the 'past' are dealt with: the return of the bodies of people killed in the conflict, and informers. The Gaza–Jericho Agreement and Interim Agreement both provide that both sides shall cooperate in assisting the other to find missing Israelis and Palestinians and their bodies.[98]

Both the Gaza–Jericho and Interim Agreement, in what is an implicit reference to informers in their confidence-building measures sections, provide that the Palestinian side will not prosecute or harm those 'Palestinians who were in [or have maintained (Interim Agreement)] contact with the Israeli authorities.'[99]

The only other measure directed at the past is Annex 6 to the Interim Agreement, which talks of Israeli/Palestinian cooperation with the stated aim of peace-building and *reconciliation*.

Bosnia Herzegovina

The ICTFY was set up during the conflict, less as a way of dealing with the past (for the conflict was not of course past) than as a way of 'ensuring that such violations [of humanitarian law] are halted and effectively redressed.'[100]

However, its mandate continued through the peace negotiations and into the Dayton Peace Agreement (DPA). In so continuing it played some part in shaping Dayton—Bosnian Serbs Karadžić and Mladić, as indicted war criminals, were excluded from the Dayton negotiations. The ICTFY was also given a role in the Dayton framework, and the DPA underwrites the continued functioning of the ICTFY affirming the duty to cooperate with the tribunal.[101]

---

[97] 151 Palestinian Prisoners were released pursuant to the agreement on 15 Oct. 1999.

[98] Article XIX Gaza–Jericho Agreement. The obligation is not symmetrical. The PA is to provide 'all necessary assistance in the conduct of searches by Israel . . . as well as by providing information about missing Israelis.' Israel is to provide 'necessary information about, missing Palestinians'; Article XXVIII Interim Agreement.

[99] Article XX(4) Gaza–Jericho Agreement; Article XVI(2) Interim Agreement (also providing that 'ongoing measures will be taken, in coordination with Israel, in order to ensure their protection'). On the issue of 'collaborators', see further Rigby (1997).

[100] UN SC Res 827 (1993).

[101] Preamble and Article IX (impliedly) of The General Framework Agreement for Peace in Bosnia and Herzegovina, 4 December 1995 (hereafter Dayton Peace Agreement or DPA). This is emphasized even more clearly by accompanying UN SC Res 1022 (1995), which notes that 'compliance with the requests and orders of the [ICTFY] constitutes *an essential aspect* of implementing the Peace Agreement' (emphasis added). See generally Jones (1996).

The agreement contemplates the fact of indictment before the ICTFY as barring individuals from Dayton institutions providing for a form of limited lustration. Article IX of Annex 4 Constitution provides that

[n]o person who is serving a sentence imposed by the International Tribunal for the Former Yugoslavia, and no person who is under indictment by the Tribunal and who has failed to comply with an order to appear before the Tribunal, may stand as a candidate or hold any appointive, elective or other public office in the territory of Bosnia and Herzegovina.

Secondly, while prisoner release and amnesty is provided for by the DPA, in each case a clear exception is provided for those who are charged with serious violations of international humanitarian law as defined by the ICTFY statute. Article IX of Annex I, dealing with the immediate military arrangements post-ceasefire, provides for prisoner exchanges. The parties are to 'release and transfer without delay all combatants and civilians held in relation to the conflict . . . in conformity with international humanitarian law . . .' This is to be facilitated by the International Committee of the Red Cross (ICRC). However, any order by the ICTFY for 'the arrest, detention, surrender of or access to persons who would otherwise be released and transferred under this Article but who are accused of violations within the jurisdiction of the Tribunal' is to be complied with notwithstanding the prisoner release provisions.

Similarly, Annex 7, Agreement on Refugees and Displaced Persons, provides for an amnesty for 'any returning refugee or displaced person charged with a crime, other than a serious violation of international humanitarian law as defined in the Statute of [the ICTFY].'[102] This annex also provides that parties are to 'provide information through the tracing mechanisms of the ICRC on all persons not accounted for, and to cooperate fully with the ICRC in its efforts to determine the identities, whereabouts and fate of the unaccounted for.'[103]

These exceptions from amnesty for serious violations for humanitarian law had the capacity to unravel the political deal, through the spectre of concurrent domestic jurisdiction for such violations. Some way into implementation an agreement had to be signed to ensure that domestic war crimes prosecutions were not used in an ethnically motivated way to prevent return (or, more cynically, to ensure that political figures key to sustaining the peace were not 'accidentally' arrested). The agreement provided that in order for any domestic arrest or prosecution to proceed, the International Tribunal had to have reviewed the relevant legal papers.[104]

---

[102] Article VI, Annex 7 DPA.   [103] Article V, Annex 7 DPA.

[104] Procedures and Guidelines for Parties for the Submission of Cases to the International Criminal Tribunal for the Former Yugoslavia under Agreed Measures of February 18, 1996 ('Rules of the Road' Agreement).

As Akhavan notes, the initial impetus for the establishment of the ICTFY was as 'an instrument for appeasing a troubled conscience [of Western Powers]' based on the unrealistic assertion that it could put an end to the worst horrors of the conflict.[105] However, since the conflict the ICTFY potentially has a different context and therefore a different role. First, it can act as a general deterrent, contributing to the evolution of individual accountability for war crimes. And secondly, in beginning to piece together a 'truth' to the conflict the ICTFY can perhaps create a basis for reconciliation. The focus of the court on individual culpability means that it may be less well equipped to carry out this second function, and interestingly some local Bosnian non-governmental organizations are pushing for a parallel Truth and Reconciliation Commission to be established which would be more focused to this end.

CONCLUSIONS

International law, through both human rights and humanitarian law branches, is moving towards an increased notion of individual accountability and punishment during and after conflict, in cases of both internal and international conflict. Indeed the issue of accountability is contributing to a breakdown of the internal–international division, as the *Tadić* case illustrates. However, the notion of accountability meshes somewhat uneasily with the issue of prisoner release, which is provided for in humanitarian law but not in human rights instruments. In recent times there has also been increased international interest in how to address the victims of conflict. Again this interest has begun to challenge distinctions between international and internal conflict and between state and non-state violations. International law also contains a right to compensation or reparation for victims of certain human rights abuses.

Peace agreements must address the issues posed by the past in a focused way, and connect them to the political realities of the compromise between old and new orders struck in the deal. The resulting mechanisms are affected by three factors, which are broadly similar to those affecting forward-looking human rights institutions: first, the 'deal' and the resulting balance of power between old and new order; secondly, the socio-legal legacy of the past, including what types of mechanism have been tried before; and thirdly, international legal provision.[106]

---

[105] Akhavan (1998: 744).   [106] Cf. Huyse (1995: 71–7).

Balance of Power

Just as the forward-looking human rights institutions link to the central deal cut, so too do the backward-looking ones. As Huyse notes, the widest scope for prosecutions arises in the case of an overthrow or 'victory' where virtually no political limits on retributive punishment pertain.[107] In contrast, where a peace agreement fashions a compromise between political elites, then both sets of elites influence the options for dealing with the past. It is unsurprising that in such a situation amnesties for those elites are standard fare. Holistic mechanisms aimed at providing a measure of accountability tend not to figure in framework–substantive peace agreements for this reason. In contrast, although most agreements address aspects of the past, the issue of prisoner release is often dealt with in the pre-negotiation stage, or by the framework stage at the latest. Where holistic mechanisms do figure at the framework stage, this is often because the international community plays a part in putting them there, as in BiH. Holistic mechanisms tend to emerge, if at all, in the post-framework agreement implementation stage, particularly as a balance of power continues to shift, as the case of South Africa illustrates.

Domestic Context

A second factor influencing the policy decision on how to deal with the past is the specific domestic context. Significant to the mechanism chosen for dealing with the past is the country's past experience with such mechanisms. In Northern Ireland historically IRA ceasefires had been followed by prisoner release.[108] In South Africa the immediate context of past amnesties was influential in shaping Interim Constitution provision for amnesties and reconciliation, and the resultant TRC. Similarly, the scope of the TRC and notion of reconciliation which it promoted presumed that economic justice and reconstruction would be provided elsewhere through the Constitution.[109] In the Israeli/Palestinian context, both imprisonment and release had been used historically as political bargaining chips. The mechanism of the ICTFY, as an internationally designed body, was not influenced by domestic institutional context but by past international experience of such mechanisms.

International Law

International law's movement towards accountability influences the design of mechanisms to deal with the past. The case-studies reveal a vital

---

[107] Huyse (1995: 76).   [108] See further McEvoy (1999: 1541–8).   [109] Hamber (1998*b*).

role for international law standards in shaping these models, albeit not a 'hard law' regulation. As noted earlier, domestic mechanisms for dealing with the past have, arguably under the influence of international law, moved towards tighter notions of accountability.[110] Blanket amnesties have tended to give way to more nuanced processes. International law's move towards accountability can also play a useful role in mediating and eliminating some of the traditional dilemmas of transitional justice.[111] For example, dilemmas over whether to judge according to positivist notions of law or naturalist notions of law can be transcended by judging according to standards of international customary law or 'crimes against humanity' jurisprudence, so providing a positivist basis upon which to introduce 'natural law' standards. This interaction of peace process mechanisms with international law is mutually reinforcing. The case of BiH and the ICTFY provides a good example. While an international legal response to the conflict, it at the same time provided impetus to international law's evolutionary direction.

In addition to this broad moral shaping of domestic mechanisms, international law lends a moral discourse to the technical decisions that have to be made in implementing any mechanism. Where, as in Northern Ireland, South Africa, and Israel/Palestine, imprisonment was effected through (emergency) criminal law processes, this creates post-conflict problems over which prisoners, if any, to release. The technical debates over which categories of prisoner should be released often play out a deeper debate about the extent to which the conflict was a 'just war', about the types of military action which were justified, the types which were not, and the extent to which parity of treatment between armed opposition groups and government accountability can be expected. Even when international law standards are not accepted by all sides as relevant, they can obliquely inform this debate by providing categories of offence and suggesting when individual accountability is appropriate and when it is not. The morality behind international law's distinctions and categorizations coincide with the distinctions between types of armed action that people seek to make after conflict. The case of South Africa provides an example of the role which international standards can have at different stages of the process. Humanitarian law was used as a basis for the ANC to judge itself in internal processes of accountability; comparative law on political offences provided a basis upon which to categorize prisoners with a view to prisoner release mechanisms; and international human rights and humanitarian law helped provide definitions of gross violations of human rights for the TRC, even while providing standards by which to judge the TRC mechanism itself.[112]

---

[110] See above, p. 272.   [111] See Teitel (1997: 2028–9).   [112] See Dugard (1997b, c).

Lessons from Peace Agreements for International Law

While international law plays a part in shaping mechanisms for the past, it points primarily towards a model of individual accountability and punishment. Peace processes and agreements demonstrate more diverse and less tidy models. Such models often seem untidy owing to political compromise. However, such compromises can also produce experimental and innovative solutions to a broad set of interlocking, and at times inconsistent, demands. Peace process models should not therefore be evaluated or dismissed solely in terms of traditional models of penal justice. Such traditional models revolve around assigning guilt or innocence to individuals as regards specific crimes. The production of any type of 'truth' is at best a side product, but certainly not the main end of peace process attempts to deal with the past.

In contrast to traditional penal models, as Teitel notes, transitional criminal processes are characterized by the partial criminal sanction—a sanction which 'prosecutes past regime wrongs but does not necessarily culminate in individual culpability and punishment.'[113] This partiality is justified in terms of the demands of transition, such as the need for stability or the difficulty of finding appropriate legal procedures and systems. However, transitional criminal justice is not partial merely because full justice is logistically or politically difficult. It is partial because this best serves the transition. Even though the transitional criminal sanction does not fully recognize individual guilt, the transitional sanction 'enables societies to recognise and condemn past wrongdoing perpetrated under repressive rule.'[114] It provides a mechanism for societies to come to some form of agreed 'truth' about the causes and worst abuses of the conflict and marks a line between regimes. Viewed this way, such transitional justice is neither better nor worse than the traditional model; it is just different. It serves a different notion of the state, and occupies a different role as regards social change and social order from traditional justice.

In other words, while international law and traditional criminal processes focus on individuals, the demands of transition include competing communal demands concerning the past. As Cohen notes, central to coming to terms with the past is 'to know exactly what happened, to tell the truth, to face the facts.'[115] While important at an individual level for families of victims, this is important too at the communal level. While individuals demand truth and justice for themselves and for relatives, a society may search for a truth about the conflict more generally. This type of truth is often seen as a necessary precursor to intercommunal reconciliation.

[113] Teitel (1997: 2049).   [114] Teitel (1997: 2051).   [115] S. Cohen (1995: 12).

What is often being sought under the banner of truth is a form of social history which will underwrite the peace agreement's meta-bargain as to what the conflict was 'about' in its broadest sense. The TRC, quoting Albie Sacks, described this 'social truth' as 'the truth of experience that is established through interaction, discussion and debate.'[116] The broad conclusions of the South African TRC regarding culpability in the conflict provide a good example of this type of 'agreed history'. The civic society pressure for a truth and reconciliation process in BiH also marks the fact that the international criminal processes, even if they were effective, are not designed for, nor capable of arriving at, this type of truth.[117] The nature of the deal is crucial to any attempt to reach a social history which will be officially endorsed, or even shared among divided communities. Where the peace agreement has not reached a meta-bargain as to the cause of the conflict, then it is unrealistic to expect that a mechanism addressing the past will reach an agreed history. Such a history can only be reached, if at all, when the conflict has been substantively transformed.

International law's emphasis on criminal law models of accountability and punishment should not, of course, be dismissed. International law has played and will continue to play an important part in setting out a moral statement. The trickle-down effect of such a moral statement on future domestic processes will be as important as, and probably more so than, the number of people international criminal trials put behind bars. However, international lawyers should remain aware that the demands of communities do not start and end with the punishment of individuals. Domestically designed mechanisms for dealing with the past respond also to communal demands for truth which cannot be delivered by traditional criminal models. While domestic models for dealing with the past typically use a partial criminal sanction, they often aim to deliver a broader range of goals than criminal processes. These goals are focused on the need for a transition from a situation of human rights abuses to a future rule of law. Such models should be evaluated not merely in terms of the measure of punishment they provide, but in terms of how effective they are in facilitating this transition. Consideration of the different contexts in which mechanisms for dealing with the past function may provide a way of reconciling international duties to punish with domestic use of the partial criminal sanction. For example, Cassese attempts to justify differences between the TRC's approach to amnesty in South Africa and

---

[116] Truth and Reconciliation Commission (1998, vol. 1, ch. 5, paras. 39–40) (the TRC identifies this type of truth as where 'the closest connection between the Commission's process and its goal was to be found'). See further the different notions of 'truth' set out in Truth and Reconciliation Commission (1998, vol. 1, ch. 5, paras. 29–45).

[117] Cf. Akhavan (1998: 783–6).

the ICTFY's approach in former Yugoslavia, with reference to the different stages of democracy that the processes have led to.[118]

Interestingly, during the drafting of the International Criminal Court statute, the drafters considered whether to give any special protection to alternative methods of accountability, such as truth commissions, and decided not to. It may be that the court itself may well find 'loopholes' in the statute that will, in practice, enable it to respect 'legitimate' amnesties, such as those of the South African Truth and Reconciliation Commission, while dismissing 'illegitimate' ones, such as that of Pinochet.[119] However, this remains to be seen.

Moreover, punishment is not the only way to achieve accountability. Domestic models for dealing with the past can and do incorporate notions of 'restorative justice' which have gained currency in domestic criminal legal systems. The TRC in South Africa, with its notion of truth-telling for amnesty, provides a good example. In Northern Ireland, also, prisoners were not given amnesties but qualified for 'early release' on 'licence', meaning that they can be recalled in certain circumstances to finish their sentence in the event of a breakdown in the process and consequent reoffending. The distinction between amnesty and early release was useful to those who sought to answer opponents of prisoner release that people were merely 'getting off'. However, it indicates yet another way to reconcile (albeit imperfectly) prisoner release with international notions of accountability in that both past conviction and the potential for future reimprisonment remain. The introduction of notions of restorative justice to international criminal processes might provide a way of fusing goals of accountability with broader political goals, although it could also undermine attempts to move towards punishment as accountability.

Interestingly *The Basic Principles and Guidelines on the Right to Reparation for Victims of [Gross] Violations of Human Rights and International Humanitarian Law*, prepared in 1997 by Theodore Van Boven for the Human Rights Commission, evidences a beginning to how the broader demands of a peace process can be accommodated in international legal frameworks.[120] While judicial sanctions against violators are provided for, also provided for as part of the 'Satisfaction and guarantees of non-repetition' for victims are

    (a) Cessation of continuing violations;
    (b) Verification of the facts and full public disclosure of the truth;

---

[118] Cf. Cassese (1998*a*), in effect arguing that the notion of accountability operates differently in different transitions, depending on what is being transitioned from and to.

[119] See e.g. Article 17(1)(d) Rome Statute (which says that the court shall declare inadmissible a case that is not of 'sufficient gravity'. This could potentially be applied where there has already been a satisfactory domestic effort at accountability). I am indebted to Professor Bill Schabas for raising this point with me.   [120] E/CN.4/1997/104.

(c) An official declaration or a judicial decision restoring the dignity, reputation and legal rights of the victim and/or of persons closely connected with the victim;

(d) Apology, including public acknowledgement of the fact and acceptance of responsibility;

(e) Commemorations and paying tribute to the victims;

(f) Judicial or administrative sanctions against persons responsible for the violations;

(g) *Inclusion in human rights training and in history or school textbooks of an accurate account of the violations committed in the field of human rights and international humanitarian law* . . . (emphasis added)

These begin to address the need for broader notions of truth and justice rather than merely assignation of guilt or innocence to individuals.

In conclusion, while international law can ground and shape mechanisms for dealing with the past, the provision in peace agreements can also play a creative and experimental role in how to satisfy the needs of victims, the demands of transition, and more flexible notions of both accountability and 'punishment'. While the tensions between justice and peace, law and politics, raised at the start of this book apparently come into stark relief when mechanisms for dealing with the past are considered, the case-studies reveal a 'jurisprudence of transition' which helps explain how and why they are mediated.[121] This jurisprudence of transition is useful to understanding how the relationship between human rights and peace is mediated, not just in this area, but in the others we have look at thus far, and will be addressed further in the final chapter.

[121] Cf. Teitel (1997).

10

'Back to the Future': Human Rights and Peace Agreements

This book set out to examine, first, the place and role of human rights provisions in peace agreements, and secondly, their relationship to international law. Throughout the book, a narrative has emerged which can now be summarized and expanded.

The human rights component of a peace agreement is shaped by three main factors. First, the central deal providing for access to power and, if relevant, territory. This deal itself can be seen as part of the human rights component of the peace agreement, as it aims to address the self-determination and minority rights issues at the heart of the conflict. Yet this central 'deal' also profoundly affects institutional provision for individual rights. Secondly, both individual and human rights provisions are also shaped by the contextual history of past human rights abuses. They do not emerge as 'ideal-type' institutions, but as a response to specific claims of abuse, and this both shapes their design and affects their role. Thirdly, both group and individual human rights provisions are shaped by international human rights law. These factors will be considered in turn and used to return to some of the underlying theoretical questions about the relationship between justice and peace, and law and politics, raised at the start of the book.

HUMAN RIGHTS AND THE DEAL

The book began by asking, what are peace agreements and what are human rights, and exploring what it meant therefore to talk about the 'human rights component of a peace agreement'. Examination of the framework agreements in the four case-studies has indicated just how impossible it is to separate the 'human rights' component of a peace agreement from the overall political package that is the peace agreement. It is impossible to separate the law from the politics. Individual and group rights mesh together to form complex constitutional arrangements. These arrangements form, in essence, a contract between competing groups regarding access to power and, depending on the conflict, territorially based control.

Individual human rights provisions (both forward-looking and backward-looking) are crucially shaped by the deal at the heart of the peace agreement. The central deal controls whether human rights protections are addressed at all. Where the deal in essence moves towards a complete 'divorce' between peoples and partition of territory, as in the case of Israel/Palestine, then the political elites of both sides may not have an interest in seeing human rights protections written into the text of that divorce agreement.

Conversely, where complete territorial separation is not contemplated, then human rights institutions may be crucial to enabling agreement on access to government. Human rights protections can address past allegations of lack of legitimacy. They can also provide for future safeguards against abuse of power under the new governmental and territorial arrangements. In Bosnia Herzegovina (BiH) it is the preservation of a unitary state and the vision of an ethnically mixed BiH which necessitates the human rights mechanisms of the Dayton Peace Agreement (DPA). The human rights protections in turn give the unitary state substance (or not, depending on their implementation). The strength of the human rights protections and the unitary state are integrally linked—they thrive or fail together. For without human rights protections people will remain within areas where their ethnic group controls power.

In Northern Ireland the Belfast Agreement provides a political arrangement for devolving power to a Northern Ireland power-sharing Assembly and Executive, together with a North–South executive dimension. Human rights protections form a safeguard against dominance and discrimination for both communities. Like the political institutions, the human rights dimension signals a fundamental change in the nature of the state. It is to be a state which recognizes both nationalist and unionist aspirations and identities as equally legitimate. In South Africa human rights protections are central to what is in essence a transfer of power. Human rights provide a new legitimacy to a new regime, but also aim to establish the new regime as multiracial or pluralist, and capable of protecting rights regardless of ethnicity, rather than a mirror image of its predecessor.

In all these examples provision for the protection and promotion of individual human rights is part of a bigger constitutional picture. Conversely, the political arrangements which form the other dimension of that picture are equally addressed to remedying past human rights abuses such as exclusion and domination. The overlap between politics and law does not evidence a lack of principle. Rather it indicates that peacemaking is often in fact constitution-making. The 'deal' and specific human rights institutions and protections together constitute 'the human rights component' of a peace agreement, although for the sake of clarity the term 'human rights' will be used to refer to specific provision other than self-determination provision throughout the remainder of this chapter.

Typical Human Rights Dynamics

Understanding the relationship between political issues of access to power and human rights issues helps to explain some typical negotiation dynamics as regards human rights. It helps to explain characteristic sequencing in which such issues are addressed, and complex constitutional arrangements developed. It also helps to explain why some human rights issues are more difficult to reach agreement on than others.

Sequencing

As regards sequencing, Table 10.1 indicates a typical sequencing of human rights issues in pre-negotiation, framework, and implementation agreements.

Pre-Negotiation Agreements

Human rights institutions often enter a peace agreement as a result of principled demands based on experience of past human rights abuses. The pressure for a human rights component within a peace agreement usually comes from one side's analysis of the causes of the conflict. Human rights therefore require to be addressed in any attempt to resolve the conflict by negotiation. Given that many conflicts are asymmetrical, the demand for human rights protections is usually initiated by the weaker party, which sees human rights as addressing a status quo against which it is battling.

During the pre-negotiation stage of negotiations, however, the human rights issues which come to be addressed are usually confined to discrete issues which impinge on the negotiating context itself. This is because human rights issues go to the heart of the substance of the dispute, and to address them substantively involves addressing the conflict substantively. Pre-negotiation human rights provision therefore tends only to include measures to limit the waging of violent conflict so that face-to-face negotiations can take place, and measures to ensure that such negotiations will not be used as cover to achieve a military defeat. Depending on the conflict, measures typically include ceasefires and/or governmental commitments to cease certain types of human rights abuse, such as use of the death penalty or aspects of emergency law such as administrative detention.

However, in other conflicts a substantive–framework peace agreement may be negotiated while the conflict is being pursued unabated and unlimited by human rights constraints. The pressure for a peace agreement may come from primarily external forces rather than internal ones. Both the Israel/Palestine peace process and the Dayton process for BiH

TABLE 10.1. *Sequencing of human rights issues*

Peace agreement	Human rights issues typically addressed
Pre-negotiation	Provisions to limit the conflict: • ceasefires • scaling back of emergency legislation • compliance with humanitarian and human rights standards • monitoring of compliance
	Humanitarian relief to victims of conflict
	Ad hoc addressing of past: • partial prisoner release • partial amnesties • independent commissions to investigate alleged abuses • return of bodies disappeared
Framework	Arrangements for access to power and territory
	Provision of a human rights agenda: • bill of rights • human rights commission • other commissions • reform of policing • reform of criminal justice • reform of judiciary
	Provision for an agenda for undoing the past: • return of refugees • return of land
	Ad hoc measures addressed at the past: • amnesties • prisoner release • measures for reconciliation • measures addressed at helping 'victims' • embryonic and partial truth processes
	Provision for civic society to become involved in implementation
Implementation–renegotiation	Refinement/clarification/renegotiation of central deal
	If agreement continues to move forward:
	Demilitarization: • monitoring Taking forward of human rights commitments: • establishment of institutions • institutions engage with society and continue to define human rights
	Increased involvement of civic society in human rights agenda (and process generally)
	More measures to deal with past human rights abuses, including perhaps a unified holistic mechanism

provide examples. In the Israeli/Palestinian peace process a secretly negotiated deal arrived into a violent conflict which was continuing. In BiH international attempts to negotiate peace took place simultaneously with the waging of conflict and gross violations of humanitarian and human rights standards, which the international community had failed to limit. The framework agreements, particularly in BiH, were in essence complex constitutional packages aiming to deal with many dimensions of the conflict simultaneously, thus eliminating underlying reasons for violence.

Framework Agreements

Unlike the pre-negotiation agreement, human rights rhetoric only takes hold in a framework agreement if it serves the interests of both sides for it to do so. Although the less powerful often articulate their claims in human rights terms, the generality, abstract impartiality, and international basis of human rights standards mean that, as the process progresses, both sides may turn to the language of human rights.

At the framework or substantive agreement stage an arrangement regarding access to government and territory aims to address the self-determination issues at the heart of the deal. At this point the language of human rights can provide a vital negotiating tool by helping to carve out win–win solutions from zero sum demands. Individualized human rights protections can address fears of annihilation, domination, and discrimination that motivate claims to territory and statehood, potentially diffusing such claims.[1] Institutions for protecting human rights can soften a power allocation at the centre of the deal by providing protections against its abuses. If the deal is one where political institutions and a unified territory are to be shared between different groups, then both sides may have an interest in seeing human rights language used, despite radically different notions of what human rights are, and of what their implementation will lead to in practice. In the text of a peace agreement such differences can often be masked and postponed by the general and universal language of rights.

More cynically, the language of rights may be rhetorically useful to those who do not contemplate conceding the human rights demands of the other side. Those who have not framed their demands in human rights language during the conflict will often come to do so during the peace process, recognizing it as an internationally endorsed language. Rights language may signal the satisfaction of the human rights claims at the heart of the conflict, even where substance has not been conceded. Human rights institutions may stamp an agreement with the badge of

---

[1] Cf. Fisher and Ury (1991); see Bell (1999).

democracy, giving it international legitimacy. In other words, human rights mechanisms can be conceded as the universally recognized chic language in which to write peace agreements.[2] Bosnia Herzegovina, and arguably Northern Ireland, provide two very different cases where human rights language was conceded by those who had not traditionally subscribed to such language, for some of these reasons.

Whatever the reasons, human rights institutions are typically included as integral to the central deal, as it emerges as a constitution-making project. These provisions include bills of rights, national institutions for protecting rights, and reform of the criminal justice system, including the judiciary and police. Often provision is not complete, but provides for broad statements of principle and a process of development and implementation. Both South Africa and Northern Ireland illustrate this type of staging. While making substantive provision for human rights, the peace agreements also provide for the further development and negotiation of this provision. This both avoids having to reach full and final agreement on everything at once, and enables a wider section of society to become involved in the negotiation of fundamental institutions, thus broadening and deepening the process.

Framework or substantive agreements may also include measures aimed at undoing the conflict, such as return of refugees, adjudication of land claims, and release of prisoners. These may be accompanied by other measures aimed at the past, such as provision for victims, and preliminary inquiries into certain past atrocities. However, a more holistic mechanism for adjudicating on past human rights abuses is rarely agreed at this stage. Only in BiH was a broad mechanism in place at the time of the signing of the peace agreement, and this was only because the mechanism—the Ad Hoc International Criminal Tribunal for Former Yugoslavia (ICTFY)—was in fact a pre-Dayton wartime mechanism aimed at limiting the conflict and inducing settlement through deterrence.

Implementation: Winners and Losers

At the implementation stage, as noted in Chapter 2, a measure of renegotiation often takes place as parties explicitly renege on earlier commitments or more subtly try to reshape the agreement in their own image. Depending on how the agreement holds, the human rights institutions will continue to be implemented and begin their adjudicative and integrative functions. Often this is the point at which civic society can become more involved in a structural way in the peace process through

---

[2] Cf. Pogany (1996) (noting that while recent constitution-making in Eastern European countries has followed Western liberal/international law patterns, genuine constitutional transformation has often remained elusive).

the new institutions. However, as described in Chapter 7, the nature of the 'deal' also helps to predict some of the difficulties which will arise.

In particular, implementation is affected by the balance of power between the parties as documented in the deal. Negotiated settlements are usually based on trying to avoid the appearance of winners and losers. If one side is going to lose in negotiation, then it is likely to continue violent conflict in the hope that military victories will change the negotiating dynamics, or even deliver a victory directly. As noted in Chapter 2, ethno-political conflict often typically involves a meta-conflict, or conflict about what the conflict is about. Negotiations therefore involve 'meta-bargaining', or bargaining around the analysis of the conflict.[3] The meta-bargain which emerges in the subtext of a peace agreement will usually not be evenly balanced. It is likely to be more consistent with one side's analysis than the other's. Where the international community is providing the main impetus for deal-making, as in BiH and the Israeli/Palestinian conflict, then the bargain struck in the agreement will reflect less a meta-bargain between the parties, and more the international community notion of what the meta-bargain should be, however incomplete or confused that notion is. The international positions adopted during the conflict crucially affect the power relations between the parties to the conflict, and the shape of any peace agreement, as illustrated in Chapters 3 and 4.

The implementation of human rights measures is largely dependent on some type of meta-bargain having been reached. In BiH it is clear from the text of the DPA that the human rights institutions which aim to cement the unitary state stand at odds with the Entities and the scope of their autonomy. Given the lack of ethno-national consent to the unitary structure it is not surprising that there is resistance to implementing the decisions of the human rights institutions. In the Israeli/Palestinian agreements the failure of the international community to set limits on how the conflict was waged makes meta-bargaining difficult and increases the likelihood that Israeli analysis of the 'solution' to the conflict will prevail. The absence of rights protections to the process also means that the negotiating positions and actions of Palestinian elites can become increasingly separated from the interests of the people they supposedly represent. Both factors would seem to reduce the chances that the process will result in a permanent reduction, or end, to violence.

In Northern Ireland, while the reaching of an agreed text reflects the fact that a meta-bargain has begun to be reached, this bargain is incomplete. The agreement is compatible with both British unionist and Irish nationalist sovereign aspirations for the future. The agreement contains

---

[3] Cf. Du Toit (1989)

the potential for either vision to be achieved, although also on another view, for a transcendent non-state centred 'third way'.[4] The human rights dimension of the agreement is likely to be a key site for a debate over the nature of the deal reached (especially if political institutions break down). This debate is likely to evidence tension around the extent to which human rights institutions should address the ability of the state to provide equality to Irish nationalists or not.

In South Africa, where a meta-bargain can be identified involving, in essence, a clear transfer of power with human rights constraints, implementation of the human rights provisions of the Interim and Final Constitutions has confirmed the nature of the transition. However, the failure of the new regime to deliver decisive movement towards socio-economic equality, and the accompanying high crime rate, indicate that, while the conflict has been transformed, it has not been eliminated.[5] Implementation of the human rights provisions is likely to be affected in particular by pressure for economic justice, both within the human rights institutions, and also paradoxically in calls for the limitations of human rights in the name of economic stability.

Reaching Agreement

The relationship between the central deal and the human rights provisions, as evidenced by their sequencing, helps to explain why some types of human rights provision are easier to reach agreement on than others. In short, some types of human rights provision are more crucially dependent on a meta-bargain having been reached than others.

Forward-looking human rights provisions may be fairly easy to get agreement on in general terms, as they are often consistent with different views of the bargain at the heart of the deal. Bills of rights, national human rights institutions, impartial judiciary, and impartial police are fairly easy to agree on in principle at a general and abstract level. In South Africa, for example, disagreement on the scope of affirmative action was ultimately resolved by turning to the general and abstract language of international human rights provision.[6] In Northern Ireland general statements regarding principles of policing avoided the central question of whether the pre-agreement Royal Ulster Constabulary did or could comply with those principles. While Irish nationalists signed up to the principles as a precursor to radical reform of policing, British unionists

---

[4] See further p. 314.   [5] Hamber (1998*b*).
[6] Initial drafts of section 8(3)(a) of the Constitution of the Republic of South Africa Act 200 of 1993 (hereafter Interim Constitution) were modelled on Article 1(4) of the International Convention on the Elimination of all Forms of Racial Discrimination. See Corder and Du Plessis (1994: 47, 144–5), and Ch. 7, p. 207.

signed up on the basis that the existing police force largely complied already. In BiH human rights were inserted in the agreement by adopting wholesale a raft of international conventions, avoiding the need to get agreement on every provision, but at the same time avoiding engagement with radically different notions of how much implementation would be necessary or possible.

In contrast, the detail of what is in a bill of rights, how those rights play out in application, composition of national institutions, or what constitutes impartiality—all much more difficult to resolve—often do not have to be resolved until the implementation stage. During implementation what was fairly easy to agree in the abstract will often be revealed in all its controversy. In South Africa the Constitutional Court, interpreting the equality provision of the Interim Bill of Rights, found that, given the country's context, 'equality' should be asymmetrical and thus justified different treatment of whites and blacks.[7] In Northern Ireland, when the Patten Commission on policing finally made its recommendations, it was the recommendation to rename the Royal Ulster Constabulary, thus providing a symbolic break with both the past and a British ethos, which proved most difficult for unionists to accept.[8]

In contrast to the relative ease with which agreement can be achieved on forward-looking human rights provisions, the extent to which a society is able or willing to address past human rights abuses depends entirely on the balance of power struck in the deal, and the extent to which the deal itself has produced a meta-bargain on what the conflict was 'about'. Until there is substantial agreement about the causes of the conflict, it is almost impossible to reach agreement on how the divided society can account for the past, because the parties are still essentially waging the conflict. Out of the four case-studies, only in South Africa has a comprehensive attempt to deal with the past been made. Even there its detail was not agreed at the framework stage. The fact that the Truth and Reconciliation Commission was possible at all reflects the fact that a meta-bargain had been reached.[9]

---

[7] *City Council of Pretoria* v. *Walker* (1998) (2) SA 363 (CC); 1998 (3) BCLR 257 (CC). Cf. also *President of the Republic of South Africa* v. *Hugo* 1997 (4) SA 1 (CC), 1997 (6) BCLR 708 (CC).

[8] Recommendation 150, Independent Commission on Policing for Northern Ireland (1999: 121).

[9] See e.g. Hamber (1998b) (who in essence argues that the focus of the Truth and Reconciliation Commission on gross violations of individuals rather than the structural benefactors of apartheid reflected the fact that the meta-bargain involved a compromise between political change and economic instability which was at odds with the reconciliation it aimed to promote—which requires economic justice). Cf. also the harsher assessment of the deal by Pilger (1998: 604–10).

THE CONTEXT OF THE PAST: THE JURISPRUDENCE OF TRANSITION

Human rights institutions are shaped not only by the context of the 'deal', but also by the particular context of past abuses. Individual rights protections signal a transition from a less liberal to a more liberal regime. The particular human rights issues addressed, and the institutions established to address them, are shaped by notions of past injustice. The role of such institutions can therefore be understood as inherently transitional—mediating between past and future. This view of the role of law is useful for re-evaluating the tension between justice and peace, law and politics outlined at the start of the book.

In the first chapter examination of human rights and peace agreements was presented as a lens through which to examine the relationship between justice and peace, or between law and politics.[10] These disputes can be jurisprudentially restated as a philosophical dispute about the boundaries between law and politics. There are two main competing versions of this relationship: that articulated by Kantian liberalism and that articulated by a range of utilitarian, critical and/or communitarian theories.[11]

From the Kantian liberal position, questions of rights are prior to questions of the good; in other words, a framework for justice based on individual rights and freedoms must be prior to any attempt to prescribe communal values for living. Liberal theorists argue that ensuring a basic level of equality and rights enables political society to facilitate a multiplicity of personal life choices and that communal values must then be negotiated in political life, as subject to those rights. In human rights terms this translates to the argument that questions of rights are universal in application and so their protection should not be contingent on showing that they lead to another end (such as 'peace') but are a prior matter. In other words, 'justice is not merely one important value among others, to be weighed and considered as the occasion requires, but rather the *means* by which values are weighed and assessed.'[12] As with the human rights activist's defences to the 'peace first' argument, the liberal asserts, first, that justice is the primary organizing principle of any society, in other words prior to the 'good' (in this case 'peace'); and secondly, that in a deeper sense justice is peace, if peace is understood as the presence of fair processes rather than any particular political vision. In contrast, a broad range of opposing positions denies that matters of justice are prior

---

[10] Although human rights are not being equated with 'justice', it is chiefly through the human rights component of peace agreements that questions of 'justice' are addressed.

[11] For classic articulation of liberalism, see Kant (1781); Rawls (1971, 1993); for a critical legal approach, see e.g. Unger (1975, 1986).   [12] Sandel (1982: 15–16).

to matters of politics, but that they must be negotiated as part and parcel of political matters.[13]

The case-studies reveal that the tension between justice and peace is often misconceived for two reasons: first, because, as we have seen, in practice political processes often assign value to human rights language and institutions for intensely pragmatic reasons.[14] In other words, in practice the tension between justice and peace can be overstated in the abstract: human rights provisions are included in peace agreements precisely because without them peace cannot be achieved or has no content.[15]

More fundamentally, the tension between justice and peace, and, thus, the relevance of distinctions between different jurisprudential conceptions of their relationship, is misconceived because it fails to recognize the peculiar role of law in times of transition. Both forward- and backward-looking human rights provisions play a role in the processes of transition which is different from their role in times of less cataclysmic social change. Rather than evaluating human rights provisions in terms of whether they comply with liberal conceptions of justice or not, and bemoaning the subjection of justice to peace when they do not, it can be useful to evaluate the human rights provisions of peace agreements in terms of what Teitel has termed a 'jurisprudence of transition'.[16]

Teitel suggests that '[l]egal practices in such periods reveal a struggle between two points, between settled and revolutionary times, as well as a dialectically induced third position.'[17] This dialectically induced third position comprises the transitory structures of the peace agreement. In ordinary times law and constitutions aim to provide stability and order, and forward-looking adjudication. Notions of the rule of law and of the constraints of constitutional interpretation are shaped by the demands of stability and order. In contrast, during times of transition law aims to mediate between the old regime and the new political arrangements. Law and constitutions in such times draw their sense of justice from past human rights abuses, and notions of the rule of law and constitutional interpretation are shaped by the attempt to construct a different future. As a result, during transition '[p]ersistent dichotomous choices arise as to

---

[13] Opposition to Kantian liberalism ranges from utilitarian critiques (Mill 1859) to communitarian critiques (e.g. Sandel 1982) to Southern challenges (e.g. wa Mutua 1995), the 'Asian values' challenge to human rights (see Ghai 1994; Kausikan 1993); the Islam and human rights debate (An Na'im 1990, 1992), and feminist and critical perspectives (e.g. Fraser 1999; Fraser and Lacey 1994; Rorty 1993).

[14] Cf. Kaufman and Bisharat (1998*a*, *b*).

[15] Constitutional theory based on empirical accounts of constitutionalism have interestingly come to similar conclusions; see e.g. Castiglione (1996) (arguing that while republican and liberal constitutionalism represent two different conceptions of the constitution, and, more generally, of the nature of politics, in fact historically the two paradigms were combined). [16] Teitel (1997).

[17] Teitel (1997: 2077).

law's role in periods of political change: backward versus forward, retroactive versus prospective, continuity versus discontinuity, individual versus collective.'[18]

This transitional dynamic can be illustrated by a brief analysis of the distinctive legal nature of peace agreements. The difficulty of classifying peace agreements as legal documents testifies to a role which is simultaneously constitution-making and transitional. Their function as 'transitional constitutions' in turn helps to explain the characteristic difficulties for the human rights institutions established by peace agreements, difficulties which revolve around the above dichotomies.

The Legal Nature of Peace Agreements

Throughout this book framework peace agreements have been described as encapsulating a central 'deal' or 'contract' or set of political arrangements or 'constitution'. This variety of terms reflects the difficulty with classifying peace agreements as legal documents. The peace agreements themselves at times are called 'constitutions' or include a constitution. They often involve both domestic and international actors. Where they involve only state parties they comprise treaties, but often they involve both states and groups who have a status short of statehood but beyond that of internal political party. It is suggested that peace agreements are best thought of as distinctively transitional constitutions.[19]

Peace agreements provide a constitutional-type 'power map' for the state. They set out the organs of government and the other institutions of the society, and the nature of the relationship between the individual and the state. However, peace agreements have a transitional quality which means that they do not fit within traditional accounts of constitutionalism in either their form or their substance.

Traditional accounts of constitutionalism understand it as 'unidirectional, forward-looking, and fully prospective.'[20] The traditional constitution as social contract looks forward from its fictional point zero and regulates future conflict within a set of accepted power arrangements. If (as is usual) it is in the form of a legal text, it is intended to be more lasting than ordinary legislation (as evidenced by entrenchment), with clear mechanisms for judicial interpretation (key to separation of powers), and stands superior to other laws.[21]

In contrast, peace agreements can only be understood in terms of what has gone before, and what will come after, sharing the characteristics of

[18] Teitel (1997: 2077).
[19] This section uses Teitel's analysis (1997) of 'transitional constitutionalism', adapting it to peace agreements.   [20] Teitel (1997: 2077).
[21] See e.g. Castiglione (1996).

'transitional constitutions'.[22] Peace agreements are distinctively partial and temporary. They balance continuity with discontinuity; they reference past constitutional structures and claim a degree of continuity with those structures, whilst simultaneously claiming legitimacy from the fact that they herald a new beginning. They tend to be produced outside prior mechanisms for constitutional reform, although often also draw on them partially.

Furthermore, unlike traditional constitutions, peace agreements tend to be neither purely domestic, nor international legal documents. Constitutions traditionally form the ultimate domestic legal document—in essence founding and defining the state. Peace agreements, however, form transitional documents which redefine the territorial, political, and power boundaries of the state. In doing so, they incorporate transnational mechanisms and signatories, which in some cases are states, but in others are not. Yet, often they do not classify as traditional treaties, even while a clear international dimension can be identified. They establish the future for what are essentially domestic power arrangements, but often internationalize those power arrangements by involving other states in internal structures, by acknowledging the international status of some non-state entities, and by providing a role for international actors in their implementation.

Peace agreements are further distinctive from traditional constitutions in depending for enforcement not primarily on the courts (who nevertheless may have some role), but on more overtly political processes. In particular they depend for enforcement upon the notion that the deal reached was the only deal that could be reached. The deal is sustained by 'enlightened self-interest', that is the knowledge that any attempt to renegotiate would result in the same net gains and losses for the parties involved. Where that notion is not persuasive, the agreement often breaks down, and constitutional adjudication, or reliance on international law adjudication, cannot save it. Agreements tend to be enforced by notions of reciprocity, by fluid mechanisms for arbitration, review, and renegotiation, or by the involvement of international guarantors, as well as, or instead of, court processes.

The Case-studies

The peace agreements of the case-studies illustrate arrangements which are both constitutional and transitional. The South Africa Interim Constitution, while called a 'constitution', significantly differs from traditional notions of constitutions. It is at the same time a peace agreement. It

---

[22] Cf. Teitel (1997).

claims constitutional status and a new dispensation, but is established as an Act of the apartheid legislature. It speaks of legal continuity of past laws and the South African state,[23] but also of discontinuity and a 'new order'.[24] In the words of its section on National Unity and Reconciliation, the Constitution 'provides a historic bridge' between a past characterized by injustice and a future 'founded on the recognition of human rights, democracy and peaceful co-existence and development opportunities for all South Africans, irrespective of colour, race, class, belief or sex.'

The Interim Constitution complies with definitions of constitutions as providing the basic rules of society, including the framework for government operating according to the rule of law—or a 'power map'. However, this power map is for an interim phase only; the Constitution provides for its own demise and replacement with a Final Constitution. Despite the Interim Constitution's interim status, binding constitutional principles aim to project an image onto the more lasting new Constitution. The detail of its provisions reads more like an insurance contract than the type of general institutional framework normally found in a constitution.

As regards enforcement, the Constitutional Court is given power to enforce the provisions of the Interim Constitution.[25] Unusually for a Constitutional Court it is also given the role 'founding' the Final Constitution; it has to certify whether the Final Constitution complies with the Constitutional Principles of the Interim Constitution. Through this provision the Constitutional Court is tasked with formulating a uniquely transitional judgment—forming both the continuity and discontinuity with the past regime and past constitution-making processes. It is a once-off politico-legal task, through which the court must simultaneously establish its own legitimacy and independence from political processes (in a truly wonderful piece of jurisprudence).[26]

The main body of the Belfast Agreement in Northern Ireland has no apparent domestic legal status. The agreement is signed by the British and Irish governments and the political parties who participated in the talks— a mixture of international and domestic parties. It may well constitute a form of international agreement. The end section, consisting of an agreement between the British and Irish governments alone, clearly constitutes a treaty. Yet, its content is addressed primarily at Northern Irish structures and institutions. The agreement contains no legal

---

[23] Sections 229 and 231 Interim Constitution (providing for continuation of laws and international legal personality).   [24] Preamble Interim Constitution.

[25] Section 98 Interim Constitution.

[26] A process enhanced by the rejection of the first version of the Final Constitution (Constitution of the Republic of South Africa Act 108 of 1996) as not in compliance with the Constitutional Principles. See *Ex Parte Chairperson of the Constitutional Assembly: In Re Certification of the Constitution of the Republic of South Africa, 1996*, 1996 (4) SA 744 (CC), 1996 (10) BCLR 1253 (CC).

enforcement mechanism, neither does it provide a basis for judicially reviewing other legislation. It does, however, provide for political processes of review by the British government alone, the British and Irish governments jointly, and by the institutions themselves.[27]

Although the agreement is not presented as a constitution, it is implemented largely through the Northern Ireland Act, which sets out the detail of devolution and in effect amounts to a Northern Ireland Constitution. The Northern Ireland Act 1998 documents the parameters of devolution, the relationship of the institutions to the overarching British (and Irish) Constitutions, and the principles (of equality and non-violence) which constrain the political structures. In form the Northern Ireland Act 1998 provides continuity with past devolution measures, such as the Northern Ireland Constitution Act 1973. However, in substance it marks a further break from a past British constitutional tradition of 'pragmatic empiricism' (the Constitution as a traditional working arrangement) moving towards 'constitutional idealism' (the Constitution as embodying values and ideals).[28] The Belfast Agreement and Northern Ireland Act 1998 encapsulate an overtly value-driven constitutionalism. They set out a number of values which the institutions are to promote. Decision-making is evaluated and constrained by the extent to which it conforms with those values.[29] Furthermore, the values deal not just with the relationship between individual and state, but with the relationship between groups of individuals. This discontinuity with traditional constitutional processes is marked by the fact that it is an all-Ireland referendum which grants the new arrangements legitimacy rather than previously accepted domestic processes of British constitution-making or law-making. This signals that the Belfast Agreement and Northern Ireland Act 1998 do not codify an existing consensus, but aim to effect that consensus.

The Israeli/Palestinian Declaration of Principles does not claim to be a constitution but, as its title suggests, a 'declaration of principles' within which future negotiations should take place. Subsequent agreements claim to be implementing these principles. The principles and arrangements found within the agreements contain copious detail delimiting the devolution of power to the Palestinian Authority in language which is

[27] Belfast Agreement (hereafter BA), Review Procedures Following Implementation, Validation, Implementation, and Review.

[28] For further explanation of these terms in the Northern Ireland context, see McCrudden (1994). While current developments throughout the United Kingdom, in particular the incorporation of the European Convention on Human Rights in the Human Rights Act 1998, are also moving towards a form of constitutional idealism, at present it is at the level of process more than substance.

[29] Cf. McCrudden (1994) (noting that prior to the peace process this was the direction of constitutionalism in the Northern Irish context).

more contractual than constitutional. The agreements concentrate on logistics rather than values, yet in providing for logistics they aim to provide the framework for how Palestinians are to be governed in the interim period, and in that sense are still 'constitutional'. They establish the form, composition, and powers of Palestinian institutions, together with commitments regarding Israeli deployment.

The Israeli/Palestinian peace agreements seem to be international legal documents.[30] They are signed by the parties, and also (like the Camp David Accords before them) witnessed by other states. Potentially they are treaties, but only if the Palestinian Liberation Organization (PLO) has signed on behalf of an existing Palestinian state; but the current existence of a Palestinian state which satisfies criteria for statehood is, at best, debatable.[31]

If they are not treaties, it seems that, given the PLO's status as an international organization, they are at least international agreements, and as such capable of being legally binding.[32] Yet, even were international legal processes capable of producing binding adjudication on breaches of these agreements, which is unlikely, evaluating when a clear breach has occurred is difficult, as a detailed discussion by Watson indicates.[33] This is largely because of the agreements' extreme ambiguity. However, it is also because the early agreements set out a framework for future progress, and this staging of the process means that drawing a tight distinction between a mere slowing of the process and a 'breach' of an agreement can be unclear. While there is a dispute resolution mechanism built into the agreement, it is essentially a political mechanism dependent on cooperation from both sides.[34] If such cooperation has not sustained the agreement itself, it seems unlikely that it will produce a successful resolution of any dispute.

In BiH the DPA comprises a central agreement with a number of attached agreements (as annexes), several of which are signed by different permutations of parties.[35] The central General Framework itself, signed on behalf of the Republics of BiH and Croatia and the Federal Republic of Yugoslavia, has treaty status with commitments given by the signatories as regards implementation of the annexes. However, as

[30] For a detailed discussion of the status of the agreements, see Watson (2000: 55–102). See also Alting von Gesau (1995: 91–5); Malanczuk (1996: 488–92).

[31] See Boyle (1990); cf. Crawford (1990).

[32] See Article 3 Vienna Convention on the Law of Treaties. See also Alting von Gesau (1995: 91–5); Malanczuk (1996: 488–92); Watson (2000: 92–102).

[33] Watson (2000: 201–64).

[34] Article XV Declaration of Principles 1993 provides that disputes are to be resolved by 'negotiations' through the Joint Israeli–Palestinian Liaison Committee established by the agreement. This provision also talks of the parties agreeing to a mechanism of conciliation and also a possible arbitration mechanism   [35] See Chs. 3 and 7 n. 133.

an international treaty it contains several distinctive aspects, in particular what has been described as a unique 'hypertrophy of international guarantees'.[36] While the three republics signed the General Framework Agreement, only the Republic of BiH is party to its central annexes. Thus, the treaty seems to be one of 'guarantee', with the Republic of Croatia and Federal Republic of Yugoslavia undertaking to ensure compliance with the various annexes.[37] While the Federal Republic of Yugoslavia seems in places to be signing on behalf of the Republika Srpska, no legal mechanism of agency was established, reflecting a compromise between preventing the participation of indicted war criminals at Dayton and failing to represent Bosnian Serbs at all. As with the Israeli/Palestinian agreements, the witnessing of the DPA by other states and by the European Union can be seen as a form of political underwriting and influenced by the Camp David Accords, which the Dayton process seems to have been modelled on.[38] Other annexes are signed by the Federation of BiH and the Republika Srpska, which under the new arrangements are sub-state Entities. Again a mix of international and internal parties characterizes the peace agreement.

The method of concluding the treaty was also unusual. The DPA was only initialled at Dayton and later signed in Paris. While initialling indicated consent to be bound, the agreement itself only entered into force with signature—in other words signature was a suspensive condition, and this was underlined by UN SC Res 1022, which made suspension of sanctions conditional on signature.[39] Also distinctive is the placing of the power of interpretation of the treaties not with the parties, but with international actors, namely the Office of the High Representative and the multinational force (IFOR) commander.

To describe the DPA in its entirety as a transitional constitution might seem strange, given that a sub-section of it, Annex 4, comprises a 'Constitution'. However, if this annex is examined, it has several unique aspects as a Constitution.[40] First, it does not stand alone, but must be read with the rest of the agreement if it is to make sense. This is not just a matter of interpretative context, but of obtaining a complete constitutional text. For example, as regards refugees and displaced persons, according to

[36] Gaeta (1996: 155) (emphasized in original) (the discussion in this section is drawn more generally from Gaeta's analysis).
[37] See Gaeta (1996: 153). Both the Republic of Croatia and the Federal Republic of Yugoslavia also directly sign Annex 1B (regional stability) and Annex 10 (civilian implementation) of the General Framework Agreement for Peace in Bosnia and Herzegovina, 4 Dec. 1995 (hereafter Dayton Peace Agreement or DPA).
[38] Holbrooke (1998: 204–5).
[39] See Agreement on Initialling the General Framework Agreement for Peace in Bosnia and Herzegovina, 21 Nov. 1995.   [40] Cf. Gaeta (1996: 160–2).

Annex 4, 'they have a right in accordance with Annex 7. . . . to have restored to them property of which they were deprived . . .'. In other words, Annex 7, it would seem, is incorporated in some fashion in the Constitution. Similarly, the Human Rights Commission is referred to in Article II(1) Annex 4, but provided for in Annex 6. The Constitution is also striking in its purported direct incorporation of a large number of international human rights conventions.

The 'constitutional' status of Dayton is also unusual as having been a product of international processes rather than internal processes. It was initially framed in English rather than any of the indigenous languages.[41] It incorporates the previously negotiated Constitution of the Federation of BiH but also requires it to be modified. It claims to promote the legal continuity of the Republic of BiH, but does not use the procedures of, or even refer to, previous Bosnian Constitutions (discontinuity): 'The Republic of Bosnia and Herzegovina . . . shall continue its legal existence under international law as a state, with its internal structure modified as provided herein and with its present internationally recognized borders . . .'.[42]

The means of enforcement of the agreement also reflects its peculiar international status. As regards the agreement as a whole, the Office of the High Representative is given a political role of interpretation (unusual as regards treaties), but has no clear enforcement arm. International actors hold the balance of power in key domestic institutions, such as the Constitutional Court, which has the power to interpret the Constitution, including 'the relationship between the Entities or between Bosnia and Herzegovina and an Entity or Entities, or between institutions of Bosnia and Herzegovina . . .'.[43] These mechanisms give it a continuing role in shaping the deal.

Understanding peace agreements as forms of transitional constitution acknowledges their constitution-making role. It also explains why, unlike traditional liberal-democratic constitutions, they are distinctively partial, temporary, and international, and why their interpretation and implementation is more overtly political. However, understanding the transitional dynamics of peace agreements and their role in social change also sheds light on the relationship between constitutionalism and social change more generally. Contemporary explanations of constitutionalism are increasingly focusing on the constitution as fluid, dialogic, and political, rather than relatively static, prescriptive, and legal. These explanations, interestingly, are prompted by analysis of examples which

---

[41] See Gaeta (1996: 169). [42] Article I(1), Annex 4 DPA.
[43] Article VI(3), Annex 4 DPA.

are in some way transitional, such as that of the European Union, but also by less obviously transitional attempts to find a constitutionalism capable of responding to the dynamic claims of multicultural societies, claims which have proved difficult to accommodate within traditional constitutional models.[44]

This 'jurisprudence of transition' helps to explain the role of human rights institutions negotiated into the text of a peace agreement, and the characteristic dilemmas which face them. Although divided into forward- and backward-looking measures for the sake of analysis, the descriptions of the case-studies in Chapters 6 to 8 illustrate the indivisibility of forward- and backward-looking measures.

The forward-looking human rights institutions aim to provide a new legitimacy and a new order for the future, by looking to the abuses of the past and preventing their recurrence. Human rights institutions in the future are shaped by the abuses of the past rather than any free-floating notion of best practice. In implementation the human rights institutions must continue to construct the shape of the new order, and this will characterize their decision-making. They play a role in mediating between past and future.

Likewise, mechanisms for dealing with past human rights abuses aim not only to deal with the past, but in doing so to legitimize the new order. Partial criminal sanctions—partial in applying only to certain categories of person and crime, and partial in that they often do not require punishment—often emerge as a transitional tool as Teitel has demonstrated. The partial criminal sanction provides an adjudication of the past which at the same time enables the transition to future legitimacy. The idea of undoing the past also provides an illustration. Specific measures aim to reverse the effects of the conflict by providing that refugees return home, that land is returned to those dispossessed, and that prisoners are released. In attempting to undo the past, they aim to reconstruct a future.

The role of the human rights provisions of transition is not therefore to replicate the liberal order, and cannot be evaluated in terms of whether it does or not. Rather the role of human rights provisions is to effect a transition from less to more liberal regimes. A transitional account of the role of law better explains the types of constitution, human rights institution, and mechanisms for dealing with the past which emerge, and the dilemmas which characterize their operation.

---

[44] See generally Bellamy and Castiglione (1996), and in particular, Bellamy (1996); Shaw (1999); Tully (1995).

Transition from What to What?

Any transitional account of the role of law must, however, acknowledge that in many instances, as human rights institutions attempt to negotiate one type of transition, the very goals of transition may still be up for grabs. New human rights institutions appear to signal a transition from a less liberal regime to a more liberal regime and from a regime in which a party feels excluded to one where all are included. However, in at least three of the peace processes examined—Northern Ireland, BiH, and Israel/Palestine—there is still a struggle over what the transition is, in fact, from and to. Is the transition from a less liberal to a more liberal regime? Is it from a majoritarian regime to a more inclusive regime? Is it from an ethnically shared territory to ethnically divided territories? Is it from the sovereignty of one state to the sovereignty of another? Or is it merely transition from violence to non-violence, but leaving the nature of the regime substantively untouched? Time alone will tell what the transition in the case-studies has been from and to, as, certainly in three out of four cases, it is still unclear which vision of the future will prevail.

What is clear is that the ability or not of the deal to deliver on human rights commitments will significantly affect, and even determine, the nature of the transition.[45] Without effective human rights institutions, the transitions in each of these three situations will at best be from more violent to less violent conflict.[46] In South Africa majority power without majority social and economic justice is unlikely to lead to stability. In Northern Ireland power-sharing without the human rights agenda is likely merely to transfer ethno-nationalist struggles to the capsule of the devolved Assembly, leaving root causes of conflict unaddressed. In BiH the (current) failure of human rights institutions seems to point to either prolonged international involvement, or international exit and concurrent moves towards partition and instability. In Israel/Palestine the absence of human rights constraints means that it looks increasingly as if, while the actors might change, the lives of ordinary Palestinians will not.

---

[45] This is especially the case when political institutions collapse, as human rights institutions often can continue to function in such situations.

[46] Cf. Roniger and Sznajder (1999: 267–71) (who conclude after a review of the long-term human rights implications of 'Southern Cone' Latin American peace processes that, while acceptance of human rights language had occurred in the peace process, implementation of human rights practices had largely failed to follow, leading to past trends being re-enacted, and ultimately to continued threats to stability and new forms of human rights violations).

THE ROLE OF INTERNATIONAL LAW

While constitutional arrangements and specific human rights institutions are produced as a result of inter-group bargaining, and shaped by both the experience of past abuses and visions of a better future, international law also plays a crucial role.

International Law Shaping Peace Agreements

Most crucially, the international legal positions taken during the conflict shape the central deal, perhaps more than is often given credit. As illustrated in Chapters 3 to 6, an important part of the context for the deal is the international law positions adopted during the conflict. This shaping can be positive—a set of minimum standards set out with which any solution must comply, as in South Africa or Northern Ireland. Or it can be negative—a failure to set and/or enforce such minimum standards which results in the deal incorporating the conflict, as in Israel/Palestine or BiH. The nature of the deal in turn affects provision for human rights mechanisms, as described above. The international community's willingness and ability to enforce a human rights framework is therefore crucial. To put it starkly, human rights are an integral part of the DPA and an absent part of the DoP, in part because in BiH the United States required their inclusion, while in the Israeli/Palestinian process it did not.

Secondly, when it comes to choosing and designing human rights institutions, international law influences the process. While the particular context of past abuses shapes the human rights provisions, prevailing international law notions of best practice also are influential. Thus the institutional mechanisms have a superficial similarity—judicial reform, policing reform, bills of rights, and human rights commissions. This similarity in part arises from modern notions of constitutionalism as involving judicial protection for enumerated rights. But this notion is reinforced by the move of international law towards a particular set of institutions as necessary to realizing the abstract and general rights which governments commit to. International law can inform negotiations, while providing standards external to any of the parties to the conflict which command a degree of moral force.

International law may also continue to shape a deal during implementation. International human rights institutions may be used to adjudicate on the compliance of transitional provisions with human rights law. Thus, domestic truth and reconciliation processes may well be challenged by international law, and new institutions, such as police, will be monitored through the mechanisms of human rights conventions which have often been ratified as part of the peace agreement package.

Peace Agreements Shaping International Law

Conversely, peace agreements shape international law. This can be illustrated by each of the types of human rights issue addressed. In the case of self-determination, peace agreements play out current normative trends towards robust internal self-determination and accommodation of minorities through group measures such as autonomy, power-sharing, and cross-border contacts. The peace agreements currently pose a question for international legal regulation concerning whether self-determination disputes can be resolved by a move away from sovereign statehood in its traditional sense.[47] Arrangements such as that in the Belfast Agreement may be best understood as 'transitional' either from violence to peace, or even from union with Britain to united Ireland. But could it be possible that the transitional arrangements could transcend the pull towards absolute statehood and form a lasting way of mediating conflicting notions of Irishness and Britishness, and a Northern Ireland which is under the sovereignty of neither or both? The very nature of peace agreements, as neither entirely domestic nor entirely international documents, points to their capacity to impact on traditional accounts of statehood.

In the case of human rights institutions, by drawing on international law notions of 'best practice', peace agreements underwrite international legal movement towards ideal-type institutional arrangements. In the case of undoing the past, as domestic mechanisms move towards greater accountability, they underwrite the moral stance of international criminal law as important but also as practical. However, they also address the wider notions of social truth and the needs of victims in ways that international law has only recently also begun to address.

As this last example illustrates, there are some areas where peace agreements have resorted to arrangements not emphasized in international human rights law (soft or hard). In other areas, examination of peace agreements reveals areas where international law is unclear and where the lack of clarity flows more from incoherence among legal instruments, than from deep controversy as to justiciability, as in the case of self-determination. These areas suggest further lessons which international law could learn from the arrangements in peace agreements.

---

[47] Cf. Gottlieb (1993) (arguing that self-determination disputes can be dealt with by separating notions of nationhood and statehood). Cf. also MacCormick (1996) (arguing that in the European context constitutionalism should combine ties of ethnicity, religion, and nationalism with a liberal respect for persons, and that this has been made possible by the weakening of state sovereignty entailed by the European Union).

The Balancing of Human Rights Institutions according to Ethnic Make-up

Soft law international standards on institutional best practice often do not address the question of ethnic balance in such institutions.[48] New standards dealing with minority rights have begun to address balance in institutions of government through the idea of 'effective participation'.[49] Peace agreements tend also to provide for ethnic balance in human rights commissions, the police, and the judiciary, and for the symbols of each to be neutral as between competing nationalisms. Further international consideration should be given to the fairly unexplored notion of ethnic balance in national human rights institutions, and how this affects the functioning of each institution. This opens up, in particular, the difficulties of reconciling the integrative function of these institutions with their enforcement or legitimizing functions.

Restorative Justice Concepts for Dealing with the Past

While international law's move towards a normative statement against impunity for serious human rights violations is important, the arrangements found in peace agreements testify to other important goals for mechanisms for dealing with the past, and the possibility of reconciling these goals with international law's imperative against impunity, through notions of restorative justice. The mechanism in South Africa provides a good example. Drawing on international law, it incorporated a notion of restorative justice aimed at reconciling the social needs and needs of victims for truth with notions of accountability and justice. Recent international legal initiatives on the rights of victims of gross human rights abuses acknowledge a range of victim needs which include accountability, but also go much broader. Notions of restorative justice deserve further consideration at the level of international law.

A Structural Place for Civic Society

The peace agreements providing the most hopeful human rights regimes are ones where civic society was involved in the peace process, and where civic society is given a structural place in the negotiations and/or the deal. As noted in Chapter 7, internationally mediated deals, for different reasons, often exclude civic society from the process of deal-making. In

---

[48] As noted in Ch. 7, a possible example is the Principles Relating to the Status of National Institutions 1992. These principles provide that selection procedures shall 'afford all necessary guarantees to ensure the pluralist representation of the social forces (of civilian society) in the promotion and protection of human rights . . .' (although this seems to relate to balance of professional and human rights background rather than of ethnicity).

[49] See e.g. UN General Assembly Declaration on the Rights of Persons Belonging to National or Ethnic, Religious, and Linguistic Minorities, 18 Dec. 1992, GA Res 47/135, UN doc A/Res/47/135 (1992); Council of Europe's Framework Convention on the Rights of National Minorities, 1 Feb. 1995, ETS No. 148.

contrast in more domestically based processes civic society often finds a way of claiming a place in the process. In a divided community civic society plays a crucial role in mediating the positions of political elites. It provides a space for creative thinking. It provides a link with other conflicts and with international institutions—a resource for political elites which they often cannot directly access themselves. It provides an agenda which goes beyond the traditional political divisions, and so enables those traditions to be reconceived. Civic society can supplement an impoverished political sector with a narrow focus.[50]

To use one example, ethno-nationalism is a process which is deeply gendered, but whose gendered aspects are often ignored. A peace process based on political elites is often a peace process designed by men for men. Journalistic accounts of the four peace processes are striking for their absence of female characters. Addressing gendered divisions often involves a radical reconception of the nature of the state just as much as addressing the traditional divisions.[51] Yet women are drawn from across the traditional divisions and often have local experience in addressing those divisions. Addressing gender equality can therefore transform both the meaning and the processes of addressing other inequalities.

In an interesting and provocative account of modern constitutionalism Tully identifies identity politics as the challenge for modern constitutionalism.[52] He suggests that modern constitutions should be 'dialogic'—they should provide ongoing ways of mediating a series of challenges on mainstream constitutionalism by women, minorities, and indigenous peoples. Peace agreements already have this dialogic quality, and can be improved if they deal with more than one attribute of identity. The peace agreements in Northern Ireland and South Africa not only deal with a broad range of rights issues, including provision for gender rights, but use the agreements to provide for a specific space for civic society.[53] In doing so they acknowledge the importance of civic society to implementation.[54]

---

[50] See e.g. Baranyi (1998); R. A. Wilson (1997).

[51] See Yuval-Davis (1997); Cockburn (1998).

[52] Tully (1995). Cf. also Bellamy (1996) (also noting the dialogic ambition of modern constitutionalism); Shaw (1999).

[53] In South Africa the Final Constitution process itself included substantial input from civic society. Furthermore, the Interim Constitution provides for both law-making and political processes to be open (section 67), while the Final Constitution provides more proactively that the National Assembly 'facilitate public involvement in the legislative and other processes of the Assembly and its committees' and that civic society be involved in the selection of members of the Commissions (sections 59 and 193(6)). In Northern Ireland civic society receives explicit references in the Belfast Agreement, with provision for a civic forum, a possible North–South civic forum, and extensive civic participation through human rights mechanisms.

[54] In contrast the provision for civic society is very limited in BiH and Israel/Palestine. In BiH Annex 6 of the DPA provides that 'the Parties shall promote and encourage the

International lawyers could consider whether standards should exist on who should be at peace talks, drawing on the same notions of legitimacy, accountability, and representation which more internally driven processes use. They could also consider whether it would be useful for international institutions to assert a place for civic society in constitutional or peace agreement arrangements. Finally, international organizations could also consider more consciously the impact of their own implementation operations on the development of local civic society.[55]

Areas where International Law could Helpfully be Clarified

Finally, the study has revealed areas where international law could helpfully be clarified. First, human rights law standards and the law of armed conflict diverge in places, as illustrated by Table 10.2.[56]

Given the difficulty in classifying ethnic conflict as internal or international, and the resistance which states have to applying humanitarian law standards to ethnic conflict within their borders, these distinctions are problematic. Indeed the dialectical evolutionary relationship between international law and such conflict has contributed to a breaking-down of distinctions between international and internal matters, and between state and non-state actors. While many of the distinctions relate to the conduct of violent conflict, they continue to be relevant during the peace process, in particular when mechanisms for dealing with the past are considered. It would seem possible to eliminate at least some of these inconsistencies, if not to provide a coherent legal regime scaled according to scale of conflict.[57]

The continued distinction drawn by international law and practice

activities of non-governmental and international organizations for the protection and promotion of human rights (Article XIII(1)). In Israel/Palestine civic society is provided for as regards limited reconciliation measures such as a 'people to people' programme (see generally Cairo Article II, Annex II; Interim Agreement Article XXII, and Annex 6).

[55] This finds some support in UN GA RES 53/144 of 8 Mar. 1999, which incorporates the Declaration on the Rights and Responsibility of Individuals, Groups, and Organs of Society to Promote and Protect Universally Recognized Human Rights and Fundamental Freedoms (this protects human rights defenders and groups which promote human rights, although its focus is on the obligations of states and does not include international organizations). Cf. also codes of ethics of non-governmental organizations regarding participation of civic society, for example International Alert (1998); cf. also SANGOCO (1998: 68–79).

[56] Table reproduced from work of colleagues Tom Hadden and Colin Harvey with permission.

[57] For example, the South African Truth and Reconciliation Commission included the recommendation that renewed international consideration be given to the way in which liberation wars and civil wars are to be conducted, and the treatment of participants in armed combat in circumstances of war, civil war, revolutions, insurgency, or guerrilla warfare. In particular it recommended looking at 'whether it is acceptable for deserters or traitors to be executed, even if they have been tried by a tribunal', especially given the difficulties of such tribunals in complying with present international requirements. Truth and Reconciliation Commission (1998, vol. 5, ch. 8, Recommendation 112).

TABLE 10.2. *Divergence between human rights law and law of armed conflict*

Human rights law	Law of armed conflict
Right to life granted high degree of protection	Right to shoot combatants formally recognized
Right to be tried rather than detained	Right of combatants to be detained but not tried is protected
Appears to be a continuing obligation to prosecute human rights violations	Obligation to grant amnesty when conflict is over for many conflict-related crimes
Primary responsibility for compliance imposed on states	Individuals as well as states may be held responsible for ensuring compliance

between international and internal conflict reduces the coherence of international legal provision in cases where what is international and what is internal is under dispute. Table 10.3 illustrates. Again, it would seem possible and useful to eliminate some of these inconsistencies, even without solving underlying controversies.

Law and Power Revisited

The mutually shaping relationship between international law and peace agreements can inform traditional accounts of the regulative power of international law. Much in the same way that accounts of domestic human rights are often caught between idealist (justice) and realist (peace or pragmatist) positions, so are accounts of the role of international law in international relations.[58]

Koskenniemi has summarized international relations discourse on law as having two opposite strands, one which accuses 'international law of being too political in the sense of being too dependent on states' political power'; and one which argues that 'the law is too political because it is founded on speculative utopias':

From one perspective, this criticism highlights the infinite flexibility of international law, its character as a manipulable facade for power politics. From another perspective, the criticism stresses the moralistic character of international law, its distance from power politics. According to the former criticism, international law

[58] There is a large and varied international relations literature; for overviews, see Brown (1997); Hollis and Smith (1990). For overviews of the specific connections between international relations and international legal scholarship, see Byers (1999: 21–34); Koskenniemi (1990a); Slaughter Burley (1993); Scott (1994). Cf. also attempts to link international law philosophically to the Kantian and Rawlsian traditions: Franck (1992); Tesón (1992a, b).

TABLE 10.3. *Examples of continuing significance of international–internal divide*

International	Internal
Self-determination debates focus around the inviolability of borders and the sovereignty and independence of states. Little focus during the peace process on the accountability or representativeness of negotiators	Emerging focus on 'internal self-determination' as including transnational arrangements and accountable, representative government with effective participation of minorities
Persons displaced across borders may classify as refugees	Persons displaced internally do not classify as refugees
Obligation to punish grave breaches of humanitarian law	Less clear discretion to punish breaches of humanitarian law

is too *apologetic* to be taken seriously in the construction of international order. According to the latter, it is too *utopian* to the identical effect.[59]

International lawyers, he argues, tend to counter these claims either by stressing the normativity of law, and being consequently vulnerable to charges of utopianism, or by stressing the close connection between international law and state behaviour, thus diluting their normative claims. This book has fallen within a more 'liberal' international law tradition by examining the impact of international law not just on how states interact with each other, but also on the internal constitutional arrangements of states.[60]

The description of the role of international law built up through examination of the case-studies indicates a relationship of interchange. As parties use international law to articulate their claims, so international law responds to their claims evolving in the process, as with South African or Palestinian or Yugoslav–republic self–determination claims. As Berman notes, 'the power of international law to shape the identity of the protagonists of such conflicts cannot be separated from even its principled activities to remedy them.'[61]

Similarly, as parties come to design political and legal institutions, so international law informs and facilitates the negotiation process. More recently, as negotiators come to design mechanisms to address past violations, international law sets out a moral standard as regards impunity. Yet, peace agreements also play a part in shaping international human rights law. They take the abstract moral baseline of international human rights standards and build around them practical institutions aimed at

---

[59] Koskenniemi (1990*b*: 9).   [60] See Slaughter Burley (1993).   [61] Berman (1998: 28).

mediating between the legacy of the past and a new future. In doing so they impact on the evolutionary direction of international law.

Thus, the relationship of international law to the human rights provision of peace agreements is neither one of traditional legal regulation, nor one of irrelevance.[62] The relationship is perhaps best understood as one of dialectical evolution. It is an evolution which continues into the implementation stage, as international law and practice draw on the arrangements in peace agreements, even while adjudicating on the human rights performance of the institutions established therein.

CONCLUSIONS

In conclusion, the role of human rights in a peace process is revealed as neither wholly principled nor completely unprincipled political barter. Similarly, the role of international law with relation to the human rights component of a peace agreement is accordingly also revealed as more complex than traditional debates of realist and idealist allow.

In both cases this observation contains both limits on and opportunities for the role of law in peace agreements. The human rights component of an agreement should not be dismissed by politicians, domestic or international, as an add-on to the political institutions agreed. The place, role, and scope of human rights institutions should be understood to be largely determinative of the type of transformation of both conflict and society which will be possible. This observation should inform future institutional design and implementation. Appropriate expertise should be fully utilized in negotiations, and if possible built in to mediation processes.

Conversely, even strong human rights language and well-designed institutions in a peace agreement cannot be taken by human rights activists as a victory. It signals merely the start of another process—that of making the language a reality. It is hoped that this account of the tensions between the political and the legal, and between peace and justice, can inform that struggle.

As regards international law, while its traditional regulative function may seem particularly susceptible to political vagaries, this observation is not new. However, the facilitative impact of a broad range of soft and hard law standards indicates a greater role for international law than might have been imagined, and a need for international law to rise to the occasion. Politicians agreeing to human rights measures in the heat of negotiations often draw on international standards. Continued evolution of the

---

[62] Cf. Byers (1999) (arguing from a review of customary law-making that international law is neither strictly political nor strictly legal).

facilitative function of international law does not necessarily depend on a hardening of law, but more on international law remaining creatively connected to notions of 'good practice' and capable of commanding a moral normativity.

In conclusion, one final influence on the human rights component of peace agreements should not be forgotten; that is, the influence of other peace processes and peace agreements. Clear examples of exchange between processes can be mapped. The resulting transplants usually take on a different dynamic in their new context. In this book I have largely concentrated on trying to unpack the specific negotiating dynamics which resulted in how human rights were dealt with in the four different sets of peace agreements. I have done this because comparison across agreements is often reduced to a comparison of particular institutions and mechanisms, rather than the processes by which they are negotiated and their place and role within an agreement. However, it is also clear that such processes of comparison, whatever their form, can stimulate creative imaginings for difficult situations. For those who would wage peace, this is an important tangible and spiritual resource. The stories of the peace processes should continue to be told.

Appendix. A Decade of Peace Agreements

Christine Bell
Elizabeth Craig

CONTENT

The following is an alphabetical table of peace agreements signed in the last decade. It is intended to show the large number of peace agreements signed, their varying contexts, their differences, and some of their similar patterns and themes. While 1990 is somewhat artificial as a starting-point, it loosely marks the end of the cold war, which was influential in enabling some of the peace agreements below. This is not meant to imply that the following peace processes all started after 1990—most of them did not, and in some the key framework agreement may have been many years earlier. In many cases the post-1990 agreements built on earlier agreements. Pre-1990 agreements have not been included here for reasons of space, but are referred to where possible in the description of the conflict. A thumbnail description of the conflict and in most cases the key elements of the agreements are provided. Summaries have not been provided, where the peace agreement proved unavailable, or when its content was adequately described by the agreement's title.

The agreements are drawn from both internal and international conflicts and include conflicts with clear ethno-national dimensions, conflicts involving the claims of indigenous groups, and political conflicts with no ethnic dimension but revolving around power struggles and/or struggles for rights and democracy. The term 'peace agreement' is broadly used to cover agreements aimed at ending conflict (even those essentially imposed after a military victory). The term 'conflict' is also broadly used and includes conflicts which have not had overtly physically violent manifestations, such as some of the conflicts involving indigenous peoples. As can be seen from this Appendix, peace agreements take different forms and include agreed land settlements (with indigenous groups), constitutions, and draft constitutions. Where legislation (such as a constitution or land settlement) itself constitutes an agreement between parties in conflict, it is included. However, other implementing legislation has not been included.

FORMAT

Within each conflict, the agreements are listed chronologically. They follow the typology in Chapter 1 of pre-negotiation agreements, substantive–framework agreements, and implementation agreements. However, they also indicate the capacity of the peace processes to unravel and stall with a series of framework agreements that reflect the difficulties of implementation. While the agreements could be categorized into different types of conflict, this was avoided as, despite the differences in the nature of the conflicts, patterns across all peace agreements emerge.

SOURCES

Many can be obtained through the Internet at the following sites: www.usip.org/library/pa.html (last visited 20 Jun. 2000); www.c-r.org/ (last visited 20 Jun. 2000) (see also Conciliation Resources' excellent series Accord: An International Review of Peace Initiatives); www.incore.ulst.ac.uk/cds/agreements/index.html (last visited 20 Jun. 2000). Many of the rest are on file with the author. This attempt to provide a comprehensive list proved surprisingly long, and is still inexhaustive. Accounts of the conflicts were put together from a variety of publications and newspaper sources.

AFGHANISTAN

A communist coup took place in 1978 and was followed by an uprising against the new government. After eighteen months the Soviet Union invaded, set up a puppet government, and took on the Mujahidin rebels. In 1988 the Soviet Union finally withdrew. A series of agreements was signed normalizing relations between Afghanistan and Pakistan and guaranteed by the United States and the Soviet Union. The remaining Communist government was defeated in 1992 against a background of violence. However, a multi-party civil war continued, with a strong tribal basis. In 1993 a Peace Accord was signed between the government of Afghanistan and a faction of the Hezb-e-Islami, and six Mujahidin leaders. In 1994 the Islamic-based Taliban emerged from refugee camps and occupied Kabul in September 1996, causing a realignment in the conflict. Groups who had militantly opposed the government united in opposition to the Taliban. The conflict continues. Approximately 200,000 people have been killed since 1989.

Peshawar Accord (Islamabad Accord), March 1993. Peace Accord between government and Islamic leaders. Brokered by Pakistan and actively supported by Iran and Saudi Arabia. Agreement provided for a transitional government with leadership from the Islamic groups.

Afghan Peace Accord (Islamabad Accord), 7 March 1993. Provided for formation of government and delimited powers of president and prime minister. Provided for a ceasefire, opening of roads, and release of detainees.

Tashkent Declaration on Fundamental Principles for a Peaceful Settlement of the Conflict in Afghanistan, 19 July 1999. Signed by governments of China, Iran, Pakistan, Tajikistan, Turkmenistan, Uzbekistan, Russian Federation, United States, and United Nations. Concluded there was no military solution to the conflict, which must be settled through peaceful, political negotiation in order to establish a broad-based, multi-ethnic, and fully representative government. Urged Afghan parties to resume political negotiations and agreed not to provide military support to any Afghan party. Outlined two stages to the negotiation process. First stage to include adoption of measures for building mutual confidence, including signing of agreement on immediate and unconditional ceasefire, and direct negotiations between the United Front and the Taliban movement aimed at reaching agreements on exchange of prisoners of war and lifting of internal blockades.

Second stage to involve Afghans in drawing up principles for future state structure and to establish a fully representative government. Also expressed commitment to take measures to combat drug-trafficking and to encourage Afghan parties to respect fully human rights and freedoms of all Afghans. Expressed readiness to cooperate with the new Afghan government and called upon the international community to respond to the Inter-Agency Consolidated Appeal for Emergency Humanitarian and Rehabilitation Assistance for Afghanistan.

ALGERIA

A civil war has been fought since 1992 between the Front de Libération National (FLN), which has ruled Algeria since independence in 1962, and fundamentalist Islamic groups. Between 50,000 and 100,000 people have been killed since 1992. In 1990 the Front Islamique du Salut (FIS) won the first democratic elections for local councils, and in December 1991 they won the first round of national elections. Before the second round took place the FLN dissolved the Parliament and suspended the Constitution and the army council took over government. FIS protested and the new military regime imposed a state of emergency. Civil war has raged ever since. The FIS itself split, and the breakaway Groupe Armé Islamique (GAI) became known for some of the most violent anti-government acts. In 1995 a conference including moderate members of both the government and FIS agreed on a platform of conciliation, which was then turned down by the government. In 1995 the military regime held a presidential election judged by international observers to be relatively fair, in which the acting president won 61 per cent of the votes. The civil war continues.

Platform of National Consensus: Text Adopted by the Conference, 1994

Communication of the State Presidency on the evolution of dialogue between the State and the ex-FIS 1995

Document on 'the Principles of Dialogue' 1995

Platform adopted by the participating parties of the Conference of the National Settlement 1996

ANGOLA

See Chapter 2 for description of the conflict and peace agreements.

ARGENTINA—UNITED KINGDOM

War fought in 1982 after Argentina invaded the Falkland Islands–Malvinas (over which they have always claimed sovereignty). The UK achieved military victory, but it was not until 1990 that an agreement to normalize relations was signed. Since the agreement below, other agreements for cooperation have been signed. In all the agreements both states preserve their sovereign claims to the islands.

Argentina–United Kingdom: Joint Statement on Confidence-Building Measures, Including an Information and Consultation System and Safety Measures for Air and Maritime Navigation, 15 February 1990

ARMENIA–AZERBAIJAN–NAGORNO-KARABAKH

In February 1988 demonstrators in Armenia demanded the transfer of the autonomous region of Nagorno-Karabakh in Azerbaijan to Armenia, and the regional assembly in Nagorno-Karabakh voted for secession from Azerbaijan. At that time 77 per cent of the people in the region were Armenians. Since then there has been conflict between the Armenians and the Azeri population over the future of the region. Provision was made for a ceasefire in 1994, but agreement has not yet been reached on the political future of the area. The Armenian army and political leaders want the permanent annexation of Nagorno-Karabakh; the Azeris (who have Russian support) do not; while some in Nagorno-Karabakh claim independence, which they see as a compromise. The conflict continues.

The Bishkek Protocol, 27 July 1994. Pursuant to a Conference on Security and Cooperation in Europe (CSCE) initiative, an informal ceasefire was negotiated. This agreement formalizing it was signed between the defence ministers of Armenia and Azerbaijan, together with the commander of the Nagorno-Karabakh army.

BANGLADESH–CHITTAGONG HILL TRACT

See Chapter 2 for description of conflict and peace agreement.

BOSNIA HERZEGOVINA

See Chapter 3 for description of conflict and peace agreements.

BURUNDI

A conflict between Hutus and Tutsis, related to the conflict in Rwanda, and dating from the murder of Rwandan and Burundian presidents in 1994 (which sparked the genocide in Rwanda). See further Rwanda.

Declaration of the Agreed Political Parties and the Government against war and in favour of peace and security 1994

Protocol of agreement between political 'families' on the reallocation of responsibilities in the territorial administration, foreign service, and immigration service 1994

Agreements endorsed by the government, between the forces of democratic change and political parties of the opposition 1994

Final Declaration and Press Release 1998

CAMBODIA

The Khmer Rouge (KR) won the civil war (1970–5) and set about the mass destruction of the better-off sections of the population. The Vietnamese invaded the area in December 1978, establishing a puppet government in Phnom Penh and forcing the KR to retreat. For ten years the Vietnamese waged war against the KR and finally withdrew in 1989. A ceasefire was mediated by the UN in 1991 and was accepted by the National United Front for an Independent, Neutral, Peaceful, and Cooperative Cambodia (FUNCINPEC), the Cambodian People's Party (CPP), the KR, and the Vietnamese. The KR withdrew from the peace process in 1992, resumed civil war, and boycotted the 1993 elections. The CPP entered into a power-sharing agreement with FUNCINPEC. The subsequent break-up of the KR strengthened the CPP's position, and in July 1997 the FUNCINPEC co-prime minister was overthrown. The CPP and its leader Hun Sen have since consolidated their position, and become increasingly authoritarian.

Final Act of the Paris Conference on Cambodia, 23 October 1991. Participating states committed themselves to promote and encourage respect for and observance of human rights and fundamental freedoms. Requested the International Committee of the Red Cross (ICRC) to facilitate the release of prisoners of war and civilian internees, expressing their readiness to assist the ICRC in this task, and urged the international community to provide economic and financial support for the measures set forth in the Declaration on the Rehabilitation and Reconstruction of Cambodia.

Agreement on a Comprehensive Political Settlement of the Cambodia Conflict, 23 October 1991. Called for establishment of UN Transitional Authority (UNTAC) and made provision for free and fair elections and for the drafting of a new Constitution. Affirmed ceasefire, expressed commitment to respect for human rights, and urged international community to support rehabilitation and reconstruction. Also provided for withdrawal of foreign forces and the creation of conditions for the return of refugees–displaced persons and the release of all prisoners of war and civilian internees. Five annexes provide for: UNTAC mandate; withdrawal, ceasefire, and related measures; elections; repatriation of Cambodian refugees and displaced persons; five principles for a new Constitution for Cambodia.

Agreement concerning the Sovereignty, Territorial Integrity and Inviolability, Neutrality, and National Unity of Cambodia, 23 October 1991

Declaration on the Rehabilitation and Reconstruction of Cambodia, 23 October 1991

Accord between the Cambodian People's Party (CPP) and the National United Front for Independent, Neutral, Peaceful and Cooperative Cambodian (FUNCINPEC), 20 November 1991. Provided for conduct of cooperative relations between the two parties.

The Four Pillars Peace Plan, 15 February 1998. An international peace plan put forward by Japan providing for no cooperation with KR, a ceasefire of forces of deposed Prime Minister Prince Ranaridh, and provision for his trial and security.

CANADA–NISGA'A

For almost a century aborigines in Nisga'a have campaigned for recognition of their territorial rights. In 1973 the Supreme Court of Canada unanimously recognized the possible existence of aboriginal rights to land and resources, and in 1976 Canada began negotiations with the Nisga'a Tribal Council (NTC). In 1989 a bilateral framework agreement was signed between Canada and the NTC setting out the scope, process, and topics for bilateral negotiations, and the British Columbia (BC) government joined the negotiations in 1990.

Tripartite Framework Agreement 1991. Set out the scope, process, and topics for negotiation.

Agreement-in-Principle 1996

Final Agreement 1999. Based on provisions of the agreement-in-principle. Nisga'a would be governed by the Nisga'a Lisims government (central government) and four village governments. They would continue to be an aboriginal people and to enjoy the same rights and benefits as other Canadian citizens. Agreement also addresses lands; land titles; forest resources; access; roads and rights of way; fisheries; wildlife and migratory birds; environmental assessment and protection; administration of justice; capital transfer and loan repayment; fiscal relations; taxation; cultural artefacts and heritage; and local and residual government relations. The Nisga'a in return agreed to release any aboriginal rights not set out in the treaty.

CANADA–NUNAVUT

The Inuit population accounts for 85 per cent of the population in the Nunavut area in the central and eastern part of the Northwest Territories (NWT). In 1973 the government of Canada established its first Comprehensive Land Claims Policy to exchange undefined aboriginal rights for a clearly defined package of rights and benefits set out in a land claim settlement, and in 1976 the Inuit Tapirisat of Canada (ITC) called for the creation of a Nunavut territory as part of a comprehensive settlement of Inuit land claims in the NWT. The Nunavut land claim was settled in 1993, and first elections to the new Legislative Assembly were held on 15 February 1999.

Nunavut Land Claim Agreement-in-Principle 1990. Affirmed Inuit, territorial, and federal government support for the creation of the territory of Nunavut 'as soon as possible.'

Nunavut Final Land Claim Agreement between the Inuit, the Government of Canada, and the Government of the NWT 1993. Outlined Nunavut settlement area and recommended establishment of a new Nunavut territory with its own Legislative Assembly. Clarified rights to ownership and use of lands and resources and of rights for Inuit to participate in decision-making concerning use, management and conservation of land, water, and resources. Also made provision for wildlife harvesting rights and right to participate in decision-making concerning wildlife harvesting and for financial compensation and means of participation in economic opportunities.

Nunavut Land Claim Agreement Act 1993. Ratified agreement.
Nunavut Act 1993. Established territory of Nunavut.

CENTRAL AFRICAN REPUBLIC

French troops and troops from neighbouring countries intervened in 1996 and 1997 to end a mutiny by part of the army in the capital, Bangui. The fighting was along tribal lines, with southern tribes in revolt against the 'northern' government. The president of Mali arranged a truce in 1996 ('Bangui Agreements') but renewed fighting broke out the following June. An Inter-African Mission to Monitor the Implementation of the Bangui Agreements was replaced with a UN mission in 1998.

Truce Agreement 1996 ('Bangui Agreements')

Mandate established by the countries designated by the 19th Summit of France and Africa, for the Inter-African Supervision Mission for the Bangui Agreements 1997

Solemn Declaration of the Heads of African States who are members of the 'Comité du Suivi', and the Central African President, on the Preliminary Accord to a pact of national reconciliation 1997

CHAD

Internal civil war saw two partial ceasefire agreements reached: **Peace Accord 1997,** and **Reconciliation Pact 1998.** However, fighting continues.

CHAD–LIBYA

Conflict between the Arab north and the non-Arab south has been long-standing, and violence also broke out between rival factions in the north after Libya annexed the Aozou, a strip of territory in northern Chad, in 1976. Libya and France both intervened in 1983, and the leader of one of the northern factions, Hissène Habré, began to drive Libyans out of Chad. A ceasefire organized by the Organization of African Unity took effect on 11 September 1987, but fighting resumed in March 1988. By the 1990s Chad and Libya agreed to submit the dispute to the International Court of Justice, who ruled in favour of Chad. Libya accepted the ruling and the UN monitored its withdrawal from the strip in 1994. However, hostilities still exist and it is disputed whether full withdrawal has taken place.

Fundamental Agreement on the Peaceful Settlement of the Territorial Dispute between the Republic of Chad and Libya, 31 August 1989. Parties undertook to settle their territorial dispute by political means within a one-year period. They agreed to submit their claims to the ICJ for judgment. Agreement provided that prisoners of war would be liberated; that the parties would cease hostile media campaigns; and that a commission to implement the agreement would be put in place.

Agreement between the Great Socialist People's Libyan Arab Jamahiriya and the Republic of Chad concerning the practical modalities for the Implementation of the Judgment delivered by the International Court of Justice on 3 February 1994. Provided for the withdrawal of Libya from Aozou, supervised by a joint team, and observed by the UN. Provided for mine disposal, future delimitation of borders, and work towards strengthening bilateral relations.

COLOMBIA

In the 1970s the Communist opposition and its military wing, the Revolutionary Armed Forces of Colombia (FARC), began an insurrection against the power-sharing Conservatives and Liberals. There was a short-lived ceasefire in 1984, but by the late 1980s the war had resumed and included a number of different groups. Towards the end of the cold war a series of armed leftist groups entered peace negotiations, and in 1990 and 1991 signed similar peace agreements (FARC did not) according to which they would disarm in exchange for entry to political and civic life. However, internal civil war has continued, fuelled by drugs trade issues and growing inequalities brought about by the neo-liberal economic policies followed during the 1990s.

Political Agreement between the National Government, the Political Parties, M-19, and the Catholic Church as Moral and Spiritual Guardian of the Process, 9 March 1990. Attempted to reinvigorate a Political Pact of 1989 and add new elements. Provided for a return to civilian life for the guerrillas, and for community programmes in areas where the guerrillas were demobilizing. Provided for electoral reform to increase political participation in particular for minorities. Provided for a Commission to look at reform of Criminal Justice. Established an Academic Non-Governmental Commission to look at the different dimensions of drug-trafficking. The government undertook to fulfil its obligations by the date on which M-19 committed to demobilizing and disarming. The signatories undertook to form an Implementation Commission to firm up the compromises in the agreement. A 1989 Security Plan was also reactivated.

Final Agreement, 25 January 1991. Signed between the national government and the Revolutionary Workers' Party (PRT). This agreement guaranteed participation for the PRT in the National Constitutional Assembly in return for PRT decommissioning. The government undertook to legalize the PRT as a political party and to give it media space to promote itself. Provided for a decree to annul prison sentences for political offences. Agreement included a human rights dimension, and a government commitment to create a nominated Office for the Atlantic Coast to Advise the President on the Defence and Promotion of Human Rights. The government also committed to creating a government-sponsored Commission for Human Rights. Agreement also provided for an indigenous police service, a plan for reconciliation and peace, a regional plan for political normalization, and implementation issues.

Final Agreement—Popular Liberation Army (EPL), 15 February 1991. Agreement again built on the 1990 negotiation process. Similar to the agreements with other groups, it dealt with representation in the National Assembly; promotion of the peace process (financing of a House of Peace and regional operative committees); promotion of the politicization of EPL, and publicity; provision for guarantors; a plan for the reinsertion of the guerrillas; a security plan; a section dealing with Human Rights and Factors Relating to Violence; provision for a regional development plan; and EPL decommissioning.

Final Agreement between the National Government and the Movimiento Armado Quintín Lame (MAQL), 27 May 1991. Building on the 1990 negotiations, provided for arrangements similar to above agreements.

Agreement between the Commandos 'Ernesto Rojas' (CER) and the National Government, 20 March 1992. A very short agreement according to which the CER subscribed to the agreement of February 1991 between the government and the EPL.

Pact to Consolidate the Peace Processes (no date provided). The parties to the above agreements largely affirmed their commitments therein.

Final Political Agreement between the National Government and the Corriente de Renovación Socialista (CRS), 9 April 1994. Provided for a social investment programme to improve standards of living in peace zones. Also provided for citizen participation in politics; urban development; human rights; a reinsertion programme; consideration of pardons for CRS members; support for the politicization of the CRS; security programmes; decommissioning; and a Commission of Verification.

Agreement for City Coexistence, between the National Government, the Popular Militias of the People and for the People, the Independent Militias of the Valley of Aburra, and the Metropolitan Militias of the City of Medellín (Militias de Medellín (MM)), 26 May 1994. Provided for social investment in communities; normalization of citizen life (with special community programmes); a programme of reinsertion in political life for the MM; consideration of pardons; a protection programme; and support for the politicization of MM.

Final Agreement between the National Government and the Frente 'Francisco Garnica' de la Coordinadora Guerrillera, 20 June 1994. Provided for economic and social insertion for the Frente; for consideration of pardons for Frente members; a programme of security; and support for politicization.

CONGO (BRAZZAVILLE)

President Pascal Lissouba was overthrown by a savage but brief civil war in 1997. The conflict involved the forces of President Lissouba against the forces of Denis Sassou-Neguesso, who was supported by Angola. Violence erupted again in 1998 between Lissouba's militiamen and the army of Sassou-Neguesso's government (still supported by Angola). A ceasefire agreement was reached between government and rebels in 1999.

Agreement of Cessation of Hostilities, 16 November 1999. Agreement providing for a ceasefire: for demilitarization; that amnesty will be given to those who decommission and denounce violence; that steps will be taken to protect peoples in specified forest areas; and that democratic life will be returned to normal. Logistics for this are provided for, with an implementation committee.

CROATIA–FEDERAL REPUBLIC OF YUGOSLAVIA

For description of conflict, see Chapter 4. Both parties were party to the Dayton Peace Agreement, the two agreements below, one prior to and one subsequent to Dayton.

Draft Agreement on the Krajina, Southern Baranja, and Western Sirmium, January 1994 ('Zagreb Four Plan'). This constituted an attempt to broker a deal between Serbia and Croatia. Provided a model for de facto confederalization of Croatia. The Serb-held Krajina area would have its own government, currency, and insignia, and dual citizenship with Serbia (in effect a mini state within a state). While negotiations were pending, President Tudjman of Croatia announced that he would not extend the mandate for the United Nations Protection Forces (UNPROFOR) in Croatia. While he accepted the plan as a basis for negotiation, Milošović refused to endorse it until Croatia reversed its UNPROFOR decision. The plan was dropped until some Serb leaders announced unqualified acceptance on the eve of Croatia's full-scale military recapture of the Krajina, by which time it was too late.

Basic Agreement on the Region of Eastern Slavonia, Baranja, and Western Sirmium, 12 November 1995 ('Erdut Agreement'). Signed by Serbs and Croatian government, it built on earlier basic principles (see Chapter 4). Provided for a transitional period with a Transitional Administration. UN Security Council to be requested to authorize an international force to assist in implementation. This force to assist in right of refugees and displaced persons to return and receive back property and compensation. At end of transitional period elections to take place. Serbian community to have a joint Council of Municipalities.

Agreement on the Normalization of Relations, 23 August 1996. Agreement between Croatia and Federal Republic of Yugoslavia. Provides for basic principles of independence, sovereignty, and equality of states; mutual recognition; provision for missing persons; repatriation of refugees and displaced persons; human rights guarantees; and cooperation in various other matters.

DEMOCRATIC REPUBLIC OF CONGO (FORMERLY KNOWN AS ZAIRE)

The Democratic Republic of Congo (DRC), then Zaire, experienced insurrection between October 1996 and May 1997, when Tutsi rebels supported by Rwanda and Uganda overthrew President Mobuto Sese Seko. The rebel Tutsi army took control, and Laurent Kabila, head of a minor Zairean opposition group, made himself president. A new insurrection started in 1998 sparked by ethnic tension in the eastern part of the country and by the expulsion in July of Rwandan troops who had helped Kabila to power. From August 1998 neighbouring countries were involved in the dispute. A ceasefire agreement was signed on 10 July 1999. This conflict clearly has a regional dimension.

Ceasefire Agreement, Lusaka, 10 July 1999. Signatories included the Democratic Republic of Congo (DRC), Rwanda, Uganda, Congolese Rally for Democracy (RCD), and Movement for the Liberation of the Congo (MLC). Provided for cessation of hostilities. Parties expressed their commitment to addressing security concerns of DRC and neighbouring countries and to the exchange of prisoners of war and release of other detainees. Provision was also made for the facilitation of humanitarian assistance; a UN peacekeeping force; a Joint Military Commission; the final withdrawal of foreign forces; re-establishment of state administration and open dialogue; formation of a national, integrated army; and a mechanism for disarmament and measures to facilitate repatriation of militias. Reaffirmed the sovereignty and territorial integrity of DRC and acceptance of the idea of equal rights for all citizens. Annexes gave further details on the implementation of various parts of the agreement and provided a timetable for implementation.

DJIBOUTI

A conflict between the government and the Front pour la Restauration de l'Unité de la Démocratie' (FRUD).

Agreement for Peace and National Reconciliation, 26 December 1994. Provided for an agreement according to which FRUD agreed to adopt the Djibouti Constitution, and government agreed to future revision of the Constitution. Agreement provided for measures aimed at freedom of movement, return of refugees and displaced persons, and repair of infrastructure. Provided for measures aimed at fairness of forthcoming elections and at education of children affected by war. Provided assurances of reintegration of combatants; a general amnesty for FRUD combatants and exiles; transformation of FRUD into a political party. Also provided for decentralization and economic reconstruction.

Framework Agreement for Civil Reform and Concord, 7 February 2000. Agreement between the government of the Republic of Djibouti and the FRUD, aimed at democratic reform following an election. Provided for reparations and indemnities for reintegration of refugees, and for victims; decentralization and autonomy; democracy and human rights; openness and transparency in public life; civil peace and security.

EAST TIMOR–INDONESIA

The Portuguese withdrew from East Timor in 1975 following a brief civil war. The dominant political party, the Revolutionary Front for an Independent East Timor (Fretilin), proclaimed the Democratic Republic of East Timor, but on 7 December Indonesia invaded the area and set up a puppet regime. East Timor was annexed to Indonesia in 1977 (although this was not recognized by many states) and the Indonesian troops began to massacre the Timorese. Full-scale war broke out, and from 1978 onwards the Fretilin army conducted a guerrilla campaign against the Indonesian government. In 1992 the National Council of Maubere Resistance (an umbrella organization of pro-independence movements and activists) put forward a three-point peace proposal. The UN arranged for Indonesia and Portugal to resume negotiations in 1997. By 1999 Indonesia had accepted a referendum on East Timorese autonomy, with the understanding that if autonomy was rejected, independence would follow. However, after the referendum supporters of Indonesia attempted to massacre those supporting independence, while the government of Indonesia was accused of complicity through inaction. The UN intervened.

Dili Peace Accord, 21 April 1999. Parties agreed to stop all kinds of hostilities, intimidation, acts of terror and violence, and to assist efforts to create an atmosphere of peace and tranquillity. Expressed support for efforts of the government, the National Human Rights Commission, and the Catholic Church to achieve reconciliation in order to uphold dignity, protection of human rights, and the law in East Timor. Also agreed on establishment of a Commission for Peace and Stability to supervise the implementation of the accord.

Agreement between the Republic of Indonesia and the Portuguese Republic on the Question of East Timor, 5 May 1999. Parties agreed to request that a UN mission carry out a referendum on autonomy for the East Timorese. The Indonesian government agreed to maintain peace and security to ensure that the referendum was carried out fairly and peacefully and to take the necessary constitutional measures if the result of the referendum was positive. If the proposed framework for autonomy was not accepted by the people, the Indonesian government undertook to take the constitutional steps necessary to terminate its links with East Timor and to make arrangements for the transfer of authority to the UN and for the transition to independence. An annex outlined the constitutional framework for autonomy with regard to respective areas of competence; East Timorese identity, residence, and immigration; powers and institutions of the Special Autonomous Region of East Timor (SARET); promotion and protection of human rights; relationship between central government and government of the SARET; relations between SARET and other entities; role of UN; a Basic Law for SARET; and transitional provisions.

Agreement regarding the Modalities for the Popular Consultation of the East Timorese through a Direct Ballot, 5 May 1999. Outlined practical arrangements for a ballot to be held on 8 August 1999 with voters being asked either to accept or to reject the proposed special autonomy for East Timor within the Unitary State of the Republic of Indonesia.

East Timor Popular Consultation Agreement regarding Security, 5 May 1999. It was agreed that a peaceful environment was prerequisite for the holding of a ballot, with responsibility resting with the Indonesian security authorities. Provision was made for the drafting of a code of conduct for the parties by the Commission on Peace and Stability and for the UN Secretary-General to ascertain if the necessary security situation existed for a ballot to take place peacefully.

UN SC Res 1236 (1999), 7 May 1999. Welcomed conclusion of agreements and intention to establish a UN presence in East Timor to assist in their implementation, and stressed responsibility of Indonesian government to maintain peace and security.

UN SC Res 1246 (1999), 11 June 1999. Decided to establish a UN Mission in East Timor (UNAMET) to organize a ballot, and authorized the deployment of 280 civilian police officers to act as advisers to the Indonesian police and to supervise transportation of ballot papers, and of fifty military liaison officers to maintain contact with the Indonesian armed forces.

UN SC Res 1257 (1999), 3 August 1999. Provides extension to UNAMET mandate.

ECUADOR–PERU

Conflict followed the annexation of a substantial part of Ecuador's territory by Peru in 1941. The subsequent peace treaty, which ceded eastern Ecuador to Peru, was later repudiated by Ecuador in 1960. In 1995 the two countries fought a three-week war over a section of the border, in the wake of which the following agreements were signed.

Declaración de Paz de Itamaraty, 17 February 1995

Acta Presidencial de Brasilia, 26 October 1998. Builds on earlier agreements and establishes the series of accords and memoranda which deal with commercial arrangements such as provision of services and joint development plans for border regions. The eleven agreements can be found at insert www.usip.org/library/pa.html (last visited 6 Jun. 2000).

EL SALVADOR

The civil war lasted from 1979 to 1992. In the early 1980s it had appeared that rebels would instigate a communist revolution, but following US intervention the Christian Democratic candidate was elected as president in democratic elections. However, by the late 1980s the central government had collapsed, and the Republican National Alliance (Arena), a right-wing party, came to power. The US supported Arena and the Salvadorean army because it wanted to defeat the communist Farabundo Martí National Liberation Front (FMLN) and its army, who opposed the government. On 13 March 1990 the rebels announced a suspension of their attacks against non-military targets and suggested entering negotiations with the government. A peace agreement was signed in January 1992. Arena won all elections in April 1994, but in March 1997 the FMLN won a considerable number of seats at congressional elections.

Geneva Agreement, 4 April 1990

General Agenda and Schedule for the Comprehensive Negotiation Process (Caracas Agreement), 21 May 1990. Set initial objective so as to achieve political agreements to halt armed confrontation and any acts that infringe rights of civilians, including agreement on armed forces; human rights; judicial system; electoral system; constitutional reform; economic and social issues; and verification by the UN. Agenda also to include establishment of necessary guarantees and conditions for reintegrating members of the FMLN into civilian institutional and political life, and agreements for the consolidation of the objectives of earlier Geneva Agreement. Agreed on schedule and set deadline for achievement of initial paragraph 1 of the Geneva Agreement, for middle of September.

Agreement on Human Rights, 26 July 1990. Agreed on respect for and guarantee of human rights, including steps to avoid any attempt on life, integrity, security, or freedom of the individual and certain immediate measures to guarantee the freedom and integrity of persons arrested. Provided for determination of procedures and timetables for release of political prisoners and guarantees of right to associate freely with others; freedom of expression and of the press; and freedom of movement. Agreed to provide displaced persons and returnees with identity documents; to guarantee their freedom of movement; freedom to carry out economic activities; to exercise their political and social rights; as well as to consider guaranteeing effective enjoyment of labour rights. Also agreed on terms of reference for the UN human rights verification mission.

Press Communiqué Issued Following the Geneva Meeting Presided over by the Secretary-General between Representatives of the Government of El Salvador and of the Frente Farabundo Martí para la Liberación Nacional (Geneva Agreement) 1990

Understandings regarding the New York Agreement, 25 September 1991

New York Act, 31 December 1991. Parties declared they had reached definitive agreements which would put the armed conflict to an end. Agreement reached on all technical and military aspects relating to separation of warring parties and cessation of the armed conflict, including end to FMLN military structure and reintegration of its members into civil, political, and institutional life. Cessation of armed conflict to take effect on 1 February 1992 and to conclude on 31 October 1992. Further meeting scheduled to negotiate timetable for implementing agreements with Final Peace Agreements to be signed on 16 January 1992.

New York Act II, 13 January 1992. Stated parties had reached agreements which complete negotiations on all issues outstanding when New York Act was signed, opening way for signing of the Peace Agreement in Mexico City on 16 January 1992.

Complementary Agreement of 22 December 1992. Parties expressed intention to ensure strict compliance with commitments on the collection of weapons; transfer of lands in non-conflict zones and of lands exceeding the constitutional limit; and financing and deployment of a National Civil Police (PNC) (replacing the National Police). Outlined government commitments to programmes for reintegration of former FMLN combatants, and for FMLN political participation. Commitment to promoting pending legislation and recognition of need to negotiate for establishment of Group of Donor Countries.

Supplementary Agreement of 5 February 1993. Outlined criteria and procedures for transfer of land of economic significance. FMLN agreed to present to the government a list of persons to be given protection under the Law to Protect Persons Subject to Special Security, and government agreed to develop plan for reintegration of FMLN officers.

Agreement of the Tripartite Meeting of 8 September 1993. Agreed on collection of weapons and property of the Armed Forces of El Salvador (AFES) held by civilians or retired military personnel and agreed to abstain from using the AFES as preventive measure or in ordinary course of events for the maintenance of public security. Provided for gradual winding down of the National Police, closure of the National Police Academy, and the dissolution of the Fiscal Battalion, and on further measures to guarantee the civilian character of the PNC. UN secretary-general to present report to Security Council on compliance with recommendations of a previously established Truth Commission. Agreement also reached on economic and social matters, including transfer of lands and implementation of reintegration programmes; the assignment of television and radio frequencies to FMLN; electoral matters and funding. Also provided for publication of Doctrine of AFES, and issue of customs duty-free permits for the importation of vehicles for the FMLN.

Timetable for the Implementation of the Most Important Outstanding Agreements, 19 May 1994. Set timetable for: collection and replacement of weapons and parties agreed to reschedule deployment of the PNC; demobilization of National Police; restructuring of the Ministry of the Interior and Public Security; and the provision of regulatory machinery. UN to verify granting of ranks and assignment of duties in PNC and functioning of National Public Security Academy. Also agreed on measures to promote recruitment to PNC and on timetable for land transfer and reintegration programmes and for approval of legislative measures reflecting recommendations of the Truth Commission. UN to verify compliance with the agreement. Annex I listed present status of draft laws and of international instruments, and Annex II outlined action arising from the Peace Accords to be concluded and set timetable for reintegration of FMLN.

Joint Declaration Signed on 4 October 1994 by the Representatives of the Government of El Salvador and of the Frente Farabundo Martí para la Liberación Nacional (FMLN) 1994. Agreed to cooperate closely to ensure compliance with all peace accords by 30 April 1995 and to establish joint mechanisms with participation of government, FMLN, and the UN Observer Mission in El Savador (ONUSAL) to determine measures necessary for fulfilment of commitments. Also agreed to keep Salvadorean people and international community informed of any decisions and steps taken, and to reiterate their requests to the UN to extend ONUSAL mandate.

ERITREA—ETHIOPIA

A complicated conflict involving secessionist claims, with Eritreans fighting to secede from Ethiopia; 'internal' conflict between ethnically different Eritrean groups; and conflict between the Ethiopian government and Ethiopian opposition groups which at times has had separatist and at times more leftist ambitions. In 1991 the Eritrean People's Liberation Front (EPLF) defeated the military junta (the 'Derg') of Ethiopia, proclaiming independence for Eritrea. At the same time the Ethiopian Peoples Revolutionary Democratic Forces (EPRDF) overthrew the Derg, and a transitional government was established in Ethiopia. Agreement was reached between most of the groups who had engaged in armed opposition, to a charter for Ethiopia's development. This charter provided that Eritrea should have the right to vote on its independence. In Eritrea an internationally monitored referendum resulted in a 99.8 per cent pro-independence vote. A democratic Constitution was promulgated in Eritrea. However, Ethiopia–Eritrea border tensions and profound differences between EPRDF and the EPLF (now the People's Front for Democracy and Justice) on economic policies and the constitutional rights of national minorities led to renewal of fighting in 1998. While a mediation effort by the US administration led to agreement to halt air strikes, no further peace agreement has been negotiated, although plans have been produced by US–Rwanda and the Organization of African Unity.

Communiqué Commun des Groupes Rebelles Ethiopiens, 1991. Agreed on a way forward for the country, including a vote on Eritrean independence.

Déclaration de reconnaissance de l'Erythrée 1993. Recognized Eritrean independence.

Constitutional Commission of Eritrea, July 1996. Elaborate Constitution providing for state structures, government, judiciary, public service, economic, and social development, national culture, national defence and security, and foreign policy. A bill of rights including economic, social, and cultural rights was included.

US–Rwandan Proposals, 30–1 May 1998. Recommended both parties to commit to finding a solution by peaceful means, proposed sending an observers mission to the border region, and request redeployment of Eritrean forces from this region. Recommended a 'swift and binding' delimitation of the border and its demilitarization.

OAU High Level Delegation Proposals for a Framework Agreement for a Peaceful Settlement of the Dispute between Eritrea and Ethiopia, 8 November 1998. Recommended a cessation of hostilities, redeployment of armed forces in border region, to be supervised by a group of military observers provided by OAU with support of UN. Recommended assistance of UN Cartographic Unit to delimit border, and an investigation of the origins of the conflict and sources of misunderstandings between the parties.

FEDERAL REPUBLIC OF YUGOSLAVIA (SERBIA, FRY)—KOSOVO—NATO

Conflict between Serbs and Kosovar Albanians involving territorial dispute with ethno-political, cultural, and language factors. Most recent phase of the war began in November 1997 when the Albanian Kosovo Liberation Army (KLA or UCK) began their campaign for the independence of Kosovo from the Federal Republic of Yugoslavia (Serbia and Montenegro). Later conflict included NATO against Yugoslavia and Serbians. The main agreements were both internationally driven, with NATO threatening air strikes against Serbs if they did not sign. The first agreement was not accepted by the Serbs, resulting in NATO air strikes. The second was not an 'agreement' but a Security Council resolution imposing a post-conflict arrangement in the wake of what was essentially a NATO military victory.

Interim Agreement for Peace and Self-Government ('Rambouillet Agreement'), 23 February 1999. A comprehensive agreement of fifty pages covering the following matters: principles including equality, respect for human rights and right to democratic self-government; confidence-building measures, including an end to the use of force and return of refugees; a Constitution; police and civil public security; conduct and supervision of elections; economic issues; humanitarian assistance, reconstruction, and economic development; and ombudsman. Included information on the implementation of the agreement with reference to a cessation of hostilities, demilitarization of forces, and prisoner releases.

Kosovo Peace Plan, approved by Serb Parliament, 3 June 1999. Outlined areas on which agreement should be reached, including the deployment of international civilian and security presence; establishment of an interim administration under which the people of Kosovo would enjoy substantial autonomy within the FRY; return of all refugees and displaced persons under United Nations High Commissioner for Refugees supervision, and undisturbed access for humanitarian organizations; political progress towards an interim political agreement which would secure autonomy for Kosovo taking the Rambouillet Agreement into full consideration; and an approach to economic development.

Military Technical Agreement between the International Security Force (KFOR) and the Governments of the Federal Republic of Yugoslavia and the Republic of Serbia, 9 June 1999. Made provision for cessation of hostilities, phased withdrawal of all FRY forces, and establishment of a joint implementation commission.

UN SC Res 1244 (1999), 10 June 1999. Resolution passed to mark the end of the conflict. Demanded end to violence and complete withdrawal of all forces and decided on deployment of international civil and security presence. Responsibilities of the civil presence to include promotion of establishment of autonomy and self-government taking into account Rambouillet accords; organizing and overseeing elections; maintaining civil law and order; and protecting and promoting human rights. Responsibilities of the security presence to include maintaining ceasefire, demilitarizing the KLA, and establishing secure environment for return of refugees–displaced persons. Also authorized UN Secretary-General to provide interim administration while overseeing development of democratic institutions.

Undertaking of Demilitarization and Transformation by the UCK [KLA], 21 June 1999. Gives details of arrangements for the KLA ceasefire in accordance with the UN Security Council Resolution and the Rambouillet Agreement, including a timetable for demilitarization. The KLA agreed that the International Security Force (KFOR) and Civil Presence would operate without hindrance, and provision was made for the establishment of a joint commission with senior KFOR and KLA commanders within two days to monitor the implementation of the provisions in the undertaking.

FEDERAL REPUBLIC OF YUGOSLAVIA—MACEDONIA

Agreement on the Regulation of Relations and Promotion of Cooperation between the Republic of Macedonia and the Federal Republic of Yugoslavia, 8 April 1996. Agreement dealing with post-war normalization. Both republics agree to respect each other as independent states within their national borders.

FIJI

Primary conflict is between Fiji's indigenous population and the Indian Fijian community. Opposition to a post-independence elected government which was allegedly sympathetic to Indo-Fijians led to two ethnically motivated military coups in the late 1980s. In 1990 a new Constitution contained weightings in favour of the indigenous Fijian community, and banned Indians from the post of prime minister. In 1994, under international pressure, the Fijian government established a Constitution Review Commission (CRC) to examine the Constitution and recommend an appropriate form of representation. A new Constitution (accepting some but not all CRC recommendations) was the eventual result. In June 2000 George Speight initiated a coup against the government, holding the (Indian) prime minister prisoner. He claimed this was in protest at the new Constitution's removal of indigenous Fijian weightings. The army took over administration of the country, the prime minister was released, and George Speight arrested. At time of writing instability continues.

Constitution (Amendment) Act 1997 of the Republic of the Fiji Islands, 25 July 1997. This Constitution implemented some of the recommendations of the government-established Constitution Review Commission's 1996 Report 'The Fiji Islands: Towards a United Future' (Parliamentary paper no. 34 of 1996, Parliament of Fiji, Suva). This was an attempt to establish an entirely new non-racial Constitution to replace the 1990 constitution with its racial weighting and under-representation of the minority Indo-Fijian community as regards the indigenous Fijian community. The new Constitution did not make the recommended move away from communalism, with two-thirds of all seats in the new seventy-seat Parliament still to be elected on a communal basis, leaving only one-third of seats free for inter-ethnic competition.

FRANCE—NEW CALEDONIA

Déclaration commune de Matignon, 26 June 1988. A declaration acknowledging escalating conflict as rooted in a clash between French sovereignty and an independence movement. Sets out a joint commitment to resolve the dispute and provides for a peace initiative.

Agreement on New Caledonia 1998. Preamble acknowledging the wrongs of French colonialism and its effect on the Kanak people. Agreement contains provisions dealing with customary law, language, and cultural heritage aimed at protecting Kanak identity more fully. Agreement envisages gradual transfer of power to proportionally representative Assembly and Executive and 'communes' which involve customary authorities. A section is devoted to economic and social development. Implementation is provided for in the form of a French Constitutional Revision Bill and a referendum on the agreement.

GABON

Serious riots broke out in 1993, when the president staged a fraudulent election to remain in power. An **Accord de Paris 1994** was signed in 1994.

GEORGIA—ABKHAZIA

Conflict broke out in 1989 between Georgians and ethnic Abkhaz in a dispute over territory and rights. In 1993 the Abkhaz (then forming a 1.8 per cent minority in the territory as a whole) dealt a humiliating defeat on the Georgian troops, taking control of Abkhazia with many Georgians fleeing. UN-sponsored talks led to a ceasefire in December 1993, and later an agreement to deploy a peacekeeping force in April 1994 and to help repatriate those who had fled. Negotiations have alternated between dialogue and deadlock, and in May 1998 full-scale war almost resumed (as the resultant agreements reflect).

Ceasefire Agreement, 3 September 1992. Parties agreed to a ceasefire and affirmed territorial integrity of Georgia. Provided for establishment of a monitoring and inspection commission; an agreed level of armed forces, exchange of detainees, hostages, and prisoners, and prohibition and prevention of all terrorist acts or taking of hostages. Also made provision for removal of obstacles to free movement; creation of conditions for return of refugees and steps to search for those who have disappeared, as well as steps to rehabilitate the area and to ensure availability of humanitarian assistance. Reaffirmed need to respect human rights and rights of national minorities, to prevent discrimination, and to hold free and democratic elections. Parties also agreed to assist legitimate authorities in Abkhazia to resume their normal functions and appealed for fact-finding missions and observers.

Ceasefire Agreement, 14 May 1993. Did not hold.

Ceasefire, 27 July 1993 ('Sochi Agreement'). Re-established the ceasefire and envisaged the arrival of international observers. Made provision for a trilateral Joint Commission to include the Russian Federation, which would assume responsibility for maintenance of ceasefire and establishment of interim monitoring groups. Agreed on demilitarization of the conflict zone; establishment of multinational police force to maintain public order; and measures to return refugees to their home. Also agreed to invite international peacekeeping forces to the area and to the immediate resumption of negotiations.

Memorandum of understanding between the Georgian and Abkhaz sides at the negotiations held in Geneva, 1 December 1993. Commitment not to use force or threat of force for period of negotiations. Maintenance of peace to be promoted by increase in international observers and use of peacekeeping forces. Also provided for exchange of prisoners of war before 20 December in gesture of good will; urgent measures to find missing persons; creation of conditions for return of refugees and return of land and property. Parties expressed hope for participation of United Nations High Commissioner for Refugees and appealed for humanitarian assistance. Agreed a group of experts would prepare recommendations on the political status of Abkhazia and set date for next round of negotiations.

Communiqué on the second round of negotiations between the Georgian and Abkhaz sides, Geneva, 13 January 1994. Noted that provisions of the last memorandum were for the most part being implemented, and reaffirmed commitment not to use force. Appealed to UN to extend mandate of UN Observer Mission in Georgia (UNOMIG) and to intensify the international civilian presence. Provided for withdrawal of armed units from lines of confrontation and complete disarmament and made provision for a Russian military contingent in a UN peacekeeping force. Agreed to continue to work out agreement on voluntary return of refugees–displaced persons, to establish special commission on refugees, and to begin implementation of phased process of their return to Abkhazia. Also agreed to continue discussion of problem of political status of Abkhazia and expressed interest in establishment of an international commission to assist economic recovery.

Declaration on measures for a political settlement of the Georgian–Abkhaz conflict, 4 April 1994. Commitment to a formal ceasefire and reaffirmation of commitment to non-use of force. Also reaffirmed request for development of peacekeeping operation and appealed for expansion of UNOMIG mandate. Parties agreed Abkhazia would have its own Constitution, legislation, and state symbols, and reached mutual understanding on powers for joint action in various fields, including foreign policy, customs, ecology, and human rights, and the rights of national minorities. Agreed to continue efforts to achieve a settlement and to intensify efforts to investigate war crimes.

Quadripartite agreement on voluntary return of refugees and displaced persons, 4 April 1994. Agreed to guarantee safety of refugees–displaced persons and to respect their right to return peacefully. Also made provision for freedom of movement; return of property; role of UNHCR; and establishment of a commission to create conditions for refugee return and of a mechanism to reunify families.

Agreement on a ceasefire and separation of forces, Moscow, 14 May 1994. Formalized commitment to ceasefire and made provision for separation of forces and deployment of peacekeeping force of the Commonwealth of Independent States (CISPKF) to monitor compliance. Also appealed to UN to expand mandate of military services to provide for their participation.

Proposal for the establishment of a coordinating commission, Moscow, 11 May 1994. Agreed to establish a commission to discuss practical matters of mutual interest for a transitional period.

UNOMIG Mandate adopted by Security Council Resolution 937, 21 July 1994. Mandate to monitor and verify implementation of Ceasefire Agreement.

Decision on measures for the settlement of the conflict in Abkhazia, Georgia, and the resolution on the extension of the mandate of the Collective Peacekeeping Forces in the zone of conflict, The Council of Heads of State of the Commonwealth of Independent States, 19 January 1996

Decision on the expansion of the operation for maintaining peace in Abkhazia, Georgia, The Council of Heads of State of the Commonwealth of Independent States, 28 March 1997. Expanded CISPKF mandate.

Statement on the meeting between the Georgian and Abkhaz parties, Tbilisi, 14 August 1997. Expressed determination to end conflict and commitment to resolving differences of opinion by peaceful political means. Noted there were substantial differences on key issues and agreed on need to maintain contact.

Protocol of the meeting of the Georgian and Abkhaz parties, Sukhumi, 20 August 1997

Concluding statement on the outcome of the resumed meeting between the Georgian and Abkhaz parties, Geneva, 17–19 November 1997. Welcomed proposals to strengthen involvement of UN and noted progress had not been made on the pivotal issues. Reaffirmed commitment to non-use of force and condemned acts of violence by armed groups or placement of mines. Agreed to take measures to halt any activity by illegal armed formations, terrorist and other 'subversive groups and individuals', and to take measures to convene a joint commission to resolve any practical issues. Also provided for establishment of a Coordinating Council and placed emphasis on need to resume process of voluntary return of refugees–displaced persons. Agreed to refrain from dissemination of hostile propaganda.

Record of the first session of the Coordinating Council of the Georgian and Abkhaz parties, Sukhumi, 18 December 1997. Adopted Statute of the Coordinating Council to take forward negotiations. Council would include three representatives each from Georgian and Abkhaz parties, and decisions would be binding. Agreed programmes for three working groups: Working Group I, to deal with issues related to the lasting non-resumption of hostilities and security problems; Working Group II, with refugees–displaced persons; and Working Group III, with economic and social problems.

Record of the first extraordinary session of the Coordinating Council of the Georgian and Abkhaz parties, Tbilisi, 22 January 1998. Instructed Working Group I to set up mechanism whereby parties, UNOMIG, and CISPKF could participate in the investigations and prevention of violations of the 1994 Moscow Agreement (see above).

Record of the second session of the Working Group I of the Coordinating Council of the Georgian and Abkhaz parties on issues related to the lasting non-resumption of hostilities and to security problems, Tbilisi, 22 January 1998. Agreed to cooperate in eliminating terrorist–banditry activities; to establish contact points and exchange information; and to form a joint investigation team on receipt of information. Also agreed to put forward proposals on preventive measures; to continue dialogue, and to develop a Plan of Action for the effective control of such activity.

Decision of 28 April 1998 on additional measures for the settlement of the conflict in Abkhazia, Georgia, The Council of Heads of State of the Commonwealth of Independent States, 28 April 1998. Decided to extend stay of Collective Peacekeeping Forces (CPF). Agreed to draw up plan to redeploy CPF and called on members of CPF to take more active part in peacekeeping. Expressed concern that decision of 28 March 1997 (expansion of peacekeeping forces) remained unimplemented, and agreed any further delay in process of return of refugees–displaced persons was inadmissible. Parties also agreed to seek cooperation of international community in resolving socio-economic and humanitarian problems.

Protocol of the fourth (second special) session of the Coordinating Council of the Georgian and Abkhaz sides, Tbilisi, 22 May 1998. Decided to take steps to halt armed confrontation in Gali district and to instruct UN Secretary-General to hold consultations on development of mechanism to investigate and prevent incidents in violation of Moscow Agreement. Agreed to refrain from steps that could exacerbate situation and to take measures to promote peace process.

Protocol on the ceasefire, separation of armed units, and guarantees for the prevention of acts involving force, Gagra, 26 May 1998 ('Gagra Protocol'). Provided for immediate ceasefire and withdrawal of both parties from Gali district and for establishment of special groups to monitor compliance. Abkhaz party obliged to prevent illegal acts involving force against the civilian population, and Georgian party obliged to take steps to halt infiltration of terrorist and subversive groups.

Concluding statement on the results of the second meeting of the Georgian and Abkhaz sides, Geneva, 23–25 July 1998. Welcomed implementation of 1997 Geneva Agreement, but noted several provisions had not been implemented. Expressed concern that parties were far from agreement on key issues, and stressed importance of bilateral contacts and direct dialogue as well as need for immediate implementation of the Coordination Council decision. Reaffirmed determination to put an end to conflict and agreement to refrain from hostile propaganda. Expressed commitment to rights of refugees–displaced persons, and to freedom of movement and security of humanitarian aid workers, and supported strengthened UN involvement. Annexes outlined position of both sides on violence in the Gali district and on the return of refugees.

Protocol of the fifth session of the Coordinating Council of the Georgian and Abkhaz sides, Sukhumi, 2 September 1998. Agreed to take effective steps to stop violence and to establish joint group to investigate and prevent terrorist acts and other offences. Pledged to examine and respond to protests made by UNOMIG and CISCPF about violations of Moscow Agreement, and agreed to request the UN Special Representative to resume negotiations on the elimination of consequences of May's events, return of refugees, and measures to rehabilitate Abkhazia's economy. In an annex the Special Representative, representatives of the Russian Federation, and others appealed to sides to refrain from actions that might exacerbate the situation, especially with regard to construction of military engineering installations.

Minutes of the meeting between the Georgian and Abkhaz sides on stabilization of the situation along the line separating the sides, 24 September 1998. Confirmed statements on halting armed conflict and overcoming differences by peaceful means, and agreed to bring military strength in security and restricted zones into line with Moscow Agreement, and to complete work defining line separating armed formations in Nabakevi-Khurcha and Otobaya-Ganmukhuri villages. Agreed to establish effective communications between heads of administration in Gali and Zugdidi districts, and between leaders of armed groups in the two villages. Also provided for the establishment of working groups to draw up regulations governing procedure for joint investigation of criminal cases involving acts of terrorism and subversion committed in security zone.

Athens meeting of the Georgian and Abkhaz sides on confidence-building measures, 16–18 October 1998. Reaffirmed commitment on right of refugees–displaced persons to voluntary return. Agreed to speed up conclusion of work on relevant documents; to provide for full implementation of 24 September Protocol, and to create joint mechanism to investigate violations of May 1994 Ceasefire Agreement. Also agreed to ensure link between leaders of military structures; to promote conclusion of working contracts in areas of energy, trade, agriculture, etc., and to investigate cases involving missing persons.

Protocol of the sixth session of the Coordinating Council of the Georgian and Abkhaz sides, Geneva, 17–18 December 1998

Decision on the further measures on settlement of the conflict in Abkhazia, Georgia, The Council of the Heads of State of the Commonwealth of Independent States, 2 April 1999

Istanbul statement of the Georgian and Abkhaz sides on confidence-building measures, 7–9 June 1999. Agreed to address issue of exchange of hostages and prisoners, to support joint investigations of incidents threatening stability, and to ensure implementation of 24 September 1998 Protocol. Provided for the revival of activities of working groups within framework of the Coordinating Council, and the development of mechanisms for exchange of information, especially between mass media and law-enforcement organs.

GUATEMALA

The civil war began after the failure of a nationalist uprising by military officers in 1960, and formally ended on 29 December 1996 with the signing of the agreement on a firm and lasting peace. Estimates suggested that 180,000 people died, 40,000 were disappeared, and 100,000 became refugees in Mexico. The war involved the related ingredients of colonialism, cold war left–right politics, injustice in distribution of land and socio-economic resources, and increasingly the treatment of indigenous peoples.

Basic Agreement on the Search for Peace by Political Means, 30 March 1990 ('Oslo Agreement'). Sets out arrangements for facilitation of future dialogue and confirms appointment and mandate of National Reconciliation Committee (CNR) conciliator and invitation of UN monitoring force. Outlines plans for series of consultations involving Guatemalan National Revolutionary Unity (URNG) and a range of civil and political groups leading to direct dialogue with the government at an unspecified future date.

Agreement on the Procedure for the Search for Peace by Political Means ('Mexico Agreement'), 26 April 1991. Agreed to discuss, first, substantive issues, such as democracy, human rights, refugees, truth commission, indigenous rights, the economic, social, and agrarian situation, the role of the army, strengthening of civil authorities and institutions, and constitutional reform. Procedural issues, such as arrangements for ceasefire, demobilization, and reintegration of the URNG into normal political life, to be discussed later. Confirmed functions of conciliator and UN observer, and both parties pledged not to abandon the negotiation process unilaterally.

Agreement on a General Agenda, 26 April 1991

Framework Agreement on Democratization in the Search for Peace by Political Means, 25 July 1991 ('Querétaro Agreement'). Outlined meaning and implications of a democratic regime. Agreed on importance of ending political repression, electoral fraud, and illegal manipulation of elections, and on need to promote citizen participation in development, implementation, and assessment of government policies.

Framework Agreement for the Resumption of Negotiations between the Government of Guatemala and the URNG, 10 January 1994. Agreed to negotiate on agenda of the Mexican Agreement, and laid ground rules for subsequent negotiations. Also agreed to promote establishment of an Assembly open to participation of non-governmental sectors, to discuss the substantive issues of negotiations, to transmit non-binding recommendations and guidelines, and to consider and endorse bilateral agreements concluded by the parties. Requested Colombia, Mexico, Norway, Spain, United States, and Venezuela to form a group of friends to support the process. Also agreed to request a UN representative to act as a moderator of the talks and gave UN responsibility for verifying the agreements. Expressed commitment to concluding a peace agreement in 1994.

Agreement on a Timetable for Negotiations on a Firm and Lasting Peace in Guatemala, 29 March 1994. Set December 1994 as the anticipated completion date.

Comprehensive Agreement on Human Rights, 29 March 1994. Commitment to observe fully human rights and to improve mechanisms for their protection. Verification role of UN mission to be defined to encompass all human rights violations committed after its inauguration.

Agreement on the resettlement of population groups uprooted by the armed conflict, 17 June 1994. Government committed to guaranteeing conditions necessary for safe return of internally displaced, to promote return of land, and to involve returnees in design and implementation of a comprehensive reintegration plan. Government assumed responsibility for decentralization and strengthening of municipal government. Parties requested UN help to fund projects resulting from the accord.

Agreement for the establishment of the commission to clarify past human rights violations and acts that have caused the Guatemalan population to suffer, 23 June 1994. Defined process for investing human rights abuses and for producing recommendations to contribute to national reconciliation. Agreed findings would not attribute responsibility to any individual, and recommendations would not be legally binding. Proceedings would be confidential, and content and sources of information would not be made public.

Agreement on the identity and rights of indigenous peoples, 31 March 1995. Outlined wide-ranging commitments to recognize the identity of indigenous peoples, to eliminate discrimination against them, and to guarantee their cultural, civil, political, economic, and social rights. Provided for establishment of three joint commissions on education reform, participation, and rights relating to land with equal numbers of government and indigenous people's representatives. Also provided for establishment of two commissions to address granting of official status of indigenous languages and definition and preservation of sacred areas.

Agreement on socio-economic aspects and the agrarian situation, 6 May 1996. Contained four chapters. (I) Democratization and Participatory Development: government committed itself to increasing citizen participation. (II) Social Development: promised high levels of government growth and restructuring of public expenditure to increase social investment. Included sections on education and training, health, social security, housing, and work. (III) Agrarian Situation and Rural Development: government agreed to strengthen provisions for consultation, to establish a trust fund to redistribute undeveloped land, to develop a land register, to raise new taxes on land, and to implement speedy resolution of land conflicts. (IV) Modernization of Government Services and Fiscal Policy.

Agreement on the strengthening of civilian power and the role of the armed forces in a democratic society, 19 September 1996. Provided for strengthening of democratic government. Under a reformed Constitution: civil patrols would be abolished; various police units restructured and unified to form the National Civil Police; reform of the penal code promoted; operations of private security firms regulated; forced conscription ended; and role of army limited to external defence.

Agreement on a definitive ceasefire, 4 December 1996. Set sixty-day timetable for separation and assembly of forces and for URNG disarmament. Demobilization to commence with a definitive ceasefire on date on which the UN verification mechanism was in place with full operational capacity.

Agreement on constitutional reforms and the electoral regime, 7 December 1996. Government to place proposals for reform before Congress within sixty days of signing of the Agreement on a Firm and Lasting Peace. Main focus of proposals to be on the recognition of the identity and rights of indigenous peoples and the mandate and structure of the country's security forces. Provision made for establishment of an Electoral Reform Commission to review the electoral process.

Agreement on the basis for the legal reintegration of the Guatemalan National Revolutionary Unity (URNG), 12 December 1996. Enabled the establishment of a joint government–URNG Integration Commission, and contained provisions to be included in a National Reconciliation Act.

Agreement on the implementation, compliance, and verification timetable for the peace agreements, 29 December 1996. Provided guide for implementation of all commitments undertaken since 1994. Mandate of the Commission for Historical Clarification set for six months, with possibility of one extension. Requested that the UN establish a mission to verify all agreements.

Agreement on a Firm and Lasting Peace, 29 December 1996. Triggered implementation of all previous agreements and bound them into an agenda for peace.

GUINEA-BISSAU

Former army chief of staff Ansumane Mare rebelled in June 1998, and was supported by most of the armed forces. His aim was to remove President Joao Bernardo Vieira and to hold new elections. An agreement was signed at Cape Verde, but sporadic fighting continued. A second agreement was signed, but sporadic clashes were still reported.

Ceasefire Agreement, Praia, 26 August 1998. Ceasefire agreed.

Agreement between the Government of Guinea Bissau and the Self-Pro-claimed Military Junta, Abuja, 1 November 1998. Brief agreement reaffirming ceasefire; providing for withdrawal of foreign troops to be replaced by Economic Community of West African States Ceasefire Monitoring Group (ECOMOG) to monitor the Guinea-Bissau–Senegal border and guarantee free access to humanitarian organizations and agencies; putting in place a government of national unity, to include members of the self-proclaimed junta; and agreeing to general and presidential elections not later than end of March 1999.

Final Communication of the Meeting of the Seven of the CEDEAO (Economic Community of the States of Western Africa) and the Contact Group for the CPLP (Community of the Portuguese-speaking countries), 25 August 1998. Provides for a coordinated mediation approach between the CEDEAO and the Contact Group for the CPLP, aimed at bringing peace to Guinea-Bissau. Meeting included an exchange of views between the participants and the government of Guinea-Bissau, and the self-proclaimed military junta, on the permanence and monitoring of the ceasefire, the reopening of the airport, return of refugees, international aid. Agreed on future meeting.

HAITI

Haiti's President Aristide was ousted from power in a coup in 1993. A series of agreements preceded a return to constitutional order in 1994.

Protocole d'accord entre le Président Jean-Bertrand Aristide et le Premier Ministre désigné 1992

Accord de Governors Island 1993

Protocole d'accord entre le Président Jean-Bertrand Aristide et la Commission parlementaire de négociation 1993

INDIA–ASSAM

The Bodo are a tribal peoples of about 2 million living in the mountain regions of eastern Assam. They want their own state, and several thousand have been killed in conflict since 1986. A truce was signed in 1989, and negotiations began with the Assam government. However, conflict was resumed by some Bodo elements. New attempts to reach settlement were not successful.

Memorandum of Settlement (Bodo Accord), 20 February 1993. Built on earlier agreements. Provided for establishment of a Bodoland Autonomous Council (BAC) within the state of Assam, to include villages with 50 per cent and more of tribal population: thirty-five members to be elected by adult suffrage and five members nominated by the Government. Council to be consulted before law made in three areas: law affecting religious or social practices of Bodos; Bodo customary laws and procedures; and the ownership and transfer of land within BAC area. Also provided for establishment of Special Courts to deal with cases between parties who belong to scheduled tribes, and for changes in the geographical areas of the BAC. Agreed the General Council could lay down policy with regard to use of Bodo languages as medium of official correspondence within the BAC area, and that correspondence with offices outside the area would be in bilingual form. Agreement also reached on powers to regulate trade and commerce; employment opportunities with BAC having power to reserve jobs for scheduled tribes; civil and police services, with the central government agreeing to hold special recruitment drives within the BAC area; relief and rehabilitation, including the surrender of arms and protection of rights of non-tribals. An Interim Bodoland Executive Council was to be established for the transitional period. An appendix listed subjects and departments over which the BAC would have control.

The Bodoland Autonomous Council Act 1993. Provided that the BAC would have maximum autonomy within the framework of the Constitution, and outlined requirements for membership of General and Executive Council. Also gave details of election and administrative procedures and the powers and functions of both councils.

INDIA–DARJEELING

Gorkhas in the state of West Bengal have waged guerrilla war against the central government for a number of years. Anti-foreign riots started in 1979 after a steady infiltration of people, both Hindu and Muslim, from other parts of Bengal. Tension continued until a peace agreement was concluded in 1988. **The Accord of Darjeeling, 25 July 1998,** provided for an autonomous Gorkha district around Darjeeling, which would remain part of West Bengal, with control over matters such as education, health, finance, and transport. This accord was implemented in **The Darjeeling Gorkha Hill Council (Amendment) Act 1994.**

INDIA–MIZORAM–HMAR

Mizoram was formerly a part of the state of Assam. A revolt led by the Mizo National Front (MNFP) began in February 1966 and continued until 25 June 1986, when Rajiv Gandhi signed an agreement meeting many of the rebels' demands in exchange for their acceptance of the permanency of the Indian Union **(Memorandum of Settlement, 1986 (The Mizo Accord)).** Mizoram became a separate state, and the MNF leader became prime minister. In February 1987 the MNF won a majority of seats in the state Assembly. The peace agreements below were internal agreements between the government of Mizoram and the indigenous Hmar.

Five Point Agreement between the Government of Mizoram and the Hmar People's Convention, 29 September 1993. Agreed to bring out an amicable solution to problem arising out of demands of Hmar People's Convention; to give adequate autonomy to the council for social, economic, cultural, and educational advancement of the people; to initiate measures for use of the Hmar language as a medium of instruction up to primary level, and recognition of the Hmar language as one of the major languages of the state of Mizoram.

INDIA–PAKISTAN

India has fought several wars with Pakistan since independence in 1947, and there has been constant hostility between the two sides over that period, not least with respect to Kashmir. The following agreements were signed after the escalation of hostilities and nuclear testing incidents.

The Lahore Declaration, 21 February 1999. Both sides agreed to intensify efforts to resolve all issues; to refrain from intervention in the other's internal affairs; and to intensify dialogue. Also agreed to take steps to reduce the risk of accidental or unauthorized use of nuclear weapons and to discuss confidence-building measures in the nuclear and conventional fields. Affirmed commitment to the promotion and protection of human rights and fundamental freedoms.

Joint Statement, 21 February 1999. Decided foreign ministers would meet periodically to discuss issues of mutual concern, and agreed to undertake consultations on World Trade Organization-related issues; to determine areas of cooperation in information technology; and to hold consultations on liberalizing the visa and travel regime. Also agreed to appoint a two-member committee to examine humanitarian issues relating to civil detainees and missing prisoners of war.

Memorandum of Understanding, 21 February 1999. Agreed to engage in consultations to develop confidence-building measures; to give notification of ballistic missile flight tests; and to conclude a bilateral agreement on this. Also agreed to reduce risks of accidental or unauthorized use of nuclear weapons and to give notification of any incident that could create the risk of fallout. Parties would conclude an agreement on prevention of incidents at sea, review the implementation of existing confidence-building measures and existing communication links, and engage in bilateral consultations on security, disarmament, and non-proliferation issues.

INDIA–TRIPURA

In 1980 a group called the Tripura National Volunteer (TNV) began fighting for the state's independence, in part at protest against the large number of immigrants from Bengal in the area, which meant that the tribal people were in the minority. In 1988 agreement was reached according to which the rebels agreed to surrender their arms and give up violence in return for reservation of seats in the Tripura Legislative Assembly, restoration of alienated lands to tribals, and redrawing of the boundaries of Autonomous District Council Areas **(Memorandum of Settlement, 2 August 1988).** However, the TNV also demanded the expulsion of Bengalis who had settled there.

Memorandum of Settlement, 23 August 1993. The All-Tripura Tribal Force (ATTF) covenanted to deposit arms and ammunition and to end underground activities. The government of Tripura covenanted to take steps for resettlement and rehabilitation of ATTF personnel; to take action in respect of sending back Bangladeshi foreign nationals who arrived after 25 March 1971; and to take steps to restore land acquired from tribals. Also agreed on inclusion of tribal majority villages in Autonomous District Council (ADC) areas; village police force for the ADC; increase in numbers of seats for scheduled tribe candidates in the ADC. Provision also made for establishment of a cultural development centre; improvement of Kok Borak and other tribal languages; presentation of Ujjayanta Palace as a historical monument; and shifting of Tripura Legislative Assembly; renaming of villages, rivers, etc.; Jhumia resettlement and industrial development of ADC area. Housing and drinking water facilities and government employment or economic package to be provided for ATTF personnel with secured accommodation and escorts for ATTF office-bearers.

IRAQ–UN

In the aftermath of the Iraq–UN conflict over Kuwait international monitoring of Iraq's weapons capacity was provided for, together with enforcement of no-fly zones. UN inspection teams (UNSCOM) entered Iraq and stayed there until October 1997 when its American members were ordered to leave after reports that secret facilities for making biological weapons had been discovered. The US began to build up its air and naval forces in the region, and the UN Secretary-General went to Baghdad on 20 February 1998 to conduct negotiations with Saddam Hussein. Both parties agreed on 22 February that UNSCOM would be allowed unfettered inspections of 'presidential sites' if accompanied by neutral diplomats appointed by the Security Council.

Memorandum of Understanding between the United Nations and the Republic of Iraq, 23 February 1998. Iraq confirmed its acceptance of all relevant Security Council resolutions and the commitment of UN member states to respect the sovereignty and territorial integrity of Iraq was expressed. Iraq undertook to cooperate fully with UNSCOM and the International Atomic Energy Agency, and UNSCOM undertook to express its concerns relating to national security, sovereignty, and dignity. Special procedures for entry to presidential sites were also agreed, and the Secretary-General undertook to bring the matter of sanctions to the full attention of Security Council members.

ISRAEL–JORDAN

See Chapter 4.

Treaty of Peace between the State of Israel and the Hashemite Kingdom of Jordan, 26 October 1994. See Chapter 4.

The Washington Declaration, Israel–Jordan–United States, 25 July 1994. Affirms a common commitment to peace. Affirms the Common Agenda programmes and takes steps to further normalize relations between Israel and Jordan.

Israel–Jordan–Palestine Liberation Organization: Declaration on Cooperation on Water-Related Matters, 13 February 1996. Detailed provision on water matters.

ISRAEL–LEBANON

Israel has operated what it termed a 'security zone' in southern Lebanon since 1978. The zone suffered twenty years of war. In May 2000 Israel unilaterally withdrew from this area.

Israel–Lebanon Ceasefire Understanding, 26 April 1996. Negotiated by the United States. Provides for a ceasefire and a monitoring group consisting of the United States, France, Syria, Lebanon, and Israel. The United States undertakes to convene an international group to look at Lebanon's reconstruction needs.

ISRAEL–PALESTINE

See Chapter 4 for conflict description and peace agreements.

LIBERIA

See Chapter 2 for conflict description and implementation agreements.

ECOWAS Peace Plan—Banjul Communiqué, 7 August 1990. Called for immediate ceasefire and announced establishment of the Economic Community of West African States Ceasefire Monitoring Group (ECOMOG) to keep peace, restore order, and ensure ceasefire was respected. Also called for a national conference of all Liberian political parties and other interest groups to establish a civilian-dominated interim; and for elections to government to be held within twelve months.

Bamako Ceasefire, 28 November 1990. Expressed commitment to Economic Community of West African States (ECOWAS) Peace Plan and to immediate ceasefire.

Lomé Agreement, 13 February 1991. Built on earlier accords and specified modalities for implementation of the ceasefire.

Yamoussoukro I Accord, 30 June 1991

Yamoussoukro II Accord, 29 July 1991

Yamoussoukro III Accord, 17 September 1991

Yamoussoukro IV Accord, 30 October 1991. A culmination of work on previous three accords. Parties agreed timetable for disarmament and affirmed mandate of ECOMOG to supervise implementation of the agreement. They also noted the nomination of the five-member Elections Commission and five-member ad hoc Supreme Court from ranks of NPFL and Interim Government of National Unity (IGNU), and agreed that elections would be held within six months. An enclosure outlined ECOMOG tasks.

Geneva Ceasefire, 17 July 1993

The Cotonou Accord, 25 July 1993. Provided a framework for resolving the dispute, dealing with ceasefire, disarmament, demobilization, the structure of the transitional government, election modalities, repatriation of refugees, and a general amnesty.

For later agreements, see Chapter 2.

MALI

The nomadic Tuaregs in the north have been in long-standing revolt against a government dominated by the south.

Agreement on a cessation of hostilities between the Government of the Republic of Mali, and the 'Mouvement Populaire de l'Azaouad' together with the 'Front Islamique Arabe', 6 January 1991. Provides for the logistics of a cease-fire with a commission to monitor, presided over by Algeria as mediator. Prisoners will be released.

MEXICO

Conflict between Mexico government and Chiapas people (through the Zapatista National Liberation Army, EZLN) over indigenous rights and culture and self-rule.

Actions and Measures for Chiapas Joint Commitments and Proposals from the State and Federal Governments, and EZLN, 17 January 1996. Addresses: guarantees of access to justice (review of imprisonment, human rights; translation facilities; and education in legal structures); situation, rights, and culture of indigenous women; access to the communication media; education and culture; institutions for the promotion, development, and diffusion of indigenous cultures (legislation, and restructuring of development, educational, and cultural institutions).

Joint Declaration [between EZLN and federal government], 16 February 1996. General commitment by government to combating poverty and marginalization of indigenous peoples and combating discrimination. Specific commitments to recognizing indigenous peoples in general Constitution; broadening political participation and representation; guaranteeing full access to justice; promoting cultural manifestations of indigenous peoples; ensuring education and training; guaranteeing satisfaction of basic needs; promoting production and employment; protecting indigenous migrants. Establishes governing principles of pluralism, sustainability, comprehensiveness, and 'free determination'. Sets out a new legal framework including indigenous rights.

Joint Proposals [between EZLN and federal government], 16 February 1996. Lists specific proposals to be remitted to national debating and decision-making bodies addressing, in chief, the legal framework and autonomy for indigenous peoples.

Commitments for Chiapas by the State and Federal Government and the EZLN under paragraph 1.3 of the Rules of Procedure, 16 February 1996. Provides for amendment of state of Chiapas Constitution to reflect indigenous rights. Sets out a loose framework of principles and structures for autonomy designed 'to best represent the different and legitimate aspirations and situations of the indigenous peoples.' Some details of the amendments are provided in the text of the agreement, as is a commitment to amend secondary legislation so as to bring it into line with the amended Constitution.

MOLDOVA—TRANSDNIESTRIA

In 1994 conflict focused on whether and when the Russian army would withdraw from the Transdniestria region of Moldova (where it had been since Soviet times). Russia wanted to wait until the self-proclaimed Transdniestria Republic had been given 'special political status'. An agreement was reached in 1994 but not implemented. While ceasefires more or less held, the underlying conflict between Transdniestria separatists and the Moldovan government continued to simmer. During 1997 Russia made effort to broker agreement, resulting in the agreements below. However, differences over their interpretation led to difficulties. Further Russian mediation saw the parties agreeing to negotiations on a form of autonomy for Transdniestria. Then in October 1997 an agreement on principles of social and economic cooperation was signed. In 1997 the unimplemented 1994 agreement on Russian withdrawal was addressed, reportedly leading to agreement for withdrawal.

Agreement on the Withdrawal of Russian Forces, 21 October 1994

Memorandum on the Bases for Normalization of Relations between the Republic of Moldova and Transdniestria, 8 May 1997. Signed by Moldovan President Petru Lucinschi, and Igor Smirnov, the leader of the breakaway Transdniestria region. Reaffirmed commitment not to use or threaten force and to resolve differences through peaceful means with the assistance of the Russian Federation and Ukraine, the Organization for Security and Cooperation in Europe (OSCE), and the Commonwealth of Independent States (CIS). Agreed to continue the establishment of state–legal relations between them. Document defining these relations and the status of Transdniestria to be based on the principles of mutually agreed decisions, including the division and delegation of competencies and mutually assured guarantees. Agreed Transdniestria would participate in conduct of foreign policy of the Republic of Moldova on questions touching its interests, and would have the right to establish unilaterally and to maintain international contact in the economic, scientific–technical, and cultural spheres, and in other spheres by agreement of the parties. Also requested the Russian Federation, Ukraine, and the OSCE to continue their mediating efforts and reaffirmed continuance of activities for maintaining peace carried out by the joint peacekeeping forces in the security zone.

Joint Statement of the Presidents of the Russian Federation and Ukraine in Connection with the Signing of the Memorandum on the Bases for Normalization of Relations between the Republic of Moldova and Transdniestria, 8 May 1997. Welcomed signing of the memorandum as an important step towards settlement of the Transdniestrian problem and towards strengthening mutual trust, stability, and security. Declared that its provisions could not contradict generally accepted norms of international law and would not be interpreted or acted upon in contradiction to existing international agreements recognizing the sovereignty and territorial integrity of the Republic of Moldova. Also noted the intention to intensify mediation efforts and called upon parties to initiate negotiations immediately to complete a comprehensive document on the final settlement of the conflict and a mechanism of appropriate guarantees. Affirmed readiness to act as guarantors for the compliance with the provisions on the status of Transdniestria as a component part of a united and territorially whole Republic of Moldova.

Agreement between Chisinau and Tiraspol, 26 September 1997. Agreed to future talks.

Chisinau–Tiraspol Cooperation Agreement, 11 November 1997. Agreement on organizational principles of social and economic cooperation signed by Moldovan prime minister and Transdniestria leader, Igor Smirnov.

MOZAMBIQUE

A Marxist government came to power after Mozambique gained its independence on 25 June 1975. The Mozambique National Resistance Organization (Renamo) was set up in 1976 and began a campaign of disruption against the new government. The conflict intensified in the 1980s, and at least 100,000 people were killed between 1984 and 1988, despite peace accords signed in 1984. When international support for the government declined at the end of the cold war, moves were made towards peace, with peace accords in 1989 paving the way for the Rome process. A ceasefire was called in August 1992 and elections were held in October 1993.

'Rome Process'

Joint Communiqué, 10 July 1990. Parties expressed their willingness to do everything possible to search for peace, and agreed to engage in dialogue in a spirit of mutual understanding.

Agreement on a Partial Ceasefire in Mozambique, 1 December 1990. Renamo agreed to end all offensive military operations in agreed areas, and both parties undertook to avoid any activities that could violate the spirit or letter of the agreement and renewed their commitment to discussing remaining points on the peace agenda. Provision was also made for the creation of a Joint Verification Commission to ensure the implementation of the agreement.

Protocol on Detailed Agenda, 28 May 1991

Protocol I—Basic Principles, 18 October 1991. The government undertook to refrain from any action contrary to the protocols, and Renamo agreed to refrain from armed struggle. Both parties affirmed their commitment to concluding the General Peace Agreement as soon as possible and agreed that the protocols would form an integral part of that agreement. They also agreed in principle to establish a Commission to supervise and monitor compliance with the agreement.

Protocol II—Criteria and Arrangements for the Formation and Recognition of Political Parties, 13 November 1991. Agreed that Renamo would commence its activities as a political party immediately after the signing of the General Peace Agreement and agreed to establish a timetable for the implementation of the protocol.

Protocol III—Principles of the Electoral Act, 12 March 1992. Electoral Act to be drafted by the government in consultation with Renamo and all other political parties. Drafters to be guided by principles of freedom of press and access to the media; freedom of association, expression, and political activity; liberty of movement and freedom of residence; return of refugees–displaced persons and social reintegration; system of democratic, impartial, and pluralistic voting; and guarantees for the electoral process and role of international observers.

Agreed Minute on Rearrangement of Agenda, 19 June 1992

Declaration on the Guiding Principles for Humanitarian Assistance, 16 July 1992. Agreed to permit and facilitate the relief operation, to be coordinated and supervised by a committee presided over by the UN; not to derive military advantages from it; and to cooperate with the international community in Mozambique in formulating action plans.

Joint Declaration, 7 August 1992. Expressed commitment to guaranteeing conditions for complete political freedom and personal safety of all citizens and all members of political parties. Agreed to accept the role of the international community in monitoring the implementation of the General Peace Agreement and to respect the principles set forth in Protocol I.

Protocol IV Military Questions, 4 October 1992. Agreed on the formation of the Mozambique Defence Force with 50 per cent of troops from each side and on the withdrawal of foreign troops from Mozambican territory. Also agreed on the function of the National Service for People's Security; on the depoliticization and restructuring of the police forces; and on the economic and social reintegration of demobilized soldiers.

Protocol V Guarantees, 4 October 1992. Agreed on timetable for the conduct of the electoral process and on the composition and powers of the National Elections Commission, with government, Renamo, and UK representatives, to supervise the ceasefire and monitor respect for and implementation of the agreements. Government agreed to make legal instruments incorporating the protocols, the guarantees, and the General Peace Agreement for adoption into Mozambique law.

Protocol VI Ceasefire, 4 October 1992. Agreed on cessation of armed conflict and on operational timetable for the ceasefire and the release of prisoners.

Protocol VII Donors' Conference, 4 October 1992. Agreed to ask the Italian government to convene a donors' conference to finance the electoral process and emergency and reintegration programmes, and to request that an appropriate share be available to political parties.

The General Peace Agreement, 4 October 1992. Accepted the protocols as binding and other documents listed as integral parts of the General Peace Agreement, and undertook to do everything within their power for the achievement of genuine national reconciliation.

NAMIBIA–SOUTH AFRICA

Walvis Bay is a port on the coast of South West Africa which became part of the South African government's Mandate over South West Africa. In 1977, when Namibian independence became a possibility, South Africa placed the administration of Walvis Bay under Cape Town province. On Namibian independence Namibia claimed sovereignty over Walvis Bay, and South Africa resisted those claims. In 1992, when the South African peace process was developing, South Africa and Namibia agreed to administer the area jointly, pending a settlement. This settlement was expedited by the South African peace process and was reached in the treaty below, which transferred Walvis Bay (and offshore islands) to Namibia.

Agreement on the Joint Administration of Walvis Bay and the Offshore Islands, 9 November 1992
Treaty on Walvis Bay, 1 March 1994

NIGER

Conflict between the government and the Coordination de la Résistance Armée (CRA).

Agreement between the Government of the Republic of Niger and the 'Coordination de la Résistance Armée' (CRA), 9 October 1994 ('Ouagadougou Accord'). Set out a framework for agreement providing for devolution of power to 'territorial collectivities'; the territorial division to be agreed by a special commission of which the CRA were to be members. Power to be devolved to include budget, organization, and programmes, with a special emphasis on economic development. Agreement provided for state representatives on all devolved bodies, to protect state interests. Also provided for urgent rehabilitation and economic reconstruction of conflict areas; return and reintegration of refugees; a ceasefire; the creation of an international commission of inquiry to look at past actions; a joint committee to oversee implementation; and international finance. Parties commit to further negotiations on points not addressed, notably on armed forces and economic, social, and cultural development.

Agreement establishing a lasting peace settlement between the Government of the Republic of Niger and the 'Organisation de la Résistance Armée' (ORA), 15 April 1995. Affirms and slightly revises the first agreement, establishing a new ceasefire, and a joint peace committee. Deals with security logistics such as ceasefire monitoring and future decommissioning (which is to be tied to government economic development). Agreement provides for an amnesty for some ORA and state defence members for acts in the conflict; a day of national reconciliation dedicated to victims; reintegration of ORA civil servants and students into state institutions. Agreement also deals with armed forces (integrating ORA into special new units); and decentralized social and economic development. A time line is provided.

Additional Peace Protocol between the Government of the Republic of Niger and the United Forces of the Resistance Army (FPLS, MUR, FAR) and the Armed Revolutionary Forces of the Sahara, 28 November 1997. Establishes a ceasefire, release of prisoners, and de-mining, and future uniting of forces, and disarmament of ex-combatants.

PAPUA NEW GUINEA–BOUGAINVILLE

For description of the conflict and pre-negotiation agreements, see Chapter 2.

The Lincoln Agreement on Peace, Security and Development on Bougainville, Lincoln, Christchurch, New Zealand, 23 January 1998. An agreement to a 'permanent and irrevocable ceasefire, and a framework for normalization. Provided for a peace monitoring group, a transition to civilian policing, promotion of reconciliation, removal of bounties and free movement, amnesty to persons involved in 'crisis-related activities on all sides', and cooperation for restoration and development. Provided for further annexes to add further detail.

Permanent and Irrevocable Ceasefire Agreement, Arawa, 30 April 1998

Buin Declaration, 20–2 August 1998. Reconfirmed Bougainvillean commitment to Bougainville Reconciliation Government.

Bougainville Reconciliation Government Basic Agreement, 15–16 January 1999. Agreement among Bougainville parties for a new government, given breakdown in negotiations with the PNG. Also adopted a Constitution.

Matakana and Okataina Understanding, 14–22 April 1999. Understanding among Bougainville parties for government. Paved way for formation of interim advisory body.

Hutjena Minute, 10 July 1999. Agreement on a set of principles governing Bougainville's political future.

Nehan Resolution, 29 October 1999. Agreement between Bougainville parties to discuss issues of full automony and a referendum with the PNG government.

The Buka Resolution, 16 November 1999. Adopted by members of Parliament and Bougainville leaders. Endorsed a timetable for political negotiations and agreed on identifying a negotiating team.

Bougainville Negotiating Position, Buka, 29 November 1999. Outlined a position on autonomy, mechanisms for implementation and guarantee, and options for a deferred referendum, to form the basis for any negotiations with the PNG.

The Arawa Resolution, 2 December 1999. Agreement between ex-combatant members of BRA and Resistance Commanders to a way forward for negotiations with the PNG.

Hutjena Record, 16 December 1999. Set out a Bougainville common negotiating position between PNG government and the Bougainville People's Congress.

Loloata Understanding, 17–23 March 2000. Culminated the third round of political negotiations between PNG delegation and Bougainville leaders. Committed to establishing an autonomous Bougainville province within the Constitution of Papua New Guinea. Leaves open question of independence and commits parties to discussing matter.

PHILIPPINES–MINDANAO

The conflict on this island under the jurisdiction of the Philippines began in 1970, when Philippine President Marcos declared martial law, and the Moro (or Muslim) National Liberation Front (MNLF) resorted to a war of independence. The Moros were granted a degree of autonomy following the signing of the Tripoli Agreement between the MNLF and government representatives in 1976. However, the agreement unravelled within a matter of months. The conflict has been between Moros, involving three main factions (the largest, the MNLF, the Bangasa Moro Liberation Organization, and the Moro Islamic Liberation Front, MILF) and the Filipino government. Exploratory talks were held between the government of the Philippines (GRP) and the MNLF in 1992, and a peace agreement was signed on 19 August 1996, but the other two groups continued to fight. Agreements were later signed between the GRP and the MILF. Approximately 120,000 are estimated to have died in the civil war.

Peace Agreements

Statement of Understanding between the GRP and the MNLF, first round of the GRP–MNLF exploratory talks, Tripoli, Libya, 4 October 1992

Statement of Understanding on the Second Round of the Exploratory Talks between the GRP and the MNLF, Cipanas, Indonesia, 16 April 1993

Interim Ceasefire Agreement between the GRP and the MNLF with the Participation of the OIC [Organization of Islamic Conference], Jakarta, Indonesia, 7 November 1993

Joint Guidelines and Ground Rules for the Implementation of the 1993 Interim GRP–MNLF Ceasefire Agreement—GRP–MNLF Panels, Zamboanga City, Philippines, 20 January 1994

Interim Agreement, second round of formal peace talks between the GRP and the MNLF with the participation of the OIC, Jakarta, Indonesia, 5 September 1994

Interim Agreement, third round of formal peace talks between the GRP and the MNLF with the participation of the Ministerial Committee of Six and the Secretary-General of the OIC, Jakarta, Indonesia, 1 December 1995

Davao Accord, Points of Consensus of the 8th GRP–MNLF Mixed Committee Meeting with the participation of the OIC Ministerial Committee of Six, Davao City, Philippines, 23 July 1996

Final Peace Agreement, Manila, 2 September 1996. See Chapter 2.

Interim Cessation of Hostilities in Buldon, Maguindanao, 27 January 1997. Provincial governor of Maguindanao to provide assistance to ensure the return to office of the mayor of Buldon, and to assist government agencies in relief and rehabilitation of evacuees and the reopening of schools in the affected areas. Agreed that the GRP and MILF forces would maintain 'as is, where is' positions within the area of conflict prior to discussions on the matter, and that Philippine National Police (PNP) would continue its mandated role to enforce all laws and maintain peace and order. MILF agreed to move and not establish checkpoints, road blocks, etc. along the road networks from Parang to Buldon, and the Armed Forces of the Philippines (AFP) and MILF agreed to refrain from provocative actions. Provided for the withdrawal of all AFP forces at the option of the AFP based on its evaluation of the peace and order situation.

GRP–MILF General Cessation of Hostilities Agreement, Cagayan de Oro City, Philippines, 18 July 1997. Agreed to commit armed forces to a general cessation of hostilities; to direct their respective Subcommittees on Cessation of Hostilities to meet on 30 July 1997 to draw and finalize guidelines and ground rules for the implementation of the agreement, and to resume and proceed with formal peace talks.

GRP–MILF Agreement (Supplemental) on repositioning troops and the display of fire arms, Cotabato City, Philippines, 3 September 1997

Implementing Administrative Guidelines of the GRP–MILF Agreement on the General Cessation of Hostilities, 12 September 1997. Provided for creation by the GRP and MILF of Coordinating Committees on Cessation of Hostilities (CCCH) to implement the administrative guidelines; of a joint Independent Fact-Finding Committee (IFFC) to make inquiries on matters referred to it for appropriate action; and of a GRP–MILF Coordination Committees Secretariat by the coordinating committees. Outlined composition and functions of the CCCH, the IFFC, and the Coordination Committees Secretariat, as well as administrative and support arrangements and conduct of public information concerning cessation of hostilities. Also listed areas of coverage of the cessation of hostilities.

Implementing Operational Guidelines of the GRP–MILF Agreement on the General Cessation of Hostilities, Marawi City, Philippines, 14 November 1997. Listed prohibited hostile and provocative acts, and actions exempted from cessation of hostilities. Also outlined ground rules and provided for observation of cessation of hostilities and conduct of inquiry by the GRP–MILF CCHC and action to be taken by the GRP and MILF if their forces violate the guidelines and ground rules. Other provisions dealt with security of the GRP and MILF panels and CCCH members, and relationships between the CCCH and the GRP and MILF forces.

Agreement to Sustain the Quest for Peace, 6 February 1998. GRP agreed to commence immediately to reposition its forces in Buldon, Maguindanao; to use its utmost efforts to resolve the issue involving Upper Minabay–Banganan–Ambal rivers in Buldon, and to propose the immediate suspension of logging operations of the Cotabato Timber Company and other logging concessionaires until final resolution of the conflict. GRP and MILF Technical Committees agreed that operationalization of the Monitoring Office of the Coordinating Committees on Cessation of Hostilities would be determined later; agreed on expansion of IFFC membership; and on formation of a Quick Response Team (QRT) composed of representatives from GRP, MILF, and the IFFC to address alleged violations of the Agreement on the General Cessation of Hostilities immediately. Both parties confirmed their strict adherence to the Implementing Operational Guidelines of the Agreement on the General Cessation of Hostilities signed on 14 November 1997.

Agreement to Sustain the Quest for Peace, 11 March 1998. Agreed on the location, composition, and operation of the QRT. QRT to address immediately a reported conflict–confrontation between the GRP and MILF panel and GRP and MILF CCCH to convene immediately to assess and respond to the reports and findings of the QRT.

GRP–MILF General Framework of Agreement of Intent, 27 August 1998. Commitment to pursue peace negotiations on substantive issues as soon as possible, and to continue until political settlement reached. Pledged to implement the joint agreements previously signed and to refrain from use or threat of force. Affirmed commitment to protect and respect human rights, and recognized that there would be lasting peace when there was mutual trust, justice, freedom, and tolerance for identity, culture, way of life, and aspirations of all the peoples of Mindanao.

Resolution Creating a Joint Monitoring Contingent (JMC) to Oversee the Peace Situation in Upper Minabay, Buldon, Maguindanao, 16 October 1998. GRP–MILF Subcommittees on Cessation of Hostilities agreed on establishment of a Joint Monitoring Contingent to monitor the implementation of the 6 February 1998 Agreement to sustain the Quest for Peace with twenty-three personnel each from the PNP and the MILF. Also resolved that GRP would reposition its forces, that MILF would not occupy the vacated area, and that GRP would implement paragraph 2 of the Agreement to Sustain the Quest for Peace regarding the suspension of logging operations by the Cotabato Timber Company in the vacated area.

Joint Acknowledgement, 10 February 1999. Acknowledged two MILF camps to be covered by the cessation of hostilities for the duration of the peace talks and tasked GRP and MILF CCCH to schedule at its first meeting the determination of the limits of the two camps, to be submitted to GRP and MILF peace panels for confirmation. Also acknowledged that CCCH would proceed to determine and verify other MLF camps.

Rule and Procedures in the Administration of the Joint Secretariat of the Joint GRP–MILF Coordinating Committees on Cessation of Hostilities, 18 May 1999. Established and outlined functions of various offices of the secretariat.

Rules and Procedures in the Determination and Verification of the Coverage of Cessation of Hostilities, 18 May 1999. Agreed on general provisions for the identification and verification of MILF camps/positions, including scheduling and the designation of an MILF camp/position coordinator initially to identify camps–positions to be verified, to act as a guide of the verifying party, and to provide maps and demographic data. Prohibited ground movement of troops and surveillance devices or gadgets. Also outlined scope of verification, procedures for verification and post-verification activities. Joint CCCH to proceed with verification and identification of five camps as set forth in joint statement; verification of other camps/positions to be conducted upon agreement of the other parties.

September 1999 Agreement, 2 September 1999. Agreed to hold opening ceremony of formal peace talks on 20 October 1999. Also agreed that all inspections, verifications, and acknowledgement of the remaining MILF identified areas would continue until its completion on 31 December 1999.

PHILIPPINES–NDF

Conflict between government of the Philippines and communist National Democratic Front–New People's Army (NDF), who were engaged in a long-running communist insurgency in Luzon. A series of peace agreements were reached in 1998.

Agreement on Additional Implementing Rules on Safety and Immunity Guarantees (JASIG), 16 March 1998. Agreed on security for duly accredited persons, and organization of their respective security committees to agree on guidelines for the implementing rules and their implementation. Agreed to prior notice on holding of consultations and disclosure of appropriate information. Security committees also to agree on necessity of declaring mutual ceasefire in areas where consultations were being conducted; on determination of safety areas and adequate protection for routes of safe passage. Also provided for formation of central and regional security forces. Duly accredited persons and members of security forces authorized to carry sidearms–firearms to act in a manner that would promote objective of negotiations.

Comprehensive Agreement on Respect for Human Rights and International Humanitarian Law between the Government of the Republic of the Philippines and the National Democratic Front of the Philippines, 16 March 1998.

Parties agreed to adhere to and be bound by the principles and standards in international instruments on human rights, and the principles of international humanitarian law to protect the civilian population as well as persons with no direct part or who had ceased to take part in the armed hostilities. Also provided for establishment of a Joint Monitoring Committee to monitor implementation of the agreement. Committee to investigate complaints of violations of human rights and international humanitarian law and to make report and recommendations to the parties.

Joint Agreement in Support of Socio-Economic Projects of Private Development Organizations and Institutes, 16 March 1998. GRP agreed to respect, encourage, and extend appropriate support to private development organizations and institutes carrying out various programmes, projects, and activities, including those aimed at promoting a just and lasting peace; to engage in research and planning for the Filipino people's empowerment and development; to promote respect for human rights and relief and undertaking relief and rehabilitation programmes. Agreed that development organizations would raise, manage, and use such financial resources as necessary, and would have access to such sources of funding and resources as are available to similar organizations in the Philippines and abroad.

RUSSIA–CHECHNYA

Chechnya proclaimed its independence in August 1991, but in December 1994 President Yeltsin ordered the Russian army to occupy Grozny, the capital of Chechnya, in an attempt to curb Chechen nationalism and its use as a base for criminal activity in Russia. This proved more difficult than the Russians had anticipated, and by March 1996 the conflict was continuing. In March 1996 Yeltsin ordered the Russian military to cease offensive military operations, and set out a proposal for negotiations. In May a ceasefire agreement was signed, but it broke down in July. In August a humiliating defeat for the Russians at Grozny saw Yeltsin appoint Aleksandr Lebed as special envoy to Chechnya. Negotiating from a position of weakness, he reached the Khasavyurt Accord. Yeltsin took some time to associate himself with the agreement, and while the ceasefire largely held and the process continued, it did so with divergent Russian and Chechen notions of what the final status of Chechnya would be, and indeed different notions of what the agreements provided on this. In 1999 a series of attacks on civilians in Russia were attributed by Russians to Chechens and sparked a Russian offensive on Chechnya aimed at retaking territory and in particular Grozny. The conflict continues at the time of writing.

Protocol of the Meeting of Delegations on the Issue of Peaceful Resolution of the Crisis in the Chechen Republic with OSCE Support, 20 June 1995

Protocol of the Meeting of Delegates for the Peaceful Resolution of the Crisis in the Chechen Republic with the Cooperation of the OSCE, 21 June 1995

Agreement on the Peaceful Regulation of the Situation in the Chechen Republic (on a set of military issues), 30 July 1995. Provided for ceasefire, freeing of prisoners of war, disarmament, and withdrawal of troops.

Agreement on the Basic Principles of Relations between the Russian Federation and the Chechen Republic, 3 December 1995.

Decree of the President of the Russian Federation on the Resolution of the Chechen Crisis, 31 March 1996 ('Yeltsin's Peace Plan'). Initiative from Yeltsin with two main aspects: the gradual withdrawal of federal troops, and signals of a readiness to negotiate. Loose process sketched out as including free and democratic elections in the republic; devolution of power; culmination in a treaty delimiting powers with the possibility of eventual resolution of Chechnya's status. At this time Yeltsin issued an order to the Russian military to cease offensive military operations.

Agreement on a Ceasefire, the Cessation of Military Activities, and on Measures for a Settlement of the Armed Conflict on the Territory of the Chechen Republic, 27 May 1996. Ceasefire agreement signed by acting Chechen President Yandarbiev and Russian Prime Minister Chernomyrdin with the two protocols below, fleshing out the other commitments.

Draft Treaty on the Delimitation of Subjects of Jurisdiction and Powers between the Russian Federation Organs of State Power and the Chechen Republic Organs of State Power, 31 May 1996. Provides for 'the special status within the Russian Federation of the Chechen Republic as a sovereign, democratic, rule-of-law, social state'. Provides for a delimitation of Russian and Chechen competencies.

Protocol of the Meeting of the Commissions on the Negotiations regarding a Ceasefire and Cessation of Hostilities and on Measures to Settle the Armed Conflict on the Territory of the Chechen Republic, 10 June 1996. Provided for the withdrawal of Russian troops by the end of August 1996 with surrender of Chechen weapons.

Protocol of the Meeting of the Working Groups, Formed under the Negotiations Commissions, to Locate Missing Persons and to Free Forcibly Detained Persons, 10 June 1996. Provided for the establishment of a joint working group to locate missing persons and to free prisoners of war, and set date for exchange of twenty-seven military personnel from each side.

Agreement on Urgent Measures to Stop Fire and Combat Operations in the City of Grozny and on the Territory of Chechnya, 22 August 1996

Russian–Chechen Truce Agreement and Principles for Clarifying the Basis for Mutual Relations between the Russian Federation and the Chechen Republic, 25 August 1996 (Khasavyurt Accord). Postponed a decision on the status of Chechnya, calling for an agreement on a treaty for regulating Russian–Chechen relations to be made before 31 December 2001. Also stipulated the creation of a joint commission of Russian and Chechen representatives to prepare for the withdrawal of Russian forces from Chechnya, to combat 'crime and terrorism', to draw up proposals for economic reconstruction, implement programmes for rebuilding of infrastructure, and control supply and distribution of food and medical aid. Joint commitment to agreement made by parties on 31 August 1996.

Russian–Chechen Agreement, 23 November 1996.

Chernomyrdin Agreement, 3 October 1997. Setting up joint commission to implement Khasavyurt Agreement.

Treaty on Peace and the Principles of Mutual Relations between the Russian Federation and the Chechen Republic of Ichkeria, 12 May 1997. Brief agreement with three provisions: that both sides had 'renounced for ever the use of force and the threat to use force in resolving all disputed issues'; that both sides agreed 'to construct relations in accordance with the generally recognized principles and norms of international law, and to deal with one another on the basis of specific agreements'; and that the treaty would 'serve as the basis for additional treaties and agreements on the entire complex of mutual relations.' Treaty was accompanied by two intergovernmental agreements, one dealing with economic cooperation, and the second with the mechanism for effecting financial transfers between the Russian central bank and Chechen government.

RWANDA

The Tutsi minority was oppressed by the Hutu government installed after Rwanda gained its independence from Belgium in 1961–2. In October 1990 Tutsi guerrillas, under the name of the Rwandese Patriotic Front (RPF), invaded Rwanda from Uganda, and fierce fighting followed. The Arusha Accords seemed to provide a possible basis for peace, but just as their acceptance by the Rwandan president seemed imminent, both he and the president of Burundi (see above) were assassinated on 6 April 1994, by Hutu factions in the government and army, in a strike against the agreements. These groups then began a campaign of genocide against the Tutsi people. In July 1994 the Hutu government was forced to flee to Zaire (now Democratic Republic of Congo, see above), and a new government was established by the RPF. However, the RPF victory did not end the violence, as forces from the ousted government, former Rwandan armed forces, and Hutu Interhamwé militias continued attacks. The Arusha Accords did, however, continue to provide a framework for government.

Arusha Accords

N'Sele Ceasefire Agreement, 29 March 1991, between the Government of the Republic of Rwanda (GRR) and the RPF as amended at Gbadolite on 16 September 1991 and at Arusha, 12 July 1992. Recognized ceasefire as the first stage of a peace process to culminate in a peace agreement, and agreed that verification was to be conducted by a neutral military observer group under Organization for African Unity (OAU) supervision. Provided for the establishment of a Joint Political Military Commission composed of five representatives of the GRR and five representatives of the RPF to follow up the implementation of the agreements. Also provided for the formation of a national army with government and RPF forces, and for the establishment of power-sharing within the framework of a broad-based transitional government, and set a timetable for further negotiations.

    Protocol of Agreement between the GRR and the RPF, 18 August 1992. Consisted of four parts. (I) Agreement that national unity was to be based on equality, equal opportunities, and respect for fundamental rights; rejection of exclusion and discrimination; and undertaking not to hinder the free exercise of the right of refugees to return to their country. (II) Agreement that democracy was to be expressed through regular, free, transparent, and fair elections, and acceptance of the implications of the fundamental principles of democracy. (III) Recognition that democratic society is founded on pluralism, which is the expression of individual freedoms, and must respect national unity and the fundamental rights of the citizen. (IV) Provided for the establishment of an independent National Commission on Human Rights to investigate human rights violations, to educate the population about human rights, and to institute legal proceedings where necessary. Established an International Commission of Inquiry to investigate human rights violations committed during the war.

Protocol of Agreement on Power-Sharing within the Framework of a Broad-Based Transitional Government between the GRR and the RPF, 30 October 1992 and 9 January 1993. Reaffirmed acceptance of principle of power-sharing within the framework of a broad-based transitional government, and agreed on modalities for its implementation. Provided for the establishment of a Commission for National Unity and National Reconciliation, a Legal and Constitutional Commission and an Electoral Commission. Also agreed on the implementation of a programme comprising democracy; defence and security; national unity and national reconciliation; post-war rehabilitation, repatriation, and reintegration of refugees, and the economy.

Protocol of Agreement between the GRR and RPF on the Repatriation of Refugees and the Resettlement of Displaced Persons, 9 June 1993. Outlined the basic principles for the voluntary return and repatriation of Rwandan refugees including the provision of land by the GRR, and recognition of the right to property for all the people of Rwanda, and of the principle of dual citizenship. Also provided for the establishment of a Commission for Repatriation with GRR, UN High Commissioner for Refugees OAU, and refugee representatives, and outlined modalities for the integration of refugees with regard to employment, housing, and access to services and education. Outlined timetable for implementation of the Overall Programme for Repatriation as well as measures for the return of persons displaced by war and social strife.

Protocol of Agreement between the GRR and RPF on the Integration of the Armed Forces of the Two Parties, 3 August 1993. Consisted of three chapters. Chapters I and II outlined missions and principles; size, structure, and organization; types of service and discipline procedures; and process for the formation of the National Army and the National Gendarmerie. Chapter III provided details on the demobilization process.

Protocol of Agreement between the GRR and the RPF on Miscellaneous Issues and Final Provisions, 3 August 1993. Consisted of two chapters. Chapter I outlined arrangements for state security services, including communal police, prison services, and the Public Prosecution Department. Chapter II consisted of miscellaneous provisions giving details concerning oaths of office and violations of the fundamental law, by the president, prime minister, other ministers and Supreme Court judges, and outlining modalities for resignations by the president, prime minister and other ministers. Also provided for the ratification of international instruments on human rights; the deletion of reference to ethnic origin in official documents; and precedence for the principles of the Universal Declaration of Human Rights over the corresponding principles in the Constitution. Also set out procedure for amendments to the peace agreement, and provided that the duration of the transition period was to be twenty-two months, with the possibility of one extension.

Peace Agreement between the GRR and the RPF, 4 August 1993. Declared that the war was thereby brought to an end, and provided that the documents above were an integral part of the peace agreement. Also provided that the transitional government would be set up within thirty-seven days, operating under the Constitution of 10 June 1991 and the Arusha Peace Agreement during the transition period.

SIERRA LEONE

The Revolutionary United Front (RUF) began a rebellion in March 1991, and in November 1996 their leader agreed to a ceasefire with the new democratically elected president, Ahmad Tejan Kabbah. However, a coalition of the Armed Forces Revolutionary Council (AFRC) and the Revolutionary United Front (RUF) overthrew President Kabbah in a coup in May 1997, taking power together. Economic Community of West African States Ceasefire Monitoring Group (ECOMOG) troops and local militia reinstalled President Kabbah in March 1998. The conflict continued with systematic terror against the civilian population. In 1999 an agreement was reached with the RUF which included, among other things, provisions for prisoner release. This agreement broke down and fighting escalated again in 2000. Again conflict has a regional dimension.

Peace Agreement between the Government of the Republic of Sierra Leone and the Revolutionary United Front of Sierra Leone (RUF/SL), Abidjan, 30 November 1996. Agreement to a ceasefire. A national Commission for the Consolidation of Peace to supervise and monitor the implementation of compliance with agreement. The commission is to establish a socio-economic forum; citizens' consultative conferences; multi-partisan council; trust fund for the consolidation of peace; a demobilization and resettlement committee; and a national budget and debt committee. The Commission is to consist of representatives of both sides drawing on state and civic institutions. A Citizens' Consultative Conference is also to be organized. Combatants are to be disarmed 'upon their entry into the designated assembly zones', with demobilization and reintegration as soon as practicable thereafter.

ECOWAS Six-month Peace Plan for Sierra Leone (Conakry Peace Plan), 23 October 1997. Provided a seven-point peace plan aimed at the early return of constitutional governance to Sierra Leone. It provided for: cessation of hostilities with immediate effect; disarmament, demobilization and reintegration of combatants; humanitarian assistance; return of refugees and displaced persons; restoration of the constitutional government and broadening of the power base; immunities and guarantees.

Agreement on a Ceasefire in Sierra Leone, 18 May 1999. Included a commitment to start negotiations in good faith, a decision to guarantee access for humanitarian aid, and a request to the UN to deploy military observers to the area. Also provided for the immediate release of all prisoners of war and non-combatants.

Statement by the Government of Sierra Leone and the Revolutionary United Front of Sierra Leone on the Release of Prisoners of War and Non-Combatants, 2 June 1999. Provided for the implementation of the provision of the Ceasefire Agreement relating to the release of prisoners of war as soon as possible, and for the establishment of an appropriate committee by the UN to handle the release of all prisoners of war and non-combatants.

Statement by the Government of Sierra Leone and the Revolutionary United Front of Sierra Leone on the Delivery of Humanitarian Assistance in Sierra

Leone, 3 June 1999. Outlined details for the safe and unhindered access of humanitarian agencies and provided for the establishment of an Implementation Committee with representatives from the government and the RUF to assess the security situation, to provide information on proposed routes, and to receive and review complaints.

June 1999 Peace Agreement between the Government of Sierra Leone and the Revolutionary United Front of Sierra Leone, Lome, 7 July 1999. Consisted of seven parts. Part I dealt with cessation of hostilities, and provided for a ceasefire and for the establishment of a Ceasefire Monitoring Committee at provincial and district levels, as well as a Joint Monitoring Commission at national level to be chaired by the UN Observer Mission in Sierra Leone (UNOMSIL) together with representatives of the government of Sierra Leone and RUF/SL. Part II dealt with governance and outlined formulas for the transformation of the RUF/SL into a political party enabling it to join a broad-based government of national unity through cabinet appointment. Provision was also made for the establishment of a Commission for the Consolidation of Peace to implement a post-conflict programme and to ensure that all structures for national reconciliation and peace were operational; and for a Commission for the Management of Strategic Resources, National Reconstruction, and Development to secure and monitor the legitimate exploitation of Sierra Leone's gold and diamonds and other resources of strategic importance. Part III dealt with other political issues, and the government agreed to grant pardon and amnesty to all combatants. Also provided for a review of the present Constitution and the establishment of a National Electoral Commission by the government in consultation with all political parties. Part IV dealt with post-conflict military and security issues, including the new mandates of ECOMOG and UNOMSIL, and provided for disarmament, demobilization, and reintegration of RUF as well as for the restructuring and training of the Sierra Leone armed forces. Part V addressed humanitarian and human rights and socioeconomic issues including the release of prisoners and abductees and the voluntary repatriation and reintegration of refugees and displaced persons, and guarantees of their security. Provision was also made for humanitarian relief; post-war rehabilitation and reconstruction; a special fund for war victims; child combatants; free compulsory schooling and affordable health care; and for the establishment of a Truth and Reconciliation Commission to address human rights violations. Part VI provided details concerning the implementation of the agreement, including the establishment of a Joint Implementation Committee, and included a request for international involvement. Part VII dealt with moral guarantors and international support. Annexes provided a definition of ceasefire violations and a schedule for the implementation of the peace agreement.

SOLOMON ISLANDS

Conflict between indigenous groups on the main island of Guadalcanal. The pro-Guadalcanal Isiantabu Freedom Fighters (IFF) spearheaded a campaign to drive ethnic Malaitan settlers from other islands off Guadalcanal. A peace deal was signed between the IFF and the government in June 1999. However, the resulting exodus of Malaitans from Guadalcanal caused tensions in the neighbouring island of Malaita, and tensions on that island flared between the Malaitan Eagles Force (MEF) and another ethnic group, the Isatabu Freedom Movement (IFM). In June 2000 the MEF seized the capital, Honiara, in a coup, demanding the resignation of the prime minister (whom they temporarily held hostage) for failing to deal with the ethnic conflict. The fighting continues, and connections with Bougainville and Fiji have been suggested.

Memorandum of Understanding between the Solomon Islands Government and the Guadalcanal Provincial Government, 13 June 1999. Made provision for payments into a reconciliation trust account to be held by the Guadalcanal province in recognition of the social costs being borne by the indigenous people of Guadalcanal as a result of the capital being located in Honiara.

Honiara Peace Accord, 28 June 1999. Resolved to eschew violence and to cooperate with the Commonwealth special envoy. Identified issues at the root of the crisis, including the demand for return of lands to the people of Guadalcanal; demand for compensation for the murders of the Guadalcanal people by individual Malaitans; and the demand that a state government be established in Guadalcanal and other provinces. Called on the government and provincial government to take action to honour commitments in the Memorandum of Understanding, and suggested further action that could be taken to alleviate the suffering by the Guadalcanal people as a result of the capital being located in the territory. For example, a review of the Lands and Titles Act was suggested so as to compensate original landowners adequately when central government or industrial projects are located in their territory. Also provided that the committee set up to review the provincial government system should endeavour to conclude its work within six months, and that all organizations formed to push for the demands of the people of Guadalcanal through force were to be dissolved, and for groups to surrender their weapons with no amnesty. The government agreed to assist victims forced to relocate, and to establish mechanisms to pay adequate compensation to those who had lost properties. Parties also agreed that there should be equal and fair representation of all provinces in the national civil service and the police force, to promote a sense of national unity.

Panatina Agreement between Solomon Islands National Government, the Guadalcanal Provincial Government, and the Police High Command, 12 August 1999. Reaffirmed commitment to implementation of Honiara Peace Accord and recognized that its successful implementation was the responsibility of all sections of the community. Agreed to discuss the security situation in Guadalcanal in view of the problems of implementation, and to note the concerns of the provincial government about the manner in which the police had been maintaining law and order in Guadalcanal. Also resolved that the police would promote a concept of community policing in all parts of the Solomon Islands; would continue to ensure the minimum use of force; and would mount a public relations campaign. The police undertook to scale down activities of the Field Force and the Rapid Response Unit, and the government agreed to lift the state of emergency in due course. Also provided that the IFF would return to their villages; refrain from activities likely to affect adversely the operations of major national economic infrastructures; begin a systematic laying down of arms under the terms agreed.

Agreed that all other illegal organizations formed with the aim of affording protection for and advancing the interest of other ethnic groups in and around Honiara and other parts of the country would be disbanded.

SOMALIA

Conflict between the government and four rebel groups (Somali National Movement, United Somali Congress, Somali Patriotic Movement, and a group of Marehan clansmen), each representing one of the Somali clans, began in 1988. The UN intervened in December 1992 but withdrew in March 1994 following attacks on its forces. Smaller-scale fighting continued, not by original parties, but by warlords, focused mostly around private gains rather than governmental power. Two different peace initiatives which emerged in 1997 negotiated with different clans; one resulted in the Sodere Declarations, backed by Ethiopia (as mandated by the Inter-Governmental Authority on Development, IADG), and the other resulted in the Cairo Accord, brokered by Egypt. To some extent these agreements worked against each other. However, an increased emphasis on civic society restored a measure of peace. A new peace deal was reached in 1998 between rival leaders, who agreed to set up joint administration in certain areas. However, the future of this deal seemed insecure.

Addis Ababa Agreement concluded at the first session of the Conference on National Reconciliation, Somalia, 27 March 1993. Framework agreement dealing with disarmament (to UN forces) and crime; rehabilitation and reconstruction; restoration of property and settlement of disputes; transitional arrangements, including a Transitional National Council with specified representation for certain groups and for women, central administrative departments, regional, and district councils. It also establishes a peace delegation to travel the country and advance the agreement.

Declaration de paix signée par les différentes parties 1994

Sodere Declarations, January 1997. Brokered by twenty-six Somali factions creating a climate of negotiation.

Cairo Declaration on Somalia signed by the political leaders of the Republic of Somalia, 22 December 1997. Provided for a ceasefire, cessation of hostilities, and disengagement of forces. Recognized need for a transitional mechanism of national authority and agreed to preserve Somalia as an independent and indivisible state. Reiterated belief in principles of democracy, equality, social justice, and constitutional guarantees of individual human rights. Also provided details of arrangements for a National Reconciliation Conference on 15 February 1998 to be held to elect a Presidential council and a prime minister, and to adopt a transitional charter. Agreed the agenda would include a Declaration of National Commitment to the formation of a constitutional transitional government guaranteeing individual freedoms and to the creation of the democratic national government; a Declaration of Peace and Cooperation for the people of Somalia to work with the transitional government towards the establishment of a constitutional federal government; and adoption of a transitional charter to serve as a framework for the national transitional government. Agreed that transitional

Presidential Council would consist of three members from each of the four major social groups in Somalia and one of the remaining Somali social group, and that forty-six seats in the Constituent Assembly would be allocated to each of four Somali social groups and three and two to the remaining social groups respectively. The existence of the transitional government was to be limited to a period of three years, with a possible extension of an additional two years. Also made provision for a national census from which an electoral system could be implemented, and for the approval of a permanent Constitution enshrining fundamental rights through a national referendum.

SOUTH AFRICA

See Chapter 3 for an account of the conflict and peace agreements.

SOUTH AFRICA / THE ≠KHOMANI SAN

The indigenous ≠Khomani San, based in Mier, lodged a land claim in August 1995, claiming traditional 'use' (i.e. hunting and gathering) rights in and to a substantial area of the Kalahari Gemsbok National Park (KGNP) and the northern Mier, and claiming ownership rights of 25,000 hectares. This claim was negotiated by the San, the South African National Parks (SANP), the Mier Transitional Local Council, and the state represented by the Department of Land Affairs. In December 1998 the Mier community lodged a separate land claim to land lost within Mier and in the KGNP due to apartheid. Negotiations began in May 1999 on symbolic rights (e.g. right to a park name change and to an access gate for the San) and commercial rights (e.g. right to establish a San cultural village and a permanent rest camp for tourists and the right to receive a community gate levy).

Final Agreement, 20 March 1999. The SANP accepted terms of the San land claim and agreed to release 50,000 hectares to the San and the Mier, who were to reach an informal agreement that the land would be shared equally. Parties undertook to negotiate a further agreement on the commercial and symbolic rights of both parties.

SRI LANKA

See Chapter 2 for description of conflict and agreements.

SUDAN

Long-standing conflict between Muslim Arabs in the north and Christian and non-Christian in the south. In May 1988 the Islamic Front became a part of the government and began to adhere more strictly to the Koran and shariah law. In November 1988 a ceasefire was agreed, along with agreement that any imposition of Islamic shariah would be postponed. This condition was ignored by the government, which developed into a military regime in the early 1990s. In 1994 many of the different groups accepted the role of the Inter-Governmental Authority on Development (IGAD) as mediator. The government signed a peace agreement with a dissident faction of the southern Sudan People's Liberation Army/Movement (SPLA/M) in April 1997. In 1998 peace talks resumed, and agreement was reached on an internationally supervised referendum on self-determination for the south of the country at an unspecified date. However, the SPLA/M found the proposal of a concurrent referendum on a nationwide constitution to be an unacceptable affirmation of a federated country based on Islamic shariah law. Fighting continued, with agreements for truces and humanitarian relief. Again the conflict has a regional dimension, leading to agreements with Somalia and Uganda.

Political Charter between Sudan Government and the SPLA (United) 1995

Political Charter of 10 April 1996 between the Sudan Government, the South Sudan Independence Movement (SSIM), and the Sudan People's Liberation Movement (SPLM). Agreed that the unity of Sudan would be preserved and that a referendum would be held by the people of the southern Sudan to determine their political aspirations after the full establishment of peace and stability. Also provided that the Sudanese people should be encouraged to express freely their different values; that freedom of religion and belief should be observed; and that power and national wealth should be shared equitably for the benefit of the citizens. Agreed that citizenship would further the values of justice, equity, freedom, and human rights, and that the shariah and custom would be the sources of legislation. A coordination council was to be formed between southern states to implement the agreement, and the parties agreed to work together for stability and improvement of living conditions in war-affected areas.

Sudan Peace Agreement, 21 April 1997. Between the government of Sudan and the South Sudan United Democratic Front (UDSF) comprising the SSIM, the Union of Sudan African Parties, SPLM, the Equatorial Defence Force, and the South Sudan Independents Group. Provided for the exercise of the right of self-determination through a referendum by the people of south Sudan. Dealt with constitutional and legal matters, including constitutional guarantees and fundamental rights and freedoms; powers to be exercised by the federal institutions and by the state and economic matters, including the establishment of a Revenue Allocation Commission. Included provisions on the balanced participation of southern citizens in federal institutions. Also outlined the activities, functions, and powers of the Coordinating Council of the Southern States, and outlined security arrangements for the four-year interim period.

Communiqué final sur la poursuite des initiatives de paix de l'IGAD du Soudan et en Somalie 1997

Déclaration solennelle d'engagement national 1997

SUDAN–UGANDA

Agreement between the Governments of Sudan and Uganda, 8 December 1999. An agreement to 'enhance relations' between the two countries and 'to promote peace in the regions'. Each commits to respecting the sovereignty and territorial integrity of each other. They renounce use of force and commit to taking steps to prevent hostile acts, to disband and disarm terrorist groups, to promote regional peace on own initiative, and not to prejudice or interfere with the role of the Inter-Governmental Authority on Development in bringing an end to the civil war in Sudan. Prisoners of war will be returned. Steps are to be taken to prevent attacks on civilians and to facilitate return or resettlement of refugees. Amnesty and reintegration is offered to all former combatants who renounce use of force. Parties commit to re-establishing normal relations if commitments are honoured.

TAJIKISTAN

A five-year civil war between the Tajik government and the United Tajik Opposition (UTO) based on inter-ethnic rivalry, rivalry between the clans and regions of Tajikistan, and ideological differences. A peace process was mediated by Iran, Russia, and UN, and resulted in a series of agreements in 1997, culminating in a general framework agreement. While it did not bring fighting to a complete end (not least because the peace agreement had alienated other groups), it did provide a framework for ongoing negotiations.

Agreement on a Temporary Ceasefire and the Cessation of Other Hostile Acts on the Tajik–Afghan Border and within the Country for the Duration of the Talks 1994

Protocol on the Fundamental Principles for Establishing Peace and National Accord in Tajikistan, 23 August 1995. Government commits to refrain from acting counter to agreement. Tajik opposition undertakes exclusively peaceful means. Both agree to future negotiations to aim at a series of protocols on political problems, military problems, repatriation and reintegration, verification, guarantees for implementation, donors' conference.

Agreement between the President of the Republic of Tajikistan, E. S. Rakhmonov, and the leader of the UTO, S. A. Huri, on the results of the meeting held in Moscow on 23 December 1996 (Annex I), 27 December 1996. Sets a timetable of twelve to eighteen months for completion of inter-Tajik talks, and notes establishment of Commission on National Reconciliation (see protocol below), and also the 'need to implement a universal amnesty and reciprocal pardoning of persons who took part in the military and political confrontation.'

Protocol on the Main Functions and Powers of the Commission on National Reconciliation Moscow, December 1996 (Annex II), 23 December 1996. Establishes a Commission on National Reconciliation to implement the agreements, to create an atmosphere of trust and mutual forgiveness, and to institute broad dialogue among the various political forces in the country. Specific tasks are assigned the Commission, such as implementing measures for 'safe and appropriate' return of refugees, and designing proposals for amending legislation on political parties, movements, and the mass media. The Commission is given the power to submit to referendum proposals for amendments and additions to the existing Constitution; to prepare a new law on elections; and to establish a transitional Central Commission on Elections and the Conduct of the Referendum.

Protocol on Refugees, Tehran, January 1997. Commits to mutual efforts to ensure 'the voluntary return, in safety and dignity, of all refugees and displaced persons to their homes.' Calls on the Organization for Security and Cooperation in Europe and United Nations High Commissioner for Refugees (UNHCR) to become involved. Government commits to reintegration. Reinvigorates a joint commission on refugees.

Joint Statement by the Delegation of the Government of Tajikistan and the Delegation of the United Tajik Opposition, 5–19 January 1997. Agreed on structure, composition, and specific functions and powers of Commission on National Reconciliation and on the procedure for the adoption of the Reciprocal Pardon Act and Amnesty Act. Agreement was also reached concerning the Central Election Commission the conduct of a referendum for the transition period, and mechanism for including UTO representatives in the government power structures. Agreement on continuing discussions on the question of the renewal of activity of the political parties and movements forming part of the UTO.

Protocol on Military Issues, Moscow, March 1997. Commitments to 'reintegration, disarmament and disbandment of armed units of United Tajik Opposition, as well as reform of governmental power structures,' to be carried out by the president, the commission on National Reconciliation, and with cooperation of UN observers. The detail of four stages is provided, leading from a UTO inventory to UTO reintegration into governmental power structures. Joint crime measures are to be taken as 'confidence-building' measures.

Joint Statement by the delegation of the Government of the Republic of Tajikistan and the delegation of the United Tajik Opposition on the outcome of the Inter-Tajik talks held in Moscow from 26 February to 8 March 1997

The Bishkek Memorandum, 18 May 1997. Affirmed previous peace agreements, and noted progress of agreements below.

Protocol on Political Issues, 18 May 1997. Provided for concrete agreement on political issues addressed earlier, namely that the president and the Commission on National Reconciliation should adopt a 'reciprocal forgiveness and amnesty law'; that 25 per cent of the members of the Central Election Commission should be UTO members during the transition period; for reform of government in accordance with a UTO quota; and that all prohibitions and restrictions on the activity of political parties and movements of the UTO be lifted after the completion of phase two of the implementation of the protocol on military issues.

UNITED KINGDOM—NORTHERN IRELAND—REPUBLIC OF IRELAND

See Chapter 3 for description of conflict and peace agreements.

WESTERN SAHARA—MOROCCO

Conflict over Western Sahara between Morocco and a group of Saharawis forming the Polisaro Front. A large amount of the territory had been given to Morocco and a small amount to Mauritania following an agreement with Spain in November 1975. The Polisaro Front and its military wing, the Saharawi People's Liberation Army (SPLA), initially launched guerrilla attacks against Mauritania, forcing

Mauritania to abandon the desert area of Tiris al-Gharbia in July 1979. Morocco annexed the area on 14 August 1979, and the SPLA continued its campaign against Morocco. In August 1988 the UN proposed a truce, followed by a referendum, and a plan was approved by the UN Security Council on 29 April 1991. The referendum was originally scheduled for early 1992, but there was disagreement over whether Moroccan settlers were entitled to vote. The referendum was rescheduled for late 1998 after an agreement was brokered by UN Special Envoy James Baker.

Compromise Agreement on Outstanding Identification Issues, 19 and 20 July 1997. Parties agreed not to sponsor or present for identification anyone from certain tribal groupings other than persons included in the 1974 Spanish census and immediate family members. Also agreed that persons from all other tribal groups could come forward to be identified, and that the special representative of the secretary-general would notify the parties of the results of the identification process to date. Oral testimony to be received and considered by the Identification Commission as provided for in the settlement plan.

Compromise on Outstanding Refugee Issues, 19 and 20 July 1997. Office of the UNHCR to begin steps towards process of repatriation of refugees in accordance with the settlement plan, and parties agreed to cooperate in implementation of the repatriation programme.

Compromise Agreement on Troop Confinement, 29 August 1997. Provided for reduction and confinement of Moroccan armed forces in accordance with the settlement plan, and the confinement and containment of Frente Polisario armed forces in locations and numbers as designated by the special representative of the secretary-general. Included statement that this compromise would in no way change, alter, or affect the internationally recognized boundaries of Western Sahara. Also provided for repatriation of all prisoners of war in accordance with the settlement plan and the continuation of full cooperation with International Committee of the Red Cross until completion of the repatriation process, and for release of all Saharan political prisoners or detainees before the referendum campaign.

1997 Houston Declaration, 14–16 September 1997. Parties agreed to comply with earlier commitments. Recognized role of UN in organizing and conducting referendum and powers and authorities of the UN during the transitional period. Agreed that the special representative of the secretary-general would be authorized to issue regulations prohibiting behaviour that could interfere with the organization and conduct of the referendum. Included a Code of Conduct for the Referendum Campaign in Western Sahara and a list of Practical Measures to be Taken for the Resumption of Identification.

YEMEN

In 1990 North and South Yemen agreed to form a unified Republic of Yemen, thereby ending twenty years of tension, border disputes, civil wars, tribal conflicts, and ideological differences.

Yemen Arab Republic (North Yemen) and People's Democratic Republic of Yemen (South Yemen): Agreement on the Establishment of the Republic of Yemen, 21 May 1990

REFERENCES

ABBAS, M. (ABU MAZEN) (1995), *Through Secret Channels* (Reading: Garnet).

ABDO, N., and N. YUVAL-DAVIS (1995), 'Palestine, Israel and the Zionist Settler Project', in D. Stasiulis and N. Yuval-Davis (eds.) *Unsettling Settler Societies: Articulations of Gender, Race, Ethnicity and Class* (London: Sage), 291–322.

ABDUL HADI, M. F. (1997a), *Palestine Documents, I: From the Pre-Ottoman/Ottoman Period to the Prelude of the Madrid Middle East Peace Conference* (Jerusalem: Palestinian Academic Society for the Study of International Affairs).

—— (1997b), *Palestine Documents, II: From the Negotiations in Madrid to the Post-Hebron Agreement Period* (Jerusalem: Palestinian Academic Society for the Study of International Affairs).

ABEL, R. (1995), *Politics by Other Means: Law in the Struggle against Apartheid, 1980–1994* (New York: Routledge).

ABURISH, S. (1998), *Arafat: From Defender to Dictator* (London: Bloomsbury).

AFRICAN NATIONAL CONGRESS (1991), 'A Bill of Rights for a Democratic South Africa—Working Draft for Consultation' 7 *South African Journal on Human Rights* 110–23.

AFRICAN NATIONAL CONGRESS DEPARTMENT OF POLITICAL EDUCATION (1996), *The Road to Peace: Resource Material on Negotiations* (Marshalltown: African National Congress, Department of Political Education).

AKENSON, D. H. (1992), *God's Peoples: Covenant and Land in South Africa, Israel, and Ulster* (Ithaca, NY: Cornell University Press).

AKHAVAN, P. (1996a), 'The International Criminal Tribunal for Rwanda: The Politics and Pragmatics of Punishment' 90 *American Journal of International Law* 501–10.

—— (1996b), 'The Yugoslav Tribunal at a Crossroads: The Dayton Peace Agreement and Beyond' 18 *Human Rights Quarterly* 259–85.

—— (1997), 'Justice and Reconciliation in the Great Lakes Region of Africa' 7 *Duke Journal of Comparative and International Law* 325–48.

—— (1998), 'Justice in the Hague, Peace in the Former Yugoslavia?' 20 *Human Rights Quarterly* 737–816.

ALBERT, S. (1997), 'The Return of Refugees to Bosnia and Herzegovina: Peacebuilding with People' 4 *International Peacekeeping* 1–23.

AL QASEM, A. (1996), 'The Draft Basic Law for the Palestinian National Authority during the Transitional Period', in E. Cotran and C. Mallat (eds.), *The Arab–Israeli Accords: Legal Perspectives* (London: Kluwer Law International), 101–36.

ALSTON, P. (ed.) (1999), *Promoting Human Rights through Bills of Rights: Comparative Perspectives* (Oxford: Oxford University Press).

—— and M. DARROW (1999), 'Bills of Rights in Comparative Perspective', in Alston (ed.) (1999: 465–524).

ALTING VON GESAU, F. A. M. (1995), 'Breaking Away towards Peace in the Middle East' 8 *Leiden Journal of International Law* 81–101

AMIEN, W., and P. FARLAM (eds.) (1998), *Basic Human Rights Documents for South Africans* (Cape Town: Law, Race, and Gender Research Unit, University of Cape Town).

AMNESTY INTERNATIONAL (1994), *Political Killings in Northern Ireland* (London: Amnesty International).

ANDERSEN, E. (1996), 'Promoting Safe and Peaceful Repatriation under the Dayton Agreements' 7 *European Journal of International Law* 193–206.

AN-NA'IM, A. A. (1990), 'Human Rights in the Muslim World' 3 *Harvard Human Rights Journal* 12–52.

—— (ed.) (1992), *Human Rights in Cross-Cultural Perspectives: A Quest for Consensus* (Philadelphia: University of Pennsylvania Press).

ANONYMOUS (1996), 'Human Rights in Peace Negotiations' 18 *Human Rights Quarterly* 249–58.

ARNON, A., and A. SPIVAK (1998), 'The Olso Peace Process: The Economic Dimension', in *Is Oslo Alive?* (Jerusalem: Konrad Adenauer Foundation, Harry S. Truman Research Institute for the Advancement of Peace, Palestine Consultancy Group), 40–54.

ARONSON, G. (1996), *Settlements and the Israel–Palestinian Negotiations* (Washington, DC: Institute for Palestinian Studies).

ARURI, N. H. (1995), 'Early Empowerment: The Burden Not the Responsibility' 24/2 *Journal of Palestine Studies* 33–9.

ASH, T. G. (1997), *The File: A Personal History* (New York: Random House).

ASHRAWI, H. (1995), *This Side of Peace: A Personal Account* (London: Simon & Schuster).

ASMAL, K. (1992), 'Victims, Survivors and Citizens–Human Rights, Reparations and Reconciliation' 8 *South African Journal of Human Rights* 491–511.

—— L. ASMAL, and R. S. ROBERTS (1997), *Reconciliation through Truth: A Reckoning of Apartheid's Criminal Governance* (Cape Town: David Philip).

ATKINSON, D. (1994), 'Principle Born of Pragmatism? Central Government in the Constitution', in Friedman and Atkinson (ed.) (1994: 92–120).

AZAR, E. (1990), *The Management of Protracted Social Conflict: Theory and Cases* (Aldershot: Dartmouth).

—— and J. BURTON (1986), *International Conflict Resolution: Theory and Practice* (Boulder, Colo.: Lynne Reinner).

AZZAM, F. (1998), 'Update: The Palestinian Independent Commission for Citizens' Rights' 20 *Human Rights Quarterly* 338–47.

BAGSHAW, S. (1997), 'Benchmarks or Deutschmarks? Determining the Criteria for the Repatriation of Refugees to Bosnia and Herzegovina' 9 *International Journal of Refugee Law* 566–92.

BANAC, I. (1984), *The National Question in Yugoslavia: Origins, History, Politics* (Ithaca, NY: Cornell University Press).

BASIĆ, N., D. J. FLEMING, and W. M. VAUGHN (1999), 'International Legal Order and Minority/Government Conflict', in P. Cumper and S. Wheatley (eds.), *Minority Rights in the 'New' Europe* (Dordrecht: Martinus Nijhoff, Kluwer Law International), 285–304.

BARANYI, S. (1998), *The People's Peace: Civil Society Organisations and the Peace Processes in the South* (London: Catholic Institute for International Relations).

BARDON, J. (1992), *A History of Ulster* (Belfast: Blackstaff Press).

BASSIOUNI, M. C. (1998), *Report of the Independent Expert on the Right to Restitution, Compensation and Rehabilitation for Victims of Grave Violations of Human Rights* and *Fundamental Freedoms, Submitted Pursuant to Commission on Human Rights Resolution 1998/43*, UN doc. E/CN.4/1999/65 (n.p.: UN).

—— (1999), *Crimes against Humanity in International Criminal Law*, 2nd edn. (Dordrecht: Kluwer Law International).

BATTERSBY, J. (1993), 'NP/ANC Pact' 19/3 *South Africa Foundation Review* 1–3.

BAWA, N. (1998), *Human Rights and South Africa: Lessons for Building Institutions*, Occasional Paper Series, no. 5 (Belfast: Centre for International and Comparative Human Rights Law, Queen's University, Belfast).

BAYEFSKY, A. (1995), 'Israel and the United Nations' Human Rights Agenda: The Inequality of Nations Large and Small' 29 *Israel Law Review* 424–58.

BEINART, W. (1994), *Twentieth Century South Africa* (New York: Oxford University Press).

BEININ, J. (1999), *The Demise of the Oslo Process*, Press Information Note 1, 26 Mar. (Washington, DC: Middle East Research and Information Project).

—— (2000), *'Camp David II'*, 26 July 2000, Press Information note 26 (Washington, DC: Middle East Research and Information Project).

BELL, C. (1999), 'Minority Rights and Conflict Resolution in Northern Ireland', in P. Cumper and S. Wheatley (eds.), *Minority Rights in the 'New' Europe* (Dordrecht: Martinus Nijhoff, Kluwer Law International), 305–23.

—— and K. CAVAUNAUGH (1999), 'Constructive Ambiguity or Internal Self-Determination? Self-Determination, Group Accommodation and the Belfast Agreement' 22 *Fordham International Law Journal* 1345–71.

BELLAMY, R. (1996), 'The Political Form of the Constitution: The Separation of Powers, Rights and Representative Democracy', in Bellamy and Castiglione (eds.) (1996: 25–44).

—— and D. CASTIGLIONE (eds.) (1996), *Constitutionalism in Transformation: European and Theoretical Perspectives* (Oxford: Blackwell).

BENEDEK, W. (ed.) (1999), *Human Rights in Bosnia and Herzegovina after Dayton: From Theory to Practice* (Dordrecht: Martinus Nijhoff).

BENVENISTI, E. (1993), 'The Israeli–Palestinian Declaration of Principles: A Framework for Future Settlement' 4 *European Journal of International Law* 542–54.

—— (1994a), 'The Influence of International Human Rights Law on the Israeli Legal System: Present and Future' 28 *Israel Law Review* 136–53.

—— (1994b) 'Responsibility for the Protection of Human Rights under the Interim Israeli–Palestinian Agreements' 28 *Israel Law Review* 297–317.

—— (1996), 'The Status of the Palestinian Authority', in E. Cotran and C. Mallat (eds.), *The Arab–Israeli Accords: Legal Perspectives* (London: Kluwer Law International), 47–65.

BERAT, L. (1995), 'South Africa: Negotiating Change?', in N. Roht-Arriaza (ed.) (1995: 267–80).

BERESFORD, D. (1987), *Ten Men Dead: The Story of the 1981 Irish Hunger Strike* (London: Grafton).

BERMAN, N. (1998), 'The International Law of Nationalism: Group Identity and Legal History', in Wippman (ed.) (1998b: 25–57).

BEVIS, L. (1994), *The Applicability of Human Rights Law to Occupied Territories: The Case of the Occupied Palestinian Territories* (Ramallah: Al Haq).

BEW, P., and G. GILLESPIE (1996), *The Northern Ireland Peace Process 1993–1996: A Chronology* (London: Serif).

—— —— (1999), *Northern Ireland: A Chronology of the Troubles 1968–1999* 2nd edn. (Dublin: Gill & Macmillan).

—— P. GIBBON, and H. PATTERSON (1996), *Northern Ireland 1921–1996: Political Forces and Social Classes*, 2nd edn. (London: Serif).

BINDER, G. (1988), *Treaty Conflict and Political Consideration: The Dialectic of Duplicity* (New York: Praeger).

BLOOMFIELD, K. (1998), *We will Remember Them*, Report of the Northern Ireland Victims Commissioner, Sir Kenneth Bloomfield KCB, Apr. 1998.

BLUM, Y. (1968), 'The Missing Reversioner: Reflections on the Status of Judea and Samaria' 3 *Israel Law Review* 279–301.

BOAL, F., T. HADDEN, and C. IRWIN (1996), *Separation or Sharing: The People's Choice* (Belfast: Fortnight Educational Trust).

BOETANG, P., and J. STRAW (1997), 'Bringing Rights Back Home: Labour's Plans to Incorporate the European Convention on Human Rights into U.K. Law' 1 *European Human Rights Law Review* 71–80.

BORAINE, A., and J. LEVY (1995), *The Healing of a Nation?* (Cape Town: Justice in Transition, Institute for a Democratic South Africa).

BOTHE, M. (1996), 'War Crimes in Non-International Armed Conflicts', in Dinstein and Tabory (eds.) (1996: 293–304).

BOURANTONIS, D., and J. WIENER (eds.) (1995), *The United Nations in the New World Order: The World Organisation at Fifty* (New York: St Martin's Press).

BOUTROS-GHALI, B. (1992), *An Agenda for Peace: Preventative Diplomacy, Peacemaking and Peace-Keeping*, Report of the Secretary-General Pursuant to the Statement Adopted by the Summit Meeting of the Security Council on 31 January 1992 (New York: United Nations).

—— (1995), Supplement to an Agenda for Peace, Position Paper of the Secretary-General on the Occasion of the Fiftieth Anniversary of the United Nations (New York: United Nations).

BOYLE, F. (1990), 'The Creation of the State of Palestine' 1 *European Journal of International Law* 301–6.

—— (1995), 'The Decolonization of Northern Ireland' 4 *Asian Yearbook of International Law* 25–46.

—— (1996), 'Negating Human Rights in Peace Negotiations' 18 *Human Rights Quarterly* 515–16.

BOYLE, K., and T. HADDEN (1985), *Ireland: A Positive Proposal* (Harmondsworth: Penguin).

—— —— (1989), *The Anglo-Irish Agreement: Commentary, Text and Official Review* (London: Sweet & Maxwell).

—— —— (1994), *Northern Ireland: The Choice* (New York: Penguin).

—— —— (1995), 'The Peace Process in Northern Ireland' 71 *International Affairs* 269–83.

—— —— (1999), 'Northern Ireland', in R. Blackburn and R. Plant (eds.), *Constitutional Reform: The Labour Government's Constitutional Reform Agenda* (London: Longman), 282–306.

BREWER, J. (1998), 'A Prolegomenon towards a Sociology of the Peace Process in Northern Ireland and South Africa', unpub., copy on file with the author.

—— A. GUELKE, I. HUME, E. MOXON-BROWNE, and R. WILFORD (1996), *The Police, Public Order and the State: Policing in Great Britain, Northern Ireland, the Irish Republic, the USA, Israel, South Africa and China*, 2nd edn. (Basingstoke: Macmillan).

BRILMAYER, L. (1991), 'Secession and Self-Determination: A Territorial Interpretation' 16 *Yale Journal of International Law* 177–202.

BROWN, C. (1997), *Understanding International Relations* (Basingstoke: Macmillan).

BRYNEN, R. (1997), 'Much Ado about Nothing? The Refugee Working Group and the Perils of Multilateral Quasi-Negotiation' 2 *International Negotiations* 279–302.

—— and J. TANSLEY (1995), 'The Refugee Working Group of the Middle East Multilateral Peace Negotiations' 2/4 *Palestine–Israel Journal* 53–8.

BRYSK, A. (1994), *The Politics of Human Rights in Argentina: Protest, Change, and Democratisation* (Stanford, Calif.: Stanford University Press).

B'TSELEM (1997*a*), *Israeli Settlement in the Occupied Territories as a Violation of Human Rights: Legal and Conceptual Aspects* (Jerusalem: B'Tselem, Israeli Information Center for Human Rights in the Occupied Territories).

—— (1997*b*), *A Policy of Discrimination: Land Expropriation, Planning and Building in East Jerusalem* (Jerusalem: B'Tselem, Israeli Information Center for Human Rights in the Occupied Territories).

—— (1998*a*), *Divide and Rule: Prohibition on Passage between the Gaza Strip and the West Bank* (Jerusalem: B'Tselem, Israeli Information Center for Human Rights in the Occupied Territories).

—— (1998*b*), *The Quiet Deportation Continues: Revocation of Residency and Denial of Social Rights of East Jerusalem Palestinians* (Jerusalem: B'Tselem, Israeli Information Center for Human Rights in the Occupied Territories).

—— (1999), *Oslo, Before and After: The Status of Human Rights in the Occupied Territories* (Jerusalem: B'Tselem, Israeli Information Center for Human Rights in the Occupied Territories).

BURGENTHAL, T. (1994), 'The United Nations Truth Commission for El Salvador' *Vanderbilt Journal of Transnational Law* 497–544.

BURGERMAN, S. D. (1998), 'Mobilising Principles: The Role of Transnational Activists in Promoting Human Rights Principles' 20 *Human Rights Quarterly* 905–23.

BUTLER, A. (1997), 'The Constitutional Court Certification Judgements: The 1996 Constitution Bills, their Amending Provisions and the Constitutional Provisions' 114 *South African Law Journal* 703–23.

BYERS, M. (1999), *Custom, Power and the Power of Rules: International Relations and Customary International Law* (Cambridge: Cambridge University Press).

CAMPBELL, B., L. McKEOWN, and F. O'HAGAN (eds.) (1994), *Nor Meekly Serve my Time: The H Block Struggle 1976–1981* (Belfast: Beyond the Pale Publications).

CAMPBELL, C. (1996), 'A Problematic Peace: International Humanitarian Law and the Israeli/Palestinian Peace Process', in K. Schulze, M. Stokes, and C. Campbell (eds.), *Nationalism, Minorities and Diasporas: Identities and Rights in the Middle East* (London: Tauris Academic Studies), 39–54.

CAMPBELL, C. (1999), 'Two Steps Backwards: The Criminal Justice (Terrorism and Conspiracy) Act 1998' *Criminal Law Review* 941–59.

CAPORTORTI, F. (1991), *Study on the Rights of Persons Belonging to Ethnic, Religious and Linguistic Minorities* (New York: United Nations).

CAREY MILLER, D. L. (1999), 'A New Property?' 116 *South African Law Journal* 749–59.

CARTY, A. (1996), *Was Ireland Conquered? International Law and the Irish Question* (London: Pluto Press).

CASSESE, A. (1986), *International Law in a Divided World* (Oxford: Clarendon Press).

—— (1990), *Human Rights in a Changing World* (Cambridge: Polity Press).

—— (1998*a*), 'Reflections on International Criminal Justice' 61 *Modern Law Review* 1–10.

—— (1998*b*), *Self Determination of Peoples: A Legal Reappraisal* (Cambridge: Cambridge University Press).

CASTIGLIONE, D. (1996), 'The Political Theory of the Constitution', in Bellamy and Castiglione (eds.) (1996: 6–24).

CATTAN, H. (2000), *The Palestine Question* (London: Sequi Books).

CENTRE FOR THE INDEPENDENCE OF JUDGES AND LAWYERS (1990), *The Independence of Judges and Lawyers: A Compilation of International Standards* 25–6 Centre for the Independence of Judges and Lawyers Bulletin, special issue, Apr.–Oct.

CHANOCK, M. (1999), 'A Post-Calvinist Catechism or a Post-Communist Manifesto? Intersecting Narratives in the South African Bill of Rights Debate', in Alston (ed.) (1999: 392–428).

CHIMNI, B. S. (1999), 'From Resettlement to Involuntary Repatriation: Towards a Critical History of Durable Solutions', Working Paper no. 2, May 1999, UNHCR Refworld (available at www.unhcr.ch/refworld/, last visited 4 Jan. 2000).

CHOMSKY, N. (1983), *The Fateful Triangle: The United States, Israel and the Palestinians* (London: Pluto Press).

CHURCHILL, R. R., and J. R. YOUNG (1992), 'Compliance with Judgments of the European Court of Human Rights and Decisions of the Committee of Minister: The Experience of the United Kingdom: 1975–1987' 62 *British Yearbook of International Law* 283–346.

COCKBURN, C. (1998), *The Space between Us: Negotiating Gender and National Identities in Conflict* (London: Zed Books).

COHEN, L. J. (1995), *Broken Bonds: Yugoslavia's Disintegration and Balkan Politics in Transition*, 2nd edn. (Boulder, Colo.: Westview Press).

COHEN, S. (1995), 'State Crimes of Previous Regimes: Knowledge, Accountability and the Policing of the Past' 20 *Law and Social Enquiry* 7–50.

COLES, G. (1988), 'The Human Rights Approach to the Solution of the Refugee Problem: A Theoretical and Practical Enquiry', in A. E. Nash (ed.), *Human Rights and the Protection of Refugees under International Law* (Nova Scotia: Institute for Research on Public Policy), 195–221.

CONCILIATION RESOURCES (1997), *Negotiating Rights: The Guatemalan Peace Process*, 2: *Accord: An International Review of Peace Initiatives* (London: Conciliation Resources).

Coogan, T. P. (1996), *The Troubles: Ireland's Ordeal and the Search for Peace 1966–1996*, rev. and updated edn. (London: Arrow).

Cook, R. (ed.) (1994), *Human Rights of Women: National and International Perspectives* (Philadelphia: Pennsylvania University Press, Pennsylvania Studies in Human Rights).

Cooper, C., R. Hamilton, H. Mashabela, S.MacKay, E. Sidiropolous, C. Gordon-Brown, S. Murphy, and C. Markham (1993), *Race Relations Survey 1992/1993* (Johannesburg: South African Institute of Race Relations).

Corder, H. (ed.) (1989), *Democracy and the Judiciary* (Cape Town: Institute for a Democratic Alternative for South Africa).

—— (1994), 'Towards a South African Constitution' 57 *Modern Law Review* 491–533.

—— (1996), 'South Africa's Transitional Constitution: Its Design and Implementation' *Public Law* 291–308.

—— (1998), 'The Law and Struggle: The Same but Different' 16 Mar. 1998, unpub., copy on file with the author.

—— and L. Du Plessis (1994), *Understanding South Africa's Transitional Bill of Rights* (Kenwyn: Juta).

Cotran, E. (1996), 'Some Legal Aspects of the Declaration of Principles: A Palestinian View', in E. Cotran and C. Mallat (eds.), *The Arab–Israeli Accords: Legal Perspectives* (London: Kluwer Law International), 67–77.

Cox, M. (1997), 'Bringing in the "International": The IRA Cease-Fire and the End of the Cold War' 73 *International Affairs* 671–93.

Craig, E., and T. Hadden (2000), *Integration and Separation: Rights in Divided Societies* (Belfast: Fortnight Educational Trust).

Craven, M. (1995), 'The European Community Arbitration Commission on Yugoslavia' 66 *British Yearbook of International Law* 333–413.

Crawford, J. (1990), 'The Creation of the State of Palestine: Too Much too Soon?' 1 *European Journal of International Law* 307–13.

—— (1993), 'Democracy and International Law' 64 *British Yearbook of International Law* 113–33.

Crawshaw, R., B. Devlin, and T. M. Williamson (1998), *Human Rights and Policing: Standards for Good Behaviour and a Strategy for Change* (The Hague: Kluwer Law International).

Criminal Justice Review Group (2000), *Review of the Criminal Justice System in Northern Ireland: A Guide* (Belfast: Stationery Office).

Cristescu, A. (1981), *The Rights of Self-Determination: Historical and Current Developments on the Basis of United Nations Instruments*, UN doc. A2 E/CN.4/Sub. 2/404/Rev. 1-1981 (n.p.: UN).

Curran, D., F. Hill, and E. Kostritsyna (1997), *The Search for Peace in Chechnya: A Sourcebook 1994–1996* (Cambridge, Mass.: Harvard University, Strengthening Democratic Institutions Project).

D'Amato, A. (1994), 'Peace v. Accountability in Bosnia' 88 *American Journal of International Law* 500–6.

Davenport, T. R. H. (2000), *South Africa: A Modern History*, 5th edn. (Basingstoke: Macmillan; New York: St Martin's Press).

Davis, D. (1996), 'The Underlying Theory that Informs the Wording of our Bill of Rights' 113/3 *South African Law Journal* 385–94.

Davis, R. H., and S. Johns (eds.) (1991), *Mandela, Tambo, and the African National Congress: The Struggle against Apartheid, 1948–1990. A Documentary Survey* (New York: Oxford University Press).

de Búrca, G. (1995), 'The Language of Rights and European Integration', in J. Shaw and G. More (eds.), *New Legal Dynamics of European Union* (Oxford: Clarendon Press), 29–54.

Democracy and Workers' Rights Center (1996), *Report on the Effects of Closures Imposed by Israel on Palestinian Workers* (Ramallah: Democracy and Workers' Rights Center).

Deng, F. (1993), *Protecting the Internally Displaced: A Challenge for the United Nations*, Report by the Special Representative of the Secretary-General on Internally Displaced Persons to the UN Commission on Human Rights (Washington, DC: Brookings Institution).

Department of Health and Social Services Registrar-General (1993), *The Northern Ireland Census 1991: Religion Report* (Belfast: HMSO).

Dickson, B. (1996), 'The European Convention in Northern Irish Courts' 5 *European Human Rights Law Review* 496–510.

—— (1997), 'Northern Ireland and the European Convention', in B. Dickson (ed.), *Human Rights and the European Convention* (London: Sweet & Maxwell), 169–82.

—— (1999), 'Northern Ireland', in Lord Lester of Herne Hill and D. Pannick (eds.), *Human Rights Law and Practice* (London: Butterworths), 287–308.

Dinstein, Y., and M. Tabory (eds.) (1996), *War Crimes in International Law* (Dordrecht: Martinus Nijhoff).

Doder, D. (1979), *The Yugoslavs* (London: Allen & Unwin).

Dolgopol, U. (1997), 'A Feminist Appraisal of the Dayton Peace Accords' 19 *Adelaide Law Review* 59–71.

Domb, F. (1996), 'Treatment of War Crimes in Peace Settlements — Prosecution or Amnesty?', in Dinstein and Tabory (1996: 305–20).

Donnelly, J. (1989), *Universal Human Rights in Theory and Practice* (Ithaca: Cornell University Press).

—— (1994), 'International Human Rights after the Cold War', in M. T. Klare and D. C. Thomas (eds.), *World Security: Challenges for a New Century* (New York: St Martin's Press), 236–55.

Drew, C. (1997), 'Self-Determination, Population Transfer and the Middle East Peace Accords', in S. Bowen (ed.), *Human Rights, Self-Determination and Political Change in the Occupied Palestinian Territories* (The Hague: Kluwer Law International), 119–68.

Dugard, J. (ed.) (1973), *The South West Africa/Namibia Dispute: Documents and Scholarly Writings on the Controversy between South Africa and the United Nations* (Berkeley, Los Angeles: University of California Press).

—— (1980), 'South Africa's Independent Homelands: An Exercise in Denationalization' 10 *Denver Journal of International Law and Policy* 11–36.

—— (1986), 'The Conflict between International Law and South African Law: Another Divisive Factor in South African Society' 2 *South African Journal of Human Rights* 1–28.

—— (1992a), 'Enforcement of Human Rights in the West Bank and the Gaza Strip', in Playfair (ed.) (1992: 461–87).

—— (1992b), 'Secession: Is the Case of Yugoslavia a Precedent for Africa?' 5 *African Journal of International and Comparative Law* 163–75.

—— (1994a), *International Law: A South African Perspective* (Kenwyn: Juta).

—— (1994b), 'The Role of Enforcement in Interpreting the Bill of Rights' 10/2 *South Africa Journal of Human Rights* 208–15.

—— (1997a), 'International Law and the South African Constitution' 1 *European Journal of International Law* 77–92.

—— (1997b), 'Is the Truth and Reconciliation Process Compatible with International Law? An Unanswered Question' 13 *South African Journal on Human Rights* 258–68.

—— (1997c), 'Retrospective Justice: International Law and the South African Model', in McAdams (ed.) (1997: 269–90).

—— (1998), 'The South African Judiciary and International Law in the Apartheid Era' 14 *South African Journal of Human Rights* 110–26.

DUMPER, M. (2000), 'Jerusalem and the Illusion of Israeli Sovereignty', 4 Aug. 2000, Press Information note 27 (Washington, DC: Middle East Research and Information Project).

DUNNE, T., and N. WHEELER (eds.) (1999), *Human Rights in Global Politics* (Cambridge: Cambridge University Press).

DU PLESSIS, L. (1996), 'Evaluative Reflections on the Final Text of South Africa's Bill of Rights' 3 *Stellenbosch Law Review* 283–306.

DU TOIT, T. (1989), 'Bargaining about Bargaining: Inducing the Self-Negating Prediction in Deeply Divided Societies: The Case of South Africa' 33 *Journal of Conflict Resolution* 210–33.

DYSENHAUS, D. (1998), *Judging the Judges, Judging Ourselves: Truth, Reconciliation and the Apartheid Legal Order* (Oxford: Hart).

EBRAHIM, H. (1998), *The Soul of a Nation: Constitution-Making in South Africa* (Cape Town: Oxford University Press).

ECONOMIDES, S., and P. TAYLOR (1996), 'Former Yugoslavia', in J. Mayall (ed.), *The New Interventionism 1991–1993: United Nations Experience in Cambodia, Former Yugoslavia and Somalia* (Cambridge: Cambridge University Press), 59–93.

EIDE, A. (1993), 'In Search of Constructive Alternatives to Secession', in C. Tomuschat (ed.) *Modern Law of Self-Determination* (Dordrecht: Martinus Nijhoff), 139–76.

—— (1995), *New Approaches to Minority Protection*, Minority Rights Group International Report 93/4 (London: MRG International).

—— (1996), *A Review and Analysis of Constructive Approaches to Group Accommodation and Minority Protection in Divided or Multicultural Societies*, Consultancy Studies, no. 3, Forum for Peace and Reconciliation, July 1996, Dublin Castle (Dublin: Forum for Peace and Reconciliation).

ELMUSA, S. S., and M. EL-JAAFARI (1996), 'Power and Trade: The Israeli–Palestinian Economy Protocol', in E. Cotran and C. Mallat (eds.), *The Arab–Israeli Accords: Some Legal Perspectives* (London: Kluwer Law International), 173–95.

EMERSON, P. J. (1998), *Beyond the Tyranny of the Majority: Voting Methodologies in Decision-Making and Electoral Systems* (Belfast: De Borda Institute).

—— (2000), *From Belfast to the Balkans: Was 'Democracy' Part of the Problem?* (Belfast: De Borda Institute).

ENGLE, K. (1993), 'After the Collapse of the Public/Private Distinction: Strategising Women's Rights', in D. G. Dallmeyer (ed.), *Reconceiving Reality: Women and International Law* (Washington: American Society of International Law), 143–55.

ENSALACO, M. (1994), 'Truth Commissions for Chile and El Salvador: A Report and Assessment' 16 *Human Rights Quarterly* 656–75.

EPSEILL, H. G. (1980), *The Right of Self-Determination: Implementation of United Nations Resolutions*, (UN doc. E/CN.4/Sub2/405/Rev. 1 (n.p.: UN).

ERASMUS, G., and J. DE WAAL (1996), 'The Constitutional Jurisprudence of South African Courts on the Application, Interpretation and Limitation of Fundamental Rights during the Transition' 7 *Stellenbosch Law Review* 179–209.

ESMAN, M., and S. TELHAMI (eds.) (1995), *International Organisations and Ethnic Conflict* (Ithaca: Cornell University Press).

EUROPEAN COMMISSION FOR DEMOCRACY THROUGH LAW (Venice Commission) (1999), *Preliminary Proposal for the Restructuring of Human Rights Protection Mechanisms in Bosnia and Herzegovina*, Adopted by the Commission at its 39th Plenary Meeting, Venice, 18–19 June 1999, Council of Europe doc. CDL (99) 19 final.

EUROPEAN STABILITY INITIATIVE (1999), *Reshaping International Priorities in Bosnia and Herzegovina*, pt. 1: *Bosnian Power Structures* (Sarajevo: European Stability Initiative).

EVANS, G. (1993), *Cooperating for Peace: The Global Agenda for the 1990s and Beyond* (London: Allen & Unwin).

FALK, R. (1995), *On Humane Governance: Toward a New Global Politics* (Cambridge: Polity Press).

—— and B. WESTON (1991), 'The Relevance of International Law to Palestinian Rights in the West Bank and Gaza: In Defence of the Intifada' 32 *Harvard International Law Journal* 129–57.

FASSBERG, C. W. (1996), 'Legal Aspects of Israeli–Palestinian Economic Relations', in E. Cotran and C. Mallat (eds.), *The Arab–Israeli Accords: Legal Perspectives* (The Hague: Kluwer Law International), 157–72.

FAY, M. T., M. MORRISSEY, and M. SMYTH (1999), *Northern Ireland's Troubles: The Human Costs* (London: Pluto Press).

FESTE, K. (1991), *Plans for Peace* (New York: Praeger).

FISHER, R., and W. URY (and B. PATTON for 2nd edn.) (1991), *Getting to Yes: Negotiating Agreement without Giving In*, 2nd edn. (London: Century Business).

FITZPATRICK, J. (1994), *Human Rights in Crisis: The International System of Protecting Rights During States of Emergency* (Philadelphia: University of Pennsylvania Press).

FORGERY, H., A. JEFFERY, E. SIDIROPOULOS, C. SMITH, T. CORRIGAN, T. MOPHUTHING, A. HELMAN, J. REDPATH, and T. DIMANT (1999), *South Africa Survey 1999–2000* (Johannesburg: South African Institute of Race Relations).

FORSYTHE, D. P. (1993), *Human Rights and Peace: International and National Dimensions* (Lincoln: University of Nebraska Press).

FOSTER, R. F. (1988), *Modern Ireland 1600–1972* (London: Penguin).

FRANCK, T. M. (1992,) 'The Emerging Right to Democratic Governance' *American Journal of International Law* 46–91.

FRASER, E. (1999), *The Problems of Communitarian Politics* (Oxford: Oxford University Press).

—— and N. LACEY (1994), *The Politics of Community: A Feminist Critique of the Liberal-Communitarian Debate* (London: Harvester Wheatsheaf).

FRIEDMAN, S. (ed.) (1993), *The Long Journey: South Africa's Quest for a Negotiated Settlement* (Johannesburg: Centre for Policy Studies, University of Witwatersrand).

—— and D. ATKINSON (eds.) (1994), *South African Review, special issue: The Small Miracle South Africa's Negotiated Settlement* (Johannesburg: Ravan Press).

GAETA, P. (1996), 'The Dayton Agreements and International Law' 7 *European Journal of International Law* 147–63.

GALTUNG, J. (1994), *Human Rights in Another Key* (Cambridge: Polity Press).

GAVISON, R. (1985), 'The Controversy over Israel's Bill of Rights' 15 *Israel Yearbook on Human Rights* 113–54.

GERSON, A. (1973), 'Trustee-Occupant: The Legal Status of Israel's Presence in the West Bank' 14 *Harvard International Law Journal* 1–49.

—— (1978), *Israel, the West Bank and International Law* (London: Cass).

GHAI, Y. (1994), 'Human Rights and Governance and the Asia Debate' 15 *Australia Year Book of International Law* 1–34.

GILBERT, G. (1993), 'Root Causes and International Law: Refugee Flows in the 1990s' 4 *Netherlands Human Rights Quarterly* 413–36.

GILIOMEE, H., and J. GAGIANO (eds.) (1993), *The Elusive Search for Peace: South Africa, Israel, Northern Ireland* (Oxford: Oxford University Press).

GLENY, M. (1996), *The Fall of Yugoslavia: The Third Balkan War*, 3rd edn. (Harmondsworth: Penguin).

GOLDSTONE, R. (1995a), 'Exposing Human Rights Abuses—A Help or a Hindrance to Reconciliation, The Matthew O. Tobriner Memorial Lecture of 18 January 1995' 22 *Hastings Constitutional Law Quarterly* 607–21.

—— (1995b), 'The International Tribunal for the Former Yugoslavia: A Case Study in Security Council Action' 6 *Duke Journal of Comparative and International Law* 5–10.

—— (1996), 'Justice as a Tool for Peace-Making: Truth Commissions and International Criminal Tribunals' 28 *New York University Journal of International Law and Politics* 485–503.

—— (1997a), 'Assessing the Work of the United Nations War Crimes Tribunals' 33 *Stanford Journal of International Law* 1–8.

—— (1997b), 'Prosecuting International Crimes: An Inside View. Symposium' 7 *Transnational Law and Contemporary Problems* 1–260.

—— (1997c), 'The South African Bill of Rights' 32 *Texas International Law Journal* 451–69.

GOODMAN, J. (1998), 'Post Cold-War Self-Determination: Ireland and Timor' 3 *Geopolitics* 53–82.

GOODWIN-GILL, G. S. (1996), *The Refugee in International Law*, 2nd edn. (Oxford: Clarendon Press).

GORLICK, B. (1999), 'The Convention and the Committee against Torture: A Complementary Protection Regime for Refugees' 11 *International Journal of Refugee Law* 479–95.

GORMLEY, B., and K. MCEVOY (1995), *The Release of Politically Motivated Offenders in Northern Ireland: A Comparative Study of South Africa, Israel/Palestine, Italy, Spain, the Republic of Ireland and Northern Ireland* (Belfast: Northern Ireland Association for the Care and Resettlement of Offenders).

GOTTLIEB, G. (1993), *Nation against State: A New Approach to Ethnic Conflicts and the Decline of Sovereignty* (New York: Council on Foreign Relations Press).

GOW, J. (1997), *Triumph of the Lack of Will: International Diplomacy and the Yugoslav War* (London: Hurst).

GREENWOOD, G. (1996), 'International Humanitarian Law and the *Tadić* Case' 7 *European Journal of International Law* 265–83.

GUELKE, A. (1985), 'International Legitimacy, Self Determination, and Northern Ireland' 11 *Review of International Studies* 37–52.

—— (1991), 'The Political Impasse in South Africa and Northern Ireland' 23 *Comparative Politics* 143–62.

—— (ed.) (1994a), *New Perspectives on the Northern Ireland Conflict* (Aldershot: Avebury).

—— (1994b), 'The Peace Process in South Africa, Israel, and Northern Ireland: A Farewell to Arms?' 5 *Irish Studies in International Affairs* 93–106.

—— (1996a), 'Dissecting the South African Miracle: African Parallels' 2 *Nationalism and Ethnic Politics* 141–54.

—— (1996b), 'The Impact of the End of the Cold War on the South African Transition' 14 *Journal of Contemporary African Studies* 87–100.

—— (1996c), 'The Influence of the South African Transition on the Northern Ireland Peace Process' 3 *South African Journal of International Affairs* 132–48.

—— (1997), 'Comparatively Peaceful: The Role of Analogy in Northern Ireland's Peace Process' 11 *Cambridge Review of International Affairs* 28–45.

—— (1999), *South Africa in Transition: The Misunderstood Miracle* (London: I. B. Tauris).

HADDEN, T. (1988), 'The Application of the Principle of Self-Determination to Northern Ireland', Submission to Northern Ireland Human Rights Assembly, unpub., copy on file with the author.

—— (1996), 'The Rights of Minorities and Peoples in International Law', in K. Schulze, M. Stokes, and C. Campbell (eds.), *Nationalism, Minorities and Diasporas: Identities and Rights in the Middle East* (London: Tauris Academic Studies), 3–22.

—— (1999), 'Human Rights Abuses and the Protection of Democracy during States of Emergency', in E. Cotran and A. O. Sherif (eds.), *Democracy, the Rule of Law and Islam* (The Hague: Kluwer Law International), 111–31.

HADFIELD, B. (1989), *The Constitution of Northern Ireland* (Belfast: Servicing the Legal System).

—— (1992), *Northern Ireland: Politics and the Constitution* (Buckingham: Open University Press).

—— (1998), 'The Belfast Agreement, Sovereignty and the State of the Union' *Public Law* 599–616.

HAILBRONNER, K. (1986), 'Non-Refoulement and "Humanitarian" Refugees: Customary International Law or Wishful Legal Thinking?' 26/4 *Virginia Journal of International Law* 857–96.

HAJJAR, L. (1997), 'Cause Lawyering in Transnational Perspective: National Conflict and Human Rights in Israel/Palestine' 31 *Law and Society Review* 473–504.

HALBERSTAM, M. (1989), 'Self Determination in the Arab–Israeli Conflict: Meaning, Myth and Politics' 21 *International Law and Politics* 465–87.

HAMBER, B. (ed.) (1998a), *Past Imperfect: Dealing with the Past in Northern Ireland and Societies in Transition* (Derry/Londonderry: INCORE).

—— (1998b), 'Who Pays for Peace? Implications of the Negotiated Settlement for Reconciliation, Transformation and Violence in a Post-Apartheid South Africa', Public lecture at the Annual General Meeting of the Catholic Institute for International Relations, Voluntary Sector Resource Centre, London, 30 Oct. 1998, unpub, copy on file with author.

HAMOKED (1998), *1998 Annual Report of Activities* (Jerusalem: HaMoked, Centre for the Defence of the Individual).

HANNUM, H (1990), *Autonomy, Sovereignty and Self-Determination: The Accommodation of Conflicting Rights* (Philadelphia: University of Pennsylvania Press).

HARRIS, P., and B. REILLY (1998), *Democracy and Deep-Rooted Conflict: Options for Negotiators* (Stockholm: International Institute for Democracy and Electoral Assistance).

HARVEY, C., and S. LIVINGSTONE (1998), 'Human Rights and the Northern Ireland Peace Process' 2 *European Human Rights Law Review* 162–77.

HARVEY, R. (1990), 'The Rights of the People of the Whole of Ireland to Self Determination, Unity, Sovereignty, and Independence' 11 *New York Law School Journal of International and Comparative Law* 167–206.

HATHAWAY, J. C. (1991), *The Law of Refugee Status* (Toronto: Butterworths).

—— (1997), 'The Meaning of Repatriation' 9 *International Journal of Refugee Law* 551–8.

HAYNER, P. (1994), 'Fifteen Truth Commissions: 1974–1994. A Comparative Study' 16 *Human Rights Quarterly* 597–655.

HEATON, J. (1997), 'A Comparison of the Bill of Rights in the Interim and Final Constitutions' 352 *De Rebus* 331–41.

HELSINKI RIGHTS WATCH (1991), *Human Rights in Northern Ireland* (New York: Human Rights Watch).

—— (1992), *Children in Northern Ireland: Abused by Security Forces and Paramilitaries* (New York: Human Rights Watch).

HENDERSON, A. (1996), 'Cry, the Beloved Constitution? Constitutional Amendments, the Vanished Imperative of the Constitutional Principles and the Controlling Values of Section 1' 113 *South African Law Journal* 542–55.

HOLBROOKE, R. (1998), *To End a War* (New York: Random House).

HOLLIS, M., and S. SMITH (1990), *Explaining and Understanding International Relations* (Oxford: Clarendon Press).

HOROWITZ, D. (1985), *Ethnic Groups in Conflict* (Berkeley: University of California Press).

—— (1991), *A Democratic South Africa? Constitutional Engineering in a Divided Society* (Berkeley: University of California Press).

HOUGH, M., and A. DU PLESSIS (eds.) (1994), *Selected Documents and Commentaries on Negotiations and Constitutional Development in the RSA 1989–1994* (Pretoria: Institute for Strategic Studies UP Pretoria).

HUMAN RIGHTS PROGRAM, HARVARD LAW SCHOOL (1996), *Truth Commissions: A Comparative Assessment* (Cambridge, Mass.: Harvard Law School).

HUMAN RIGHTS WATCH (1998), *An Analysis of the Wye River Memorandum*, Press release (New York: Human Rights Watch, Nov.).

HUMPHRIES, R., T. RAPOO, and S. FRIEDMAN (1994), 'The Shape of the Country', in Friedman and Atkinson (eds.) (1994: 148–81).

HUYSE, L. (1995), 'Justice after Transition: On the Choices Successor Elites Make in Dealing with the Past' 20 *Law and Social Inquiry* 51–78.

INDEPENDENT COMMISSION ON POLICING FOR NORTHERN IRELAND (1999), *A New Beginning: Policing in Northern Ireland* (Sept.).

INSTITUTE FOR PUBLIC POLICY RESEARCH (1998), *A Human Rights Commission: The Options for Britain and Northern Ireland* (London: Institute for Public Policy Research).

INTERNATIONAL ALERT (1998), *Code of Conduct: Conflict Transformation Work* (London: International Alert).

INTERNATIONAL COMMISSION ON THE BALKANS (1996), *Unfinished Peace* (Washington, DC: Aspen Institute, Carnegie Endowment for International Peace).

INTERNATIONAL CRISIS GROUP (1996), *Elections in Bosnia Herzegovina* (Sarajevo: International Crisis Group).

—— (1999), *Is Dayton Failing? Bosnia Four Years after the Peace Agreement* (Sarajevo: International Crisis Group).

JOINET, L. (1997), *Question of Impunity of Perpetrators of Human Rights Violations (Civil and political): Final Report. Prepared by Mr Joinet pursuant to Sub-Commission Decision 1996/119*, UN doc. E/CN.4/Sub.2/1997/20 (n.p.: UN).

JONES, P. (1999), 'Human Rights, Group Rights and People's Rights' 21 *Human Rights Quarterly* 80–107.

JONES, R. W. D. (1996), 'The Implications of the Peace Agreement for the International Criminal Tribunal for the Former Yugoslavia' 7 *European Journal of International Law* 226–44.

JOULWAN, G. A., and C. C. SHOEMAKER (1998), *Civilian–Military Cooperation in the Prevention of Deadly Conflict: Implementing Agreements in Bosnia and Beyond* (Washington DC: Carnegie Commission on Preventing Deadly Conflict).

KÄLIN, W. (ed.) (1994), *Human Rights in Times of Occupation: The Case of Kuwait* (Beirne: Law Books in Europe).

KALSHOVEN, F. (1987), *Constraints on the Waging of War* (Geneva: International Committee of the Red Cross).

KANT, I. (1781), *Critique of Pure Reason*, 1st edn., trans. N. Kemp Smith (London: Macmillan, 1929).

KAUFMAN, E., and I. BISHARAT (1998a), 'Bringing Human Rights into the Israeli–Palestinian Peace Process' 6 *Palestine–Israel Journal* 8–13.

—— —— (1998b), 'Human Rights and Conflict Resolution: Searching for Common Ground Between Justice and Peace in the Israeli/Palestinian Conflict', NIDR Forum, 16–23 Dec.

KAUSIKAN, B. (1993), 'Asia's Different Standard' 92 *Foreign Policy* 24–41.

KEIGHTLEY, R. (1995), 'Political Offences and Indemnity in South Africa' 9 *South African Journal of Human Rights Law* 334–57.

KENNEDY, D. (1987), *International Legal Structures* (Baden-Baden: Nomos).

DE KIEWIET, C. E. (1950), *A History of South Africa: Social and Economic* (London: Oxford University Press).

KLIEMAN, A. (1999), *Constructive Ambiguity in Middle East Peace-Making*, Research Report Series, no. 10 (Tel Aviv: Tami Steinmetz Center for Peace Research).

KLUG, H. (1990), 'Self-Determination and the Struggle against Apartheid' 8 *Wisconsin International Law Journal* 251–99.

KOSKENNIEMI, M. (1989), *From Apology to Utopia: The Structure of International Legal Argument* (Helsinki: Lakimiesliiton Kustannus).

—— (1990a), 'The Pull of the Mainstream' 88 *Michigan Law Review* 1946–62.

—— (1990b), 'The Politics of International Law' 1 *European Journal of International Law* 4–32.

—— (1994), 'National Self-Determination To-day: Problems of Legal Theory and Practice' 43 *International and Comparative Law Quarterly* 241–69.

KRETCHMER, D. (1996), 'The New Basic Laws on Human Rights: A Mini-Revolution in Israeli Constitutional Law?' 14 *Netherlands Quarterly of Human Rights* 173–83.

—— (1999), 'Basic Laws as a Surrogate Bill of Rights: The Case of Israel', in Alston (ed.) (1999: 75–92).

KRITZ, N. J. (ed.) (1995), *Transitional Justice: How Emerging Democracies Reckon with Former Regimes,* 3 vols. (Washington, DC: United States Institute of Peace Press).

KUMAR, R. (1997), *Divide and Fall? Bosnia in the Annals of Partition* (London: Verso).

KUTTAB, J. (1992), 'Avenues Open for Defence of Human Rights in the Israeli-Occupied Territories', in Playfair (ed.) (1992: 489–504).

LAMBERT, H. (1999), 'Protection against *Refoulement* from Europe: Human Rights Law Comes to the Rescue' 48 *International and Comparative Law Quarterly* 515–44.

LAPIDOTH, R. (1997), *Autonomy: Flexible Solutions to Ethnic Conflicts* (Washington, DC: US Institute of Peace Press).

—— and M. HIRSCH (eds.) (1992), *The Arab–Israeli Conflict and its Resolution: Selected Documents* (Dordrecht: Martinus Nijhoff).

LAQUER, W. (1969), *The Israel–Arab Reader: A Documentary History of the Middle East Conflict* (London: Weidenfeld & Nicolson).

—— and B. RUBIN (eds.) (1984), *The Israel-Arab Reader: A Documentary History of the Middle East Conflict* (New York: Penguin).

LAW (1998a), *Apartheid, Bantustans, Cantons: The ABC of the Oslo Process* (Jerusalem: LAW, Palestinian Society for the Protection of Human Rights and the Environment).

—— (1998b), *Israel's House Demolition Policy in the West Bank since the Signing of the Oslo Agreements* (Jerusalem: LAW, Palestinian Society for the Protection of Human Rights and the Environment).

—— (1999a), *Bulldozed into Cantons: Israel's House Demolition Policy in the West Bank Since the Signing of the Oslo Agreements* (Jerusalem: LAW, Palestinian Society for the Protection of Human Rights and the Environment).

LAW (1999b), *Land and Settlement Policy in Jerusalem* (Jerusalem: LAW, Palestinian Society for the Protection of Human Rights and the Environment).

—— (1999c), *Palestinians Dispossessed: 50 Years of Human Rights Violations. Law's Annual Report 1998* (Jerusalem: LAW, Palestinian Society for the Protection of Human Rights and the Environment).

LIJPHART, A. (1968), *The Politics of Accommodation: Pluralism and Democracy in the Netherlands* (Berkeley: University of California Press).

—— (1969), 'Consociational Democracy' 21 *World Politics* 207–25.

—— (1977), *Democracy in Plural Societies: A Comparative Exploration* (New Haven: Yale University Press).

—— (1989), 'Democratic Political Systems: Types, Cases, Causes, and Consequences' 1 *Journal of Theoretical Politics* 33–48.

LIVINGSTONE, S. (1990), 'Using Law to Change a Society: The Case of Northern Ireland', in S. Livingstone and J. Morison (eds.), *Law, Society and Change* (Aldershot: Dartmouth), 51–70.

—— (1995), 'Reviewing Northern Ireland in Strasbourg 1969–1994', in G. Quinn (ed.), *Irish Human Rights Yearbook 1995* (Dublin: Round Hall, Sweet & Maxwell), 115–30.

—— (1999), 'The Northern Ireland Human Rights Commission' 22 *Fordham International Law Journal* 1465–98.

—— and J. MORISON (1995), *Reshaping Public Power: Northern Ireland and the British Constitutional Crisis* (London: Sweet & Maxwell).

LOCKMAN, Z., and J. BEININ (eds.) (1990), *Intifada: The Palestinian Uprising against Israeli Occupation* (London: I. B. Tauris).

LODGE, T., and B. NASSON with S. MUFSON., K. SUBANE, and N. SITHOLE (1991), *All, Here, and Now: Black Politics in South Africa in the 1980s* (London: Hurst).

LUSTICK, I. S. (1990), 'Changing Rationales for Political Violence in the Arab–Israeli Conflict' 20 *Journal of Palestinian Studies* 54–79.

—— (1993), *Unsettled States, Disputed Lands: Britain and Ireland, France and Algeria, Israel and the West Bank–Gaza* (Ithaca, NY: Cornell University Press).

MCADAMS, A. J. (ed.) (1997), *Transitional Justice and the Rule of Law in New Democracies* (Notre Dame, Ind. : University of Notre Dame Press).

MACCORMACK, T. L. H., and G. J. SIMPSON (eds.) (1997), *The Law of War Crimes: National and International Approaches* (The Hague: Kluwer Law International).

MACCORMICK, N. (1996), 'Liberalism, Nationalism and the Post-Sovereign State', in Bellamy and Castiglione (eds.) (1996: 141–56).

MCCORQUODALE, R. (1992), 'Self-Determination beyond the Colonial Context and its Potential Impact on Africa' 4 *African Journal of International and Comparative Law* 592-608.

—— (1994a), 'Self Determination: A Human Rights Approach' 43 *International and Comparative Law Quarterly* 857–85.

—— (1994b), 'South Africa and the Right of Self-Determination' 10 *South African Journal on Human Rights* 4–30.

—— (1995), 'Negotiating Sovereignty: The Practice of the United Kingdom in Regard to the Right of Self-Determination' 66 *British Yearbook of International Law* 283–331.

McCoubrey, H., and N. D. White (1995), *International Organisations and Civil Wars* (Aldershot: Dartmouth).

McCrudden, C. (1994), 'Northern Ireland and the British Constitution', in J. Jowell and D. Oliver (eds.) *The Changing Constitution* (Oxford: Clarendon Press) 323–75.

—— (1999a), 'Human Rights Codes for Transnational Corporations: What can the Sullivan and MacBride Principles Tell Us?' 19 *Oxford Journal of Legal Studies* 167–201.

—— (1999b), 'Mainstreaming Equality in the Governance of Northern Ireland' 22 *Fordham International Law Journal* 1696–1775.

McEvoy, K. (1998), 'Prisoner Release and Conflict Resolution: International Lessons for Northern Ireland' 8 *International Criminal Justice Review* 33–61.

—— (1999), 'Prisoners, the Agreement and the Political Character of the Northern Ireland Conflict' 22 *Fordham International Law Journal* 153—76.

McGarry, J. (1998), 'Political Settlements in Northern Ireland and South Africa' 46 *Political Studies* 853–70.

—— and B. O'Leary (1990), *The Future of Northern Ireland* (Oxford: Clarendon Press).

—— —— (1993), *The Politics of Ethnic Conflict Regulation* (New York: Routledge).

—— —— (1995), *Explaining Northern Ireland: Broken Images* (Oxford: Blackwell).

McGoldrick, D. (1999), 'From Yugoslavia to Bosnia: Accommodating National Identity in National and International Law' 6 *International Journal on Minority and Group Rights* 1–63.

McKittrick, D. (1996), *The Nervous Peace* (Belfast: Blackstaff Press).

—— S. Kelters, B. Feeny, and C. Thornton (1999), *Lost Lives: The Stories of the Men, Women and Children who Died as a Result of the Northern Ireland Troubles* (Edinburgh: Mainstream).

Mageean, P., and M. O'Brien (1999), 'From the Margins to the Mainstream: Human Rights and the Good Friday Agreement' 22 *Fordham International Law Journal* 1499–1538.

Maguire, P. (1981), 'The Standing Advisory Commission on Human Rights 1973–1980' 32 *Northern Ireland Law Quarterly* 31–61.

Makovsky, D. (1996), *Making Peace with the PLO: The Rabin Government's Road to the Oslo Accord* (Boulder, Colo.: Westview Press).

Malamud-Goti, J. (1990), 'Transitional Governments in the Breach: Why Punish State Criminals?' 12 *Human Rights Quarterly* 1–16.

—— (1996), *Game without End: State Terror and the Politics of Justice* (Norman, Okla.: University of Oklahoma Press).

Malanczuk, P. (1995), 'Israel: Status, Territory and Occupied Territories' 2 *Encyclopaedia of Public International Law* 1468–1508.

—— (1996), 'Some Basic Aspects of the Agreements between Israel and the PLO from the Perspective of International Law' 7 *European Journal of International Law* 485–500.

Mallie, E., and D. McKittrick (1996), *The Fight for Peace: The Secret Story behind the Irish Peace Process* (London: Heinemann).

Mandela, N. (1995), *Long Walk to Freedom: The Autobiography of Nelson Mandela* (London: Abacus).

MARAIS, D. (1989), *South Africa: Constitutional Development, A Multi-Disciplinary Approach* (Johannesburg: Southern Book Publishers).

MAR'I, M. (1997), *Guarantees for Respect of Human Rights in Palestine: Present Problems and Future Prospects* (Jerusalem: LAW, Palestinian Society for the Protection of Human Rights and the Environment).

MARX, A. W. (1992), *Lessons of Struggle: South African Internal Opposition 1960–1990* (New York: Oxford University Press).

MAYIBUYE CENTRE FOR HISTORY AND CULTURE IN SOUTH AFRICA (1994), *Apartheid and the History of the Struggle for Freedom in South Africa* (Bellville: Mayibuye CD-ROM Publications).

MBEKI, G. (1992), *The Struggle for Liberation in South Africa: A Short History* Mayibue History Series, no. 13 (Bellville: Mayibuye Centre).

MELI, F. (1988), *A History of the ANC: South Africa Belongs to Us* (Zimbabwe: Zimbabwe Publishing House).

MERON, T. (1989), *Human Rights and Humanitarian Norms as Customary Law* (Oxford: Clarendon Press).

—— (1998), *War Crimes Law Comes of Age: Essays* (Oxford: Clarendon Press).

MILL, J. S. (1859), *On Liberty* (London: J. W. Parker).

MILLER, D. (1994), *Don't Mention the War: Northern Ireland, Propaganda and the Media* (London: Pluto Press).

MILTON-EDWARDS, B. (1996), 'Policing the Peace: Northern Ireland and the Palestinian Case' 2 *Contemporary Politics* 1–22.

MITCHELL, C. R. (1981), *The Structure of International Conflict* (London: Macmillan).

MOHAMED, J. (1991), 'Collective Rights, Transformation and Democracy', in G. Naidoo (ed.), *Reform and Revolution: South Africa in the Nineties* 54–78.

MOORE, L. (1999), 'Policing and Change in Northern Ireland: The Centrality of Human Rights' 22 *Fordham International Law Journal* 1577–1607.

—— and M. O'RAWE (1997), *Human Rights on Duty: Principles for Better Policing— International Lessons for Northern Ireland* (Belfast: Committee on the Administration of Justice).

—— —— (1998), 'International Lessons for the Transformation of Policing in Northern Ireland' 2 *International Journal of Human Rights* 66–86.

MORRIS, B. (1987), *The Birth of the Palestinian Refugee Problem, 1947–1949* (Cambridge: Cambridge University Press).

MOTSUENYANE COMMISSION (1993), *Report of the Commission of Enquiry into Certain Allegations of Cruelty and Human Rights Abuse against ANC Prisoners and Detainees by ANC Members, 20 August 1993*.

MÜLLERSON, R. (1997), *Human Rights Diplomacy* (London: Routledge).

MUREINIK, E. (1994), 'A Bridge to Where? Introducing the Interim Bill of Rights' 10 *South Africa Journal of Human Rights* 31–48.

MUSGRAVE, T. (1997), *Self Determination and National Minorities* (Oxford: Clarendon Press).

MUTTUKAUMARU, C. (1999), 'Reparation to Victims', in R. S. Lee (ed.), *The International Criminal Court: The Making of the Rome Statute* (The Hague: Kluwer Law International in Cooperation with the Project on International Courts and Tribunals), 262–70.

NGCOKOVANE, C. (1989), *Demons of Apartheid: A Moral and Ethical Analysis of the NGK, NP and Broederbond's Justification of Apartheid* (Braamfontein: Skotaville).

NÍ AOLÁIN, F. (1995), 'The Emergence of Diversity: Differences in Human Rights Jurisprudence' 19 *Fordham International Law Journal* 101–42.

—— (2000), *The Politics of the Force: Conflict Management and State Violence in Northern Ireland* (Belfast: Blackstaff Press).

NICOL, M. (1997), *The Making of the Constitution: The Story of South Africa's Constitutional Assembly, May 1994–December 1996* (Cape Town: Churchill Murray).

NINO, C. S. (1991), 'The Duty to Punish Past Abuses of Human Rights Put into Context: The Case of Argentina' 100 *Yale Law Journal* 2619–40.

NORMAND, R. (2000), 'The Final Approach to Final Status', 7 July 2000, Press Information note 25 (Washington, DC: Middle East Research and Information Project).

NORTHERN IRELAND HUMAN RIGHTS COMMISSION (1999), *Draft Strategic Plan* (Belfast: Northern Ireland Human Rights Commission).

NUR, M. (1992), *Expulsion of the Palestinians: The Concept of 'Transfer' in Zionist Political Thoughts* (Washington, DC: Institute for Palestine Studies).

NUTTALL, T., J. WRIGHT, J. HOFFMAN, N. SISHI, and S. MKHANDLELA (1998), *From Apartheid to Democracy: South Africa, 1948–1994* (Pietermaritzburg: Shuter & Shooter).

O'BRIEN, B. (1995), *The Long War: The IRA and Sinn Féin from Armed Struggle to Peace Talks* (Dublin: O'Brien Press).

O'BRIEN, C. C. (1998), *Memoir: My Life and Themes* (Dublin: Poolbeg Press).

O'DOWD, L., B. ROLSTON, and M. TOMLINSON (1981), *Northern Ireland: Between Civil Rights and Civil War*, 2nd edn. (London: CSE Books).

OFFICE OF THE HIGH REPRESENTATIVE (1998), *Bosnia and Herzegovina: Essential Texts*, 2nd edn. (Sarajevo: Office of the High Representative).

OFFICE OF THE UNITED NATIONS SPECIAL COORDINATOR IN THE OCCUPIED TERRITORIES (1999), *Rule of Law Development in the West Bank and Gaza Strip: Survey and State of the Development Effort May 1999* (Gaza: United Nations Special Coordinator in the Occupied Territories).

O'LEARY, B. (1999), 'The Nature of the Agreement' 22 *Fordham International Law Journal* 1628–60.

O'MALLEY, P. (1990), *Biting at the Grave: The Irish Hunger Strikes and the Politics of Despair* (Belfast: Blackstaff Press).

O'MEARA, D. (1996), *Forty Lost Years: The Apartheid State and the Politics of the National Party, 1948–1994* (Randburg: Ravan Press).

ORENTLICHER, D. F. (1991), 'Settling Accounts: The Duty to Prosecute Human Rights Violations of a Prior Regime' 100 *Yale Law Journal* 2537–615.

OWEN, D. (1996), *The Balkan Odyssey* (London: Indigo).

OYEDIRAN, J. (1997), *Plunder, Destruction and Despoliation: An Analysis of Israel's Violations of the International Law of Cultural Property in the Occupied West Bank and Gaza Strip* (Ramallah: Al Haq).

PAJIĆ, Z. (1998), 'A Critical Appraisal of Human Rights Provisions of the Dayton Constitution of Bosnia and Herzegovina' 20 *Human Rights Quarterly* 125–38.

PALESTINIAN CENTRE FOR HUMAN RIGHTS (1995), *The Israeli Policy of Closure: Legal, Political and Humanitarian Evaluation* (Gaza City: Palestinian Center for Human Rights).

PALESTINIAN CENTRE FOR HUMAN RIGHTS (1996), *A Comprehensive Survey of Israeli Settlements in the Gaza Strip* (Gaza: Palestinian Centre for Human Rights).

PALESTINIAN INDEPENDENT COMMISSION FOR CITIZENS' RIGHTS (1996), *First Annual Report*, 1 Jan. 1997–31 Dec. 1997 (Ramallah: Palestinian Independent Commission for Citizens' Rights).

—— (1997), *Second Annual Report*, 1 Jan. 1996–31 Dec. 1996 (Ramallah: Palestinian Independent Commission for Citizens' Rights).

—— (1998), *Third Annual Report*, 1 Jan. 1997–31 Dec. 1997 (Ramallah: Palestinian Independent Commission for Citizens' Rights).

—— (1999), *Fourth Annual Report*, 1 Jan. 1998–31 Dec. 1998 (Ramallah: Palestinian Independent Commission for Citizens' Rights).

PAPPÉ, I. (1994), *The Making of the Arab–Israeli Conflict, 1947–51* (London: I. B. Tauris).

PARKER, P. (1996), 'The Politics of Indemnities, Truth Telling and Reconciliation in South Africa: Ending Apartheid Without Forgetting' 17 *Human Rights Law Journal* 1–13.

PELLET, A. (1992), 'The Opinions of the Badinter Arbitration Committee: A Second Breath for the Self-Determination of Peoples' 3 *European Journal of International Law* 178–85.

PILGER, J. (1998), *Hidden Agendas: Wars and the Media* (London: Vintage).

PITYANA, B. (1996), *Towards a Rationalisation of Human Rights Institutions in South Africa: A Proposal* (Johannesburg: Human Rights Commission).

PLAYFAIR, E. (ed.) (1992), *International Law and the Administration of Occupied Territories: Two Decades of Israeli Occupation of the West Bank and Gaza Strip* (Oxford: Clarendon Press).

POGANY, I. (1996), 'Constitution Making or Constitutional Transformation in Post-Communist Societies?', in Bellamy and Castiglione (eds.) (1996: 157–79).

POMERANCE, M. (1982), *Self-Determination in Law and Practice: The New Doctrine in the United Nations* (Dordrecht: Martinus Nijhoff).

POSEL, D. (1991), *The Making of Apartheid 1948–1961: Conflict or Compromise* (Oxford: Clarendon Press).

PRICE, R. M. (1991), *The Apartheid State in Crisis: Political Transformation in South Africa 1975-1990* (New York: Oxford University Press).

PUGH, M. (eds.) (1997), *The UN, Peace and Force* (London: Cass).

QUIGLEY, J. (1989), 'David v. Goliath: Humanitarian and Human Rights Law in the Light of the Palestinian Right of Self-Determination and Right to Recapture Territory Taken by Force' 21 *International Law and Politics* 489–525.

—— (1997), 'Mass Displacement and the Individual Right to Return' 68 *British Yearbook of International Law* 65–125.

—— (1998), 'Displaced Palestinians and a Right to Return' 39 *Harvard International Law Journal* 171–229.

QUPTY, M. (1992), 'The Application of International Law in the Occupied Territories as Reflected in the Judgments of the High Court of Justice in Israel', in Playfair (ed.) (1992: 87–124).

RAMET, S. P. (ed.) (1985), *Yugoslavia in the 1980s* (Boulder, Colo.: Westview Press).

—— (1992), *Nationalism and Federalism in Yugoslavia 1962–1991*, 2nd edn. (Bloomington: Indiana University Press).

—— (1996), *Balkan Babal: The Distintegration of Yugoslavia from the Death of Tito to Ethnic War*, 2nd edn. (Boulder, Colo.: Westview Press).

RAUSCHNING, D. (1987), 'Mandates' 10 *Encyclopedia of International Law* 288–95.

RAWLS, J. (1971), *A Theory of Justice* (Oxford: Oxford University Press).

—— (1993), *Political Liberalism* (New York: Columbia University Press).

REILLY, B., and A. REYNOLDS (1999), *Electoral Systems and Conflict in Divided Societies*, Papers on International Conflict 2 (Washington, DC: National Academy Press).

REISMAN, M. (1994), 'Introductory Remarks' 19 *Yale Journal of International Law* 189–92.

—— (1995), 'Institutions and Practices for Restoring and Maintaining Public Order' 6 *Duke Journal of Comparative and International Law* 175–86.

RICH, R. (1993), 'Recognition of States: The Collapse of Yugoslavia and the Soviet Union' 4 *European Journal of International Law* 36–65.

RIGBY (1997), *The Legacy of the Past: The Problem of Collaborators and the Palestinian Case* (Jerusalem: PASSIA).

ROBERTS, A. (1987), 'The Applicability of Human Rights Law during Military Occupations' 13 *Review of International Studies* 39–48.

—— (1992), 'Prolonged Military Occupation: The Israeli-Occupied Territories 1967–1988', in Playfair (ed.) (1992: 25–86).

—— and B. KINGSBURY (eds.) (1998), *United Nations, Divided World: The UN's Roles in International Relations* (Oxford: Clarendon Press).

—— B. JOERGENSEN, and F. NEWMAN (1984), *Academic Freedom under Israeli Military Occupation* (London: World University Services (UK) and International Commission of Jurists).

ROBERTS, B. (ed.) (1995), *Order and Disorder after the Cold War* (Cambridge, Mass.: MIT Press).

ROBERTSON, G. (1999), *Crimes against Humanity: The Struggle for Global Justice* (London: Penguin).

ROBINSON, G. E. (1997), *Building a Palestinian State: The Incomplete Revolution* (Bloomington: Indiana University Press).

RODRÍQUEZ, L. V. (1993), *Report on the Right of Everyone to Own Property Alone as Well as in Association with Others*, 1993, UN doc. E/CN.4/1994/19 (23 Nov.).

ROHT-ARRIAZA, N. (ed.) (1995), *Impunity and Human Rights in International Law and Practice* (New York: Oxford University Press).

—— and L. GIBSON (1998), 'The Developing Jurisprudence on Amnesty' 20 *Human Rights Quarterly* 843–85.

ROLSTON, B. (1996), *Turning the Page without Closing the Book: The Right to Truth in the Irish Context* (Dublin: Irish Reporting Publications).

ROMANY, C. (1993), 'Women as *Aliens*: A Feminist Critique of the Public/Private Distinction in International Human Rights Law' 6 *Harvard Human Rights Journal* 87–125.

RONIGER, L., and M. SZNAJDER (1999), *The Legacy of Human Rights Violations in the Southern Cone: Argentina, Chile and Uruguay* (Oxford: Oxford University Press).

RORTY, R. (1993), 'Human Rights, Rationality, and Sentimentality', in S. Shute and S. Hurley (eds.), *On Human Rights: The Oxford Amnesty Lectures 1993* (New York: Basic Books), 111–34.

ROSENBERG, T. (1995), *The Haunted Land: Facing Europe's Ghosts after Communism* (London: Vintage).

ROSTOW, E. V. (1979), 'Palestinian Self-Determination: Possible Futures for the Unallocated Territories of the Palestine Mandate' 5 *Yale Studies in World Public Order* 147–72.

ROWAN, B. (1996), *Behind the Lines: The Story of the IRA and Loyalist Ceasefires* (Belfast: Blackstaff Press).

ROY, S. (1995), *The Gaza Strip: The Political Economy of De-Development* (Washington, DC: Institute for Palestinian Studies).

ROY, S. (1996), 'U.S. Economic Aid to the West Bank and Gaza Strip: The Politics of Peace' 4/4 *Middle East Policy* 50–76.

RUPESINGHE, K. (ed.) (1995), *Conflict Transformation* (London: Macmillan).

—— (1998), *Civil Wars, Civil Peace: An Introduction to Conflict Resolution* (London: Pluto Press).

RUSINOW, D. I. (1977), *The Yugoslav Experiment, 1948–74* (London: C. Hurst for the Royal Institute of International Affairs).

RUSSETT, B. (1990), 'Politics and Alternative Security: Toward a More Democratic, therefore More Peaceful, World', in B. H. Weston (ed.), *Alternative Security: Living without Nuclear Deterrence* (Boulder, Colo.: Westview Press), 107–36.

—— (1993), *Grasping the Democratic Peace* (Princeton: Princeton University Press).

SADIKOVIĆ, C. (1999), *Human Rights without Protection* (Sarajevo: Bosanskaknijiga).

SAID, E. (1995a), *Peace and its Discontents: Gaza–Jericho 1993–95* (London: Vintage).

—— (1995b), *Politics of Dispossession: The Struggle for Palestinian Self-Determination 1969-94* (London: Vintage).

SALAND, P. (1999), 'International Criminal Law Principles', in R. S. Lee (ed.), *The International Criminal Court: The Making of the Rome Statute* (The Hague: Kluwer Law International in cooperation with the Project on International Courts and Tribunals).

SANDEL, M. J. (1982), *Liberalism and the Limits of Justice* (Cambridge: Cambridge University Press).

SANGOCO (1998), 'Guildelines for Good Practice for Northern Non-Governmental Organisations (NGOs) Working in South Africa' 2 *Development Update* 78–9.

SARAKINSKY, I. (1994), 'Rehearsing Joint Rule: The Transitional Executive Council', in Friedman and Atkinson (eds.) (1994: 68–91).

SARKIN, J. (1997), 'The Political Role of the South African Constitutional Court' 114 *South African Law Journal* 134–50.

SCHEFFER, D. J. (1998), 'U.N. Engagement in Ethnic Conflict', in Wippman (ed.) (1998a: 147–77).

SCOTT, S. V. (1994), 'International Law as Ideology: Theorizing the Relationship between International Law and International Politics' 5 *European Journal of International Law* 313–25.

SEGAL, N. (1998), 'Israel, Palestinians Rely on CIA to Negotiate Prisoner Releases', Jewish Telegraphic Agency, 21 Dec. 1998.

SEIDL-HOHENVELDERN, I. (1982a), 'Reparations' 4 *Encyclopaedia of Public International Law* 178–80.

—— (1982b), 'Reparations after World War II' 4 *Encylopaedia of Public International Law* 180–4.

SESAY, M. A. (1996), 'Bringing Peace to Liberia' 1 *Accord: An International Review of Peace Initiatives* 9–26.

SHAH, S. (1997), *The By-Pass Road Network in the West Bank* (Ramallah: Al Haq).

SHAMGAR, M. (1971), 'The Observance of International Law in the Administered Territories' 1 *Israel Yearbook of International Law* 262–77.

SHAW, J. (1999), 'Postnational Constitutionalism in the European Union' 6 *Journal of European Public Policy* 579–97.

SHEHADEH, R. (1988), *Occupier's Law: Israel and the West Bank*, rev. edn. (Washington, DC: Institute of Palestinian Studies).

—— (1996), 'The Weight of Legal History: Constraints and Hopes in the Search for a Sovereign Legal Language', in E. Cotran and C. Mallat (eds.), *The Arab–Israeli Accords: Legal Perspectives* (London: Kluwer Law International), 3–20.

—— (1997), *From Occupation to Interim Accords: Israel and the Palestinian Territories* (The Hague: CIMEL and Kluwer Law International).

SHESTACK, J. J. (1998), 'The Philosophical Foundations of Human Rights' 20 *Human Rights Quarterly* 202–34.

SHUQAIR, R. (1994), *Criminal Jurisdiction under the Gaza–Jericho Agreement* (Ramallah: Al Haq).

—— (1996), *Jerusalem: Its Legal Status and the Possibility of a Durable Settlement* (Ramallah: Al Haq).

SIEGEL, R. L. (1998), 'Transitional Justice: A Decade of Debate and Experience' 20 *Human Rights Quarterly* 431–54.

SILBER, L., and A. LITTLE (1996), *The Death of Yugoslavia*, rev. edn. (London: Penguin, BBC Books).

SINGLETON, F. (1976), *Twentieth Century Yugoslavia* (New York: Columbia University Press).

—— (1983), *A Short History of the Yugoslav Peoples* (Cambridge: Cambridge University Press).

SISK, T. (1995), *Democratization in South Africa: The Elusive Social Contract* (Princeton: Princeton University Press).

—— (1996), *Power Sharing and International Mediation in Ethnic Conflicts* (Washington DC: United States Institute of Peace Press).

SKWEYIYA COMMISSION (1992), *Report of the Commission of Enquiry into Complaints by Former African National Congress Prisoners and Detainees, August 1992* (Bellville: Centre for Development Studies).

SLAUGHTER, A. (1998), 'Pushing the Limits of Liberal Peace: Ethnic Conflict and the "Ideal Polity"', in Wippman (ed.) (1998a: 128–44).

SLAUGHTER BURLEY, A. (1993), 'International Law and International Relations Theory: A Dual Agenda' 87 *American Journal of International Law* 205–39.

SLOAN, J. (1996), 'The Dayton Peace Agreement: Human Rights Guarantees and their Implementation' 7 *European Journal of International Law* 207–25.

SLOVO, J. (1992), 'Negotiations: What Room for Compromises' *African Communist* 36–40.

SOUTH AFRICAN LAW COMMISSION (1989), *Project 58: Group and Human Rights*, Working Paper 25 (Pretoria: South African Law Commission).

—— (1991), *Project 58: Group and Human Rights*, Interim Report (Pretoria: South African Law Commission).

SOUTHALL, R. (1990), 'Negotiations and Social Democracy in South Africa' 28 *Journal of Modern African Studies* 487–509.

SPARKS, A. (1996), *Tomorrow is Another Country* (Cape Town: Stuik Book Distributors).

STAVROS, S. (1992), 'The Right to Fair Trial in Emergency Situations' 41 *International and Comparative Legal Quarterly* 343–65.

STEELE, S. (1998), 'Island Troubles: Keating's Irish Visit', in J. Aubrey (ed.), *Free East Timor: Australia's Culpability in East Timor's Genocide* (Sydney: Random House), 177–89.

STEINER, H. (1991), 'Ideals and Counter-Ideals in the Struggle over Autonomy Regimes for Minorities' 66 *Notre Dame Law Review* 1539–60.

STEWART, A. T. Q. (1977), *The Narrow Ground: Aspects of Ulster 1609–1969* (London: Faber & Faber).

STOTZKY, I. P. (ed.) (1993), *Transition to Democracy in Latin America: The Role of the Judiciary* (Boulder, Color.: Westview Press).

STRYDOM, H. A. (1993–4), 'Self-Determination and the South African Constitution' 19 *South African Yearbook of International Law* 43–64.

SZASZ, P. C. (1995), 'Peacekeeping in Operation: A Conflict Study of Bosnia' 28 *Cornell International Law Journal* 685–99.

TACSAN, J. (1992), *The Dynamics of International Law in Conflict Resolution* (Dordrecht: Martinus Nijhoff).

TAKKENBERG, L. (1998), *The Status of Palestinian Refugees in International Law* (Oxford: Clarendon Press).

TAMARI, S. (1996), 'Return, Resettlement, Repatriation: The Future of Palestinian Refugees in the Peace Negotiations' *FOFOGNET Digest* (22 Apr.).

TAYLOR, R. (1994), 'A Consociational Path to Peace in Northern Ireland and South Africa?', in Guelke (ed.) (1994a: 161–74).

TEITEL, R. (1997), 'Transitional Jurisprudence: The Role of Law in Political Transformation' 106 *Yale Law Journal* 2009–80.

TESÓN, F. R. (1992a), 'The Kantian Theory of International Law' 92 *Columbia Law Review* 53–102.

—— (1992b), 'Realism and Kantianism in International Law' 86 *American Society of International Law Proceedings* 113–18.

TESSLER, M. (1994), *A History of the Israeli–Palestinian Conflict* (Bloomington, Indianapolis: Indiana University Press).

THOMPSON, M. (1992), *A Paper House: The Ending of Yugoslavia* (London: Vintage).

THORNBERRY, P. (1989), 'Self-Determination, Minorities, Human Rights: A Review of International Instruments' 38 *International and Comparative Law Quarterly* 867–89.

—— (1991), *International Law and the Rights of Minorities* (Oxford: Clarendon Press).

—— (1993), 'The Democratic or Internal Aspect of Self-Determination with Some Remarks on Federalism', in Tomuschat (ed.), *Modern Law of Self-Determination* (Dordrecht: Martinus Nijhoff), 101–38.

TOMUSCHAT, C. (1993), 'Self-Determination in a Post-Colonial World', in C. Tomuschat (ed.), *Modern Law of Self-Determination* (Dordrecht: Martinus Nijhoff), 1–20.

TRIFUNOVSKA S. (1994), *Yugoslavia through Documents from its Creation to its Dissolution* (Dordrecht: Martinus Nijhoff).

TRUTH AND RECONCILIATION COMMISSION (1998), *Final Report* (Cape Town: Juta).

TULLY, J. (1995), *Strange Multiplicity: Constitutionalism in an Age of Diversity* (Cambridge: Cambridge University Press).

ULLMAN, R. H. (ed.) (1996), *The World and Yugoslavia's Wars* (New York: Council on Foreign Relations).

ULSTER UNIONIST PARTY (1994), *A Blueprint for Stability, 28 February 1994* (Belfast: Ulster Unionist Party).

UNGER, R. M. (1975), *Knowledge and Politics* (New York: Free Press; London: Collier Macmillan).

—— (1986), *The Critical Legal Studies Movement* (Cambridge, Mass.: Harvard University Press).

UNITED NATIONS (1995), *National Human Rights Institutions: A Handbook on the Establishment and Strengthening of National Institutions for the Promotion and Protection of Human Rights* (New York: United Nations).

—— (1997), *Human Rights and Law Enforcement: A Manual on Human Rights Training for the Police* (New York: United Nations).

UNITED NATIONS HIGH COMMISSIONER FOR REFUGEES (1996a), *Post Conflict Solutions: UNHCR Programme in Bosnia and Herzegovina and Other Countries in the Region*, Press Statement, 14 (10 Jan. 1996).

—— (1996b), *Update on Ex-Yugoslavia: UNHCR Presents Bosnia Repatriation Plan* (Geneva: UNHCR, Public Information Section, 16 Jan.).

—— (1996c), *Voluntary Repatriation: International Protection* (Geneva: UNHCR).

—— (1997), *The State of the World's Refugees: A Humanitarian Agenda* (Oxford: Oxford University Press).

UNITED NATIONS MISSION IN BOSNIA AND HERZEGOVINA (1999a), *Building Civilian Law Enforcement in Stolac and throughout the Herzegovina-Neretva Canton*, HRO 2/99 (n.p.: Human Rights Office, Dec. 1998–May 1999).

—— (1999b), *Interrogation Techniques Employed by Republika Srpska Law Enforcement Officials in the Srdjan Knezevic Murder Investigation*, HRO 1/99 (n.p.: Human Rights Office, 21 Jan.).

VAN MAARSEVEEN, H., and G. VAN DER TANG (1978), *Written Constitutions: A Computerised Comparative Study* (Alphen aan den Rijn: Sitjhoff & Noordhoff).

VAN WYK, D. (ed.) (1994), *Rights and Constitutionalism: The New South African Legal Order* (Cape Town: Juta).

VENTER, F. (1985), 'Perspectives on the Constitutions of Transkei, Bophutatswana, Venda and Ciskei', in M. P. Vorster, M. Wiechers, and D. J. Van Vuuren (eds.), *The Constitutions of Transkei, Bophuthatswana, Venda and Ciskei* (Durban: Butterworths) 1–19.

—— (1995), 'Requirements for a New Constitutional Text: The Imperatives of the Constitutional Principles' 112 *South Africa Law Journal* 32–44.

VINCENT-DAVISS, D. (1989), 'The Occupied Territories and International Law: A Research Guide' 21 *International Law and Politics* 575–665.

WALDMEIR, P. (1997), *Anatomy of a Miracle* (London: Penguin).

WALZER, M. (1992), *Just and Unjust Wars*, 2nd edn. (New York: Basic Books).

WA MUTUA, M. (1995), 'The Banjul Charter and the African Cultural Fingerprint: An Evaluation of the Language of Duties' 35 *Virginia Journal of International Law* 339–80.

—— (1997), 'Hope and Despair for New South Africa: The Limits of Rights Discourse' 10 *Harvard Human Rights Journal* 63–114.

WATERS, T. W. (1999), 'The Naked Land: The Dayton Accords, Property Disputes, and Bosnia's Real Constitution' 40 *Harvard International Law Journal* 517–93.

WATSON, A. (1993), *Legal Transplants: An Approach to Comparative Law*, 2nd edn. (Athens: University of Georgia Press).

WATSON, G. R. (2000), *The Oslo Accords: International Law and the Israeli–Palestinian Peace Agreements* (Oxford: Oxford University Press).

WEINER, R. O. (1995), 'Trying to Make Ends Meet: Reconciling the Law and Practice of Human Rights Amnesties' 26 *St Mary's Law Journal* 857–75.

WELCHMAN, L. (1993), *A Thousand and One Homes: Israel's Demolition and Sealing of Houses in the Occupied Palestinian Territories* (Ramallah: Al Haq).

WELLER, M. (1992), 'The International Response to the Dissolution of the Socialist Federal Republic of Yugoslavia' 86 *American Journal of International Law* 569–607.

WESCHLER, L. (1991), *A Miracle, a Universe: Settling Accounts with Torturers* (Chicago: University of Chicago Press).

WHYTE, J. (1990), *Interpreting Northern Ireland* (Oxford: Clarendon Press).

WILSON, J. P. (1999), *A Place and a Name*. Report of the Victims' Commission, (Dublin: Stationery Office, July).

WILSON, R. A. (1997), *The People's Conscience: Civil Groups, Peace and Justice in the South African and Guatemalan Transitions* (London: Catholic Institute for International Relations Briefing).

WIPPMAN, D. (ed.) (1998a), *International Law and Ethnic Conflict* (Ithaca: Cornell University Press).

—— (1998b), 'Practical and Legal Constraints on Internal Power Sharing', in Wippman (ed.) (1998a: 211–41).

WOODHOUSE, D. (2000), *The Pinochet Case: A Legal and Constitutional Analysis* (Oxford: Hart).

WOODWARD, S. (1995), *Balkan Tragedy: Chaos and Dissolution after the Cold War* (Washington, DC: Brookings Institution).

WRIGHT, F. (1987), *Northern Ireland: A Comparative Analysis* (Dublin: Gill & Macmillan).

YUVAL-DAVIS, N. (1997), *Gender and Nation* (London: Sage).

INDEX